Globalization and Common Responsibilities of States

The International Library of Essays on Globalization and Law
Series Editor: Michael K. Addo

Titles in the Series:

The Globalization of International Law
Paul Schiff Berman

Globalization and International Investment
Fiona Beveridge

Globalization of Criminal Justice
Michael Bohlander

Globalization and Common Responsibilities of States
Koen De Feyter

Globalization and Intellectual Property
Alexandra George

Globalization and International Organizations
Edward Kwakwa

Globalization and Common Responsibilities of States

Edited by

Koen De Feyter

University of Antwerp, Belgium

ASHGATE

Published by
Ashgate Publishing Limited
Wey Court East
Union Road
Farnham
Surrey GU9 7PT
England

Ashgate Publishing Company
Suite 3-1
110 Cherry Street
Burlington
VT 05401-3818
USA

www.ashgate.com

British Library Cataloguing in Publication Data
Globalization and common responsibilities of states. –
(The international library of essays on globalization and law)
1. Common good. 2. Law and globalization. 3. International law. 4. Environmental responsibility. 5. Environmental law. 6. Human rights.
I. Series II. Feyter, K. de (Koen)
340.1'1-dc23

Library of Congress Control Number: 2012942735

ISBN 9780754629139

MIX
Paper from responsible sources
FSC® C018575
FSC www.fsc.org

Printed and bound in Great Britain by the MPG Books Group, UK

Contents

Acknowledgements

Ashgate would like to thank our researchers and the contributing authors who provided copies, along with the following for their permission to reprint copyright material.

American Society of International Law for the essays: Christopher D. Stone (2004), 'Common but Differentiated Responsibilities in International Law', *American Journal of International Law*, **98**, pp. 276–301; Carsten Stahn (2007), 'Responsibility to Protect: Political Rhetoric or Emerging Legal Norm?', *American Journal of International Law*, **101**, pp. 99–120.

Brill for the essay: Michael Byers (1997), 'Conceptualising the Relationship between *Jus Cogens* and *Erga Omnes* Rules', *Nordic Journal of International Law*, **66**, pp. 211–39. Copyright © 1997 Kluwer Law International.

Cambridge University Press for the essays: Werner Scholtz (2008), 'Custodial Sovereignty: Reconciling Sovereignty and Global Environmental Challenges amongst the Vestiges of Colonialism', *Netherlands International Law Review*, **55**, pp. 323–41. Copyright © 2008 T.M.C. Asser Instituut and Contributor; Roger O'Keefe (2004), 'World Cultural Heritage: Obligations to the International Community as a Whole?' *International and Comparative Law Quarterly*, **53**, pp. 189–209.

Canadian International Council for the essay: Alexandre Kiss (1985), 'The Common Heritage of Mankind: Utopia or Reality?' *International Journal*, **40**, pp. 423–41.

Jimena Murillo Chávarro for the essay: Jimena Murillo Chávarro (2008), 'Common Concern of Humankind and Its Implications in International Environmental Law', *Macquarie Journal of International and Comparative Environmental Law*, **5**, pp. 133–47.

Columbia Journal of International Law for the essay: Balakrishnan Rajagopal (2003), 'International Law and Social Movements: Challenges of Theorizing Resistance', *Columbia Journal of Transnational Law*, **41**, pp. 397–433.

Edward Elgar for the essay: Upendra Baxi (2010), 'Writing about Impunity and Environment: The '"Silver Jubilee" of the Bhopal Catastrophe', *Journal of Human Rights and the Environment*, **1**, pp. 23–44. Copyright © 2010 The Author.

Elsevier for the essay: Paul J. Nelson (2007), 'Human Rights, the Millennium Development Goals, and the Future of Development Cooperation', *World Development*, **35**, pp. 2041–55. Copyright © Elsevier Ltd. All rights reserved.

The Johns Hopkins University Press for the essays: Adeno Addis (2009), 'Imagining the International Community: The Constitutive Dimension of Universal Jurisdiction', *Human Rights Quarterly*, **31**, pp. 129–62. Copyright © 2009 The Johns Hopkins University Press;

Sigrun I. Skogl, and Mark Gibney (2002), 'Transnational Human Rights Obligations', *Human Rights Quarterly*, **24**, pp. 781–98. Copyright © 2002 The Johns Hopkins University Press.

Oxford University Press for the essay: Gorik Ooms and Rachel Hammonds (2008), 'Correcting Globalisation in Health: Transnational Entitlements versus the Ethical Imperative of Reducing Aid-Dependency', *Public Health Ethics*, **1**, pp. 154–70. Copyright © 2008 The Authors.

Pázmány Péter Catholic University for the essay: Dinah Shelton (2009), 'Common Concern of Humanity', *Iustum Aequum Salutare*, **V**, pp. 33–40.

Manchester Journal of International Economic Law for the essay: Gbenga Oduntan (2005), 'Imagine There are No Possessions: Legal and Moral Basis of the Common Heritage Principle in Space Law, *Manchester Journal of International Economic Law*, **2**, pp. 30–58.

Melbourne Journal of International Law for the essays: Edward Guntrip (2003), 'The Common Heritage of Mankind: An Adequate Regime for Managing the Deep Seabed?', *Melbourne Journal of International Law*, **4**, pp. 376–405; Angela Williams (2009), 'Solidarity, Justice and Climate Change Law', *Melbourne Journal of International Law*, **10**, pp. 493–508.

Taylor & Francis for the essay: Simon Caney (2009), 'Justice and the Distribution of Greenhouse Gas Emissions', *Journal of Global Ethics*, **5**, pp. 125–46. Copyright © 2009 Taylor and Francis. Taylor & Francis Ltd, www.tandfonline.com

University of Michigan Press for the essays: Anne Orford (2009), 'Jurisdiction without Territory: From the Holy Roman Empire to the Responsibility to Protect', *Michigan Journal of International Law*, **30**, pp. 981–1015; Francesco Francioni (2004), 'Beyond State Sovereignty: The Protection of Cultural Heritage as a Shared Interest of Humanity', *Michigan Journal of International Law*, **25**, pp. 1209–28.

Virginia Journal of International Law Association for the essay: Anthony J. Colangelo (2006), 'The Legal Limits of Universal Jurisdiction', *Virginia Journal of International Law*, **47**, pp. 149–200.

Every effort has been made to trace all the copyright holders, but if any have been inadvertently overlooked the publishers will be pleased to make the necessary arrangement at the first opportunity.

Publisher's Note

The material in this volume has been reproduced using the facsimile method. This means we can retain the original pagination to facilitate easy and correct citation of the original essays. It also explains the variety of typefaces, page layouts and numbering.

Series Preface

Globalization is as much a process as a phenomenon of our age with forceful transformative qualities that affect conventional knowledge of politics, economics and the law. In most cases, but not always, globalization has led to an increasing convergence of values that affect different sectors of society unequally. Of the diverse dimensions of globalization, its tangible impact on economic processes is illustrative of the transformative potential and impact. Economic globalization has so fundamentally affected the roles and relationships of national and international actors that conventional rules of law have come under intense scrutiny. With economic globalization comes the confirmation of neo-classical economic doctrine as a dominant theme in policy-making and with it the diminution of the State and other symbols of sovereignty, coupled with a noticeable empowerment of actors such as transnational corporations, civil society groups and intergovernmental economic organizations. In this rapidly changing environment the law continues to play its usual defining and facilitative role but with a responsive twist to the demands of the phenomenon and processes of globalization. As a thematic collection of essays put together by experts in different fields transformed by globalization, the International Library of Essays on Globalization and Law seeks to capture the changing role of the law in modern society. In addition to containing key articles, each volume has an authoritative introduction which explains the context and significance of the essays which have been selected. Considerable care and attention have gone into selecting essays for each volume and I am grateful to each editor for this.

MICHAEL K. ADDO
Series Editor
University of Exeter, UK

Introduction

Globalization and the Nature of International Law

Globalization is a contested[1] notion used to describe increasing cross border flows in trade, investment, communication and people, facilitated by technological innovation. It can be conceived:

> as a process, or set of processes, that embodies a transformation in the spatial organization of social relations, engendering a shift in the spatial reach of networks and systems of social relations to transcontinental patterns of human organization, activity and the exercise of social power. (Perraton, 2011, p. 69)

At the individual level, the process implies that people develop social networks and activities that are no longer contained by the borders of the State of which they are a national. Similarly, consumers prefer to have access to goods and services regardless of where they are produced. The process may have significant implications for the self-identification of individuals: they may identify not only with a specific national or ethnic community, but also with a global class or a global cause (cf. Sklair, 2002). Clearly, not all individuals have the means to enjoy these choices: the life of a peasant in the interior of China remains very much confined by the territorial space in which she lives, while the life of her compatriot who is a member of China's urban elite internationalizes rapidly. As the UN Millennium Declaration states:

> For while globalization offers great opportunities, at present its benefits are very unevenly shared, while its costs are unevenly distributed … . Thus, only through broad and sustained efforts to create a shared future, based upon our common humanity in all its diversity, can globalization be made fully inclusive and equitable.[2]

The increasing interconnectedness of people challenges the sovereignty of States, since sovereignty is deeply rooted in territory. Governments exercise power within their territory, but are also obligated to respect the territorial integrity of other States. As a consequence of globalization, domestic policies in economic and other realms are increasingly influenced by events elsewhere, while local decisions may have a global impact. Governments of industrialized countries may find it difficult to prevent the delocalization of industry to low wage countries, while at the same time they may be reluctant to take into account the adverse

---

1 For the purposes of this section, I have used Jonathan Michie's *The Handbook of Globalisation* (2011) as a reference book on globalization.

2 UN Millennium Declaration (18 September 2000), UN General Assembly resolution 55/2, par. I.5.

extraterritorial impact of their economic activity on the environment of other countries or on areas beyond national control.

Globalization as a process is a descriptive term. Trade, investment and migration are globalized to varying degrees. Nevertheless, globalization is also normatively charged: the impact of globalization on peace and security, economic growth, social justice or the environment may be evaluated as positive or negative. Globalism is the ideology that supports globalization as a positive process. Intergovernmental organizations such as the World Trade Organization and the international financial institutions, and transnational corporations adopt a globalist perspective. Such actors encourage States not to use their sovereign powers in order to impede free flows into and out of their territory. States should create a space where domestic and foreign companies can compete freely and fairly. International economic law provides legal security to those entering domestic markets, by ensuring that State decisions to open up to the international economy cannot simply be reversed by a change of direction in national politics.

Governments that pursue globalist policies – in power in the large majority of States today – tend to take a more nuanced view. Their enthusiasm for globalization is tempered by the particular responsibility governments owe to their own population, the political community that – at least in the ideal scenario – entrusted them with decision-making power. The interests of these political communities, defined by State borders, differ, due to inter alia historical and geographical circumstances. Domestic sovereignty remains important, because it enables these communities to participate in decision-making. A true globalist might favour a world government that is entrusted with the ideal distribution of production and labour, but from a democratic perspective, the localization of political power remains attractive.

Given this background, it is unlikely that States will disappear as an organizational structure in the near future, but the large majority of States may have to coordinate action through intergovernmental organizations or international regulation even in order to effectively realize their domestic agendas. Hegemonic States may maintain the capacity to take unilateral decisions, although they too are well-advised to consult and seek coalitions (Hirst and Thompson, 2011, p. 24). Due to the emphasis on free cross-border flows, globalization also creates the space for non State actors to significantly impact on global policy issues. In political science literature, the hypothesis that the State is the most powerful actor is no longer necessarily taken for granted (Woodward, 2011, p. 381). The impact of non-State actors raises questions about the accountability of these actors to the communities affected by their actions.

Increased cross border activity also heightens awareness within societies and at the governmental level that there are global issues that arise at the level of the entire world, and that threaten the stability of the global system. International organizations, such as the United Nations (UN), have pushed hard to convince States and non-State actors that in order to protect their interests global coordinated action is a necessity.

One suggested list of global issues requiring international cooperation and reflecting UN concerns was compiled by Kaul and others in their 2003 study on global public goods:

- basic human dignity for all people, including universal access to basic
- education and health care;
- respect for national sovereignty;
- global public health, particularly communicable disease control;

- global security or, put differently, a global public domain free from crime and violence;
- global peace;
- communication and transportation systems harmonized across borders;
- institutional infrastructure harmonized across borders to foster such goals as market efficiency, universal human rights, transparent and accountable governance, and harmonization of technical standards;
- concerted management of knowledge, including worldwide respect for intellectual property rights;
- concerted management of the global natural commons to promote their sustainable use;
- availability of international arenas for multilateral negotiations between States as well as between State and non-State actors.

In theory, these global common concerns could be effectively addressed by supranational institutions with coercive powers and powers to redistribute more equitably (Hirst and Thompson, 2011, p. 23). In reality, the principle of the sovereign equality of States remains a cornerstone of international law. The challenge is to devise legal instruments within international law that take sovereign equality into account, but that are nevertheless effective in addressing global interests requiring concerted action.

States are sovereign, and thus they are capable to both exercise domestic jurisdiction over persons, objects and resources on their territory, and to enter into relations with other States. States are also equal in law (even if they differ hugely in terms of population, or military and economic power), and are therefore not subject to the authority of any other State.

State sovereignty implies that, while States are fully capable to commit to international obligations across the whole field of international relations, they are not under an obligation to do so. As the Permanent Court of International Justice held:

> International law governs relations between independent States. The rules of law binding upon States therefore emanate from their own free will as expressed in conventions or by usages generally accepted as expressing principles of law and established in order to regulate the relations between these co-existing independent communities or with a view to the achievement of common aims. Restrictions upon the independence of States cannot therefore be presumed.[3]

In a system that divides sovereignty on the basis of territory, a government is responsible for and accountable to the population on that territory. Inevitably, the decision on whether to commit to international obligations 'with a view to the achievement of common aims' is determined primarily by the government's assessment of whether such a commitment serves the interest of its own population.

State consent is also the point of departure in Article 38 of the Statute of the International Court of Justice[4] that lists the sources of international law. Treaties are only binding on States after they have expressed their consent to be bound.[5] Customary law requires evidence of a

---

3 Permanent Court of International Justice, *The case of the S.S. Lotus*. France v. Turkey (7 September 1927), par. 44.

4 ICJ Statute annexed to the UN Charter (26 June 1945), 1 UNTS xvi.

5 Article 34, Vienna Convention on the law of treaties (23 May 1969), 1155 UNTS, 331 (No. 18232).

substantial State practice by a substantial number of States, supported by a general conviction that the practice amounts to a legal obligation (see, for instance, Aust, 2010, pp. 6–7). States that are not in agreement with a customary rule can escape application by acting as a persistent objector. General principles of law are common to domestic legal systems – which have been adopted by States in the exercise of their sovereign powers.

The principle of sovereign equality has further important consequences for the review of the conformity of State conduct with international obligations. In principle, the courts of State A cannot judge the conduct of State B, because State A cannot place itself above State B. When disputes between States need to be settled judicially at the international level, both parties enjoy equal rights. International courts, however, can usually only exercise jurisdiction if a State consents. A State that has undertaken an international obligation can thus validly decide not to enable an international court to assess compliance.

Finally, international law remains strongly focused on States as the primary subjects of international law, possessing the totality of rights and duties recognized by this system of law. Intergovernmental organizations enjoy more limited rights and duties.[6] The mainstream view today still is that multinational corporations and non-governmental organizations do not enjoy international legal personality at all, and that their conduct needs to be regulated at the domestic level.

The situation is problematic, since non-State actors acting across borders increasingly impact on issues of global concern, and may be able to escape the reach of domestic law, given its territorial nature. As explained above, there is a growing awareness that addressing global concerns requires the cooperation of the international community as a whole. In this approach, the international community encompasses not only all States, but also non-State actors that have an impact on the achievement of the common aim. States and non-State actors are perceived of as a community that strives after the realization of common aims that go beyond the minimum consensus that can be achieved through the 'accidental' ad hoc convergence of national interests of States.

Traditional international law as described above thus appears ill-equipped to deal with global common interests.

In the different fields of international law that are relevant to the realization of these aims, and notwithstanding the limitations of this system of law identified above, legal developments have taken place that attempt to respond to the identification of global concerns. The following sections contain examples of such techniques. Several treaties have been drafted that use the language of 'common heritage of mankind' or 'common concern of humanity' and attempt to draw the consequences by setting up a system of shared responsibilities. As Dinah Shelton points out in Chapter 1, neither term refers to States – suggesting that they reflect a global set of values and interests independent of the interests of States.

Soft law efforts focus on carving out a responsibility or accountability for non-State actors in this regard, but there also interesting examples of binding multi-stakeholder agreements that are brought under the realm of international law. Some progress has been made in defining extraterritorial obligations of States and duties of cooperation. The UN Security Council has referred situations to the International Criminal Court without the consent of the State where

[6] International Court of Justice, *Reparations for injuries suffered.* Advisory Opinion (11 April 1949), p. 174.

these situations occurred. In legal writings, general principles of law are rediscovered as principles inherent to the international legal order that may serve to protect global interests.

In the final section, the sources of international law are revisited. The sources of international law determine the process through which international law is created, or found. In the end, it is through the process of norm creation or norm change that global interests will need to be protected in international law.

The focus of this book is on common responsibilities within the realm of international public law. As an earlier volume in this series demonstrated (Schiff Berman, 2005), international public law is not the only normative system that is relevant to the protection of global interests. Other pertinent normative systems include international private law, domestic law and rules produced by stakeholders other than governments. The debate on internet governance thus focuses on whether regulation of the internet is best achieved within a specific normative system or through a combination of legal instruments from different normative systems (consider, for instance, Svantesson, 2012; Segura-Serrano, 2006).

Common Responsibilities in Various Fields of International Law

The Law of the Sea

In a system based on territorial sovereignty, the legal techniques developed to deal with areas beyond national jurisdiction are of special interest from a common interest perspective. These spatial areas include Antarctica and outer space, and also – in the UN Convention on the Law of the Sea (10 December 1982)[7] – the high seas and the Area (that is, the seabed and ocean floor and its subsoil that is not part of the continental shelf of any State). All these common areas lie outside State boundaries and cannot be appropriated by States, and therefore require international regulation. International regulation can, however, come in various shapes and sizes. Policy decisions determine the aims of such regulation (ranging on a scale from allowing free use of the areas to all to prohibition of access), and the nature of the international regime that can be either fragmented (that is, consist of a jigsaw of domestic, regional and international rules) or comprehensive (establishing one international regime without referral to other levels of regulation).

The two contrasting regimes in the UN Convention on the Law of the Sea offer a case in point. The high seas regime combines non-appropriation by States with free use – even if the exercise of these freedoms is subject to a number of conditions, including that the high seas are reserved for peaceful purposes. The high seas are 'open to all States', for the purposes of navigation and fishing. Every state has the right to sail ships flying its flag on the high seas, and those ships are generally subject only to the jurisdiction of the state whose flag they fly (resulting in the applicability of a plethora of domestic legal rules that incorporate international or regional law to varying degrees – hence the problem of flags of convenience). States also have the right for their nationals to engage in fishing.

The Area and its resources however are 'the common heritage of mankind'. All rights in the resources of the Area are vested in mankind as a whole, and mining activities are to be

7 UN Convention on the law of the sea, 1833 UNTS, 3 (No. 31363).

carried out for the benefit of mankind as a whole, taking into account in particular the needs of developing countries. The International Seabed Authority is the organization through which State parties to the Convention organize and control activities in the Area, specifically with regard to the prospecting, exploration and exploitation of marine minerals. The use of the Area is also exclusively for peaceful purposes.

The starting point of the two regimes is fundamentally different: the high seas regime combines non-appropriation by States with multiple flag state jurisdictions and the protection of private interests, while exploitation of resources in the Area is governed by an international body for the benefit of mankind, including an element of positive discrimination in favour of the developing countries. Due to subsequent developments, the distinction between both regimes is less clear-cut.

Even on the high seas, States have a duty to cooperate with each other to preserve their common interest in the conservation and management of living resources by agreeing the allowable catch, which may 'as appropriate' require the establishment of sub-regional or regional fisheries organizations. In fact, high seas resources are managed mainly through regional fishery organizations. The UNCLOS Convention was later supplemented with the UN Fish Stocks Agreement (4 December 1995)[8] and with the FAO Compliance Agreement.[9] Both instruments call for more effective enforcement by flag states, port states and coastal states of the conservation and management measures adopted for such stocks. As in other treaties dealing with conservation, the UN Fish Stock Agreement recognizes the special requirements of developing States, and provides measures of assistance. The 1995 FAO Code of Conduct for Responsible Fisheries[10] was adopted by the FAO Conference, and is a voluntary instrument. The Code addresses States but also non-State actors such as 'fishing entities, sub-regional, regional and global organizations, whether governmental or non-governmental, and all persons concerned with the conservation of fishery resources and management and development of fisheries'.[11]

Nothing in these rules prevents fishing for private gain and in practice most of the fishing on the high seas is by private actors, not by States. The role of States is mainly to ensure that their nationals can fish on the high seas, but do so in a responsible way. In the UNCLOS Convention minerals recovered from the Area are, however, 'not subject to alienation'.[12] Ownership of these resources is vested in mankind. The Authority holds the monopoly over activities in the area, and is obliged to ensure equitable benefit-sharing derived from these activities. As Alexandre Kiss states in Chapter 5, the Authority acts as the trustee of the

---

8 Agreement for the Implementation of the provisions of the United Nations Convention on the law of the sea of 10 December 1982 relating to the conservation and management of straddling fish stocks and highly migratory fish stocks available at http://www.un.org/depts/los/convention_agreements/convention_overview_fish_stocks.htm.

9 FAO Agreement to promote compliance with international conservation and management measures by fishing vessels on the high seas (24 November 1993), available at http://www.fao.org/docrep/meeting/003/x3130m/X3130E00.HTM.

10 FAO Code of Conduct for responsible fisheries (31 October 1995), available at http://www.fao.org/docrep/005/v9878e/v9878e00.HTM.

11 Article 1, par. 2, FAO Code of Conduct for responsible fisheries.

12 Article 137, par. 2, UN Convention on the law of the sea.

international community to ensure the peaceful use, rational management and conservation of the resources that are the common heritage of mankind.

Developed States opposed the Area regime, and in order to pacify their concerns and ensure global ratification of the UNCLOS treaty, a 1994 Agreement[13] was adopted by the UN General Assembly that was to be interpreted and applied as a single instrument with the relevant part IX of UNCLOS, but that prevailed over UNCLOS in case of inconsistencies between both texts. Although the common heritage of mankind principle remains applicable to the Area, the 1994 Agreement provided that the Enterprise, the organ of the Authority empowered to engage in mining operations, should do so through joint ventures with contractors 'in accord with sound commercial principles'.[14] The decision-making system applicable to the Authority was also amended, resulting, in the assessment of Edward Guntrip in Chapter 11, in 'a regime that allows the individual interests of States to override the interests of mankind'.[15] The International Seabed Authority has concluded contracts with eight contractors for the exploration (not exploitation) of Polymetallic Nodules in the Area. The contractors include State institutions, State enterprises and a private company. The large majority of contractors are from industrialized countries, but also from China and India.

In Chapter 10 on outer space exploration and exploitation, Gbenga Oduntan, drawing lessons from developments in the law of the sea and relating to Antarctica, expresses concerns often voiced in the Global South. Future outer space exploitation, he argues, should not benefit only a few States and companies domiciled in those States. Commercial exploitation should not take place until a solid international regime is set up including a proportionate financing scheme and the establishment of a committee on environmental protection. The author's preferred solution, however, is that no regime of commercial exploitation is ever developed on celestial bodies in order to avoid the risk of severe environmental damage.

The Protection of World Cultural Heritage

The UNESCO Convention concerning the world cultural and natural heritage[16] offers protection to sites that are not in a common area, but that are situated within the territory of a State. The point of departure therefore is that the relevant cultural and natural sites are subject to the exercise of sovereignty by the territorially competent State. According to the Convention, cultural heritage includes monuments and groups of buildings 'of outstanding universal value from the point of view history, art or science' and sites 'of outstanding universal value from the historical, aesthetic, ethnological or anthropological point of view'.

---

[13] Agreement relating to the Implementation of Part XI of the United Nations Convention on the law of the sea of 10 December 1982 (28 July 1994), 1836 UNTS 42 (No. 31364).

[14] Annex IV, Article 1, par. 3, Agreement relating to the Implementation of Part XI of the United Nations Convention on the law of the sea.

[15] For a scathing critique of the 1994 Agreement, see Pureza (2005).

[16] UNESCO Convention concerning the protection of world cultural and natural heritage (16 November 1972), 1037 UNTS 151.

Although these heritage sites belong to a people, their safeguarding is nevertheless important to all peoples of the world.[17]

As Derek Gillman points out, the UNESCO Convention reflects the tension between two ways of thinking about cultural property (Gillman, 2010, p. 42). One is to look at cultural property as local: that is, as belonging and contributing to the identity of persons belonging to specific communities. The other view is cosmopolitan, encouraging the sharing of cultural objects beyond the source country and the exhibition of achievements of local cultures to a global audience.

The UNESCO Convention takes the traditional approach in international law of representation of communities by their States. Although the sites may belong to a people, it is the State that acts on the people's behalf, both in terms of rights and responsibilities. It is the State that identifies and delineates the cultural and natural heritage on its territory. The State also has the 'primary' duty to ensure protection, conservation and presentation. Only the State of the territory where the site is situated can submit an application to the World Heritage Committee[18] for inscription on the World Heritage List,[19] and no property can be included on this list without the relevant State's consent.

On the other hand, since the protection of world heritage is in the interest of all peoples, Article 6 of the Convention provides that:

> Whilst fully respecting the sovereignty of the States on whose territory the cultural and natural heritage … is situated, and without prejudice to property right provided by national legislation, the State Parties to this Convention recognize that such heritage constitutes a world heritage *for whose protection it is the duty of the international community as a whole to co-operate* [emphasis added].

The UNESCO Convention establishes a system of international cooperation that consists of two components: assistance and monitoring.

Requests for assistance with respect to properties included in the World Heritage List can be formulated by States Parties and are addressed to the World Heritage Committee. The Committee takes into account the importance of the property, the urgency of the work, but also the extent to which the State is able to safeguard the property from its own means. Assistance takes various forms: studies, training, and also loans or subsidies. A Fund has been established that supports the work of the World Heritage Committee, with resources consisting of both compulsory[20] and voluntary contributions of the States Parties and any other funds raised, including from private actors.

---

[17] Article 1 of the UNESCO Convention concerning the Protection of world cultural and natural heritage.

[18] The World Heritage Committee is an intergovernmental committee composed of 15 State parties to the Convention.

[19] The criteria for inscription on the list are contained in Operational Guidelines for the Implementation of the World Heritage Convention (November 2011), available at http://whc.unesco.org/pg.cfm?cid=57 (checked March 2011).

[20] Subject to a declaration to the contrary, see Article 16, par. 2, UNESCO Convention concerning the protection of world cultural and natural heritage.

The World Heritage Committee also engages in monitoring of the state of conservation of world heritage sites. States Parties are required to submit reports to the UNESCO General Conference through the World Heritage Committee on the legislative and administrative provisions they have adopted and other actions which they have taken for the application of the Convention. The Committee also engages in 'reactive monitoring' on the state of conservation of specific World Heritage properties that are under threat. States Parties to the Convention should inform the Committee, through the Secretariat, of their intention to undertake or to authorize in an area protected under the Convention major restorations or new constructions which may affect the outstanding universal value of the property. The Committee may inscribe a property on the List of World Heritage in Danger – in cases of urgency, also without the relevant State's consent. The Committee annually reviews the state of conservation of properties on the List of World Heritage in Danger. Properties can be deleted from the World Heritage list in cases where the property has deteriorated to the extent that it has lost those characteristics which determined its inclusion in the World Heritage List; and where the intrinsic qualities of a World Heritage site were already threatened at the time of its nomination by action of man and the necessary corrective measures were not taken.

In the context of the Convention, the duty of international cooperation is organized via an international treaty body that monitors States Parties' duties and provides assistance. But the World Heritage Committee is not the only means of enforcement of the Convention.

The duty of international cooperation complements the primary duty of the State exercising territorial sovereignty to ensure conservation of the heritage on its territory. The State owes this duty to all other States Parties to the Convention; at the time of writing the Convention was ratified by 188 States. An argument can be made under the Articles on the Responsibility of States for Internationally Wrongful Acts[21] that the State owes this duty to all States, including to the few States that are not party to the Convention, since the duty is owed to the international community as a whole.[22] In any case, States parties to the Convention have the right to invoke the primary State Party's responsibility for breach of its treaty obligations. According to Roger O'Keefe in Chapter 16, the implication is that other States are entitled to scrutinize, comment and criticize a State's treatment of its heritage. Such actions do not constitute an impermissible interference in the State's domestic affairs.

In Chapter 15, Francesco Francioni points out that the expression 'international community' is not limited to States only: it certainly includes international organizations (such as UNESCO itself) that are equally entitled to scrutinize a State's behavior in terms of protecting heritage of significant value for humanity. In the UNESCO Convention for the Safeguarding of the Intangible Cultural Heritage[23] the 'international community' further includes non-State actors. The 2003 Convention defines intangible cultural heritage as 'the practices, representations, expressions, knowledge, skills – as well as the instruments, objects, artifacts and cultural

---

[21] Draft Articles on the responsibility of States for internationally wrongful acts, Report of the ILC on the Work of its Fifty-third Session, UN General Assembly, 56th Sess., Supp. No. 10, p 43, UN Doc. A/56/10 (2001).

[22] See Article 48, par. 1a of the Draft Articles on the responsibility of States for internationally wrongful acts.

[23] UNESCO Convention for safeguarding of the intangible cultural heritage (17 October 2003), 2368 UNTS 1.

spaces associated therewith – that communities, groups and, in some cases, individuals recognize as part of their cultural heritage'.[24] and approaches the safeguarding of intangible cultural heritage as a common concern of humanity. Since communities and groups are the guardians of intangible heritage, State obligations at the national level include obligations to ensure the participation of communities and groups in the identification of the elements of the intangible cultural heritage, in safeguarding activities, and in specific educational and training programmes. International cooperation needs to respect not only national legislation, but also customary law and practices.[25] Non-governmental organizations can be accredited with the International Committee for the Safeguarding of the Intangible Cultural Heritage in an advisory capacity.[26]

The designation of intangible cultural heritage as a common concern of humanity, thus results in rights and duties for various actors. The State that exercises sovereignty has the primary duty to protect the heritage on its territory. Other States are entitled to monitor and criticize the fulfillment of this duty through the treaty body or by other means; they also have a duty of international cooperation. Non-State actors are entitled to participate in decision-making at the domestic level, and to take up an advisory role at the international level.

In Chapter 14, Werner Scholtz introduces the term custodial sovereignty to describe this type of approach. International law, he argues, should not abandon the emphasis on sovereignty, but should promote the use of sovereignty to protect the interests of all peoples. Custodial sovereignty perceives of a State as the custodian of world heritage or global environmental resources on its territory. Other States have a legitimate expectation that the relevant state will offer protection for the whole of mankind, but they also have a joint responsibility to offer support to the relevant State to fulfill its obligations. In Scholtz's approach, custodial sovereignty thus entails the implementation of differential treatment in relation to developing countries.

Sustainable Development

Sustainable development was defined in the Brundtland Report (World Commission on Environment and Development, 1987) as development that meets the needs of the present without compromising the ability of future generations to meet their own needs. Many treaties and soft law documents contain preambular or operative paragraphs referring to the concept – usually without offering a definition. Clearly the concept requires the integration of economic and social development and environmental protection, and in legal terms, the integration of the relevant fields of international law. Philippe Sands (2003, p. 253) identifies four elements of sustainable development:

- the need to preserve natural resources for the benefit of future generations;
- the aim of exploiting natural resources in a manner which is 'sustainable';

---

[24] Article 2, par. 1, UNESCO Convention for the safeguarding of the intangible cultural heritage (17 October 2003).

[25] Article 19, par. 2, UNESCO Convention for the safeguarding of the intangible cultural heritage (17 October 2003).

[26] Article 9, UNESCO Convention for the safeguarding of the intangible cultural heritage (17 October 2003).

- the 'equitable' use of natural resources, which implies that use by one State needs to take into account the needs of other States;
- the need to ensure that environmental considerations are integrated into development plans, and that development needs are taken into account in applying environmental objectives.

Uncertainty remains about the legal status of 'sustainable development' in international law. The International Court of Justice has famously referred to sustainable development as a 'concept' in the *Gabcikovo-Nagymaros* case:

> Throughout the ages, mankind has, for economic and other reasons, constantly interfered with nature. In the past, this was often done without consideration of the effects upon the environment. Owing to new scientific insights and to a growing awareness of the risks for mankind – for present and future generations – of pursuit of such interventions at an unconsidered and unabated pace, new norms and standards have been developed, set forth in a great number of instruments during the last two decades. Such new norms have to be taken into consideration, and such new standards given proper weight, not only when States contemplate new activities but also when continuing with activities begun in the past. This need to reconcile economic development with protection of the environment is aptly expressed in the concept of sustainable development.[27]

'Concepts' are not a source of international law in Article 38 of the Statute of the International Court of Justice. The use of the term 'concept' by the Court may suggest that the majority did not believe that there was a legal definition of 'sustainable development' in international law. References to sustainable development in international treaties dealing with specific subjects usually serve the purpose of identifying the rationale underlying the treaty, and of connecting the treaty to a global common concern agenda (such as the agenda defined at the Rio Conference on Environment and Development[28]). References to sustainable development in treaty provisions are important in terms of the interpretation of the treaty, but they may not create separate, stand alone legal obligations.[29]

In his separate opinion in *Gabcikovo-Nagymaros*, Judge Weeramantry took issue with the majority, and held that sustainable development was more than a concept. In his view, it was a principle of customary international law, resting on a basis of worldwide acceptance:

> Evidence appearing in international instruments and State practice (as in development assistance and the practice of international financial institutions) likewise amply supports a contemporary general acceptance of the concept.[30]

---

27 International Court of Justice, *Gabcikovo-Nagymaros Project.* Hungary v. Slovakia, Judgment, *I.C.J. Reports* 1997, par. 140.

28 The United Nations Conference on Environment and Development was held in Rio de Janeiro from 3 to 14 June 1992.

29 For example, see Article 3 of the UN Framework Convention on climate change (9 May 1992), 1771 UNTS 1907 (No. 30822).

30 International Court of Justice, *Gabcikovo-Nagymaros Project.* Hungary v. Slovakia, Separate Opinion Weeramantry, *I.C.J. Reports* 1997, par. 92.

The Permanent Court of Arbitration held in the *Iron Rhine Railway* case that the duty to integrate environment and development had become a principle of general international law:

> Today, both international and EC law require the integration of appropriate environmental measures in the design and implementation of economic development activities. Principle 4 of the Rio Declaration on Environment and Development, adopted in 1992 …, which reflects this trend, provides that 'environmental protection shall constitute an integral part of the development process and cannot be considered in isolation from it.' Importantly, these emerging principles now integrate environmental protection into the development process. Environmental law and the law on development stand not as alternatives but as mutually reinforcing, integral concepts, which require that where development may cause significant harm to the environment there is a duty to prevent, or at least mitigate, such harm … This duty, in the opinion of the Tribunal, has now become a principle of general international law. This principle applies not only in autonomous activities but also in activities undertaken in implementation of specific treaties between the Parties.[31]

Article 38, par. 1,c of the Statute of the International Court of Justice refers to general principles of law as a source of international law. Christina Voigt argues that sustainable development can now be classified as a general principle of law because its use in many legal systems and in international law, and in the jurisprudence of international courts and tribunals is widespread (Voigt, 2009, p. 186). Consequently, the principle can be relied on in the course of treaty interpretation, but also autonomously as a balancing principle to ensure coherence in a fragmented system of international law. She argues that general principles are necessarily broad and open-textured, enabling a construction of the law that is dynamic and responsive to evolving problems (ibid., p. 151–2).

In Voigt's view, general principles obtain from the common legal conscience as recognized by the international community.[32] Today, general principles derive from a wider acceptance than just that of States: they reflect an *opinio juris communis,* supported by a wider spectrum of actors, including actors at sub-national, cross-national or international levels, such as indigenous peoples, communities, NGOs and intergovernmental organizations.

If understood in this sense, general principles can serve as a useful instrument for the promotion of global common concerns. They act:

> as correctives to the written law. They help bridge the gap between the law as it is to the law as it ought to be, by introducing a communal sense of justice and dynamism where it is lacking in the respective norms … (Ibid., p. 164)

In *Gabcikovo-Nagymaros* the International Court of Justice further acknowledged that concerns for the natural environment could constitute an essential interest of the State. The Court endorsed the International Law Commission's earlier comments that in the last two

[31] Permanent Court of Arbitration, *Iron Rhine Railway*. Belgium v. The Netherlands. Award of 24 May 2005, par. 59.

[32] In contrast with customary law that reflects only the legal conviction (and general practice) of States. In the context of general principles, the requirement of general practice is absent (see Voigt, 2009, p. 158).

decades safeguarding the ecological balance had become an essential interest of all States.[33] In Chapter 13, Jimena Murillo Chávarro infers from the Court's statement that the safeguarding of the earth's ecological balance has now become a stand-alone *erga omnes* obligation owed to the international community as a whole. As Michael Byers explains in Chapter 4, *erga omnes* rules expand the scope of possible claimants in certain situations, to protect key common interests where traditional rules of standing are insufficient to do so.

Biological Diversity and Climate Change: Differentiated Responsibility

International environmental treaties that differentiate the responsibilities of States take inspiration from Principles 6 and 7 of the Rio Declaration on Environment and Development (14 June 1992).[34] Principle 6 indicates that the special situation and needs of developing countries, particularly the least developed and the most environmentally vulnerable, should be given priority. Principle 7 notes that States contribute differently to global environmental degradation; that developed States and their societies place higher pressures on the global environment, and that they command more technological and financial resources. It is notable that the United States issued an interpretive statement to Principle 7, stating that the country accepted that the principle highlighted the leadership role of the developed countries, but did not accept an interpretation of the principle that would imply a recognition or acceptance by the US of any international obligations or liabilities, or any diminution in the responsibilities of developing countries.

Principles 6 and 7 acknowledge in broad terms that developing and developed countries have different needs; that they impact differently on the environment, and that they have different capabilities to address the problem. Such differences provide the justification for a differentiated responsibility that is intended to reflect a concept of substantive, rather than of formal equality of States. As Christopher Stone points out in Chapter 3, differential treatment between States takes various forms, including non-uniform obligations, a more favourable compliance timetable or forgiving non-compliance altogether, the permission of special defences, or differentiation in financial and technical contributions to international cooperation for the achievement of the objectives of an agreement.

According to the Preamble of the Convention on Biological Diversity (5 June 1992),[35] the conservation of biological diversity is a 'common concern of humankind'. This is because of the intrinsic value of biodiversity, but also due to its benefit and use to humans (of present and future generations). The Convention provides for sustainable use of biodiversity – and not simply for preservation. The integrated approach of different concerns inherent in the concept of sustainable development fully applies.

The Convention constructs a network of rights and duties of various actors, similar to the UNESCO World Heritage Convention. A State has sovereign rights over the biological resources on its territory, but also the duty to conserve and use biological resources in a

---

[33] International Court of Justice, *Gabcikovo-Nagymaros Project.* Hungary v. Slovakia, Judgment, *I.C.J. Reports* 1997, par. 53.

[34] Available at http://www.unep.org/Documents.Multilingual/Default.asp?documentid=78.

[35] The Convention on biological diversity (5 June 1992), 1760 UNTS 79 (No. 30619) is currently ratified by 193 States.

sustainable manner. Several provisions stress the need for international cooperation, taking into account the special needs of developing countries, and, within that group, of the least developed countries and small island States. There is some recognition of the role of non-State actors, as actors to be taken into account at the domestic level – the preamble refers to the need to involve women in policy-making on biodiversity and recognizes the dependence of indigenous and local communities on biological resources – and also stresses the importance of involving the non-governmental sector in international cooperation.

Of particular interest to the issue of differentiation of State responsibilities within the context of a common concern approach is Article 20 of the Convention on financial assistance. Each Contracting Party is required to provide financial support to activities at the national level that are intended to achieve the objectives of the Convention 'in accordance with its capabilities'. The developed States commit to provide additional financial resources to enable developing countries to meet the full incremental costs of implementing the obligations in the Convention. These costs are agreed between the developing country and the Convention's financial mechanism. Since 1996, the Global Environment Facility (GEF)[36] is the institutional structure that operates the financial mechanism.

As there is no generally applicable definition of developing and developed countries in international law, treaties including non-uniform obligations need to provide their own mechanism for distinguishing between States having different obligations. In the Biodiversity Convention, the Conference of the Parties is entrusted with the task to adopt and review the list of developed countries that are under an obligation to provide the enabling financial resources.[37]

Article 20, par. 4 further adds:

> The extent to which developing country Parties will effectively implement their commitments under this Convention will depend on the effective implementation by developed country Parties of their commitments under this Convention related to financial resources and transfer of technology and will take fully into account the fact that economic and social development and eradication of poverty are the first and overriding priorities of the developing country Parties.

The provision makes developing country implementation of the Convention as a whole conditional on the fulfillment by the developed countries of their obligation to provide enabling resources. Developing countries are not defined in the Convention, but GEF funding modalities now apply. The wording of Article 20, par. 4 opens the door for protracted debates between developed and developing countries on attributing blame for lack of achievement of the Convention's objectives.

---

[36] GEF was established as an independent financial organization in 1994 under the Instrument for the Establishment of the Restructured Global Environment Facility, adopted by the three implementing agencies of the Facility: UNEP, UNDP and the World Bank. The GEF currently operates as a mechanism for international cooperation for the purpose of providing new and additional grant and concessional funding to meet the agreed incremental costs of measures to achieve agreed global environmental benefits in the areas of: biological diversity, climate change international waters; land degradation, primarily desertification and deforestation; ozone layer depletion; and persistent organic pollutants.

[37] For the current list, see annex to Conference of the Parties 8 (2006) Decision VIII/18.

The ultimate objective of the UN Framework Convention on Climate Change (9 May 1992)[38] is the stabilization of greenhouse gas concentrations in the atmosphere at a level that would prevent dangerous anthropogenic interference with the climate system. The preamble to the Convention acknowledges that change in the Earth's climate and its adverse effects are a common concern of humankind. The climate is a shared resource, and thus the designation of climate change as a common concern is more straightforward than with regard to the conservation of biodiversity.

Although climate change is a common responsibility, the attribution of responsibility among States varies. Non-uniform obligations are a striking component of the Kyoto Protocol to the UN Framework Convention on Climate Change (11 December 1997).[39] In attributing different responsibilities, the treaty avoids use of the developing/developed country dichotomy. Provisions either refer to 'all States Parties' or to 'Parties listed in Annex I' (to the Framework Convention). During negotiations on the Protocol and on a potential post-2012 successor treaty, debates on which countries were to be included in Annex I, and were thus subject to quantified emission limitation, proved extremely contentious. National interests obviously play an important role, but there is also a substantive debate on which criteria should be used to determine responsibility, and on the relative weight these criteria should have, as discussed by Simon Caney in Chapter 2. The various criteria include: historical contribution to the emission of greenhouse gasses; current emission levels; capacity to pay; impact of climate change commitments on economic development or on poverty reduction; limiting permissible emissions to basic needs satisfaction; and the need to provide preferential treatment to those immediately and disproportionately affected (particularly with respect to adaptation measures). Depending on the priority given to these criteria, a different list of countries required to carry the heaviest burden for addressing adverse impacts of greenhouse gasses emerges.

Parties included in Annex I – currently only industrialized States, including countries in transition to a market economy in former Eastern Europe – are under an obligation to ensure that they reduce their overall greenhouse gas emissions by at least 5 per cent below 1990 levels in the commitment period 2008 to 2012. In addition, a system of differentiated targets was agreed among the major industrialized countries. The EU agreed to reduce emissions by 8 per cent, and internally agreed further differentiated targets for its Member States. Developing countries, including China and India that currently emit significant amounts of greenhouse gasses, are not subject to quantified reductions of emissions. All States party to the Protocol are required to formulate cost-effective national programmes to improve the quality of local emission factors, and to keep a national inventory of anthropogenic emissions. Article 3, par. 4 of the Framework Convention on Climate Change offers a justification for the differentiation by referring of the right of States to promote sustainable development: climate change measures should be 'appropriate for the specific conditions of each Party' and integrated into national development plans 'taking into account that economic development is essential for adopting measures to address climate change'.

The climate change instruments stress the need for international cooperation. International cooperation implies first that unilateral actions (such as trade policy measures) to deal with

38 UN Framework Convention on climate change, 1771 UNTS 1907 (No. 30822).

39 UN Doc FCCC/CP/1997/7/Add.1 (6 March 1998).

environmental challenges in other countries should be avoided[40] and international action in a spirit of global partnership is the preferred approach. An interesting innovation in the field of international cooperation in the Kyoto Protocol is the clean development mechanism (Article 12). Parties to Annex I can support project activities in non-Annex I parties, through sponsoring investment (including by private companies) or through technology transfer, resulting in certified emissions reductions. Annex I parties may use these emission reductions in non-Annex I parties as credits for reaching their own targets. Efforts in cooperation thus contribute to the realization of the assisting State's own obligations.

The polluter pays principle (included as Principle 16 in the Rio Declaration) is of particular interest in determining the responsibility of private actors. In essence the principle is about holding actors that pollute or cause harm to the environment responsible for the consequences of their actions. In the Rio Declaration the burden is on States 'to endeavor to promote' the principle. The provision suggests that, if the polluter is a private actor, the principle should be implemented mainly through national torts law. The OECD Guidelines for Multinational Enterprises (25 May 2011)[41] are also adhered to by States and not by companies, but they are nevertheless phrased as recommendations to multinational enterprises. The OECD Guidelines provide that enterprises should take due account of the need to protect the environment, and conduct their activities in such a way as to contribute to the goal of sustainable development.[42] This implies that, where there are threats of serious damage to the environment, companies should engage in cost-effective measures to prevent or minimize such damage. In the same chapter on the environment, the Guidelines also provide that enterprises should contribute, for example through partnerships, to the development of environmentally meaningful and economically efficient public policy.[43]

Human Rights

Human rights law is a particular branch of international law because its main focus is not on reciprocal obligations between States, but on the internal relationship between a State and the people within its jurisdiction. Individuals hold a legal claim to human rights protection vis-à-vis the State where they are situated.

Human rights treaties do not generally provide for a common responsibility, but rather for a division of responsibility on the basis of territorial sovereignty. Neither do human rights treaties provide for differentiation in State responsibility. All States have the same legal obligations in civil and political rights (although all of them also have the right to make certain reservations to the treaties), even if protection of these rights may be resource intensive. All States also have to progressively realize economic, social and cultural (ESC) rights, but only to the maximum of their available resources. According to the UN Committee on Economic, Social and Cultural Rights, the reference to progressive realization was a 'necessary flexibility device, reflecting the realities of the real world and the difficulties involved for any country

40 Principle 12 of the Rio Declaration on environment and development (14 June 1992).

41 Available at http://www.oecd.org/dataoecd/43/29/48004323.pdf.

42 Preambular paragraph, chapter VI, OECD Guidelines Multinational Enterprises (25 May 2011).

43 Chapter VI, par. 8, OECD Guidelines Multinational Enterprises (25 May 2011).

in ensuring full realization of economic, social and cultural rights'.[44] But the Committee was also of the view that a minimum core obligation to ensure the satisfaction of, at the very least, minimum essential levels of each of the rights was incumbent upon every State party:

> Thus, for example, a State party in which any significant number of individuals is deprived of essential foodstuffs, of essential primary health care, of basic shelter and housing, or of the most basic forms of education is, *prima facie*, failing to discharge its obligations under the Covenant.[45]

In international human rights treaties, public interest concerns appear most visibly in limitation clauses. Restrictions to rights that are formulated in a non-absolute way may be permissible, if it can be demonstrated that such restrictions are provided for by law, and are necessary to achieve a legitimate aim. Among the aims regularly included are concepts such as the protection of public order, health or safety, the rights of others, or the general welfare in a democratic society. Limitation clauses allow balancing the individual interest against the interest of society as a whole. As States act or purport to act as custodians of the general interest, the practical effect of limitation clauses is usually not to curtail sovereignty, but to provide a justification for sovereign decision-making that overrides the human rights claim. It should also be pointed out that in the context of limitation clauses, the public interest is not necessarily the common interest of humankind (all societies), but the interest of a specific domestic society. Domestic and common interest may or may not coincide.

Although international human rights law is essentially based on division of responsibility on the basis of State sovereignty, the regime does have some cross-border dimensions. International cooperation for human rights appears in Article 1, par. 3 of the United Nations Charter as one of the purposes of the organization. In the UN Charter, human rights are not a matter exclusively within the domestic jurisdiction of States, but a legitimate concern of all Member States of the United Nations. The inclusion of human rights as a purpose of the UN enables the integration of human rights into other main concerns of the organization, such as peace and security and economic and social cooperation, or its modern variety, sustainable development. Human rights protection is not only intrinsically valuable, but also contributes to other UN objectives, and therefore should be fully integrated in international cooperation efforts. Article 28 of the Universal Declaration of Human Rights[46] expresses this idea when it states that everyone is entitled to a social and international order in which human rights can be fully realized. A practical application has been the emergence of the so-called rights-based approach to different fields of international cooperation such as development, trade and climate change, as discussed by Paul Nelson in Chapter 18.

Perhaps the most explicit human rights treaty provision on duties of cooperation is Art. 2, par.1 of the International Covenant on Economic, Social and Cultural Rights.[47] The article provides explicitly that ESC rights should be realized not only by States individually, but

---

[44] UN Committee on Economic, Social and Cultural Rights, General Comment No. 3: The Nature of States Parties Obligations, UN doc. E/1991/23, par. 9.

[45] Ibid., par. 10.

[46] UN General Assembly resolution 217 A (III) (10 December 1948).

[47] International Covenant on Economic, Social and Cultural Rights (19 December 1966), 993 UNTS 3 (No. 14531).

also through international assistance and cooperation. Arguably, duties of cooperation as a minimum imply the duty of States to abstain from any policy that impedes on the protection of at least the core content of the economic, social and cultural rights of the affected peoples of another State,[48] as Sigrun Skogly and Mark Gibney argue in Chapter 19.

The reference to international assistance and cooperation triggered a fascinating scholarly debate on whether the developed States also have an extraterritorial duty to assist in the realization of economic, social and cultural rights (and by extension, also in other human rights) in developing countries.[49] Do donor States have human rights obligations towards persons outside their territories, and are they legally responsible when their acts or omissions lead to human rights violations elsewhere? The notion of extraterritorial obligations has a certain appeal, as it deconstructs the duty of the international community to cooperate into a bundle of unilateral individual State responsibilities that international law can more easily define. Nevertheless, extraterritorial obligations are also controversial, precisely because they do not result from an agreement between the relevant countries – the relevant countries are not necessarily a party to the same human rights treaties – and because they apply within the legal realm of another State.

According to the UN Committee on Economic, Social and Cultural Rights, the treaty monitoring body under the Covenant, 'where a State party is clearly lacking in the financial resources and/or expertise required … the international community has a clear obligation to assist'.[50] In its review of State reports, the Committee has started questioning developed States gently on whether their participation in intergovernmental organizations is in conformity with their duties of international co-operation under the Covenant, and in its concluding observations has encouraged them to ensure that it is. The ESC Rights Committee argues that:

> in accordance with Articles 55 and 56 of the Charter of the United Nations, with well-established principles of international law, and with the provisions of the Covenant itself, international cooperation for development and thus for the realization of economic, social and cultural rights is an obligation of all States. It is particularly incumbent upon those States which are in a position to assist others in this regard.[51]

---

[48] UN Committee on Economic, Social and Cultural Rights, General Comment No. 8: The relationship between economic sanctions and respect for economic, social and cultural rights, UN doc. E/C.12/1997/8 par. 7. In international environmental law, the do no harm principle similarly applies extraterritorially.

[49] A recent development are the Maastricht Principles on extraterritorial obligations of States in the area of economic, social and cultural rights (28 September 2011) available at www.icj.org. See generally Coomans and Kamminga (2004); Skogly (2006); Gondek (2008).

[50] UN Committee on Economic, Social and Cultural Rights, General Comment No. 11: Plans of action for primary education. UN doc. E/C.12/1998/24, par. 9.

[51] UN Committee on Economic, Social and Cultural Rights, General Comment No.3: The nature of States parties obligations, UN doc. E/1991/23, par. 14. See also the Committee's views on the justiciability of economic, social and cultural rights in the domestic legal order, notwithstanding the reference to available resource in the Covenant in Committee on Economic, Social and Cultural Rights, General Comment No. 9: The domestic implementation of the Covenant, UN doc. E/C.12/1998/24, par. 10.

The statement above, however, does not offer a criterion for identifying States that are in a position to assist, nor does the text explain what the connection is between the duties of the State that is territorially responsible and the duties of other States to assist. In Chapter 17, Gorik Ooms and Rachel Hammonds think through the possible practical consequences of the Committee's approach with regard to the right to health. They argue that the right to health entitles everyone to a minimum essential level that translates into core obligations of all States. They then calculate the cost of providing this core content of the right (minimum health care), and what can reasonably be expected in terms of public spending on health from a domestic government, depending on how much a government tax its people, and the maximum percentage of the budget that can be spent on health. The result (according to the authors, 3 per cent of the GDP) constitutes the maximum of the available resources at the domestic level. If the amount falls below what is required for minimum health care, other States have a duty to assist, ideally through a global health fund.

In addition, in its general comments on specific articles of the Covenant, the Committee addresses the direct responsibility of intergovernmental organizations, such as the international financial institutions. General Comment No. 14 on the right to health may serve as an example. The General Comment contains a separate section on 'obligations of actors other than State parties'. As part of its monitoring activities, the Committee vows to consider the effects of the assistance provided by all other actors, including United Nations specialized agencies, programmes and bodies, and the role of health professional associations and other non-governmental organizations in relation to the States' obligations.[52]

Another instrument developed within international human rights law expressing the idea that human rights can only be achieved fully across the globe through international cooperation is the right to development. The right to development is included in Article 22 of the African Charter on Human Rights and People's Rights, but at the global level, only appears in non-binding documents. In paragraph 11 of the Millennium Declaration, the world heads of state and government thus declare that they 'are committed to making the right to development a reality for everyone and to freeing the entire human race from want'.[53] The idea of a human right to development was originally launched in the early 1970s by two scholars/practitioners, Karel Vasak (1972) and Keba M'Baye (1972). Vasak argued that a new category of human rights was needed, called 'solidarity rights'. These rights would seek to infuse the human dimension into areas where it had been missing, such as development, peace and the environment. This view resonates with Angela Williams' in Chapter 12 on the concept of solidarity in current international law. She clarifies that solidarity goes beyond cooperation in that it includes a dimension of support and redistribution so as to ensure that less fortunate members of the community are provided for.

In Vasak's view, the active holders of the right to development were individuals, States and also sub-national groups such as local collectivities and national, ethnic and linguistic communities. The duty holders included not only territorially responsible States but the international community as a whole. The desired effect was to humanize the international

---

[52] UN Committee on Economic, Social and Cultural Rights, General Comment No. 14: The right to the highest attainable standard of health. UN doc. E/C.12/2000/4, par. 64.

[53] UN General Assembly resolution 55/2 (8 September 2000).

economic order. Only if all actors on the social scene participated both as holders and duty bearers would the objective be realized.

The 1986 UN Declaration on the Right to Development[54] represented a much watered down version of the original idea. The non-binding Declaration perceived of the right to development as a human right of every human person and all peoples to economic, social, cultural and political development. The text identifies the human person as the central subject of development, and offers little clarification on the collective component of the right. As far as duties are concerned, the primary responsibility lies with the national State. The Declaration is cautious on international responsibilities for development: States collectively have a responsibility for the creation of 'favourable international conditions' for the realization of the right. The United States opposed the Declaration, and a number of developed countries abstained. Perhaps the main substantive influence of the Declaration has been in mainstreaming human rights in the UN specialized agencies.

On 30 March 2007, the United Nations Human Rights Council enabled its Working Group on the Right to Development to gradually move towards the consideration of 'an international legal standard of a binding nature' on the right to development,[55] but progress has been exasperatingly slow. A subsidiary expert body of the Working Group, the High Level Task Force (HLTF), proposed criteria for assessing development agreements on whether or how they contribute to the realization of the right to development. In its final report, the HLTF also proposed a clarification of the content of the right to development (the 'core norm'), three attributes of the right and illustrative indicators.[56]

Arguably, the potential merit of the right to development resides in the idea that developing and developed countries (and perhaps non-State actors as well: see De Feyter, 2008, p. 97) accept mutual obligations – possibly on a subject-by-subject conventional basis – for the realization of human rights.

International Crimes, Universal Jurisdiction and the Responsibility to Protect

Crimes that are classified as international include piracy, slavery, genocide, crimes against humanity, war crimes, aggression and torture. In addition, treaties impose State obligations to prosecute or extradite for a number of other crimes related to terrorism[57] and drug offences.[58]

Different reasons may explain why certain crimes are labelled international crimes. The preamble of the Genocide Convention (9 December 1948)[59] states that genocide is an international crime because it is contrary to the spirit and aims of the United Nations

---

54 UN General Assembly resolution 39/11 (12 November 1986).

55 UN Human Rights Council resolution 4/4 (30 March2007), par. 2,d. The resolution was adopted without a vote.

56 See UN doc. A/HRC/WG.2/TF/2/Add 2 (8 March 2010). See also Marks (2011).

57 For example, see Articles 5–8, Convention for the suppression of unlawful acts against the safety of civil aviation (23 September 1971), 974 UNTS 178 (No. 14118).

58 See articles 4 and 6, UN Convention against illicit traffic in narcotic drugs and psychotropic substances (19 December 1988), 1582 UNTS 165 (No. 27637).

59 Convention on the prevention and punishment of genocide (9 December 1948), 78 UNTS 277 (No. 1021).

and condemned by the civilized world. This is so because genocide inflicts great losses on humanity and requires international cooperation if mankind is to be liberated from it. The preamble of the Statute of the International Criminal Court (17 July 1988)[60] notes that international crimes shatter the mosaic of cultures that binds all peoples; that they shock the conscience of humanity; and, again, that their effective prosecution requires both measures at the national level and enhanced international cooperation. In Chapter 8, Adeno Addis reviews the reasons why crimes are eligible for universal jurisdiction. He lists the power of practice, the heinousness of the crimes; the risk that crimes might go unpunished, and the fundamental nature of the norm that is threatened by these crimes. In her book on the Eichmann trial, Hannah Arendt argued that the persecution of the Jews by Germany during the Second World War was a crime 'against humanity', because the Nazi regime went beyond cleansing Germany of Jews, and wished to make the entire Jewish people disappear from the face of the earth. In her view, this was an attack upon human diversity as such: 'that is, upon a characteristic of the "human status" without which the very words "mankind" or "humanity" would be devoid of meaning' (Arendt, 2006, p. 269). With considerable foresight she predicted that genocide was an actual possibility of the future that could be directed against other peoples, who would only be able to feel reasonably sure of their continued existence, with 'the help and the protection of international law' (ibid., p. 273).

International law places criminal responsibility for international crimes on the individual who committed them, although the State on whose behalf the international crime was done, may also incur responsibility.[61]

Every State has a duty to exercise its criminal jurisdiction over those responsible for international crimes. Article VI of the Genocide Convention provides for trials either by a tribunal of the State in the territory of which the act was committed, or by an international penal tribunal that may have jurisdiction. In the context of the ICC Statute, the domestic State that is expected to exercise jurisdiction is either the State on the territory of which the conduct occurred, or the State of which the person accused of the crime is a national. In both situations, the regulated person or act is closely connected to the relevant State. That State is expected to prosecute international crimes on behalf of the international community. State sovereignty is conceived of as responsibility: once again, the State acts as the guardian of the interests of the international community as a whole.

The ICC Statute provides that if the relevant State fails to exercise its responsibility, the International Criminal Court may act with regard to the limited list of international crimes within its jurisdiction: that is, genocide, crimes against humanity, war crimes and the crime of aggression. The International Criminal Court is complementary to national criminal jurisdictions. The Court needs to show that the State that has jurisdiction is unwilling or

---

60 Statute of the International Criminal Court (17 July 1988), 2187 UNTS 91 (No. 38544).

61 For example, in the *Bosnia and Herzegovina v. Serbia and Montenegro* case, the International Court of Justice held that, under the Genocide Convention, States are not only under an obligation to legislate on individual criminal responsibility, but that they also have a direct obligation not to commit genocide themselves. See International Court of Justice, *Application of the Convention on the Prevention and Punishment of Genocide.* Bosnia and Herzegovina v. Serbia and Montenegro. Judgment. *I.C.J. Reports* 2007, par. 142–201.

unable to investigate or genuinely prosecute.[62] Unwillingness implies that either the domestic State is shielding a person from criminal responsibility or that there is no real intent to bring the person concerned to justice, or that the proceedings are not independent and impartial. Inability is determined in the light of the collapse or unavailability of the relevant national judicial system.

The ICC Statute provides for a possible referral by the UN Security Council to the ICC of situations where crimes under the jurisdiction of the Court appear to have been committed.[63] Referrals by the UN Security Council occur in the context of Chapter VII of the United Nations Charter.[64] When the Security Council referred the situation in Libya 'since 15 February 2011' to the Prosecutor of the ICC, the Council argued that the highest level of the Libyan government was involved in gross and systematic violations of human rights, and that widespread and systematic attacks against the civilian population 'may amount to crimes against humanity'.[65] Libya is not a party to the ICC Statute, but this is not a requirement when the Security Council refers a situation to the ICC.

A further issue is whether *all* States are allowed to assert jurisdiction over international crimes, even if they have no connection with the alleged perpetrator or act. In Chapter 6, Anne Orford discusses the gradual shift in European legal history away from universal jurisdiction based on the authority of the Pope or the Emperor to a concept of jurisdiction that depended on de facto control over territory and the capacity to ensure protection. Nevertheless, in current international law, universal jurisdiction for (certain) international crimes requires no territorial or national nexus to the alleged act or actor. As Anthony Colangelo explains in Chapter 9, with regard to these crimes, every State has both prescriptive jurisdiction (that is lawmaking authority) and adjudicative jurisdiction (that is, the power to subject the alleged perpetrator to its judicial process). In current international customary law, States are allowed (but not necessarily required) to assert universal jurisdiction over some international crimes as defined in international law: piracy, slavery, genocide, crimes against humanity, war crimes and torture.

In Chapter 8, Addis argues that the current exercise of universal jurisdiction, by transcending boundaries of traditional political communities (i.e. the populations of States) is constitutive of the international community as a community of interest. It is by classifying certain acts as being beyond commonly held international norms, that the international community provides itself within an identity that is based on solidarity across borders and needs to be protected against, in Hannah Arendt's phrase, the *hostis generis humani*, the enemy of human kind.

The concept of the responsibility to protect is also linked to certain international crimes. According to the General Assembly resolution incorporating the 2005 World Summit Outcome, the responsibility to protect doctrine applies to genocide, war crimes, ethnic cleansing and crimes against humanity.[66] Each individual State has the responsibility to protect

62 Article 17, Statute of the International Criminal Court (17 July 1998).

63 Situations can also be referred to the ICC by a party to the Statute or by the Prosecutor, but in those instances only if the State on whose territory the conduct occurred or the State of the nationality of the accused person is a party to the Statute.

64 Article 13, b, Statute of the International Criminal Court (17 July 1998).

65 UN Security Council resolution 1970 (26 February 2011), par. 4.

66 UN General Assembly resolution 60/1 (24 October 2005), par. 138–9.

its populations from those crimes, and the international community should, as appropriate, encourage and help States to exercise this responsibility. In this instance, the responsibility of the international community is a concurrent one; it stands next to the responsibility of the territorially responsible State. The international community should use appropriate diplomatic, humanitarian and other peaceful means, in accordance with Chapters VI and VIII of the Charter, to help to protect populations from these crimes. Collective use of force, however, can only be authorized by the Security Council when peaceful means are inadequate and national authorities are manifestly failing to protect their populations from the relevant crimes. In the General Assembly resolution, the international community declares that it is prepared to take such collective action whenever these conditions apply, but, as Carsten Stahn points out in Chapter 7, no sanctions or remedies have as yet been provided in case of a failure of the international community to take up its responsibility. The World Summit Outcome document provides no justification for unilateral military action by a State to protect the population of another State.

The determination that a State is manifestly failing to protect the populations on its territory needs to be made by the UN Security Council. In resolution 1973 (2011), the UN Security Council reiterated the responsibility of the Libyan authorities to protect the Libyan population, and condemned the authorities' failure to provide such protection. The Security Council consequently authorized Member States to take all necessary measures to protect civilians and civilian-populated areas under threat of attack in Libya, including the city of Benghazi, while excluding a foreign occupation force of any form or on any part of Libyan territory.[67]

Revisiting the Sources of International Law

This final section reviews the extent to which each of the three main sources of international law – treaties, custom and general principles – can contribute to the protection of the common interest.

Although treaty law is dependent on individual State consent, it remains the source most frequently used in current international law for the protection of the common interest. Initial treaties relevant to the common interest legislated for areas beyond national jurisdiction, establishing a variety of regimes focusing either on user rights or on global management.

Of all sources of international law, treaties provide the most adequate tools for clearly determining the responsibility of each State party in the context of a common interest regime. Most treaties concerned with the common interest acknowledge the territorial sovereignty of States. In these treaties, however, sovereignty is not only understood as decision-making power, but also as responsibility. The sovereign State is under a duty to protect the common interest on its territory as a custodian acting on behalf of the international community. Other State parties have the right to monitor and criticize the State's conduct, but they also accept the duty to assist the State (through various means) in circumstances defined by the treaty.

Apart from distinguishing between the responsibilities of the State exercising territorial sovereignty and the responsibilities of other States, treaties may also differentiate among the

67 UN Security Council resolution 1973 (17 March 2011), par. 4.

States exercising territorial sovereignty – usually on the basis of a categorization of countrie as either developed or developing. As there is no general definition of these categories i international law, and as the relevance of the developing/developed country dichotomy to th protection of the specific common interest that the treaty aims to protect may be disputed, th creation of non-uniform obligations and the linkage between these obligations and duties o assistance by other States remain controversial. Decisions on treaty-making on these issue are very much ad hoc.

Treaties create international organizations or bodies that may be intergovernmental i nature or consist of experts. Treaty bodies take on an existence that is separate from the Stat parties to the treaties. They are somewhat removed from the State parties' national interests and thus potentially well-geared to promote a common interest perspective. Typically suc international bodies take up both monitoring and technical/financial assistance functions. I the area of peace and security, their role extends to sanctions and the use of armed force.

Treaties are not useful tools for directly creating responsibilities for private actors, sinc treaties are not accessible to these actors. This is problematic to the extent that the protection o common interests may require an effort by the international community as a whole, includin both public and private actors. Treaties do, however, provide for State obligations to regulat the behaviour of private actors, mainly through domestic law. A clear example from the la of the sea is the requirement that States ensure that masters of a ship flying their flag abide b the duty to provide assistance to persons in distress at sea, without regard to their nationalit status or the circumstances in which they are found.[68] The treaty provision creates a Stat obligation, but the primary addressee of the norm is a private actor who is responsible unde domestic law.

It should be noted, however, that Article 3 of the Vienna Convention on the Law o Treaties (23 May 1969) explicitly provides that international agreements concluded betwee States and other subjects of international law or between such other subjects can have leg force in international law. Subjects of international law are defined as entities capable o possessing rights and duties in international, and having the capacity to maintain rights (an to be held responsible for their duties) at the international level.[69] Both rights and duties an standing will however usually be provided in agreements, so the reference to subjects i Article 3 VCLT is somewhat circular. In recent literature therefore, the trend is to give priorit to the autonomy of the parties to determine the applicable law (Lindblom, 2005, p. 492). I agreements with non-State actors are placed under international law, then they will govern by international law, even if these agreements are technically not treaties.[70] Such agreement involving non State actors are binding under international law if the parties intended to creat obligations under international law. The intention of the parties will need to be shown by th terms of the instrument and the circumstances of conclusion (cf. Aust, 2010, pp. 53–5). I

[68] See, for instance, Chapter V, Regulation 33, par. 1, International Convention for the safety of li at sea (1 November 1974), 1184 UNTS 3 and article 98, par. 1 United Nations Convention on the law the sea (10 December 1982).

[69] International Court of Justice, *Reparations for injuries suffered.* Advisory Opinion (11 Ap 1949), 174, 179–80.

[70] See International Court of Justice, *Anglo-Iranian Oil Co.*, United Kingdom v. Iran, Judgme (22 July1952), 112.

short, if the conclusion of multi-stakeholder agreements proves a necessity for the protection of global interests in the future, such agreements can have legal force under international law, if the parties so desire. Multi-stakeholder agreements may become more frequent as a result of a move away from a purely intergovernmental diplomacy to a diplomacy that involves all relevant stakeholders. Today, international multi-stakeholder instruments that include private parties are mostly of a soft law nature.[71]

Customary international law, building on the twin elements of substantial State practice and the recognition that the practice amounts to a binding obligation (*opinio juris*) also has a role to play in the protection of the common interest. As shown above, customary law is particularly relevant in the context of the permissibility of establishing universal jurisdiction for international crimes – an area where the international rule is created as a consequence of the cumulative effect of decisions to exercise universal jurisdiction taken at the domestic level.

Nevertheless, establishing the existence of a customary law in the context of the protection of the common interest remains a cumbersome process, and one that is open to a divergence of views. The O'Keefe/Francioni discord (included in this Reader) – on whether a State's duty during peace time to preserve the world's heritage on its territory has now evolved into a customary rule – offers a case in point. O'Keefe argues, in Chapter 16, that the duty has not evolved into a customary obligation owed to all States, because the practice of non-State actors (such as IGOs (including UNESCO) and NGOs) is irrelevant for the establishment of a customary rule; because even the near-universal ratification of the 1972 World Heritage Convention does not suffice; and because the diplomatic practice of States does not clearly demonstrate the necessary *opinio juris*. On the other hand, Francioni, in Chapter 15, criticizes O'Keefe's view as being reductionist and too State-oriented. The disagreement shows that the use of an argument based on customary law vis-à-vis a State that has not consented to a treaty obligation to protect a common interest, may be far from straightforward.

General principles of law, when interpreted along the lines suggested by Voigt, may offer a more promising avenue. General principles can be derived not only from the opinions of States, but also of intergovernmental and non-governmental actors that are directly concerned with protecting the common interest. Soft law instruments that are drafted with the participation of non-State actors are relevant in determining the content of these general principles. As a further step, the application of general principles could also be extended to all actors, whether public or private, that have contributed to their emergence.[72] In such an approach, the finding that 'the responsibility to respect human rights is a global standard of expected conduct for

[71] An interesting hybrid is the Global Fund to Fight Aids, Tuberculosis and Malaria. According to Article 1 of its By-Laws (as amended 21 November 2011), the Fund is 'a multi-stakeholder international financing institution duly formed as a non-profit foundation under the laws of Switzerland and recognized as an international organization by various national governments'. Voting members include both developing and developed States, and actors from civil society and the private sector.

[72] In its advisory opinion on Interpretation of the agreement of 25 March 1951 between the WHO and Egypt, the International Court of Justice accepted that as subjects of international law, international organisations were bound by 'any obligation incumbent upon them under general rules of international law'. See International Court of Justice, Interpretation of the Agreement of 25 March 1951 between the WHO and Egypt. Advisory opinion, *I.C.J. Reports* 1980, 89–90.

all business enterprises wherever they operate'.[73] would suffice for the establishment of an international obligation of companies to respect human right. The process of discovery of general principles depends to a large extent on judicial intervention.

The major benefit of general principles of law is that they enable the integration of otherwise fragmented areas of international law. Issues of common concern are often impacted upon by conflicting norms in different areas of international law, and therefore they stand to benefit from protection through the mechanism of general principles.

When a global interest cannot be sufficiently protected through balancing principles, reliance on *jus cogens* norms serves as a last resort. According to Article 53 of the Vienna Convention on the Law of Treaties (23 May 1969), the effect of a *jus cogens* norm is to invalidate the treaty that conflicts with the norm. In Chapter 4, Michael Byers offers a more general description of the term as norms that limit the ability of States to create or change rules of international law, and prevent States from violating fundamental rules of international public policy, when the resulting rules or violations of rules would be seriously detrimental to the international legal system and how that system, and the society it serves, define themselves. The Vienna Convention does not list the norms that fall within the *jus cogens* category, but some of the generally accepted examples of *jus cogens* norms relate to common concerns discussed above, such as the prohibition on the use of genocide, slavery, racial discrimination, torture and crimes against humanity.

The final chapters in this volume return to the theme of whether international law's concern with global issues also serves the interests of the less privileged within society. In Chapter 21, Balakrishnan Rajagopol argues that international law should place much more significance on the consequences of particular legal rules and doctrines for those who do not have a voice or power in the legal system. International should be reinterpreted in order to account for their interests, and texts of resistance should find a place within the system of sources of international law. In his review of legal actions with regard to the Bhopal catastrophe in Chapter 20, Upendra Baxi brushes a bleak picture of the impact on the victims of a 'trade-related, market friendly and environmentally hostile human rights' global law. Nevertheless, he also discerns in the continuing movement of the Bhopal victims a new jurisprudence of human solidarity that is fully differential to the perspectives of the movements-on-the ground.

---

[73] The sentence is taken from the commentary to Principle 11 in The Guiding Principles on Business and Human Rights [contained in UN doc. A/HRC/17/31 (21 March 2011), and endorsed by the UN Human Rights Council in HRC resolution 17/4 (16 June 2011)]. In the view of the Special Representative of the Secretary-General on the issue of human rights and transnational corporations and other business enterprises, John Ruggie, the responsibility of corporations to respect human rights is 'not an obligation that current international human rights law generally imposes directly on companies, although elements may be reflected in domestic laws. At the international level, the corporate responsibility to respect is a standard of expected conduct acknowledged in virtually every voluntary and soft-law instrument related to corporate responsibility' (see UN doc. A/HRC/14/27, par. 55). In the approach to general principles proposed above, a standard of expected conduct in every voluntary and soft-law instrument, endorsed by international organizations and incorporated in the domestic legislation of many states would suffice to establish an international legal obligation.

Bibliography[74]

Aguirre, D. (2008), *The Human Right to Development in a Globalized World* Aldershot: Ashgate.

Arendt, H. ([1963] 2006), *Eichmann in Jerusalem*, New York: Penguin Books.

Aust, A. (2010), *Handbook of International Law*, Cambridge: Cambridge University Press.

Brunnée, J. (2007), 'Common Areas, Common Heritage, and Common Concern', in D. Bodansky, J. Brunnée and E. Hey (eds), *The Oxford Handbook of International Environmental Law*, New York: Oxford University Press, pp. 550–71.

Brunnée, J. (2007), 'International Law and Collective Concerns: Reflections on the Responsibility to Protect', in T. Ndiaye and R. Wolfrum (eds), *Law of the Sea, Protection of the Marine Environment and Settlement of Disputes: Liber Amicorum Judge Thomas A. Mensah*, Boston: Martinus Nijhoff, pp. 35–51.

Coomans, F. and Kamminga, M. (eds) (2004), *Extraterritorial Application of Human Rights Treaties*, Antwerp: Intersentia.

De Feyter, K. (2008), 'Towards a Multi-stakeholder Agreement on the Right to Development', in S. Marks (ed.), *Implementing the Right to Development. The Way Forward*, Berlin: F. Ebert Stiftung, pp. 97–104.

De Sousa Santos, B. and Rodriguez-Garavito, C. (2005), *Law and Globalization from Below*, Cambridge: Cambridge University Press.

Fastenrath, U., Geiger, R., Khan, D.-E., Paulus, A., von Schorlemer, S. and Vedder, C. (eds) (2011), *From Bilateralism to Community Interest: Essays in Honour of Bruno Simma*, Oxford and New York: Oxford University Press.

Fishman, J. (2010), 'Locating the International Interest in International Cultural Property Disputes', *Yale Journal of International Law*, **35**, pp. 347–404.

Gillman, D. (2010), *The Idea of Cultural Heritage*, Cambridge: Cambridge University Press.

Glanville, L. (2012), 'The Responsibility to Protect beyond Borders', *Human Rights Law Review*, Online Advance Access. Available at: http://hrlr.oxfordjournals.org/content/early/2012/01/23/hrlr.ngr047.short?rss=1 (accessed 15 February 2012).

Gondek, M. (2008), *Extra-territorial Application of Human Rights Treaties*, Antwerp: Intersentia.

Hakimi, M. (2010), 'State Bystander Responsibility', *European Journal of International Law*, **21**, pp. 341–85.

Hey, E. (2009), 'Global Environmental Law: Common Interests and the (Re)constitution of Public Space, *Iustum Aequum Salutare*, **1**, pp. 41–57.

Hirst, P. and Thompson, G. (2011), 'The Future of Globalisation', in J. Michie (ed.), *The Handbook of Globalisation*, Cheltenham: Edward Elgar, pp. 19–38.

Honkonen, T. (2009), *The Common but Differentiated Responsibility Principle in Multilateral Environmental Agreements: Regulatory and Policy Aspects*, Alphen aan de Rijn: Kluwer Law International.

Kaul, I., Conceiçao, P., Le Goulven, K. and Mendoza, R. (2003), *Providing Global Public Goods: Managing Globalization*, New York: Published for the United Nations Development Project [by] Oxford University Press, p. 44.

Lindblom, A.-K. (2005), *Non-Governmental Organizations in International Law*, Cambridge: Cambridge University Press.

[74] The bibliography includes materials for further reading compiled by Claire Buggenhoudt.

M'Baye, K. (1972), 'Le droit au développement comme un droit de l'homme', *Revue des droits de l'homme*, **51**, pp. 505–34.

Marks, S. (ed.) (2008), *Implementing the Right to Development. The Way Forward*, Berlin: F. Ebert Stiftung.

Marks, S. (2011), *The Politics of the Possible. The Way Ahead for the Right to Development*, Berlin: F. Ebert Stiftung.

Matz, N. (2002), 'Comment: The Common Interest in International Law: Some Reflections on Its Normative Content', *Heidelberg Journal of International Law*, **62**, pp. 17–19.

Michie, J. (ed.) (2011), *The Handbook of Globalisation*, Cheltenham: Edward Elgar.

Molenaar, E. and Oude Elferink, A. (2010), *The International Legal Regime of Areas beyond National Jurisdiction*, Leiden and Boston: Martinus Nijhoff.

Orford, A. (2011), 'From Promise to Practice? The Legal Significance of the Responsibility to Protect Concept', *Global Responsibility to Protect*, **3**, pp. 400–424.

Paulus, A. (2005), '*Jus cogens* in a Time of Hegemony and Fragmentation – An Attempt at a Re-appraisal, *Nordic Journal of International Law*, **74**, pp. 297–334.

Perraton, J. (2011), 'The Scope and Implications of Globalisation', in J. Michie (ed.), *The Handbook of Globalisation*, Cheltenham: Edward Elgar, pp. 60–86.

Pureza, J.M. (2005), 'Defensive and Oppositional Counter-Hegemonic Uses of International Law: From the International Criminal Court to the Common Heritage of Mankind', in B. de Sousa Santos and C. Rodriguez-Garavito (eds), *Law and Globalization from Below*, Cambridge: Cambridge University Press, pp. 276–7.

Salomon, M. (2007), *Global Responsibility for Human Rights: World Poverty and the Development of International Law*, Oxford and New York: Oxford University Press.

Sands, P. (2003), *Principles of International Environmental Law*, Cambridge: Cambridge University Press.

Sands, P. (2004), 'Sovereignty Bounded: Public Trusteeship for Common Pool Resources?', *Global Environmental Politics*, **4**, pp. 47–71.

Schiff Berman, P.S. (2005), *The Globalization of International Law*, Aldershot: Ashgate.

Segura-Serrano, A. (2006), 'Internet Regulation and the Role of International Law', *Max Planck Yearbook of International Law*, **10**, pp. 191–272.

Shackelford, S. '2009', 'The Tragedy of the Common Heritage of Mankind', *Stanford Environmental Law Journal*, **28**, pp. 109–69.

Shelton, D. (2006), 'Normative Hierarchy in International Law', *American Journal of International Law*, **100**, pp. 291–323.

Simma, B. and Paulus, A. (1998), 'The "International Community": Facing the Challenge of Globalization', *European Journal of International Law*, **9**, pp. 266–77.

Sklair, L. (2002), *Globalization. Capitalism and Its Alternatives*, Oxford: Oxford University Press.

Skogly, S. (2006), *Beyond Borders. States' Human Rights Obligations in International Cooperation*, Antwerp: Intersentia.

Stec, S. (2010), 'Humanitarian Limits to Sovereignty: Common Concern and Common Heritage Approaches to Natural Resources and Environment', *International Community Law Review*, **12**, pp. 361–89.

Svantesson, D. (2012), *Private International Law and the Internet*, Alphen aan de Rijn: Kluwer Law International.

Tams, C. (2005), *Enforcing Obligations erga omnes International Law*, Cambridge: Cambridge University Press.

Tuerk, H. (2012), *Reflections on the Contemporary Law of the Sea*, Leiden; Boston: Martinus Nijhoff Publishers.

Vasak, K. (1972), 'Le droit international des droits de l'homme', *Revue des droits de l'homme*, **51**, pp. 43–51.

Villalpando, S. (2010), 'The Legal Dimension of the International Community: How Community Interests Are Protected in International Law', *European Journal of International Law*, **21**, pp. 387–419.

Voigt, C. (2009), *Sustainable Development as a Principle of International Law*, Leiden: Martinus Nijhoff Publishers.

Woodward, R. (2011), 'Governance in a Globalised World', in J. Michie (ed.), *The Handbook of Globalisation*, Cheltenham: Edward Elgar, pp. 381–92.

World Commission on Environment and Development (1987), *Our Common Future*, London: Oxford University Press.

Part I
Conceptual Issues

[1]

COMMON CONCERN OF HUMANITY

DINAH SHELTON
Manatt/Ahn Professor of International Law
(The Geroge Washington University Law School)

Alexandre Kiss believed deeply in the interdependence of all persons and in the dependence of humanity on nature and its processes. In his lifetime, and partly through his work, he saw these beliefs spread and environmental protection emerge as a fundamental value of society. He concluded that, like other fundamental values in a society, environmental protection must be recognized as a common concern, and ensured through law, especially superior norms of constitutional or international law. While he was skeptical of the concept of jus cogens as it has been expanded by writers,[1] he accepted the need for recognition of fundamental substantive rules to protect the global environment in the common interest. This paper explores briefly the origin, recognition, and legal consequences of the notion of a "common concern of humanity."

1. Why and What is a Common Concern?

The phrase common concern of humanity is rich in implications. As an international law term, it is notable, first for what it does not include, which is a reference to states. It is rather humanity as a whole, the multitude of individuals whose concerns are at issue.[2] Justice Weeramantry, in his separate opinion in the *Gabcikovo/Nagymaros* case,[3] speculated that "we have entered an era of international law in which international law subserves not only the interests of individual States, but looks beyond them and their parochial concerns to the greater interests of humanity and planetary welfare…

---

1 See, e.g. EVA KORNICKER UHLMANN: State Community Interests, Jus Cogens and Protection of the Global Environment: Developing Criteria for Peremptory Norms. 11 *Geo. Int'l Envt'l L. Rev.* 101 (1998)

2 Contrast the definition of jus cogens, as set forth in the Vienna Convention on the Law of Treaties, as a norm recognized and accepted as such by "the international community *of states* as a whole." Vienna Convention on the Law of Treaties, art. 53 (emphasis added.).

3 Case concerning the Gabcikovo-Nagymaros Project (Hungary/Slovakia) 1997 ICJ Rep. 7 (25 Sept.).

International environmental law will need to proceed beyond weighing the rights and obligations of parties within a closed compartment of individual State self-interest, unrelated to the global concerns of humanity as a whole."[4] In fact, there are long-standing precedents reflecting the notion of common concerns or a global set of values and interests independent of the interests of states. The entire subject of "humanitarian" law rests on the concept of humans protected as such and not by and because of their nationality. The Martens Clause in the Preamble to the 1907 Hague Convention (IV)[5] is perhaps the best known early example of this idea, referring to "the laws of humanity, and the dictates of the public conscience" as the sources of principles of the law of nations. The development of human rights law to protect individuals beyond the context of armed conflict, and international criminal law, in which individuals are prosecuted for the most serious crimes against the international community, can also be seen as reflections of some common concerns of humanity.

What makes a concern a "common" one? Alexandre Kiss suggested it was the importance of the values at stake. This idea is also implicit in the Martens Clause and in the ICJ's recognition that erga omnes obligations arise "by their very nature" "in view of the importance of the rights involved."[6] Supporting this notion, it is suggested later in this paper that issues of common concern are linked to the recognition of erga omnes obligations and the formation of collective compliance institutions and procedures that reinforce the erga omnes obligations imposed in the common interest. Indeed, in its advisory opinion on the Legality of the Threat or Use of Nuclear Weapons, the ICJ implicitly recognized the existence of erga omnes environmental obligations on the part of states:

[T]he environment is not an abstraction but represents a living space, the quality of life and the very health of human beings, including generations unborn. The existence the general obligation of States to ensure that activities within their jurisdiction and control respect the environment of other States or of areas beyond national control is now part of the corpus of international alw relating to the environment.[7]

Certainly, the importance of an issue may make it a concern, but it does not necessarily make it a "common" one. Instead, it may be suggested that issues of common concern are those that inevitably transcend the boundaries of a single state and require collective action in response; no single state can resolve the problems they pose or receive all the benefits they provide. Harm to a matter of common concern is often widespread and diffuse in origin, making it difficult if not impossible to rely on traditional bilateral notions of state responsibility to enforce international norms. When that harm is mitigated, all or at least large parts of the community benefit.

Common concern is related to, but different from the concepts of commons areas and the common heritage of mankind. International law has long recognized that

---

4 Id. Separate opinion of Vice-President Weeramantry, at 115.

5 Convention (No. IV) Respecting the Laws and Customs of War on Land, with Annex of Regulations (The Hague, Oct5. 18, 1907), 36 Stat. 2277 (1911).

6 Case Concerning the Barcelona Traction, Light and Power Company, Limited (Belgium v. Spain), Second Phase, 1970 ICJ Resp. 3, para. 33.

7 Legality of the Threat or Use of Nuclear Weapons, Advisory Opinion [1996] ICJ Rep. 226 at para. 29.

there are common areas, like the high seas, Antarctica and outer space, which lie outside national boundaries, are not reducible to national or private appropriation, and where coherent and comprehensive regulation must be international. International law also recognizes certain resources, such as those on or under the deep seabed, as belonging to the common heritage of mankind by virtue of their location in commons areas.

Common concerns are different because they are not spatial, belonging to a specific area, but can occur within or outside sovereign territory. The 1972 World Heritage Convention uses the term heritage in referring to cultural and natural resources, but treats them as a common concern, not as common heritage. The preamble declares that certain natural areas or sites should be "preserved as part of the world heritage of mankind as a whole" but the Convention is primarily concerned with ensuring the duty of "the international community as a whole to participate in the protection of …natural heritage of outstanding universal value"[8] within the territory of states parties.

Environmental issues are common ones because they often cannot be managed effectively by national or regional efforts; moreover, environmental benefits and burdens are shared by all persons. The climate, the stratospheric ozone layer, the oceans, and indeed the entire physical world form an interdependent ecological system, much of which can only be protected at the global level, making it a common concern for all humanity. The modalities of protection and preservation are formulated in law and policy and enforced by national and international institutions.

2. Recognition of the Common Concern

During the second half of the twentieth century, states aimed to create a universal political organization to maintain international peace and security and improve the well-being of all humanity. This ambitious effort could only proceed by defining domains of common concern. The international recognition of human rights and fundamental freedoms constituted a first step of paramount importance in developing the concept of an international community built upon the fundamental values of humanity. Similarly, knowledge that the biosphere is the only known place in the universe where life is possible led to the emergence of protection of the human environment as a common concern of humanity.

The term "common interest" appeared early in international treaties concerning the exploitation of shared natural resources. The International Convention for the Regulation of Whaling (Washington, Dec. 2, 1946) recognized in its preamble the "*interest of the world* in safeguarding for future generations the great natural resources represented by the whale stocks" and that it is in the common interest to achieve the optimum level of whale stocks as rapidly as possible. Soon thereafter states began to recognize that it was in their common interest to take conservation measures to protect exploited fish stocks. The 1952 Tokyo Convention for the High

[8] Preamble, Convention for the Protection of the World Cultural and Natural Heritage (UNESCO 1972). See FRANCESCO FRANCIONI: Beyond State Sovereignty: The Protection of Cultural Heritage as a Shared Interest of Humanity. 25 *Mich. J. Int'l L.* 1209 (2004).

Seas Fisheries of the North Pacific Ocean (May 9, 1952) expressed the conviction of the parties that it would best serve the "common interest of mankind," as well as the interests of the contracting parties, to ensure the maximum sustained productivity of the fishery resources of the North Pacific Ocean.

Further international recognition of the environment as a "common concern of humanity" came with conclusion of the 1959 Antarctic Treaty (Washington, Dec. 1, 1959). Its preamble affirms that "it is in the interest of all mankind that Antarctica shall continue forever to be used exclusively for peaceful purposes." Article IX authorizes the adoption of measures for the preservation and conservation of living resources in Antarctica "in furtherance of the principles and objectives of the Treaty." The Antarctic Treaty system further developed with adoption of the Canberra Convention on the Conservation of Antarctic Marine Living Resources (CCAMLR) which made express reference to the "interest of all mankind to preserve the waters surrounding the Antarctic continent for peaceful purposes only."[9] The most recent addition to the Antarctic Treaty system, the 1991 Madrid Protocol on Environmental Protection to the Antarctic Treaty[10] achieved full recognition of the common interest. Its preamble expresses the conviction that the development of a comprehensive regime for the protection of the Antarctic environment and dependent and associated ecosystems is in the interest of mankind as a whole and for this purpose it denominates Antarctica a nature reserve, devoted to peace and science.[11]

Such evolution must be seen as reflecting awareness of the general depletion of natural resources and of the threats to the environment, awareness that is increasing the pressure to adopt broad measures in the interest of present and future generations. Even before the 1972 Stockholm Conference, the 1968 African Convention on the Conservation of Nature and Natural Resources had expressed the desire of the contracting states to undertake individual and joint action for the conservation, utilization and development of natural resources by establishing and maintaining their rational utilization for the present and future welfare of mankind.[12] With the words "future welfare" the temporal dimension of the common interest of humanity has appeared.

Other international environmental treaties similarly recognize the common concern of mankind. The 1979 Bonn Convention on the Conservation of Migratory Species of Wild Animals recognizes in its preamble that "wild animals in their innumerable forms are an irreplaceable part of the earth's natural system which must be conserved for the good of mankind ...[E]ach generation of man holds the

---

19 May 20, 1980, preamble, 19 I.L.M. 837 (1980). See also DANIEL VIGNES: Protection of the Antarctic Marine Fauna and Flora. The Canberra Convention and the Commission Set up by It. *In International Law for Antarctica*. (eds. F. FRANCIONI–T. SCOVAZZI) 1996, 159.

10 Oct. 4, 1991, 30 I.L.M. 1461 (1991). See also, LAURA PINESCHI: The Madrid Protocol on the Protection of the Antarctic Environment and its Effectiveness. In FRANCIONI–SCOVAZZI op.cit. 261.

11 See also the UN General Assembly Resolution on the Question of Antarctica, Dec. 6, 1991, G.A. Res 46/41, UN GAOR, 46th Sess. Supp. No 49 at 83, UN Doc. A/46/49 (1992) which implicitly expresses that Antarctica constitutes a common concern for all the states.

12 Algiers, Sept. 15, 1968, 1001 U.N.T.S. 3.

resources of the earth for future generations and has an obligation to ensure that this legacy is conserved and, where utilized, is used wisely."[13] The Convention on the Conservation of European Wildlife and Natural Habitats, adopted several months after the Bonn Convention joins the concepts of general interest and future humanity by recognizing that wild flora and fauna constitute a natural heritage that "needs to be handed on to future generations."[14] Similarly, the World Charter for Nature states that the preservation of the species and of the ecosystems should be ensured "for the benefit of present and future generations."[15] The World Charter opened the door for the 1992 Convention on Biological Diversity which explicitly proclaims the principle of common concern of humanity[16] by stating "the importance of biological diversity for evolution and for maintaining life sustaining systems in the biosphere," and by "affirming that the conservation of biological diversity is a common concern of humankind..." The Framework Convention on Climate Change similarly affirms in the first paragraph of its preamble that "change in the Earth's climate and its adverse effects are a common concern of humankind."

The formulations of the last two instruments are significant. It is neither biological diversity nor the climate in isolation that are common concerns. It is rather the conservation of biological resources and climate change and adverse effects therefrom that are a common concern. The theme of sovereignty and sovereign rights remains important to both conventions, but the language suggests recognition that international cooperation is necessary to address loss of biodiversity and climate change.

The inclusion of smaller areas in the common concern is seen in the Paris Convention for the Protection of the Marine Environment of the North-East Atlantic, adopted several months after the Convention on Biological Diversity. It recognizes that "the marine environment and the fauna and flora which it supports are of vital importance to all nations."[17] More recently, the UN Convention to Combat Desertification in those Countries Experiencing Serious Drought and/or Desertification, Particularly in Africa referred to "the urgent concern of the international community, including states and international organizations, about the adverse impacts of desertification and drought," although only some parts of the world are directly concerned.[18]

3. The Legal Implications of Recognizing the Environment as a Common Concern of Humanity

The notion of common concern leads to the creation of a legal system whose rules impose duties on society as a whole and on each individual member of the community. Almost all national constitutions proclaim fundamental human rights and freedoms

[13] June 23, 1979, 19 I.L.M. 15 (1980)

[14] Bern, Sept. 19, 1979, E.T.S. 104, EMuT 979: 70.

[15] Oct. 28, 1982, Res. 37/7, UN Doc. A/37/51.

[16] See on the replacement of the concept of "common heritage of mankind" by "common concern": N. SCHRIJVER: Sovereignty over Natural Resources, Balancing Rights and Duties. 246, 389 (1997).

[17] September 22, 1992, 32 I.L.M. 1069 (1993).

[18] Paris, June 17, 1994, 33 I.L.M. 1328 (1994).

and require the government to respect and ensure those rights. Increasingly, similar provisions are included to secure environmental protection. National regulatory systems are built upon this foundation. Again, common interest may be contrasted with common ownership.

National legal systems and international law have long recognized common ownership of or equitable interests in shared resources. The concept of *res communis* is a form of common ownership that precludes individual appropriation but allows common use of a resource. It contrasts with *res nullius,* which most systems extends to wild animals and plants. *Res nullius* belong to no one and can be freely used and appropriated when taken or captured; it is the absence of a common interest. The concept of common heritage of mankind, which emerged in the 1960s, is distinct from both earlier concepts, in part because inclusion of the word "heritage," connotes a temporal aspect in the communal safeguarding of areas or resources incapable of national appropriation. Based on this concept, special legal regimes have been created for the deep seabed[19] and the Moon.

The nature of the common heritage is a form of trust, whose principal aims include restricting use to peaceful purposes, rational utilization in a spirit of conservation, good management or wise use, and transmission to future generations. Benefits derived from the common heritage may be shared through equitable allocation of revenues, but this is not the essential feature of the concept. Benefit-sharing can also mean sharing scientific knowledge acquired in common heritage areas like Antarctica.

In contrast, the common concern, *l'intérôt général,* is a general concept which does not connote specific rules and obligations, but establishes the general basis for the concerned community to act. The conventions cited imply a global responsibility to conserve disappearing or diminishing wild fauna and flora, ecosystems, and natural resources in general in danger. Language to this effect can be found in the Oct. 30, 1980 resolution of the UN General Assembly on the draft World Charter for Nature, which asserts the "supreme importance of protecting natural systems, maintaining the balance and quality of nature and conserving natural resources, in the interests of present and future generations."[20]

The right and duty of the international community to act in matters of common concern must be balanced with respect for national sovereignty. States retain sovereignty subject to the requirements of international law developed to ensure the common interest. Other domains of international law, including trade and diplomatic relations, are instrumental to achieving this common interest of humanity. They do not constitute in themselves the ultimate goals of international society but are means to improve the moral and economic well-being of humanity as a whole. The terms of the United Nations Charter indicate that international peace and security must be coupled with

---

[19] See: UN, Division for Ocean Affairs and the Law of the Sea, The Law of the Sea, Concept of the Common Heritage of Mankind (1996).

[20] G.A.Res. 35/7 on the Draft World Charter for Nature, UN GAOR, 35th Sess., Supp.No 48 at 15, UN Doc. A/35/7, Nov. 5, 1980, 20 I.L.M. 462 (1981).

economic and social advancement of all peoples and individuals in order to ensure overall advancement of humanity. Respect for human rights, economic development and environmental protection have been unified in the concept of sustainable development as a common concern of humanity.

One avenue to explore is the link between common concern and *erga omnes* obligations. Both concepts relate to matters which touch the interests of people throughout the world. It may very well be that one of the consequences of denoting a subject a common concern of humanity is that it gives rise to *erga omnes* obligations that may be pursued by any party. At the same time, it must be recognized that traditional dispute settlement mechanisms are unlikely to be utilized to enforce such obligations. States rarely use them to pursue their own interests, and it may be idealistic to assume they will litigate in the broad public interest. Instead, cooperation in law-making has been coupled with innovative compliance mechanisms, as discussed further below.

The various treaties that refer to common interest have much in common. They do not establish explicit rules of conduct, but do limit states' freedom of action, even when other states rights are not directly implicated. Certain environmental harm is identified as of concern to all, widening the scope of *erga omnes* obligations and imposing a duty to cooperate, a duty that has shown itself to be enforceable. In the *Mox Plant Case* (Ireland v. United Kingdom), the International Tribunal on the Law of the Sea, in its order on provisional measures issued Dec. 3, 2001, *reprinted* 41 ILM 405 (2002), opined that the duty to cooperate is a fundamental principle in general international law, as well as one contained in the relevant treaty provisions, and that rights may arise therefrom which the Tribunal may protect. The ITLOS provisional order mandated that the parties cooperate to exchange further information about the environmental consequences of the proposed project and devise measures to prevent harm resulting from proceeding with the project.

In general, institutional and procedural arrangements are required to implement the duty to cooperate on matters of common concern. And indeed, various treaty regimes today reflect the specific requirement to cooperate and take action. The treaty regimes establish principles, norms, and procedures which evolve over time to ensure collective action and can be considered the institutional dimension of the common concern of humanity. They ensure that scientific knowledge, the views of non-governmental organizations and the business sector, and other technical bodies are taken into account. The participatory and transparent processes that exist in the best of the treaty regimes enhance legitimacy and the possibility of adopting effective responses to common concerns. The norm-creating process is supplemented by innovative compliance mechanisms and dispute settlement procedures. As Jutta Brunnee has described it "cooperative facilitation of compliance is the primary objective of the majority of existing compliance procedures."[21] This is certainly clear in the Montreal Protocol procedures.

[21] JUTTA BRUNNEE: Common Areas, Common Heritage, and Common Concern. In *Handbook of International Environmental Law*. (eds. BODANSKY–BRUNNEE–HEY) 2007, 550 at 571.

Conclusions

The emergence of environmental protection as a common interest of humanity has altered the traditional role of state sovereignty, what Louis Henkin calls the "s-word". At the very least, agreement that a topic is a common concern of humanity must mean that it is no longer in the reserved domain and under the exclusive domestic jurisdiction of states. By definition, a common concern requires international action and necessitates new forms of law-making, compliance techniques and enforcement. Other consequences include the importance of participation by non-state actors and management of environmental resources at all levels of governance. As international law continues to struggle with collective action in the face of the s-word, treaty regimes provide examples of practical action in the common interest to further those fundamental values that Alexandre Kiss held so dear.

[2]

Justice and the distribution of greenhouse gas emissions[1]

Simon Caney*

Department of Politics and International Relations and Magdalen College, University of Oxford, Oxford, UK

The prospect of dangerous climate change requires Humanity to limit the emission of greenhouse gases. This in turn raises the question of how the permission to emit greenhouse gases should be distributed and among whom. In this article the author criticises three principles of distributive justice that have often been advanced in this context. He also argues that the predominantly statist way in which the question is framed occludes some morally relevant considerations. The latter part of the article turns from critique and advances a new way of addressing the problem. In particular, first, it proposes four key theses that should guide our normative analysis; and, second, it outlines how these four theses can be realised in practice.

Keywords: equality; grandfathering; greenhouse gas emissions; justice; historical responsibility

Introduction

The scientific consensus is very clear that the continued emissions of high levels of greenhouse gases are causing fundamental changes to the earth's climate. These will lead to severe threats to fundamental human rights – including the human right to life, the human right to health, and the human right to subsistence (see Caney 2009c,d). There is, therefore, a moral imperative to prevent dangerous climate change from occurring. This, in turn, requires limiting the emission of greenhouse gases. Given that there must be a limit on the total volume of greenhouse gases emitted there is a paramount need to arrive at a fair way of distributing the right to emit greenhouse gases.

The importance of arriving at an equitable solution is recognised by the United Nations Framework Convention on Climate Change (UNFCCC 1992). As Article 3.1 states:

> The Parties should protect the climate system for the benefit of present and future generations of humankind, on the basis of *equity* and in accordance with their common but differentiated responsibilities and respective capabilities. Accordingly, the developed country Parties should take the lead in combating climate change and the adverse effects thereof. (UNFCCC, Article 3.1; emphasis added)

What, then, would be a fair way of distributing rights to emit greenhouse gases? I shall break this question down into two further questions – namely:

(1) What distributive principle should govern the distribution of the right to emit greenhouse gases? What is or are the fairest distributive criterion or criteria? Should it or they be equality or sufficiency or something else? (Q1)
(2) Which entities should possess emission rights? Who is entitled to possess rights to emit greenhouse gases? Should they be states or firms or individuals or some other entity? (Q2)

*Email: simon.caney@googlemail.com

These two questions do not, of course, exhaust the questions of justice that we face. Other important questions include:

(3) May emission rights be permissibly traded? (Q3)
(4) Is it permissible for some to receive additional emission rights through flexibility mechanisms such as the Clean Development Mechanism and Joint Implementation? (Q4)
(5) What would be a just procedure for deciding how greenhouse gas emissions should be distributed? (Q5)

In what follows I shall concentrate on Q1 and Q2 (though what I say will have implications for Q3 and Q4).

Background

Prior to beginning the analysis, it is worth making three preliminary points. First, it is helpful to provide an empirical background. Three salient facts should be borne in mind. The first concerns the historical record. The Pew Center on Global Climate Change reports that '[f]rom 1850 to 2000, the United States and the European Union were responsible for about 60% of energy-related CO_2 emissions, while China contributed 7% and India 2%'.[2] Furthermore, according to a recent report by Michael Raupach and his co-authors published in 2007, '[t]ogether, the developing and least-developed economies (forming 80% of the world's population) accounted for ... only 23% of global cumulative emissions since the mid-18th century' (Raupach et al. 2007, 10288). The second point concerns the current distribution of emissions. The Netherlands Environmental Assessment Agency (2008) reports that in 2007, the USA's per capita emissions were 19.4 metric ton CO_2, Russia's were 11.8, and the EU-15's were 8.6. China, which now emits 24% of global CO_2 emissions, emits only 5.1 metric ton CO_2 per person, and India's figure is 1.8. Developing countries thus have low per capita emissions. It is with these first two points in mind that we should draw attention to a third point – namely, that the greatest increases in greenhouse emissions are now coming from developing countries. Raupach and his authors report, for example, that 'the developing and least-developed economies ... accounted for 73% of global emissions growth in 2004' (Raupach et al. 2007, 10288). The Netherlands Environmental Assessment Agency (2008) further reports that '[i]n 2007, global CO_2 emissions increased by 3.1%, compared to 3.5% in 2006. China's emissions accounted for two thirds of this increase.' As stressed above, it is crucial that this point not be taken in isolation. China's cumulative and current per capita emissions are still a fraction of the cumulative and per capita emissions of North Americans and Europeans. Nonetheless, it is relevant for when we think of future emissions policies.

A second point: it is very important to put the question of the fair distribution of emissions into context. The prospect of dangerous climate change generates a number of different imperatives. First, there are a variety of different mitigation responsibilities. It is essential that there is (1) a reduction in the emission of greenhouse gases, (2) the creation and maintenance of carbon sinks, and (3) increased use of alternative energy sources and the creation and transfer of clean technology. Second, in addition to these mitigation responsibilities, there are also adaptation responsibilities. That is, there is a need to enable those who will be threatened by dangerous climate change to cope with the changes to which we are already committed. It bears noting here that mitigation and adaptation may not be sufficient. This entails that there is a third set of responsibilities – compensation responsibilities – that is, the responsibility to aid those whose rights have been violated by dangerous climate change. The full set of responsibilities is set out in Table 1.[3]

Table 1. Climate-related responsibilities.

Type of responsibility	Content of responsibility
Mitigation[1]	Lowering greenhouse gas emissions (M-1) Creating and maintaining greenhouse gas sinks (M-2) Developing and transferring safe and clean energy (M-3)
Adaptation[2]	Designing natural and social arrangements so that people are able to cope with climate-related threats and exercise their legitimate entitlements without loss (A-1)
Compensation	Making recompense for a failure to fulfil the responsibility to mitigate and the responsibility to enable others to adapt (C-1)

Notes: 1. The Intergovernmental Panel on Climate Change (IPCC) defines mitigation as '[a]n *anthropogenic* intervention to reduce the anthropogenic forcing of the *climate system*; it includes strategies to reduce *greenhouse gas sources* and emissions and enhancing *greenhouse gas sinks*' (Parry et al. 2007, 878).
2. This differs slightly from that employed by the IPCC. The latter defines adaptation as an '[a]djustment in natural or *human systems* in response to actual or expected climatic stimuli or their effects, which moderates harm or exploits beneficial opportunities' (Parry et al. 2007, 869). One very important limitation of the IPCC's definition is that it does not say what this adjustment in natural or human systems will achieve or enable people to do. It is instructive here to consider Gerald MacCallum's famous 'triadic' analysis of freedom. In his celebrated article MacCallum argues that conceptions of freedom can be defined as follows '*x* is (is not) free from *y* to do (not do, become, not become) *z*' (MacCallum 1967, 314). In a similar fashion one might say that adaptation enables an agent (*x*) to be protected from a climate related threat (*y*) so that they can do or become (*z*). This raises the question as to how we should think of (*z*). My proposal is that we define it as 'being able to exercise one's legitimate entitlements without loss'. If adaptation is successful people will be able to exercise their legitimate entitlements without suffering some kind of loss.

Now the point here is that a fair share of emissions should be seen in the context of a fair share overall. What matters is that the relevant actors bear their fair share of the total burden. Given this, it is misplaced to focus simply on an actor's emission rights in isolation from their other responsibilities. This is an important methodological point to which I will return later.

Finally, it is worth underscoring the importance of devising a fair distribution of the burdens of combating climate change. The necessity of preventing dangerous climate change is widely recognised. This view is, rightly, motivated by a concern for the potential victims of climate change. As such, it is concerned with what one might term entitlement-bearer justice; that is, its focus is on people's rights that are jeopardised by climate change. It is, however, also crucial to distribute the responsibilities to combat climate change fairly. This point is frequently overlooked. Many interesting and important policy proposals focus exclusively on the entitlement-bearer's concerns and do not explore the question of whether the sacrifices involved are distributed in a fair way.[4] This, however, is of fundamental importance. A policy that averted dangerous climate change would nonetheless be unfair if the duties to mitigate and adapt were unfairly distributed. It is not enough to devise efficient policy proposals, for they might be thoroughly unjust in their distribution of costs. We might term this second value 'duty-bearer justice'. This article is an attempt to make a contribution to the issues of duty-bearer justice: how should emissions be distributed?

Distributive criterion 1: grandfathering

Let us now consider various possible criteria for distributing emissions. I shall examine four different proposals. The distributive criterion that is most often applied in practice is 'grandfathering'. This has two features. It stipulates, first, that the fair share of emissions for any actor should be a function of its past share of emissions, and, second, that these emission rights should be handed out free of charge to these actors. As such, it is a particular kind of historical principle. The EU Emissions Trading Scheme (EU ETS) that came into effect on

1 January 2005 initially distributed emissions according to a grandfathering rule (though it is now moving towards an auction-based scheme). A partial commitment to grandfathering can also be found in the Kyoto Protocol. By requiring Annex I countries to make cuts with respect to 1990 levels, it takes the latter as an appropriate benchmark for the distribution of emissions (among industrialised countries). (Of course, its treatment of developing countries does not have a grandfathering component.) A commitment to grandfathering is also presupposed in any argument to the effect that everyone should make proportionate cuts in their greenhouse gas emissions. The latter assumes that the existing share of emissions is just but that the total level is too high and so cuts should be made that preserve the initial distribution of emissions.

No moral and political philosopher (to my knowledge) defends grandfathering, presumably assuming that it is unjust. Given, however, that negotiators for major emitters routinely invoke it and that it is also generally embodied in environmental policy making, it is worth discussing it, if only briefly. It is vulnerable to two serious objections. First, it is insensitive to people's needs and would lock members of developing countries into a permanent state of poverty and underdevelopment. Any adequate principle governing the emission of greenhouse gas emissions should take into account other ethical concerns and fundamental human rights. And it is implausible to deny that eradicating great poverty is an ethical concern of paramount importance. Persons have human rights to meet their most basic needs. At the moment, though, many lack those most fundamental human rights. The United Nations Development Programme reports, for example, that currently 20% of the world's population live on less than $1 per day and a further 1.5 billion people survive on $1–$2 per day; in addition to this, a third of preschool children and 850 million people in total suffer from malnutrition (UNDP 2005, 24). Many also lack adequate access to energy. Consider the situation faced by China and India – both countries which would be allocated low emissions on any per capita grandfathering rule. Shonali Pachauri and Leiwen Jiang report that '[o]f the world's estimated 1.6 billion people without access to electricity ..., over a billion reside in these two countries [China and India], most of them in India' (Pachauri and Jiang 2008, 4022).[5] They add that 'in India only about half of the rural population has access to electricity and close to 10% of the urban population also still lacks access' (Pachauri and Jiang 2008, 4033). Grandfathering would entail that both China and India receive radically fewer emission rights per capita than North American, Japanese and European citizens, and as such would thwart the former's legitimate interests in development and the realisation of fundamental human rights to meet basic needs.

Second, grandfathering runs contrary to another deeply held principle of justice – namely, the principle of historical responsibility. It is widely held that those responsible for creating an environmental problem should bear a commensurate cost. If, for example, some release toxic waste into a river or create a mess in the street we expect them to make good the harms they have created. Grandfathering, however, violates this deeply entrenched principle. It does not make those who cause a problem bear a corresponding burden. In fact, it remunerates people for behaviour that has caused the problem.[6]

For these reasons, we should conclude that grandfathering represents a profoundly unfair way of distributing emission rights.

Note, though, that to affirm that grandfathering is an unfair principle for the distribution of greenhouse gas emissions does *not*, of necessity, entail that policymakers motivated by a commitment to justice should reject a scheme that employs grandfathering. For that we need further argumentation. Consider two pragmatic justifications of grandfathering:

(1) *The longhaul argument*: this holds that it is necessary to include grandfathering at the start of a scheme designed to lower total emissions because the scheme can then be reformed over time to produce a more equitable distribution of emissions. On this

view, grandfathering is a necessary first step in order to move, after time, to a fairer distribution.

(2) *The priority argument.* This holds that humanity's most urgent priority is to avert dangerous climate change. It reasons that major emitters need to be involved in a programme of mitigation for it to succeed and that the major emitters will refuse to engage in any mitigation without grandfathering. Thus, it argues, we should accede to the demands of major emitters in order to secure people's entitlement to be protected from the threats posed by climate change.

One could endorse either of these arguments and still hold that the distribution of emission rights according to grandfathering is an unfair way of distributing such rights. A proponent of the first argument can accept that it is unfair but argue that it is a necessary price for attaining a fairer distribution in the end. A proponent of the second argument can also accept that it is unfair but argue that this is an acceptable price to pay because the goal of preventing dangerous climate change is more important. It does not deny (or affirm) that grandfathering is distributively unfair: it contends that in this case entitlement-bearer justice should take priority over duty-bearer justice.

To put the point another way round, it would be a category mistake to think that either of these pragmatic arguments could show that grandfathering is a fair distributive principle. The first argument concedes that it is not just because it endorses as a long-term goal an alternative putatively fairer distributive principle. It is thus predicated on the assumption that grandfathering is in fact unjust and should be rejected in the long term. And the second argument simply downplays the relevance of the issue of the fair distribution of greenhouse gases.

With these points duly noted, it is nonetheless worth adding that it would be inappropriate to endorse either pragmatic argument as they stand without any further comment. In the case of the *longhaul argument*, one would want to add that though a policymaker who endorsed this argument might be acting justly, the high emitters who insist that a mitigation programme must adopt a grandfathering principle before they will comply with it are acting unjustly.[7] Others can say, 'You/we had better give them (the major emitters) grandfathered rights because otherwise they will not join up and then there will be no prospect for arriving at an equitable emissions agreement. So, in the name of achieving justice, you/we had better agree to their requests.' However, those with high emissions cannot themselves employ the *longhaul argument* to argue that grandfathering is required by a commitment to justice. *They* cannot say that without granting grandfathered rights to major emitters it would not be possible to arrive at the fair outcome because *they* themselves could, by lowering their own emissions, arrive at the antecedently defined fair outcome. All they can say is, 'Give us the grandfathered rights otherwise we will not move towards a fair distribution (even though we could do so now)', and if that is the only reason they can give in defence of a scheme that grants them grandfathered rights, then they are evidently acting unjustly.[8]

Consider now the *priority argument*. The weak point in this argument is the assumption that preventing climate change should necessarily take priority over any possible distribution of the burdens involved in combating climate change. Suppose that one could avert dangerous climate change but only through systematic and extensive violation of human rights. There is a point at which the injustice involved in the distribution of burdens may be so great that it trumps the fact that the policy in question prevents dangerous climate change. The cure may be worse than the disease. This is not to deny that one may have to make some trade-offs between entitlement-bearer justice and duty-bearer justice. However, to do this one needs to have some idea of the fair share of those burdens (including the fair share of greenhouse gases). It is only with this in mind that one could gauge whether any proposed compromise represents an 'acceptably' unjust as opposed to an 'unacceptably' unjust price to pay.[9] The question as to what is a fair distribution of emission rights thus remains pertinent.

Distributive criterion 2: equality

Let us turn now to consider a second view. Many propose an egalitarian approach to greenhouse gas emissions (and in particular to carbon emissions). They hold that all persons have a right to emit an equal amount of greenhouse gases. This idea was given powerful expression by Anil Agarwal and Sunita Narain in their seminal 'Global Warming in an Unequal World'. They write that the earth's ability to absorb greenhouse gases is a 'global common' and they maintain that 'this vital global common should be shared equally on a per capita basis' (Agarwal and Narain 1991, 13). The egalitarian principle is also defended by Dale Jamieson, who writes:

> In my opinion the most plausible distributive principle is one that simply asserts that every person has a right to the same level of GHG emissions as every other person. It is hard to see why being American or Australian gives someone a right to more emissions, or why being Brazilian or Chinese gives someone less of a right. (Jamieson 2005, 231)[10]

A variant of the equal per capita principle is also affirmed in the proposal known as 'contraction and convergence' (see Meyer 2000).[11] This idea, which was developed by the Global Commons Institute, allows industrialised countries gradually to reduce their emissions and for developing countries gradually to increase their emissions until, after a transition period, everyone has the same emission rights as others. So although it seeks to realise a state of affairs in which everyone has the same emission rights, it proposes a transition period in which industrialised countries have a marked more-than-equal quota of emissions.

The 'equal per capita' view has considerable intuitive appeal. The global atmosphere is plausibly seen as a global public good and one might at first glance think that, as such, use of it should be shared out equally between all of humanity. This view is, however, vulnerable to a number of objections.

First, one puzzling aspect of this approach is that it fixes on one good (the ability to emit greenhouse gases) and treats it in isolation from people's access to all other goods. But why should we treat this one good separately from all other goods? Why not consider someone's entitlements as a whole, taking into account their access to all the relevant 'primary goods' (Rawls) or 'resources' (Dworkin)?[12] In other words, why should this one particular good (emitting carbon dioxide) have its own principle regulating it? Why single this out for special (equal) treatment? Why not put it into the general pot of all goods to be distributed and then have a distributive rule applying to the whole package of goods contained therein?[13] It is true that there are some goods (for example, voting rights) which we do think should be treated in isolation from the distribution of other goods, and which do have their own distributive rule. But this is because those goods have a special social significance (it would, for example, be humiliating to allocate some unequal civil liberties even if those with the lesser civil liberties were given some extra money instead), and the distribution of emission rights does not have this kind of social significance.

A second problem with the equal per capita approach follows from a point made by Amartya Sen. Sen has long argued that it is wrong for theories of distributive justice to focus on 'resources' or Rawlsian 'primary goods'. Sen's claim is that this is a kind of 'fetishism', for it wrongly focuses its attention on what has value only as a means to an end (Sen 1997, 366). The same can be said of focusing on emission rights. For the latter have value only as means to an end – what matters is people's ability to pursue various goals and to enjoy certain 'capabilities'. Emissions have value only insofar as they serve these goals. It is therefore implausible to focus on distributing one particular resource equally if doing so will leave people *un*equal in their ability to pursue various goals.

The importance of this argument to the issue at hand is apparent when we consider the fact that people have different needs. Some have a greater need of emissions because they are more physically frail or sick. Others have a need for greater emissions than others because they live in a cold and inhospitable climate. A regime of equal emissions is thus unfair on those with unequal needs.[14]

Third, a further, and related, flaw in the equal per capita view is that it ignores the fact that people have differential access to acceptable non-fossil-fuel energy sources. The capacity to employ fossil fuels is valuable as a means of creating energy, but given this, it makes sense to focus on people's access to energy as a whole, rather than their access to fossil fuels. Hence, if some have greater access to other acceptable energy sources then they have less need of fossil-fuel-based energy sources. (By an acceptable energy source, I mean one that [a] is neither dangerous nor too costly for the user, and [b] does not impose an unfair burden on others.)

The second and third considerations above are of considerable practical relevance. A recent analysis of the determinants of greenhouse gas emissions concludes that: 'geography matters when it comes to explaining variation in CO_2 emissions. Cold climates and the availability of renewable energy sources exert a statistically significant impact upon such emissions that is also substantively important' (Neumayer 2004, 39).[15]

A further, fourth flaw in the equal per capita approach is apparent if we consider the concept of mitigation in further detail. Reducing emissions matters, and has the significance it does, because it reduces anthropogenic forcing. It should be understood then as one kind of mitigation. However, as was stressed earlier, mitigation can take various forms. Recall the definition of mitigation by the Intergovernmental Panel on Climate Change (IPCC) (given above in Table 1) as '[a]n *anthropogenic* intervention to reduce the anthropogenic forcing of the *climate system*; it includes strategies to reduce *greenhouse gas sources* and emissions and enhancing *greenhouse gas sinks*' (Parry et al. 2007, 878). One can mitigate then either by reducing greenhouse gas emissions or by promoting greenhouse gas sinks. Given this, however, it is not clear why we should formulate a distributive principle for greenhouse gas emissions rather than formulate one that applies to people's anthropogenic forcing as a whole. Suppose, for example, that some support carbon sinks that absorb large quantities of carbon dioxide; why should they have the same emission rights as some who (though they have the opportunity to do so) do not engage in such a project? To allocate both groups equal emission rights is both theoretically unsatisfying (should not duties to mitigate be considered all together?) and unfair (some are engaged in more anthropogenic forcing than others). In short: isolating greenhouse gas emissions when our focus should be on anthropogenic forcing as a whole is a mistake.

This has significance not only when there are natural greenhouse gas sinks. Suppose the technology to create artificial trees that capture CO_2 from the air is developed.[16] Those who employ these devices might reasonably be able to argue that they are entitled to greater-than-equal emission rights because when their 'carbon capture' records are also taken into account they result in less anthropogenic forcing than that by other people (including those who emit less).

This fifth point can be developed further if we consider the other climate-related duties listed earlier. Table 1 draws attention to five kinds of climate change-related responsibilities. We have discussed the duties to create and maintain greenhouse gas sinks, but there is also the duty to incentivise and transfer clean technology. The latter is required in order to meet people's energy needs in a way which does not cause climate change and which does not also expose their users and others to other unreasonable risks. If people in industrialised countries are to cut their emissions and if people in developing countries are to develop without causing dangerous climate change, it is paramount that cheap, safe, clean technologies are developed and transported. There is thus a duty to bring about such technological innovation (M-3 in Table 1). And there are, moreover, duties to fund adaptation (A-1) and to provide compensation

(C-1). Given all this, it is appropriate to ask why we should focus on emission rights without taking into account the broader picture. If X engages in much more adaptation than Y, and/or develops clean technologies for others to use, whereas Y does not, then should this not inform the distribution of emissions?

Finally, it is worth noting that some versions of the equal per capita view start with the greenhouse gas budget and propose to divide that equally. This, however, is vulnerable to the objection that it wrongly ignores the historical record. As was noted in the section above entitled 'background', some countries, including the USA and those in Western Europe, have contributed disproportionately to the cumulative level of greenhouse gases because they have been emitting ever-increasing amounts since the Industrial Revolution. They have, moreover, derived great benefit from this. It thus seems quite implausible to ignore this historical record and distribute the remainder equally among humanity regardless of whether they enjoy the benefits produced by the previous 150 years of economic growth or whether they possess none of the benefits produced by the history of high emissions growth and are among the 20% living on less than a dollar a day.

At this point it is worth recording that some of the above criticisms are more intractable than others. In some cases, it might be argued, the appropriate response is not to jettison the equal per capita view but to revise it. To take one recent example, Steve Vanderheiden responds to the fact that some people have greater needs than others (which was raised in the second objection above (see pp. 130–1) but does not exhaust the point being made there) by defending what he terms a 'modified equal shares model' (Vanderheiden 2008, 226). This holds that 'subsistence emissions' should be distributed so as to meet everyone's basic needs and then remaining 'luxury emissions' should be distributed on an equal per capita basis (Vanderheiden 2008, 226–7, 249).[17] This would not fully meet Sen's concern with the 'fetishistic' character of focusing on resources, but would address the particular concern about poverty and would retain an egalitarian character. To take a second example, some respond to the final objection (see previous paragraph) by starting from the claim that each person has an equal per capita entitlement and then adjusting it to reflect their country's prior record of emissions.[18] One might, in similar spirit, retain a commitment to the equal per capita view and then revise it to reflect the fact that some have differential access to energy sources which do not emit greenhouse gases (replying to the third objection listed above).[19] Someone motivated by a commitment to the equal per capita view might also deal with some of the other objections by sticking to the equal per capita view (as duly modified in the light of the second, third and final objections listed above) and then deriving a separate principle to deal with the creation and maintenance of greenhouse gas sinks (thus responding to the fourth objection)[20] and a separate principle to deal with other climate-related responsibilities (thus responding to the fifth objection).

The resulting principle would no doubt issue in quite unequal allocations of greenhouse gases but can legitimately be seen as a variant of the equal per capita view (if perhaps a distantly related variant) since it takes that as its starting point and then adds qualifications and supplementary principles.

Three points can be made about the proposal to adopt a revised equal per capita view. First, it is not clear that the equal per capita view can always be revised to meet the objections mentioned above. For example, the equal per capita view is a resourcist view and Sen's argument cited in the second objection gives us reason to reject resourcism. Second, the modified egalitarian principle would be tremendously complex and unwieldy and this is a considerable disadvantage. There is, however, a third much more fundamental problem. The problem is this: Even though it might be possible to adopt an approach that takes the form of '*(a)* equal greenhouse gas emissions + *(b)* revisions + *(c)* additional principles', this is not sufficient to justify taking such an approach. It does not show that it is desirable. We need a positive reason as to why this is an appropriate way of thinking about greenhouse gas emissions and other entitlements. Consider, for example, the first objection listed above. This remains unanswered and its challenge to the equal per capita view retains its bite against a modified equal per capita view. For it is not clear what the rationale would be for retaining a focus on equal greenhouse gas emissions (and then making the above additions and alterations), as opposed to abandoning the exclusive focus on greenhouse gases and concentrating instead on the total package of goods. To refer to the formulation above: there is no rationale for adopting component *(a)* – starting with equal greenhouse gas emissions. Consider now the fourth objection above. This too retains its force. Why one would want to have a separate principle for one kind of component of anthropogenic forcing (carbon dioxide emissions or greenhouse gas emissions more generally) and then a second separate one for the second component of anthropogenic forcing (maintaining greenhouse gas sinks)? It is peculiar to single out one aspect of anthropogenic forcing and then identify another one and treat them separately rather than consider them in conjunction. After all, they (greenhouse gas emissions and sinks) matter only insofar as they come under the heading of anthropogenic forcing. Consider finally the fifth objection. This also remains a forceful challenge. It might be *possible* to have one principle for the distribution of greenhouse gas emissions and then other ones (jointly or separately) for other aspects of mitigation, adaptation and compensation. But why do this? What is the rationale? Why not take an integrated view? To refer to the formulation above: we have no reason to adopt an approach that starts with *(a)* and adds *(c)*, as opposed to one that combines the distribution of greenhouse gas emissions with all other climate-related burdens and benefits.

In short: we have seen that there are a number of serious problems with the equal per capita approach. Many of the weaknesses share a common feature – namely, that the per capita approach focuses on greenhouse gas emissions in isolation from other goods and without putting matters into the relevant context. Thus we saw that the equal per capita approach overlooks the fact that principles of justice focus on people's overall package of goods and not on each individual component; it focuses on some people's entitlements without accommodating those with greater needs; and it focuses on one energy source without considering how inequalities in fossil fuel energy sources might be counterbalanced by inequalities in other energy sources. And we also saw that it overlooks the fact that the duty to limit greenhouse gas emissions is only one aspect of mitigation, thereby overlooking the relevance of differential support of carbon sinks. And finally we saw how it ignored the historical record.

Distributive criterion 3: historical responsibility

Thus far we have discussed two proposals for the equitable distribution of emissions. I now wish to consider a third. Many approach the question of the fair distribution of emission rights from a historical angle. They adopt what I shall call the principle of historical responsibility. This holds that the appropriate distribution of greenhouse gases should reflect the historical fact that industrialised countries have been emitting greenhouse gases since the Industrial Revolution. Drawing on this, they argue that the industrialised countries should make radical cuts and developing countries may permissibly increase their greenhouse gas emissions. One version of this is the proposal famously made by the Brazilian governmental delegation in the international climate negotiations in 1997 (Brazilian Party 1997).[21] This adopts a particular version of the principle of 'common but differentiated responsibilities' (UNFCCC Article 3.1; Kyoto Protocol, Article 10), apportioning differentiated responsibilities on the basis of a differentiated contribution to causing climate change.

Several objections might be pressed against the historical view:

(1) First, some might argue that humans did not have good reason to think that greenhouse gas emissions caused climate change until some point around, say, 1990. Prior to this time, the argument runs, people were excusably ignorant of the effects of their actions and it is therefore wrong to hold them morally responsible for those emissions. To make people liable for their emissions when they could not have known of the consequences of their actions is, this argument contends, deeply unfair on them.

Of course, this objection has little force against the most recent emission of greenhouse gases. It is not clear at what point we can say that ignorance about the link between greenhouse gases and climate change is inexcusable – 1990? – but this does not undermine the point that many greenhouse gas emissions have occurred in a period in which it was known that doing so would have harmful effects. In addition to this first point, two additional arguments can be made in reply. First, even when we lacked sure knowledge of the effects of the emission of greenhouse gases there was a long period during which many climate scientists argued that there was a not insignificant *possibility* that this could result in global warming. Accordingly, one might argue that major industries and governments of industrialised countries should have acted in a 'precautionary' manner. Clearly, however, they did not and so they may be required to pay for failing to adopt a sufficiently circumspect policy. Second, it bears noting that those who emitted high levels of greenhouse gases also benefited greatly from those emissions. One might grant for the sake of argument that the fact that someone's actions caused harm to others is not on its own sufficient to obligate them if they were excusably ignorant of the effects of their actions. However, the situation is different if they also benefit from the act that inflicts harm on others. The charge that it is unfair to burden them loses its force if they have gained considerably from the harmful activities and if one insists that the burden placed upon them should not exceed the benefits they have derived (see Caney 2009a in press).[22]

(2) Second, some might argue that it is fair to make people pay for the emissions which they caused, but, they add, many of the greenhouse gas emissions in the atmosphere have been emitted by previous generations – and not by them.

Although members of earlier generations who emitted greenhouse gases clearly cannot now pay for the cost, it does not follow that no one is duty-bound to make up for these emissions. For as a number of thinkers have argued, one might respond that this duty should be borne by those who are currently alive whose current holdings have arisen because of these past emissions. Since their wealth is built on this history of high emissions (and consequent overuse of a shared resource), they have a diminished claim on this wealth and may be liable to contribute to the costs of combating climate change (Shue 1999, 536–7; Neumayer 2000, 189; Gosseries 2004, 42ff; Caney 2009d).

(3) The first two objections are thus unpersuasive. A third point is, however, more significant. The principle of historical responsibility maintains that persons in the past used more than their 'fair' share and hence that their descendants should have a reduced quota that reflects the excess emissions of their ancestors. As such, however, it is a necessarily incomplete account of the fair distribution of emissions, for it presupposes an antecedently defined 'fair' share. It requires, that is, a second principle (or more) specifying what a fair share of emissions is. The principle of historical responsibility thus needs to be supplemented.

Many, but not all, of those who have affirmed the historical approach have assumed an equal per capita view and then sought to distribute emissions between people today on the basis of the level of emissions of their fellow-nationals in the past.[23] The principle of historical responsibility is not, however, committed to such a view about what constitutes a fair share. It simply requires some principle of fair shares – which might be that everyone has a sufficient amount of emissions to survive or that everyone has a sufficient amount to attain a decent standard of living.

This third point is *not* an objection to the principle of historical responsibility; it is simply a recognition of the fact that it is insufficient on its own to tell us how emissions should now be distributed.

(4) Let us turn now to one final question. The principle of historical responsibility requires us to identify who the actor is who is responsible for the emissions. This, however, is often not straightforward and raises complex issues about causation. Consider three cases. First, consider the case of firms that consume high levels of fossil fuels but then export the products (or services) to foreign consumers. Who is responsible for the emissions? One might focus on the process of production and ascribe the emissions to those who actually burn the fossil fuels or produce cement. On the other hand, one might argue that responsibility should be accorded to the consumers because it is their demand that, at least in part, leads to the process that causes emissions. We thus have a producer-based and a consumer-based approach. This is of considerable practical importance. For example, Bin Shui and Robert Harriss calculate that in the period from 1997 to 2003, '[a]bout 7%–14% of China's current CO_2 emissions were a result of producing exports for US consumers' (Shui and Harriss 2006, 4063). They further report that in this same period, 'US CO_2 emissions would have increased from 3% to 6% if the goods imported from China had been produced in the US' (Shui and Harriss 2006, 4063).[24] Moreover, in addition to considering the respective roles of consumers and producers, it would seem reasonable to ascribe some responsibility to government actors. Suppose, for example, that they could have passed regulations prohibiting the use of certain kinds of greenhouse gases but they chose not to. Presumably they are in part responsible for the resultant emissions. So the responsibility may be attributed to consumers, producers, and government officials – but how can we apportion it?

Consider now a second kind of case. Suppose that companies with their headquarters in one country locate some of their power plants in another country. Do we attribute the emissions to the owner of the companies? Or do we chalk them up to the countries in which the physical process resulting in emissions occurred? Or do we ascribe it to the consumers of the products?

Consider, finally, a third case. Suppose that a country hosts an airport which is heavily used by the airlines of other countries. Should the emissions be accorded to the country containing the airport or to the owners of the airlines or to the consumers?[25] My point is *not* that these problems are sufficient reason to reject any historical view, merely that there are some thorny issues concerning its application and that these need to be addressed.

Who are the rights-bearers?

Having considered three accounts of how emissions rights might be equitably shared, I now want to turn to the question of who should be deemed the rights-bearers. What kind of entities should own the permission to emit greenhouse gases – states, firms, individuals, humanity at large? It is striking that much of the discussion of climate change adopts a statist perspective, focusing on the aggregate emissions of different countries and treating states as if they were the rights-holders.

Before commenting on this statist approach it is crucial to distinguish between two separate questions. First, there is the philosophical question – what kind of entity (or entities) holds (or hold) the moral right to greenhouse gases? Are individuals morally entitled to emit greenhouse gases or is this moral right the possession of the state? Second is the practical question – what kind of entity should, in practice, be attributed the legal right to emit greenhouse gases? When designing legal and political systems for mitigating climate change (including, for example, carbon trading schemes), to whom should we accord the legal rights?

In what follows I shall assume that the answer to the philosophical question is that individuals are the moral right-holders. It is individuals who benefit from emissions and need access to energy sources (including fossil fuels) to meet their needs and pursue their conceptions of the good. Individuals have vital material needs (for heating, food, transportation, cooking and so on) that require energy sources, and these facts can help ground a right to energy sources (which for many requires access to fossil fuels). To hold that individuals are the owners of the moral rights to emit greenhouse gases does not, of course, commit one *either* to holding that the legal right to emit should be allocated to individuals *or* to denying that states should be accorded the legal right to hold these emissions. In what follows, however, I want to draw attention to three problems with according states the legal right to possess the greenhouse gas emissions of their members.

(i) First, we need a positive argument as to why states, as opposed to other entities, should be the (legal) rights-bearers. It is not self-evident that they should own emission rights. Consider, for example, the discussion of this issue by the highly distinguished climate economist, Michael Grubb. He starts by saying that 'every human being has an equal right to use the atmospheric resource' (Grubb 1992, 37; cf. also 40) but he then concludes that 'governments' should own permits (Grubb 1992, 34) and proposes that they should be allocated emission rights in accordance with their population size (Grubb 1992, 37–41). Clearly, however, an argument is required to show why such individualist premises yield the conclusion that states are entitled to pool all these individual rights. Suppose, for example, that someone says, following John Locke, that each individual has a right to decide how to use their labour power (Locke 1986 [1690], chapter 5, §27): it would obviously be grotesque to infer from this that their state has the right to sell this labour power to others and receive the benefits from the sale. If we start with a commitment to each individual's human rights then we need a very good argument to show why the state is then entitled to pool these rights and decide whether to sell these rights to others.[26]

(ii) Second, to treat states as the fundamental owners of emission rights (and to focus solely on ensuring that states receive a certain quota of emissions) ignores the vast differences in emission levels within states and can thus give a very misleading picture. Some developing countries may include some people who are high emitters and with a great ability to pay, and some Annex I countries may include some who are low emitters and desperately poor. Focusing on states does not enable us to pick this up. Consider, for example, the disparities that exist within China:

> Shanxi province, to the west of Beijing, is the leading consumer of coal, primarily for the production of coke, and has the highest per capita emissions in the country. Per capita emissions from China as a whole have risen to 1.1 tonnes C/person, but in Shanxi province, a leading coal producer, this rate is 3.3 tonnes C/person, equivalent to per capita emissions rates in Western Europe. (Gregg, Andres, and Marland 2008, 3)

Striking disparities also exist in the USA, India, and within European countries. To treat states as the owners of emission rights overlooks these important inequalities within states. It has the implausible implication that justice could be done so long as emission rights were shared appropriately between states – even if it is the case that some in a state may lack sufficient emissions to survive whilst others possess emissions of which they have no need. Treating states as (legal) rights-holders thus comes at a moral cost.

(iii) Finally, and on a more practical note, to treat states as the owners of emission rights has morally problematic consequences. For example, the leaders of unjust states may simply use these carbon permits to enrich themselves and without any intention to benefit their own subjects. This point can be related to an argument developed by Thomas Pogge. Pogge has forcefully criticised what he terms the 'international resources privilege', where the latter is the practice whereby states recognise all other states as the legitimate owners of the natural resources in their own jurisdiction even if they are thoroughly unjust (Pogge 2008, 29–30, 119–21, 168–72). Now granting states this extra resource privilege (the ownership of emission rights) has two malign effects. First, corrupt leaders of some states can benefit themselves and further strengthen their position. Second, there is a high chance the poor in their country may receive neither the emissions nor the revenues generated. If there is a system of carbon trading which allocates rights to states it would allow some unjust states to deprive their own people of emission rights and sell the rights to foreigners (for related concerns, see Nordhaus 2008, 159–60).

For these three reasons, a statist approach to the distribution of emissions is profoundly troubling. Given a commitment to the moral rights of individuals, there is an urgent need *either* for reforms that improve the statist approach *or* for non-statist mitigation programmes that more reliably distribute emission rights (or the benefits of emission rights) directly to individuals.

An alternative approach: theory

Thus far I have criticised three different distributive criteria and have drawn attention to the problems in statist and individualist accounts of who should bear emission rights. In the next two sections I outline the beginnings of a new approach. This section outlines three normative claims. The next section outlines how the normative theory could be applied in practice.

The first thesis that I wish to advance holds that:

> **Thesis I: The Rejection of the Assumption that there is a Distributive Principle for everything:** The fact that there are activities which involve greenhouse gas emissions does not entail that there should be a principle of distributive justice specifying a fair distribution for these greenhouse gas emissions.

Thesis I is supported by two arguments. First, it is grounded in the more general point that it is wrong to suppose that if there is some 'stuff' then there must be a distributive principle that specifies a fair distribution of that stuff. There are many scarce resources – from plutonium to aluminium – but we do not think that there is a distributive principle that applies just to plutonium, say.[27] Second, and in addition to this, Tim Hayward has correctly pointed out that emissions of greenhouse gases have value because, and to the extent that, they contribute to a good – namely, they are involved in the creation of some energy which meets important human needs (Hayward 2007, especially 441–4 and 446–7). They do not have value in and of themselves; they only have value because they serve valuable goals. Moreover, fossil fuels are obviously not the only source of energy and they are substitutable by other energy sources (such as renewable energy). What matters, then, is that there is a fair distribution of energy. Therefore what we should seek are principles for the fair distribution of *energy use* (and its burdens) – not greenhouse gas emissions.

This first thesis sets the scene for a second thesis. This holds that:

> **Thesis II: The anti-Atomist Principle:** With the exception of some special cases, distributive justice requires the fair distribution of a combined set of goods. As such, the distribution of greenhouse gases (or energy use) can be fair if it is part of fair package of goods.

This second thesis states that there is no such thing as a fair distribution of greenhouse gas emissions per se. Rather, there are fair principles which govern a person's overall set of goods (one, but only one, of which is the good of engaging in activities which emit greenhouse gases). Thesis II stands opposed to the 'atomist' view which says that there must be a distributive principle for each benefit. It holds that a person's fair share involves a combination of different benefits (access to health, education, income) and burdens (arduous jobs, less income, hazards), but there is no uniquely best combination of them. In practical terms, this means that there can be unequal emissions if one person's shortfall with respect to emissions is made up by their greater access to either other energy sources or some other goods (and if the combination is reasonable).[28]

Note that Thesis II is *not* committed to holding that every good can be traded off against other goods. It allows that there are cases where this is impermissible.[29] One example, given earlier, is of voting rights. These should be distributed equally. One might also say that some access to the natural world is also not *substitutable* with other goods.[30] Thesis II simply contends that for many goods, including the ability to emit greenhouse gases, what matters is the fair distribution of the overall set of resources.

Let us turn now to a third, distinct, normative claim. My third proposed claim asserts that:

> **Thesis III: The Revenue Principle:** A fair distributive principle governing greenhouse gases need not take the form of, (a), distributing permits to emit greenhouse gases, and can take the form of, (b), distributing the revenues raised by selling greenhouse gases.[31]

The preceding theories have assumed that permits to emit greenhouse gases should themselves be distributed, but, as a number of other proposals have brought out, another approach is to distribute *not* the actual permits to use greenhouse gases but *rather* the proceeds from the sale of greenhouse gases. Four examples may illustrate this point. Consider first the example of the Permanent Alaska Fund. Article IX section 15 of the Alaska State Constitution specifies that a proportion of the revenues raised from a number of sources (most notably from the sale of oil) should be collected by the state and then each citizen of Alaska should receive an annual dividend.[32] Under this scheme, it is not the case that each citizen privately owns a proportion of the oil; rather, he or she owns a proportion of the revenue raised by the sale of the oil. A second example of the same kind of idea comes from Thomas Pogge. Pogge has argued that there should be a global resources dividend. Under this scheme, those who use natural resources should pay a small fee for doing so. These fees should be collected together under the heading of the global resources dividend and then the payments will be disbursed to all members of the world. Under Pogge's scheme, then, humanity might be said to have a claim on all the world's natural resources. However, Pogge does not interpret this to mean that the earth's natural resources should be shared among everyone. Rather, he interprets it, in line with Thesis III above, to mean that everyone should have a share of the revenues raised by charging for use of the earth's natural resources (Pogge 2008, chapter 8).[33] A third example can be found in the Commission on Global Governance's report, *Our Global Neighbourhood*. This too argues that there should be 'charges for use of the global commons' (Commission on Global Governance 1995, 220). Under this heading it suggests: charging for use of the ocean for sea travel and for fishing; charging for the permission to release non-toxic levels of waste into the sea; levying fees for the use of Antarctica; 'parking fees (or auction revenues) for geostationary satellites'; and 'charges for user rights of the electromagnetic spectrum' (Commission on Global Governance 1995, 220–1). In each case the proposal is not that all citizens of the world own a private share of the ocean or the electromagnetic spectrum or some other stuff. The thought is rather that humanity owns it as a whole and user rights can be charged or auctioned which then raise revenue for valuable goals. One other proposal made by the Commission on Global Governance is that fees be levied on air flight (Commission on Global Governance 1995, 220). This idea is developed in much greater length in my fourth illustration of Thesis III. For Benito Müller and Cameron Hepburn have proposed that there should be an International Air Travel Adaptation Levy (IATAL) (Müller and Hepburn 2006). This would involve charging a levy on air travel and the funds would then be devoted to adaptation. In short, then, a fair emissions policy may take the form of disbursing the revenues raised from selling permits rather than allocating permits. This point will be illustrated further in the next section.

Before doing so, however, I wish to introduce a fourth thesis. This additional thesis introduces a qualification to the preceding two theses. It states:

> **Thesis IV: The Subsistence Emissions Principle:** Each person is entitled to that level of emissions required for them to attain a minimal decent standard of living.

This claim holds that persons have a right to 'subsistence emissions' (Shue 1993). It thus endorses the proposal that there should be greenhouse development rights (Baer, Athanasiou, and Kartha 2007). Thesis IV is grounded in a recognition that everyone is entitled to a basic standard of living and that for very many this will require access to greenhouse gas emissions.[34]

Thesis IV qualifies the preceding three theses and sets parameters that they must all honour. Consider Thesis I: taken to its logical extreme, Thesis I suggests that *any* distribution of greenhouse gas emissions can be fair. And Thesis II similarly suggests that *any* shortfall in emission rights can be compensated for by having extra goods. There are, however, limits to both theses. Regarding Thesis I: at some point, *if a person lacks access to other energy sources*, then he or she will need to be able to emit a certain amount of greenhouse gases. Fairness thus requires some minimal standard of distribution of greenhouse gases. This point also qualifies Thesis II. In a world where many lack access to renewable energy sources, greenhouse gas permits are not perfectly substitutable. It is therefore not the case that *all* distributions of greenhouse gases are fair and it is also not the case that *all* shortfalls in emissions can be made up by the addition of other goods.

Consider now Thesis III: what Thesis IV shows here is that there are limits to the extent to which one can adopt option (b) rather than option (a). One might decide to sell a large proportion of the emission rights and then (in line with [b]) distribute the revenues among the members of the world. However, option (a) cannot be disregarded altogether. For many people (those without access to clean energy sources), there is a need for fossil fuels to meet their basic energy needs.

In short, then, I have argued that:

(1) everyone should have access to whatever level of greenhouse gas emissions is essential for a minimum standard of living (Thesis IV).[35]
    Once everyone has the emissions necessary to attain a minimum standard of living, then:
(2) there is no uniquely correct distribution of greenhouse gas emission rights (Thesis I);
(3) there can be different levels of greenhouse gas emissions for different persons if their overall package of resources (and the combination of resources) is fair (Thesis II); and
(4) distributive justice can be served by selling emission rights and distributing their revenues to individuals (Thesis III).

An alternative approach: practice

The last section advanced four key components of a theory of fair emissions. This section moves from theory to practice, and considers what this might mean in practice. I do so by outlining *one* way of distributing emissions which would satisfy Theses I, II, III and IV. I do not say that this is the only way of doing so, but I outline it to show that the abstract principles stated above can be translated into practice.

The model in question has the following features. *First*, it starts from a commitment to the cosmopolitan view that the atmosphere belongs to humanity at large. In the words of one of the leading proponents of the approach I am outlining, this approach 'recognizes the atmosphere as a "global commons" – a resource that is the common property of humanity' (Tickell 2008, 68). Or, as another puts it, 'the atmosphere belongs to everyone equally' (Barnes 2008, 56). On this view, the atmosphere does not belong to firms or countries or to any private individual. This constitutes its answer to Q2. In this respect it agrees strongly with the starting point adopted by proponents of the equal per capita view, for they too think of the world's atmosphere as a 'common resource' (Vanderheiden 2008, 104) and as a 'global common' (Agarwal and Narain 1991, 13).[36]

Second, the view to be discussed holds that an international body should determine a fair level of greenhouse gas emissions – a carbon budget – and that the size of this budget should decrease over time to prevent dangerous climate change. However, in contrast to all the views considered so far, under this scheme permits to emit greenhouse gases should be sold at an auction and those who wish to emit greenhouse gases, such as firms, must purchase permits to do so. This scheme thus employs what economists call an 'upstream' approach because the distribution (via auction) of permits takes place closer to the point of production. 'Downstream' systems, by contrast, distribute permits directly to consumers. We now then have an answer to Q1. Emissions are distributed at an auction to the highest bidder.

The *third*, and final, core feature of this system concerns the revenues raised from the auctions. For on this proposal, the proceeds raised are to be spent on efforts to combat climate change – funding mitigation projects, fostering technological development, enabling adaptation in developing countries and compensating those who have already been harmed.

This kind of approach has been defended at length by Oliver Tickell in his book *Kyoto2* (2008), and Peter Barnes has defended similar ideas in a number of publications (2001, 2006, especially Part 2, and 2008, especially Part 3).[37] Barnes gives a crisp formulation of his version of this approach in an article in *Science* co-authored with Robert Costanza, Paul Hawken, David Orr, Elinor Ostrom, Alvaro Umaña and Oran Young (Barnes et al. 2008). The latter defend what they term an 'Earth Atmospheric Trust' in which there is an ever-decreasing carbon budget and permits are auctioned off. On their view, half of the dividend should be distributed to everyone on an annual basis. The remaining half should be spent on combating climate change (through incentivising clean technology, developing renewable energy and funding carbon sequestration) (Barnes et al. 2008, 724).[38]

Let us turn now to the four theses introduced in the last section. Note, first, that the approach sketched above clearly accepts Thesis III. By contrast with the proposals considered earlier, it does not distribute emission rights to individuals so much as distribute *the proceeds* of selling emission rights to people. Note too that it honours Thesis I, for it does not treat greenhouse gases as a 'stuff' with its own distributive principle. Consider now Thesis II. This requires principles of justice to apply (in general) to people's overall package of goods (and not, in normal cases, to one single burden or benefit). The upstream auction will honour this principle because the revenues raised from the auction are to be spent (in part or in their entirety) on mitigating and adapting to climate change. By doing so they protect a number of different kinds of human interests – including life, health, subsistence, and autonomy. The auction scheme thus does not single out one particular good and apply a particular distributive principle to it. Rather, its use of revenues advances a number of different goods.[39] Finally, we can observe that this approach can be designed to honour Thesis IV. That is to say, it can exempt certain necessary emissions from the auction system. Alternatively, it can ensure that revenues from the auction are distributed to the least advantaged to ensure that they have access to the energy sources they need to attain a minimum standard of living. The scheme outlined above can, then, honour each of the four theses stated earlier.

More generally, this approach has a number of virtues. First and foremost, it simultaneously performs two tasks, for it both lowers the total amount of greenhouse gases being emitted, thereby contributing to the mitigation of climate change, and it also generates revenue which can be employed to fund adaptation and sponsor attempts that further lower anthropogenic forcing (Barnes et al. 2008; Tickell 2008). This is of vital importance because money is required to assist developing countries to adapt to the climate change to which the world is already committed. In addition to this, it is widely recognised that to prevent further climate change it is essential to develop and transfer clean technology to all, especially to developing countries. Without this, they lack the possibility of developing without contributing further to the problem. The revenues raised by an auction can thus be employed to fund (i) adaptation and (ii) technological innovation needed to engage in successful mitigation.

Second, this proposal avoids the problems that beset both individualist and statist accounts considered earlier. Allocating individual permits to all the world's citizens is utopian. However, as noted earlier, allocating permits to states is also morally problematic. One problem is simply that doing so treats states as homogeneous units, but emission levels vary enormously within states. Some states, like India, have a low per capita emissions level but nonetheless contain many people who are high emitters and who ought to pay. Allocating rights to states will not do anything to make sure that the highest emitters within that country pay the appropriate cost. It is true that a state might choose to do so but it might not. The auction-based scheme is, however, more sensitive to this issue. Since firms are likely to buy these emission rights they will pay the cost for their emissions and to the extent that the costs are passed onto consumers then those who choose to purchase will bear the costs of their decisions. The auction-based scheme is thus much more discriminating and nuanced.

Conclusion

There has been a long-standing debate about how emission rights should be distributed and to whom they should be distributed. In this article I have examined and criticised several leading approaches. In their place I have defended an alternative view that changes the terms of the debate. This both has sound normative foundations (see the section above entitled 'A Different Approach') and can be realised in practice (see 'An Alternative Approach: Practice', above).

Notes

1. This article was written while I held an ESRC Climate Change Leadership Fellowship (2008–2011) and I am very grateful to the Economic and Social Research Council (ESRC) for its support. The article has been presented as a paper at the conference on 'Ethics and Climate Change: Scenarios for Justice and Sustainability' at Padova (23–25 October 2008), at the Oxford-Princeton workshop on 'Global Norms and Global Justice' (30 October 2008), at the seminar at the Warwick Centre for Ethics, Law and Public Affairs (4 February 2009), at the Smith School for Enterprise and the Environment (23 February 2009), and at the 'Environmental Norms, Institutions, and Policy' seminar series at Stanford (5 March 2009). I am grateful to the audiences at these occasions and am particularly grateful to Robin Attfield, Göran Duus-Otterström, Dave Frame, Lauren Hartzell, David King, David Miller, Ed Page, Debra Satz, Steve Schneider, Kai Spiekermann, Zosia Stemplowska, Victor Tadros, Andrew Walton, and Andrew Williams for their questions. I owe a special debt to Bob Keohane, my commentator at the Oxford-Princeton workshop, and to Avia Pasternak, my commentator at Stanford, for their illuminating suggestions; to Aubrey Meyer for his helpful comments and discussion; to Don Maier for his lengthy written comments; to Narasimha Rao for advice about empirical material on India and China; and to Jay Gregg for helpful correspondence about measurements of China's carbon emissions.
2. Pew Center on Global Climate Change, 'Cumulative CO_2 Emissions'. Available at http://www.pewclimate.org/facts-and-figures/international/cumulative.
3. Table 1 is not fully comprehensive. A number of scientists and economists have proposed 'geo-engineering' solutions, so this should arguably be added to the set of responsibilities. Geo-engineering has been challenged on scientific and ethical grounds and so I shall set it aside here. I have discussed it elsewhere (Caney forthcoming).
4. See, for example, S. Socolow and R. Pacala's important and influential article (Socolow and Pacala 2004). This is not intended as a criticism of this important paper. The point is that before deciding whether to implement their proposal for 15 separate 'wedges' one needs to ascertain how the costs associated with this programme would be distributed and whether their scheme can be designed so that the burden is distributed equitably.
5. They cite the International Energy Agency (2002).

6. This historical principle should be distinguished from another historical principle that some might invoke to criticise grandfathering. Some might argue that if one group of people have already enjoyed access to a scarce good (in this case, using the earth's absorptive capacity), it is reasonable to require them to give way so that others can now have access to it. The thought is simply that standard accounts of the acquisition of some scarce resource invoke some kind of proviso. The best-known example of this kind of view is, of course, John Locke's 'proviso' governing the use of natural resources. See Locke (1986 [1690]), chapter 5 ('Of Property'), §27.
7. The point is expressed nicely by John Rawls's famous statement: 'to each according to his threat advantage is not a conception of justice' (Rawls 1999, 116).
8. My argument here is indebted to G.A. Cohen's critique of Rawls's treatment of talented people. Cohen first expressed this critique in 'Incentives, Inequality, and Community' (Cohen 1991), especially section 3 and Cohen's 'kidnapper' argument in section 4. The argument is restated in his recent *Rescuing Justice and Equality* (2008, chapter 1).
9. Of course some might seek to give more principled (as opposed to pragmatic) arguments for grandfathering, hoping to show that it is in fact a fair distributive principle. For example, some might try to defend grandfathering on the grounds that people are entitled not to have their expectations thwarted. For discussion, see Gosseries (2005, 297–301).
10. See also Neumayer 2000, 185–92, Singer 2002, 43; Attfield 2003, 179–80.
11. See also http://www.gci.org.uk/.
12. See Rawls (1999, 78–81) for Rawls's account of primary goods, and Dworkin (2000, 65–119) for Dworkin on equality of resources.
13. This point has also been forcefully made by Derek Bell (2008, 250) and David Miller (forthcoming). See also Caney (2009b).
14. See again Miller's (forthcoming) incisive critique of the equal per capita view.
15. See also Neumayer (2002, 7–12). It might be argued that those who live in hot countries also need high levels of energy to cool themselves. Neumayer (2004, 37–9) finds, however, that this is not the case.
16. See on this the discussions by Lackner, Grimes, and Ziock (2001) and by Keith, Ha-Duong, and Stolaroff (2006, 17–45). See also the discussion of the work by Klaus Lackner by Kunzig and Broecker (2008), especially chapters 14 and 15.
17. The terminology of 'subsistence emissions' and 'luxury emissions' comes from Shue (1993).
18. Neumayer, for example, starts from the claim that each person has a right to emit an equal per capita amount carbon dioxide but then seeks to adjust each person's entitlements in light of their country's 'Historical Emission Debt' (Neumayer 2000, 186). This presupposes that countries are a morally significant unit such that if a nineteenth-century Briton emits more than his allotted quota then a later Briton is entitled to a correspondingly smaller quota. Why 'nations' or 'states' should be the appropriate reference group is unclear. Which entities should be treated as the rights-holders of emission rights is discussed later.
19. Note that differential access to clean energy sources matters not simply in cases where it entails that people have unequal ability to meet basic needs. The issue is a more fundamental one: why should one equalise one energy source without regard to access to other energy sources?
20. Perhaps those who maintain greenhouse gas sinks could be given extra emission permits.
21. This proposal was referred to the Subsidiary Body for Scientific and Technological Advice (SBSTA). See Secretariat of the Subsidiary Body for Scientific and Technological Advice (2001).
22. For other versions of this third point, see Singer 2002, 34; Gosseries 2004, 40–1; and Baer 2006, 136.
23. Cf. Neumayer 2000, especially 186; and Bode 2004.
24. For further pertinent analysis of China's emissions embodied in international trade, see Wang and Watson 2007; Leggett, Logan and Mackey 2008, 14–16; and Weber et al. 2008. See also, more generally, Peters and Hertwitch 2008). For discussion of consumer-based and producer-based perspectives (and its application to Denmark), see Rothman 1998; and Munksgaard and Alsted Pederson 2001.
25. This third example was suggested by the FAQs section of the Carbon Dioxide Information Analysis Center (CDIAC). See question 11 (http://cdiac.ornl.gov/faq.html#Q11) and Tom Boden's response. Boden (director of CDIAC) writes, 'Many small island nations have military bases that are used for re-fueling or have large tourist industries. Who do you assign the emissions to; the US whose military planes are re-fueling on the Wake Island with aviation and jet fuel or the Wake Island?'
26. I am not saying that no argument could be given that could justify this pooling. My point is just that we need an argument for this inference. (I do doubt, though, that any human rights based argument could establish that the citizens' individual rights could legitimately be held by their state independently of how unjust and illiberal it is.)

27. I owe this point to Cameron Hepburn.
28. See, again, the points made by Bell 2008, especially 250–1 and 254; Caney 2009b; and Miller forthcoming.
29. See James Tobin's interesting discussion of 'specific egalitarianism' (Tobin 1970, 264: cf. further 263–77).
30. There have been extensive debates about whether the destruction of natural goods can be compensated for by the creation of human capital; for discussion, see Dobson 1998.
31. This possibility is noted by Axel Gosseries. He, though, does not explore option (b) and adopts an (a)-like approach (Gosseries 2005, 296). Gosseries says that (a) is closer to what is being applied by the Kyoto Protocol. It is not clear why, however, we should be guided here by what is actually happening in practice. Furthermore, if we are to be guided by what is occurring in practice, then it bears noting that recent developments in the EU ETS fit well with option (b) (see section on 'An alternative approach: practice'). Gosseries also suggests that (a) fits better with egalitarian thinking (2005, 296), but this is not self-evident. I can see no reason why egalitarians cannot endorse (b).
32. For information, see http://www.apfc.org/home/Content/home/index.cfm and https://www.pfd.state.ak.us/. The content of Article IX section 15 can be found at http://www.apfc.org/home/Content/fundlaw/constAndLaw.cfm. For further information about the Alaskan Permanent Fund, see Anderson 2002.
33. For a contrary view (and defence of his preferred alternative), see Steiner 1999.
34. In Henry Shue's nice phrase, emitting greenhouse gases is an 'avoidable necessity' (Shue 1995). It is 'necessary' because many people need to be able to emit greenhouses gases to achieve a minimum standard of living. And it is 'avoidable' because this necessity arises because major political and economic actors have designed and perpetuated an energy regime that it is heavily reliant on the use of fossil fuels. Those elites could redesign our energy regime in ways that are more energy efficient and utilise other energy sources.
35. This is compatible with some people being entitled to none where they have secure access to renewable energy sources.
36. For analysis of the global commons and the common ownership of the atmosphere, see Risse (2008).
37. See also http://www.earthinc.org/. For my own defence of an auction system, see Caney (forthcoming).
38. An auction scheme is also defended by Ross Garnaut in Garnaut (2008, chapter 14, especially 331–2). The case for auctioning permits to emit greenhouse gases has also been advanced by Hepburn et al. 2006.
39. One might go one step further and argue that the revenues raised should be spent wherever they would have the greatest effect. We thus face a choice between hypothecating the funds and using them to address climate change or spending them in those ways which result in the greatest benefit. The latter might seem to be the most rational. However, against this it is arguable that hypothecation produces stable supplies of money and, moreover, that spending the revenues on other areas will simply result in a decrease in the other funds being spent on those other areas. For good discussions of the rationale for hypothecation, see Müller (2008) and Oxfam and WWF (2008).

References

Agarwal, Anil, and Sunita Narain. 1991. *Global warming in an unequal world: A case of environmental colonialism.* New Delhi: Centre for Science and Environment.

Anderson, Jonathan. 2002. The Alaska Permanent Fund: Politics and trust. *Public Budgeting & Finance* 22, no. 2: 57–68.

Attfield, Robin. 2003. *Environmental ethics.* Cambridge: Polity.

Baer, Paul. 2006. Adaptation: Who pays whom? In *Fairness in adaptation to climate change*, ed. W. Neil Adger, Jouni Paavola, Saleemul Huq and M.J. Mace, 131–53. Cambridge, MA: MIT Press.

Baer, Paul, Tom Athanasiou, and Sivan Kartha. 2007. *The right to development in a climate constrained world: The greenhouse development rights framework.* Berlin: Heinrich Böll Foundation.

Barnes, Peter. 2001. *Who owns the sky? Our common assets and the future of capitalism.* Washington, DC: Island Press.

Barnes, Peter. 2006. *Capitalism 3.0: A guide to reclaiming the commons.* San Francisco, CA: Berrett Koehler Publishers.

Barnes, Peter. 2008. *Climate solutions: A citizen's guide.* White River Junction, VT: Chelsea Green Publishing.

Barnes, Peter, Robert Costanza, Paul Hawken, David Orr, Elinor Ostrom, Alvaro Umaña, and Oran Young. 2008. Creating an earth atmospheric trust. *Science* 319, no. 5864 (8 February): 724.

Bell, Derek. 2008. Carbon justice? The case against a universal right to equal carbon emissions. In *Seeking environmental justice*, ed. Sarah Wilks, 239–57. Amsterdam: Rodolphi.

Bode, Sven. 2004. Equal emissions per capita over time – a proposal to combine *responsibility* and *equity of rights* for post-2012 GHG emission entitlement allocation. *European Environment* 14, no. 5: 300–16.

Brazilian, Party. 1997. Proposed elements of a protocol to the United Nations Framework Convention on Climate Change, presented by Brazil in response to the Berlin mandate. (Item 3 of the provisional agenda of the seventh session of the ad hoc group on the Berlin mandate, FCCC/AGBM/1997/MISC.1/Add.3.). Paper no. 1, Brazil, presented at the United Nations Framework Convention on Climate Change (UNFCCC), May 30.

Caney, Simon. 2009a. in press. Climate change and the duties of the advantaged. *Critical Review of International Social and Political Philosophy* 12, no. 2.

Caney, Simon. 2009b. Justice, morality and carbon trading. *Ragion Pratica* 32, no. 1, (June): 203–27.

Caney, Simon. 2009c. Climate change, human rights and moral thresholds. In *Climate change and human rights*. ed. Stephen Humphreys. Cambridge: Cambridge University Press.

Caney, Simon. 2009d. Human rights, responsibilities and climate change. In *Global basic rights*, ed. Charles Beitz and Robert Goodin, 227–47. Oxford: Oxford University Press.

Caney, Simon. Forthcoming. Climate change, energy rights and equality. In *Ethics, energy and climate change*. ed. Denis Arnold.

Cohen, G.A. 1991. Incentives, inequality, and community. The Tanner Lectures on Human Values, delivered at Stanford, CA, 21 and 23 May. http://www.tannerlectures.utah.edu/lectures/documents/cohen92.pdf.

Cohen, G.A. 2008. *Rescuing justice and equality*. Cambridge, MA: Harvard University Press.

Commission on Global Governance. 1995. *Our global neighbourhood*. Oxford: Oxford University Press.

Dobson, Andrew. 1998. *Justice and the environment: Conceptions of environmental sustainability and dimensions of social justice*. Oxford: Oxford University Press.

Dworkin, Ronald. 2000. *Sovereign virtue: The theory and practice of equality*. Cambridge, MA: Harvard University Press.

Garnaut, Ross. 2008. *The Garnaut climate change review: Final report*. Cambridge: Cambridge University Press.

Gosseries, Axel. 2004. Historical emissions and free-riding. *Ethical Perspectives* 11, no. 1: 36–60.

Gosseries, Axel. 2005. Cosmopolitan luck egalitarianism and the greenhouse effect. *Canadian Journal of Philosophy* 31 (suppl. vol., 'Global Justice, Global Institutions'): 279–309.

Gregg, Jay S., Robert J. Andres, and Gregg Marland. 2008. China: Emissions pattern of the world leader in CO_2 emissions from fossil fuel consumption and cement production. *Geophysical Research Letters* 35, no. L08806: 1–5.

Grubb, Michael. 1992. *The greenhouse effect: Negotiating targets*. 2nd ed. Chatham House, London: Royal Institute of International Affairs.

Hayward, Tim. 2007. Human rights versus emissions rights: Climate justice and the equitable distribution of ecological space. *Ethics and International Affairs* 21, no. 4: 431–50.

Hepburn, Cameron, Michael Grubb, Karsten Neuhoff, Felix Matthes, and Maximilien Tse. 2006. Auctioning of EU ETS Phase II allowances: How and why?. *Climate Policy* 6, no. 1: 137–60.

International Energy Agency. 2002. *World energy outlook 2002*. Paris: OECD/IEA.

Jamieson, Dale. 2005. Adaptation, mitigation, and justice. In *Perspectives on climate change: Science, economics, politics, ethics*, ed. Walter Sinnott-Armstrong and Richard B. Howarth, 217–48. Amsterdam: Elsevier.

Keith, David W., Minh Ha-Duong, and Joshua K. Stolaroff. 2006. Climate strategy with CO_2 capture from the air. *Climatic Change* 74, nos. 1–3: 17–45.

Kunzig, Robert, and Wallace Broecker. 2008. *Fixing climate: The story of climate science – and how to stop global warming*. London: Profile Books.

Lackner, Klaus S., Patrick Grimes, and Hans-J. Ziock. 2001. Capturing carbon dioxide from air. Paper presented at First National Conference on Carbon Sequestration, May 14–17, Washington, DC, http://www.netl.doe.gov/publications/proceedings/01/carbon_seq/7b1.pdf.

Leggett, Jane A., Jeffrey Logan, and Anna Mackey. 2008. Congressional research service report for Congress: China's greenhouse gas emissions and mitigation policies. September 10. http://fas.org/sgp/crs/row/RL34659.pdf.

Locke, John. 1986 [1690]. Second treatise of government. In *Two treatises of government*. London and Melbourne: Dent.

MacCallum, Gerald. 1967. Negative and positive freedom. *Philosophical Review* 76, no. 3: 312–34.

Meyer, Aubrey. 2000. *Contraction and convergence: The global solution to climate change*. Foxhole, Devon: Green Books.

Miller, David. Forthcoming. Global justice and climate change: How should responsibilities be distributed? Lecture 2, Tanner Lectures 2008.

Müller, Benito. 2008. To earmark or not to earmark? A far-reaching debate on the use of auction revenue from (EU) emissions trading. Oxford Institute of Energy Studies EV43, November. http://www.oxfordenergy.org/pdfs/EV43.pdf.

Müller, Benito, and Cameron Hepburn. 2006. IATAL – an outline proposal for an international air travel adaptation levy. Oxford Institute for Energy Studies, EV 36, October. http://www.oxfordenergy.org/pdfs/EV36.pdf.

Munksgaard, Jesper, and Klaus Alsted Pederson. 2001. CO_2 accounts for open economies: Producer or consumer responsibility? *Energy Policy* 29, no. 4: 327–34.

Netherlands Environmental Assessment Agency. 2008. Global CO_2 emissions: increase continued in 2007. http://www.mnp.nl/en/publications/2008/GlobalCO2emissionsthrough2007.html. .

Neumayer, Eric. 2000. In defence of historical accountability for greenhouse gas emissions. *Ecological Economics* 33, no. 2: 185–92.

Neumayer, Eric. 2002. Can natural factors explain any cross-country differences in carbon dioxide emissions? *Energy Policy* 30, no. 1: 7–12.

Neumayer, Eric. 2004. National carbon dioxide emissions: Geography matters. *Area* 36, no. 1: 33–40.

Nordhaus, William. 2008. *A question of balance: weighing the options on global warming policies*. New Haven, CT and London: Yale University Press.

Oxfam and World Wildlife Fund (WWF). 2008. Cash to tackle climate change – the role of revenues from EU emissions trading scheme auctions, November. http://assets.wwf.org.uk/downloads/auctioning_revenues.pdf

Pachauri, Shonali, and Leiwen Jiang. 2008. The household energy transition in India and China. *Energy Policy* 36, no. 11: 4022–35.

Parry, Martin, Osvaldo Canziani, Jean Palutikof, Paul van der Linden, and Clair Hanson. 2007. Appendix I: Glossary. In *Climate change 2007: Impacts, adaptation and vulnerability. Contribution of Working Group II to the Fourth Assessment Report of the Intergovernmental Panel on Climate Change*, ed. Martin Parry, Osvaldo Canziani, Jean Palutikof, Paul van der Linden and Clair Hanson, 869–83. Cambridge: Cambridge University Press.

Peters, Glen P., and Edgar G. Hertwitch. 2008. CO_2 embodied in international trade with implications for global climate policy. *Environmental Science & Technology* 42, no. 5: 1401–07.

Pogge, Thomas. 2008. *World poverty and human rights: Cosmopolitan responsibilities and reforms*. 2nd ed. Cambridge: Polity.

Raupach, Michael R., Gregg Marland, Philippe Ciais, Corinne Le Quéré, Josep G. Canadell, Gernot Klepper, and Christopher B. Field. 2007. Global and regional drivers of accelerating CO_2 emissions. *Proceedings of the National Academy of Sciences of the United States of America* 104, no. 24: 10288–93.

Rawls, John. 1999. *A theory of justice*. rev. ed. Oxford: Oxford University Press.

Risse, Mathias. 2008. Who should shoulder the burden? Global climate change and ownership of the earth. Faculty Research Working Paper Series, Working Paper No. RWP08-075.

Rothman, Dale S. 1998. Environmental kuznets curves: Real progress or passing the buck? A case for consumption-based approaches. *Ecological Economics* 25, no. 2: 177–94.

Secretariat of the Subsidiary Body for Scientific and Technological Advice (SBSTA). 2001. Progress report on the review of the scientific and methodological aspects of the proposal by Brazil. Item 4 of the provisional agenda of the fourteenth session of the SBSTA, FCCC/SBSTA/2001/INF.2, July 10, Bonn, Germany.

Sen, Amartya. 1997. Equality of what?. In *Choice, welfare and measurement*, 353–69. Cambridge, MA: Harvard University Press.

Shue, Henry. 1993. Subsistence emissions and luxury emissions. *Law and Policy* 15, no. 1: 39–59.

Shue, Henry. 1995. Avoidable necessity: Global warming, international fairness, and alternative energy. In *Theory and practice: NOMOS XXXVII*, ed. Ian Shapiro and Judith Wagner DeCew, 239–64. New York and London: New York University Press.

Shue, Henry. 1999. Global environment and international inequality. *International Affairs* 75, no. 3: 531–45.
Shui, Bin, and Robert C. Harriss. 2006. The role of CO_2 embodiment in US-China trade. *Energy Policy* 34, no. 18: 4063–8.
Singer, Peter. 2002. *One world: The ethics of globalization*. New Haven, CT and London: Yale University Press.
Socolow, S., and R. Pacala. 2004. Stabilization wedges: Solving the climate problem for the next 50 years with current technologies. *Science* 305, no. 5686: 968–72.
Steiner, Hillel. 1999. Just taxation and international redistribution. In *Global justice: Nomos XLI*, ed. Ian Shapiro and Lea Brilmayer, 171–91. New York and London: New York University Press.
Tickell, Oliver. 2008. *Kyoto2: How to manage the global greenhouse*. London: Zed Books.
Tobin, James. 1970. On limiting the domain of inequality. *Journal of Law and Economics* 13, no. 2: 263–77.
United Nations Development Programme (UNDP). 2005. *Human Development Report 2005: International cooperation at a crossroads – aid, trade and security in an unequal world*. New York: Oxford University Press.
United Nations Framework Convention on Climate Change (UNFCCC). 1992. http://unfccc.int/resource/docs/convkp/conveng.pdf
Vanderheiden, Steve. 2008. *Atmospheric justice: A political theory of climate change*. New York: Oxford University Press.
Wang, Tao, and Jim Watson. 2007. Who owns China's carbon emissions? Tyndall Briefing Note no. 23, October.
Weber, Christopher L., Glen P. Peters, Dabo Guan, and Klaus Hubacek. 2008. The contribution of Chinese exports to climate change. *Energy Policy* 36, no. 9: 3572–7.

[3]

COMMON BUT DIFFERENTIATED RESPONSIBILITIES IN INTERNATIONAL LAW

*By Christopher D. Stone**

> [T]he majestic equality of the laws . . . forbid[s] rich and poor alike to sleep under the bridges, to beg in the streets, and to steal their bread.
>
> —*Anatole France*

The concept of "common but differentiated responsibilities" (CDR) is receiving increasing recognition in international law.[1] "Common" suggests that certain risks affect and are affected by every nation on earth.[2] These include not only the climate and the ozone shield, but all

* J. Thomas McCarthy Trustee Professor of Law, University of Southern California; cstone@law.usc.edu. This article is based on a paper originally presented at the Fourth International Symposium of the International Center for Environmental Compliance Assessment at Kagawa University, Takamatsu, Japan, (Dec. 13–15, 2002). The author would like to acknowledge the value of comments by Daniel C. Esty, Daniel E. Farber, David Freestone, Michael Guttentag, Gregory C. Keating, Bentley Macleod, Kal Raustiala, Todd Sandler, Eric Talley, David G. Victor, Jake Werksman, Mark Weinstein, and Farhana Yamin. Law students Michael Fern and Joseph Tadros provided valuable research assistance. The epigraph to this article is taken from ANATOLE FRANCE, THE RED LILY 91 (Winifred Stephens trans., Dodd, Mead & Co. 1925) (1894).

[1] Conventions that adopt the expression explicitly include the United Nations Framework Convention on Climate Change, *opened for signature* June 4, 1992, 31 ILM 849 (1992) [hereinafter FCCC]. Other conventions do not adopt the term, but do differentiate explicitly, including the Adjustments and Amendments to the Montreal Protocol on Substances That Deplete the Ozone Layer, June 29, 1990, 30 ILM 537, 541 (1991) [hereinafter Amendments to Montreal Protocol]. Several of the more veiled or encoded variants are illustrated in the United Nations Framework Convention on Biological Diversity, *opened for signature* June 5, 1992, 31 ILM 818 (1992) [hereinafter CBD]: for example, that each party do something "as far as possible and as appropriate," *id.*, Arts. 5, 7–11, 14; that the benefits of resources be shared "in a fair and equitable way," *id.*, Art. 15(7); and that for the purposes of financing, "[c]onsideration . . . be given to the special situation of developing countries." *id.*, Art. 20(7). *See generally* PHILIPPE SANDS, PRINCIPLES OF INTERNATIONAL ENVIRONMENTAL LAW 225–28 (2d ed. 2003); Duncan French, *Developing States and International Environmental Law: The Importance of Differentiated Responsibilities*, 49 INT'L & COMP. L.Q. 35 (2000); Daniel Barstow Magraw, *Legal Treatment of Developing Countries: Differential, Contextual, and Absolute Norms*, 1 COLO. J. INT'L ENVTL. L. & POL'Y 69 (1990); Lavanya Rajamani, *The Principle of Common but Differentiated Responsibility and the Balance of Commitments under the Climate Regime*, 9 REV. EUR. COMMUNITY & INT'L ENVTL. L. 120 (2000). Other conventions use close cognates. For example, the preamble to the 1982 UN Convention on the Law of the Sea, references "the special interests and needs of developing countries." United Nations Convention on the Law of the Sea, *opened for signature* Dec. 10, 1982, 1833 UNTS 397 [hereinafter LOS Convention]. In trade law, where conditions of trade access rather than provisions regarding public goods are typically at issue, "special and differential treatment" (S&DT) is ordinarily used. But even in the WTO context, CDR, in those terms, has made an appearance. *See infra* note 41. For a critique of S&DT, see Michael Hart & Bill Dymond, *Special and Differential Treatment and the Doha "Development" Round*, 37 J. WORLD TRADE 395, 395 (2003) (deeming "misguided and perverse" the theory that the economies of developing countries require sheltering from full application of liberalized trade rules; and arguing that differential trade treatment is "more likely to retard than aid economic development").

[2] The term thus has a common root with such international law expressions as "common heritage" and "common concern of mankind." Note that, at least under the FCCC, *supra* note 1, not every country that faces the *common problem* shares in a *common responsibility* to fix it. The Kyoto Protocol to the FCCC divides the parties into four groupings. Kyoto Protocol to the United Nations Framework Convention on Climate Change, 3d Sess., Dec. 11, 1997, 37 ILM 32 (1998), *available at* <http://unfccc.int/resource/docs/convkp/kpeng.html> [hereinafter Kyoto Protocol]. Annex II includes the Organisation for Economic Co-operation and Development countries. *See infra* text at notes 23–26. Annex I includes the Annex II countries, plus some countries in Central and Eastern Europe (CEE) and the newly independent states that resulted from the Soviet breakup. In 1995, the parties exempted non–Annex I countries from any new commitments (leaving, for example, reporting obligations untouched), but leaving further responsibilities to be divided among the richer (Annex I) parties exclusively. United Nations FCCC Conference of the Parties, 1st Sess. U.N. Doc. FCCC/CP/1995/7/Add 1, Decision 1/CP.1, at 4–6 (June 6, 1995) [hereinafter Berlin Mandate].

There is even a further qualification embedded in Annex B of the Kyoto Protocol that gives special consideration to the Annex I–listed "economies in transition." Annex B differs from Annex I by the addition of Croatia, Liechtenstein, Monaco, and Slovenia and the removal of Belarus and Turkey. The non–Annex I parties' "common

risk-related global public goods, including peace, public health, and terrorism. In reducing the mutual risks, all nations should "cooperate in a spirit of global partnership."[3] Responsibilities are said to be "differentiated," however, in that not all countries should contribute equally. CDR charges some nations, ordinarily the Rich, with carrying a greater share of the burden than others, ordinarily the Poor.[4]

The meaning of "differentiated" is problematic. In some manner of speaking, every agreement *differentiates.* In an ordinary contract, one side undertakes to deliver coal, the other, to pay for it. If a group of nations agree that each shall decommission the same percentage of its fleet, the *impact*, measured in tons or vessels, may be different, depending on the relative size of each fleet to begin with.[5] Nonetheless, differentiation in the CDR literature appears to be reserved for multilateral agreements that are nonuniform in how the undertakings are formally verbalized,[6] not in how they affect each party.

The arbitrariness of the distinction can be illustrated by comparing two hypothetical air quality conventions. In the first, the agreement, in its terms, orders curtailments in the ratio of 4:2:1, but the baseline emissions are such that the quantity that each party is required to eliminate is the same. The expressly differentiated ratio marks it as a case of CDR. In the second agreement, nations with different levels of emissions agree to reduce by the same percentage with the consequence of differentiated cutbacks, in tons, in the ratio of 4:2:1. One could certainly argue that the second treaty should be considered no less an illustration of CDR than the first, and drawn into a unifying analysis. Nonetheless, because virtually every convention will have different effects on different parties, it seems prudent to follow the literature and restrict our focus to agreements that display their disparities in their wording, leaving aside variances that show up only "incidentally" in impacts.[7]

We can comb through existing conventions to illustrate the several dimensions along which differential terms can be provided. An agreement can make differential substantive

responsibilities" are nominal, such as reporting requirements, thereby making the term somewhat misleading as applied to the FCCC. *But see infra* pp. 11–12 (discussing the possible obligation of the Poor to make low-cost abatement opportunities available to the Rich).

[3] The phrase appears in the Report of the World Summit on Sustainable Development, ch. I, pt. 2, Annex, para. 81, UN Doc. A/CONF.199/20 (2002), *available at* <http://www.johannesburgsummit.org/html/documents/summit_docs/131302_wssd_report_reissued.pdf>, *revised by* UN Doc. A/CONF. 199/20/Corr. 1 (2003) [hereinafter Johannesburg Declaration].

[4] Not all differentiating agreements favor the Poor. One example is the Washington Treaty apportioning total permissible capital ships among the United States, the United Kingdom, (525,000 tons each), Japan (315,000 tons), France, and Italy (175,000 tons each). Multilateral Limitation of Naval Armament (Five-Power Treaty or Washington Treaty), Feb. 6, 1922, Art. 4, TS No. 671, 2 Bevans 351 (entered into force Aug. 17, 1923) [hereinafter Washington Treaty]. The 1972 London Convention illustrates obligations adjusted by reference to the "scientific, technical and economic capabilities" of the parties. Convention on the Prevention of Marine Pollution by Dumping of Wastes and Other Matter, Dec. 29, 1972, Art. 2, 26 UST 2403, 1046 UNTS 120 (entered into force Aug. 30, 1975). Even within the framework of the FCCC and Kyoto Protocol, which generally soften demands on the poor, some comparatively rich countries, such as Kuwait, Saudi Arabia, and Singapore, have no emissions target while other comparatively poor countries, such as Greece and Portugal, do.

[5] Note that arms limitations agreements, like climate change agreements, are responses to the problem of providing a public good: a reduced risk of war and its damages.

[6] Some differentiations are arrived at as informal extensions of the original agreement, for example, the "burden sharing" in replenishment funds of the Global Environment Facility (GEF) and the International Development Association (IDA). *See* Global Environment Facility, Summary of Negotiations on the Third Replenishment of the GEF Trust Fund (Nov. 5, 2002), *at* <http://www.gefweb.org/Replenishment/Joint_Summaries/joint_summaries.html>; International Development Association, The IDA Deputies: An Historical Perspective (Nov. 2001), *at* <http://siteresources.worldbank.org/IDA/Resources/Seminar%20PDFs/deputS.pdf>. For informal (voluntary) differential contributions in the area of global public health, see Joint United Nations Programme on HIV/AIDS, *at* <http://www.unaids.org/html/pub/Governance/PCB01/Core_1995-2003_en_xls.htm>.

[7] Other scoping questions remain. What about a nation that agrees to the same standards as the other parties but is subject to a common understanding that it will not really be held to them? Is a nation that signs a nondifferentiating treaty subject to a reservation unilaterally bringing about a de facto CDR? I incline to regard both as CDR, but others may disagree. The questions are only definitional and will not affect the analysis.

requirements;[8] subject some parties to a more favorable compliance timetable;[9] permit special defenses;[10] make noncompliance, if not forgiven, overlooked;[11] or afford qualified nations financial and technical contributions, either to absorb the costs of compliance,[12] or as a precondition for their own participation.[13]

Although the term CDR is recent,[14] the practice of differentiating responsibilities in multilateral agreements is not. Differential demands appear no later than the Treaty of Versailles (1919) in which the International Labour Organisation (ILO) recognized "that differences of climate, habits and customs, of economic opportunity and industrial tradition, make strict uniformity in the conditions of labour difficult of immediate attainment."[15] The post–World War I naval agreements were explicitly nonuniform in the tonnage permitted national fleets.[16] In 1965, the Contracting Parties of the General Agreement on Tariffs and Trade (GATT) added provisions to encourage nonreciprocal trade concessions in favor of developing countries and even, in 1979, expressly enabled "differential and more favorable" tariff treatment.[17]

[8] *See, e.g.*, Washington Treaty, *supra* note 4; Treaty on the Non-Proliferation of Nuclear Weapons, July 1, 1968, Art. III(2), 21 UST 483, 729 UNTS 161 (entered into force Mar. 5, 1970) (imposing different obligations on non-nuclear-weapon and weapon-possessing state parties, for example, regarding the right to acquire special fissionable material); Kyoto Protocol, *supra* note 2; *infra* text at note 23. Kyoto Protocol Annex I parties have a joint goal (reduction of 5% of 1990-level emissions by 2008–2012), but the allocation required to meet the joint target is negotiated inter se and varies. Non–Annex I parties currently have no obligation to commit themselves to quantity limits. Annex II parties have further special obligations beyond those of other Annex I parties relating to the provision of financial resources, technology transfer, and capacity building. The European Union directive on combustion boilers, Council Directive 88/609/EEC, on the limitation of Emissions of Certain Pollutants into the Air from Large Combustion Plants, as amended, 1988 O.J. (L336), provides that four of the wealthier member states (Belgium, Germany, France, and the Netherlands) must reduce their sulfur dioxide emissions by 70% of 1980 levels by 2003; three of the poorer member states (Greece, Ireland, and Portugal) were allowed to increase their emissions over the same period by 6-, 25-, and 79%, respectively. *See* SANDS, *supra* note 1, at 337. Variations in demands are not always so express; they can be insinuated, for example, through clauses requiring performance "in so far as possible and as appropriate," or the equivalent. *See* Magraw, *supra* note 1, at 91.

[9] Article 5 of the Amendments to the Montreal Protocol, *supra* note 1, while not adopting the term "CDR" or a cognate, requires industrialized countries to halt production and import of chlorofluorocarbons (CFCs) in 1996, while developing countries, identified by their low levels of CFC and halon use (<0.3 kg per/cap), are given until 2002 to eliminate 50% CFC production and consumption, 2007 to eliminate 85%, and 2010 for complete elimination. Report of the Eleventh Meeting of the Parties to the Montreal Protocol on Substances that Deplete the Ozone Layer, Dec. 17, 1999, UNEP/OzL.Pro.11/10, *available at* <http://www.unep.org/ozone/11mop-report.htm>.

[10] LOS Convention, *supra* note 1, Art. 71 ("The provisions of articles 69 and 70 [establishing fishing rights for landlocked and geographically disadvantaged states] do not apply in the case of a coastal State whose economy is overwhelmingly dependent on the exploitation of the living resources of its exclusive economic zone.").

[11] The double standard is most discussed in the human rights area. *See generally* Oona A. Hathaway, *Do Human Rights Treaties Make a Difference?* 111 YALE L.J. 1935 (2002). *See also* Daniel Vice, *Implementation of Biodiversity Treaties: Monitoring, Fact-Finding, and Dispute Resolution*, 29 N.Y.U. J. INT'L L. & POL. 577, 631 (1997) ("State governments may feel that they can ratify . . . [environmental] treaties without fulfilling all of the treaty obligations, presenting the public image of an environmental commitment without having to dedicate resources to implementation.").

[12] *See* French, *supra* note 1, at 42–45.

[13] Article 4(7) of the FCCC, *supra* note 1, suggests that "[t]he extent to which developing country Parties will effectively implement their commitments . . . will depend on" receipt of financial and technology transfers from the developed country parties. Article 20 of the CBD, *supra* note 1, adopts the same requirement. *See* Mark A. Drumbl, *Northern Economic Obligation, Southern Moral Entitlement and International Environmental Governance*, 27 COLUM. J. ENVTL. L. 363, 367 (noting that demands by the South for financial and technological support as a condition of participation in international environmental agreements has become widespread).

[14] *See infra* note 22 and corresponding text.

[15] Constitution of the International Labour Organisation, June 28, 1919, Art. 427, 49 Stat. 2712, 2733–34, 225 CONSOL. T. S. 188, 385; *see also id.*, Art. 405.

[16] For example, under the Washington Treaty, *supra* note 4, Japan was limited to 60% of the tonnage allotted to either the United States or the United Kingdom.

[17] *See* General Agreement on Tariffs And Trade, *opened for signature* Oct. 30, 1947, Part IV, TIAS No. 1700, 55 UNTS 187. For the waiver of discriminatory tariffs (the General System of Preferences), see Decision of the Contracting Parties to GATT of 28 November 1979 on Differential and More Favorable Treatment Reciprocity and Fuller Participation of Developing Countries, GATT B.I.S.D. (26th Supp.) at 203 (1980). *See* Hart & Dymond, *supra* note 1, at 400–04 (maintaining that some differentiations proved counterproductive); *see also* GATT Art. XVIII (providing special dispensations for "contracting parties . . . the economies of which can only support low standards of living and are in the early stages of development"). Notwithstanding these exceptions, the overall thrust of GATT, as evidenced in Article I's national treatment mandate, is certainly toward uniformity.

Both the World Bank[18] and the United Nations[19] have adopted formulas for assessing individual members that significantly discriminate in their demands.[20]

The environment is emerging as the most fertile field for nonuniform obligations. The LOS Convention (1982) is permeated with special privileges for developing[21] and fish-dependent nations.[22] The landmark Stockholm Declaration of the United Nations Conference on the Human Environment (1972) endorsed "taking into account the circumstances and particular requirements of developing countries and any costs which may emanate from their incorporating environmental safeguards into their development planning and the need for making available to them, upon their request, additional international technical and financial assistance for this purpose."[23]

Consistently with the Stockholm Declaration, several ensuing multilateral environmental agreements (MEAs) began to differentiate in fact, without adopting the term. Among these are the 1991 protocol to the 1979 Convention on Long-Range Transboundary Air Pollution (LRTAP),[24] and, even more dramatically, the 1987 Montreal Protocol to the Vienna Convention for the Protection of the Ozone Layer.[25] The Montreal Protocol gave less-developed countries (LDCs) a grace period for coming into compliance, and established a fund to provide them with the incremental costs of implementation.[26]

The first unambiguous adoption by a multilateral environmental agreement of "common but differentiated responsibilities," in those words, was the United Nations Framework Convention on Climate Change (FCCC).[27] Article 3(1) provides that "[t]he Parties should protect the climate system . . . on the basis of equity and in accordance with their common but differentiated responsibilities and respective capabilities." In accordance with Article 3(1), the Convention has evolved along lines that allocate different responsibilities among different groups of parties. Under the Kyoto Protocol to the FCCC,[28] the Annex I parties (developed countries)[29] are obligated (as a group) to reduce their collective greenhouse gas (GHG)

[18] World Bank Group, General Information About Membership (Mar. 2003), *at* <http://www.worldbank.org/>.

[19] United Nations Association of the United States of America, The New UN Assessment Scale, *at* <http://www.unausa.org/programs/scale.asp> (last visited July 24, 2003).

[20] Moreover, even without express formulas, it appears that the "burden sharing" in furtherance of other agreements has evolved informally. *See supra* note 9.

[21] *E.g.*, LOS Convention, *supra* note 1, Arts. 61(3), 62(3), 69(4), 70(5), 82, 140, 144, 148, 150, 152.

[22] *See id.*, Art. 71.

[23] United Nations Conference on the Human Environment, Stockholm Declaration, June 16, 1972, UN Doc. A/CONF.48/14 (1972), princ. 12, *reprinted in* 11 ILM 1416, 1419 (1972) [hereinafter Stockholm Declaration]; *see also id.*, princ. 23, at 1420:

> Without prejudice to such criteria as may be agreed upon by the international community, or to standards which will have to be determined nationally, it will be essential in all cases to consider the systems of values prevailing in each country and the extent of the applicability of standards which are valid for the most advanced countries but which may be inappropriate and of unwarranted social cost for the developing countries.

[24] For example, under the 1991 Geneva Protocol to the 1979 Convention on Long-Range Transboundary Air Pollution Concerning the Control of Emissions of Volatile Organic Compounds or Their Transboundary Fluxes, U.N. Doc. ECE/EB.AIR/30 (1991), *reprinted in* 31 ILM 568 (1992), almost all signatories have taken on a commitment to reduce emissions by 30% from 1988 levels, and Hungary and Bulgaria have only committed themselves to "stabilize" at 1988 levels. *See* United Nations Economic Commission for Europe, Convention on Long-Range Transboundary Air Pollution: Executive Summary, *available at* <http://www.unece.org/env/lrtap/conv/conclusi.htm> (last updated Mar. 22, 2004).

[25] *See* Montreal Protocol on Substances That Deplete the Ozone Layer, Sept. 16, 1987, 1522 UNTS 3, 26 ILM 1550 (1987) (entered into force Jan. 1, 1989).

[26] *See* Amendments to Montreal Protocol , *supra* note 1, Art. 10.

[27] FCCC, *supra* note 1, Art. 3(1).

[28] Kyoto Protocol, *supra* note 2.

[29] *See id.*, note 2.

emissions at least 5 percent below 1990 levels by 2008–2012;[30] the non–Annex I (developing) countries are under no such obligation.[31]

This differentiation, in particular the failure to extract reduction commitments from China and India, became a basis for the United States to sideline itself from Kyoto and therefore from much of the FCCC regime's progress.[32] Interestingly, the sense of the Senate does not appear to oppose CDR in principle. In fact, many senators are agreeable to subjecting developing countries to less restrictive constraints, not ruling out even an *increase* in emissions over the commitment period, as long as they make *some* commitment on paper.[33] However, the eighth Conference of the Parties (COP–8) in 2002 ended with a declaration that clearly sidesteps any obligation by developing countries to declare emission targets, much less to reduce them.[34]

The FCCC regime has thus reached a stalemate—some would say collapse[35]—while the world continues to warm.[36] Disputes over the scope of CDR are a primary cause.[37] And while

[30] Notice that there are "differentials" even among the Annex I countries inter se. *See supra* note 2. Another sort of differential is illustrated by Article 2 of the Sulphur Dioxide Protocol to LRTAP, which provided for the parties to reduce their national annual sulfur emissions or their transboundary fluxes by at least 30% from 1980 levels by 1993; the same nondifferentiating percentage reduction may differentiate in terms of quantity or required level of effort. 1979 Convention on Long-Range Transboundary Air Pollution on the Reduction of Sulphur Emissions or Their Transboundary Fluxes by at Least 30 Percent, July 8, 1985, 27 ILM 698, 707 (entered into force Sept. 2, 1987). Depending on how we measure equality, the distinction between differentiating and nondifferentiating becomes ambiguous.

[31] *See supra* note 2. Indeed, Arts. 3(5)–3(6) of the Kyoto Protocol, *supra* note 2, displays further differentiation in providing the "economies in transition" listed in Appendix 1 with the option of selecting a base year from which to make reductions more favorable than 1990.

[32] *See* P. G. Harris, *Common but Differentiated Responsibility: The Kyoto Protocol and United States Policy*, 7 N.Y.U. ENVTL. L.J. 27 (1999). A secondary reason is the present administration's determination not to accept any measure that would undermine the U.S. economy. *See* Letter to Members of the Senate on the Kyoto Protocol on Climate Change, 37 WEEKLY COMP. PRES. DOC. 11 (Mar. 13, 2001) [hereinafter Bush Letter on Kyoto]. The *Weekly Compilation of Presidential Documents* is available online at <http://www.whitehouse.gov>. It is unclear what degree of emissions reduction, if any, the administration deems consistent with the economic welfare of the United States, or even whether, at this point, the United States would sign the Kyoto Protocol under any conditions.

[33] *See* Harris, *supra* note 32. President Bill Clinton intimated that it would be acceptable if commitments were made only by the "key" developing countries. *See* Rajamani, *supra* note 1, at 120, 120 n.1. In 2001, however, President George W. Bush omitted even these qualifications in indicating his determination to oppose the Kyoto Protocol "because it exempts 80 per cent of the world, including . . . China and India from compliance, and would cause serious harm to the U.S. economy." Bush Letter on Kyoto, *supra* note 32. A more current presentation of President Bush's position can be found in the Clear Skies and Global Climate Change Initiative, 38 WEEKLY COMP. PRES. DOC. 232 (Feb. 14, 2002). Developed countries fear that if they tolerate the LDCs' development to follow lax, environmentally destructive lines—possibly repeating the errors of developing countries—in fifteen or twenty years, when we hope that their economies will have changed, they may find bad habits hard to break. *See* Richard B. Stewart, *Environmental Regulation and International Competitiveness*, 102 YALE L.J. 2039, 2080 (1993); Michael Weisslitz, *Rethinking the Equitable Principle of Common but Differentiated Responsibility: Differential Versus Absolute Norms of Compliance and Contribution in the Global Climate Change Context*, 13 COLO. J. INT'L ENVTL. L. & POL'Y 473, 488–99 (2002). The environmental Kuznets curve argument suggests that with rising wealth, the LDCs will clean up naturally, but the effect is less clear when it involves remedying transboundary emissions.

[34] The final text can be found in the Eighth Conference of the Parties to the UN Framework Convention on Climate Change, 12 EARTH NEGOTIATIONS BULL., No. 209, *available at* <http://www.iisd.ca/linkages/download/asc/enb12209e.txt>. The *New York Times* reported that "the wording was a victory for the developing countries which fought hard to insure that the declaration did not include any possible future measures they might have to abide." *Proposal to Reduce Greenhouse Gases Loses Momentum*, N.Y. TIMES, Nov. 2, 2002, at A4. Farhana Yamin, a close observer of the FCCC negotiations, observed that

> many LDCs are very hesitant to accept targets because they feel they have too little control over their economies. Even more basically, they do not have the institutional capacity to monitor and track their own emissions. And of course, finally, many LDCs have not taken on more quantitative targets because they just want to see whether the LDCs meet their own targets—not very well thus far.

E-mail from Farhana Yamin, Fellow in Environment, Institute of Development Studies, University of Sussex, to Christopher D. Stone (Mar. 26, 2002, 09:24 PST) (on file with author).

[35] *See generally* DAVID G. VICTOR, THE COLLAPSE OF THE KYOTO PROTOCOL (2001), which provides a succinct critical examination of the breakdown at Kyoto and makes suggestions for getting the process back on a more realistic footing.

[36] *See Temperature in 2002 Warmer Than 2001; Underlying Trend Continues, Scientists Say*, 26 Int'l Env't Rep. (BNA) 37 (2003).

[37] Speaking at the closing plenary meeting of COP–8, Steen Gade, who headed the European Union delegation, quoted a statement from Samoa's representative: "We cannot just sit here through meeting after meeting, year after year, with one side of the room saying we cannot act alone, and the other side saying we cannot accept obligations." *Declaration Emphasizes Development Plan, Urges Swift Ratification of Kyoto Protocol*, 25 Int'l Env't Rep. (BNA) 1055

the FCCC is the most dramatic stage for CDR debate, the issues are not limited to climate change or even to the areas of global environment and resources. CDR is now being put forward by some developing countries—implausibly, I believe[38]—as a "principle" of international law[39] that should selectively relieve them from standards that the World Trade Organization may impose on the more developed countries.[40] A certain momentum is thus building, notwithstanding the charge that "this so-called principle" is neither necessary nor "helpful . . . [t]here [being] no agreement on what it means" and "no agreement on when it applies."[41]

I. The General Background

On first acquaintance, the wide appeal of CDR seems unsurprising. Is it not right that the law should subject the rich to higher demands than the poor? But a moment's reflection will show that the principle is neither universal nor self-evident. True, the rich pay a higher marginal tax rate than the poor. But differentiations in municipal legal systems are the exception. Poverty does not excuse theft. Domestic environmental regulations do not hold marginally profitable polluters to lower standards than their wealthy competitors.[42]

Why should our posture be different—that is, why should we differentiate more liberally—in the international arena?

To begin with the principles of "customary international law,"[43] I can think of none that *does* differentiate on the basis of wealth. Surely, the customary rules against piracy and abusing diplomats carve out no exceptions for the needy.

One might expect treaties and conventions to provide more fertile ground for differentiations because no nation can be compelled to join a convention; dangling "softer" commitments before marginally motivated parties is one way to broaden participation. The likelihood of nonuniform terms is increased in agreements, such as framework conventions, the details of which are typically worked out in sequential, multilateral negotiations—first for a broad general set of terms, then for increasingly detailed protocols. The complex, seriatim process should provide each potential party, particularly the *n*-th signer of a requisite *n*-party

(2002). Indeed, Article 3(9) of the Kyoto Protocol, *supra* note 2, appears to force opening negotiations on commitments beyond 2012, by 2005 at the latest. At this point, however, it is doubtful that the Bush administration would sign onto the Kyoto Protocol under any conditions.

[38] Daniel Bodansky, *The United Nations Framework Convention on Climate Change: A Commentary*, 18 YALE J. INT'L L. 451, 451, 501–02 (1993) (indicating the express disavowal of industrialized countries that they were accepting CDR as a customary principle); *see also* Philippe Cullet, *Differential Treatment in International Law: Towards a New Paradigm of Inter-state Relations*, 10 EUR. J. INT'L L. 549, 579 (1999) (expressing skepticism that CDR has risen to customary international law); Rajamani, *supra* note 1, at 124 ("[CDR] cannot technically be termed a 'principle'"). However, Edith Brown Weiss submits that "[t]hough nonbinding, CDR has significantly affected international legal discourse." Edith Brown Weiss, *Common but Differentiated Responsibilities in Perspective*, 96 ASIL PROC. 366, 366 (2002).

[39] That is to say, applicable to all nations independently of their acceptance of treaties endorsing it.

[40] *See* Committee on Trade and the Environment, World Trade Organization, The Effects of Environmental Measures on Market Access, Especially in Relation to Developing Countries, in Particular the Least-Developed Among Them, WTO Doc. WT/CTE/W/207 (May 21, 2002), *available at* <http://www.dfat.gov.au/trade/negotiations/environment/pdf/wt_cte-w_207_market_access.pdf>. Paragraph 17, for example, states: "The CTE needs to further debate the ways in which the negative effects of environmental measures on the market access of developing countries can be mitigated so as to achieve the objective of sustainable development in a manner consistent with the principle of common but differentiated responsibilities."

[41] Susan Biniaz, Remarks (on common but differentiated responsibility), 96 ASIL PROC. 359, 361 (2002). Biniaz argues that the "so-called principle . . . is over-argued; and . . . breeds laziness in the negotiating process." *Id.*

[42] The disregard of wealth is not without exceptions. *See* Gregory C. Keating, *Pressing Precaution Beyond the Point of Cost-Justification*, 56 VAND. L. REV. 653, 687–97 (2003) (identifying several regulatory schemes that reject cost-benefit analysis in favor of "feasible risk reductions," in which the costs of measures imposed to eliminate significant risks are constrained by the requirements of continued viability of the industry). *The Restatement (Second) Torts* makes an element in exacting damages for nuisance whether "the financial burden of compensati[on] . . . would . . . make the continuation of the conduct not feasible." RESTATEMENT (SECOND) OF TORTS §826(b) (1979).

[43] That is, principles generally accepted as law based on general and consistent practices states have followed from a sense of legal obligation. RESTATEMENT (THIRD) OF THE FOREIGN RELATIONS LAW OF THE UNITED STATES §102(2) (1987) [hereinafter RESTATEMENT (THIRD)].

protocol, considerable temptation to jockey away from the "standard" terms and extract some tailored advantage as the price of keeping the momentum moving.[44] For these reasons, we should expect "selective incentives," as Mancur Olson termed them, to be rife.[45] Indeed, a Realist critique of international law would predict selectivity that favored the powerful.[46]

Nonetheless, despite the inducements to differentiate, uniform terms remain the rule. Under the conventions governing the conduct of war, a belligerent's use of poison gas is not excused because it cannot afford canonry. The Stockholm Declaration's principle 21 speaks in universal terms that "States have . . . the responsibility to ensure that activities within their jurisdiction or control do not cause damage to the environment of other States or of areas beyond the limits of national jurisdiction."[47] There is no qualification that a lack of resources to mitigate damage constitutes a defense.[48] No one proposes adjusting the international standards for radioactive emissions to account for a nation's difficulties in meeting them.[49]

In fact, the real puzzle about differentiations is not why we have them, but why they emerged so late and appear no more frequently than they do. Differences in power and different "demands" for participation being so typical, it is curious that negotiators have not responded more regularly by offering different "products" in the form of tailored terms.

There are a number of possible explanations why differential obligations are the exception, rather than the rule. To begin with, some conventions, such as those opposed to torture, genocide, and piracy, are too morally unambiguous to admit exceptions (openly)—to agree, for example, that some torture is acceptable until the party in question reaches a higher level of economic development.

Second, one should not dismiss the force of good citizenship in international politics; for one nation to hold out and demand special treatment because its participation was required as the *n*-th signer would be considered "bad form."[50]

[44] *See* Timothy Swanson, *Negotiating Effective International Environmental Agreements: Is an Objective Approach to Differential Treatment Possible?* 1 INT'L ENVTL. AGREEMENTS: POLITICS, LAW AND ECONOMICS 125 (2001).

[45] MANCUR OLSON, THE LOGIC OF COLLECTIVE ACTION: PUBLIC GOODS AND THE THEORY OF GROUPS 51 (1965); *see also* TODD SANDLER, COLLECTIVE ACTION: THEORY AND APPLICATIONS 56–60 (1992) (analyzing Olson's position that impediments to providing public goods can be addressed by selectively tying some parties' provision with private benefits as inducement). But as pointed out in the following text, the benefit need not be a favorable clause.

[46] Richard H. Steinberg, *In the Shadow of Law or Power? Consensus-Based Bargaining and Outcomes in the GATT/WTO*, 56 INT'L ORG. 339 (2002). Steinberg raises the very issue in questioning why powerful entities, like the European Union and the United States, so often support consensus decision-making rules. *Id.* at 340. Steinberg's answer is that, in fact, the powerful states have not been restrained by formally "equal" rules from imposing their wills on the weak. *Id.*

[47] Stockholm Declaration, princ. 21. The language of the principle, as endorsed by the *Restatement (Third) of Foreign Relations Law* is interesting in adding the italicized (by the author) qualification to a state's obligation "to take such measures as may be necessary, *to the extent practicable under the circumstances*, to ensure that activities within its jurisdiction or control (a) conform to generally accepted international rules and standards for the prevention, reduction, and control of injury to the environment of another state." RESTATEMENT (THIRD), *supra* note 43, §601(1)(a). It is uncertain whether this was intended to make an excuse for poorer nations as such; more likely a crude cost-benefit qualification was intended, one that might excuse the United States from responsibility in some circumstances.

[48] The difficulties the Scandinavian countries have encountered stanching Russia's transboundary sulfur dioxide (SO_2) fluxes from its nickel smelters on the Kola Peninsula may suggest that, in practice, principle 21 recognizes economic hardship de facto; but no one is suggesting that such hardships legitimate the damage. *See generally* Vladimir Kotov & Elena Nikitina, *Norilsk Nickel: Russia Wrestles with an Old Polluter*, ENV'T, Nov. 1996, at 6.

[49] At the 1998 Stockholm International Symposium on Hazardous Waste Disposal, a great range of issues was brought up, including intergenerational equity and the impact such wastes have on nonhuman life—but no one raised CDR. *See* Stockholm Environment Institute, Proceedings of the International Symposium on Hazardous Waste Disposal: Health and Environmental Criteria and Standards (Apr. 1999), *available at* <http://www.sei.se/dload/1999/Proceedings.pdf>.

[50] The rules of the Kyoto Protocol, *supra* note 2, do not go into force until ratified by nations whose emissions aggregate 55% of the global total. *See id.*, Art. 25. With ratifications up to 44%, Russia, with its 17%, is capable of putting the Protocol over the top; sitting in the *n*-th signer's catbird seat, it enjoys strong courting from those most anxious for Kyoto to succeed. But, as of this writing, and even in the face of favorable side inducements in the form of technical assistance, it has not signed on. *See EU Should Step up Efforts to Cajole Russia into Ratifying Kyoto Pact, Italian Official Says*, 26 Int'l Env't Rep. (BNA) 669 (2003).

Third, favoritism even for good-faith bargainers expends the cooperative gains that motivated the original signers. At some point, a cumulation of special-pleading exceptions, marking a movement toward the lowest common denominator of demands, will be unacceptable to the major forces. In the many cases where the participation of weak countries is only minimally required, special treatment is out of the question; nations whose impact is marginal may have to take the standard terms or leave them.

Fourth, even where the participation of weak, or of weakly motivated countries, is desirable, cooperation may be purchased through side payments less "expensively" without diluting the treaty's demands.[51] Side payments can take the form of developmental aid, for example, light-water reactors to keep North Korea within the Nuclear Non-Proliferation Treaty,[52] or a diplomatic "credit"—for example, toward gaining admission to the European Union.[53]

And of course, laws of universal application are probably less costly both to organize and to enforce.[54] Scaling obligations may bring more players on board, but it also invites fracas over bad faith and rent seeking. How do the negotiators judge when a holdout's demands reflect legitimate claims, such as particularly high costs of compliance, or opportunistic posturing?[55] It may be better to hold all parties to the same terms in the text and settle up, ex ante or ex post, outside it.

II. THREE VERSIONS OF CDR

There are thus several factors pressing for, and others against, the appearance of differentiated responsibilities in international agreements. But what more exactly are the normative stakes? Does CDR deserve support, if not, perhaps, as a principle of international law, then at least as a "guide to negotiations"? At this point, we have to divide CDR into its three possible versions.

In the first version, a proponent might simply be saying that some nonuniformities—what might be called *rational bargaining CDR*—should be expected and welcomed as natural outcomes

[51] To seal the 1911 North Pacific Fur Seal Treaty, the United States made immediate side payments of $100,000 to both Great Britain and Japan. SCOTT BARRETT, ENVIRONMENT AND STATECRAFT 34 (2003). But as Barrett notes, the efficacy of ex ante side payments in the international arena is undermined by obvious enforcement difficulties; the signatory can accept the payment, join the agreement—and then withdraw. *Id.* at 336.

[52] In 1994, the "price" for North Korea's continued participation in the Nuclear Non-Proliferation Treaty (abandonment of its nuclear weapons production and opening to inspection) was that the United States supply it with fuel oil and construct two light-water reactors. Alan Riding, *U.S. and North Korea Sign Pact to End Nuclear Dispute,* N.Y. TIMES, Oct. 22, 1994, at A5. There are widespread reports that the inducement for certain nonwhaling nations to join the International Whaling Convention (and to vote sympathetically with Japan) has been the lure of Japanese assistance in reducing depletion of the ozone shield. *See* Elizabeth DeSombre, *Distorting Global Governance; Membership, Voting, and the IWC, in* TOWARD A SUSTAINABLE WHALING REGIME 183, 187–88 (Robert L. Friedheim ed., 2001).

[53] *See* David G. Victor, *The Regulation of Greenhouse Gases: Does Fairness Matter? in* FAIR WEATHER? EQUITY CONCERNS IN CLIMATE CHANGE 193, 197 (Ferenc L. Tóth ed., 1997) (suggesting that Poland's expenditure on pollution abatement increased with an eye toward acceptance into the European Union).

[54] *See* James E. Krier, *On the Topology of Uniform Environmental Standards in Federal System—and Why It Matters,* 54 MD. L. REV. 1226, 1230 (1995); Weisslitz, *supra* note 33, at 486. Weisslitz, citing Richard Stewart, also maintains that imposing less stringent rules on developing countries may come back to haunt all parties, the weak practices becoming disentrenchable. *Id.* at 489.

[55] Swanson, *supra* note 44, at 129. In view of the added costs of differentiation, Swanson would approve it only in exceptional circumstances, where recognition of a criterion will not encourage opportunistic behavior; for example, recognizing geographic distinctions and predominant skin color in the context of ozone negotiations will not result in parties altering their location and skin color. *Id.* at 132–33. Swanson would admit developmental stage on the same basis, viz., the unlikelihood that a state will strategically elect to remain undeveloped in order to improve its future bargaining hand. But of course, once stage of development is admitted to be relevant, there are costs of sorting out who is "developed," particularly if no single metric, such as per capita gross national product, can command consensus. Such an issue has already broken out in the FCCC. Issues in the Negotiating Process, Request from a Group of Countries of Central Asia and Caucasus, Albania and Moldova Regarding Their Status under the Convention, *at* <http://unfccc.int/issues/cacam.html> (updated Mar. 17, 2003) (documenting request by Armenia and others at the COP-6, pt. II (Bonn, July 2001), regarding the definition of the term "developing countries" as used in the Convention, the Protocol, and COP decisions to determine recipients of financial, technological, and capacity-building support).

of mutually beneficial negotiations among negotiants pursuing their own advantage in the most narrowly self-interested way. Such outcomes, with one party contributing or receiving more than another, could be supported as "efficient" in the sense of being Pareto-improving: they leave at least one party better off, and no party worse off than at the status quo's no-agreement point.

A second version, what I will call *equitable CDR*, goes a step further, introducing constraints on unbridled bargaining, but without departing from the commitment to Pareto-improve. After all, the negotiators' choice set typically includes a number of potential Pareto-improving outcomes, and CDR might be understood simply as constraining the parties to choose, from within this set, treaty terms that tilt the cooperative surplus more favorably toward a designated group of parties, paradigmatically the Poor.

A third position, what might be called *inefficient CDR*, goes a step still further in advantaging one group—again, say, the Poor. It would carry differentiation beyond the point of awarding them the entire net surplus of cooperation. In the interests of "righting" the inequity of the status quo ante, the Rich-Poor transfers would leave the Rich worse off than before negotiations began. The idea (as reflected in the Johannesburg summit) is that environmental negotiations, like any others, should be conscripted into the service of the overarching goal, wealth equalization.[56]

The three positions can be illustrated by imagining two adjacent coastal nations which jointly exploit a stock of fish that straddles their economic zones. The one country, R, is Rich, and enjoys a wide range of food sources. P is Poor, and heavily dependent on the sea for protein. By cooperating, the two nations can increase the value of the harvest. Cooperation could take the form of monitoring to diminish unlawful catches by third parties, restoring nursery areas, and so on. Suppose that for a mutual $100 investment they can increase the value of the harvest by $200; in other words, there is a potential $100 net gain from cooperation, perhaps in the form of raising maximum economic yield an additional one hundred fish per annum. How are they to divide the gain?

To accept CDR in the first sense of rational bargaining CDR is to accept whatever division of the net increase the parties hammer out. Of course, each party will require that, at a minimum, it be repaid the value of its investment. If they each put in $50, they would each have to get at least that amount in return. But to focus on the cooperative gain is to distribute the one hundred fish surplus. R and P could decide on a nondifferentiating 50:50 split, but R and P could also divide in the ratios 90:10, 10:90, or 99:1. Much depends on their bargaining skills, although the Nash solution to the bargaining problem suggests that, in rational (self-interested) bargaining between a Rich and a Poor bargainer, Rich, for whom failure to reach agreement would be less onerous (it needs the fish less than Poor does), will emerge with a more than equal share of the net benefit in dollar value.[57] Rich in effect leverages its lower urgency into a higher payoff.[58] The result is that if we rely on rational bargaining, unfettered by normative constraint, Rich might emerge with a 90:10 advantage.

CDR understood in the second sense, equitable CDR, would block Rich from such a one-sided, self-favoring result. A "fairness" norm would constrain Rich to accept 10:90 or even 1:99. Poor would get the lion's share of the surplus, but Rich would be no worse off.

[56] *See, e.g.*, Johannesburg Declaration, *supra* note 3, para. 89 (urging debt relief and, as appropriate, debt cancellation).

[57] J. F. Nash, *The Bargaining Problem*, 18 ECONOMETRICA 155, 155–62 (1950). The Nash solution locates the outcome at the point that maximizes the product of Rich and Poor's utilities, which, assuming declining marginal utility of wealth, will not accord with a 50:50 division of the wealth-measured gains. The fact that Poor would be expected to draw less than 50:50 division is not, in and of itself, a moral argument that Poor ought to get less, without demonstrating that the "just" division is that which replicates the solution the parties would have achieved through rational bargaining. This is consistent with the Realist position that powerful states will dominate weak states. *See* Steinberg, *supra* note 46.

[58] This explication of Nash owes to John Harsanyi. *See* BRIAN BARRY, THEORIES OF JUSTICE 12–24 (1989).

The third, more extreme version, inefficient CDR, would commit Rich to favor Poor to an extent that not only improved Poor's welfare position, but also set Rich's back. For example, the agreement might give Poor the entire one hundred fish surplus, plus some fishing technology, plus a right to a fraction of the catch that was Rich's prior to the negotiation.

When we review the differentiating treaties recorded in the introductory pages, it is impossible to specify which version is reflected in which treaty. Plenty of literature suggests that some notion of fairness—on which the second and third versions rely—is a crucial consideration in concluding multilateral agreements.[59] If true, that would diminish the scope of rational bargaining CDR and enlarge the scope of fairness/equity constraints. But the effective strength of fairness/equity concerns is controversial,[60] and in all events unresolvable. Did the major players in the Montreal Protocol negotiations make concessions to LDCs to be "fair," or because it secured them the best deal available?

The notion of "national self-interest" is so ill-defined that it is hard to interpret where the force of self-interest ran out and equity or some softer value took hold. But let us demonstrate that most of the differentiations that we have seen thus far are at least *consistent with* the parties' engagement in rational bargaining unbridled by "fairness." To the extent a rational bargaining explanation holds, it undermines the claim that CDR has been operating as a normative constraint widely adopted in state practice.

Rational Bargaining CDR

Any claim about the pervasiveness of "rationality" risks its own oversimplification. The fact that there are so many sorts of multilateral negotiations makes it as difficult to generalize about what is "rational" as about what is fair.[61] Some multilateral arrangements, typified by the World Health Organization's efforts to eliminate globe-spanning diseases, aim at the provision of pure public goods. There, each contributor's costs (contributions) are borne privately, while the benefits are conferred on the public at large. That is, the derived benefits of an AIDS-free world are available to all, whether they contributed or not. In still another set of negotiations, aimed at overcoming overuse of an open access commons, the costs (of congestion or reduced fish stocks) fall on the public in common, while the derived benefits of the corrective collective action (the reduced congestion, the added fish) are in the form of privately captured benefits.[62] The level of some public goods, such as freedom from terrorism, tends to be set by the "weakest links."[63] The "rational" bargaining reaction shifts accordingly.

While there is thus no single model for multilateral agreements, we can take, as a crucial and typical illustration, negotiations aimed at reducing the risk of climate change, ozone shield

[59] A representative host of authorities (e.g., "It is almost axiomatic that an effective international agreement to limit CO_2 [carbon dioxide] emissions (or other greenhouse gases) will not be undertaken unless it is perceived as fair") is gathered in BENITO MÜLLER, JUSTICE IN GLOBAL WARMING NEGOTIATIONS: HOW TO OBTAIN A PROCEDURALLY FAIR COMPROMISE 5 (1998).

[60] Evidence to support the claim that fairness exercises a pervasive influence is presented in THOMAS M. FRANCK, FAIRNESS IN INTERNATIONAL LAW AND INSTITUTIONS (1995). *But see* Victor, *supra* note 53 (doubting the influence in the climate change negotiations). *See also* FRANCESCO BOSELLO ET AL., CAN EQUITY ENHANCE EFFICIENCY? SOME LESSONS FROM CLIMATE NEGOTIATIONS, (Discussion Paper No. 3606, Centre for Economic Policy Research Feb. 2003). "[A]lbeit intuitive, there is no substantial analysis that a more equitable distribution of the burden of reducing GHG emissions would induce more countries to sign and ratify the Kyoto Protocol or another climate agreement." *Id.* at 4.

[61] Is the United States being "unfair" to insist that China and India take on responsibilities under the Kyoto Protocol, or are China and India being "unfair" for refusing to commit to it?

[62] The implications of this distinction are developed in Todd Sandler & Daniel G. Arce, *Pure Public Goods Versus Commons: Benefit-Cost Duality*, 79 LAND ECON. 355 (2003). The authors demonstrate that while game theorists have traditionally represented both financing public goods (eliciting contributions) and governing open access commons (restraining overgrazing) as alike expressions of the Prisoner's Dilemma, closer attention to this benefit-cost duality reveals basic underlying differences that lend to independent representations, and different policy implications, for each.

[63] *See* Todd Sandler, *Collective Action and Transnational Terrorism*, 26 WORLD ECON. 779 (2003).

depletion, or the crash of a common pool fish stock. The prevailing level (of carbon, ozone-depleting agents, or fish) is a public good in that all parties "take" the supply that prevails, whether the country contributes to the improvement effort or not. Inasmuch as different nations attach a different value to each level of the good (each level of risk purged), differential contributions may be a perfectly rational outcome of self-interested negotiations, without any pressures of fairness.

To illustrate, let us again start with two countries, Rich and Poor, confronting the risks of climate change. The negotiating landscape is detailed in figure 1 (p. 287). In essence, it assumes that for Poor, with its lower level of wealth, reducing risk is of lower priority than other items on its agenda.[64] The analysis demonstrates that if each party were to act solely in its own self-interest, the result would be for Rich to pay the entire cost of mutually desired risk reduction; the amount of protection that Poor would underwrite in its own interests would be underwritten by Rich independently, in its interests. As a result, Poor free rides on the supply Rich buys. The differentiation is total without any independent pressures of "fairness."

Let us take the analysis a step further. Surely, if the parties cooperate rather than act independently, there is room for mutual gain. Cooperation can take several forms.

Cooperation in the form of pooling marginal costs. At any point in time, some countries (characteristically, Rich) will have made further investments than others (characteristically, Poor) in providing for a regional or global public good. As we have just illustrated, in some cases, all measures taken may have been undertaken by Rich. We know, too, from the increasing marginal costs of abatement, that the cheapest measures will have been taken first: Rich will have eliminated the ton of emissions it can eliminate at $1 before it advances on the ton it takes $2 to eliminate, and so on. At each level of elimination, Rich's most effective step is to "pick off" the least costly ton it can find not only in its own territory, but on any territory, including those of the less-developed Poor. At some point, $1 spent at home will remove fewer global pollutants than an equivalent amount spent on the best opportunity abroad.

The negotiating space is illustrated in figure 2 (p. 289). What it demonstrates is that it is mutually beneficial for Poor to permit Rich to pick up Poor's costs of abatement; in effect, to "lease" access to Poor's supply of low-cost abatement opportunities. (Think of Poor's lower costs as a valuable "resource" to the industrialized, like its oil.)

Notice that Rich gets further risk reduction, paying a lower unit price (P^{R*}) than it would have paid at home. Because the good (the reduced risk of climate change) is public, Poor shares the benefits of the further reduction. And it has paid nothing for it. Once again, what emerges—this time from an agreement—is a differentiation, but not one that requires departure from unalloyed, self-interested bargaining.

The strategy of figure 2 is in fact widespread. It underlies environmental agreements such as that establishing the Global Environment Facility (GEF) and the Montreal Protocol's multilateral fund. These provide a vehicle for the Rich to pay the Poor, via multilateral funds, the "agreed full incremental costs" of certain risk-reducing projects.[65] The idea is for Rich to

[64] A number of factors could lower Poor's demand, including situational considerations (distance from equator in the case of ozone-shield-depleting agents) and differences in and marginal utility of wealth being tapped for amelioration of the risk. It is imagined that Poor, lagging behind Rich in stage of development, would not be at the same point on the environmental Kuznets curve, that is, would not have put as high a share of its national income into pollution abatement (amenities supply). It should be remembered that some risks, such as those of sea level rise from climate change, are especially severe for some Poor countries even in the medium term, e.g., island states.

[65] *See* Kyoto Protocol, *supra* note 2, Art. 11(2)(b) (providing such financial resources, including for the transfer of technology, needed by the developing parties to meet the agreed full incremental costs of advancing the implementation of certain commitments); Amendments to Montreal Protocol, *supra* note 1, Art. 10(1) (providing that the multilateral fund, funded by the developed parties, "shall meet all agreed incremental costs of such Parties in order to enable their compliance with the control measures of the Protocol"). The theoretical background of transferring money versus in-kind technology is examined in Simon Vicary & Todd Sandler, *Weakest-Link Public Goods: Giving In-Kind or Transferring Money*, 46 EUR. ECON. REV. 1501 (2002).

Figure 1.
Noncooperative Supply of Public Good: Rich and Poor Act Independently

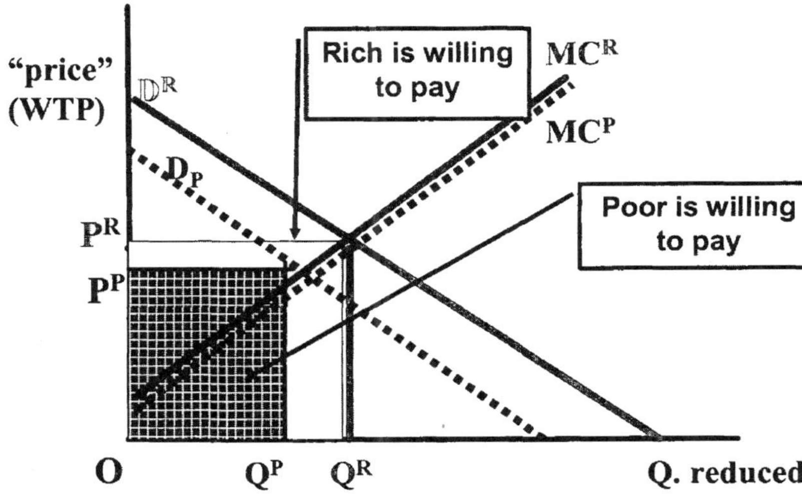

The *x*-axis represents the units of accumulated carbon reduced from the atmosphere; the origin is set at the present level of congestion; further right, further reductions. The *y*-axis represents the price each party is willing to pay (WTP) to achieve each unit of reduction. The demand (marginal benefit) curve for a Rich country is D^R. The curve slopes downward because the more congestion has been lowered—the more perils quelled—the less it is worth to eliminate the remaining risks. Poor's demand, D^P, is represented as lower than Rich's. The benefits curves are depicted as crossing the *x*-axis—falling to zero—based on the fact that some level of atmospheric blanket is a value crucial, indeed, to life on earth. How much of the current blanket is a risky "excess," the removal of which each country will finance, depends strongly on its social rate of discount which I presume to be steeper in Poor than in Rich. Rich's and Poor's upward sloping marginal costs reflect the fact that the costs of eliminating pollutants rise, the more units have already been removed. The effluents that are least costly to eliminate are selected for purging first (coal-fired plants or whatever); hence the costs increase with each additional unit. By positioning the two curves as virtually identical, we recognize that the shape and location of national marginal costs curves are subject to so many variables, including access to technology and capital, that it is impossible to generalize whose curve is higher or lower, Rich's or Poor's. In fact, the location "in general" does not matter, for we will see that some Rich, having already eliminated the emissions that are purged most costlessly in their own jurisdictions, will, in seeking further reduction opportunities, select as "partner" a (typically) Poor country that is facing lower reduction costs. Here, Rich will seek Q^R (at a unit price P^R) that is beyond the reduction that Poor would finance from its own pocket, Q^P. But R "covers" P.

absorb any costs that Poor incurs to reduce the risks over the level that is cost-beneficial from Poor's own, noncooperative perspective.[66] The differentiation that results requires no notion of fairness to drive it.

Cooperation in the form of pooling marginal benefits and dividing costs. But agreeing to exploit the lowest cost abatement opportunities—pooling marginal costs—does not exhaust the zone of mutually beneficial cooperation. There remains some action that Rich would no longer find rational to pay for exclusively, but that would be rational if (and only if) Poor contributed *something* as well.

To illustrate, imagine a large-scale geo-engineering project to reduce carbon congestion, such as constructing a network of giant lasers to "scrub" greenhouse gases from the atmosphere.[67] Assume that the economies of scale are such that the minimum feasible project costs $10 billion. The public goods benefits are such that at *some* division of costs it is to both Rich's and Poor's advantage to undertake the project; but neither will go ahead without assurances that the other party will put up some threshold portion.[68]

The bargaining field is depicted graphically in figure 3 (p. 289). The parties recognize that because the reduction of carbon congestion is a public good, they should not only pool their marginal costs, but consider the prospect of pooled benefits. The parties identify an area (the shaded triangle C-D-E) that offers mutual benefits—if they can cooperate in providing the costs (the checkered quadrilateral). This requires agreeing on a formula for dividing the costs. The problem is that if each party is "rational" in the narrowest sense, neither will make a concession. They are stuck, in the language of game theory, in a dominant Nash equilibrium in which, although cooperation would be Pareto-improving, neither party will unilaterally alter its noncooperative strategy.[69]

As in the illustration of the neighboring fishing nations, their progress toward the optimal solution, if any, and the division of the burden, is indeterminate.

Here, we reach a point where rational bargaining CDR might be adjudged inferior to equitable CDR—one in which there is an understanding that when bargaining gets "stuck," it is Rich who should budge, abjuring hard bargaining, and perhaps accepting any outcome that leaves it no less well-off. What can be said about such an "equitable" understanding of CDR?

Equitable CDR

CDR might be understood to mean (say, as a soft principle of international law) that the Rich(er) at least concede the lion's share or perhaps even all of the cooperative gains to the Poor(er).[70] I want to put aside the question, Is it *likely* Rich would agree? and instead examine the normative question, Is placing the heavier burden on Rich *morally persuasive*? The moral grounding of CDR has been intuitive and vague from the start. As we have seen, it was not until the 1992 UN Conference on Environment and Development (UNCED) in Rio de Janeiro

[66] A nice illustration of such cooperation is the GEF-backed Latvian waste management project. The target waste site in Riga not only pollutes groundwater, it generates methane, a greenhouse gas with far greater blocking power than CO_2. GEF funds will support installation of technology that captures the methane and uses it to generate electricity, thereby reducing GHG emissions both directly, to the extent methane is replaced by more benign atmospheric input, and indirectly, to the extent the electricity provided through the captured methane relieves demand that would have been met through fossil fuels. *See* World Bank, Latvia—Solid Waste Management and Landfill Gas Recovery Project (GEF Project) (Feb. 28, 1998), *at* <http://www-wds.worldbank.org/servlet/WDS_IBank_Servlet?pcont=details&eid=000009265_3980429110806>.

[67] *See* William J. Broad, *Scientists Dream up Bold Remedies for Ailing Atmosphere*, N.Y. TIMES, Aug. 16, 1988, at C1.

[68] *See* SANDLER, *supra* note 45, at 42–44.

[69] *See* TODD SANDLER, ECONOMIC CONCEPTS FOR THE SOCIAL SCIENCES 40 (2001); Sandler & Arce, *supra* note 62, at 357 (absent special circumstances, such as the game being played indefinitely and repeatedly with some threat-based strategy, the mutual contribution Pareto-optimal will not be achieved).

[70] I put aside for a moment the more demanding alternative that the Rich redistribute even to the point of emerging less well-off (see below).

Figure 2.
Cooperative Supply of Public Good: Pooling of Marginal Costs

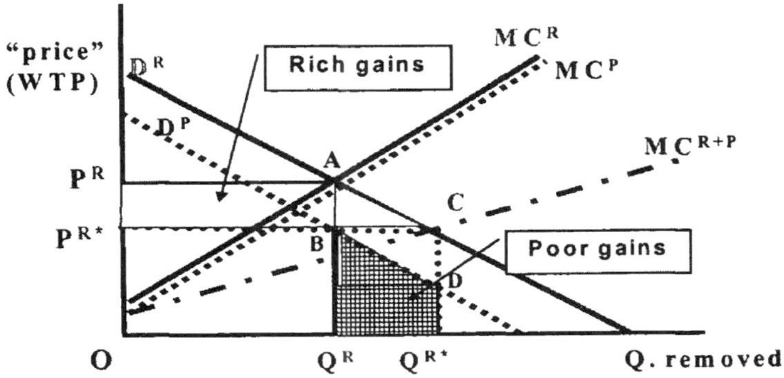

The two countries' marginal costs, MC, curves are added horizontally to provide a social (combined) MC curve. Rich's self-interest is now revised to advance out to the level Q^{R*}—marked by the intersection of its demand curve with the now-available social costs curve. The associated price is P^{R*}, less than the original price, P^R. Rich's potential gain is depicted in the shaded quadrilateral, P^R-A-C-P^{R*}. Poor's benefit is the checkered area, Q^R-B-D-Q^{R*}. How far the combined curve rotates down is a function of the MC curve of the Poor partner and the countries' relative production of pollutants.

Figure 3.
Cooperative Supply of Public Good: Pooling of Benefits and Costs

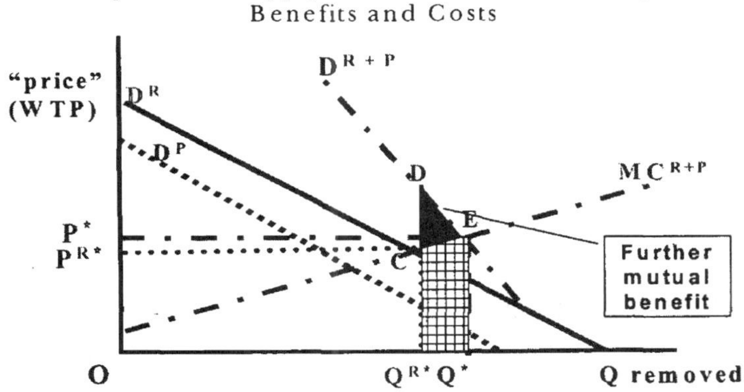

The parties' demand curves, D^P and D^R, are summed vertically to reveal their mutual benefits, D^{R+P}. This is what they are rationally willing to pay between them for each level of improvement. The marginal costs, MC^{R+P}, remain pooled, as in figure 2. Rich, of its own, will not underwrite reduction beyond Q^{R*}, located by the intersection of its own demand with the pooled costs. But when they consider the combined benefits, Q^* is the efficient outcome. If additional investment—the checkered area—is forthcoming, R and P will realize the benefit, C-D-E, by extending reduction to Q^*. But to achieve C-D-E they must cooperate in providing the costs Q^{R*}-C-E-Q^*.

that CDR emerged as a distinct normative principle, complete with its own term.[71] But the Rio Declaration alluded to several normative positions on which differentiation might be based.

Principle 6 introduced the theme: "The special situation and needs of developing countries, particularly the least developed and those most environmentally vulnerable, shall be given special priority."[72]

Principle 7 fleshed it out, stating:

> In view of the different contributions to global environmental degradation, States have common but differentiated responsibilities. The developed countries acknowledge the responsibility that they bear in the international pursuit of sustainable development in view of the pressures their societies place on the global environment and of the technologies and financial resources they command.[73]

These principles, taken together, advance at least three arguments for differentiation. Principle 6, in alluding to the undeveloped and vulnerable, suggests (1) differentiation in accordance with *needs*. Principle 7 begins on a note of differentiations in accordance with (2) the *pressures* each country places on the environment, and concludes with (3) differential *capabilities* in terms of wealth and technology.

One problem with these criteria is that they may conflict. A ranking of the most *needy* nations, generated under (1), does not necessarily mirror a ranking of the nations *most responsible for damage*, generated under (2); nor yet again are the states most responsible for damage necessarily those with (3) the superior *capabilities*.[74]

But let us put this problem aside and ask, How coherent and convincing are any of these rationales for "equitable" differentiation?

Differentiation in Accordance with Needs

Principle 6 calls attention to the fact that although some risks fall across all nations, some nations are more needful of help than others. For example, one consequence of climate change might be inundation of low-lying coastal areas. (Bangladesh and the Alliance of Small Island States (AOSIS) come to mind.) Some fear that the melting of Andean glaciers, a crucial source of freshwater for Bolivia and Peru, will shrivel them to critical levels in a matter of decades.[75]

One might imagine that the need-based claims for differentiation require little justification. The position wins recognition, albeit nebulously, in the FCCC.[76] But the normative implications of need are not self-evident.

To begin with, need, per se, is not ordinarily a sufficient moral condition for wealth transfers. Ordinarily, the person who needs something more is expected to pay more, not to be

[71] Rio Declaration on Environment and Development, UN Conference on Environment and Development, UN Doc. A/CONF.151/5/Rev. 1 (1992), 31 ILM 874 (1992) [hereinafter Rio Declaration]. The principles are probably but guides to negotiation, not legally binding even as instantiated in the FCCC. *See* David Freestone, *The Road from Rio: International Environmental Law After the Earth Summit*, 6 J. ENVTL. L. 193 (1994). However, Freestone later ventures that

> the Declaration reflects a real consensus of developed and developing states on the need for generally agreed norms of international environmental protection. Despite certain reservations on the part of the United States, the principles and rules it contains have a universal significance and cannot be dismissed as the work of one segment of international society.

INTERNATIONAL LAW AND SUSTAINABLE DEVELOPMENT: PAST ACHIEVEMENTS AND FUTURE CHALLENGES 4 (Alan Boyle & David Freestone eds., 2001).

[72] Rio Declaration, *supra* note 71, princ. 6.

[73] *Id.*, princ. 7.

[74] Consider, in regard to this last point, the states of the former Soviet Union, which include some nations that are historically heavy GHG-emitters—high-ranking "causers"—but are relatively lower in capacity to remediate.

[75] *See* Juan Forero, *As Andean Glaciers Shrink, Water Worries Grow*, N.Y. TIMES, Nov. 24, 2002, at A3.

[76] FCCC, *supra* note 1, Art. 4(8) (enjoining the parties to "give full consideration to what actions are necessary . . . to meet the specific needs and concerns of developing country Parties"). Article 4(9) is similar.

subsidized by the person who needs it less.[77] A person who lives on Los Angeles's fire-prone hillsides needs fire insurance more than the flatlanders—and pays a higher premium.

Principle 6, therefore, probably stands on its firmest moral ground when it is understood as favoring the needful, not in the sense of high-risk exposure, per se, but of exposure that is high in light of limited resources to mitigate the risks. In other words, to find moral support (Why *ought* we to favor them over us?) the "need" argument has to appeal to the same foundations that may oblige the wealthy to relieve victims of famine or earthquake in a distant, impoverished land.[78]

Respectable philosophical arguments have been made for a duty to rescue strangers, from both neo-Kantian[79] and utilitarian bases.[80] But even if such arguments were accepted, the implications for any present international policy, using multilateral environmental agreements as "rescue" vehicles, for example, would remain unclear. In general, the poorer countries are probably more vulnerable to a broad range of climate change perils for the same reason they are more vulnerable to almost any perils—they have fewer resources with which to defend their assets and to adapt. But beyond that, we know so little about how, when, or where the perils of climate change might unfold (through droughts, freezing, desertification, pests, and so on) that it is hard to judge what differentiated measures a needs-regarding equitable CDR would call for.

Differentiation in Accordance with Harm Caused

Rio principle 7, in calling for the assignment of heavier contributions to developed countries in response to "the pressures their societies place on the global environment,"[81] shifts the focus from Poor's needs to Rich's wrongs. If we agreed to put the principle into action, it would mean that the Rich (and everyone else) should be confronted with the full social costs of their emissions. Thus understood, the principle is no more controversial, or peculiarly equitable, than declaring that the polluter should pay.[82]

Principle 7 represents an equitable departure from efficiency, and becomes controversial, only when understood not as written, in the present tense ("their societies *place*"), but as past tense ("their societies *placed*"), so as to count against a polluter its historically cumulated emissions. If that is the claim, then it has indeed to appeal to some notion of fairness truly distinct from efficiency, which has nothing to say about past harms.

Claims for an accounting based upon past conduct are not unknown in the MEA context.[83] Consider India's 1989 demand that the developed nations transfer $2 billion as a precondition

[77] Consider the negotiations over ozone-depleting substances. The thinning of the ozone shield poses its gravest risks to light-skinned populations living at high latitudes. That is because the thinning is most pronounced toward the magnetic poles and its principal direct human health hazard is skin cancer to which fair-skinned people are most susceptible. Therefore, it was not surprising, at the London ozone negotiations most markedly, to find (in the Northern Hemisphere) the Scandinavian countries, Germany, and Canada, and (in the Southern) New Zealand and Australia, taking the lead in pressing for the most rapid phaseout of ozone-depleting agents. Their citizens needed the agreement more than the Indians and Chinese, who resisted signing onto the phaseout unless they were compensated by side agreement for the higher costs of substitute refrigerants. The more vulnerable were expected to pay the less vulnerable.

[78] The obligations of the Rich to succor the Poor are especially strong to the extent the Rich may be the cause of the Poor's plight, and not merely bystanders to erratic nature.

[79] *See* ONORA O'NEILL, FACES OF HUNGER: AN ESSAY ON POVERTY, JUSTICE AND DEVELOPMENT 144–163 (1986).

[80] *See* PETER SINGER, *Famine, Affluence and Morality*, *in* WRITINGS ON AN ETHICAL LIFE 105, 105–24 (2000).

[81] Rio Declaration, *supra* note 71, princ. 7.

[82] Many would ground a polluter pays principle on "fairness," but in its welfare economic version an ideally efficient (Pigovian) tax is set at a level that induces efficient adjustments by the "victims" as well as by the polluters. Efficiency concerns dominate corrective justice. Unlike recovery in tort, the state, not the victim, collects the fee.

[83] The concept emerged as the "main responsibility principle" at a Beijing symposium in 1991. *See* Bodansky, *supra* note 38, at 479. One Marshall Islander dismissed at COP–7 suggestions that island nations should adapt to changing conditions by building surge barriers and storm drains by noting: "Whoever caused the problem has to clear [it] up." AP, *Amid Rising Waters, Island Nations Plead Case at Climate Conference*, Nov. 17, 2000, *available at* <http://www.cnn.com/2000/NATURE/11/17/climate.conference.ap>.

for it to sign the Montreal Protocol, on the grounds that "it is the Western nations that caused the ozone depletion."[84] Such a demand could find support in Locke's "proviso" that asserts the right of each person to appropriate from the commons, viz., that the right exists only insofar as the appropriator leaves "enough and as good for others."[85] Conscripting this reasoning, a developing country might liken the risk-free absorptive capacity of the atmosphere to a "good" in the global commons. It could thereupon argue that the pressures it faces to reduce its emissions came about because the early industrializers had been congesting the atmosphere—over the past two centuries "taking" its safe-level absorptive capacities—without leaving, in the terms of Locke's proviso, "enough and as good" for the late bloomers.

Carrying out this line of argument is not without difficulties. For one thing, it is not clear why a contemporary U.S. citizen should make amends for the overuse of the global commons during the stretch before her forebears had immigrated. The demand opens complex issues akin to those raised in demands that white people in the United States and Europe pay African nations for damages done during the slave-trade period.[86]

Moreover, against the Poor's imperfect argument for historical blame must be weighed the ironic argument for adverse possession and prescription available to the Rich, that after a long period of wrongfully occupying (or trespassing across) another's land, the "wrongdoer" wins recognizable rights based on, among other things, morally salient reliance interests.[87] Indeed, the Kyoto Protocol might be viewed as recognizing the force of such interests in allocating targets among the Annex I countries; targets are expressed as a percentage decrease from a baseline year, thereby legitimating the rights of the heaviest polluters to continue the heaviest pollution.[88] Polluters are awarded, in effect, easements to continue to commit global nuisance based upon the hardship of surrendering "rights" won from historical "wrongs."

Differentiation in Accordance with Technological and Financial Resources

To justify the second branch of principle 7, that the burden should be slanted toward those parties with greater resources, nothing is required beyond utility maximization coupled with the assumption of declining marginal utility of wealth. If a beggar and a millionaire each lose a dollar in the park, the loss represents a lesser reduction in utility to the millionaire. Similarly, demanding a differentiated, viz., heavier, contribution from the rich states *in dollars* may be (depending upon the level) asking no more than a ratable or even lighter contribution by the Rich in welfare measured by *utility*. It is such thinking that gives rise to the cry of developing countries that, in addressing reduction in GHG outputs, "luxury emissions" should not be treated on a par with "subsistence emissions."[89] Whether or not the Rich can be made to accept the argument—not the issue here—surely, equitable CDR can command strong intuitive moral appeal. At least as long as the Rich are made no less well off, why *not* shunt the lion's share of cooperative gains to the Poor?

[84] *India Wants $2 Billion from Others to Sign Ozone Depletion Montreal Protocol*, 12 Int'l Env't Rep. (BNA) 389 (1989).

[85] In other words, the fisher's ownership of the fish taken from a common pool is recognized, as long as the fisher leaves for others all that the others can use. *See* JOHN LOCKE, SECOND TREATISE ON GOVERNMENT §27 (Thomas P. Peardon ed., 1952) (1690).

[86] It is tempting to sidestep these conundrums by refocusing the argument away from the damage formerly imposed and toward the continuing benefits received. The Poor can charge that those of us with the good fortune to have been born in the developed world are the beneficiaries of bygone extravagances, wherever our forebears were living in their lifetimes at the time of the conduct. We have (it may be argued) a differentiated responsibility rooted not as much in the duty to pay damages for consummated wrongs as, alternatively, in either the duty to make restitution of inequitable gains or to compensate for the higher costs that late industrializers face under the more confining legal targets required by the early industrializers' appropriations.

[87] Oliver Wendell Holmes rooted adverse possession in the claimant's "deepest instincts" of resentment at having to relinquish property she had used as her own over a long period of time. Oliver Wendell Holmes, *The Path of the Law*, 10 HARV. L. REV. 457, 477 (1897).

[88] Kyoto Protocol, *supra* note 2, Art. 3(3), (5), (7) and Annexes referred to therein.

[89] *See* Henry Shue, *Subsistence Emissions and Luxury Emissions*, 15 LAW & POL'Y 39 (1993).

Inefficient CDR: Should Welfare and the Environment be Coupled?

But should we go further to alleviate the plight of the Poor? In *bargaining outcome* CDR (above), absent procedural defects such as information asymmetries, what is "legitimate" is whatever agreement (with its differentiations) emerges. In *equitable* CDR (above), the range of legitimate outcomes is confined to the set of Pareto-improvements, but within that set, distribution of cooperative benefits is allocated more heavily (or wholly) toward the Poor. This can easily command support. Controversy is more likely with *inefficient* CDR, which would advance Poor's welfare unconditioned by mutual, if even marginal, advances for Rich. Such a position underlies the demand, already alluded to, that Rich retroactively amend for damages, or unpaid-for advantages.[90] The limits are to be set by some sort of corrective justice, not efficiency. The idea likewise underlies the calls, most recently at the Johannesburg summit, for debt relief, debt cancellation, and grants.[91] After all, among the Poor, appeals to "efficiency" and "Pareto-possible improvements," which accept the status quo's (mal)distribution of wealth and proceed from there, ring hollow.[92] In their minds, the starting point—the way things are—is not off the negotiating table but remains the key issue. That is the significance of elevating development to "an inalienable human right";[93] efficiency is out of court.[94] The conviction that equity and fairness override efficiency runs so strong that proposals to award developed countries abatement credits for foreign-soil investments have been stalled by objections that those who caused the problem ought not to be permitted so to buy their way out on foreign soil—even if "leasing" low-cost opportunities is, as we have shown, mutually beneficial.[95]

As for finding a moral foundation for a "tilt" toward the Poor not constrained within the limits of Paretian efficiency, one approach would be through a "veil of ignorance" thought experiment.[96] We might ask, What rules and institutions would be selected by an embryo who did not know whether its fortune would be to be born in the United States or in Bangladesh?[97] Surely, even without the presumption of risk aversion, it is not hard to imagine that we would be attracted to institutions that leveled gross wealth disparities, perhaps grounded on economic or social "rights to development."[98]

But even if we suppose that the present worldwide distribution of wealth is so unsupportable that some Rich to Poor redistributions are in order, it is an additional leap to defend redistributions within the matrix of a particular framework, such as a multilateral environmental agreement. Why should redistribution be sought through exempting the Poor from

[90] *See supra* pp. 291–92.

[91] Johannesburg Declaration, *supra* note 3, Art. 89.

[92] Daniel C. Esty & Robert Mendelsohn, *Moving from National to International Policy*, 31 POL'Y SCI. 225, 228 (1998). Esty and Mendelsohn tout efficiency, as many northern scholars would do, "as a step toward credibility." But whether demonstrating that a solution is efficient adds to credibility among the Poor is uncertain. *See* A. Dan Tarlock, *Environmental Protection: The Potential Misfit Between Equity and Efficiency*, 63 U. COLO. L. REV. 871, 876–81 (1992) (tracing "the historical roots of the subordination of equity to efficiency").

[93] *See* Declaration on the Right to Development, GA Res. 128, UN GAOR, 41st Sess. (1986).

[94] Tarlock observes that since the 1992 UNCED meeting in Stockholm, "developing countries have generally urged that they have an 'equitable' right to pollute." Tarlock, *supra* note 92, at 871 n.3.

[95] *See* World Council of Churches, Press Release, WCC Challenges Rich Countries at Climate Change Conference in The Hague (Nov. 14, 2000), *available at* <http://www.wcc-coe.org/wcc/news/press/00/34pre.html>. At COP–6, the discussions ended up with a decision that "the use of [credit from investment on foreign soil] mechanisms shall be supplemental to domestic action," with the facilitative branch of the compliance committee being charged "to assess" the information provided. Summary of the Resumed Sixth Session of the Conference of the Parties to the UN Framework Convention on Climate Change, EARTH NEGOTIATIONS BULL., July 30, 2001, at 6, *available at* <http://www.iisd.ca/vol12/enb12176e.html>.

[96] JOHN RAWLS, A THEORY OF JUSTICE 12 (1971).

[97] *See* BRIAN M. BARRY, THE LIBERAL THEORY OF JUSTICE 133 (1973).

[98] A good and concise exposition of the daunting area of transnational and international distributive justice is found in Allen Buchanan & David Golove, *Philosophy of International Law*, OXFORD HANDBOOK OF JURISPRUDENCE AND PHILOSOPHY OF LAW 868, 897–902 (Jules Coleman & Scott Shapiro eds., 2002).

efficient environmental and resource standards—giving them a "right to pollute"—rather than through a more straightforward step-up in aid and development assistance?

In fact, while coupling clean air or other environmental policies with welfare goals may appear to be an obvious solution to the duality of the problems—pollution and poverty—coupling has drawbacks, which explains why it is so infrequently adopted. Put another way, should the fight against poverty extend to making poverty a defense against laws against pollution?[99] The alternative is to entrust environmental aims to the environmental laws, and welfare to the welfare system. One reason to decouple is that the merging may lead to an outcome suboptimal to the achievement of both.[100] To make matters worse, combining the two reduces transparency and accountability.

The California Motor Vehicle Code's provisions for inspection and maintenance of catalytic converters provides a provocative illustration of what can go wrong when environmental and welfare policies are cobbled into one well-intentioned regime. The law caps the dollar cost of repairs that an owner may be required to pay, depending largely on the age of the car.[101] The idea is to shoulder less economic burden onto the Poor, who are presumed to be the owners of the old cars. The problem is that from an air-quality perspective, the older cars are the dirtiest polluters, the ones we should be most concerned to repair or drive off the roads, not coddle. And from a welfare perspective, the law fares hardly better. The age of an owner's car is an imperfect indicator of poverty. Vintage cars may be collector's items for the very rich; and the most needy among us do not own a car at all. That is why no one who set out to attack poverty would go about it by distributing $400 to every Californian with a car thirty years old or older.

The ideal solution would be to devise the best auto emissions policies, with eyes on the worst polluters, and the best antipoverty policies, with eyes on the most needy. Of course, the world is not California.[102] But there are real parallels. In MEA negotiations that combine environment with "need," the countries that can extract the largest concessions in, say, transfers of technology, are not apt to be the poorest countries. Rather, the "winnings" will go to those poor countries that can most credibly threaten industrialization along "dirty" paths from which they must be diverted, or that are richest in biological hot spots.[103]

[99] However, institutional sympathy for variations in wealth may turn up at sentencing. *See* U.S. SENTENCING GUIDELINES MANUAL §8(C)(3.3) (finding applicable to convicted organizations whose fine in strict accordance with the guidelines might "substantially jeopardiz[e] the continued viability of the organization").

[100] The position in the text is in accord with the Louis Kaplow and Steven Shavell warning that if independent weight is given to a notion of morality under a measure of social welfare, in some situations the utility of every individual will be lowered. Louis Kaplow & Steven Shavell, *Any Non-Welfarist Method of Policy Assessment Violates the Pareto Principle*, 109 J. POL. ECON. 281, 284 (2001).

[101] The maximum repair bill that the owner can be forced to pay is $450, with caps declining for cars by age of vehicle, down to $50 for the oldest (1971 and earlier vintage). CAL. HEALTH & SAFETY CODE §44016 (2003). In practice, the administration is complex, providing for consumer assistance centers that enable repairs by picking up some portion of the bill in accordance with owner's income. Cal. Dep't of Consumer Affairs—Bureau of Automotive Repair, "Smog Check Consumer Assistance Application Package" *at* <http://www.smogcheck.ca.gov/ftp/pdfforms/cap_app.pdf> (last visited Apr. 2, 2004). In some cases, excess repair bills of the Poor are shared by or picked up by the state, while in other cases, cars that cannot be brought into compliance may receive exemptions. *See id.*

[102] Perhaps most crucially, California can tax and the United Nations cannot. *See* Louis Kaplow & Steven Shavell, *Should Legal Rules Favor the Poor? Clarifying the Role of Legal Rules and the Income Tax in Redistributing Income*, 29 J. LEGAL STUD. 821 (2000) (arguing that, assuming taxes are available, it is generally more efficient to transfer a dollar simply through raising taxes than through skewing regulatory regimes toward redistributive goals). *But see* Daniel A. Farber, *What (If Anything) Can Economics Say about Equity?* 101 MICH. L. REV. 1791 (2003) (maintaining that in some circumstances legal (regulatory) rules can be superior redistributive mechanisms, even from an efficiency perspective). Whoever is right, if taxation as an alternative is moot internationally, the case for "coupling" in the international arena, though complex, must be considered alive.

[103] *See* Drumbl, *supra* note 13, at 379. Drumbl adds that transfers under international environmental agreements may exacerbate the developmental gap because, first, they may divert funds to resolve global-scale problems, thereby overlooking some of the worst environmental problems facing the very poorest countries, such as dirty water, which are local; and second, donors are likely to favor transfers to those nations with the best-developed regulatory and market institutions, and are therefore apt to provide a better return on the donors' investments with lower transactions costs. *Id.* at 379–80.

Moreover, from the Poor nation's perspective, there is no assurance that the bigger slice of gains that cooperation would enable in the environmental area will be handed back to the Poor as a bigger slice of aid, rather than be consumed by the Rich. That is an impediment to dividing negotiations into "pure environmental" and "pure aid" fora. And it explains why, at Johannesburg, while lip service was paid to the environment, development and elimination of poverty, pure and simple, were what dominated the LDCs' agenda.[104]

This is not to imply that the developing countries are indifferent to global-scale environmental problems. But development is more urgent. Recall, too, that as far as the global environment goes, the Poor already get considerable free-ride "cover" from public goods investments that the Rich will make, such as research and development to pave into a hydrogen economy, whether the Poor cooperate or not (figure 1).[105] It is true that Poor could do better, environmentally speaking, by cooperating as figure 3 suggests. But the benefits Poor anticipates from the contribution that collective action requires, beyond what Rich will provide independently, may appear lower than what Poor would get from returns on investment in education, public health, and other infrastructure.

The trouble is this: from Rich's point of view, as the share of cooperative contribution by the Poor diminishes (or turns negative!), it becomes increasingly attractive to identify and embrace environmental policies that are second-best.[106] We can illustrate by returning to the lost inertia of the Kyoto negotiations.

Kyoto: The "Coupling" Dilemma Illustrated

It was the hope of many that the Kyoto Protocol would set up a capped-emission, permit-trading mechanism that would reduce climate change risks efficiently, within the bounds of mutually beneficial gains (figure 4, p. 296).[107] But efforts to blend fairness into the architecture, under the banner of CDR, threaten to undermine the motivations that optimal cooperation, and welfare of the parties, require. This can be gleaned by considering the procedures from the perspective of the United States, whose potential gains from cooperation face gutting as the Poor are excused from contributing.

The U.S. dilemma is vividly demonstrated in table 1 (p. 297), which reflects global CO_2 contributions of the top sixteen emitters, which together account for 74 percent of the world total.[108]

[104] Johannesburg Declaration, *supra* note 3. Of course, they had always been part of the agenda; as the FCCC recites, "economic and social development and poverty eradication are the first and overriding priorities of the developing country Parties." FCCC, *supra* note 1, Art. 4(7). But at Stockholm (1972), *supra* note 23, and Rio (1992), *supra* note 71, the environmentalists had lead, rather than shared, billing.

[105] The Poor might want the Rich to do more to clean up the global environment. But this does not mean that, given the choice of the Rich putting another dollar into the cleanup and putting it into developmental aid, the Poor would prefer the former.

[106] The theory of "second best" is that if policies are ranked in order of preference under certain conditions, and if those conditions are unrealized, the best alternative to the "first-best" choice is not necessarily the alternative that was next best under the unrealizable conditions, had they been obtained. The circumstances that make "first best" unrealizable may make it imperative to rerank all options from the start; the most viable of the new set of alternatives may be an option—the second best—that is other than the next ranked choice in the original ranking. *See generally* Richard G. Lipsey & Kelvin Lancaster, *The General Theory of Second-Best*, 24 REV. ECON. STUD. 11 (1956).

[107] As illustrated by figure 4 and the accompanying text.

[108] The table is composed from data presented in G. Marland et al., *Global, Regional, and National Fossil Fuel CO_2 Emissions*, *in* ONLINE TRENDS: A COMPENDIUM OF DATA ON GLOBAL CHANGE (Carbon Dioxide Information Analysis Center & U.S. Dep't of Energy 2003), *available at* <http://cdiac.esd.ornl.gov/trends/emis/em_cont.htm>. Note that the table reflects not all GHGs, but only CO_2 from activities other than land clearing. Putting water vapor aside, CO_2 constitutes about 60% of total GHG accumulation, referenced by radiative forcing power. Calculated from INTERGOVERNMENTAL PANEL ON CLIMATE CHANGE, CLIMATE CHANGE 2001: THE SCIENTIFIC BASIS, CONTRIBUTION OF WORKING GROUP I TO THE THIRD ASSESSMENT REPORT, tbl. 6.1, *available at* <http://www.grida.no/climate/ipcc_tar/wg1/221.htm> (last visited Aug. 12, 2003).

Figure 4
Rich-Poor Emissions Trading

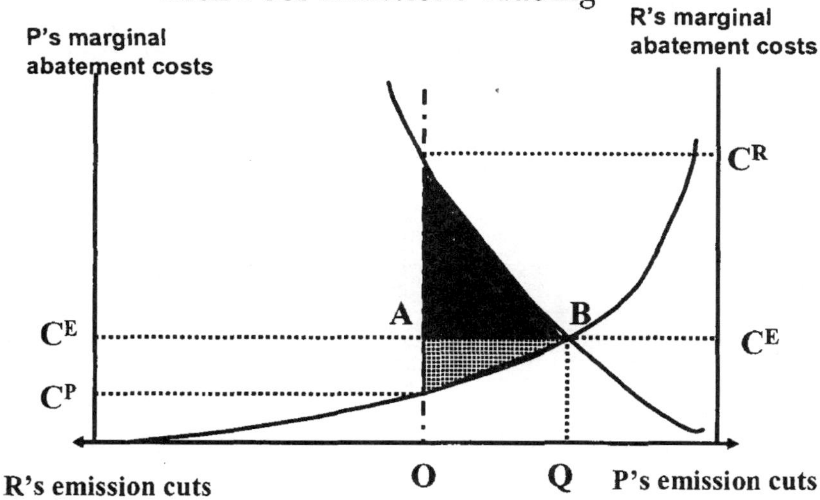

Another cooperative differentiating technique is to adopt mutual restrictions on effluents hinged on tradable permits. Imagine the original level for the onset of trading to be O, in figure 4, which we can identify with Q^{R*} in figure 2. (We have exhausted the benefits of Rich's "leasing" of Poor's marginal costs at Rich's expense.) Permits for trading under the confined regime have been established and allocated between the parties. Because at the origin O the costs to Rich of purging a unit, C^R, exceed that to Poor, C^P, Poor will sell permits to Rich until the marginal costs of the emissions equate, at the equilibrium level Q. At that point Rich will have paid Poor O-A-B-Q for Poor's rights it has acquired. Poor's gain from trade is represented by the checkered, lower triangle; Rich's, by the upper, shaded triangle. If the cap and allocation have been well established, Q will be the sought-for target of figure 3, Q^*. Note that at the equilibrium both Rich and Poor are paying the same price for permits, C^E, but the scheme is based upon the parties being able to agree upon differentiated contributions arising from the negotiation over the cap and original allocations. Depending on the concessions on original entitlements, the regime could fall into any of the three versions of CDR.

TABLE 1: CO_2 EMISSIONS

ALL COUNTRIES/COUNTRIES SUBJECT TO KYOTO TARGETS				
	Country	CO_2 (1000 metric tons)	% among all countries	% among countries subject to Kyoto impact*
1	United States	1,486,801	23.81%	51.60%
2	China	858,490	13.75%	
3	Russian Federation	391,535	6.27%	
4	Japan	309,353	4.95%	10.74%
5	India	289,587	4.64%	
6	Germany	225,208	3.61%	7.82%
7	United Kingdom	148,011	2.37%	5.14%
8	Canada	127,517	2.04%	4.43%
9	Italy	113,238	1.81%	3.93%
10	Mexico	102,072	1.63%	
11	France	100,951	1.62%	3.50%
12	South Korea	99,260	1.59%	
13	Ukraine	96,510	1.55%	
14	South Africa	93,808	1.50%	
15	Australia	90,470	1.45%	3.14%
16	Poland	87,807	1.41%	
	All Others	1,623,019	25.99%	9.71%
	Global Total	**6,243,637**	**100%**	
	Derived from: Carbon Dioxide Information Analysis Center, 2002.			

*Assuming ratification. Neither the United States nor Australia has ratified. Excludes both countries not subject to target under Annex B and "economies in transition" whose targets are fixed at nonconstraining levels in the First Compliance Period (2008–2012).

The United States is the largest with 24 percent. In the far right column we have restated the percentages subject to cutback when we have eliminated both the Poor (non–Annex I) countries that are under no obligation, and some "nations in transition" from socialism which, because of their industrial contraction from baseline years, do not face constraint from business-as-usual paths. (Indeed, they may stand to reap huge "hot air" windfalls.)[109]

In the restated figures, with China, India, the Russian Federation, and other similarly situated countries pulled out, the U.S. share—what the United States is being asked to bring to the table—rises to more than 50 percent. Of the 186 nations that started out as FCCC ratifiers, only 25 of the Annex I countries, which alone are on the line for curtailment, have signaled willingness to remain in play by ratifying the Protocol. Of the top 16 emitters, only 6, representing merely 16.4 percent of the global total, are still "in." The national shares of countries not on the chart are insubstantial.

In other words, from the U.S. vantage point, the first-best outcome may well have been a fully cooperative trading regime with all (major) polluters participating. But as emitters defect, its second best is less likely to be to remain in a broad multilateral framework. To take other, second-best measures does not (hopefully) imply a business-as-usual scenario for U.S. policymakers.[110] But it almost certainly will encourage the United States, in determining the magnitude and timing and mode of *its* response, to make fewer accommodations aimed at salvaging reciprocal advantages from collective efforts.

To illustrate, consider how the United States is likely to divide its efforts, such as they may be, between cooperative preventive measures, in the Kyoto spirit, and adaptations that are deferred until a future time when local threats have become better defined. Measures that aim at *preventing* GHGs from invading the atmosphere, such as switching to alternative energy sources, require a nation to clean up at its own expense for a benefit that will inure in large part to others, whether they participate or not. Such measures are therefore hard to motivate on a broad scale, as we anticipate from theory and know from the Kyoto experience. Of every \$1.00 we spend on prevention, \$.50 goes to the benefit of others.

By contrast, the benefits of adaptive techniques, such as water conservation programs, micro-irrigation, and seawalls, are typically fully internalized by the state that invests in them, and can be pinpointed to those areas that will need the interventions if, when, and where trouble develops. Viewed by the global community, \$1.00 spent on adaptation may be less effective than \$1.00 spent on prevention; but because there are adaptation opportunities whose benefits are largely internalized, a well-aimed adaptation investment of the same \$1.00 may pay its investor \$1.25 in benefit.

Diminished emphasis on prevention would not entail that all U.S. investments be at home, adaptive, and unilateral. Some selective preventive measures taken abroad might be highly beneficial, perhaps, for example, a bilateral agreement to pay for, and provide technology for, plugging leaks in the gas delivery system of the Commonwealth of Independent States and reducing its flaring of associated gas at oil wellheads.[111] The United States might well

[109] By some estimates, Russia and Ukraine, whose carbon-generating industries have collapsed since their Kyoto baseline years, could turn around and sell their "hot air" entitlements, which they could not use anyway, for \$20 to \$170 billion. *See* Victor, *supra* note 35, at 10.

[110] For an excellent review of the options, see Scott Barrett & Robert N. Stavins, *Increasing Participation and Compliance in International Climate Change Agreements* (John F. Kennedy School of Government, Harvard University, Working Paper No. RW P02–031, Aug. 14, 2002), *at* <http://ksgnotes1.harvard.edu/research/wpaper.nsf/rwp/RWP02-031?OpenDocument>.

[111] *See* OGANES TARGULIAN & HELMUT HIRSCH, RUSSIA: NO OIL AND GAS LEAKS, NO NUCLEAR POWER PLANTS (Apr. 2000), *available at* <http://greenpeace.no/3media/pr/rapport.pdf> (assessing savings that could be realized, perhaps quite cost-effectively, with jump-starting efforts). Pipeline leaks alone in Russia are estimated to generate some 35 million tons of methane emissions annually—the figure corresponding to Germany's annual CO_2 emission level. IRINA BARANOVA & CEE BANKWATCH NETWORK, LEAKING OPERATIONS: ENVIRONMENTAL CONSEQUENCES OF WORLD BANK AND EBRD INVOLVEMENT IN THE RUSSIAN OIL SECTOR, *available at* <http://www.bankwatch.org/publications/studies/leakingop/index.html> (last updated Apr. 20, 2001).

undertake some such measures through modest multilateral frameworks, which is a way it can get other developed countries to "match," and therefore amplify, its own contributions.[112]

My impression is that the multilateral fund established under the Montreal Protocol to underwrite phasing out emissions of ozone-depleting agents has been successful.[113] But such funds will not extend much beyond the level where there is payoff for the donors—if at all. At that boundary, the donors may prefer channeling assistance through frank and (hopefully) well-tailored aid and development programs, rather than through concessions in environmental accords.

Unfortunately, the Poor recognize that the "ideal" separate welfare system is just that—an ideal. The reality is that global development and welfare transfers are miserly.[114] And, for that matter, the "aid" that is provided is all too often designed to address donor priorities.[115] In this context, efforts of the Poor to extract "inefficient" benefits under the cover of MEAs—or through any other means—are not surprising. Nor do they appear likely to meet with much success.

III. Conclusion

"Common but differentiated responsibilities" puts a fresh label on a longstanding practice. The idea is that some countries should contribute more than others to the provision of global public goods, usually but not inevitably divided along a Rich-Poor axis. CDR is being pressed most vigorously in regard to the repair of the global environment. But the same issues arise in all areas that may benefit from collective action, ranging from peace and control of terrorism to regulation of epidemics and trade.

The practice of differentiating responsibilities has not, despite occasional claims by its proponents, been elevated to the status of a customary principle of international law. In general, the terms of customary international law and multilateral conventions apply universally.

In fact, the institutional framework for addressing the problem bilaterally is already in place in the form of the U.S./Gazprom Working Group, a joint initiative between Gazprom and the U.S. Environmental Protection Agency and Department of Energy. *See* Ilya Popov & Pacific Northwest National Laboratory, Estimating Methane Emissions from the Russian Natural Gas Sector, PNNL 13462 (Mar. 2001), *available at* <http://www.pnl.gov/aisu/pubs/Gazprom.pdf>.

[112] In 2002, the Bush administration increased its contribution to the Global Environment Facility, the premier multilateral funding mechanism for global environmental protection, by $70 million, pledging $500 million over four years, as part of a $2.92 billion replenishment to further the GEF through June 2006. *See* Eryn Gable, *Development: Nations Agree to $3b Enviro Fund Replenishment*, Greenwire, Aug. 8, 2002, §International.

[113] *See* Timothy Swanson & Robin Mason, *The Impact of International Environmental Agreements: The Case of the Montreal Protocol* (Fondazione Eni Enrico Matte Note di Lavoro, Working Paper No. 81, 2002), *available at* <http://www.feem.it/NR/rdonlyres/5542BA50-4119-4546-8989-3D4CC55CEA37/184/8102.pdf> (arguing that the cooperative path promoted by the regime has significantly diminished CFC emissions from their precooperative trajectory, and also suggesting that developing countries bear disproportionately larger costs). The wheels for success are greased by side payments organized under the multilateral fund, *see* Amendments to Montreal Protocol, *supra* note 1, Art. 10, which eases developing countries away from ozone depleting agents (ODAs) through a combination of tailored investment, noninvestment, policy, and regulatory support measures. As of the close of 2001, the World Bank and its country partners had phased out more than 80% of the total amount of ODAs to be phased out under the multilateral fund, with grant financing of over U.S.$420 million (about 45% of the funding available for investment projects). *See World Bank to Finance Projects in Four Countries to Fight Global Warming: Projects Worth USD35 Million will Protect the Ozone Layer*, Dec. 7, 2001, M2 Presswire (Ozone Depletion Network Online Today). *See generally* World Bank Montreal Protocol: 2002 Group Business Plan, *at* <http://www.worldbank.org/montrealprotocol>). Whether the marginal cost of the reductions, $3.81/kg/ODA, *id.* at 16, is efficient, is of course harder to say.

[114] *See* William B. Gould IV, *Labor Law for a Global Economy: The Uneasy Case for International Labor Standards*, 80 Neb. L. Rev. 715, 721 (2001).

[115] "USAID appears to have established as a priority the importance of influencing domestic policy in the recipient countries." Benjamin F. Nelson, International Affairs Budget: Framework for Assessing Relevance, Priority and Efficiency (Washington, DC: General Accounting Office, Oct. 30, 1997) (statement of Benjamin F. Nelson, director, international relations and trade issues, National Security and International Affairs Division, General Accounting Office, before the Senate Committee on the Budget), *at* <http://www.conginst.org/resultsact/PDF/NS98018.PDF>.

Lack of resources is no more a defense to transboundary pollution or trading in endangered species than it is to abusing ambassadors or practicing piracy.

It appears that as the number and reach of multilateral treaties has increased, so, too, has the incidence of obligation-differentiating agreements. But that falls short of proof that a new normative "principle" is in play. Different nations anticipate different costs and benefits from any single set of terms. Thus, one would expect some heterogeneity in terms just from rational, self-interested bargaining among parties with heterogeneous interests and resources.

Indeed, the fact that negotiations produce different burdens is less in need of explaining than why we do not see differences more frequently. Part of the answer is that we just do not *see* them, because they commonly occur in ways that preserve formal equality within the instrument's four corners and leave the discriminating to the margins. These extratextual discriminatory devices include reservations; unilateral "understandings"; side payments; de facto, informally differentiated commitments to agencies and funds; and clauses that, while formally equal, are known to be uneven in impact. The two routes are not equivalent. Side payment, for example, invites free riding—which party will pay the holdout?—and recipients may pocket an ex ante payoff and drop out. Universal terms are presumably easier to negotiate and administer than equality-riddling exceptions.

Sometimes, however, inequalities do find their way into the text. Those are the cases that present technical CDR, with its coinage of candidly differentiated formal terms. But even then, CDR is not a single notion. The form and scope may vary in ways not well marked in the literature. One version is rational bargaining CDR. It holds nothing more than that we accept as legitimate the outcome of unrestricted bargaining, notwithstanding that the burden falls unevenly, for example, by giving Poor countries a free ride on the contributions of Rich. Such outcomes, with one party contributing or receiving more than another, are "efficient" in the sense of being Pareto-improving: they leave at least one party better-off and no party less well-off than under the status quo. This version can hardly be controversial.

A second position, equitable CDR, would also confine the range of legitimate outcomes to a Pareto-improving set. But within that set, considerations of "fairness," based on differences in wealth or perhaps historical responsibilities, constrain distribution of cooperative gains more favorably toward the Poor than would occur under unfettered bargaining. The legitimacy of such an appeal, if hard to prove, is hard to deny.

The third version, however, inefficient CDR, demands that Poor's welfare be advanced unconditioned by mutual, if even marginal, reciprocal advances for Rich. In this view, given the global disparity in wealth and opportunity, there is no reason to protect Rich from emerging worse off than at the nonagreement point. The language of "efficiency" and "Pareto," which accept the status quo, is considered irrelevant or premature. The inequity (perhaps "iniquity") of the status quo is the very top item on the agenda.[116]

The stronger the version of CDR, and the more it seeks to override unbridled national self-interest and even to reshuffle wealth, the more resistance can be expected. The more the resistance, the heavier the burden on its proponent to come up with some "efficiency"-countervailing force, either in moral theory or in human understanding.

Moreover, even assuming that a moral or a humane (or even a pragmatic) argument can be made for some global wealth redistribution, it is not clearly wise to accomplish the transfers under the umbrella of multilateral negotiations aimed at other goals, such as environment or health. Such coupling may produce results that are suboptimal from both their

[116] And there is the ominous prophesy of the Johannesburg Declaration, *supra* note 3, Art. 12: "The deep fault line that divides human society between the rich and the poor and the ever-increasing gap between the developed and developing worlds pose a major threat to global prosperity, security and stability."

wealth-equalizing and substantive perspectives. The ideal would be to have one set of institutions focused on optimal substantive policies and another group focused on poverty and development. Coupling the ambitions threatens to produce suboptimal outcomes for each.

But the first best is not always achievable, less often so in the international than in the domestic arena. In the international arena, the realization of cooperative maxima is undermined by state sovereignty; free riding; the absence of any integrated, accountable government to tax, spend, and make and enforce rules; and the fragmentation and impotence of international governmental organizations that have been inserted to fill in the gaps. Moreover, from Poor's perspective, there is no assurance that the Rich will redirect their share of cooperative gains into higher budgets for development and aid.

We have not, by any means, heard the last of CDR, nor should we have. But we should proceed to address the issues it raises with greater clarity and understanding.

[4]

Conceptualising the Relationship between *Jus Cogens* and *Erga Omnes* Rules

MICHAEL BYERS*
Fellow, Jesus College, Oxford; Visiting Fellow, Max-Planck-Institut für ausländisches öffentliches Recht und Völkerrecht, Heidelberg, Germany

Abstract. Few concepts in international law have attracted as much attention or created as much controversy as *jus cogens* and *erga omnes* rules. This article attempts to show that *jus cogens* rules are rules of customary international law, and then to elucidate the relationship between these customary rules and the concept of *erga omnes*.

This article explains that: in contrast to *jus cogens* rules, *erga omnes* rules may arise either as customary rules or through treaties; a *jus cogens* or *erga omnes* rule could apply to only a limited number of States; although *jus cogens* rules are necessarily *erga omnes* rules, *erga omnes* could exist which were not of a *jus cogens* character.

1. Introduction

Few concepts in international law have attracted as much attention or created as much controversy as *jus cogens* and *erga omnes* rules. *Jus cogens* rules, otherwise known as "peremptory rules", are non-derogable rules of international "public policy". They render void other, non-peremptory rules which are in conflict with them. *Erga omnes* rules, on the other hand, are rules which, if violated, give rise to a general right of standing – amongst all States subject to those rules – to make claims.

Although it is widely assumed that the concepts of *jus cogens* and *erga omnes* are related, international lawyers have yet to agree on the character of that relationship. Some have asserted that there are important differences between the two types of rules, while others have argued that the two concepts refer to different aspects of the same rules, and are therefore coterminous.

It is also widely assumed that the special characteristics of *jus cogens* and *erga omnes* rules are not the result of one or more of the "voluntarist" (i.e., consent-based) sources of international law, in particular treaties and custom, but rather of "natural law" or some entirely new, *sui generis* mechanism of

* I wish to thank James Crawford, Anne Denise, Emanuela Gillard, Heike Krieger, Claus Kress, Georg Nolte and Jayaprakash Sen for their helpful comments on earlier drafts.

law creation. This latter assumption has created problems for international lawyers by making it difficult to account for such rules in a manner which is consistent with mainstream conceptions of international law. Philip Allott has gone so far as to assert that the existence of such rules is impossible to explain "except through the intervention of a Hammurabi or a Solon, through the adoption of a constitution, or through the systematic acceptance of an appropriate social theory, such as a theory of so-called natural law".[1]

This article addresses these theoretical problems, responding to and building on Allott's assertion by conceptualising the relationship between *jus cogens* rules, *erga omnes* rules, and the "voluntarist" sources of international law. It agrees with Allott that *jus cogens* rules could be explained as a consequence of the adoption of an international constitution, and argues that this development has already occurred. *Jus cogens* rules are constitutional rules: they limit the ability of States to create or change rules of international law, and prevent States from violating fundamental rules of international public policy, when the resulting rules or violations of rules would be seriously detrimental to the international legal system and how that system, and the society it serves, define themselves.

More specifically, this article attempts to show that *jus cogens* rules are derived from the "process of customary international law", which is itself part of an international constitutional order. The process of customary international law involves the development, by way of State practice and within a structure of shared understandings and virtually immutable principles, of informal but nevertheless binding rules. The shared understandings and virtually immutable principles define and control how legally relevant instances of supporting, ambivalent and opposing behaviour are weighed against one another, thus ensuring that customary rules protect or promote the common interests of most if not all States.[2]

This article then turns its attention to the relationship between *jus cogens* and *erga omnes* rules. It explains how, in contrast to *jus cogens* rules, *erga omnes* rules may be created either through the process of customary international law or by treaty. It also shows how, conceptually at least, a *jus cogens* or *erga omnes* rule could apply to only a limited number of States. Finally, this article demonstrates that *jus cogens* rules are necessarily *erga omnes* rules, but that *erga omnes* rules could exist which were not of a *jus cogens* character. Unlike *jus cogens* rules, *erga omnes* rules operate to expand the scope of possible claimants in those situations where traditional rules of standing do not

[1] Allott, "Reconstituting Humanity – New International Law", (1992) 3 *E.J.I.L.* 219, 250.

[2] See generally Michael Byers, "Custom, Power, and the Power of Rules: An Interdisciplinary Perspective on Customary International Law", (1995) 17 *M.J.I.L.* 109.

suffice to ensure that all rules of international law are capable of supporting effective inter-State claims.

2. *Jus Cogens* Rules

The concept of *jus cogens* has long been part of international law. Grotius, for instance, relied heavily on the Roman law distinction between *jus strictum* (obligatory law) and *jus dispositivum* (voluntary law) in *De Jure Belli et Pacis*.[3] Vattel distinguished between "le Droit des Gens *Naturel*, ou *Nécessaire*" and "le Droit *Volontaire*".[4] Even in the early twentieth century, when thinking about international law was heavily dominated by voluntarist approaches, several prominent scholars clung to the idea of *jus cogens* rules.[5] Oppenheim asserted that a number of "universally recognised principles" of international law existed which rendered any conflicting treaty void, and that the peremptory effect of such principles was itself a "unanimously recognised customary rule of International Law".[6] Similarly, the eighth edition of Hall's *International Law* stated:

> The requirement that contracts shall be in conformity with law invalidates, or at least renders voidable, all agreements which are at variance with the fundamental principles of international law and their undisputed applications, and with the arbitrary usages which have acquired decisive authority.[7]

During the same period the concept of *jus cogens* twice found favour in a judicial context: first in the decision of the French-Mexican Claims Commission in the 1928 *Pablo Nájera Case*[8]; and then by Judge Schücking

[3] (1625) See William Whewell (ed. and trans.) (Cambridge: C.U.P., 1853).

[4] (1758) See Emer de Vattel, *Le Droit des Gens* (Washington: Carnegie Institution, 1916) Préliminaires, §§9 and 27.

[5] On the apparent incompatibility of voluntarist approaches and *jus cogens* rules, see discussion *infra*, text accompanying notes 43–44.

[6] Lassa Oppenheim, *International Law (Vol. 1: Peace)* (London: Longmans, 1905) 528. Oppenheim gave the example of a treaty supporting piracy, which he claimed would be void.

[7] William Hall, *A Treatise on International Law* (8th ed., edited by Pearce Higgins) (Oxford: Clarendon, 1924) 382. The following examples were given of treaties which would be void: treaties for "the subjugation or partition of a country", for the "assertion of proprietary rights over the open seas" or to "establish slave trade", or any agreement "at variance with such principles, not immediately applicable to the relations of states, as it is incumbent on them as moral beings to respect". Ibid., 383. See also Friedrich v.d. Heydte, "Die Erscheinungsform des Zwischenstaatlichen Rechts: jus cogens und jus dispositivum im Völkerrecht", (1932) 16 *Z. Völkerrecht* 461.

[8] (1928) 5 *R.I.A.A.* 466, 472.

of the Permanent Court of International Justice in his individual opinion in the 1934 *Oscar Chinn Case*.[9] Later, a number of separate or dissenting opinions of judges of the International Court of Justice made similar references to *jus cogens* rules.[10]

In recent years, most of the attention paid to the *jus cogens* concept has resulted from its inclusion in two separate provisions of the 1969 *Vienna Convention on the Law of Treaties*.[11] The first of these provisions, Article 53, deals with the effect of existing *jus cogens* rules on treaties which, at the time of their conclusion, conflict with those rules. It reads:

> A treaty is void if, at the time of its conclusion, it conflicts with a peremptory norm of general international law. For the purposes of the present Convention, a peremptory norm of general international law is a norm accepted and recognized by the international community of States as a whole as a norm from which no derogation is permitted and which can be modified only by a subsequent norm of general international law having the same character.

The second of these provisions, Article 64, deals with those situations where such a *jus cogens* rule emerges, and comes into conflict with a pre-existing treaty. It reads:

> If a new peremptory norm of general international law emerges, any existing treaty which is in conflict with that norm becomes void and terminates.

In both instances, the *jus cogens* rule trumps the relevant treaty, rendering it void in its entirety.

Today, there is widespread acceptance among international lawyers of the concept of *jus cogens*. It has been widely discussed by scholars and was included in the 1986 *Vienna Convention on the Law of Treaties Between States and International Organizations or Between International Organizations*.[12]

[9] (1934) *P.C.I.J. Rep.*, Ser. A/B, No. 63, 61, 149–150.

[10] See, e.g., Judge Quintana in *Case Concerning the Application of the Convention of 1902 Governing the Guardianship of Infants* (1958) *I.C.J. Rep.* 55, 106–107; Judge *ad hoc* Fernandes in *Case Concerning Right of Passage over Indian Territory* (1960) *I.C.J. Rep.* 6, 135; Judge Tanaka in *South West Africa Case, Second Phase* (1966) *I.C.J. Rep.* 6, 298; Judge Nervo in *North Sea Continental Shelf Cases* (1969) *I.C.J. Rep.* 3, 97.

[11] 1155 U.N.T.S. 331; reproduced in (1969) 8 *I.L.M.* 679 (hereinafter "1969 *Vienna Convention*").

[12] For scholarly support for the concept see, e.g., Alfred Verdross, "Jus Dispositivum and Jus Cogens in International Law", (1966) 60 *A.J.I.L.* 55; Michel Virally, "Réflexions sur le «jus cogens»", (1966) 12 *A.F.D.I.* 5; Hermann Mosler, "Jus Cogens im Völkerrecht", (1968) 25 *Schw. J.i.R.* 9; Nicholas Onuf and Richard Birney, "Peremptory Norms of Internation-

The International Court mentioned the concept in its judgment in the 1969 *North Sea Continental Shelf Cases*[13] and, in its judgment in the 1986 *Nicaragua Case (Merits)*, quoted with approval the following statement by the International Law Commission:

> [T]he law of the Charter concerning the prohibition of the use of force in itself constitutes a conspicuous example of a rule in international law having the character of *jus cogens* . . . .[14]

There has also been a growing trend of thought which considers that *jus cogens* rules have unusual effects on more than just conflicting treaties. This trend is consistent with Article 53 of the 1969 *Vienna Convention*, which states that *jus cogens* rules permit "no derogation".[15] For instance, the International Law Commission may have adopted the concept, or at least some variant of it, in distinguishing between international crimes and international delicts in its work on State responsibility. International crimes are breaches by States of obligations which are "essential for the protection of fundamental interests of the international community", whereas international delicts are all other "internationally wrongful" acts.[16]

al Law: Their Source, Function and Future", (1974) 4 *Denver J.I.L. & Pol'y* 187; Ronald Macdonald, "Fundamental Norms in Contemporary International Law", (1987) 25 *C.Y.I.L.* 115; Lauri Hannikainen, *Peremptory Norms (Jus Cogens) in International Law* (Helsinki: Lakimiesliiton Kustannus, 1988); Karen Parker and Lyn Neylon, "*Jus Cogens*: Compelling the Law of Human Rights", (1989) 12 *Hastings I. & Comp. L.R.* 411; Gennady Danilenko, "International *Jus Cogens*: Issues of Law-Making", (1991) 2 *E.J.I.L.* 42; Stefan Kadelbach, *Zwingendes Völkerrecht* (Berlin: Duncker & Humblot, 1992). For scepticism see, e.g., Georg Schwarzenberger, "International *Jus Cogens*?" (1965) 43 *Texas L.R.* 455; Jerzy Sztucki, *Jus Cogens and the Vienna Convention on the Law of Treaties* (Vienna: Springer-Verlag, 1974); Prosper Weil, "Towards Relative Normativity in International Law?" (1983) 77 *A.J.I.L.* 413 (originally published in French: "Vers une normativité relative en droit international?" (1982) 86 *R.G.D.I.P.* 5); Gode Hartmann, "Internationales jus cogens?" (1983) 11(4) *Demokratie und Recht* 390; Mark Weisburd, "The Emptiness of the Concept of *Jus Cogens*, As Illustrated by the War in Bosnia-Herzegovina", (1995) 17 *M.J.I.L.* 1. The 1986 *Vienna Convention* is reproduced in (1986) 25 *I.L.M.* 543. Articles 53 and 64 of this treaty are identical to Articles 53 and 64 of the 1969 *Vienna Convention*, reproduced *supra*, text following note 11.

[13] *Supra*, note 10, 42 (para. 72).

[14] (1986) *I.C.J. Rep.* 14, 100 (para. 190) (quoting from the commentary of the I.L.C. to Article 50 of its "Draft Articles on the Law of Treaties", in *Report of the I.L.C. on the Work of Its 18th Session* (1966) 2 *Yb.I.L.C.* 172, 247). For scholarly support for this conclusion see, e.g., Verdross (1966), *supra*, note 12, 60; Virally, *supra*, note 12, 28; James Crawford, *The Creation of States in International Law* (Oxford: Clarendon, 1979) 106; Hannikainen, *supra*, note 12, 323–356.

[15] For the text of Article 53, see *supra*, text following note 11.

[16] See Article 19, "Draft Articles on State Responsibility (Part One)", in *Report of the I.L.C. on the Work of Its 32nd Session*, (1980) 2(2) *Yb.I.L.C.* 26, 32; Joseph Weiler et al. (eds.), *International Crimes of State: A Critical Analysis of the I.L.C.'s Draft Article 19 on State Responsibility* (Berlin: de Gruyter, 1989). The distinction is important in terms of the scope of

It has also been suggested that treaty provisions which potentially limit the application of *jus cogens* rules without being in violation of them might not apply in such situations.[17] Similarly, an action which, although taken pursuant to a legal treaty, is nonetheless in violation of a *jus cogens* rule would clearly be contrary to international law notwithstanding the legality of the treaty.[18] It was on the basis of such reasoning that Judge *ad hoc* Lauterpacht, in his 1993 separate opinion on a request for provisional measures in the *Case Concerning Application of the Convention on the Prevention and Punishment of the Crime of Genocide*, applied the concept of *jus cogens* to the question of the legality of the arms embargo which had been imposed on Bosnia-Herzegovina by the United Nations Security Council.[19] The Security Council had been acting under Chapter VII of the *Charter of the United Nations*. Lauterpacht wrote:

> The concept of *jus cogens* operates as a concept superior to both customary international law and treaty. The relief which Article 103 of the Charter may give the Security Council in case of conflict between one of its decisions and an operative treaty obligation cannot – as a matter of simple hierarchy of norms – extend to a conflict between a Security Council

injury in the event of a breach. In short, only international crimes constitute violations of *erga omnes* rules. It is, therefore, probably more accurate to describe the concept of international crimes as a variant of the concept of *erga omnes*. See Article 5(3), "Draft Articles on State Responsibility (Part Two)", in *Report of the I.L.C. on the Work of Its 37th Session*, (1985) 2(2) *Yb.I.L.C.* 25; discussion, *infra*, text accompanying note 73. The I.L.C. clearly did not consider international crimes and *jus cogens* rules to be exactly the same thing. In its commentary to Article 19 it wrote (ibid., 120):

> [O]bligations whose breach is a crime will "normally" be those deriving from rules of *jus cogens*, though this conclusion cannot be absolute ... the category of international obligations admitting of no derogation is much broader than the category of obligations whose breach is necessarily an international crime.

It is perhaps significant that Article 19 of the "Draft Articles on State Responsibility (Part One)" does not refer explicitly to the concept of *jus cogens* (or "peremptory norm"), whereas Articles 18(2), 29(2) and 33(2)(a) do. In addition, it is unclear whether the concept is required with respect to unilateral acts. *Jus cogens* rules are essentially "conflict of law" rules which operate between customary rules of a fundamental, public policy character and treaties and other objective regimes. They are not needed to control the actions of individual States because States cannot create treaties and objective regimes on their own. See Krystyna Marek, "Contribution à l'étude du *jus cogens* en droit international", in *Recueil d'études de droit international en hommage à Paul Guggenheim* (Tome 2) (Geneva: University of Geneva, 1968) 426, 441.

[17] See Ian Brownlie, *Principles of Public International Law* (4th ed.) (Oxford: Clarendon, 1990) 613, fn. 49. Brownlie referred to Article 102(2) of the *Charter of the United Nations*, which reads: "No party to any such treaty or international agreement which has not been registered ... may invoke that treaty or agreement before any organ of the United Nations". He asked: "If the instrument is part of the *jus cogens*, should non-registration have this effect?"

[18] See Oscar Schachter, *International Law in Theory and Practice* (Dordrecht: Nijhoff, 1991) 343–344.

[19] (1993) *I.C.J. Rep.* 325, 407. The arms embargo extended to the rest of the former Yugoslavia.

> resolution and *jus cogens*. Indeed, one only has to state the opposite proposition thus – that a Security Council resolution may even require participation in genocide – for its unacceptability to be apparent.[20]

If Lauterpacht's analysis is correct a *jus cogens* rule may thus override even the most authoritative form of executive action known to international society, should that authority be exercised in violation of that rule.[21]

Jus cogens rules would also seem to preclude persistent objection, as well as the establishment of other legal exceptions through the creation of rules of special customary international law.[22] They may also play a role with regard to questions of statehood and territorial acquisition, such that they make it more difficult for the principles of effectiveness and extinctive prescription

[20] Ibid., 440 (para. 100). For support for the prohibition against genocide being a *jus cogens* rule see, e.g., *Report of the I.L.C. on the Work of Its 18th Session*, *supra*, note 14, 248; Virally, *supra*, note 12, 10; Roberto Ago, "Droit des traités à la lumière de la Convention de Vienne", (1971 III) *R.d.C.* 297, 324, fn. 37; Levan Alexidze, "Legal Nature of *Jus Cogens* in Contemporary International Law", (1981 III) 172 *R.d.C.* 219, 262. It might be argued that the prohibition against genocide is in this respect an unusual *jus cogens* rule and that the Security Council is explicitly authorised to act contrary to another *jus cogens* rule, namely the prohibition on the use of force. However, this latter rule is constrained in scope and only concerns the aggressive use of force, i.e., force which is used neither in self-defence nor with the authorization of the Security Council. Moreover, the Security Council was created to enforce this rule, not to act contrary to it.

[21] However, it is not clear whether Lauterpacht's analysis would apply if the Security Council were violating a *jus cogens* rule in order to prevent the violation of either that same rule, or another *jus cogens* rule. Given that most Security Council actions address the aggressive threat or use of force, and therefore violations of the *jus cogens* rule prohibiting such threats or uses, the analysis would seem to require expansion to include an examination of the effectiveness of any such action in support of one *jus cogens* rule, at the expense of another. That being said, the Security Council's actions to prevent genocide in Bosnia-Herzegovina were clearly ineffective.

[22] On the preclusion of persistent objection, see M.K. Yasseen (Chair of the Drafting Committee), *U.N. Conference on the Law of Treaties, Official Records* (1st Sess. 1968) (New York: United Nations, 1969) 472; Christos Rozakis, *The Concept of Jus Cogens in the Law of Treaties* (Amsterdam: North-Holland, 1976) 78; Alexidze, *supra*, note 20, 246–247 and 258; Brownlie, *supra*, note 17, 514; *Case 9647 (United States)* (Inter-American Commission of Human Rights), reproduced in Thomas Buergenthal and Robert Norris (eds.), *Human Rights: The Inter-American System* (Booklet 21.3) (Dobbs Ferry: Oceana, 1988) 61, 78–79. Compare: Schwarzenberger, *supra*, note 12, 459–460; Antonio Cassese, *International Law in a Divided World* (Oxford: Clarendon, 1986) 178. On persistent objection more generally, see Jonathan Charney, "The Persistent Objector Rule and the Development of Customary International Law" (1985) 56 *B.Y.I.L.* 1; Ted Stein, "The Approach of the Different Drummer: The Principle of the Persistent Objector in International Law" (1985) 26 *H.I.L.J.* 457; David Colson, "How Persistent Must the Persistent Objector be?" (1986) 61 *Wash. L.R.* 957. On special customary international law, see generally Gérard Cohen-Jonathan, "La coutume locale" (1961) 7 *A.F.D.I.* 119; Paul Guggenheim, "Lokales Gewohnheitsrecht" (1961) 11 *Ö.Z.ö.R.* 327; Anthony D'Amato, "The Concept of Special Custom in International Law" (1969) 63 *A.J.I.L.* 211; Michael Akehurst, "Custom as a Source of International Law", (1974–1975) 47 *B.Y.I.L.* 1, 28–31; Serge Sur, *La coutume internationale* (Paris: Librairies Techniques, 1990) 2e cahier, 3 and 12–13.

to operate in situations where territory has been occupied in a manner which violates one or more *jus cogens* rules.[23] Their violation might also result in the loss of certain privileges, such as the rule that belligerent States are not responsible for damage caused to subjects of neutral States by military operations.[24] Finally, the existence of *jus cogens* rules would seem to provide a strong guide to the interpretation of treaties, so that conflicts between such rules and treaties are avoided wherever possible.[25]

[23] See Robert Jennings, "Nullity and Effectiveness in International Law", in *Cambridge Essays in International Law* (London: Stevens, 1965) 64, 70–78; James Crawford, "The Criteria for Statehood in International Law", (1976–1977) 48 *B.Y.I.L.* 93, 148; Crawford, (1979) *supra*, note 14, 81–84 and 420; Brownlie, *supra*, note 17, 80; discussion (of the *East Timor Case*) *infra*, note 97.

[24] See Georg Schwarzenberger, *International Law* (3rd ed., Vol. 1) (London: Stevens, 1957) 646; Brownlie, *supra*, note 17, 514. Article 33(2)(a) of the "I.L.C. Draft Articles on State Responsibility (Part One)", *supra*, note 16, 33, reads:

> In any case, a state of necessity may not be invoked by a State as a ground for precluding wrongfulness: (a) if the international obligation with which the act of the State is not in conformity arises out of a peremptory norm of general international law.

[25] See Article 31(3)(c), 1969 *Vienna Convention*, *supra*, note 11; Arnold McNair, *The Law of Treaties* (Oxford: Clarendon, 1961) 383–385. There are at least two other instances where the effects of *jus cogens* rules might seem to extend beyond treaties. Firstly, in *Siderman de Blake* v. *Republic of Argentina* (965 F.2d 699 (9th Cir. 1992)), *Princz* v. *Federal Republic of Germany* (26 F.3d 1166 (D.C.Cir 1994), *cert. denied*, 115 S.Ct. 923 (1995)) and *Al Adsani* v. *Government of Kuwait and Others* (Court of Queen's Bench (England), 3 May 1995; Court of Appeal, 12 March 1996; both forthcoming in ILR) national courts were asked to deny State immunity in cases involving violations of the prohibition against torture in the territories of other States. However, in all three cases immunity was upheld. Moreover, strictly speaking these cases were not about international law, but rather about the jurisdiction of national courts over rights under international law. For comment on the U.S. cases, see Mathias Reimann, "A Human Rights Exception to Sovereign Immunity: Some Thoughts on *Princz* v. *Federal Republic of Germany*", (1995) 16 *M.J.I.L.* 403; Andreas Zimmermann, "Sovereign Immunity and Violations of International *Jus Cogens* – Some Critical Remarks", (1995) 16 *M.J.I.L.* 433.

Secondly, in both *Belilos* v. *Switzerland* (1988) *E.C.H.R.*, Ser. A, Vol. 132 and *Loizidou* v. *Turkey (Preliminary Objections)* (1995) *E.C.H.R.*, Ser. A, Vol. 310 the European Court of Human Rights held that a State which made an illegal reservation to a human rights treaty (or, more specifically in *Loizidou*, an illegal reservation to a declaration of acceptance under an optional clause) was bound by that treaty (or declaration) without the benefit of the reservation. A set of guidelines produced by the United Nations Human Rights Committee has adopted the same position. See "General Comment No. 24 (52)", CCPR/C/21/Rev.1/Add.6, 11 Nov. 1994, 7 (para. 18), reproduced (with the key paragraph missing) in (1995) 34 *I.L.M.* 839. This position is contrary to that of general international law, whereby an objection to an illegal reservation results in the article which is the subject of that reservation being severed from the treaty, or in the entire treaty being struck down, or whereby an illegal reservation to an acceptance of an optional clause results in the entire acceptance being rendered void. See Article 21(3), 1969 *Vienna Convention*, *supra*, note 12; *Reservations to the Convention on Genocide, Advisory Opinion* (1951) *I.C.J. Rep.* 15, 21–27; Ian Sinclair, *The Vienna Convention on the Law of Treaties* (2nd ed.) (Manchester: M.U.P., 1984) 56–63. However, these unusual effects do not appear to be the result of *jus cogens* rules – as such – but rather of human rights rules more generally speaking.

In addition to the prohibitions against the aggressive use of force and genocide, rules which are today widely accepted as being rules of *jus cogens* include the prohibitions against slavery, torture and apartheid.[26] These rules play an essential role in the international legal system by defining certain key aspects of that system and making it extremely difficult for States to change the way these rules apply to them. In this way *jus cogens* rules would appear to resemble – at least to some degree – the constitutional rules of national legal systems.

3. *Jus Cogens* Rules as Constitutional Rules

All mature legal systems contain at least some constitutional rules. Constitutional rules define the fundamental characteristics of a legal system: namely, who may participate in that system and how they may participate, and how rules, both constitutional and not, may be developed, maintained and changed. Perhaps most importantly, constitutional rules frequently limit the ability of law-makers to create or change rules in ways which would be detrimental to those human rights or civil liberties which are considered to be essential, defining aspects of the legal system and the society it serves.[27]

It is clear that a constitutional system of some sort exists at the international level.[28] Certain "secondary rules", such as the rule of *pacta sunt servanda* and the process of customary international law, have long affected how rules of international law are developed, maintained and changed.[29] The process of customary international law is itself composed of a number of shared understandings and virtually immutable principles which structure the evolu-

[26] On the prohibition against slavery, see Hannikainen, *supra*, note 12, 444–447; Brownlie, *supra*, note 17, 513; Kadelbach, *supra*, note 12, 296–297. On the prohibition against torture: Rosalyn Higgins, "Derogations under Human Rights Treaties", (1976–1977) 48 *B.Y.I.L.* 281, 282; Nigel Rodley, *The Treatment of Prisoners in International Law* (Oxford: Clarendon, 1987) 70; Hannikainen, *supra*, note 12, 499–513; Kadelbach, *supra*, note 12, 291–294. On the prohibition against apartheid: John Dugard, *Recognition and the United Nations* (Cambridge: Grotius, 1987) 156–158; Hannikainen, *supra*, note 12, 467–489; Kadelbach, *supra*, note 12, 277–282.

[27] On constitutional theory, see generally Geoffrey Marshall, *Constitutional Theory* (Oxford: Clarendon, 1971); Ernst Böckenförde, *Staat, Verfassung, Demokratie* (Frankfurt: Suhrkamp, 1991).

[28] See generally Jochen Frowein, *Reaction by Not Directly Affected States to Breaches of Public International Law*' (1994 IV) 248 *R.d.C.* 345, 355–365.

[29] See Byers, *supra*, note 2. *Pacta sunt servanda* may be considered to be one aspect of a more general rule, namely the principle of legitimate expectation. See also: Vaughan Lowe, "Do General Rules of International Law Exist?" (1983) *R.I.S.* 207; Jonathan Charney, "Universal International Law", (1993) 87 *A.J.I.L.* 529, 533–542. The concept of secondary rules was developed by H.L.A. Hart in *The Concept of Law* (Oxford: Clarendon, 1961).

tion of those informal rules which are binding upon States.[30] But unlike the constitutional rules of many national legal systems, these secondary rules of international law are themselves customary in origin.[31]

It is also sometimes asserted that the *Charter of the United Nations* is a constitution for international society, one which is binding even on non-member States.[32] Related assertions have been made with respect to other, more recent developments, such as aspects of the 1982 *United Nations Convention on the Law of the Sea*.[33]

Some of the most obvious examples of constitutional rules in international law are rules of *jus cogens*. Nowhere else in the international legal system is the ability of some rules to limit the ability of States to develop, maintain or change other rules, or to prevent them from violating fundamental rules of international public policy, so clear.

4. The Source of *Jus Cogens* Rules

There is, however, some uncertainty as to the source of *jus cogens* rules. There are serious problems associated with assertions that they could be the result of one or any of the traditional primary sources of international law (treaties,

[30] See Byers, *supra*, note 2.

[31] See Byers, *supra*, note 2, 147–149. The customary process is, therefore, essential to the current international constitutional order. A few national legal systems, such as that of the United Kingdom, also have constitutions which are primarily customary in character. See Philip Allott, "The Theory of the British Constitution", in Hyman Ross and Ross Harrison (eds.), *Jurisprudence: Cambridge Essays* (Oxford: Clarendon, 1992); Stanley de Smith and Rodney Brazier, *Constitutional and Administrative Law* (7th ed.) (London: Penguin, 1994).

[32] See, e.g., Alf Ross, *Constitution of the United Nations* (New York: Rinehart, 1950); Hans Kelsen, *The Law of the United Nations* (London: Stevens, 1951) 106–110; Alfred Verdross and Bruno Simma, *Universelles Völkerrecht* (3rd ed.) (Berlin: Duncker & Humblot, 1984) 66–220; Nicholas Onuf, "The Constitution of International Society", (1994) 5 *E.J.I.L.* 1, 16-17. Article 2(6) of the *Charter* itself states:

> The Organization shall ensure that States which are not Members of the United Nations act in accordance with these Principles so far as may be necessary for the maintenance of international peace and security.

Compare: Josef Kunz, "Revolutionary Creation of Norms of International Law" (1947) 41 *A.J.I.L.* 119; Philippe Cahier, "Le problème des effets des traités à l'égard des états tiers", (1974 III) 143 *R.d.C.* 589, 715–716; "Note Verbale from the Chargé d'affaires a.i. of the Permanent Observer Mission of Switzerland to the United Nations addressed to the Secretary-General", 22 August 1990, reproduced in Daniel Bethlehem, *The Kuwait Crisis: Sanctions and their Economic Consequences* (Cambridge: Grotius, 1991) 306–307. A constitutional role might also be ascribed to the 1957 *Treaty Establishing the European Economic Community* ((1958) 298 U.N.T.S. 11).

[33] See, e.g., Philip Allott, "*Mare Nostrum*: A New International Law of the Sea", (1992) 86 *A.J.I.L.* 764.

customary international law, general principles of law), or perhaps natural law.[34] Treaties can at best only be contributing factors in the development of *jus cogens* rules, for two reasons. Firstly, a treaty cannot bind its parties not to modify its terms, nor to relieve themselves of their obligations under it, through a subsequent treaty to which all the parties to the first treaty have consented.[35] Secondly, all existing, generally accepted *jus cogens* rules apply universally and none of the treaties which have codified these rules has been universally ratified.[36] No treaty which has not been universally ratified, not even the *Charter of the United Nations*, can establish a rule of general international law, for treaties can only create obligations as between their parties.[37]

There are some indications that *jus cogens* rules should be considered rules of customary international law. Traditional conceptions of customary international law require *opinio juris* in addition to State practice, with *opinio juris* being the belief or acceptance by States that their practice is consistent with or creative of the relevant customary rule.[38] *Opinio juris*, or something like *opinio juris*, appears to be at the root of the non-derogable character of *jus cogens* rules because States, quite simply, do not believe that it is possible to contract out of *jus cogens* rules, or persistently to object to them. They regard those rules as being so important to the international society of States, and to how that society has come to define itself, that they can conceive of no exceptions to them. As a result, State practice which would otherwise

[34] For a suggestion that *jus cogens* rules may be derived from either treaties, customary international law, or general principles of law, see *Report of the I.L.C. on the Work of Its 18th Session, supra*, note 14, 248. For assertions that they are rules of customary international law see, e.g., Brownlie, *supra*, note 17, 513; Jordan Paust, "The Reality of *Jus Cogens*", (1991) 7 *Conn. J.I.L.* 81; Kadelbach, *supra*, note 12, 186. For explanations that they are derived from natural law, see, e.g., *U.N. Conference on the Law of Treaties, supra*, note 22, statements by Italy (311); Ecuador (320); Monaco (324). See subsequently: Charles de Visscher, "Positivism et «*jus cogens*»", (1971) 75 *R.G.D.I.P.* 5. On the different sources of international law, see Article 38(1) of the *Statute of the International Court of Justice*; Brownlie, *supra*, note 17, 1–31.

[35] See Article 39, 1969 *Vienna Convention, supra*, note 11; Article 29(1), "I.L.C. Draft Articles on State Responsibility (Part One)", *supra*, note 16.

[36] See Danilenko, *supra*, note 12, 63.

[37] See Article 34, 1969 *Vienna Convention, supra*, note 11; Sur, *supra*, note 22, 1er cahier, 13.

[38] See Article 38(1)(b) of the *Statute of the International Court of Justice*; *North Sea Continental Shelf Cases, supra*, note 10, 44 (para. 77); Gennady Danilenko, "The Theory of International Customary Law", (1988) 31 *G.Y.I.L.* 9; Brownlie, *supra*, note 17, 4–11; Robert Jennings and Arthur Watts (eds.), *Oppenheim's International Law (Vol. 1: Peace)* (9th ed.) (Harlow: Longman, 1992) 25–31; Rudolf Bernhardt, "Customary International Law", in Bernhardt (ed.), *Encyclopedia of Public International Law* (Vol. 1) (Amsterdam: North-Holland, 1992) 898.

contribute to the creation of legal exceptions is consequently not regarded as relevant to the customary process and capable of generating legal effects.

A good example of this phenomenon may be international society's reaction to South Africa's former racist policies.[39] It seems that other States never contemplated the possibility of South Africa establishing itself as a persistent objector to the prohibition against apartheid, which they regarded as a *jus cogens* rule.[40] The non-derogable character of *jus cogens* rules may thus be explained in a manner which is consistent with traditional, bi-partite conceptions of customary international law.

Even if *jus cogens* rules were regarded as being in some way self-evident, rather than being derived from or evident in those instances of State practice which States consider to be legally relevant, *jus cogens* rules might nevertheless still be regarded as rules of customary international law. Since the customary process determines the common interests of most if not all States, and then protects and promotes those common interests with rules,[41] the weighing of supporting, ambivalent and opposing State practice may be a facilitative, and not an always necessary exercise. Although the interests of States will usually become clear only through a careful examination of their actions and statements, in some instances their interests may be so obvious that such a careful examination of State practice is not required.[42] Translated literally *jus cogens* means "compelling law", and many of the rules which are widely accepted as being *jus cogens* rules are quite clearly in the interests of most States, as those States see and manifest those interests to be.

Yet customary international law is problematic as a source for *jus cogens* rules because customary international law is generally considered to be based on State consent,[43] even though this consent may take the form of a diffuse consensus, or of a general consent to the process of customary international

[39] See generally Richard Bissell, *Apartheid and International Organizations* (Boulder: Westview, 1977); Özdemir Özgur, *Apartheid: The United Nations and Peaceful Change in South Africa* (Epping: Bowker, 1982).

[40] See, e.g., Article 5(3) *International Convention on the Suppression and Punishment of the Crime of Apartheid*, U.N.G.A. Res. 3068 (XXVIII) (1973), reproduced in (1974) 13 *I.L.M.* 50; U.N.G.A. Res. 33/183 (1979) (concerning policies of apartheid of the Government of South Africa); Jost Delbrück, "Apartheid", in Rudolf Bernhardt (ed.), *Encyclopedia of Public International Law* (Vol. 8) (Amsterdam: North-Holland, 1985) 37; Dugard, *supra*, note 26, 156–158.

[41] See discussion, *supra*, text accompanying note 2; Byers, *supra*, note 2, 136–147.

[42] See Byers, *supra*, note 2, 145–147.

[43] On the consensual basis of customary international law, see *Lotus Case* (1927) P.C.I.J. Rep., Ser. A, No. 9, 18; *Nicaragua Case (Merits)*, *supra*, note 14, 135 (para. 269); Percy Corbett, "The Consent of States and the Sources of the Law of Nations", (1925) 6 *B.Y.I.L.* 20; G.J.H. van Hoof, *Rethinking the Sources of International Law* (Deventer: Kluwer, 1983) 76 et seq.; Sur, *supra*, note 22, 2e cahier, 4–5; Karol Wolfke, *Custom in Present International Law* (2nd rev. ed.) (Dordrecht: Nijhoff, 1993).

law, as distinct from specific consent to individual rules.[44] Individual States, if they choose, are, therefore, able to create legal exceptions to such rules. Even a general consent does not in itself preclude the creation of such exceptions.

The creation of legal exceptions does not only occur through persistent objection, but also through the development of rules of special customary international law and the conclusion of treaties. These latter two kinds of exception operate on the basis of new rules applicable only between the States which are subject or party to them. Most scholars agree, and the 1969 *Vienna Convention* confirms, that *jus cogens* rules deny the latter of these three options, namely the creation of exceptions through treaties.[45] Many scholars consider that *jus cogens* rules also deny the first two options, namely persistent objection and the creation of rules of special customary international law.[46] Since the creation of legal exceptions is precluded, *jus cogens* rules might appear to lack the consensual basis which is generally associated with customary international law. For this reason it is frequently assumed that such rules cannot be the result of the customary process.[47]

Jus cogens rules are frequently explained as being, or at least being derived from, general principles of law, even though such principles have only rarely been invoked explicitly by international tribunals, and when invoked, have never had their basis fully explained.[48] For example, in 1953 Hersch Lauterpacht, as Special Rapporteur on the Law of Treaties, included an article on *jus cogens* rules in his report to the International Law Commission.[49] In his commentary to that article he stated:

[44] See Lowe, *supra*, note 29; Joseph Raz, *Practical Reason and Norms* (Princeton: P.U.P., 1990) 123–129; Philip Allott, *Eunomia: New Order for a New World* (New York: O.U.P., 1990) 145–177; Sur, *supra*, note 22, 2e cahier, 5 and 10.

[45] See discussion *supra*, text accompanying and notes 3–12.

[46] See discussion *supra*, text accompanying and note 22.

[47] See, e.g., Weil, *supra*, note 12, 425–429; Sur, *supra*, note 22, 1er cahier, 13 and 2e cahier, 8; Danilenko, *supra*, note 12, 47 et seq.; to some degree, Onuf and Birney, *supra*, note 12. Compare: *Report of the I.L.C. on the Work of Its 18th Session*, *supra*, note 14, 248, where the I.L.C. stated its intent to leave the full content of the *jus cogens* concept "to be worked out in State practice and in the jurisprudence of international tribunals"; "Commentary to the I.L.C. Draft Articles on State Responsibility", in *Report of the I.L.C. on the Work of Its 28th Session* (1976) 2(2) *Yb.I.L.C.* 75, 85–86 (para. 21); Brownlie, *supra*, note 17, 513; Paust, *supra*, note 34; Kadelbach, *supra*, note 12, 186; by implication, *Nicaragua Case (Merits)*, *supra*, note 14, 100–101 (para. 190).

[48] See *Chorzow Factory Case* (1928) P.C.I.J. Rep., Ser. A, No. 17, 29; the individual opinion of Judge Hudson in the *River Meuse Case* (1937) P.C.I.J. Rep., Ser. A/B, No. 70, 76–77; *Effect of Awards of Compensation made by the U.N. Administrative Tribunal, Advisory Opinion* (1954) *I.C.J. Rep.* 47, 53.

[49] (1953) 2 *Yb.I.L.C.* 90, 93. The article in question was Article 15:

> A treaty, or any of its provisions, is void if its performance involves an act which is illegal under international law and if it is declared so to be by the International Court of Justice.

> [T]he test whether the object of the treaty is illegal and whether the treaty is void for that reason is not only inconsistency with customary international law pure and simple, but inconsistency with such overriding principles of international law which may be regarded as constituting principles of international public policy (*ordre international public*). These principles need not necessarily have crystallized in a clearly accepted rule of law .... They may be expressive of rules of international morality so cogent that an international tribunal would consider them as forming part of those principles of law generally recognized by civilized nations which the International Court of Justice is bound to apply .... The voidance of contractual agreements whose object is illegal is a general principle of international law.[50]

General principles of law may be viewed in two ways. Firstly, it is possible to consider them as Lauterpacht seemed to do, as a kind of natural law.[51] From this perspective their possible status as *jus cogens* rules, or as bases for *jus cogens* rules, falls victim to the following problem. Natural law scholars generally consider that rules of international law are, at least to some degree, part of an established order which necessarily predated the development of any contemporary legal system.[52] However, societies are dynamic, even if the fundamental rules which structure their legal systems purport not to be. The international legal system is, in the absence of an overarching sovereign, a particularly dynamic legal system. It is therefore likely at some point to conceive, or to have already conceived, differently of its requirements in terms of fundamental, peremptory rules. For instance, most international lawyers would accept that *jus cogens* rules have not always existed. As a result, *jus cogens* rules cannot be rules of natural law, or based on such rules.[53]

[50] Ibid., 155. See also: Alfred Verdross, "Forbidden Treaties in International Law", (1937) 31 *A.J.I.L.* 571, 572–573.

[51] See also: Arrigo Cavaglieri, "Règles générales du droit de la paix", (1929 I) 26 *R.d.C.* 544; Gabriele Salvioli, "Observations", (1932) 40 Annuaire 314; Alfred Verdross, "Les principes généraux du droit dans la jurisprudence internationale", (1935 II) 52 *R.d.C.* 191, 195–206.

[52] See generally Alfred Verdross and Heribert Koeck, "Natural Law: The Tradition of Universal Reason and Authority", in Ronald Macdonald and Douglas Johnston (eds.), *The Structure and Process of International Law* (The Hague: Nijhoff, 1983) 17.

[53] See Commentary to Article 50, "I.L.C. Draft Articles on the Law of Treaties with Commentaries", in *United Nations Conference on the Law of Treaties: Official Records (Documents of the Conference)* (New York: U.N., 1971) 7, 68 ("[I]t would clearly be wrong to regard even rules of *jus cogens* as immutable and incapable of modification in the light of future developments"); Panos Terz, "Zum Jus Cogens in demokratischen Völkerrecht", (1978) 27 *Staat und Recht* 617, 620; Milenko Kreca, "Some General Reflections on Main Features of Ius Cogens as Notion of International Public Law", in Rafael Girardot et al. (eds.), *New Directions in International Law: Essays in Honour of Wolfgang Abendroth* (Frankfurt: Campus Verlag, 1982) 27, 27 and 32.

Secondly, it is possible to consider general principles of law as a kind of customary law based on the general principles, constitutional and statutory provisions, and court judgments of different national legal systems as forms of State practice.[54] To the degree that they concern issues of an international character, general principles of law, like rules of customary international law, usually serve to protect and promote the common interests of States. One of the clearest manifestations of a State's interests may be how it regulates itself and its citizens through its own national laws. If one State's national laws indicate that State's particular interests, the national laws of all States may, in so far as they concern an issue of an international character, collectively provide a reasonable indication of the common interests of the international society of States as a whole.[55] Since national laws have long played a role as instances of relevant State practice in the customary process, looking to national laws to determine whether States have a common interest in *jus cogens* rules would be consistent with those rules being rules of customary international law.[56]

The language of Article 53 of the 1969 *Vienna Convention* also provides evidence that *jus cogens* rules are the result of the customary process rather than derived from general principles of law (of the natural law kind) in that it conforms more closely to Article 38(1)(b) of the *Statute of the International Court* (on custom) than to Article 38(1)(c) of the *Statute* (on general principles). Although the *Vienna Convention* should not be regarded as the definitive statement concerning *jus cogens* rules, in part because it deals with those rules solely in the context of treaties, Article 53 requires that such rules be "accepted and recognized by the international community of States as a whole". Article 38(1)(b) of the *Statute* speaks similarly of "a general practice accepted as law". Article 38(1)(c), on the other hand, does not speak of acceptance as such, but of recognition. Moreover, its "general principles"

[54] See Paul Guggenheim, *Traité de Droit international public* (Geneva: Librairie de l'université, 1953) Tome 1, 149–153; Bin Cheng, *General Principles of Law as applied by International Courts and Tribunals* (London: Stevens, 1953) 23–26.

[55] With respect to some issues divergences in national laws will preclude the determination of common interests in this way. Yet comparative law studies aimed at resolving questions of international law sometimes produce convincing results. See, e.g., Greg Fox and Georg Nolte, "Intolerant Democracies", (1995) 36 *H.I.L.J.* 1 (on international law and the right of democratic States to impose limits on democratic participation).

[56] National legislation and national court judgments have been particularly important in the development, maintenance and change of customary rules concerning State immunity. See generally Sompong Sucharitkul, "Immunities of Foreign States before National Authorities: Some Aspects of Progressive Development of Contemporary International Law", in *Estudios de Derecho Internacional: Homenaje al Profesor Miaja de la Muela* (Madrid: Editorial Tecnos, 1979) 477; Claude Emanuelli, "L'immunité souveraine et la coutume internationale: de l'immunité absolue à l'immunité relative?" (1984) 22 *C.Y.I.L.* 26; Peter Trooboff, "Foreign State Immunity: Emerging Consensus on Principles", (1986 V) 200 *R.d.C.* 235.

must only be "recognised by civilised nations", a phrase which, despite its roots in a past colonial era, might still limit the requirement of recognition to something less than the "international community of States as a whole" required by Article 53.[57]

An explanation of *jus cogens* rules as being derived from the customary process would differ in only one respect from many explanations which base those rules on general principles of law. An explanation based on the process of customary international law would accommodate situations where a *jus cogens* rule, such as the prohibition against the aggressive use of force, has not been widely incorporated into national legal systems, where States have instead expressed their interests in other ways. Some issues of an essentially international character might not be dealt with at the national level, despite their importance to States.

However, this explanation still does not resolve the problem concerning State consent which was discussed earlier in this section, namely that *jus cogens* rules deny the possibility of legal exceptions.[58] In attempting to do so it is useful to distinguish between two aspects of any *jus cogens* rule: firstly, the substantive rule itself; and secondly, the imperative character of that rule, which renders it non-derogable and gives it peremptory effect.[59] It is the latter aspect which is at the heart of the problem, for it remains to be explained how the process of customary international law could give rise to the peremptory character of *jus cogens* rules, as opposed to their substantive content.

Hermann Mosler accounted for the non-derogable character of certain rules of international law in the following way:

> In any legal community there must be a minimum of uniformity which is indispensable in maintaining the community. This uniformity may relate to legal values which are considered to be the goal of the community or it may be found in legal principles which it is the duty of all members to realise. It may relate to legal rules which are binding within the community. The whole of this minimum can be called a common public order (ordre public international). The international community cannot

[57] Compare Cheng, *supra*, note 54, 25. He wrote (footnote omitted, emphasis in original):

> [T]he word *nation* was originally used in the sense of "people" rather than "State". The qualifying epithet "civilised" was, therefore, necessary in order to exclude from consideration systems of law of primitive communities which were not yet civilised. At a later stage, however, it would seem that the term was sometimes understood in the sense of States, in which case the word "civilised" must be considered as merely redundant, since any State which is a member of the international society must be considered as civilised.

[58] See discussion *supra*, text accompanying notes 43-47.

[59] See Sur, *supra*, note 22, 1er cahier, 13.

> dispense with this minimum of principles and rules as without them it would cease to exist.[60]

Mosler's argument may be challenged on the basis that it is possible to imagine an international society in which States did not have a common interest in certain rules being invulnerable to the creation of exceptions, either through treaties, rules of special customary international law, or persistent objection. The key point, however, is that in contemporary international society States may well have such common interests.

The existence and ongoing development of such common interests is implicitly recognised by Article 53 of the 1969 *Vienna Convention*, which affirms that *jus cogens* rules "can be modified only by a subsequent norm of general international law having the same character".[61] Although this fact does not address the larger issue of principle – i.e., as to whether *jus cogens* rules are inconsistent with consent based theories of international law – new or modified *jus cogens* rules will consequently not be imposed lightly on non-consenting States.

The larger issue of principle is addressed by the fact that, if States have common interests in non-derogable rules, there is no reason why the process of customary international law could not give rise to rules having a *jus cogens* character. States may, if they choose, behave in accordance with a potential or emerging *jus cogens* rule and accept that their behaviour is consistent with or creative of that rule, thus fulfilling the traditional requirements of both State practice and *opinio juris*.[62] If most or nearly all States behaved and accepted their behaviour in this way, or at least did not oppose this development, the non-derogable character – and not just the substance of the rule – would become part of customary international law.[63]

[60] Mosler, "The International Society as a Legal Community", (1974 IV) 140 *R.d.C.* 1, 33 (footnote omitted). See also: Verdross, *supra*, note 50, 572. Verdross wrote:

> [E]very judicial order regulates the rational and moral coexistence of the members of a community. No judicial order can, therefore, admit treaties between juridical subjects, which are obviously in contradiction to the ethics of a certain community.

[61] *Supra*, text following note 11. This requirement may be overly strict, for it implies that a peremptory rule can only be replaced by another peremptory rule, rather than by a non-peremptory rule of general application. As Virally (*supra*, note 12, 18–19, fn. 13) pointed out, there must be some mechanism whereby constitutional rules may be "de-constitutionalised". See also: Stefan Riesenfeld, "*Jus Dispositivum* and *Jus Cogens* in International Law: In the Light of a Recent Decision of the German Supreme Constitutional Court", (1966) 60 *A.J.I.L.* 511, 514–515; Michael Akehurst, "The Hierarchy of the Sources of International Law", (1974–1975) 47 *B.Y.I.L.* 273, 285, fn. 5. It is interesting to note that, as with changes to *jus cogens* rules, amendments to constitutional rules in national legal systems usually require larger majorities than amendments to ordinary legislation.

[62] See citations *supra*, note 38.

[63] See Virally, *supra*, note 12, 27–28.

Such rules would remain open to change, although in most instances they would have received so much support from States that such changes would be unlikely to occur.[64] This degree of resistance to change may be heightened further by the fact that there is only one kind of State practice in which States wishing to support a change to a *jus cogens* rule may legally engage, namely the making of statements. Unlike non-peremptory rules of customary international law, which only render conflicting acts illegal, the effect of *jus cogens* rules extends to treaties and other objective regimes. Although States may nevertheless choose to create such regimes, and although these regimes may then contribute as State practice to a possible change, States will consequently be less willing to engage in these particular forms of practice – forms which, in other instances, are often quite influential in the development, maintenance and change of customary rules.

Nevertheless, international lawyers have difficulty accepting that the customary process is the source of *jus cogens* rules because they assume that when a State adopts an opposing stance with respect to a potential or emerging customary rule it is withholding its consent to be bound by that rule, should that rule come into force, and certainly not conceding its ability to make certain legal exceptions (i.e., by way of treaty or special customary international law) to any such rule in the future. The answer to this apparent conundrum may be that in an international society which is based on the rule of law, at least, the members of that society recognise that certain fundamental rules must bind them all equally.[65] States, by participating in the customary process, may therefore be consenting to that process, to any existing customary rules, to any subsequently developed customary rules the development of which they have not opposed, and to any *jus cogens* rules, *even if* they have opposed their development.[66]

The principal source of *jus cogens* rules may thus be identified as the process of customary international law. One consequence of this conclusion

[64] See Byers, *supra*, note 2, 147–149. One consequence of this explanation may be that it dispels claims that *jus cogens* rules occupy a higher place than other rules in a new "normative hierarchy". See, e.g., Weil, *supra*, note 12. As Virally, *supra*, note 12, 18 explained:

> [L]es normes du droit international général se distribuent en deux classes, les normes du *jus cogens* et les normes de *jus dispositivum*, la différence entre les deux catégories tenant à la validité ou, au contraire, à la nullité des traités particuliers qui prétendraient déroger à leurs dispositions. La véritable hiérarchie qu'introduit le *jus cogens* – et elle est très nouvelle – est donc une hiérarchie entre, d'une part, les normes du droit international général, qui présentent ce caractère, et, d'autre part, les normes du droit international particulier, régional, local ou bilatéral.

[65] See *supra*, discussion accompanying and notes 60–61.

[66] Persistent objectors to rules which are not of a *jus cogens* character eventually abandon their objections for other reasons. See Byers, *supra*, note 2, 161–165.

may be that States cannot "opt out" of the concept of *jus cogens*, just as they cannot opt out of specific *jus cogens* rules. France, in particular, has asserted that it is not subject to the *jus cogens* character of any rules, if rules with such a character exist, because it never consented to the development of that concept.[67] The concept of *jus cogens*, however, is not a rule as such, but rather a description of certain characteristics held by particular rules which have themselves been developed or changed through the long accepted, and generally accepted, process of customary international law.

5. *Jus Cogens* and *Erga Omnes* Rules

Very shortly after the concept of *jus cogens* was included (in terms of its effect on treaties) in the 1969 *Vienna Convention*, the International Court of Justice brought another, related concept to the forefront of international law. In a *dictum* in the 1970 *Barcelona Traction Case* the Court referred to obligations (and therefore rules) *erga omnes*, which translated literally, means "as against all":

> [A]n essential distinction should be drawn between the obligations of a State towards the international community as a whole, and those arising vis-à-vis another State in the field of diplomatic protection. By their very nature the former are the concern of all States. In view of the importance of the rights involved, all States can be held to have a legal interest in their protection; they are obligations *erga omnes*.
>
> Such obligations derive, for example, in contemporary international law, from the outlawing of acts of aggression, and of genocide, as also from the principles and rules concerning the basic rights of the human person, including protection from slavery and racial discrimination. Some of the corresponding rights of protection have entered into the body of general international law . . . ; others are conferred by international instruments of a universal or quasi-universal character.
>
> Obligations the performance of which is the subject of diplomatic protection are not of the same category.[68]

[67] See Olivier Deleau, "Les positions françaises à la Conférence de Vienne sur le droit des traités", (1969) 15 *A.F.D.I.* 7, 14–17 and 23; Weil, *supra*, note 12, 428.

[68] (1970) *I.C.J. Rep.* 3, 32 (paras. 33–35). With this *dictum* the Court was effectively reversing its judgment in the *South West Africa Cases (Second Phase)* (1966) *I.C.J. Rep.* 6. In that case Ethiopia and Liberia had argued that they had standing to bring an action because they, as members of the (former) League of Nations, had a legal interest in the enforcement of South Africa's mandate over South West Africa. The Court responded (at 47, para. 88):

Although some of the rules which the Court identified as being *erga omnes* rules may also be considered *jus cogens* rules, the Court in this passage was clearly referring to a characteristic distinct from that of non-derogability. It focused on the fact that some rules give rise to a generality of standing – amongst all States bound by those rules – to make claims in the event of a violation. Generality of standing, rather than non-derogable character, is the essence of *erga omnes* rules.

A similar reference was made by the Court in its judgment in the 1974 *Nuclear Test Cases*, where it analyzed certain unilateral statements made by French government officials as having been made "*erga omnes*", and held those statements to be legally binding.[69] More recently, in the 1995 *East Timor Case* the Court accepted that the right of self-determination is a rule which has an "*erga omnes* character".[70] And in its 1996 judgment on preliminary objections in the *Case Concerning Application of the Convention on the Prevention and Punishment of the Crime of Genocide* the Court affirmed that "the rights and obligations enshrined by the Convention are rights and obligations *erga omnes*".[71]

The concept of *erga omnes* rules has been endorsed by numerous States, organisations and scholars.[72] For example, the International Law Commission, in Article 5(3) of Part Two of its "Draft Articles on State Responsibility", stated that "if the internationally wrongful act constitutes an international crime" the injured States include "all other States".[73] However, the relationship between *erga omnes* rules and *jus cogens* rules remains unclear. Some scholars have suggested that the concepts involve different aspects of the same rules,[74] and the terms have been used interchangeably in debates of the

[T]he argument amounts to a plea that the Court should allow the equivalent of an "*actio popularis*", or right resident in any member of a community to take legal action in vindication of a public interest. But although a right of this kind may be known to certain municipal systems of law, it is not known to international law as it stands at present; nor is the Court able to regard it as imported by the "general principles of law" referred to in Article 38, paragraph 1(c), of its Statute.

[69] (1974) *I.C.J. Rep.* 253, 269–270 (paras. 50–51).

[70] (1995) *I.C.J. Rep.* 90, 102 (para. 29). See also: dissenting opinion of Judge Weeramantry (1995) *I.C.J. Rep.* 139, 172–173 and 213-216.

[71] 11 July 1996, General List No. 91, 23 (para. 31).

[72] See generally Schachter, *supra*, note 18, 208-213; Frowein, *supra*, note 28, 405–422; Claudia Annacker, "The Legal Régime of *Erga Omnes* Obligations in International Law", (1994) 46 *Austrian J.P.I.L.* 131. For criticism of the concept, see Weil, *supra*, note 12, 431–433.

[73] See discussion *supra*, note 16.

[74] See, e.g., Bruno Simma, "Bilateralism and Community Interest in the Law of State Responsibility", in Yoram Dinstein (ed.), *International Law at a Time of Perplexity: Essays in Honour of Shabtai Rosenne* (Dordrecht: Nijhoff, 1989) 821, 825.

International Law Commission.[75] Others have suggested that the concept of *erga omnes* is wider than that of *jus cogens*.[76]

In exploring the relationship between *erga omnes* and *jus cogens* rules it is useful to begin by considering the nature of international legal rules generally.

One of the concepts normally considered fundamental to the rule of law is that the law of any society must in principle apply to all its members. In national legal systems this concept may be understood in at least two ways. Firstly, it is possible to understand law as being imposed from above by the State or sovereign and generally applicable to all citizens.[77] Secondly, it is possible to understand law as a multitude of bilateral relationships, either between individual people or between individuals and the State.[78]

In international society there is no overarching sovereign, and international law has usually been understood as a multitude of bilateral relationships between those entities which have international legal personality, i.e., predominantly States. Since there is no overarching sovereign, no part of this law necessarily has to apply to any one State, nor does this law have to apply in the same way to all States; that is, it does not need to be generalised. Instead, the application of any particular rule of international law to a State is usually regarded as being dependent on its consent, which may be accorded either to specific rules, or to legal processes more generally.[79] This consent operates bilaterally, as can be seen in the requirement of consent by States parties to reservations to multilateral treaties,[80] and in the existence of special customary international law.[81]

It may appear that this bilateralist understanding of international law is incompatible with the existence of generally applicable rules. Bruno Simma has criticised bilateralism as being "a barrier in the way of stronger solidarity in international law" and argued that *jus cogens* and *erga omnes* rules represent

[75] See, e.g., (1986) 1 *Yb.I.L.C.* 247–253.

[76] See, e.g., Theodor Meron, *Human Rights Law-Making in the United Nations* (Oxford: Clarendon, 1986) 187; Macdonald, *supra*, note 12, 138.

[77] See John Austin, *The Province of Jurisprudence Determined* (London: Weidenfeld & Nicolson, 1954) Lecture I, 9–33; A.V. Dicey, *Introduction to the Study of the Law of the Constitution* (10th ed.) (London: Macmillan, 1959) 70–76.

[78] See Wesley Hohfeld, "Fundamental Legal Conceptions as Applied in Judicial Reasoning (Part 2)", (1916-17) 26 *Y.L.J.* 710, reprinted in Hohfeld, *Fundamental Legal Conceptions* (New Haven: Y.U.P., 1923) 65. The distinction between these two understandings is reflected in civil law systems, which distinguish between duties (owed to the State) and obligations (owed to other, private parties). See generally Otto Kahn-Freund et al., *A Source-book on French Law* (3rd ed.) (Oxford: Clarendon, 1991) 10–20.

[79] See discussion *supra*, text accompanying notes 43–44.

[80] See Article 20, 1969 *Vienna Convention*, *supra*, note 11. This requirement is also part of customary international law. See McNair, *supra*, note 25, 158–177.

[81] See citations *supra*, note 22. On this point, see Lowe, *supra*, note 29, 208–209.

the "antithesis" of bilateralism.[82] However, if a bilateral legal relationship with respect to any particular rule is multiplied so that similar relationships with respect to the same rule exist between all States, the rule becomes general in application. Furthermore, the bilateral relationships which make up any general rule do not exist in isolation. The customary process adds weight to, and therefore increases the resistance to change of, the legal rule which grounds the various bilateral legal relationships.[83] The process, and the State practice which drives the process, are general in scope; the bilateral relationships which connect rights with obligations with respect to rules are not.[84]

If all rules of international law are composed of bilateral legal relationships, an *erga omnes* rule might be considered to involve a series of identical bilateral relationships between every possible pair of States. Such an explanation, however, fails to satisfy because a violation of the bilateral relationship between two States would not give other States any right to make a legal claim. The obligations existing between the violating State and those other States would remain fulfilled.

Erga omnes rules are therefore best seen as being more than just rules whose bilateral relationships have been fully generalised. As was explained by the International Court in the *Barcelona Traction Case*, there are two parts to every *erga omnes* rule.[85] Firstly, as with ordinary rules, each *erga omnes* rule contains a series of rights and corresponding obligations concerning its substantive content. It is these rights and obligations which form the principal bilateral relationships between any of the many pairs of States which are subject to the rule. Secondly, each State has, in the words of the International Court, a "corresponding right of protection". In other words, each State not only has rights and obligations with respect to the substantive content of the rule, giving rise to State responsibility *vis-à-vis* injured States in the event of a violation, but it is also subject to a series of additional, bilateralised rights and obligations. The additional rights enable it to make claims against any State which is bound by and violates the substantive rule, while the additional

[82] Simma, *supra*, note 74, 822 et seq. See also: Weil, *supra*, note 12, 432.

[83] See Byers, *supra*, note 2, 136–149.

[84] Lowe (*supra*, note 29, 209, emphasis in original) has described international law as a "network of obligations" in which:

> [A] rule may only be said to be general in the *descriptive* sense that it is a rule to which states in general subscribe, but this does not imply that it is general in any *prescriptive* sense, applying in principle to all states.

[85] See quotation *supra*, at note 68.

obligations require that it not violate that same substantive rule in its relations with any other similarly bound State.[86]

The creation of an *erga omnes* rule is, therefore, a two-step process involving: firstly, the creation of a rule; and secondly, the creation of additional bilateralised rights and obligations which confer standing, in the event of any violation, on *any* of the States subject to that rule.[87] It may be possible for these two steps to occur simultaneously.

Unlike the explanation of *jus cogens* rules advanced earlier in this article, this explanation of *erga omnes* rules does not preclude the possibility of persistent objection, nor the possibility of *erga omnes* rules which are created by treaty and limited in scope to those States which are party to the relevant treaty.[88] Similarly, this explanation does not preclude the customary development of *erga omnes* rules which are limited in applicability to a group of States. Although it is generally assumed that *erga omnes* rules apply universally, the right of protection associated with a rule having an *erga omnes* character is a right which is held by all States *bound by that rule*. Persistent objectors and any other States which might be outside the scope of that rule cannot be affected by its *erga omnes* character.[89]

As importantly, pairs (and multiple pairs) of States which are bound by a rule having an *erga omnes* character are not prevented from subsequently

[86] As with all violations of international law, violations of these additional rights and obligations engage the responsibility of the violating State and must therefore be remedied. However, as these specific violations are of rights of protection, remedies will frequently be limited to declarations of responsibility. Reparations will generally not be available.

[87] For an explanation of the concept of *erga omnes* which is very different from that provided here, see Annacker, *supra*, note 72. Annacker claimed (at 136) that the "distinguishing feature of an *erga omnes* obligation is its non-bilateralizable structure". Yet after examining the background to Article 5 of the "I.L.C. Draft Articles on State Responsibility (Part Two)" she admitted that the I.L.C. had come to the opposite conclusion. See Annacker, *supra*, note 72, 142–148. For Article 5, see *supra*, note 16.

In addition, widespread use of the phrase "obligations *erga omnes*" rather than "*erga omnes* rules" may facilitate a distinction between substantive rights and obligations and those rights and obligations which confer standing, in the event of a violation, on States which would otherwise not have a claim. And in the *East Timor Case* (*supra*, note 70) Portugal argued on the basis of "*erga omnes* rights". But as Judge Weeramantry pointed out in his dissenting opinion (*supra*, note 70, 215), an *erga omnes* right is the corollary of an obligation *erga omnes*. The terminology adopted in this article – of *erga omnes* rules – encompasses both rights and obligations.

[88] On the latter point, see Schachter, *supra*, note 18, 209–210.

[89] This (potential) limitation is reflected in Article 5(2)(e) of the "I.L.C. Draft Articles on State Responsibility (Part Two)" (*supra*, note 16), which reads, *inter alia*:

> In particular, "injured State" means:
>
> (e) if the right infringed by the act of a State arises from a multilateral treaty or from a rule of customary international law, any other State party to the multilateral treaty or bound by the relevant rule of customary international law, if it is established that:
>
> (i) the right has been created or is established in its favour,

contracting out of that rule as between themselves, although that rule will remain applicable *erga omnes* between them and all other similarly bound States. This is because the conclusion of a treaty or the development of a rule of special customary international law in an area governed by a more general rule does not normally violate that more general rule in and of itself. Instead, it creates a legal exception to that more general rule. The rights of protection held by the other States which are bound by the general rule do not come into play *unless* that general rule is actually violated, and only if the *erga omnes* rule is also a *jus cogens* rule will the creation of such legal exceptions be precluded.

It seems unlikely, but is nevertheless conceivable that a *jus cogens* rule could also apply to a limited number of States. It seems unlikely because *jus cogens* rules are the result of the process of customary international law developing constitutional rules within a society of States, and both that customary process and the legal system of which it is a part are today predominantly global in scope. It would seem conceivable because societies of States may exist or develop which are distinct and closely knit enough to want to preclude exceptions to certain rules amongst themselves, while accepting that those rules do not apply, or do not have peremptory effects, with respect to States on the "outside".[90]

It is also conceivable that such developments occurred in the past. At one point in time Latin American States had developed a number of rules of special customary international law which, potentially, could have acquired a *jus cogens* character within that limited group of States.[91] It is possible that such rules exist today, such as in the concept of a "public order" within

(ii) the infringement of the right by the act of a State necessarily affects the enjoyment of the rights or the performance of the obligations of the other States parties to the multilateral treaty or bound by the rule of customary international law, ...

[90] See Kadelbach, *supra*, note 12, 203–204. However, such a "special" *jus cogens* rule would be unable to derogate from a *jus cogens* rule which was general in application. See Virally, *supra*, note 12, 14.

[91] See the comments of Mr. Belaunde (Peru), 915 meeting of the Sixth Committee (1966) U.N.G.A.O.R., 21st Sess., A/C/.6/SR/915, 87 (para. 15); the 1987 decision of the Inter-American Commission of Human Rights, *supra*, note 22, which held that "in the member States of the OAS there is recognized a norm of *jus cogens* which prohibits the State execution of children". On Latin American special customary international law generally, see Alejandro Alvárez, *Le droit international américain* (Paris: Pedone, 1910); *Asylum Case* (1950) *I.C.J. Rep.* 266, 276–277 and dissenting opinion of Judge Alvárez, 290, 293–294; Julio Barberis, "International Law, American", in Rudolf Bernhardt (ed.), *Encyclopedia of Public International Law* (Vol. 6) (Amsterdam: North-Holland, 1983) 222.

European law,[92] and assertions by "liberal" scholars of international law may point towards such developments in the future.[93]

However, the strongest possibility of non-derogable rules which are limited in scope exists within the context of human rights treaties, as States parties appear to be unable to create legal exceptions to many of the rules set out in such treaties.

Human rights treaties may be understood as involving two kinds of rights. Firstly, there are rights which are held by individuals or groups. These rights may exist independently of the treaty (as rules of customary international law) or they may have been created by the treaty as a kind of third party right, or "stipulation pour l'autrui".[94] States have corresponding obligations – to those individuals or groups – not to violate these rights. Secondly, there are rights of protection. These rights are created by the treaty and are held by the States parties. They apply *erga omnes* and allow any State party to make a claim in the event that any other State party violates the rights of an individual or group under the treaty.

These rules appear to be non-derogable because the primary rights and obligations do not exist between States, but rather between States and individuals or groups. Consequently, legal exceptions to these rules cannot be created by States but instead require the consent of the individual or group holders of the rights. This consent is extremely unlikely to be forthcoming given the numbers of individuals or groups which are usually involved. Yet because it is at least conceivable that these individuals or groups could consent to the creation of exceptions, and because such exceptions would then appear to be valid, these rules are in fact derogable and should therefore not be referred to as *jus cogens* rules.[95]

[92] See, e.g., *Austria* v. *Italy* (*South Tyrol Case*) (1962) 4 *Yb.E.C.H.R.* 116, 140 (E.C.H.R.); *Chrisostomos et al.* v. *Turkey* (1991) 12 *H.Rts.L.J.* 113, 121 (para. 22) (E.Comm.H.Rts.); Hermann Mosler, "Der 'Gemeinschaftliche Ordre Public' in europäischen Staatengruppen", (1968) *Revista Esp. D.I.* 523, esp. 532; Verdross and Simma, *supra*, note 32, 333.

[93] See, e.g., Anne-Marie Slaughter Burley, "International Law and International Relations Theory: A Dual Agenda", (1993) 87 *A.J.I.L.* 205; Anne-Marie Slaughter, "International Law in a World of Liberal States", (1995) 6 *E.J.I.L.* 503. For a critical analysis of this approach, see Benedict Kingsbury, "The Tuna-Dolphin Controversy, the World Trade Organization, and the Liberal Project to Reconceptualize International Law", (1994) 5 *Yb.I.Envir.L.* 1.

[94] On human rights in customary international law see Theodor Meron, *Human Rights and Humanitarian Norms in Customary Law* (Oxford: Clarendon, 1989); Schachter, *supra*, note 18, 335–342. On the third party rights of individuals see Christine Chinkin, *Third Parties in International Law* (Oxford: Clarendon, 1993) 13–15 and 120–133.

[95] Some human rights are designated by treaties as being "non-derogable", in that they cannot be overridden during "states of emergency". See generally Higgins, *supra*, note 26. It is possible that these particular rights are also inalienable, although derogation with the consent of the right holder is very different from derogation in the absence of consent. On the relationship between the concept of *jus cogens* and rules which are designated by treaties as

Despite the possibility that *jus cogens* rules and *erga omnes* rules might sometimes apply to limited numbers of States, such situations are unlikely to arise. Both types of rules exist to protect and promote common interests, and although groups of States frequently have their own, unique common interests international society is today more and more defining itself as universal, at least in terms of its fundamental, constitutional rules.

It follows that particularly "weighty" rules of international law are usually both *jus cogens* and *erga omnes* in character.[96] Moreover, *jus cogens* rules necessarily apply *erga omnes*. Illegal treaties and illegal rules of special customary international law would never be struck down as being inconsistent with *jus cogens* rules unless those rules also gave standing to other States.[97] States which enter into illegal treaties or otherwise attempt to create illegal exceptions to general rules are normally not interested in challenging the

being non-derogable, see Theodor Meron, "On a Hierarchy of International Human Rights", (1986) 80 *A.J.I.L.* 1, 15–19.

[96] See Frowein, *supra*, note 28, 405–406.

[97] There is, it should be noted, an important difference between an *erga omnes* rule and the jurisdiction of international courts or tribunals. Although a State may be subject to an *erga omnes* rule it still cannot be subject to judicial proceedings in the absence of its consent. See *East Timor Case*, *supra*, note 70, 102 (para. 29); A.J.J. de Hoogh, "The Relationship between *Jus Cogens*, Obligations *Erga Omnes* and International Crimes: Peremptory Norms in Perspective", (1991) 42 *Austrian J.P.I.L.* 183, 196.

In the *East Timor Case* this issue arose because Indonesia had not consented to the jurisdiction of the Court and, as had been established in the *Monetary Gold Case* ((1954) *I.C.J. Rep.* 19, 32), the Court cannot decide issues which concern the legal interests of third States as the "very subject matter of the decision" when those third States are not themselves before it. Portugal attempted to get around this principle by arguing that Australia had violated the right of the East Timorese to self-determination, that the Court had jurisdiction because Australia had violated that right independently of Indonesia's actions, and that Portugal had standing, either as the administering Power over the non-self-governing territory, or on the basis that the right of self-determination was a "right *erga omnes*". The problem with these arguments was that any violation by Australia of the right to self-determination in this instance was still closely linked to, and highly dependent on, Indonesia's role as occupying power.

Portugal did not make any arguments based on the concept of *jus cogens*. However, it could have argued that Australia had violated Portugal's rights – as administering Power – by entering into the treaty because Indonesia's violation of the *jus cogens* rule prohibiting the use of force had prevented Indonesia from establishing effective title over East Timor, and that Indonesia consequently lacked the legal capacity to enter into a treaty concerning that territory. See discussion *supra*, text accompanying note 23. Although the legality of Indonesia's actions would still have been an issue, Australia's actions – in entering into a treaty which was in violation of Portugal's rights – would then have formed "the very subject matter of the decision", thus allowing Portugal to sidestep the principle from the *Monetary Gold Case*. This argument could perhaps have been buttressed by an argument that the *Monetary Gold Case* principle cannot serve to protect third States which have violated *jus cogens* rules, in that such rules override the principle of State consent in this context as well as in regard to attempts to create legal exceptions.

validity of those exceptions.[98] However, *erga omnes* rules are not necessarily also of a *jus cogens* character.[99] As was explained earlier in this section, there is nothing which prevents States from opting out of *erga omnes* rules unless those rules are also *jus cogens* rules, for claims by third States must be based on violations of rules and not the creation of legal exceptions.[100]

One type of situation where *erga omnes* rules might not at the same time be *jus cogens* rules is where the *erga omnes* rules in question apply to individuals, or other non-State entities, rather than to States. Rules prohibiting war crimes appear to be the best examples of rules which apply in this way.[101] In such situations the particular rule in question may be of a kind which cannot bind States, although it may give all States a right – and perhaps impose an obligation – to enforce that rule.[102]

It is true that were two States to enter into a treaty the effect of which was to assist individuals in committing war crimes, that treaty would almost certainly be rendered void for being in violation of a *jus cogens* rule. However, the *jus cogens* rule having the effect in that instance would be a rule prohibiting State complicity in those individual acts, rather than a *jus cogens* rule directed at the individuals committing them.[103] The obligation to enforce a rule prohibiting war crimes would remain unaffected by the treaty, but it would do so as an *erga omnes* rule, and not as a *jus cogens* rule.

[98] This lack of interest in challenging illegal treaties or exceptions on the part of States involved in their creation was demonstrated in the *East Timor Case* (*supra*, note 70), where it was a State not party to the relevant treaty, i.e., Portugal, which challenged its validity before the International Court of Justice.

[99] For scholarly support for this proposition, see citations *supra*, note 76.

[100] See discussion *supra*, text following note 89.

[101] See generally S/RES/827 (1993) (Security Council Resolution Establishing an International Tribunal for the Prosecution of Persons Responsible for Serious Violations of International Humanitarian Law Committed in the Territory of the Former Yugoslavia), reproduced in (1993) 32 *I.L.M.* 1203; *Report of the Secretary-General Pursuant to Paragraph 2 of Security Council Resolution 808 (1993)*, U.N. Doc. S/25704 (1993), reproduced in (1993) 32 *I.L.M.* 1163; S/RES/955 (1994) (Security Council Resolution Establishing the International Tribunal for Rwanda), reproduced in (1994) 33 *I.L.M.* 1598; "I.L.C. Draft Statute for an International Criminal Court" (and commentary), in *Report of the I.L.C. on the Work of Its 46th Session*, U.N. Doc. A/49/10 (1994) 43, reproduced in (1994) 33 *I.L.M.* 253; Cherif Bassiouni, *International Criminal Law (Vol. 1)* (Dobbs Ferry: Transnational, 1986).

[102] On the right ("universal jurisdiction"), see Michael Akehurst, "Jurisdiction in International Law", (1972–1973) 46 *B.Y.I.L.* 145, 160–166; Derek Bowett, "Jurisdiction: Changing Patterns of Authority over Activities and Resources", (1982) 53 *B.Y.I.L.* 1, 11–14. On the obligation, see *Report of the Secretary General Pursuant to Paragraph 2 of Security Council Resolution 808 (1993)*, ibid., Articles 9 and 29; S/RES/955 (1994), ibid., Articles 8 and 28; "I.L.C. Draft Statute for an International Criminal Court", ibid., Articles 58 and 63.

[103] There would be no point in having rules with a *jus cogens* character which were directed solely at individuals. Individuals cannot modify, persistently object, or otherwise create exceptions to rules of international law.

Most rules which are generally accepted as being *erga omnes* in character are rules the violations of which are not readily subject to inter-State claims by directly injured States, or by States on behalf of their own directly injured nationals. In situations involving violations of the most fundamental of human rights a claim on the basis of diplomatic protection is generally precluded because the State committing the violation is usually – although not necessarily – also the victim's State of nationality. Similarly, a State which is subjected to an armed attack may not be able to protect itself through the invocation of international law to the same extent as it might be protected by other States, were those other States to have rights of protection which were violated as a result of the attack. Although the attacked State may invite other States to come to its assistance, and the United Nations Security Council can always take action under Chapter VII of the *Charter*, the violation of an *erga omnes* rule may give those other States another option, namely that of engaging in countermeasures against the attacking State even if the victim of the aggression has not requested assistance.[104]

The International Court's of Justice's *dictum* in the *Barcelona Traction Case* seems to have been directed at redressing situations like these, on the basis that rules of international law should be capable of supporting inter-State claims and allow for effective enforcement opportunities if they are to have any effect.[105] *Erga omnes* rules expand the scope of possible claimants in certain situations, to protect key common interests where traditional rules of standing are insufficient to do so.

[104] See generally Schachter, *supra*, note 18, 196–198; Frowein, *supra*, note 28; Annacker, *supra*, note 72, 159–160. The issue of what limits necessarily exist on the rights of States, including third States, to engage in countermeasures in response to international crimes is currently the subject of much debate in the I.L.C. See, e.g., Gaetano Arangio-Ruiz, *Seventh Report on State Responsibility*, 9 May 1995, UN Doc. A/CN.4/469 (with addenda: 24 and 29 May 1995); "Symposium: Countermeasures and Dispute Settlement: The Current Debate within the ILC", (1994) 5 *E.J.I.L.* 20 (including comments from several members of the I.L.C.). This proposition might seem to have been rejected by the International Court of Justice in the *Nicaragua Case (Merits)* (*supra*, note 14, 127) when it stated that: "They [the acts of which Nicaragua was accused] could not justify counter-measures taken by a third State, the United States, and particularly could not justify intervention involving the use of force". However, it may be that the Court was merely defining limits on the right to engage in countermeasures, much as the I.L.C. is attempting to do. As Nicaragua did not launch an armed attack (in the sense of Article 2(4) of the *Charter*) but rather only supported the actions of private persons and thus violated only the rule of non-intervention, third States could not resort to countermeasures involving the use of force. For an extended analysis of the concept of *erga omnes* in the context of situations like that in the *Nicaragua Case*, see Claus Kress, *Gewaltverbot und Selbstverteidigungsrecht nach der Satzung der Vereinten Nationen bei staatlicher Verwicklung in Gewaltakte Privater* (Berlin: Duncker & Humblot, 1995) 332 et seq.

[105] See quotation *supra*, at note 68.

6. Conclusion

The concepts of *jus cogens* and *erga omnes* have become widely accepted in international law. Their developments represent important milestones in the evolution of the international legal order. The scrutiny of rules and State behaviour in terms of fundamental common interests and the expansion of standing in certain situations to improve access to justice are important indications that the international legal system is now seeking to do more than merely protect the freedoms of selfish and competitive States.

Jus cogens rules and *erga omnes* rules seek to protect and promote the common interests of States to a much more obvious degree than most rules of international law. They are constitutional rules which help define the fundamental characteristics of the international legal system: they play an important role in determining how rules of international law are developed, maintained and changed, and in protecting those human rights or civil liberties which are considered essential to the self-identity of the international legal system, and the international society it serves.

Yet *jus cogens* rules and *erga omnes* rules are not the result of a *sui generis* mechanism of law creation. Instead, *jus cogens* rules are best explained as being derived from the long-established process of customary international law. The same is true of most *erga omnes* rules, although it is possible that some such rules may be created by treaty. Although the effects of *jus cogens* rules and *erga omnes* rules are exceptional, their origins are not, and they should not be explained – or feared – on that basis.

[5]

The common heritage of mankind: utopia or reality?

ALEXANDRE KISS

The common heritage of mankind is a newly formulated concept: it has only existed in its present form since the end of the 1960s. However, ever since the beginnings of modern international law, some parts of the Earth's surface have been considered outside all national jurisdictions. At first, the only such area was the régime of the high seas. A long debate ensued between those who believed that the high seas did not belong to anyone, and thus constituted a *res nullius*, and those who believed them to be a *res communis*, belonging to all nations. In practice, however, there was general agreement that the high seas could not be appropriated by any nation and that they could be freely used by all nations.

A more rigorous legal analysis shows that in fact there is a fundamental difference between the concepts of *res nullius* and *res communis*. The former concept implies that its object can be freely used and appropriated by everyone – the classical example is wild game. But since the high seas cannot be appropriated, they cannot themselves be considered *res nullius*. However, their resources can be used by everybody, and while navigation or the laying of submarine cables or pipelines does not imply an appropriation, fish or shrimp from fishing and related activities belong from the moment of capture to the fisherman. Thus, confusion has arisen because no distinction has been made between the seas themselves and some of their resources. The former are *res communis*, be-

Directeur de recherche au Centre National de la Recherche Scientifique (France); Directeur, Centre du Droit de l'Environnement, Université de Strasbourg III (Recherches juridiques, politiques et sociales); President, European Council for Environmental Law; Secretary General, International Institute for Human Rights.

longing to everybody and not able to be appropriated, while the living and mineral resources of the high seas are *res nullius* and can freely become the property of those who exploit them.

These scholarly distinctions are of importance in tracing the development of the new concept of the common heritage of mankind. The concept of *res communis*, which was extended during the twentieth century to the new areas made accessible to humans by technological progress – that is, to the atmosphere and to outer space, certainly involves the idea that elements of the areas belong to all nations. Further technological progress – the ability to exploit the minerals lying on the deep seabed and to store weapons of mass destruction there – as well as the realization that the riches of this planet are not infinite and that therefore all the elements needed for the survival of mankind must be considered *resources* have led to the conviction that a simple régime of non-appropriation and common use of those resources – which could be freely appropriated – was not sufficient. Other considerations had to be integrated into the law governing the international system: the need to manage natural resources in a rational way so that they could be transmitted to future generations, so that their benefits are shared equitably among nations, whether rich or poor, and, last but not least, so that they will be used for exclusively peaceful purposes.

These themes were developed by Arvid Pardo of Malta in different international bodies during the 1960s. In one of his most significant statements, made before the Parliamentary Assembly of the Council of Europe on 3 December 1970, he summed up his views:

Traditionally, international law has been essentially concerned with the regulation of relations between states. In ocean space, however, the time has come to recognize as a basic principle of international law the overriding common interest of mankind in the preservation of the quality of marine environment and in the rational and equitable development of its resources lying beyond national jurisdiction. This does not imply disregard of the interest of individual states, but rather the recognition of the fact that in the long term these interests can be protected only within the framework of a stable international régime of close co-operation between states.[1]

The ambassador had suggested that such a régime of co-operation should be established first for the deep seabed and its subsoil. These regions were to be reserved exclusively for peaceful purposes, scientific research not directly related to military activities was to be allowed, and the resources of the deep seabed and of its subsoil were to be exploited in conformity with the principles of the United Nations Charter and in the interest of all mankind, taking into account particularly the needs of the poor countries. Thus, when speaking on 1 November 1967 in the First Committee, he had invited the General Assembly to proclaim that the deep seabed constitutes a common heritage of mankind.[2]

The concept of the common heritage of mankind is thus much more than the *res communis omnium*. The idea which underlies it is that certain interests of all mankind should be safeguarded by special legal régimes. Defined in this way, the concept is clearly applicable in fields other than the deep seabed. However, such suggestions have not been welcomed by many governments. One is therefore led to examine the idea of the common interest of mankind and the present concrete meaning of the concept of the common heritage of mankind.

THE COMMON HERITAGE OF MANKIND: A MATERIALIZATION OF THE COMMON INTEREST OF MANKIND

The man in the street would be sceptical about whether the foundation of the common heritage of mankind concept, the common interest of mankind, exists in the world of today. However, it is true that such an interest is expressed in various important international legal instruments and that such instruments are becoming more and more numerous. This growth can be demonstrated by

1 Arvid Pardo, *The Common Heritage; Selected Papers on Oceans and World Order, 1967-1974* (Valletta: Malta University Press 1975), 176.
2 *Ibid*, 39-41.

comparing traditional international law with the rules which today govern the life of the international community.

Traditional international law was essentially an inter-state law system ruling the relationships between states. Those relations were based mainly on reciprocity, that is, the granting of advantages to another state or states in return for equivalent advantages for oneself. However, as early as 1815, an attempt had been made to achieve an international order, and a new sort of international treaty had appeared. The Congress of Vienna set out principles which were general in scope and implied no direct advantages for the states which accepted the obligations: for example, establishing and guaranteeing freedom of navigation on international rivers. During the nineteenth century, other treaties of a similar nature were concluded concerning prohibition of the slave trade, religious freedom, and freedom of navigation on the recently constructed inter-oceanic canals.[3] At the end of that century and the beginning of the present one the first fundamental international conventions concerning humanitarian law were agreed,[4] and since the end of World War I, international conventions with worldwide scope but containing no implication of reciprocity have become more and more numerous and today form an important body of international law.

Such conventions have usually dealt with specific fields. The first of them led to the international regulation of labour conditions through conventions by which states committed themselves to guarantee minimum conditions of health, security, and assistance to workers, and to prohibit practices such as night work by women and the exploitation of young children. More recently various conventions with a much wider application have sought to ensure the protection of human rights, civil and political as well as economic, social, and cultural. At present about sixty conventions, both uni-

3 Respectively, the Treaty of London of 20 December 1841, the Treaty of Berlin of 13 July 1878 (article 44), and the Convention of Constantinople of 20 October 1888 (Suez Canal) and the treaty of 15 November 1901 between the United Kingdom and the United States (Panama Canal).

4 The most important of these were the Hague Conventions on Land Warfare of 1899 and 1907.

versal and regional, ensure respect for human life, dignity, and freedom by requiring obligations from the contracting states without any immediate reciprocal benefit. Nearly all the international instruments protecting human rights have been drafted since World War II, that is, in less than forty years. The evolution was even faster in another field, the protection of the environment. Since the late 'sixties, when the consciousness of the growing deterioration of our planet's environment became general, the number of important multilateral treaties related to environmental protection has grown to about a hundred. In most cases such conventions do not offer any direct advantage for the states which are parties to them – only obligations.

Many other examples could be cited from other fields, such as health or development. Once again, what is at stake in all these cases is not the immediate interest of a state or states, but a more remote concern: a benefit for all mankind which can be obtained only by international co-operation and the acceptance of obligations by all governments, even if they receive no immediate return. The aim is to eliminate situations which may endanger future life or which are contrary to elementary human values and to create the conditions for a better life for everyone, including future generations.

These goals may sound very idealistic. In reality, they are largely accepted and are set out in the preambles of various treaties protecting human rights, labour conditions, or the environment. In the common interest, European governments have agreed to defend themselves against individuals – often their own nationals – before the European Commission and European Court of Human Rights. At present, they risk being condemned for violations of the European Convention on Human Rights and in any event must face an international process which they generally consider a nuisance. However, in the long run, these governments understand that this is the price they pay to avoid the return of dictators – and the reign of dictators in several European countries was costly enough for the whole world to accept sacrifices to prevent a recurrence.

In some circumstances the common interest of mankind has led the states to establish international régimes: the permanent neutrality of Switzerland, the demilitarization of certain areas, the freedom of navigation on the Rhine, in the Suez Canal, or in the Panama Canal were early territorial expressions of such an international concern. However, the régime as a means for regulating the international system has reached its full flowering with the need not just to maintain peace in certain areas but also to manage the resources of such areas in concert in order to conserve them. This dual need has led to the formulation of the concept of the common heritage of mankind. In fact, the common heritage is the complete territorial expression, the materialization of the common interest of mankind. This means that the states suspend or do not assert rights or claims to territorial jurisdiction, or in some cases exercise such jurisdiction only within set limits, for the benefit of the whole human community, without any immediate return, and conserve and if necessary manage areas in conformity with the common interest for the benefit of all mankind.

Chronologically, if not explicitly, the first elements of the concept of the common heritage of mankind appeared in the Antarctic Treaty, which applied to Antarctica and the ocean around it. Signed in Washington on 1 December 1959, this treaty proclaims in its preamble that 'it is in the interest of all mankind that Antarctica shall continue forever to be used exclusively for peaceful purposes and shall not become the scene or object of international discord.'[5] Although the twelve original contracting states did not renounce previously asserted rights or claims to territorial sovereignty in Antarctica, they did accept the prohibition on any non-peaceful use (with inspection by other states to see that this provision was honoured) and freedom of scientific investigation.

In the years following the entry into force of the Antarctic Treaty, additional measures were agreed by the original contracting states in order to ensure that the uses of Antarctica are in conformity with its aims: the limitation of man's impact on the

5 For the text of the treaty, see *International Legal Materials* 19 (July 1980), 860ff.

environment, the preservation and conservation of wildlife and living resources, the facilitation of scientific research and of international scientific co-operation.[6] A real system has been established with the conclusion of two further treaties. The first, for the conservation of Antarctic seals, was adopted on 1 June 1972 and the second, the Convention for the Conservation of Antarctic Marine Living Resources, on 20 May 1980.[7] The whole system now covers not only the Antarctic continent but also large areas of the surrounding ocean. It provides not only for exclusively peaceful uses and freedom of scientific research but also for the management of living resources. Rules concerning the exploration for and exploitation of the area's mineral resources are now being drafted.[8] Thus, although the term 'common heritage of mankind' is not used, the characteristics of the Antarctic system, as it has been established by the relevant treaties and by the rules adopted inside the system, correspond to the criteria of this newly formulated concept.

The same can be said of the arrangements surrounding the use of the radio spectrum which is generally considered (in the present state of technology) a limited natural resource.[9] International regulations adopted in the framework of the International Telecommunication Union have established the principle of sharing the spectrum among all the states of the world on an equitable basis, thus avoiding the simple application of the first come, first served rule.[10] This has led to co-operative planning, in particular

6 Antarctic Treaty, *Handbook of Measures in Furtherance of the Principles and Objectives of the Antarctic Treaty* (3rd ed, April 1983).

7 For texts of these agreements see, respectively, *International Legal Materials* 11 (March 1972), 251, and 19 (July 1980), 841ff.

8 For an exhaustive study of the Antarctic system, see, the Report of the United Nations Secretary-General on the Question of Antarctica, requested under General Assembly resolution 38/77. It includes the views of a number of states. UN Doc A/39/583, parts I-III, 31 October 1984.

9 See *Intermedia*, a review issued by the International Institute of Communications (London), 13 (May 1985), 8-27.

10 A. Kiss, 'La notion de patrimoine commun de l'humanité,' *Recueil des cours de l'Académie de droit international de la Haye*, tome 175 (1982), 145-51 with references.

for the use of the high-frequency bands allocated to the broadcasting service.[11]

Until now, telecommunications were confined to space activities – the only way to maintain contact with spaceships is to use radio facilities. But the role of satellites is becoming more and more important in world telecommunications. It has therefore been advocated that the whole of outer space should be considered the common heritage of mankind. However, the system of existing international regulations with respect to space does not exhibit all the fundamental characteristics of the concept. Even if outer space is 'not subject to national appropriation by claims of sovereignty, by means of use or occupation or by any other means' and even if it is to be used for the benefit and in the interest of all countries,[12] no common management has so far been constructed and its use for military or even non-peaceful purposes is not prohibited.[13] The present outer space régime is in general thus very much like that of the high seas: it can be considered a *res communis*, but does not fulfil the criteria of the concept of the common heritage of mankind.

That said, it is true that certain elements of outer space have been granted a special régime amounting to a de facto status of common heritage – dedicated orbits, for example – or have been explicitly declared parts of the common heritage of mankind – the moon, for example.

The orbits around the earth which currently are of special interest are those used by geostationary satellites, which orbit at a height of approximatively 35,800 kilometres and always keep the same position relative to the earth. Satellites placed in this orbit

11 International Institute of Communications, World Administrative Conference for the Planning of HF Bands Allocated to the Broadcasting Service, London, November 1983.

12 Treaty on Principles Governing the Activities of States in the Exploration and Use of Outer Space, Including the Moon and Other Celestial Bodies, 27 January 1967, in United Nations, Treaty Series, vol 610, 205.

13 As a matter of fact article 4 of the space treaty prohibits, as far as all space is concerned, only the placing in orbit around the earth of objects carrying nuclear weapons or any other kinds of weapons of mass destruction. A complete demilitarization is provided for only on the moon and the other celestial bodies.

have special advantages when used for telecommunications, including direct broadcasting, for guiding ships or aircraft, for surveying the earth and its atmosphere, and for remote sensing. Despite its size, this orbit cannot be occupied by more than a limited number of satellites in order to ensure favourable conditions for radio transmissions, and in consequence international management became a necessity. The principle of planning its use based on equitable access has been embodied in the revised article 33(2) of the ITU Convention, although the details are still to be worked out.[14] Here again the emphasis is on the importance of international management in the interest of all nations and future generations. This theme seems to me the most essential characteristic of the concept of the common heritage of mankind.

The moon, another part of outer space, has actually been declared part of the common heritage of mankind. A treaty adopted by the United Nations General Assembly on 5 December 1979 proclaims (article 11) that the moon and its natural resources are the common heritage of mankind and envisages that the states parties will undertake to establish an international régime to govern the exploitation of its natural resources with the purpose of ensuring orderly and safe development, rational management, and the expansion of opportunities in the use of those resources.[15]

The most developed formulation of the common heritage concept to date is to be found in part XI of the Law of the Sea Convention signed in Montego Bay on 10 December 1982.[16] Article 136 of this convention proclaims that the 'Area,' meaning the seabed and ocean floor and subsoil thereof beyond the limits of national jurisdiction, is the common heritage of mankind. All rights in the resources of the Area are vested in mankind as a whole, and these resources are not subject to alienation, save in accordance with the rules and principles proclaimed in the convention. No state shall

14 Ram S. Jakhu, 'Legal aspects of the WARC,' *Intermedia* 13 (May 1985), 14-18.

15 Agreement Governing the Activities of States on the Moon and Other Celestial Bodies, United Nations, General Assembly, Official Records, 34th session, supplement 20.

16 Convention on the Law of the Sea, as printed in *The Law of the Sea* (New York: United Nations 1983), 1ff.

claim or exercise sovereignty or sovereign rights over any part of the Area or its resources, nor shall any state or natural or juridical person appropriate any part of it. Activities in the Area shall be carried out for the benefit of mankind as a whole, irrespective of the geographical location of states, whether coastal or landlocked, and shall take into particular consideration the interests and needs of developing states. The Area is to be used exclusively for peaceful purposes, and the marine environment is to be protected against harmful effects which may arise from activities in the Area. All objects of an archaeological and historical nature found in the Area are to be preserved or disposed of for the benefit of mankind as a whole. Marine scientific research in the Area is to be carried out exclusively for peaceful purposes and for the benefit of mankind as a whole.

A complex machinery has been invented for the implementation of these principles: in particular, activities in the Area are to be organized, carried out, and controlled by an international authority which has three principal organs – an assembly, a council, and a secretariat. An enterprise placed under the authority is to carry out activities in the Area directly, but national or private enterprises may obtain, in accordance with a rather complicated procedure and under strict conditions, the right to explore and to exploit the resources of the Area.[17] The main principle is that the revenues from exploitation of the Area should be shared inside the international community and in particular should benefit developing countries.

The Law of the Sea Convention presented the most detailed version of the concept of the common heritage of mankind to date. It was so elaborate and complex that some of the most important states considered it unrealistic and even dangerous and did not sign the convention. However, the criteria for the common heritage concept can be drawn from agreements in other fields of international co-operation.

In all the situations which have been discussed so far, the prin-

17 See, in particular, annex III of the convention, *ibid*, 113-30.

ciple of non-appropriation by states, that is, a prohibition on establishing jurisdiction over the areas concerned has been a common feature. Still, one may ask whether this is an indispensable criterion of the concept of common heritage. Without a doubt, non-appropriation is a guarantee of the free use of the area concerned – at least for certain forms of use such as navigation or scientific research. However, this is the essential characteristic of the *res communis*, not of a common heritage which our generation has received and which it has to transmit to future ones with as little damage as possible. From this point of view it would seem that the most essential criteria are non-destructive – that is, peaceful – use and good management in the interest of all mankind (in essence, a trust).

Under these criteria the concept of the common heritage appears to be broader than is usually understood. The term 'heritage' has certainly been used to encompass many things. For example, the Convention for the Protection of the World's Cultural and Natural Heritage, adopted by the United Nations Educational, Scientific, and Cultural Organization in Paris on 23 November 1972, includes monuments, groups of buildings, sites, natural features, geological and physiographical formations, and natural sites or precisely delineated areas of outstanding universal value from the point of view of history, art, science, natural beauty, or conservation. According to the convention the contracting parties recognize that their duty is to ensure the identification, protection, conservation, presentation, and transmission to future generations of that heritage and that such a heritage constitutes a world heritage for whose protection it is the duty of the international community as a whole to co-operate. As a consequence, concrete measures are provided for ensuring the achievement of the aims of the convention, in particular by creating a specific organ of co-operation, by establishing a World Heritage List, and by organizing, in certain cases, international assistance. Two regional conventions[18] also deal with the cultural heritage, and a long list

18 In its preamble, the European Convention on the Protection of the Archaeological Heritage (European Treaty Series, no 66), signed in London on 6 May 1969,

of treaties can be cited which tend to ensure the conservation and the transmission to future generations of landscapes and wild flora and fauna.[19]

All these agreements have long-term objectives and in general bring no immediate advantages to any of the contracting parties. They thus fulfil the criteria which have been proposed here as particularly important characteristics of the common heritage concept: peaceful use, rational management, conservation. However, they also differ from some of the agreements we discussed earlier in that individual elements of the world's cultural and natural heritage are quite often under national jurisdiction and may even be private property – like historic buildings in cities. However any problem this might create does not seem too difficult to manage.

---

recognizes that 'while the moral responsibility for protecting the European archaeological heritage ... rests in the first instance with the State directly concerned, it is also the concern of European States jointly,' while the preamble of the Convention on the Protection of the Archaeological, Historical and Artistic Heritage of the American Nations (OAS publication SER.A/24), signed in Santiago on 16 June 1976, proclaims that there is a basic obligation to transmit their cultural heritage to coming generations and that this heritage can only be protected and preserved by mutual appreciation and respect for such properties, within a framework of the soundest inter-American co-operation.

19 One of the most interesting examples is the African Convention on the Conservation of Nature and Natural Resources (Algiers 15 September 1968), whose preamble proclaims the necessity of undertaking individual and joint action for the conservation, utilization, and development of natural resources 'by establishing and maintaining their rational utilization for the present and future welfare of mankind.' According to article 8 when an animal or plant species is threatened with extinction or may become so and is represented only in the territory of one of the contracting states, that state has a particular responsibility for its protection (OAU Doc. CM/232). The Convention on International Trade in Endangered Species of Wild Fauna and Flora (Washington 3 March 1973) also declares that wild fauna and flora are an irreplaceable part of the natural systems of the earth 'which must be protected for this and the generations to come' (Official Journal of the European Communities, no C243 of 22/9/1980). Equivalent expressions can be found in many other treaties such as the Convention on the Conservation of European Wildlife and Natural Habitats (Berne 19 September 1979) and the Convention on Conservation of Nature in the South Pacific (Apia 12 June 1976). The preamble of the Convention on the Conservation of Migratory Species of Wild Animals (Bonn 23 June 1979) declares: '... each generation of man holds the resources of the earth for future generations and has an obligation to ensure that this legacy is conserved and, where utilized, is used wisely.' (The text of these treaties appears in A.C. Kiss, ed, *Selected Multilateral Treaties in the Field of the Environment* [Nairobi: United Nations Environment Program 1983], at 509, 463, and 500.)

The very nature of the common heritage seems to imply a form of trust under which the principal aims are rational use, good management, and transmission to future generations. These obligations have achieved common acceptance by virtue of all the treaty systems in which they have been mentioned. Whether the trustee is the international community through the intermediary of an international organ, or whether it is the concerned state which has agreed to act on the community's behalf, is a matter of policy. One may recall here the theory of the *dédoublement fonctionnel* formulated by the late Georges Scelle, according to which in given circumstances individual governments can be considered as organs in charge of the implementation of international law rules since the international community has in most cases no specific organs to ensure such implementation.[20] An extra-legal consideration could also be added. Although no one contests the sovereignty of, let us say, the Italian state over Venice or of Kenya over its wild fauna, the world's conscience would react unanimously if the Italian government decided to destroy that historic city and replace it with an industrial plant or if the Kenyan authorities enacted a law commanding destruction of all the elephants on their territory. The world would declare that the state has no right to take such drastic measures because such things belong to all human beings. In certain respects, therefore, there is a strong sense that a common heritage exists, even if all its implications have not been clearly established.

The most serious resistance to the common heritage concept has arisen over the principle of equitable sharing of benefits. While the problem is not the same in all the situations in which the concept has been applied, it is nonetheless the issue over which general principles war with the everyday realities of the international system.

THE COMMON HERITAGE CONCEPT AND PRESENT REALITIES

The idea of a common heritage of mankind is relatively new, and although the concept's fundamental characteristics are to be found in various situations, it has been officially formulated in an ex-

20 G. Scelle, *Droit international public: manuel élémentaire* (Paris 1944), 21-2.

haustive way, with its legal and institutional consequences, only recently with the Convention on the Law of the Sea. However, this convention is far from being accepted by all the states of the world; the United States, the United Kingdom, the Federal Republic of Germany, and some other powers had not signed it by the time the signature period was closed on 9 December 1984. The reason for that refusal is part XI of the convention which deals with the government of the seabed beyond national jurisdiction. It should be noted that three of the non-signatory states are among the 'happy few' with the technical and financial capacity to explore and to exploit the mineral resources of the deep seabed. The 1979 treaty which declared the moon the common heritage of mankind has been signed by only a few states. Again, none of the signatories is a participant in major space activities.

Parallel with this evolution – although the word regression might be more apt – the characteristics of the common heritage of mankind have also been contested in other fields. This was the case with the privileged orbit for geostationary satellites. On 3 December 1976 eight equatorial countries adopted a declaration in Bogota claiming sovereign rights to the orbit above their territory, because, they asserted, no boundary has been fixed between national air space and outer space. However, the World Administrative Conference on Satellite Broadcasting of 1977 did not give attention to these claims.[21]

Antarctica has been administered, in practice, by the consultative parties of the 1959 treaty, which now include the twelve original contracting parties and four others which have acquired 'consultative' status more recently.[22] The question has been raised

21 S. Gorove, 'The geostationary orbit: issues of law and policy,' *American Journal of International Law* 73 (July 1979), 450-5.

22 Full participation in the work of the consultative meetings which establish regulations for Antarctica is accorded only to original parties to the treaty and those contracting parties which demonstrate their interest in Antarctica by conducting substantial scientific research activity there, such as the establishment of a scientific station or the despatch of a scientific expedition. The original contracting parties are Argentina, Australia, Belgium, Chile, France, Japan, New Zealand, Norway, South Africa, the Soviet Union, the United Kingdom, and the United States. Poland, India, Brazil, and the Federal Republic of Germany have become consulting parties since 1959.

whether this Antarctic 'aristocracy' could be considered to be administering a part of the common heritage on behalf of the whole international community. At their seventh summit conference, held at New Delhi from 7 to 12 March 1983, the heads of state or government of the non-aligned countries considered that, in view of the increasing international interest in the Antarctic, the United Nations should undertake a comprehensive study of the subject. In fact, it was the attempt of the consultative parties to draft regulations for a hypothetical minerals régime in the Antarctic area which had attracted attention to this continent, and the precedent of the deep seabed may have played a certain role in the interest manifested in Antarctica by Third World countries. During discussions in the First Committee of the General Assembly some states asserted that Antarctica was a part of the common heritage of mankind so that the concern of the United Nations was justified, while others considered that this principle was not relevant to Antarctica and that its application to the régime governing this area was inappropriate. They argued that an effective legal system in the region that was open to all states already existed and noted that seven countries still maintain national claims in Antarctica. For those reasons, Antarctica was neither *res communis* nor *res nullius* and the application of the principle of the common heritage of mankind was not acceptable.[23]

One might conclude from these responses that the concept of the common heritage of mankind is not really accepted by the states most concerned. Following what happened with the Convention on the Law of the Sea, it also has been asserted that, after all, the international instruments which formally recognize the concept of the common heritage reserve this régime for areas to which access is extremely difficult, while the most accessible parts of the planet are or have been placed under national jurisdiction. Moreover, there has certainly been an ebb in the support for the concept of common heritage, just as there has been less support for other generous and altruistic ideas which played an important role in the developments of the 'sixties and the early 'seventies.

23 United Nations, General Assembly, A/39/583, part I, 31 October 1984, 33ff.

Although the general economic and psychological state of the world certainly plays a role in this evolution – or regression – there are, I would suggest, specific reasons for it which arise from some fundamental misunderstandings about the true nature of the common heritage concept. In the discussions surrounding the drafting of the provisions of the Law of the Sea Convention related to the Area, the benefit-sharing aspect was very strongly stressed and indeed the whole complex machinery which has been created is aimed at ensuring that developing countries receive a part of the direct economic profits which the exploitation of deep sea mineral resources is supposed to yield. Though a better sharing of resources is a fundamental condition of any successful future economic world order, this requirement should not be considered one of the principal criteria of the common heritage concept, at least not in the narrow interpretation it has been given in the context of the Law of the Sea Convention. As I have shown, the essential characteristics of the common heritage concept include exclusive use for peaceful purposes and optimum use of resources in a spirit of conservation for future generations, which means rational exploitation and, if necessary, appropriate management by or under the supervision of the international community. Benefit sharing may involve the equitable sharing of revenue, but, depending on the situation, it can also mean sharing scientific knowledge – as in Antarctica – cultural values for the cultural heritage, or the use itself, as with the orbit for geostationary satellites. The principles and mechanisms established by the space treaty in this regard which are applicable to the privileged orbit and to the moon as well as article 143 of the Law of the Sea Convention related to marine scientific research provide examples of benefit sharing relating to the dissemination of the results of scientific research and analysis. Thus, the term 'for the benefit of all mankind' is to be interpreted in a generous way to include aesthetic, cultural, and scientific benefits as well as economic revenues.

Nor does the non-appropriation of elements which can be considered parts of the common heritage of mankind seem to be an essential criterion. When discussing the régime of Antarctica, some states have clearly confused *res communis* with the common heritage, even though the two concepts are different. Although the two conventions which openly establish a régime based on the common heritage – that on the law of the sea and that on the moon – do concern areas which have not been appropriated and whose appropriation has now been prohibited by international law, the main criteria of the concept are present in other circumstances independent of appropriation – for example in agreements dealing with the cultural and natural heritage and other elements of the environment.

If non-appropriation is not a basic characteristic of the common heritage concept, then the question of who has to take care of the heritage is more easily answered. The Law of the Sea Convention foresees complex machinery for this purpose, while for the moon detailed regulations are still to be adopted. However, a worldwide international authority does exist for the management of the radio spectrum and of the privileged orbit. As far as cultural and natural heritage or the environment is concerned, individual states are charged with the implementation of internationally accepted principles. The central idea is that of a trust which is to be exercised in the common interest of mankind either by international bodies, by groups of states, or by individual states under some form of supervision by the international community – whichever seems most suitable. The trust as an institution, which seems at present to be most developed in American law,[24] is not unknown in international law. After several de facto applications,[25] it has been incorporated into the United Nations Charter in the trusteeship system. The general characteristic in all these cases was the administration of a territory or of a situation – for example, the prep-

24 In American law a trust is defined as 'a fiduciary relationship with respect to property, subjecting the person by whom the property is held to equitable duties to deal with the property for the benefit of another person,' Restatement (Second) of Trusts, par. 2 (1959), quoted by J. Dukeminier and S.M. Johanson, *Family Wealth Transactions: Wills, Trusts, Future Interests and Estate Planning* (1972), 379.

25 See, for example, A. Kiss, 'La notion de patrimoine commun de l'humanité,' 131-3.

aration of a plebiscite by an international organ – by a group of states or by one single state, not in their own interest but in that of the concerned territory, and, beyond that, of the whole international community, in order to maintain peace or to help development. Those charged with the responsibility for different elements of the common heritage of mankind work in the same way at the tasks of management and conservation of those elements, whatever their relationship to them may be: administration, exclusive territorial jurisdiction, or ownership. They act on behalf of all mankind and in its interest.

We thus come back to the starting point of the present reflections: there is very clearly a common interest of mankind expressed in a great number of treaties and the concept of the common heritage of mankind is the materialization of that interest, that is, its application to material elements. The implications which are to be drawn from this fundamental fact may be different in different situations – that is, whether this interest involves the sharing of economic and financial gains or only of scientific, technical, or cultural benefits. Similarly, the choice of the trustee may be different in different circumstances. The most essential characteristics are the maintenance of peace and the optimum use of the resource compatible with its transmission to future generations.

However, one has to recognize that the present structure of international law is such that even when numerous important international instruments are adopted which set out the interest of mankind, their implementation is not necessarily guaranteed. Indeed, in the absence of an international executive or even compulsory jurisdiction, the main guarantee of a contracting party's compliance with international legal rules has been reciprocity. In the absence of reciprocity the only sanction is a condemnation by the international community in a more or less institutional form – by individual states or by an international organ. It is clear that an infringement of the common heritage by one state cannot be dealt with by all the other states of the world responding in kind. The result is a certain weakness of the legal instruments which are based on such interest and, as a consequence, of those which establish a régime of the common heritage of mankind. The attempt to build up institutions to ensure the implementation of the principle, made in the Law of the Sea Convention, has not been welcomed with unanimous enthusiasm. (It also must be admitted that the machinery to be set up is particularly ponderous.) Still, this seems to be the only way to make sure that long-term interests can be safeguarded. The flexibility of the Antarctic Treaty system, even though – or perhaps because – it is based on the co-operation of a limited number of states which actually intervene in the management of a resource, may be an example which should receive consideration as an alternative enforcement mechanism.

Part II
Responsibility to Protect

[6]

JURISDICTION WITHOUT TERRITORY: FROM THE HOLY ROMAN EMPIRE TO THE RESPONSIBILITY TO PROTECT

*Anne Orford**

The relationship between jurisdiction and territory has long been a contested one. As the modern State gradually replaced the Holy Roman Empire to become the dominant form of political organization in Western Europe, questions about the limits and divisibility of power began to be framed as questions about the relationship between jurisdiction and territory. The emergence of the territorial State during the sixteenth and seventeenth centuries posed a challenge to the universal jurisdiction of both the Pope and the Holy Roman Emperor within Europe. Both the Pope and the Emperor claimed the right to exercise jurisdiction over the world as a matter of right, even if they had no control over particular territories as a matter of empirical fact. The relationship between jurisdiction and territory was not only an issue within Europe. During the sixteenth and seventeenth centuries, debates about the authority of European sovereigns to rule newly discovered territories in the New World also began to be articulated in terms of the relation between jurisdiction and control over territory. Disputes amongst European powers about which Christian monarchs could claim rights of *dominium* over territory

---

* Michael D. Kirby Professor of International Law and ARC Australian Professorial Fellow, Melbourne Law School, University of Melbourne. I gratefully acknowledge the generous support of the Australian Research Council, which made work on this project possible by awarding me a five-year research fellowship.

in the New World turned on whether the Pope had the authority and jurisdiction to grant such rights.[1]

The eventual triumph of the territorial State as the dominant political form globally meant that jurisdiction and territory came to be understood as closely related terms. Richard Ford, for example, argues that modern jurisdiction is always "defined by area."[2] While in theory an entity could be defined in terms of genre (for example, as an entity with "authority over 'all oil, wherever it is found'"), that entity "would not be a jurisdiction but an authority of another kind. A jurisdiction is territorially defined."[3] Yet if we look to the history of the debate over the right of external actors to determine the legitimacy of control over territory, we can see that the relation between jurisdiction and territory has never been finally determined. That debate stretches across six hundred years, from fifteenth century arguments about the extent of papal or imperial jurisdiction to decide who has authority over territories in Europe or the New World, through to contemporary debates about whether the international community has jurisdiction to intervene in situations where States are ruled by tyrants or by governments that are unable or unwilling to protect the population.

This Essay focuses upon one contemporary manifestation of that ongoing battle over the relationship between jurisdiction and control over territory—the emergence and institutionalization of the "responsibility to protect" concept. The idea that States and the international community have a responsibility to protect populations has shaped internationalist debates about conflict prevention, the use of force, and international administration since its development by the International Commission on Intervention and State Sovereignty (ICISS) in 2001.[4] The responsibility to protect concept is premised on the notion, to quote former Secretary-General Kofi Annan, that "the primary raison d'être and duty" of every State is to protect its population.[5] If a State proves unable to protect its

1. *See, e.g.*, Francisco de Vitoria, Political Writings 84–92 (Anthony Pagden & Jeremy Lawrance eds., 1991); Richard Hakluyt, A Discourse Concerning Western Planting, Written in the Year 1584, at 129–51 (Charles Deane ed., 1877); *see also* Ken MacMillan, Sovereignty and Possession in the English New World: The Legal Foundations of Empire, 1576–1640, at 64–74 (2006) (discussing the English response to papal claims of authority and jurisdiction to distribute lands in the New World).

2. Richard T. Ford, *Law's Territory (A History of Jurisdiction)*, 97 Mich. L. Rev. 843, 852 (1999).

3. *Id.*

4. Int'l Comm'n on Intervention & State Sovereignty [ICISS], The Responsibility to Protect 16 (2001), *available at* http://www.iciss.ca/pdf/Commission-Report.pdf (last visited June 6, 2009).

5. The Secretary-General, *In Larger Freedom: Towards Development, Security and Human Rights for All*, ¶ 135, *delivered to the General Assembly*, U.N. Doc. A/59/2005 (Mar. 21, 2005).

citizens, the responsibility to do so shifts to the international community. The concept was endorsed by the General Assembly in its World Summit Outcome, and has since garnered the support of States, international organizations and civil society, and informed major projects of institutional transformation at the United Nations.

Part I of the Essay sets the scene by situating the responsibility to protect concept within the longstanding debate about the relationship between jurisdiction and territory. The competition for authority between States and the Holy Roman Empire, both within and beyond Europe, has involved debates over the meaning of jurisdiction, *imperium*, territory, and possession. Those questions were not resolved with the demise of the Holy Roman Empire and the emergence of the modern State in Europe, but have continued to play out in battles over the proper relation between state jurisdiction and international jurisdiction. Part II outlines the ways in which the relation between state (or domestic) jurisdiction and international jurisdiction was defined in the Charter of the United Nations (U.N.), and traces the growing importance of the claim that authority must be constrained in particular ways in order to be legitimate in the post-United Nations era. I argue there that the drive for humanitarian action to defend the rights of individuals quickly undermined any tidy settlement of these jurisdictional questions. The jurisdiction of the United Nations to shape the way in which States are governed has long been a source of contest, as has the jurisdiction of the Security Council to police the common interest. Debates about the limits of international authority have intensified since 1989 with the growth of support for the concepts of humanitarian intervention and, more recently, the responsibility to protect. Part III examines the way in which the scope and limits of the international responsibility to protect have been expressed in jurisdictional terms. In the lead up to the 2005 World Summit, many States, particularly from the global South, were very concerned at the potential expansion of international authority that might follow from any official endorsement of the responsibility to protect concept. As a result, States looked to jurisdiction as a means of limiting the situations in which an international responsibility to protect might arise. Yet while legal determinations of jurisdiction are often thought to be about the delimitation of authority, they are also very productive sites for generating a sense of what is possible on either side of the limit.[6] It is through the institutional practices of jurisdiction that authority is made intelligible.

6. For the argument that discourses concerned with boundaries or limits have this productive quality, see R.B.J. WALKER, INSIDE/OUTSIDE: INTERNATIONAL RELATIONS AS POLITICAL THEORY (1993); Leslie J. Moran, *Placing Jurisdiction*, *in* JURISPRUDENCE OF JURISDICTION 159 (Shaun McVeigh ed., 2007).

This Part shows that the legal articulation of the triggers to international jurisdiction produced new representations of the nature and extent of both state and international authority. Part IV concludes by drawing out some of the key implications that emerge from the jurisdictional practice related to the implementation of the responsibility to protect concept.

I. Territory and Jurisdiction in the Modern World

A. *Universal Jurisdiction and the Holy Roman Empire*

How does jurisdiction ("the power of stating what is lawful"[7]) relate to control over territory? Is control over territory the source or the effect of jurisdiction? Such questions were of great importance in medieval and early modern Europe. The answers to these questions turned, among other things, on the relationship between fact and right. The debate, as with many debates over authority in Europe during that time, was framed using the language and concepts of Roman law.[8] The most important of these Roman law concepts to this debate were those of *ius*, *dominium*, *imperium*, and *iurisdictio*.

In early Roman law, the concept of *ius* was used to refer to the outcome of a "method of divine judgement."[9] Disputants were required to take an oath attesting to the righteousness of their claim, and these claims would then be tested by "ordeal or other supernatural judgement. The favorable verdict was a *ius*."[10] A *ius* was thus both "something objectively right" and something intimately connected with "private, bilateral relationships" and the "right way in which two disputants should behave towards each other . . . ."[11] A *ius* could also come into existence through agreements, such as agreements between neighbors. The objective and relational quality of *ius* distinguished it from the concept of *dominium*. Classical lawyers distinguished between "having *dominium* in something and having a *ius* in it."[12] *Dominium* was not constituted through agreements or relationships. Instead, it was "simply given by the fact, as it

7. Peter Stein, Roman Law in European History 60 (1999).

8. *See id.* at 38–67 (discussing the twelfth-century recovery of Roman law in Western Europe). For two analyses of the importance of Roman law to debates about the limits of imperial authority during the medieval and early modern periods, see David Armitage, The Ideological Origins of the British Empire 29–36 (2000); Anthony Pagden, Lords of All the World: Ideologies of Empire in Spain, Britain and France c.1500—c.1800, at 11–28 (1995).

9. Richard Tuck, Natural Rights Theories: Their Origin and Development 8 (1979).

10. *Id.*

11. *Id.*

12. *Id.* at 10.

seemed to the Romans, of a man's total control over his physical world . . . ."[13] In the later Empire, the distinction between notions of *ius* and *dominium* would become much less clean-cut. As the Emperor became more powerful and able to intervene in all aspects of life, the idea that a citizen might have "total control over his physical world" began to seem "increasingly implausible."[14] Everything, including *dominium*, was mediated through the Emperor. The Emperor was the citizen "with whom all other Roman citizens had the most extensive relationships."[15] *Dominium* began increasingly to be seen as a form of *ius*.

Nonetheless, the distinction between *ius* as an objective right that was ultimately determinable by divine judgment, and *dominium* as a form of property that was determined by control over the physical world, would reappear in medieval debates over the reach of papal or imperial authority. Central to those debates was the question of whether either the Pope or the Holy Roman Emperor could properly claim to exercise universal jurisdiction (*ius dicere*) as *dominus mundi* or lord of the world. The idea that the papacy and the Emperor exercised dual forms of universal jurisdiction shaped medieval legal thought.[16] The extent of papal and imperial jurisdiction, and the relation between jurisdiction and control (or *ius* and fact), had important implications both within and beyond Europe.

The question of the extent of papal jurisdiction was at the heart of the dispute about the legitimacy of Alexander VI's Bulls of Donation, through which the Spanish Crown claimed *dominium* over the New World. The papal bull *Inter caetera*, issued by Alexander VI in 1493, granted to "the illustrious sovereigns" King Ferdinand and Queen Isabella, and to their "heirs and successors, kings of Castile and Leon," "all islands and mainlands found and to be found, discovered and to be discovered" in the Atlantic world "towards the west and south" of a line bisecting the Atlantic ocean.[17] The proviso to this "gift, grant, and assignment" was that "no right acquired by any Christian prince, who may be in actual possession of said islands and mainlands" could be

---

13. *Id.*

14. *Id.*

15. *Id.* at 12.

16. James Muldoon, Empire and Order: The Concept of Empire, 800–1800, at 65 (1999).

17. Alexander VI, The Bull Inter Caetera (1493), *as reprinted in* European Treaties Bearing on the History of the United States and its Dependencies to 1648, at 71, 75–78 (Frances Gardiner Davenport ed., 1917).

"withdrawn or taken away."[18] By implication, *imperium* and *dominium* did not vest with indigenous peoples.[19]

The Spanish crown interpreted *Inter caetera* and the other Bulls of Donation as grants that authorized Spanish *dominium* over the lands they "discovered" in the New World. Ferdinand and Isabella appeared to believe not only that the Pope had the authority to dispose of *dominium* over lands in the New World, but that they needed a papal grant in order to acquire *dominium* over such lands.[20] The Bulls of Donation were drafted in consultation with Ferdinand and Isabella, and proof of the value that the Spanish monarchs attached to the bulls can be seen "in their anxiety that the things which they desired should be incorporated in them, and also in the revisions to which . . . they subsequently caused them to be subjected."[21] The bulls continued to be invoked both by the Spanish crown and by its imperial rivals in debates over the legal justifications for Spanish conquest of the New World until the late seventeenth century.[22] To take just one example, when Sir Francis Drake returned to England after his circumnavigation of the world in September 1580, with reports of having claimed land including Nova Albion (today's California or Oregon) and with commodities from the West Indies and South America, the Spanish ambassador Mendoza lodged a formal complaint with Queen Elizabeth.[23] Mendoza claimed "that these territories belonged to the King of Spain by virtue of first discovery and the papal bull of donation."[24]

In return, almost every "French or English attack on the claims to Spanish sovereignty overseas . . . [began] with a rejection of the validity of both the Bulls and the terms of the Treaty of Tordesillas."[25] Most challenges to the validity of the Bulls of Donation argued that the Pope did not have jurisdiction to grant rights to territory. Perhaps the most famous of these were the challenges to Spanish conquest of the New World posed by Francisco de Vitoria and his followers. Vitoria argued that "the [P]ope has no dominion (*dominium*) in the lands of the infidel" and those who think that the Pope "has temporal authority and jurisdiction over all princes in the world, are wrong."[26] According to Vitoria, "*the [P]ope has*

18. *Id.* at 77.

19. *See* ANTONY ANGHIE, IMPERIALISM, SOVEREIGNTY AND THE MAKING OF INTERNATIONAL LAW 17 (2004).

20. H. Vander Linden, *Alexander VI and the Demarcation of the Maritime and Colonial Domains of Spain and Portugal, 1493–1494*, 22 AM. HIST. REV. 1, 15–16 (1916).

21. *Id.* at 16.

22. MACMILLAN, *supra* note 1, at 66–74; PAGDEN, *supra* note 8, at 48.

23. MACMILLAN, *supra* note 1, at 52, 75.

24. *Id.* at 75.

25. PAGDEN, *supra* note 8, at 48.

26. VITORIA, *supra* note 1, at 84.

no power, at least in the ordinary course of events, to judge the cases of princes, or the titles of jurisdictions or realms . . . ."[27] While Vitoria did accept that the Pope had authority "to use temporal means" where necessary to fulfill a spiritual purpose,[28] he considered that this did not give the Pope authority "to award rights of *imperium* and *dominium* over *terra incognita*, which was within the jurisdiction of temporal, Roman law."[29] The spiritual jurisdiction of the Pope thus did not extend to the temporal world. A similar challenge to the legitimacy of the Bulls of Donation was made by the Anglican priest Richard Hakluyt the younger. Hakluyt argued that the Pope had no authority to dispose of or distribute "kingdomes and empires . . . ."[30] According to Hakluyt, ecclesiastical jurisdiction "hath nothinge to doe with absolution donation and devidinge of mere temporalities and earthly kingdomes."[31] The Bulls of Donation therefore posed no limitations upon the rights of the English to trade, settle, or plant in the New World, as "no Pope had any lawfull aucthoritie to give any suche donation at all."[32]

There were, however, some advisers to the English crown who accepted that the Pope had jurisdiction to make the donation of territory and invest the Spanish king with rights to the New World. In particular, this argument was made by the "English renaissance polymath" John Dee,[33] who was one of the advisers commissioned by Elizabeth to consider whether, and on what basis, English activities in the New World could be justified. Dee's writings drew on his training in geography and mathematics, as well as his knowledge of law and history.[34] Unlike some of his contemporaries, Dee was prepared to concede that Alexander VI had "authoretie" to "gift" land in the New World and that such an act was "of force sufficient by Gods lawe or mans lawe against all other Christian princes."[35] Dee was willing to accept that the Pope had such authority because he saw "the jurisdiction assumed by the [P]ope and his bull" as "legally analogous to that of Elizabeth" and the letters patent she issued to petitioners seeking authorization to claim *dominium* over

27. *Id.* at 87 (emphasis in original).

28. *Id.* at 92.

29. MACMILLAN, *supra* note 1, at 68.

30. HAKLUYT, *supra* note 1, at 130.

31. *Id.*

32. *Id.* at 129; *see also* MACMILLAN, *supra* note 1, at 67 (discussing Hakluyt's challenge to papal authority).

33. Ken MacMillan, *Introduction: Discourse on History, Geography, and Law*, *in* JOHN DEE, THE LIMITS OF THE BRITISH EMPIRE 1, 2 (Ken MacMillan & Jennifer Abeles eds., 2004).

34. *See generally* DEE, *supra* note 33.

35. *Id.* at 91; *see also id.* at 92–93 (challenging the Iberian interpretation of the grant as being too liberal because, according to Dee, the bull was intended by the Pope to be proscriptive and to limit Spanish domination of the New World to a particular geographically defined area); MACMILLAN, *supra* note 1, at 49–78 (providing a detailed analysis of Dee's arguments).

territories in the New World.[36] For Dee, Elizabeth, as "the leader of the Anglican Church and a holder of *imperium*," was able to "authorize settlement in the New World," in the same way that "the [P]ope, the leader of the Catholic Church and a holder of *imperium*" was able to donate territory.[37] Just as the Spanish *conquistadores* traced their rights to territory in the New World to the Bulls of Donation, English settlers and trading companies traced their rights to territory in the New World to the letters patent issued by Elizabeth. Both the papal bulls and the letters patent were represented as exercises of jurisdiction, through which the power to authorize rights to territory was expressed in writing. These documents did not simply claim jurisdiction but also *performed* jurisdiction. By this I mean that jurisdiction involves the process by which a worldly claimant to authority is transformed through the successful performance of the power to declare the law. To the extent that the Pope or Elizabeth claimed to have a form of jurisdiction that enabled them to declare rights to title in far-flung territories, they represented themselves as something other than mere tyrants or *de facto* rulers whose armies or followers were able to gain control of territory by force.

In addition to debates over the extent of the spiritual jurisdiction exercised by the Pope, the extent of the Holy Roman Emperor's jurisdiction was also contested within Europe and beyond. The secular jurisdiction of the Holy Roman Emperor was conceived of as universal. The medieval jurist Bartolus of Sassoferrato made this clear in his defense of the claim that the Emperor was lord of the world despite the fact that "foreign peoples, the cities of Italy, and the kings of France and England did not obey him."[38] Bartolus sought to show that the Emperor's universal jurisdiction could survive and co-exist with the new forms of territorial jurisdiction beginning to be exercised by princes and kings. The Emperor was lord of the world, not because he was lord of all the particular things, places, and people in the world, but rather because "he alone had *dominium* over the world considered as a single whole."[39] Bartolus defended this claim by distinguishing between the universal jurisdiction of the Emperor and the particular jurisdictions of other rulers, such as the Kings of England and France. The two could coexist because they were of a different nature. The universal jurisdiction of the Emperor involved jurisdiction "over the world considered as a single whole" rather than as a collection of "particular things," while the jurisdiction of Kings constituted jurisdiction over particular things (such as

36. MacMillan, *supra* note 1, at 73, 107.
37. *Id.* at 73.
38. Constantin Fasolt, The Limits of History 192 (2004).
39. *Id.*

England or France).[40] Jurisdiction was not an effect of power, but a form of power. The Emperor had universal jurisdiction over the world as a matter of right, not as a question of fact. However, when ambitious monarchs like Charles V or Ferdinand II succeeded to the title of Emperor, they sought to combine temporal authority with the universal rights to which they felt entitled as rulers of the Roman Empire.[41] As a result, the reach of imperial authority became far more worldly and far more threatening to peace in Europe.

The rulers of emerging States in Europe thus faced "two universal antagonists outside their own realms," in the form of the Papacy and the Empire.[42] Both claimed authority as a supranational body descended from the Roman Empire, and both alleged that this legacy gave them universal jurisdiction, understood as the power to state what is lawful for the whole world. Those who opposed medieval forms of government sought to counter papal and imperial authority with detailed arguments showing why the claim to be *dominus mundi* or lord of the world was flawed. As the next Section shows, these statist arguments were premised on the claim that sovereignty, and thus jurisdiction, depended upon *de facto* control over territory. Worldly authority, to be legitimate, must be effective.

B. *Protection, Control, and the Modern State*

As the State emerged to challenge the authority of the Holy Roman Empire, scholars like Thomas Hobbes developed detailed arguments grounding the authority of the State in its capacity to guarantee protection. Indeed, to invoke protection as the "primary raison d'être" of the State is to be in a complicated relation to a long tradition of absolutist theories such as that of Hobbes.[43] In his LEVIATHAN, Hobbes argued that the creation of a political order depended upon the establishment of a common power with the capacity to protect its subjects. This common power is "made by covenant of every man with every man."[44] Through that covenant, the commonwealth was entrusted with sovereign power for a particular end—"the procuration of *the safety of the people* . . . ."[45] According to Hobbes, the lawful authority is the one who achieves protection in the broad sense of bringing into being a condition in which the

---

40. *Id.*

41. *See id.* at 93 (discussing Ferdinand II).

42. ARMITAGE, *supra* note 8, at 33.

43. The Secretary-General, *In Larger Freedom: Towards Development, Security and Human Rights for All*, ¶ 135, U.N. Doc. A/59/2005, *supra* note 5.

44. THOMAS HOBBES, LEVIATHAN 114 (Oxford Univ. Press 1996) (1651).

45. *Id.* at 222.

safety of the people can be achieved. This was the "office," or in other words the responsibility, of the sovereign.[46]

Hobbes thus based his defense of power on its present efficacy rather than on the validity of its origins. His was a theory that spoke to conditions of conquest and of civil war. Hobbes argued that the continual debate about the legitimacy of the conditions under which authority was first constituted was radically destabilizing and ultimately irresolvable. By refusing to anchor the legitimacy of the commonwealth in its capacity to represent a romantic or historical collectivity of the people, Hobbes "pulled the rug out" from under arguments based on the nation as a "platform of resistance" to tyranny or misrule.[47] For Hobbes, the question of public authority did not turn on issues of authenticity, or on who was the true representative of God or the people. The authority of such a common power was instead grounded on its capacity in fact to ensure protection in accordance with the terms of the covenant. Indeed, Hobbes argued that the "obligation of subjects" to obey the sovereign would "last as long, and no longer, than the power lasteth, by which he is able to protect them."[48] The linkage of sovereignty and protection thus emerged alongside the modern State, as a way of distinguishing the State's *de facto* capacity to protect from *de jure* claims to authority, whether those claims were made by the peasantry (such as the revolutionary claimants to authority in seventeenth century England), the Pope, the Holy Roman Emperor, or rival claimants to territory in the new world.[49] Jurisdiction and the freedom to legislate at will were not a matter of right, but a consequence of the fact of control. The State was the form in which human beings could declare their independence from past obligations and ancient texts, and express their freedom to shape the future.[50]

With the triumph of the modern State and the demise of the Holy Roman Empire, debates over the divisibility of power ceased to be framed in terms of the competition between imperial and state jurisdic-

46. The history of linking sovereignty and protection in order to justify state authority has been invoked by Edward Luck, the U.N. Special Advisor on the Responsibility to Protect. *See* Edward C. Luck, U.N. Special Advisor, Statement to the UNSC Working Group on Conflict Resolution and Prevention in Africa, (Dec. 1, 2008), *available at* http://www.responsibilitytoprotect.org/index.php/eupdate/1965 (last visited June 6, 2009) ("From the dawn of the nation-state era, it has been the intrinsic and inherent responsibility of the sovereign to offer protection to its people. In return, they offer their loyalty. What higher purpose could sovereignty serve?").

47. ISTVAN HONT, JEALOUSY OF TRADE: INTERNATIONAL COMPETITION AND THE NATION-STATE IN HISTORICAL PERSPECTIVE 130 (2005).

48. HOBBES, *supra* note 44, at 147.

49. Anne Orford, *Lawful Authority and the Responsibility to Protect, in* LEGALITY AND LEGITIMACY IN INTERNATIONAL ORDER (Richard Falk et al. eds., forthcoming 2009).

50. FASOLT, *supra* note 38, at 7–10.

tion. However, this is not to say that the demise of the Holy Roman Empire meant that power was understood to be unified in the form of the sovereign, as the mythologizing of absolutist theorists of the State would seem to suggest. It was certainly no longer plausible to argue that the Holy Roman Emperor had universal jurisdiction as lord of the world, while princes had rights to particular jurisdiction, and that both forms of jurisdiction could apply over the same territory. However, the idea that power might be divided, or that people, places, and things might be subject to plural sources of law, did not disappear. Instead, it changed form. In particular, it persisted in two debates that inform contemporary international law.

The first debate concerns the question of whether the recognition of a government, or even of a new State, by external actors should be understood as declaratory or constitutive. According to the declaratory theory, which was dominant until at least the late eighteenth century, the "legal status" of a ruler was understood to be "derived and perfected from within."[51] As a result, "internal legality determines external legality . . . ."[52] Within Europe, the law of nature and of nations had little to say about the basis of state legitimacy. The question of whether a duly appointed or elected ruler properly had authority over territory was not treated as a question for interstate relations. If the people of a State thought a person "worthy of election to the throne of their country and useful to their welfare," that election was not "capable of being validly challenged by other States."[53] To give foreign rulers or powers "the *right to recognition* . . . would mean intervention and result in submission which would stultify the fundamental right of States to equality guaranteed by the law of nature and nations."[54] If the legitimacy of a government were understood to depend upon external recognition or championing by external powers, the uneasy peace that existed in the aftermath of the European wars of religion could quickly unravel. Thus the *de facto* existence of control over territory was sufficient to establish sovereignty.

Yet beginning in the early nineteenth century, the law of nations began to treat statehood as a question that was not determined only internally. International lawyers such as Henry Wheaton were confronted with "frequent changes in membership of the Family of Nations" as a result of revolutions in Europe and the New World,[55] and questions about

51. C.H. Alexandrowicz, *The Theory of Recognition In Fieri*, 1958 BRIT. Y.B. INT'L L. 176, 179.

52. *Id.*

53. *Id.* at 177.

54. *Id.*

55. *Id.* at 196.

the normative criteria of statehood began to appear in urgent need of resolution. Wheaton and his contemporaries began to argue that while "internal sovereignty" was a question of "factual formation[,]" "external sovereignty" of a State "was not *derived* from within," but instead required "action from without which must be taken by the existing Member States of the Family of Nations."[56] States began to treat external recognition as an act that "renders the sovereignty of a new State perfect and complete."[57] In this sense, *de facto* control over territory was no longer sufficient to ground a claim to statehood.

The second way in which an uncertainty about the relation between right and power, or jurisdiction and control over territory, persisted was in relation to the question of whether individuals within a State had fundamental rights that derived from a source other than the positive law of the State. While States were understood to have public authority over all people and things within their jurisdiction, from the seventeenth century onwards private individuals were also understood to have a form of "subjective right" to property in their persons, liberty, and estates that could coexist with, and constrain, public authority.[58] These inalienable property rights were argued to derive from a source other than social, political, or legal convention and to fix "limits on the powers of government."[59]

As the next Part shows, both the debate about the role of external actors in determining the legitimacy of governments and the debate about the extent to which fundamental rights represented a constraint on state action became linked to international jurisdiction with the creation of the United Nations.

56. *Id.* at 195; *see also* JENNIFER L. BEARD, THE POLITICAL ECONOMY OF DESIRE: INTERNATIONAL LAW, DEVELOPMENT AND THE NATION STATE 124–49 (2007) (offering a critical reading of these practices of recognition).

57. Alexandrowicz, *supra* note 51, at 195.

58. This modern division of jurisdiction and property is explained by Hugo Grotius. 2 HUGO GROTIUS, THE RIGHTS OF WAR AND PEACE 457 (Liberty Fund, 2005) (1625) (commenting that "altho' Jurisdiction and Property are usually acquired by one and the same Act, yet they are in themselves really distinct; and therefore Property may be transferred, not only to those of the same State, but even to Foreigners too, the Jurisdiction remaining as it was before."); *see also* JAMES CRAWFORD, THE CREATION OF STATES IN INTERNATIONAL LAW 56 (2d ed. 2006) (offering a contemporary differentiation of public authority and private ownership: "Territorial sovereignty is not ownership of but governing power with respect to territory.").

59. Cary J. Nederman, *Property and Protest: Political Theory and Subjective Rights in Fourteenth-Century England*, 58 REV. POL. 323, 327 (1996).

II. International Jurisdiction and Humanitarian Action

A. *International Jurisdiction Under the U.N. Charter*

International law has long treated effective control over territory as an important criterion of statehood.[60] In that sense, statehood is premised upon *de facto* authority. Yet the creation of the United Nations in 1945 saw the emergence of an international regime in which the principles of self-determination, sovereign equality, and the prohibition against acquisition of territory through the use of force were also treated as central to determining the lawfulness of particular claimants to authority.[61] These principles shaped the process of decolonization and delegitimized alien rule. The preamble of the U.N. Charter also expressed a determination "to reaffirm faith in fundamental human rights" and "the dignity and worth of the human person."[62] That faith would inform the body of international human rights law and international humanitarian law that developed over the course of the twentieth century as a constraint on state action. Under the U.N. Charter, the lawfulness of authority over a given territory was thus treated as a matter both of fact and of right.

That understanding of state authority informed the way that the U.N. Charter attempted to formulate the relationship between state and international jurisdiction. As the authority of sovereign States was understood to be an expression both of effective control over territory and of fundamental principles such as the right to self-determination, external intervention in the internal affairs of States was *prima facie* illegitimate. Yet, because the legitimacy of state authority had become a matter for international law, as overseen by an organization with supranational authority, intervention in the internal affairs of States must also, in some circumstances, be legitimate. As the earlier debates about the role of external actors in recognizing elected monarchs or revolutionary States made clear, the treatment of authority as a matter for international law opened up new possibilities for destabilizing external intervention and new threats to peace. It was the task of the U.N. Charter to articulate the jurisdictional grounds upon which the new organization might exercise its authority to police and perfect the State, while at the same time establishing a commitment to fundamental principles of sovereign equality and self-determination.

The U.N. Charter attempts to settle these jurisdictional questions by authorizing international intervention in two distinct situations. First, the

60. Crawford, *supra* note 58, at 37–89.
61. *Id.* at 96–173.
62. U.N. Charter pmbl.

preamble to the Charter provides that "armed force shall not be used, save in the common interest"[63] and all Members agree to "refrain in their international relations from the threat or use of force" in any manner "inconsistent with the Purposes of the United Nations."[64] The Charter vests the international police function in the Security Council—the organ given the "primary responsibility for the maintenance of international peace and security."[65] Like the other organs of the United Nations, the Security Council is effectively given the power to determine the extent of its jurisdiction, including its jurisdiction to authorize force when there is a "threat to the peace, breach of the peace, or act of aggression."[66] To the extent that there are limitations on Security Council jurisdiction, they have been seen to flow from Articles 24 and 39 of the Charter, which establish the scope of the police function of the Security Council and its role within the broader Charter system.[67] The Council determines whether a particular event triggers its jurisdiction under Chapter VII, and decides what measures should be taken to restore peace and security.[68] Any decision by the Security Council to authorize the use of force against a State requires its Members to submit to the discipline of a multilateral decision-making process.[69] This commitment to multilateralism has been seen as a significant bulwark against a resurgence of imperialism.[70] It means that a powerful State does not have the right to undertake police action against another State without Security Council authoriza-

63. *Id.*

64. *Id.* art. 2(4).

65. *Id.* art. 24(1); *see also* Hans Kelsen, *Collective Security Under International Law* 4, 114, 142 n.20 (Int'l Law Studies Series No. 49, 1957) (characterizing the collective security system established under the U.N. Charter in terms of international police action); Martti Koskenniemi, *The Police in the Temple: Order, Justice and the UN: A Dialectical View*, 6 EUR. J. INT'L L. 325, 344 (1995) (analyzing the Security Council as "the technician of peace, the police").

66. For the broad principle that each U.N. organ "must, in the first place at least, determine its own jurisdiction," see Certain Expenses of the United Nations (Article 17, Paragraph 2, of the Charter), Advisory Opinion, 1962 I.C.J. 151, at 168 (July 20); *see also* THOMAS M. FRANCK, RECOURSE TO FORCE: STATE ACTION AGAINST THREATS AND ARMED ATTACKS 5–6 (2002) (discussing the practice by which the political organs of the United Nations have determined their own jurisdiction).

67. U.N. Charter art. 24 (providing that "In discharging these duties the Security Council shall act in accordance with the Purposes and Principles of the United Nations"); *id.* art. 39 (granting to the Security Council the authority to "determine the existence of any threat to the peace, breach of the peace, or act of aggression" and to "decide what measures shall be taken . . . to maintain or restore international peace and security").

68. *Id.* art. 39.

69. *Id.* art. 27.

70. *See generally* Ralph Zacklin, Former Assistant Secretary-General for Legal Affairs, United Nations, Hersch Lauterpacht Memorial Lecture at the University of Cambridge: The United Nations Secretariat and the Use of Force in a Unipolar World (Jan. 22–24, 2008) (transcript available in the Lauterpacht Centre for International Law), *available at* http://www.lcil.cam.ac.uk/lectures/2007-08_ralph_zacklin.php (last visited June 6, 2009).

tion. For lawyers, the "hard" or enforceable legal regime governing peace and security is premised upon a commitment to the core principles of sovereign equality, self-determination, and territorial integrity. These principles have been seen as desirable both in achieving realist ends (preserving the *status quo* and the international order from the threat of world wars and mass destruction) and for more idealistic reasons (a commitment to international justice and the defense of newly decolonized States from hegemonic powers with imperial appetites).

The Charter also envisages a second and more expansive jurisdiction to regulate Member States. The Charter seeks to advance peace, justice, and the public good by encouraging States to protect and promote human rights and to achieve economic development. The U.N. Charter not only established a "hard" regime governing public law questions relating to territory and the use of force, but also a "soft" regime concerned with economic and social issues.[71] The soft regime was institutionally based in the more democratic organ of the General Assembly. The more expansive jurisdiction of the General Assembly was balanced against the lack of enforcement mechanisms available to it. Resolutions could be passed dealing with a wide range of issues of social and economic importance, but no real mechanisms existed for obliging States to comply with these resolutions.[72] The broad "public good" jurisdiction of the international community is also limited by Article 2(7) of the U.N. Charter.[73] Article 2(7) limits (or, more often, fails to limit) soft forms of U.N. intervention (for example, involving the work of human rights bodies or the General Assembly) in what might otherwise have been understood to be the sphere of a State's domestic jurisdiction.

The relation between hard (or public) and soft (or private) U.N. activity became the subject of contest almost as soon as it was enshrined in the U.N. Charter. Already by the 1950s, the distinction between the work of the Security Council and that of the General Assembly began to break down. The General Assembly started to concern itself with security matters, beginning with the *Uniting for Peace* Resolution passed in 1950 in response to the Soviet veto of Security Council resolutions endorsing

71. Koskenniemi, *supra* note 65, at 336.

72. *Id.* at 338–39.

73. The U.N. Charter provides that:

> Nothing contained in the present Charter shall authorize the United Nations to intervene in matters which are essentially within the domestic jurisdiction of any [S]tate or shall require the Members to submit such matters to settlement under the present Charter; but this principle shall not prejudice the application of enforcement measures under Chapter VII.

U.N. Charter art. 2(7).

U.N. intervention in the Korean War.[74] Peacekeeping thus emerged in the early 1950s, alongside the process of decolonization, as a means of responding to conflict over territory, threats to the sanctity of former colonial investments, and civil war in post-colonial States. As the General Assembly began to be dominated by newly decolonized States, it also began to pass resolutions, such as those concerned with the new international economic order, questioning the liberal distinction between public and private, order and justice.[75] The Security Council, in turn, began to concern itself with broader public good questions—both within and between States. In addition, at various times during the 1960s and 1970s, States justified their use of force against neighboring countries by reference to the notion of humanitarian intervention. Nonetheless, during the Cold War period, the notion that a powerful State or a coalition of allies might intervene to rescue or protect the people of another State could not easily be represented as an apolitical action.

B. *Humanitarian Action Under the U.N. Charter*

The jurisdictional basis for humanitarian intervention within this regime was always uncertain. Where occupation by foreign States or administration by international organizations was permitted, it was conceived of as temporary, that is, authorized for limited periods and for restricted ends. Humanitarian intervention was largely conceived of as an exceptional measure undertaken in situations of emergency and extreme human suffering, brought somewhat uneasily under an international jurisdiction to protect peace and security, or more controversially, to represent universal values. Nonetheless, the institutional and ideological conditions of the post-Cold War period led to the growth of support amongst policy makers and academics for the idea that force could legitimately be used as a response to situations of massive human rights violations within a State. The expanded vision of the meaning of international peace and security was, in part, a product of the post-Cold War revitalization of the Security Council. During the Cold War, the Security Council had been paralyzed by reciprocal use of the veto exercisable by the five permanent members. The ending of the Cold War meant an end to that deadlock. The ideological climate of the 1990s also contributed to the plausibility, for some, of the notion that military inter-

74. The Uniting for Peace Resolution, G.A. Res. 377A (V), U.N. Doc. A/RES/377A (V) (Nov. 3, 1950). For a discussion of the context in which the Uniting for Peace Resolution was passed, see William Stueck, *The United Nations, the Security Council, and the Korean War*, *in* THE UNITED NATIONS SECURITY COUNCIL AND WAR: THE EVOLUTION OF THOUGHT AND PRACTICE SINCE 1945, at 265 (Vaughan Lowe et al. eds., 2008).

75. *See, e.g.*, Charter of Economic Rights and Duties of States, G.A. Res. 3281 (XXIX), U.N. Doc. A/RES/29/3281 (Dec. 12, 1974).

vention might be benevolent and disinterested—that powerful States might really come to liberate and not to occupy. It was in this new environment that the Security Council, post-1989, proved willing to interpret its jurisdiction to authorize force so as to include situations of civil war or humanitarian crisis.

The willingness of the Security Council to expand its jurisdiction with a broad reading of "threats to the peace" was first evidenced by the statement issued from its 1992 Summit Meeting. The members of the Security Council there declared that the "absence of war and military conflicts amongst States does not in itself ensure international peace and security," and that "non-military sources of instability in the economic, social, humanitarian and ecological fields have become threats to peace and security."[76] The range and nature of resolutions passed by the Security Council in the decade following the end of the Cold War reinforced the sense that the Council was willing to treat the failure to guarantee democracy or human rights, or to protect against humanitarian abuses, as a threat to peace and security.

While these resolutions were hotly debated, they were generally thought to have "stretched the literal text of Chapter VII" rather than to have violated the Charter prohibition on recourse to force.[77] These decisions were not seen to threaten the key principles of sovereign equality, territorial integrity, and self-determination. The notion that international police action was exceptional still governed. More serious questions of legality and legitimacy arose when the enthusiastic embrace of multilateral intervention extended to support for military action undertaken by regional organizations without Security Council authorization, most notably the 1999 intervention in Kosovo by the North Atlantic Treaty Organization (NATO), but also the interventions by the Economic Community of West African States in Liberia and Sierra Leone. The gradual movement towards the acceptability of collective humanitarian intervention reached a crisis point with these actions undertaken by coalitions of States without Security Council authorization. The ensuing debate over humanitarian intervention can be seen as a breaking down of the unstable boundary between the hard and soft activities of the United Nations—between policing and justice.

In addition to the debates around humanitarian intervention, humanitarian action proceeded under the U.N. Charter in other less visible, but no less productive, ways. The soft U.N. regime overseen by the General Assembly involved lawyers in promoting human rights, protecting

76. The President of the Security Council, *Note by the President of the Security Council*, ¶ 11, *delivered to the Security Council*, U.N. Doc. S/23500 (Jan. 31, 1992).
77. FRANCK, *supra* note 66, at 137.

refugees, and introducing the "rule of law" into the economic development agenda. While the big questions of intervention and authority were debated in relation to the use of force and formal control over territory, international governance quietly expanded through the consensual involvement of the aid, human rights, development, and humanitarian communities in the administration and management of economic and social life within African, Middle Eastern, Asian, Latin American, and Eastern European States.[78] The 1990s saw the publication of subtle analyses by humanitarian actors of the problems that increased soft interventions had begun to produce, particularly in Africa. These analyses, authored by people who had been involved in development, refugee, famine assistance, and emergency relief work, were framed in terms of responsibility and protection. They explored the difficult issues raised by the involvement of the development enterprise in contributing to conditions leading to genocide,[79] the responsibility of protection agencies in situations where humanitarian spaces and refugee camps were providing safe havens for belligerents,[80] and the effects of the over-inflated claims that humanitarians made in representing their capacity to offer protection to people at risk.[81] This literature began to ask questions about the lawfulness or ethics of humanitarian internationalists, both in terms of how they represented their presence and how they understood their responsibility for the effects of their actions and decisions. It also addressed issues of effectiveness, asking whether humanitarian protection was in fact assisting populations at risk, and whether humanitarian actors were fulfilling their responsibilities to those people they claimed to be assisting. Academic commentators in turn argued that representatives of the international community were involved in governing, and suggested that the responsibility of these actors would be better addressed if international presence were recognized as an ongoing factor shaping the dynamics of conflict in the Third World rather than characterized as a series of temporary interventions.[82]

---

78. Anne Orford, *The Gift of Formalism*, 15 EUR. J. INT'L L. 179 (2004).

79. *See, e.g.*, PETER UVIN, AIDING VIOLENCE: THE DEVELOPMENT ENTERPRISE IN RWANDA (1998).

80. *See, e.g.*, FIONA TERRY, CONDEMNED TO REPEAT?: THE PARADOX OF HUMANITARIAN ACTION (2002).

81. *See, e.g.*, ALEX DE WAAL, FAMINE CRIMES: POLITICS AND THE DISASTER RELIEF INDUSTRY IN AFRICA (1997).

82. *See, e.g.*, DAVID KENNEDY, THE DARK SIDES OF VIRTUE: REASSESSING INTERNATIONAL HUMANITARIANISM (2004); ANNE ORFORD, READING HUMANITARIAN INTERVENTION: HUMAN RIGHTS AND THE USE OF FORCE IN INTERNATIONAL LAW (2003).

C. *The Emergence of the Responsibility to Protect Concept*

The responsibility to protect concept can be seen as one outcome of these converging sets of institutional and academic deliberations. As I have already noted, the concept of the responsibility to protect was propelled into the internationalist mainstream by ICISS in its report of 2001. The ICISS was an initiative sponsored by the Canadian government in response to the perceived tension between state sovereignty and humanitarian intervention in the aftermath of the NATO action in Kosovo. In 2001, the ICISS issued a report entitled *The Responsibility to Protect.*[83] The responsibility to protect report was presented as a new way of talking about humanitarian intervention, as well as a new way of talking about sovereignty.[84] Both were organized around protection. The new way of talking about sovereignty was to argue that "its essence should now be seen not as *control* but as *responsibility*."[85] If a State is unwilling or unable to meet this responsibility to protect its population, it then falls upon the international community to do so. The new way of talking about humanitarian intervention involved re-characterizing the debate "not as an argument about any *right* at all but rather about a *responsibility*—one to protect people at grave risk."[86] The people at grave risk were those "[m]illions of human beings" who, in the words of the ICISS report, "remain at the mercy of civil wars, insurgencies, state repression and state collapse."[87] With the emergence of the responsibility to protect concept, we see a movement away from that representation of intervention as an exceptional interference in the domestic affairs of States, and towards the representation of international presence as authorized, and indeed mandated, by international legal obligations. The General Assembly, in its 2005 World Summit Outcome, endorsed the notion of both an individual and an international responsibility to protect, stating that "[t]he international community, through the United Nations, also has the responsibility . . . to help to protect populations from genocide, war crimes, ethnic cleansing and crimes against humanity." [88]

The ICISS report set out a broad range of techniques envisaged as available to meet the responsibility to protect, well beyond the use of force or military intervention. According to the ICISS, the responsibility to protect encompasses a responsibility to prevent conflict, to react to

83. ICISS, *supra* note 4.

84. *Id.* at 16.

85. Gareth Evans, *From Humanitarian Intervention to the Responsibility to Protect*, 24 WIS. INT'L L.J. 703, 708 (2006).

86. *Id.*

87. ICISS, *supra* note 4, at 11.

88. 2005 World Summit Outcome, G.A. Res. 60/1, ¶ 139, U.N. GAOR, 60th Sess., 8th plen. mtg., U.N. Doc. A/RES/60/1 (Oct. 24, 2005).

conflict, and to rebuild after conflict.[89] In doing so, it expands the range of techniques legally available for meeting the responsibility to protect at a distance to include the provision of development assistance or "support for local initiatives to advance good governance, human rights, or the rule of law,"[90] the deployment of good offices missions or mediation efforts, monitoring and reporting on human rights abuses, receiving and analyzing "sensitive information from [M]ember [S]tates,"[91] promoting better terms of trade for developing economies, reforming military and state security services, and prosecuting "perpetrators of crimes against humanity" before the International Criminal Court.[92] According to ICISS, the responsibility to protect also brings with it a responsibility on the part of the international community "to build a durable peace" in the aftermath of military intervention.[93] "If military intervention is to be contemplated, the need for a post-intervention strategy is also of paramount importance."[94] In turn, ICISS envisaged that the responsibility to rebuild that accompanies military intervention "may mean staying in the country for some period of time after the initial purposes of the intervention have been accomplished."[95] The General Assembly accepted this broad vision of the kinds of techniques that might be authorized as an exercise of the responsibility to protect and accepted the ambitious scope of that responsibility.[96] U.N. members undertook to help States build "capacity to protect their populations," assist "those which are under stress before crises and conflicts break out," establish "an early warning capability," and take "collective action, in a timely and decisive manner, through the Security Council . . . should peaceful means be inadequate" to protect populations.[97]

The institutionalization of the responsibility to protect concept has led to a process of systemic integration at and around the United Nations. Throughout his campaign for U.N. Secretary-General, Ban Ki-moon made clear that he was a strong supporter of the responsibility to protect. Ban told U.S. audiences in 2006 that "the concept of the international community's responsibility to protect . . . should be further substantiated" and vowed that as Secretary-General he would "speak out in favor" of the

89. ICISS, *supra* note 4, at 19, 29, 39.
90. *Id.* at 19.
91. *Id.* at 22.
92. *Id.* at 24.
93. *Id.* at 39.
94. *Id.*
95. *Id.*
96. 2005 World Summit Outcome, G.A. Res. 60/1, *supra* note 88, ¶ 139.
97. *Id.* ¶¶ 138–39.

responsibility to protect.[98] Since his appointment as Secretary-General, Ban has said he will "spare no effort to operationalize the responsibility to protect,"[99] and has spoken of the need to "turn promise into practice, words into deeds."[100] The Secretary-General signaled the emphasis to be placed on the responsibility to protect with the creation of two senior positions to oversee its implementation. Francis Deng was appointed to the newly styled position of U.N. Special Adviser on the Prevention of Genocide in 2007 and Edward Luck was appointed to the new position of Special Adviser to the Secretary-General on the Responsibility to Protect in 2008. The two advisers "share an office on genocide prevention and RtoP [the responsibility to protect], helping the United Nations to speak and act as one."[101] According to Luck, the aim of the responsibility to protect concept is to create "interagency cooperation," "a common policy and operational strategy," and an "integrated framework" for activities in areas including conflict prevention, capacity-building, humanitarian assistance, peacekeeping, and security sector reform.[102] A range of actors, from U.S. Naval Academy counter-insurgency specialists to U.N. officials, human rights activists, and Christian aid workers, have now begun enthusiastically to re-describe and re-conceptualize their missions in terms of protection. These actors have also begun to integrate activities across a remarkable range of areas within a protection framework and to call upon States to do the same.[103] Moves to institu-

98. *Ban Ki-moon's Positions on Human Rights, The Responsibility to Protect, International Criminal Court*, UNSGSELECTION.ORG (Oct. 19, 2006), http://www.unsgselection.org/content/latest-developments/issue-34-19-october-2006-ban-ki-moon's-positions-on-human-rights-the-responsibility-to-protect-international-criminal-court/173 (last visited June 6, 2009).

99. Ban Ki-moon, U.N. Secretary-General, Address to the Summit of the African Union (Jan. 31, 2008), *available at* http://www.un.org/apps/news/infocus/sgspeeches/search_full.asp?statID=180# (last visited June 6, 2009).

100. Ban Ki-moon, U.N. Secretary-General, Address at Event Entitled "Responsible Sovereignty: International Cooperation for a Changed World" (July 15, 2008) (transcript available from the U.N. Department of Public Information), *available at* http://www.un.org/News/Press/docs/2008/sgsm11701.doc.htm (last visited June 6, 2009) [hereinafter Ki-moon, Responsible Sovereignty].

101. *Id.*

102. EDWARD C. LUCK, STANLEY FOUND., POLICY ANALYSIS BRIEF: THE UNITED NATIONS AND THE RESPONSIBILITY TO PROTECT (2008), *available at* http://www.stanleyfdn.org/publications/pab/LuckPAB808.pdf (last visited June 6, 2009).

103. *See, e.g.*, Letter from William R. Pace, Executive Director, World Federalist Movement-Institute for Global Policy, to Heads of Governments and Foreign Ministers (Sept. 22, 2008), *available at* http://www.responsibilitytoprotect.org/index.php/civil_society_statements/1859?theme=alt1(last visited June 6, 2009) (urging governments to "support the Responsibility to Protect through words and actions in the upcoming 63rd Session of the [U.N.] General Assembly"). Thirty-five non-governmental organizations signed the letter, including Human Rights Watch (U.S.), the International Crisis Group (United States), the International Refugee Rights Initiative (Uganda), the Executive Secretariat of the International Conference on the Great Lakes Region (Burundi), Coalition for the International Criminal Court (South Africa),

tionalize the responsibility to protect are thus leading to a coordinated project of intensification and rationalization of international administration.

States and regional organizations have also embraced the responsibility to protect concept, apparently with much greater willingness than was the case with humanitarian intervention. Member States voted unanimously in the General Assembly at the 2005 World Summit to adopt the responsibility to protect as an obligation both of individual Member States and of the international community.[104] Since then, representatives of States including Australia, France, Sweden, the United Kingdom, and the United States have specifically invoked the responsibility to protect to explain actions taken or proposed by their governments. In addition, regional organizations such as the African Union (A.U.) have formally endorsed the responsibility to protect concept.[105] Thus the responsibility to protect concept is increasingly being invoked as one of the purposes towards which state institutions are being directed.[106]

The responsibility to protect concept thus appears to envisage a greatly expanded scope of authority for the international community. Under the U.N. Charter, humanitarian intervention and international administration were occasionally tolerated as temporary or emergency measures, but *de jure* authority was always understood to remain with the sovereign State. In contrast, the advocates of the responsibility to protect concept seek to make an argument for the lawfulness of both state and international authority, without reference to self-determination, popular sovereignty, or other *de jure* bases for determining who should have the power to govern in a particular territory. The responsibility to protect concept rejects the automatic priority of claims to authority based on right, whether that right be understood in historical, universal, or democratic terms. Rather, the legitimacy of authority is determinable by

---

the Church of Sweden (Sweden), DanChurch Aid (Denmark), the National Council of Churches in Australia (Australia), and the World Federalist Movement (Canada).

104. 2005 World Summit Outcome, G.A. Res. 60/1, *supra* note 88, ¶ 139.

105. African Union, Executive Council, *The Common African Position on the Proposed Reform of the United Nations: The Ezulwini Consensus*, AU Doc. Ext/EX.CL/2 (VII) (Mar. 7–8, 2005) (adopting the principle of the responsibility to protect); *see also* African Commission on Human and Peoples' Rights, *Resolution on Strengthening the Responsibility to Protect in Africa*, A.C.H.P.R./Res. 117 (XXXXII) (Nov. 28, 2007) (endorsing the 2007 Security Council decision to deploy an A.U./U.N. Hybrid Operation in Darfur as an exercise of the responsibility to protect).

106. This practice is arguably contributing to a reformulation of the international law relating to nonintervention. For a reformulation of the *opinio juris* element of customary international law formation in terms of "the arguments used by political elites to drive the institutions of the [S]tate into motion," see Anthony Carty, *The Iraq Invasion as a Recent United Kingdom 'Contribution to International Law'*, 16 EUR. J. INT'L L. 143, 144 (2005).

reference to the *fact* of protection.[107] The legitimacy of authority—whether of States or of the international community—depends on the capacity to provide effective protection to populations at risk. By focusing upon *de facto* authority, the responsibility to protect concept implicitly asserts not only that an international community exists, but also that its authority to govern is, at least in situations of civil war and repression, superior to that of the State.

III. Authority, Jurisdiction, and the Responsibility to Protect

Many States were concerned at the potential expansion of international authority that might flow from the endorsement of the responsibility to protect concept, and sought to limit the scope of international protective authority with a narrow definition of the triggers to international jurisdiction. This Part explores the ways in which the World Summit Outcome articulates the nature and extent of state and international jurisdiction in relation to the responsibility to protect. Discussions about the limits of a particular jurisdiction are often the site of "law's own most self-reflexive operations."[108] Jurisdiction involves the establishment or articulation of power as and through public law. In articulating the nature and limits of power through public law, legal determinations of jurisdiction give a conventional or shared meaning to authority and to its objects. As Shaunnagh Dorsett and Shaun McVeigh suggest, "[i]t is through jurisdiction that a life before the law is instituted, a place is subjected to rule and occupation, and an event is articulated as juridical."[109] The jurisdictional practices related to the responsibility to protect are the specific techniques by which life in the new zones of protection is marked as belonging to international law; places are subjected to the rule of international law and events are articulated as legally relevant.

A. *Jurisdiction and the Territorial State*

The traditional principle that each State has jurisdiction over its territory is reinforced in the World Summit Outcome. It stresses that each "individual [S]tate" has "the responsibility to protect its populations

107. *See* Anne Orford, International Authority and the Responsibility to Protect (forthcoming 2010).

108. Bradin Cormack, A Power to Do Justice: Jurisdiction, English Literature, and the Rise of Common Law, 1509–1625, at 22 (2007).

109. Shaunnagh Dorsett & Shaun McVeigh, *Questions of Jurisdiction*, *in* Jurisprudence of Jurisdiction, *supra* note 6, at 3, 5.

from genocide, war crimes, ethnic cleansing and crimes against humanity" and that this extends to "the prevention of such crimes, including their incitement." Secretary-General Ban Ki-Moon has, in turn, emphasized that "[g]overnments unanimously affirmed the primary and continuing legal obligations of States to protect their populations," and has described this as the "bedrock" principle of the responsibility to protect.[110] The State continues to exercise primary jurisdiction over its territory and has the responsibility to protect the population within that territory. The World Summit Outcome and the officials charged with its implementation thus reaffirm that the world is divided into spatially defined units, within which politics takes place. The responsibility to protect concept takes as a given that physical space exists as a series of defined and bounded territories. Each territory can be "associated or identified with a sovereign . . . ."[111] The entity with primary control over, and responsibility for, the inhabitants of those territories is the sovereign State. If people are not protected or are at risk, this is a manifestation of the failure of the State to meet its responsibility to protect its population.

The responsibility to protect concept thus diagnoses a problem. The problem it diagnoses is the tyranny of state governments and the threat posed to security when the State has unconditional control over a territory and population. Tyranny here has a very modern meaning. Where once tyrants were those who exercised *de facto* authority by force and had a "lack of respect for law," in the modern world tyrants are those who interfere with the subjective rights of individuals to property in life, liberty, or estate.[112]

B. *Jurisdiction and the Limits of International Authority*

The responsibility to protect concept challenges the tyranny of state leaders or militias from the position or "political viewpoint" of the people and their material interests—that is, their need for protection.[113] Yet it does not propose to vest the power wrested from the State in the people, or at least not immediately. Instead, the responsibility to protect litera-

110. *See* Ban, Responsible Sovereignty, *supra* note 100.

111. Shaunnagh Dorsett, *Mapping Territories*, *in* JURISPRUDENCE OF JURISDICTION, *supra* note 6, at 137–38.

112. *See* FASOLT, *supra* note 38, at 201, 281 n.130 (discussing Bodin's assertion that "the true mark of the tyrant is not his relationship to law but his lack of respect for property" and commenting that this "is about as good a definition of tyranny as can be expected under modern circumstances."). For a discussion of the political theory of " 'subjective' property rights," see Nederman, *supra* note 59, at 324.

113. My analysis of the difference between the subject of the political viewpoint from which a problem is diagnosed, and the subject of the political practice needed to respond to that problem, is informed by LOUIS ALTHUSSER, MACHIAVELLI AND US 25–26 (François Matheron ed., Gregory Elliot trans., 1999).

ture fixes another place—"the place of the force that must be constituted" in response to the political problem it has diagnosed.[114] In the World Summit Outcome, this place is called "the international community."[115] The international community is the name given to the place of the force that must be constituted to resolve the problem of state tyranny or the failure of protection. The responsibility to protect concept provides that in certain situations, where a State manifestly fails to protect its population, state authority must give way to that of the international community.

The jurisdictional basis for an international responsibility to protect is quite different to the jurisdictional basis previously proffered for humanitarian action under the U.N. Charter, whether that action took the form of military intervention, conflict prevention, or international administration. Early reports and documents relating to the responsibility to protect had referred in very broad terms to the situations in which the international community might have jurisdiction to exercise that responsibility. For example, the ICISS report had referred to the "[m]illions of human beings" who "remain at the mercy of civil wars, insurgencies, state repression and state collapse."[116] The report discussed the need to deliver "practical protection for ordinary people, at risk of their lives, because their [S]tates are unwilling or unable to protect them."[117] According to the report, States have a responsibility to protect their populations from threats including "mass killing," "systematic rape" and "starvation."[118] Both "the [S]tate whose people are directly affected" and "the broader community of [S]tates" have a responsibility to provide "life-supporting protection and assistance to populations at risk."[119] Where there is a threat of "large scale loss of life" or "large scale 'ethnic cleansing,'" the report found that military intervention by the international community is justified.[120]

In contrast, when the World Summit of the General Assembly endorsed the responsibility to protect, it made a significant change in the formulation of jurisdiction. The World Summit Outcome describes the international responsibility to protect as a responsibility "to help to protect populations from genocide, war crimes, ethnic cleansing and crimes against humanity."[121] The proposal to link the responsibility to protect

114. *Id.* at 25.
115. 2005 World Summit Outcome, G.A. Res. 60/1, *supra* note 88, ¶ 139.
116. ICISS, *supra* note 4, at 11.
117. *Id.*
118. *Id.* at 17.
119. *Id.*
120. *Id.* at 32 (emphasis omitted).
121. 2005 World Summit Outcome, G.A. Res. 60/1, *supra* note 88, ¶ 139.

populations with the four crimes of genocide, war crimes, ethnic cleansing, and crimes against humanity was put forward by Pakistan's Ambassador to the United Nations, H.E. Akram Mounir, in the lead-up to the 2005 World Summit.[122] Pakistan, like "most countries of the South at the level of the Non-[A]ligned Movement," was strongly opposed to the concept of the responsibility to protect.[123] The introduction of the amendment linking the responsibility to protect to specific crimes was designed to address the fears of those who viewed the principle "as an instrument that could be used by the powerful countries against the weaker ones."[124]

Thus the protective jurisdiction of the international community as articulated in the World Summit Outcome is organized around the subject matter jurisdiction of international criminal law. This appears to be quite a novel use of international criminal law categories. The subject matter jurisdiction of international criminal law has traditionally been understood to represent "principles on the basis of which States can exercise criminal jurisdiction" outside their own territories "in conformity with international law."[125] It has been used to explain when a foreign State and, later, the international community, might exercise criminal jurisdiction—that is, the power to judge and to punish. There have been other moves to extend the reach of international criminal law beyond the sphere of criminal jurisdiction and punishment. In particular, in its 2007 judgment in the *Case Concerning the Application of the Convention on the Prevention and Punishment of the Crime of Genocide*, the International Court of Justice found that Contracting Parties to the Genocide Convention have a "normative and compelling" obligation to "take such action as they can to prevent genocide from occurring . . . ."[126] This interpretation of the obligation to take action to prevent genocide from occurring envisages something beyond the exercise of criminal jurisdiction and punishment—something more akin to an international responsibility to protect populations wherever they are situated. According to the Court, the obligation to prevent is not "limited by territory" and applies "to a State wherever it may be acting or may be able to act in

122. Jean Ping, Chairperson, African Union Comm'n, Keynote Address at the Round-Table High-Level Meeting of Experts on 'The Responsibility to Protect in Africa' (Oct. 23, 2008), *available at* http://www.responsibilitytoprotect.org/index.php/civil_society_statements/1910 (last visited June 6, 2009).

123. *Id.*

124. *Id.*

125. Luc Reydams, Universal Jurisdiction: International and Municipal Legal Perspectives 21 (2003).

126. Application of Convention on the Prevention and Punishment of the Crime of Genocide (Bosn. & Herz. v. Serb. & Mont.), 2007 I.C.J. 91, ¶ 427 (Feb. 26).

ways appropriate to meeting the obligations in question."[127] In addition, the Constitutive Act of the African Union treats the risk of international crimes as jurisdictional triggers for regional intervention.[128] However, it is with the emergence of the responsibility to protect concept that we see an institutionalization of this expanded role for international criminal law categories in international governance. The risk of international crimes taking place is now posited as the trigger to a broad range of governance and police functions. The jurisdiction of the international community will be triggered by the risk that certain specified crimes may be committed.

As noted above, this trigger was introduced in an attempt to limit what otherwise seemed to be an extraordinarily open-ended authorization of international involvement to take responsibility for protection wherever there was a perceived threat to populations or people. Yet the terms in which international jurisdiction is formulated still envisage an expansive role for the international community in policing the actions of governments. The situation in which that international jurisdiction may be triggered is spelled out most clearly in the context of military intervention. The World Summit Outcome provides that where "national authorities are manifestly failing to protect their populations," "we" (who this "we" refers to is not spelled out) "are prepared to take collective action, in a timely and decisive manner, through the Security Council, in accordance with the Charter, including Chapter VII." [129] In relation to the other techniques of international protection envisaged in the World Summit Outcome, it is far less clear when international jurisdiction will be triggered. For example, the World Summit Outcome provides that "[t]he international community, through the United Nations, also has the responsibility to use appropriate diplomatic, humanitarian and other peaceful means . . . to help to protect populations from genocide, war crimes, ethnic cleansing and crimes against humanity."[130] This jurisdiction "to help to protect" appears to exist alongside state jurisdiction without any specific trigger for action. Similarly, "[w]e also intend to commit ourselves, as necessary and appropriate, to helping States build capacity to protect their populations from genocide, war crimes, ethnic cleansing and crimes against humanity and to assisting

127. *Id.*, ¶ 183.

128. Constitutive Act of the African Union art. 4(h) (setting out as one of the principles of the Union "[t]he right of the Union to intervene in a Member State pursuant to a decision of the Assembly in respect of grave circumstances, namely war crimes, genocide and crimes against humanity.").

129. 2005 World Summit Outcome, G.A. Res. 60/1, *supra* note 88, ¶ 139.

130. *Id.*

those which are under stress before crises and conflicts break out."[131] That articulation of the responsibility to protect re-characterizes activities such as conflict prevention, surveillance, human rights monitoring and development as part of a normative framework of international responsibilities. Yet it is not clear under what circumstances the jurisdiction to help States build capacity and to assist "before crises and conflicts break out" will be triggered.

C. *The Encounter Between Jurisdictions*

The World Summit Outcome thus envisages two forms of authority—one in the form of the State and one in the form of the international community. Both the State and the international community are represented as having an ongoing responsibility to protect populations from specified crimes. The World Summit Outcome thus envisages the existence of complementary jurisdictions. The State has primary authority for protection of its population, and the international community has both a specific authority to take over the role of protector if the State fails in its obligations and an ongoing authority to help protect populations through diplomatic, humanitarian, and other peaceful means, and through capacity-building "before crises and conflicts break out."[132] Where two authorities have overlapping jurisdiction, it would seem necessary to provide for some means of determining which authority has jurisdiction in a given situation. Yet the World Summit Outcome does not elaborate how the encounter between these jurisdictions is to be negotiated, or according to what protocols or procedures the movement between jurisdictions will be conducted.[133] For instance, it is not clear how, and by whom, the determination will be made that a particular event or action constitutes a risk of genocide, war crimes, ethnic cleansing or crimes against humanity. What kind of information or evidence would be necessary before the international police could be called into action?

In this respect, the World Summit Outcome can usefully be contrasted with the Rome Statute of the International Criminal Court (ICC), which gives detailed treatment to the procedures for moving between complementary forms of jurisdiction over very similar crimes. The Rome Statute creates a regime in which the ICC operates in parallel to

131. *Id.*

132. *Id.*

133. For an analysis of the European tradition of international law as a source of protocols for mediating the encounter between laws, see Anne Orford, *Ritual, Mediation and the International Laws of the South*, 16 GRIFFITH L. REV. 353 (2007). On the need for protocols governing the encounter between jurisdictions, see Christine Black et. al, *Of the South*, 16 GRIFFITH L. REV. 299 (2007).

national courts, both having jurisdiction to prosecute those responsible for genocide, crimes against humanity, war crimes, or aggression. The preamble to the Rome Statute provides that "it is the duty of every State to exercise its criminal jurisdiction over those responsible for international crimes."[134] In many situations, the ICC will have jurisdiction over the same crimes. The Rome Statute sets up a mechanism for the complementary administration of criminal justice, or for the "distribution of authority between national jurisdictions, on the one hand, and the jurisdiction of the International Criminal Court, on the other."[135] The basic rule governing that distribution is that the ICC is authorized to intervene "only when, but whenever the State primarily responsible for prosecution is not able or willing to genuinely investigate and prosecute."[136] In addition, the Rome Statute contains detailed provisions dealing with "the way in which this typically delicate question—whether a State has taken serious action or not—is to be resolved."[137] The World Summit Outcome lacks any such procedures for moving or negotiating between the complementary jurisdictions of the State and the international community when it comes to the exercise of the responsibility to protect.

D. *The Nature of International Authority*

Perhaps the lack of clarity about the limits of the international jurisdiction to protect in documents dealing with the responsibility to protect is due to an implicit assumption about the nature of that jurisdiction. If international jurisdiction were by its nature unable to conflict with state jurisdiction, there would be no need to elaborate procedures for moving between these forms of jurisdiction.

This would be the case, for example, if the international jurisdiction envisaged by the responsibility to protect concept were understood as a form of jurisdiction that mirrors the spiritual jurisdiction claimed by the medieval papacy or the universal jurisdiction claimed by the Holy Roman Emperor. The responsibility to protect concept does in some ways seem to be a return to a world-view in which there exists "a single universal society functionally divided into spiritual and temporal spheres of responsibility",[138] with the role of representative of spiritual authority

134. Rome Statute of the International Criminal Court pmbl., July 17, 1998, 2187 U.N.T.S. 3; U.N. Diplomatic Conference of Plenipotentiaries on the Establishment of an International Court, June 15–July 17, 1998, U.N. Doc. A/CONF.183/9 (July 17, 1998).

135. Florian Jessberger, *Universality, Complementarity, and the Duty to Prosecute Crimes under International Law in Germany*, *in* INTERNATIONAL PROSECUTION OF HUMAN RIGHTS CRIMES 213, 220 (Wolfgang Kaleck et al. eds., 2007).

136. *Id.*

137. *Id.*

138. MULDOON, *supra* note 16, at 66.

played by the international community and that of temporal authority played by the State. With this in mind, we might understand the emergence of the responsibility to protect concept as signaling the intensification of a non-territorial form of jurisdiction that applies to the world as a whole. International jurisdiction understood in such terms, and from the perspective of those claiming to represent the universal, would necessarily take priority over merely particular authority.

The Pope reinforced that vision of the United Nations as an agent of universal jurisdiction with responsibility for overseeing the conduct of temporal authority in his address to the General Assembly in 2008.[139] In that address, the Pope embraced the responsibility to protect as a common project of the United Nations and the Catholic Church. He traced the lineage of the responsibility to protect to Francisco de Vitoria, and described the principle that those in government have a responsibility to protect the governed as "an aspect of natural reason shared by all nations," based upon "the idea of the person as image of the Creator . . . ."[140] In this view, the expression of the responsibility to protect institutes a form of spiritual jurisdiction, one premised not upon control over territory, but upon the policing of the obligations and duties of responsible subjects. Here, the international community takes up the responsibilities once claimed by the Pope of controlling princes and authenticating obedient subjects. The authority of the international community, like the Holy Roman Empire before it, derives from its direct representation of the idea of justice, unmediated by the will of States or governments.[141] The capacity to govern of the international community, like the Holy Roman Empire before it, depends not upon its control over territory, but upon the success of its officials (experts in human rights, development economics, conflict studies, or genocide prevention) in spreading the beliefs underlying Western legality throughout the world.[142]

As it is not possible to return to a period prior to the emergence of the modern territorial State, the new form of spiritual jurisdiction signaled by the responsibility to protect would have to be able to achieve redemption by moving the military machinery of powerful States into action. And this is indeed the aim of coalitions such as the Save Darfur

139. Pope Benedict XVI, Address to the General Assembly (Apr. 18, 2008) (transcript available from The Vatican) *available at* http://www.vatican.va/holy_father/benedict_xvi/speeches/2008/april/documents/hf_ben-xvi_spe_20080418_un-visit_en.html (last visited June 6, 2009).

140. *Id.*

141. *See generally* Carl Schmitt, Roman Catholicism and Political Form 30 (G.L. Ulmen trans., 1996).

142. Alain Supiot, Homo Juridicus: Essai sur la fonction anthropologique du Droit 18–20, 29–30 (2005).

campaign—to persuade the United States, in particular, to move its military into action in Darfur and elsewhere. The frustration expressed by those members of civil society who understand themselves as playing the role of the judges of States without the power to have their judgments enforced suggests that this form of universal authority is not yet realizable.

Alternatively, we might understand the turn to protection, together with the centralized and integrated form of governance envisaged by the proponents of the responsibility to protect, as indicating an ambition to fashion the international community into something resembling a really big State. If that were the case, there would be no need to provide for a system to determine when a particular state jurisdiction gives way to international jurisdiction, as territorial States would always have to answer or defer to this newly empowered international community. Indeed, there is a sense in which the turn to protection as the ground of authority, and the linking of jurisdiction with the right to judge and punish, appears to mirror the constitution of the modern State. Hobbes' argument that the capacity to provide protection was the marker of legitimate authority worked to discredit papal and imperial claims to *de jure* authority, as well as populist arguments that authority should be grounded on an authentic relation between governors and governed. His turn to protection privileged *de facto* authority over appeals to popular sovereignty, the ancient constitution, the will of the people, or the obligations of history. Something similar is being staged with the turn to protection as the ground of international authority today. The responsibility to protect concept does not consider the legitimacy of authority in relation to a third term—the people, the nation, the *Volk*. So whether or not the representatives of the international community should, say, be present in Iraq is not answerable in terms of the legitimacy of the initial acquisition of control over that territory, or in terms of whether international authority was constituted in accordance with the will of the people. The turn to protection works to delegitimize appeals to those principles of territorial integrity and self-determination that have been significant limiting factors to foreign rule.[143]

Of course, any attempt to transform the international community into a world State would face the same problems that faced various emperors who aspired to turn the Holy Roman Empire into a big centralized State. Such attempts were thwarted by "the scores of European kingdoms and other principalities that . . . had created their own legal and constitutional systems over a period of several centuries and were quite

143. Orford, *supra* note 49.

unwilling to surrender them."[144] Indeed, those who are charged with institutionalizing the responsibility to protect concept have been careful to avoid any sense that the international community is seeking to supersede state jurisdiction. As Edward Luck has commented:

> For all the public pressures to advance RtoP principles, in the end it was sovereign [S]tates that produced Article 4(h) of the [African Union] Constitutive Act and paragraphs 138 and 139 of the [World Summit] Outcome Document. It will take even closer collaboration among States, international bodies, and civil society to begin to realize the promise of RtoP.[145]

It is more likely, then, that the responsibility to protect concept will not radically alter the complex set of relations that exist between States and the varied representatives of the international community. Contemporary international relations are characterized by the existence of many overlapping jurisdictions with no accepted system for prioritizing between them. This situation is perhaps close to that which scholars now argue existed in the territories claimed as part of the Holy Roman Empire. New scholarship on the history of the Empire has challenged "the orthodox view of imperial politics as a dualism between emperor and princes."[146] That scholarship argues that it is necessary to consider the multiple components that made up the imperial political situation and that produced a complex set of overlapping forms of jurisdiction and competence. What was at stake then, as now, was how complementary jurisdictions were to be negotiated, or how one law would encounter another.

Indeed, the public international law of Europe emerged, in part, out of this need to negotiate between forms of jurisdiction. As Christian Europe fragmented into separate nation-states, mediation between estranged nation-states became one of the key aims of the social practices of war, commerce, law, and diplomacy that have since shaped the modern state system. To take one example, norms and protocols governing the movement, immunity, and privileges of diplomats were one of the earliest forms of international law to develop in Europe.[147] Ritual played a central role in diplomatic culture, particularly during the early stages of diplomacy when the modern sovereign State was still in formation. Ceremonies and rituals relating to the movement of diplomats "sanc-

---

144. Muldoon, *supra* note 16, at 119.
145. Luck, *supra* note 46.
146. Peter H. Wilson, The Holy Roman Empire 1495–1806, at 8 (1999).
147. *See generally* Garrett Mattingly, Renaissance Diplomacy (1988).

tioned the *movement across* social and political boundaries."[148] The focus on rituals and on the reciprocal exchange of letters, privileges, and obligations contributed to creating the sense of a common culture of norms and values in a Europe which could no longer rely upon a universal authority (whether imperial or religious) to guarantee the law.[149] In this sense, the international law of early modern Europe had an awareness of its limits, which has perhaps been lost with the more universalist ambitions of contemporary international law. If the relation between international and state jurisdictions is to involve something other than dominance and submission, some such attention must be paid to the procedures for moving or negotiating between the complementary jurisdictions of the State and the international community.

IV. The Limits of International Authority

As territory and jurisdiction became ever more closely intertwined with the emergence of the modern State, questions about jurisdiction increasingly came to be seen as purely technical questions. The practice of jurisdiction is now understood simply to involve determining in what circumstances a particular authority has power to declare the law in a particular territory. Yet as we watch the way that power, territory, control, and law shift and relate over time, we can see that jurisdiction is more than a technical question. When a lawful authority articulates the terms of its jurisdiction, it is forced to confront "in practice, the question of its competence over a given case."[150] The process of claiming jurisdiction is a form of alchemy. A successful claim of jurisdiction transforms power into authority, or fact into right.

Precisely what new form of "international community" will emerge from the process of transformation now taking place with the institutionalization of the responsibility to protect concept is as yet unclear. There is certainly little attention paid by those advocating the embrace of the concept to the need to articulate the legal limits to the jurisdiction of such an international protective authority. Most of the attention in internationalist literature to date has been on the ways in which the responsibility to protect concept justifies the expansion of international authority in situations where a State has failed to protect its population. That literature is concerned with ensuring that in such cases, the international community can be empowered to prevent, react and rebuild. The

148. James Der Derian, On Diplomacy: A Genealogy of Western Estrangement 34 (1987).

149. *Id.* at 36.

150. Cormack, *supra* note 108, at 4.

international community is portrayed as largely unlimited with respect to the actions it can take to achieve its universal mission.[151] In terms of the responsibility to prevent, the prospect of increased surveillance of foreign populations is welcomed as a contribution to realizing the promise that never again will genocide be allowed to occur, rather than seen as a threat to civil liberties or self-determination.[152] In terms of the responsibility to react, activists have to date focused most of their energy on arguing for military intervention or criminal prosecution, calling for decisions about the use of force to be made quickly and for the largest degree of force possible to be deployed.[153] In terms of the responsibility to rebuild, the situation seems to resemble that of the 1990s, when the effect of post-conflict governance in the aftermath of international interventions was to diminish the potential for parliamentary participation and expand the potential for executive governance in the name of achieving social and economic integration.[154] Humanitarian intervention was routinely followed by the creation and legitimization of strong international administrations, marked by an apparent distrust of local parliamentary democracy, an absence of constraints on international executive decisions, and the prioritization of economic liberalization as a policy goal.[155] The ICISS report continues to treat international administration as a technical project concerned with "protection tasks,"[156] such as security sector reform, the facilitation of repatriation, "the recreation

151. *See* Behrami v. France, 45 Eur. Ct. H.R. 85 (2007); Saramati v. France, Germany & Norway, 45 Eur. Ct. H.R. 85, 121 (2007) (holding that operations established by Security Council resolutions, such as that conducted in Kosovo, are "fundamental to the mission of the [United Nations] to secure international peace and security" and that to subject the actions carried out under U.N. authority to the scrutiny of the European Court of Human Rights would "interfere with the fulfillment of the [United Nations'] key mission in this field including, as argued by certain parties, with the effective conduct of its operations."). For a discussion of these admissibility decisions, see Anne Orford, *The Passions of Protection: Sovereign Authority and Humanitarian War*, *in* Contemporary States of Emergency: The Politics of Military and Humanitarian Interventions (Didier Fassin & Mariella Pandolfi eds., forthcoming 2009).

152. At a major conference on *The Responsibility to Protect: A Framework for Confronting Identity-Based Atrocities* held at Cardozo Law School on March 10–11, 2008, the panel of invited speakers on "Preventing Identity-Based Atrocities" included not only the Director of the Program in Holocaust and Human Rights Studies at Cardozo Law School and the Program Director of Human Rights Watch, but also a Professor Emerita at the U.S. Naval Academy, who provided a detailed insight into the way in which the widespread U.S. counter-insurgency surveillance conducted in foreign States could be understood as a form of conflict, and thus, genocide prevention.

153. For a critique of this tendency, see Alex de Waal, *Darfur and the Failure of the Responsibility to Protect*, 83 Int'l Aff. 1039 (2007).

154. Orford, *supra* note 82, at 126–43.

155. *Id.*

156. ICISS, *supra* note 4, at 65.

of markets," and the "pursuit of war criminals."[157] It is to the question of the limits of the jurisdiction of such an expansive international authority that the responsibility to protect literature must turn if the absolutist tendencies of the turn to protection and the privileging of *de facto* authority are to be avoided.

A focus upon the articulation of jurisdiction can help indicate what is at stake in this process. The attempt to give institutional expression to the concept of the responsibility to protect through articulating the triggers to international jurisdiction necessarily gives rise to questions about the nature, limits, and ends of international authority. The processes of debating, defining, and delimiting jurisdiction allow us to see the work involved in transforming an ideal like protection into institutional practice, and in transforming a conventional basis for the exercise of power into a universal claim to authority. Legal institutions are places where arguments for the legitimacy of authority are made conventional and public, and where official language goes to work to institute a collective opinion about power. Conventional or public representations of authority matter because authority, in order to be lasting, must be recognized as legitimate by rivals and subjects. Authority, in order to be profitable, must be recognized as legitimate by investors. Those who exercise international protective authority in a given territory must therefore be able to articulate that authority in terms of jurisdiction, if they are to be able to undertake the tasks necessary to governing (or protecting) effectively. Whether we think of this new form of international authority as a big State, a new Holy Roman Empire, or a more chastened authority negotiating competencies with the territorial State, it is in the articulation of its jurisdiction that the question of the limits and ends of international authority will have to be addressed.

157. *Id.* at 42, 66.

[7]

RESPONSIBILITY TO PROTECT: POLITICAL RHETORIC OR EMERGING LEGAL NORM?

*By Carsten Stahn**

The history of the concept of "responsibility to protect"[1] sounds almost like a fairy tale. The International Commission on Intervention and State Sovereignty developed this concept in its 2001 report *The Responsibility to Protect.* The central theme was "the idea that sovereign states have a responsibility to protect their own citizens from avoidable catastrophe—from mass murder and rape, from starvation—but that when they are unwilling or unable to do so, that responsibility must be borne by the broader community of states."[2]

In December 2004, this idea was taken up in the context of the debate on United Nations reform. Pointing to international responses to the "successive humanitarian disasters in Somalia, Bosnia and Herzegovina, Rwanda, Kosovo and now Darfur, Sudan," the High-Level Panel on Threats, Challenges and Change stated in its report *A More Secure World: Our Shared Responsibility* that

> there is a *growing acceptance* that while sovereign Governments have the primary responsibility to protect their own citizens from such catastrophes, when they are unable or unwilling to do so that responsibility should be taken up by *the wider international*

* Associate Legal Officer, International Criminal Court; Visiting Research Fellow, Leiden University. The views expressed in this essay are those of the author alone and do not necessarily reflect the position of the International Criminal Court. The essay is based on a presentation by the author at the Biennial Conference of the European Society of International Law held at La Sorbonne, Paris, on May 18–20, 2006.

[1] *See generally* C. F. Amerasinghe, *The Conundrum of Recourse to Force—To Protect Persons,* 3 INT'L ORGS. L. REV. 7 (2006); Laurence Boisson de Chazournes & Luigi Condorelli, *De la "responsabilité de protéger" ou d'une nouvelle parure pour une notion déjà bien établie,* 110 REVUE GÉNÉRALE DE DROIT INTERNATIONAL PUBLIC 11 (2006); Gareth Evans, *The Responsibility to Protect and the Duty to Prevent,* 98 ASIL PROC. 77 (2004); Peter Hilpold, *The Duty to Protect and the Reform of the United Nations—A New Step in the Development of International Law?* 2006 MAX PLANCK UN Y.B. 35; Gelijn Molier, *Humanitarian Intervention and the Responsibility to Protect After 9/11,* 53 NETH. INT'L L. REV. 37 (2006); Thomas G. Weiss, *The Sunset of Humanitarian Intervention? The Responsibility to Protect in a Unipolar Era,* 35 SECURITY DIALOGUE 135 (2004); Paul D. Williams & Alex J. Bellamy, *The Responsibility to Protect and the Crisis in Darfur,* 36 SECURITY DIALOGUE 27 (2005); Gareth Evans & Mohamed Sahnoun, *The Responsibility to Protect,* FOREIGN AFF., Nov./Dec. 2002, at 99; ALEX J. BELLAMY, PREVENTING FUTURE KOSOVOS AND FUTURE RWANDAS: THE RESPONSIBILITY TO PROTECT AFTER THE 2005 WORLD SUMMIT (Carnegie Council, Policy Brief 2006), *at* <http://www.cceia.org/media/Bellamy_Paper.pdf>. For comprehensive documentation on the subject, see Responsibility to Protect—Engaging Civil Society, *at* <http://www.responsibilitytoprotect.org>.

[2] INTERNATIONAL COMMISSION ON INTERVENTION AND STATE SOVEREIGNTY, THE RESPONSIBILITY TO PROTECT, at VIII (2001), *available at* <http://www.iciss.ca/report-en.asp> [hereinafter RESPONSIBILITY TO PROTECT].

> *community*—with it spanning a continuum involving prevention, response to violence, if necessary, and rebuilding shattered societies.[3]

The UN high-level panel even went so far as to speak of an "emerging norm of a collective international responsibility to protect," which encompasses not only "the 'right to intervene' of any State, but the 'responsibility to protect' of *every* State when it comes to people suffering from avoidable catastrophe."[4]

In March 2005, this finding was endorsed by the report of the UN secretary-general entitled "In Larger Freedom: Towards Development, Security and Human Rights for All," which fostered the idea that the security of states and that of humanity are indivisible and that threats facing humanity can be solved only through collective action.[5] In this report, the secretary-general made express reference to a paragraph of the High-Level Panel Report that refers to an emerging norm of a collective responsibility to protect, and reaffirmed that the idea of a "responsibility to protect" must be "embrace[d]," and, "when necessary, . . . act[ed] on."[6]

In September 2005, the concept of the responsibility to protect was incorporated into the outcome document of the high-level meeting of the General Assembly (Outcome Document).[7] The Outcome Document contains two paragraphs (paras. 138 and 139) on the responsibility to protect. The assembled heads of state and government recognized the responsibility to protect populations from genocide, war crimes, ethnic cleansing, and crimes against humanity,[8] including the responsibility of each individual state to protect its populations from such crimes, and a corresponding responsibility of the international community.[9] This document was subsequently adopted by the General Assembly in its Resolution 60/1, 2005 World Summit Outcome.

The Security Council made its first express reference to the concept in Resolution 1674 on the protection of civilians in armed conflict.[10] Not long ago, the notion of "responsibility to protect" was added as a key word to the *Wikipedia Free Encyclopedia*, where it is defined as a recently developed concept in international relations that aims at "provid[ing] a *legal* and *ethical* basis for 'humanitarian intervention.'"[11]

The articulation of the concept of responsibility to protect is a remarkable achievement. The inclusion of the concept in the Outcome Document not only marks one of the most important results of the 2005 World Summit, but is testimony to a broader systemic shift in international

[3] A More Secure World: Our Shared Responsibility, Report of the High-Level Panel on Threats, Challenges and Change, UN Doc. A/59/565, at 56–57, para. 201 (2004), *available at* <http://www.un.org/secureworld/report.pdf> (emphasis added) [hereinafter High-Level Panel Report].

[4] *Id.*, paras. 202, 201.

[5] In Larger Freedom: Towards Development, Security and Human Rights for All, Report of the Secretary-General, UN Doc. A/59/2005, paras. 16–22 (2005), *available at* <http://www.un.org/largerfreedom/contents.htm> [hereinafter Report of the Secretary-General].

[6] *Id.*, para. 135 (citing High-Level Panel Report, *supra* note 3, para. 203).

[7] 2005 World Summit Outcome, GA Res. 60/1, paras. 138–39 (Oct. 24, 2005) [hereinafter Outcome Document].

[8] *Id.*, para. 138.

[9] *Id.*, para. 139.

[10] *See* SC Res. 1674, para. 4 (Apr. 28, 2006) ("*reaffim[ing]* the provisions of paragraphs 138 and 139 of the 2005 World Summit Outcome Document regarding the responsibility to protect populations from genocide, war crimes, ethnic cleansing and crimes against humanity").

[11] WIKIPEDIA FREE ENCYCLOPEDIA, *Responsibility to Protect* (Dec. 6, 2006), *at* <http://en.wikipedia.org/wiki/Responsibility_to_protect> (emphasis added).

law, namely, a growing tendency to recognize that the principle of state sovereignty finds its limits in the protection of "human security."[12] Under the concept of responsibility to protect, matters affecting the life of the citizens and subjects of a state are no longer exclusively subject to the discretion of the domestic ruler but are perceived as issues of concern to the broader international community (e.g., third states, multilateral institutions, and nonstate actors). This development is part and parcel of a growing transformation of international law from a state- and governing-elite-based system of rules into a normative framework designed to protect certain human and community interests.

Yet the quick rise of the concept of responsibility to protect from an idea into an alleged emerging legal norm raises some suspicions from a positivist perspective. How can a concept that is labeled as a "new approach"[13] and a "re-characterization" of sovereignty[14] in 2001 turn into an emerging legal norm within the course of four years, and into an organizing principle for peace and security in the UN system one year later? None of the four main documents in which responsibility to protect has been treated in depth can be regarded as generating binding international law under the classic sources of international law set forth in Article 38 of the Statute of the International Court of Justice (ICJ) (e.g., "international conventions," "international custom, as evidence of a general practice accepted as law," and "general principles of law").[15] Contemporary understanding lends some weight to resolutions adopted by the General Assembly[16] and occasionally even to reports issued by the UN secretary-general and certain expert bodies, in particular when combined with more traditional sources (treaties or state practice).[17] However, even this broader conception of the formation of law, which takes into account the provenance and conditions of adoption of certain documents (e.g., adoption by consensus, the composition of the respective body), fails to offer conclusive guidance in this regard. A closer study of the relevant reports and documents reveals considerable divergences in opinion. Different bodies have employed the same notion to describe partly different paradigms. The text of the Outcome Document of the World Summit, which is arguably the most authoritative of the four documents in terms of its legal value,[18] leaves considerable doubt concerning whether and to what extent states intended to create a legal norm.

[12] The Outcome Document is qualified by some as a "milestone in the relationship between sovereignty and human rights." See the abstract dated July 28, 2006, of the online version of Alex J. Bellamy, *Whither the Responsibility to Protect? Humanitarian Intervention and the 2005 World Summit*, 20 ETHICS & INT'L AFF. 143 (2006), *at* <http://www.cceia.org/resources/journal/20_2/articles/5384.html>, in which Bellamy's article is described as taking a different view.

[13] RESPONSIBILITY TO PROTECT, *supra* note 2, ch. 2.

[14] *Id.*, para. 2.14.

[15] For a survey of the classic understanding of sources of law, see 1 L. OPPENHEIM, INTERNATIONAL LAW 22–23 (Hersch Lauterpacht ed., 6th ed. 1947).

[16] Law-declaring resolutions of the General Assembly, for example, may assist in the determination or interpretation of international law or even constitute evidence of international custom. Scholars differ, however, as to whether "law-declaring resolutions" of the Assembly can create law beyond their contributory role in the formation of customary international law. *See generally* GEORGES ABI-SAAB, LES RÉSOLUTIONS DANS LA FORMATION DU DROIT INTERNATIONAL DU DÉVELOPPEMENT 9 (1971). For doubts, see Hartmut Hillgenberg, *A Fresh Look at Soft Law*, 10 EUR. J. INT'L L. 499, 514 (1999).

[17] The assessment of "soft law" may be based on an analysis of such sources. *See generally* Alan Boyle, *Soft Law in International Law-Making*, *in* INTERNATIONAL LAW 141 (Malcolm D. Evans ed., 2006).

[18] The Institute of International Law found that principles and rules proclaimed in law-developing resolutions "may influence State practice, or initiate a new practice that constitutes an ingredient of new customary law," or "contribute to the consolidation of State practice, or to the formation of the *opinio juris communis.*" Institut de droit international, The Elaboration of General Multilateral Conventions and of Non-Contractual Instruments

These findings suggest that something is wrong here. Either the concept of responsibility to protect is actually not so new and innovative as portrayed,[19] or the qualification is wrong. Maybe the notion itself is so indeterminate that it does not yet meet the requirements of a legal norm.

This essay seeks to clarify the current status of the law and to identify its possible future directions. It argues in part I that the concept of responsibility to protect should be understood partly as a political catchword that gained quick acceptance because it could be interpreted by different actors in different ways, and partly as "old wine in new bottles." Some of the propositions are not novel, but grounded in established concepts of international law.[20] Other aspects of the concept are seen in part II as deserving of further clarification. It is thus fair to conclude that the concept currently encompasses a spectrum of different normative propositions that vary considerably in their status and degree of legal support.

I. INTERPRETIVE AND NORMATIVE DIVIDES: DIFFERENT BODIES, DIFFERENT MEANINGS

The concept of responsibility to protect is treated differently in the four documents associated with its genesis, namely, the report of the Commission on State Sovereignty and Intervention, the High-Level Panel Report, the Report of the Secretary-General, and the Outcome Document of the 2005 World Summit.

The Approach of the Commission on State Sovereignty and Intervention

The most comprehensive treatment of the concept was offered by the Commission on State Sovereignty and Intervention. The commission essentially developed the concept of responsibility to protect to solve the legal and policy dilemmas of humanitarian interventions. The commission focused on the relationship between sovereignty and intervention, specifically on how the international community should "respond to a Rwanda, to a Srebrenica—to gross and systematic violations of human rights that [offend] every precept of our common humanity" if "humanitarian intervention is, indeed, an unacceptable assault on sovereignty."[21]

The commission proposed dealing with this problem by recharacterizing sovereignty, that is, by conceiving of sovereignty as responsibility rather than control.[22] The commission thus used a rhetorical trick:[23] it flipped the coin, shifting the emphasis from a politically and legally undesirable right to intervene for humanitarian purposes to the less confrontational idea of a responsibility to protect.[24]

Having a Normative Function or Objective, Res. II, conclusion 22 (Cairo Conference, 1987), *available at* <http://www.idi-iil.org/idiE/resolutionsE/1987_caire_02_en.PDF>.

[19] *See* Boisson de Chazournes & Condorelli, *supra* note 1, at 11–18; Molier, *supra* note 1, at 47–52.

[20] *See* Molier, *supra* note 1, at 37–62.

[21] RESPONSIBILITY TO PROTECT, *supra* note 2, at VII (quoting Secretary-General Kofi A. Annan, Millennium Report and Annual Report on the Work of the Organization, UN Docs. A/54/2000 & A/55/1 (2000), at 48 & para. 37, respectively).

[22] *Id.*, para. 2.14.

[23] The commission found that the expressions "humanitarian intervention" and "right to intervene," which had been used in "past debates," did not "help to carry the debate forward." *Id.*, para. 2.4.

[24] *Id.*, para. 2.29.

The commission tried to distinguish the idea of responsibility to protect from the concept of humanitarian intervention[25] in three ways.[26] The report emphasized, first of all, that responsibility to protect looks at intervention from a different perspective than the doctrine of humanitarian intervention. The commission stressed that responsibility to protect addresses the dilemma of intervention from the perspective of the needs of those who seek or need support (e.g., communities in need of protection from genocide, mass killings, ethnic cleansing, rape, or mass starvation),[27] rather than from the interests and perspectives of those who carry out such action (entities asserting the "right to intervene").[28]

Second, the commission sought to bridge the gap between intervention and sovereignty by introducing a complementary concept of responsibility, under which responsibility is shared by the national state and the broader international community. The commission recognized that the main (the primary) responsibility to protect resides with the state whose people are directly affected by conflict or massive human rights abuses,[29] and "that it is only if the state is unable or unwilling to fulfill this responsibility, or is itself the perpetrator, that it becomes the responsibility of the international community to act in its place."[30]

Third, the commission expanded the conceptual parameters of the notion of intervention, declaring that an effective response to mass atrocities requires not only reaction, but ongoing engagement to prevent conflict and rebuild after the event. The commission developed a multiphased conception of responsibility, based on a distinction between responsibility to prevent and react and responsibility to rebuild. This conception of responsibility "means that if military intervention action is taken—because of a breakdown or abdication of a state's own capacity and authority in discharging its 'responsibility to protect'—there should be a genuine commitment to helping to build a durable peace, and promoting good governance and sustainable development."[31]

[25] *See generally* SIMON CHESTERMAN, JUST WAR OR JUST PEACE: HUMANITARIAN INTERVENTION AND INTERNATIONAL LAW 228 (2001); Antonio Cassese, Ex Iniuria Ius Oritur: *Are We Moving Towards International Legitimation of Forcible Humanitarian Countermeasures in the World Community?* 10 EUR. J. INT'L L. 23 (1999); Antonio Cassese, *A Follow-up: Forcible Humanitarian Countermeasures and* Opinio Necessitatis, 10 EUR. J. INT'L L. 791; Ralph Zacklin, *Beyond Kosovo: The United Nations and Humanitarian Intervention*, 41 VA. J. INT'L L. 936 (2001).

[26] RESPONSIBILITY TO PROTECT, *supra* note 2, para. 2.29. The commission was critical of the notion of "humanitarian intervention." It believed that the "humanitarian" argument could be used to disguise motives for an intervention and that it would tend "to prejudge the very question in issue—that is, whether the intervention is in fact defensible." The commission also abandoned the term in response to opposition by humanitarian agencies and organizations to the "militarization" of the word "humanitarian," which they argued could not be ascribed "to any kind of military action." *Id.*, para. 1.40.

[27] One of the particularities of the report is that it formulated specific "threshold" criteria for "military intervention for human protection purposes." *Id.*, para. 4.19. Military intervention may be

> justified in two broad sets of circumstances, namely in order to halt or avert:
>
> large scale loss of life, actual or apprehended, with genocidal intent or not, which is the product either of deliberate state action, or state neglect or inability to act, or a failed state situation; or
>
> large scale "ethnic cleansing," actual or apprehended, whether carried out by killing, forced expulsion, acts of terror or rape.

Id. (emphasis omitted).

[28] *Id.*, para. 1.40.

[29] *Id.*, para. 2.30.

[30] *Id.*, para. 2.29.

[31] *Id.*, para. 5.1.

The move from a right to intervene to a responsibility to protect was justified by the commission on the basis of a distinction between a state's internal and external responsibility. The commission recognized that states' authorities are responsible for the safety, life, and welfare of their citizens, and that they are also responsible to citizens internally.[32] However, the commission stressed that at the same time states bear an external responsibility with regard to the international community through the United Nations.[33] The commission acknowledged that violations of this dual responsibility could ultimately require "action . . . by the broader community of states to support populations that are in jeopardy or under serious threat."[34] It identified three circumstances in which this "residual responsibility" of the broader community of states is activated:

— "when a particular state is clearly either unwilling or unable to fulfill its responsibility to protect";

— "when a particular state . . . is itself the actual perpetrator of crimes or atrocities"; or

— "where people living outside a particular state are directly threatened by actions taking place there."[35]

The report of the commission managed to gather broad support because it avoided taking a final stance on the question of the legality/legitimacy of unauthorized interventions. The invention of the notion of responsibility to protect assisted in this effort by leaving flexible the choice of means (e.g., humanitarian assistance, economic assistance, military engagement) to exercise that responsibility. The commission made it clear that the "Security Council should be the first port of call on any matter relating to military intervention for human protection purposes,"[36] but it did not categorically exclude the possibility that the responsibility to protect might ultimately be assumed by the General Assembly, regional organizations, or coalitions of states if the Security Council fails to act. The commission left open whether and under what circumstances an "intervention not authorized by the Security Council or [the] General Assembly" would be valid in legal terms.[37] Nevertheless, it advised that when the Council fails to discharge what the commission would regard as its responsibility to protect, a balancing assessment should be made as to where the most harm lies: "in the damage to international order if the Security Council is bypassed or in the damage to that order if human beings are slaughtered."[38] Moreover, the commission developed five criteria of legitimacy for interventions, which were deemed to apply to "both the Security Council and [UN] member states,"[39] namely, just cause, right intention, last resort, proportionality of means, and a reasonable prospect of success.[40]

[32] *Id.*, para. 2.15.
[33] *Id.*
[34] *Id.*, para. 2.31.
[35] *Id.*
[36] *Id.*, para. 6.28.
[37] *Id.*, para. 6.37.
[38] *Id.*
[39] *Id.*, para. 4.32.
[40] *Id.*, paras. 4.18, 4.32–.48.

The High-Level Panel Report

The debate about the concept of responsibility to protect took a new turn in the High-Level Panel Report, where it was directly related to institutional reform of the United Nations. The high-level panel saw the idea of responsibility to protect as a means to strengthen the collective security system under the Charter.

The panel treated the concept in two parts of its report. It mentioned the nexus between sovereignty and responsibility in the opening pages[41] and subsequently developed the contours of the concept in the context of the "use of force," in a section entitled "Chapter VII of the Charter of the United Nations, internal threats and the responsibility to protect."[42]

The purported scope of the responsibility to protect remained unclear in the panel's report. Although the panel recognized that each individual state has a special duty vis-à-vis its citizens,[43] it spoke at the same time of a (collective) "'responsibility to protect' of *every* State when it comes to people suffering from avoidable catastrophe—mass murder and rape, ethnic cleansing by forcible expulsion and terror, and deliberate starvation and exposure to disease."[44] The reference to the responsibility of "*every* State" left room for different interpretations. It could be read as a simple reminder of the *erga omnes* nature of the international obligations (e.g., in cases of genocide, torture, and grave breaches of the Geneva Conventions) that give rise to the responsibility to protect.[45] However, the text also allowed for a broader reading that endorsed a wider concept of "responsibility" under which the responsibility of the host state shifts to every other state in cases where the former is unable or unwilling to act.[46] This reading would significantly extend the existing parameters of the law of state responsibility. It would detach the idea of responsibility of a sovereign from the traditional criteria of nationality or territoriality and establish a multilayered system of responsibility, in which the primary responsibility of the state vis-à-vis its citizens is complemented by a residual responsibility of *all* sovereign governments vis-à-vis human catastrophes.

One of the particularities of the High-Level Panel Report is the linkage of the panel's vision of shared responsibility directly to the United Nations. The idea of responsibility to protect became part and parcel of the vocabulary of UN reform. The panel associated the concept of collective responsibility, in particular, with action by the Security Council. It reiterated that

[41] High-Level Panel Report, *supra* note 3, paras. 29–30.

[42] *Id.*, paras. 199–203.

[43] *Id.*, para. 201 ("[S]overeign Governments have the primary responsibility to protect their own citizens from . . . catastrophes . . . ").

[44] *Id.*

[45] The ICJ reaffirmed in the *Barcelona Traction* case that obligations *erga omnes* "derive, for example, in contemporary international law, from the outlawing of acts of aggression, and of genocide, as also from the principles and rules concerning the basic rights of the human person, including protection from slavery and racial discrimination." Barcelona Traction, Light & Power Co. (Belg. v. Spain), Second Phase, 1970 ICJ REP. 3, 32, para. 34 (Feb. 5) [hereinafter Barcelona Traction].

[46] This understanding was challenged by the United States in the context of the drafting of the Outcome Document. The U.S. representative to the United Nations addressed this point in a letter to the UN member states dated August 30, 2005, noting that "the responsibility of the other countries in the international community is not of the same character as the responsibility of the host, and we thus want to avoid formulations that suggest that the other countries are inheriting the same responsibility that the host state has." Letter from Ambassador Bolton to UN Member States Conveying U.S. Amendments to the Draft Outcome Document Being Prepared for the High Level Event on Responsibility to Protect, at 2 (Aug. 30, 2005), *available at* <http://www.responsibilitytoprotect.org/index.php/pages/2>, <http://www.un.int/usa/reform-un-jrb-ltr-protect-8-05.pdf> [hereinafter Bolton Letter].

the Security Council has not only the authority, but also a certain *responsibility* to take action to combat humanitarian crises. The report stated that the Security Council and the wider international community have come to accept that, under Chapter VII and in pursuit of the emerging norm of a collective responsibility to protect, the Council "can always authorize military action to redress catastrophic internal wrongs if it is prepared to declare that the situation is a 'threat to international peace and security'."[47] This passage was meant as an incentive for the Council to act responsibly by giving the UN collective security system the wherewithal to work effectively in all cases of humanitarian crises.[48] The panel combined this appeal to responsibility with a plea for a more transparent and responsible use of the right of veto by the five permanent members of the Security Council. The panel urged the permanent members, in particular, "to pledge themselves to refrain from the use of the veto in cases of genocide and large-scale human rights abuses."[49] Both statements reflect the panel's intention to make the Council both a vehicle for, and an addressee of, the concept of responsibility to protect.

This goal was accompanied by an express effort to channel international intervention through the Security Council.[50] The panel took the position that UN members must resort to the collective security system in all cases of military intervention, including operations carried out by regional organizations.[51] Unlike the Commission on State Sovereignty and Intervention, the panel did not envisage that an international responsibility to protect could be invoked by coalitions of the able and willing or regional organizations in the absence of Security Council authorization.[52] The report stressed that the "emerging norm" of a "collective international responsibility to protect" was only "exercisable by the Security Council" and only if military intervention was at stake. This approach was guided by the ambition of the drafters of the report to reinforce the UN system after the 2003 intervention in Iraq.[53]

The panel's treatment of collective security culminated in the identification of "five basic criteria of legitimacy" for the use of force (seriousness of threat, proper purpose, last resort, proportional means, and balance of consequences).[54] Interestingly, in establishing these legitimacy criteria, the panel did not contemplate solving the impasse of unauthorized interventions, but intended to enhance "the effectiveness of the global collective security system."[55] The

[47] High-Level Panel Report, *supra* note 3, para. 202.

[48] This point was also made in paragraph 198 of the report, where the panel stressed that "[t]he task is not to find alternatives to the Security Council as a source of authority but to make the Council work better than it has."

[49] High-Level Panel Report, *supra* note 3, para. 256.

[50] *Id.*, para. 196. There the panel stated:

> It may be that some States will always feel that they have the obligation to [protect] their own citizens, and the capacity, to do whatever they feel they need to do, unburdened by the constraints of collective Security Council process. But however understandable that approach may have been in the cold war years, when the United Nations was manifestly not operating as an effective collective security system, the world has now changed and expectations about legal compliance are very much higher.

[51] *Id.*, para. 272. The panel stated that "[a]uthorization from the Security Council should in all cases be sought for regional operations." However, the panel left a small backdoor open by recognizing that "in some urgent situations" such an "authorization may be sought *after* such operations have commenced." *Id.* (emphasis added).

[52] *Id.*, para. 203 ("exercisable by the Security Council authorizing military intervention as a last resort"). As regards the Commission on State Sovereignty and Intervention, see text at notes 36–40.

[53] For a full discussion, see the contributions in FUTURE IMPLICATIONS OF THE IRAQ CONFLICT: SELECTIONS FROM THE *AMERICAN JOURNAL OF INTERNATIONAL LAW* (ASIL 2004).

[54] High-Level Panel Report, *supra* note 3, para. 207.

[55] *Id.*, para. 204.

criteria were primarily addressed to the Security Council and formulated to guide the Council in its decision "whether to authorize or endorse the use of military force."[56] The panel only hinted at the option of a broader application of these criteria by states, noting that "it would be valuable if individual Member States, whether or not they are members of the Security Council, subscribed to them."[57]

The Report of the Secretary-General

The tensions inherent in the notion of responsibility to protect are reflected in the subsequent report of the secretary-general on larger freedom. The secretary-general did not simply endorse the findings of an emerging norm of a collective responsibility to protect, but stressed that he was "aware of the sensitivities involved in this issue."[58] The concept was removed from the section on the use of force and placed in the section dealing with freedom to live in dignity, so as to detach the idea of responsibility from an automatic equation to armed force. Accordingly, the thematic focus of the concept changed. Responsibility to protect was no longer exclusively viewed as a surrogate for humanitarian intervention but as a strategy to promote the commitment of all nations to the rule of law and human security.[59] This focus was in line with the general theme of the secretary-general's report, which sought to combine the "imperative of collective action" with a "shared vision of development."[60]

Consequently, the secretary-general placed stronger emphasis on the need to implement the responsibility to protect through peaceful means. In the report, the international community's residual responsibility to protect became a responsibility to "use diplomatic, humanitarian and other methods to help protect the human rights and well-being of civilian populations."[61] Use of force was described as an *ultima ratio* measure that, if taken, ought to be carried out by the Security Council.[62] The notion of responsibility to protect was used to constrain, rather than to enable, the use of force. When associated with armed force, however, the concept of responsibility to protect was not viewed as a means to establish alternatives to the Security Council but as an instrument "to make it work better."[63] Moreover, the report referred to the five criteria of legitimacy for the use of force mentioned in the High-Level Panel Report as exclusively directed to the Council.[64]

Thus, from a legal point of view there was no substantive change with respect to the treatment of humanitarian interventions. The Report of the Secretary-General did not expressly rule out the possibility of unilateral action in any circumstances (e.g., where the veto is used to block action in a case of genocide). Nevertheless, the general focus of the report on the Council and the silence of the secretary-general on alternative means of carrying out interventions

[56] *Id.*, para. 207.

[57] *Id.*, para. 209.

[58] Report of the Secretary-General, *supra* note 5, para. 135.

[59] *Id.*, para. 133.

[60] *Id.*, pts. I(C), II(A), respectively.

[61] *Id.*, para. 135 ("[I]f national authorities are unable or unwilling to protect their citizens, then the responsibility shifts to the international community . . . ").

[62] *Id.*, para. 135 ("When such methods appear insufficient, the Security Council may out of necessity decide to take action under the Charter of the United Nations, including enforcement action . . . ").

[63] *Id.*, para. 126.

[64] *Id.*

for purposes of human protection indicated a general reluctance to accept military action without the Security Council's authorization.

The Outcome Document of the 2005 World Summit

The different conceptions of the notion of responsibility to protect finally became apparent in the drafting process of the Outcome Document of the 2005 World Summit. Both the form and contours of the concept were intensively debated before the high-level plenary meeting. Several states (Algeria, Belarus, Cuba, Egypt, Iran, Pakistan, the Russian Federation, and Venezuela) expressed reservations about including the responsibility to protect in the Outcome Document. Some delegations argued that the concept was too vague and open to abuse. Others doubted that it was compatible with the Charter, noting that there is no shared responsibility in international law outside the responsibility of a state to protect its own citizens and the institutional mandate of the United Nations to safeguard international peace and security.[65] Still others again questioned the legal nature of the responsibility to protect and sought to frame this idea in terms of a moral principle. U.S. ambassador John R. Bolton, for example, stated in a letter dated August 30, 2005, that the United States would "not accept that either the United Nations as a whole, or the Security Council, or individual states, have an obligation to intervene under international law."[66] Accordingly, the U.S. delegation proposed that the idea of an international responsibility to protect be defined in the form of a "moral responsibility" of the international community to "use appropriate diplomatic, economic, humanitarian and other peaceful means, including under Chapters VI and VIII of the Charter to help protect populations from . . . atrocities."[67]

The final text of the Outcome Document is a compromise solution that seeks to bridge the different positions. States avoided reducing the idea of responsibility to protect to a purely moral concept. However, paragraphs 138 and 139 of the Outcome Document represent a rather curious mixture of political and legal considerations, which reflects the continuing division and confusion about the meaning of the concept.

The two paragraphs are drafted in a discursive fashion, which is typical of political declarations. The clearest commitment is contained in paragraph 138. It opens with the straightforward statement that "[e]ach individual State has the responsibility to protect its populations from genocide, war crimes, ethnic cleansing and crimes against humanity."[68] This sentence reflects the traditional bond of duty between the host state and its citizens. This bond is expressly recognized by the respective heads of state and government by way of a collective affirmation ("We accept that responsibility . . . ").[69]

The passage on the responsibility of the international community is framed in more cautious terms. The Outcome Document relied implicitly on the distinction between responsibility to prevent, responsibility to react, and responsibility to rebuild made by the Commission on State

[65] For a survey of the statements of Algeria, Cuba, Egypt, Iran, Pakistan, Russia, and Venezuela, see Responsibility to Protect—Engaging Civil Society, Chart on Government Positions (Aug. 11, 2005), *at* <http://www.responsibilitytoprotect.org/index.php/pages/2>.

[66] Bolton Letter, *supra* note 46, at 2.

[67] *Id.* at 3 (enclosure entitled "United States Proposals: Responsibility to Protect").

[68] Outcome Document, *supra* note 7, para. 138.

[69] *Id.*

Sovereignty and Intervention. However, each of these concepts is treated in individual terms with varying degrees of support.

The idea of responsibility to prevent is phrased in terms of a general appeal ("should, as appropriate") to the international community to assist states and the United Nations in the prevention of crimes.[70] Responsibility to react is taken up in paragraph 139, which states plainly and unconditionally that "[t]he international community, through the United Nations, also has the responsibility to use appropriate diplomatic, humanitarian and other peaceful means, in accordance with Chapters VI and VIII of the Charter, to help to protect populations from genocide, war crimes, ethnic cleansing and crimes against humanity."[71] This sentence suggests that the idea of responsibility to react enjoys at least some acceptance with regard to measures falling short of the use of force.

However, the Outcome Document assumes a more reserved stance vis-à-vis responsibility to take collective action through the Security Council under Chapter VII. The second sentence of paragraph 139 places this idea under a double qualifier. First, the heads of state and government merely reaffirm their preparedness to take such action.[72] This language points toward a voluntary, rather than a mandatory, engagement. Moreover, states commit themselves to act only "on a case-by-case basis" through the Council,[73] which again stands in contrast to the assumption of a systematic duty. This dual condition distinguishes the tenor of the Outcome Document from the responsibility-driven approach of the high-level panel toward collective security[74] and appears to reflect the view of those states that questioned the proposition that the Charter creates a legal obligation for Security Council members to support enforcement action in the case of mass atrocities.[75] The idea of guidelines for the authorization or endorsement of the use of force by the Council was dropped entirely.

More fundamentally, the text of the Outcome Document does not firmly state that UN collective security action constitutes the only option for responding to mass atrocities through the use of force. Some states claimed that the concept of collective action under the umbrella of the responsibility to protect should not preclude action absent Security Council authorization. The United States, for example, argued that the Outcome Document should not foreclose the possibility of unauthorized intervention, noting that there "may be cases that involve humanitarian catastrophes but for which there is also a legitimate basis for states to act in self-defense."[76] The Outcome Document does not exclude this line of reasoning. It leaves the door open to unilateral responses through its "case-by-case" vision of collective security and a qualified commitment to act in cooperation with regional organizations ("as appropriate").[77]

[70] *Id.*

[71] *Id.*, para. 139.

[72] *Id.* ("In this context, we are *prepared* to take collective action . . . " (emphasis added)).

[73] *Id.*

[74] *See* text at notes 43–57 *supra.*

[75] *See* Bolton Letter, *supra* note 46, at 1.

[76] *Id.* at 2.

[77] The Outcome Document states:

> In this context, we are prepared to take collective action, in a timely and decisive manner, through the Security Council, in accordance with the Charter, including Chapter VII, on *a case-by-case basis* and in cooperation with relevant regional organizations *as appropriate*, should peaceful means be inadequate and national authorities are manifestly failing to protect their populations from genocide, war crimes, ethnic cleansing and crimes against humanity.

Importantly, the Outcome Document places the entire concept of responsibility to react under a final, additional proviso. The heads of state and government stressed "the need for the General Assembly to continue consideration of the responsibility to protect populations from genocide, war crimes, ethnic cleansing and crimes against humanity and its implications, bearing in mind the principles of the Charter and international law."[78] This language was inserted in the text in deference to states that felt that responsibility to protect was not yet sufficiently clear in conceptual terms and needed further consideration in the General Assembly before its implementation.[79] The express reference to the need for conformity with "the principles of the Charter and international law" creates further ambiguity. It almost seems to suggest that the drafters of the Outcome Document had some doubts whether their own proposal was consistent with international law and the Charter.

The concept of responsibility to rebuild received even less explicit support. The heads of state and government merely expressed their intention to commit themselves, *"as necessary and appropriate,* to helping States build capacity to protect their populations from genocide, war crimes, ethnic cleansing and crimes against humanity and to assisting those which are under stress before crises and conflicts break out."[80] The issue of postintervention engagement was mainly addressed in institutional terms, namely, through the creation of the Peacebuilding Commission, which was specifically established to address the challenge of helping countries make the transition from war to lasting peace.[81]

Altogether, the Outcome Document is rather confusing. The fact that responsibility to protect is treated under a separate heading indicates that the idea as such enjoys basic support. Obviously, the drafters also sought to give the concept a certain legal meaning. However, its individual components remain unclear as a result of obvious differences in opinion.

II. TRADITION VS. INNOVATION

The continuing international division raises some doubts about the status of the concept of responsibility to protect. The High-Level Panel Report qualified this concept as an emerging norm. However, this characterization is misleading, since it is overoptimistic and overpessimistic at the same time. Some of the features of the concept are actually well embedded in contemporary international law, while others are so innovative that it may be premature to speak of a crystallizing practice.

Outcome Document, *supra* note 7, para. 139 (emphasis added); *see also* Amerasinghe, *supra* note 1, at 47 ("[I]t would seem that the resolution does not rule out humanitarian intervention by other States as a means of discharging this responsibility.").

[78] Outcome Document, *supra* note 7, para. 139.

[79] See, for example, the statement of the delegate of the Russian Federation at the Security Council's open debate on December 9, 2005, on the protection of civilians in armed conflict:

> We all remember well the complex compromise that was required to reflect that issue [responsibility to protect] in the 2005 Summit Outcome document. In that connection—and the outcome document states this—we need to have a detailed discussion in the General Assembly of the issue of the responsibility to protect before we can discuss its implementation.

UN Doc. S/PV.5319, at 19 (Dec. 9, 2005) (statement of Mr. Rogachev), *reprinted in* Responsibility to Protect—Engaging Civil Society, Excerpted Statements on the Responsibility to Protect at the Security Council Open Debate on the Protection of Civilians in Armed Conflict, *at* <http://www.responsibilitytoprotect.org>.

[80] Outcome Document, *supra* note 7, para. 139 (emphasis added).

[81] *Id.*, para. 97–105. For a closer survey, see GA Res. 60/180 (Dec. 30, 2005) (Peacebuilding Commission).

Partly "Old Wine in New Bottles"

As mentioned above, the responsibility to protect is not a completely novel idea. Some of the allegedly emerging elements of the concept have surfaced in the past.

Sovereignty as responsibility. The shift from sovereignty as control to sovereignty as responsibility appears to be less radical than suggested by its history.[82]

The understanding that a state exercises the functions of an agent and trustee for the human beings who are affected by the consequences of state action is not a twentieth-century principle, but can be traced much further back. It appeared as early as the time of Hugo Grotius, whose conception of law was based on the assumption that the rules governing the organization and behavior of states exist ultimately for the benefit of the actual subjects of the rights and duties concerned, individual human beings.[83] Grotius even maintained that it would be just to resort to war to prevent a state from maltreating its own subjects.[84] A similar understanding of the state is reflected in the work of contract theorists. John Locke viewed the relationship between the state and its citizens in terms of "trust."[85] In fact, the word "trust" appears more frequently than "contract" in his most famous political work, *The Second Treatise of Civil Government.*

Similarly, in international law the state has never been exclusively considered a self-referential entity. Sovereignty and domestic jurisdiction have traditionally served as forums for the protection of the well-being and interests of human beings. Ever since the seventeenth century, attempts have been made to grant individuals and groups international protection from the arbitrary exercise of state authority.[86] Religious groups were even protected by treaty from their own sovereign. Later, this protection was extended to minorities.[87] In the external relations of

[82] *See* text at notes 22–24 *supra.* The concept of responsibility to protect builds on earlier works in peace research, notably FRANCIS M. DENG ET AL., SOVEREIGNTY AS RESPONSIBILITY: CONFLICT MANAGEMENT IN AFRICA (1996).

[83] This understanding is reflected in Grotius's conception of things that are public and common to all men. *See* HUGO GROTIUS, DE MARE LIBERUM, ch. V (Ralph Deman Magoffin trans., Oxford Univ. Press 1916) (1609); HUGO GROTIUS, DE JURE BELLI AC PACIS, bk. II, ch. 2 (Francis W. Kelsey trans., Clarendon Press 1925) (1625); *see generally* Hersch Lauterpacht, *The Grotian Tradition in International Law*, 1946 BRIT. Y.B. INT'L L. 1, 27.

[84] GROTIUS, DE JURE BELLI AC PACIS, *supra* note 83, bk. II, ch. XXV, pt. VIII(2), where Grotius states that if a ruler "should inflict upon his subjects such treatment as no one is warranted in inflicting, the exercise of the right vested in human society is not precluded." According to Lauterpacht, "[T]his is the first authoritative statement of the principle of humanitarian intervention—the principle that the exclusiveness of domestic jurisdiction stops where outrage upon humanity begins." Lauterpacht, *supra* note 83, at 46.

[85] See, for example, JOHN LOCKE, *The Second Treatise of Government*, ch. XIII, §149, *in* TWO TREATISES OF GOVERNMENT (Peter Laslett ed., Cambridge University Press 1988) (1690), where he states:

> Though in a Constituted Commonwealth, standing upon its own Basis, and acting according to its own Nature, that is, acting for the preservation of the Community, there can be but *one Supreme Power,* which is *the Legislative,* to which all the rest are and must be subordinate, yet the Legislative being only a Fiduciary Power to act for certain ends, there remains still *in the People a Supream Power* to remove or *alter the Legislative,* when they find the *Legislative* act contrary to the trust reposed in them. For all *Power given with trust* for the attaining an *end,* being limited by that end, whenever that *end* is manifestly neglected, or opposed, the *trust* must necessarily be *forfeited,* and the Power devolve into the hands of those that gave it, who may place it anew where they shall think best for their safety and security.

[86] *See* 1 GEORG SCHWARZENBERGER, INTERNATIONAL LAW 273 (3d ed. 1957).

[87] A good example is the Peace Treaty of Versailles, in which Poland agreed to "protect the interests of inhabitants of Poland who differ from the majority of the population in race, language or religion." Treaty of Peace, Art. 93, June 28, 1919, Allied & Associated Powers–Ger., 11 Martens (ser. 3) 323, 225 Consol. TS 188. The Versailles Treaty was complemented by a Treaty of Minorities of June 28, 1919, between the Principal Allied and Associated Powers and Poland, 112 Brit. Foreign & St. Papers 232.

states, citizens and subjects of other states were often perceived as capital assets or extensions of a state's dignity. However, foreigners were protected by a minimum standard of protection under international law, which came to include guarantees of equality and dignity at the beginning of the twentieth century.[88] Moreover, the classical paradigm of diplomatic protection, which is rooted in customary international law, is at least partly built on the idea of the fusion of private and public (state) interests.[89]

It is also well understood that sovereignty entails duties on the international plane. Sovereignty never meant that a state could act in its territory regardless of the effect of its acts on another state. This point was expressly made in 1928 by the arbitrator Max Huber in the award in the *Island of Palmas* case.[90] After the end of World War II, the adoption of the UN Charter and the rise of key human rights instruments eroded the classic equation of sovereignty and "power." Although the Charter was oriented toward protecting the sanctity of sovereignty, it contained important references to human rights protection. The preamble, the last sentence of Article 2(7),[91] and Articles 1(3) and 55 made it clear that the Charter was designed to "protect the sovereignty of peoples" and was "never meant as a licence for governments to trample on human rights and human dignity."[92] This reading of the Charter was recognized in legal doctrine as early as 1947.[93] It became apparent with the unleashing of Chapter VII after the Cold War. It was accompanied by the recognition of the concept of *erga omnes* obligations ("obligations of a State towards the international community as a whole") by the ICJ[94] and was later followed by the establishment of separate rules of state responsibility for "serious breaches of obligations under peremptory norms of general international law" by the International Law Commission (ILC).[95]

[88] At the beginning of the twentieth century, claims commissions invoked the minimum standard as a benchmark in cases where states failed to protect the life, property, or human dignity of foreigners. SCHWARZENBERGER, *supra* note 86, at 201.

[89] This bond was stressed more than half a century ago by the Permanent Court of International Justice in the *Mavrommatis* case, where the Court held that "[b]y taking up the case of one of its subjects and by resorting to diplomatic action or international judicial proceedings on his behalf, a State is in reality asserting . . . its right to ensure, in the person of its subjects, respect for the rules of international law." Mavrommatis Palestine Concessions, 1924 PCIJ (ser. A) No. 2, at 12 (Aug. 30).

[90] In the award, it is pointed out that "[t]erritorial sovereignty . . . . has as corollary a duty," namely, the "obligation to protect within the territory the rights of other States, in particular their right to integrity and inviolability in peace and in war, together with the rights which each State may claim for its nationals in foreign territory." Island of Palmas, 2 R. Int'l Arb. Awards 829, 839 (1928). In 1949 this understanding was reaffirmed in Article 14 of the Draft Declaration on the Rights and Duties of States, which provided that "[e]very State has the duty to conduct its relations with other States in accordance . . . with the principle that the sovereignty of each State is subject to the supremacy of international law." International Law Commission [ILC], Draft Declaration on Rights and Duties of States, Art. 14, GA Res. 375(IV), annex (Dec. 6, 1949), *available at* <http://www.un.org/law/ilc/>.

[91] The subsequent rise of regional and universal human rights instruments provided evidence that human rights could no longer be considered as "internal affairs" that fall "essentially within the domestic jurisdiction of any State" within the meaning of Article 2(7) of the Charter.

[92] Kofi Annan, UN secretary-general, Intervention, 35th Annual Ditchley Foundation Lecture (June 26, 1998), *available at* <http://www.ditchley.co.uk/page/173/lecture-xxxv.htm>.

[93] *See* OPPENHEIM, *supra* note 15, at 280 ("The Charter of the United Nations, in recognising the promotion of respect for fundamental human rights and freedoms as one of the principal objects of the Organisation, marks a further step in the direction of elevating the principle of humanitarian intervention to a basic rule of organised international society." (footnote omitted)).

[94] Barcelona Traction, 1970 ICJ REP. 3, 32, para. 33 (Feb. 5).

[95] Articles on Responsibility of States for Internationally Wrongful Acts, pt. II, ch. 3, *in* Report of the International Law Commission on the Work of Its Fifty-third Session, UN GAOR, 56th Sess., Supp. No. 10, at 43, UN

Consequently, it has been argued on numerous occasions over the last several decades that sovereignty cannot be used as a shield against intervention. Some authorities made this point in the immediate aftermath of World War II. Hersch Lauterpacht, for example, in the sixth edition of Oppenheim's *International Law*, departed from the view of his predecessor, noting that "when a State renders itself guilty of cruelties against and persecution of its nationals, in such a way as to deny their fundamental human rights and to shock the conscience of mankind, intervention in the interest of humanity is legally permissible."[96]

In the 1980s, the concept of a "duty to intervene" was invoked by groups seeking access to victims for the purpose of humanitarian assistance. Humanitarian organizations used the vocabulary of "duty" (*devoir d'ingérence*) to make the case that nongovernmental organizations should have unrestricted access to victims of humanitarian catastrophes, even without the consent of the territorial state.[97]

In the 1990s, this argument was extended to certain military interventions, specifically those in collapsed states and those styling themselves as "humanitarian interventions." In the context of Somalia, it was argued that the prohibition of the use of force does not rule out interventions in states that are unable to protect their populations because of a collapse of public authority. Such interventions, so went the argument, would not run counter to the principles of sovereignty and territorial integrity of the host state, which Charter Articles 2(4) and 2(7) are designed to protect.[98]

Later, this reasoning was more frequently applied to humanitarian interventions, and in particular to the case of Kosovo.[99] Proponents of the legality of humanitarian interventions relied on the concept of sovereignty as responsibility to justify a (limited) right to use force for humanitarian purposes. They contended that humanitarian interventions are compatible with the *telos* of the principle of nonintervention and the prohibition of the use of force under Article 2(4). Both norms, they claimed, were meant to protect the citizens of a state, rather than the state as an entity. This rationale ceases to apply in favor of the state when the domestic sovereign violates the rights of its own population.[100]

Doc. A/56/10 (2001), *reprinted in* JAMES CRAWFORD, THE INTERNATIONAL LAW COMMISSION'S ARTICLES ON STATE RESPONSIBILITY: INTRODUCTION, TEXT AND COMMENTARIES (2002) [hereinafter Articles on State Responsibility].

[96] OPPENHEIM, *supra* note 15, at 280. This conclusion is preceded by the following reasoning: "There is general agreement that, by virtue of its personal and territorial supremacy, a State can treat its own nationals according to discretion. But there is a substantial body of opinion and of practice in support of the view that there are limits to that discretion" (and that intervention is permissible when the state denies its nationals their fundamental human rights). *Id.* at 279–80 (footnotes omitted).

[97] LE DEVOIR D'INGÉRENCE (Mario Bettati & Bernard Kouchner eds., 1987); OLIVIER CORTEN & PIERRE KLEIN, DROIT D'INGÉRENCE OU OBLIGATION DE RÉACTION? (1992).

[98] *See generally* Daniel Thürer, *Der zerfallene Staat und das Völkerrecht*, 74 DIE FRIEDENS-WARTE 275 (1999).

[99] Note, however, that small and some large states (e.g., China and Russia) have strong reservations about unauthorized humanitarian intervention.

[100] For example, FERNANDO R. TESÓN, HUMANITARIAN INTERVENTION: AN INQUIRY INTO LAW AND MORALITY 217 (3d rev. ed. 2005), states:

> Force used in defense of fundamental human rights is therefore not a use of force inconsistent with the purposes of the United Nations. State sovereignty makes sense only as a shield for persons to organize themselves freely in political communities. A condition for respecting state sovereignty is, therefore, that sovereign governments (minimally) respect human rights. Delinquent governments forfeit the protection afforded by Article 4(2).

Recently, the departure from classic principles of nonintervention was codified in the Constitutive Act of the African Union.[101] Article 4(h) of the treaty recognizes an express right of intervention of the Union,[102] the "right of the Union to intervene in a Member State pursuant to a decision of the Assembly in respect of grave circumstances, namely: war crimes, genocide and crimes against humanity [as well as a serious threat to legitimate order]."[103]

The concept of responsibility to protect is rooted in the same school of thought. It relies on the axiom that sovereignty exists essentially for the purpose of protecting people. The state is conceived of as the principal guardian of the rights of its people; however, it loses this status of primacy in cases where it is unable or unwilling to ensure this protection.

Parameters of intervention. A similar point may be made with respect to the concept of intervention when used in connection with the notion of responsibility to protect.

The idea of intervention as a continuum (responsibility to prevent, responsibility to protect, responsibility to rebuild) did not come out of the blue. The need for a multiphased vision of international engagement became evident during the multidimensional UN peacekeeping of the 1990s. Secretary-General Boutros Boutros-Ghali developed a tripartite conception of peacemaking in his widely read *Agenda for Peace*, which distinguished peacemaking as preventive diplomacy and "post-conflict peacebuilding."[104] Individual aspects of this distinction were then developed in other reports, such as the Brahimi report,[105] which stressed the importance of the continuity of the process from preventive action to peace building, and the report of the secretary-general "No Exit Without Strategy," which stressed the idea of responsibility after intervention and the need for a postengagement strategy after elections.[106]

An even longer historical lineage marks the criteria for the legitimacy of intervention proposed by the Commission on State Sovereignty and the high-level panel. At least four of these criteria (just cause, right intention, last resort, and proportionality of means) hark back to the just war doctrine.

[101] *See* Constitutive Act of the African Union, Art. 4(j), (h), July 11, 2002, OAU Doc. CAB/LEG/23.15, *available at* <http://www.africa-union.org> [hereinafter AU Web site].

[102] *See generally* Ben Kioko, *The Right of Intervention Under the African Union's Constitutive Act: From Non-interference to Non-intervention*, 85 INT'L REV. RED CROSS 807 (2003).

[103] Constitutive Act of the African Union, *supra* note 101, Art. 4(h). The bracketed words regarding "a serious threat to legitimate order" are added to this provision by Article 4 of the Protocol on Amendments to the Constitutive Act of the African Union, Feb. 3, 2003, *available at* AU Web site, *supra* note 101. This Protocol has not yet entered into force. The modalities of the right to intervene are set forth in the Protocol Relating to the Establishment of the Peace and Security Council of the African Union, July 9, 2002, *available at* AU Web site, *supra*. This Protocol balances the principles of "non-interference" and respect "for the sovereignty and territorial integrity of Member States" with "respect for the rule of law, fundamental human rights and freedoms, the sanctity of human life and international humanitarian law." *See id.*, Art. 4.

[104] AN AGENDA FOR PEACE—PREVENTIVE DIPLOMACY, PEACEMAKING, AND PEACE-KEEPING, REPORT OF THE SECRETARY-GENERAL, at 2, para. 5, UN Doc. A/47/277–S/24111 (1992), UN Sales No. E.95.I.15 (1995).

[105] Report of the Panel on United Nations Peace Operations, UN Doc. A/55/305–S/2000/809.

[106] No Exit Without Strategy: Security Council Decision-Making and the Closure or Transition of United Nations Peacekeeping Operations, Report of the Secretary-General, para. 26, UN Doc. S/2001/394. In this report, the secretary-general emphasized that "[m]ission closure, as a result of the failure of the parties to abide by their agreements, does not represent an end to the responsibility of either the United Nations system or the Security Council, nor need it signal an end to the Council's involvement." The report went on to recommend that, in such situations, Council members should "individually and collectively" consider "what forms of leverage are available to address the conflict." *Id.*

All of these examples illustrate one broader point. Many of the elements of the concept of responsibility to protect are not novel, but rooted in a broader ideological or legal tradition; and it appears to be this link that allowed the concept to gain some acceptance in recent practice.

Partly Progressive Development of the Law

Other elements of the responsibility to protect, in contrast to those just reviewed, are innovative—so innovative, indeed, that it is difficult to ascribe them to the existing *acquis* of international law.

The concept of responsibility to protect appears to associate the idea of human security with certain duties, that is, a collective responsibility to act in the face of gross human rights violations (e.g., to prevent, to react, to rebuild). This vision is novel. So far, such duties have been derived (if at all) from the (rather vague) concept of solidarity. To link protection to responsibility goes a step further, in particular, if responsibility is understood in the sense of a positive obligation.

The law of state responsibility recognizes that certain violations of international law affect all states,[107] and it authorizes states to respond to such violations through claims for "the cessation of the . . . wrongful act," demands for the performance of reparation,[108] or countermeasures.[109] However, contemporary international law imposes only limited positive duties on states. The ILC Articles on State Responsibility, for instance, endorse the idea that certain breaches of international law may be so grave as to trigger not only a right, but also a certain obligation of states to foster compliance with the law. But the ILC limited this principle to the particular category of violations designated as serious breaches ("a gross or systematic failure by the responsible State"[110]) of "a peremptory norm of general international law."[111] The Commission specified that such breaches would entail two sets of consequences: (1) a positive obligation of states "to cooperate to bring [the serious breach] to an end through lawful means" (Article 41(1)); and (2) a negative obligation of states not to reçognize as lawful a situation created by the serious breach and not to render aid or assistance in maintaining that situation (Article 41(2)).

The duty of cooperation under Article 41(1) comes close to the idea of collective responsibility under the concept of responsibility to protect. The Commission made clear that the obligation to cooperate applies to states whether or not they are individually affected by the serious breach. It associated this duty, in particular, with two forms of action, which are also relevant to the responsibility to protect: "a joint and coordinated effort by all states to counteract the effects of [serious] breaches" of peremptory norms of general international law;[112] and international cooperation, which would be "organised in the framework of a competent international organization, in particular the United Nations."[113]

[107] *See* Articles on State Responsibility, *supra* note 95, Arts. 42(b) ("injured State"), 48(1) ("State other than injured State").

[108] *Id.*, Art. 48(2)(a), (b).

[109] *Id.*, Arts. 49–53. Countermeasures may be taken by "injured States."

[110] *Id.*, Art. 40(2).

[111] *Id.*, Art. 40.

[112] *Id.*, Art. 41 Commentary, para. (3).

[113] *Id.*, para. (2).

However, the Commission subjected the entire concept of an obligation to cooperate to an express caveat. It acknowledged that it is open to question whether general international law at present prescribes a positive duty of cooperation and conceded that in that respect Article 41(1) "may reflect the progressive development of international law."[114]

The concept of responsibility to protect takes the idea of responsibility even a step further than the ILC. The Outcome Document of the 2005 World Summit modifies the threshold set by the ILC articles. It does not link the idea of a collective international responsibility to a double qualifier (*serious* breaches of *peremptory* norms of general international law, such as genocide[115]), but extends that idea to all forms of "genocide, war crimes, ethnic cleansing and crimes against humanity."[116] Moreover, the targeted obligation to cooperate to end the breach is transformed into a general responsibility to "use diplomatic, humanitarian or other peaceful means" or collective (security) action to "help protect populations from atrocities." It is thus clear: if the responsibility to protect as set forth in the Outcome Document is meant to entail positive obligations in the sense of Article 41(1) of the ILC articles, it marks an even more progressive development of international law than the project of the ILC.

III. Constructional Ambiguities

These normative ambiguities are complemented by some constructional deficiencies. Some of the implications of the conception of responsibility to protect have not yet been fully contemplated from a legal perspective. Two issues deserve further attention: the concept of complementarity, and the consequences of a violation of the responsibility to protect.

The "Complementarity Trap"

Complementarity has been used as a tool to win the support of states for the concept of responsibility to protect. All of the four documents that refer to the concept rely on complementarity. They make a distinction between the primary responsibility to protect of the host state, and the fallback responsibility of the international community,[117] which is triggered if the host is unable or unwilling to secure protection.[118] This setting of priorities accords with the idea that domestic authorities are often "best placed to take action" on the ground[119] and enjoy the proper legitimacy to make fundamental choices about the future of their constituency.

However, in some cases this scheme may actually turn into a complementarity trap. The complementarity principle may create an additional threshold for collective security action,

[114] *Id.*, para. (3).

[115] The prohibition against genocide is recognized as a peremptory norm of international law. Armed Activities on the Territory of the Congo (New Application: 2002) (Dem. Rep. Congo v. Rwanda), Jurisdiction and Admissibility, para. 64 (Int'l Ct. Justice Feb. 3, 2006). This case is more difficult to make with respect to crimes against humanity and war crimes, which comprise a large bundle of individual crimes whose status of recognition varies.

[116] Outcome Document, *supra* note 7, paras. 138, 139.

[117] RESPONSIBILITY TO PROTECT, *supra* note 2, para. 2.30; High-Level Panel Report, *supra* note 3, para. 201; Report of the Secretary-General, *supra* note 5, para. 135; Outcome Document, *supra* note 7, para. 138.

[118] One may observe here a certain structural parallel to the complementarity regime of the International Criminal Court under Article 17 of the Rome Statute of the International Criminal Court, July 17, 1998, 2187 UNTS 3, *available at* <http://www.un.org/law/ilc/>.

[119] *See* RESPONSIBILITY TO PROTECT, *supra* note 2, para. 2.30.

which would burden the Security Council. The argument of states' primary responsibility may be used to constrain, rather than enable, Council involvement. This risk looms particularly large in the case of paragraph 139 of the Outcome Document, which indicates that, in principle, collective action shall be taken only if national authorities manifestly fail to protect their populations from genocide, war crimes, ethnic cleansing, or crimes against humanity. The meaning of the term "manifestly fails" is unclear. Moreover, the requirement of manifest failure may be used as an additional means to challenge the legality and timing of collective security action. Nonfailure may be invoked as a defense in a double sense, both prior to international engagement and following any such deployment. Domestic authorities may invoke their primary responsibility to argue that international actors are either not yet competent to assume control or no more entitled to exercise such protection than local actors.

The case of Darfur serves as an example in this regard. In the Security Council, some states used the argument of primacy to prevent the imposition of sanctions against Sudan. They claimed that it was premature to take collective action, since the crisis in Sudan had not yet reached a stage where the domestic government had manifestly failed to exercise its responsibility to protect.[120] This experience shows that the concept of complementarity is a double-edged sword. It preserves domestic ownership but may in some instances run counter to the very idea of strengthening collective security. To avoid any incompatibilities with the collective security system, the operation of the complementarity principle should remain subject to the Chapter VII powers of the Security Council under the Charter.

Implications of Inaction

All of the four documents examined are silent on the fundamental question of how to deal with violations of the responsibility to protect. This issue has been addressed only in cursory fashion by the architects of the concept.

Some agreement appears to have taken hold on the idea that inaction by the host state can be remedied through collective action. But what if states or international authorities do not live up to their residual responsibility to protect? Should such omissions equally be subject to some sanction; and, if so, how should they be remedied?

The four documents fail to deal with this question. If the responsibility to protect were indeed a primary legal norm of international law, it would be logical to assume that such violations should entail some form of legal sanction in case of noncompliance. But it is uncertain on what basis and under which rules such violations could be remedied. This specific type of violation, the breach of a positive duty, is not addressed as such by the regime of the law of state responsibility.[121] Nor has it been conclusively determined whether and under what conditions inaction by an international organization may entail international legal responsibility.[122] One

[120] Responsibility to protect was invoked in particular in the context of the adoption of Security Council Resolution 1556 on July 30, 2004. For a survey of statements following its adoption, see UN Doc. S/PV.5015 (July 30, 2004). *See generally* Alex J. Bellamy, *Responsibility to Protect or Trojan Horse? The Crisis in Darfur and Humanitarian Intervention After Iraq*, 19 ETHICS & INT'L AFF. 31 (2005).

[121] The ILC Articles on State Responsibility deal with omissions only briefly in the context of breaches of a "composite act." Articles on State Responsibility, *supra* note 95, Art. 15. No specific consequences are attached to a failure to act under chapter I of Part II: Content of the International Responsibility of a State.

[122] *See generally* Responsibility of International Organizations, *in* International Law Commission, Report on the Work of Its 56th Session, ch. V, UN GAOR, 59th Sess., Supp. No. 10, at 94, UN Doc. A/59/10 (2004).

might argue that a state's noncompliance with a duty "to protect" might trigger a certain right, or even duty, of third parties to protest against this inaction. Yet it is difficult to imagine what legal consequences noncompliance by a political body like the Security Council should entail. It is highly questionable whether the architects of the responsibility to protect wanted to attach any direct legal consequence to such inaction.

The uncertainty surrounding the consequences of noncompliance raises a broader question of principle. It sheds doubt on the notion that responsibility to protect was meant to be an emerging hard norm of international law at all, instead of "soft law" or a political principle.

IV. Conclusion

A comparative analysis of the report of the International Commission on State Sovereignty and Intervention, the High-Level Panel Report, the Report of the Secretary-General, and the Outcome Document of the 2005 World Summit indicates that responsibility to protect is a multifaceted concept with various elements. The core tenet of the concept (sovereignty entails responsibility) enjoys broad support among states, and in the United Nations and civil society. However, each of the four documents examined here embodies a slightly different vision of responsibility to protect. This divergence explains part of its success. The notion became popular because it could be used by different bodies to promote different goals.

The guiding theme of the concept is a sharing of responsibility by the territorial state (primary responsibility) and other actors in matters of human security. The main components of this division of responsibility may be described in five propositions that enjoy different levels of support, ranging from the most accepted to the least.

Proposition No. 1: The Host State Has a Duty to Protect Citizens on Its Territory

The most commonly accepted proposition is that the host state has a responsibility to protect citizens on its territory from large-scale atrocities. This duty is recognized in an equal fashion by all four documents and has been articulated in contemporary statements by state representatives.[123] It is rooted in the traditional obligation of the state to safeguard the well-being and security of persons under its jurisdiction, which is reflected, inter alia, in universal and regional human rights conventions,[124] and reinforced by the growing commitment to criminalizing genocide, crimes against humanity, and war crimes under domestic law.[125]

[123] See, for example, the statements by the UK representative and the representative of the Philippines after the adoption of Security Council Resolution 1556 (2004). UN Doc. S/PV.5015, *supra* note 120, at 5, 10.

[124] See, for example, Article 2, in conjunction with Article 6 (right to life) and Article 9 (liberty and security of persons), of the International Covenant on Civil and Political Rights, Dec. 16, 1966, 999 UNTS 171; and Article 1, in conjunction with Article 2 (right to life), and Article 5 (liberty and security of persons), of the European Convention for the Protection of Human Rights and Fundamental Freedoms, *opened for signature* Nov. 4, 1950, 213 UNTS 221.

[125] This process is fostered by the enactment of implementation legislation under the Rome Statute of the International Criminal Court, *supra* note 118. *See generally* Jann K. Kleffner, *The Impact of Complementarity on National Implementation of Substantive International Criminal Law*, 1 J. INT'L CRIM. JUST. 86 (2003). Paragraph 138 of the Outcome Document, *supra* note 7, makes reference to this commitment ("This responsibility entails the prevention of such crimes, including their incitement, through appropriate and necessary means.").

Proposition No. 2: States Failing the Duty to Protect Have a Weak Sovereignty Defense

Second, the documents in question reflect an emerging consensus on what one may call the negative dimension of responsibility to protect: the limited ability of the host state to invoke sovereignty against external interference. Responsibility to protect is based on the assumption that the host state has a duty to accept aid, assistance, or even the use of force from the outside.[126] This idea may be found in the final clause of Article 2(7) of the Charter. It gains a broader dimension in the context of responsibility to protect, which makes it harder for states to invoke sovereignty as a shield when they are failing to protect their populations. State sovereignty and territorial integrity are no longer a blanket defense against intervention. States will be forced to substantiate the claim that they are upholding certain norms and standards of governance vis-à-vis their own population when they invoke sovereignty as a defense against external interference.

Proposition No. 3: Foreign Entities May Intervene Nonforcibly

Third, there is growing support for the idea that both the United Nations and third states may intervene nonforcibly (i.e., through diplomatic, humanitarian, and peaceful means) in cases where the host state fails to protect citizens on its territory from genocide, war crimes, ethnic cleansing, and crimes against humanity. The Outcome Document strongly emphasizes a collective response "through the United Nations."[127] However, none of the four documents excludes state-based responses.[128] Under the ILC Articles on State Responsibility, this option finds support in the right of "injured State[s]"[129] to take countermeasures under Article 49 and the entitlement of "[a]ny state" to claim "cessation of the internationally wrongful act, and assurances and guarantees of non-repetition" when the "obligation breached is owed to the international community as a whole."[130]

Proposition No. 4: Foreign States May Intervene Forcibly

It is far more controversial whether and under what circumstances states may use force to put an end to large-scale atrocities. The use of military force is expressly excluded from the realm of possible countermeasures under the ILC articles.[131] In the context of the responsibility to protect, the approach to unauthorized uses of force varies from document to document. The High-Level Panel Report ("exercisable by the Security Council")[132] and the Report of the Secretary-General reflect continuing reservations about responses outside the collective security

[126] *See* Anne-Marie Slaughter, *Security, Solidarity, and Sovereignty: The Grand Themes of UN Reform*, 99 AJIL 619, 625 (2005).

[127] Outcome Document, *supra* note 7, para. 139.

[128] This option is contemplated, inter alia, in RESPONSIBILITY TO PROTECT, *supra* note 2, paras. 4.3–4.9.

[129] Note that several states may be "injured" in case of a violation of an *erga omnes* obligation. Articles on State Responsibility, *supra* note 95, Art. 42(b). In its commentary on Article 42, the Commission noted expressly that a broader range of states may have a legal interest in ensuring compliance with such obligations, even though none of them is individually or specially affected by the breach.

[130] *Id.*, Art. 48(1), (2).

[131] Countermeasures shall not affect "the obligation to refrain from the threat or use of force as embodied in the Charter of the United Nations." *Id.*, Art. 50(1)(a).

[132] High-Level Panel Report, *supra* note 3, para. 203.

system. At the same time, states did not categorically reject the option of (individual or collective) unilateral action in the Outcome Document. This discrepancy leaves some leeway to argue that the concept of responsibility to protect is not meant to rule out such action in the future.[133] However, all four documents subscribe to one common qualifier: they make clear that the collective security system shall remain the primary forum for military action. Unilateral responses (if contemplated at all[134]) are envisaged only as a last resort.

Proposition No. 5: Foreign Entities Have a Positive Duty to Act

Finally, there is even less agreement on the last proposition, that the United Nations or states have a positive obligation to intervene under the concept of responsibility to protect. The potential addressee of such an obligation is a matter of some confusion. All four documents adhere to the core idea of the Commission on State Sovereignty and Intervention to shift the focus from the right to intervene to a responsibility to protect. However, the consensus becomes very thin when it comes to defining to whom this responsibility shifts if a state fails to live up to its (primary) duty to protect citizens living on its territory.

The Commission on State Sovereignty and Intervention avoided taking a clear stance on this issue. It simply referred to the residual responsibility of the broader community of states[135]—a notion that lacks any legal specificity. The High-Level Panel Report, the Report of the Secretary-General, and the Outcome Document postulate that coercive collective action is to be undertaken through the Security Council.[136] This assumption, however, fails to answer the fundamental question: What if the international community, through the Security Council, fails to exercise its responsibility to protect? Does the burden then shift back to individual states, groups of states, or regional organizations; and, if so, to which states and organizations?

In addition, one finds hardly any evidence that states understand the three substantive components of responsibility to protect (responsibility to prevent, responsibility to react, responsibility to rebuild) in the sense of a positive duty to act under international law. The cautious phrasing of paragraph 139 of the Outcome Document ("[W]e are prepared to take collective action . . . on a case-by-case basis") resulted partly from the unwillingness of Security Council members to concede that the Council has a firm duty to act. States are even less inclined to accept this proposition. Under current international law, their obligations encompass at best the duties identified by the ILC in Article 41 of the 2001 Articles on State Responsibility.

The concept of responsibility to protect may gradually replace the doctrine of humanitarian intervention in the course of the twenty-first century. However, at present, many of the propositions of this concept remain uncertain from a normative point of view or lack support. Responsibility to protect is thus in many ways still a political catchword rather than a legal norm. Further fine-tuning and commitment by states will be required for it to develop into an organizing principle for international society.

133 See in this sense Amerasinghe, *supra* note 1, at 47.

134 *See* RESPONSIBILITY TO PROTECT, *supra* note 2, paras. 6.36, 6.37.

135 *Id.*, para. 2.31.

136 High-Level Panel Report, *supra* note 3, para. 203 ("by the Security Council"); Report of the Secretary-General, *supra* note 5, para. 135 ("Security Council may"); Outcome Document, *supra* note 7, para. 139 ("through the Security Council").

Part III
Universal Jurisdiction

[8]

Imagining the International Community: The Constitutive Dimension of Universal Jurisdiction

*Adeno Addis**

ABSTRACT

The assertion of prescriptive and adjudicative universal jurisdictions by some countries in relation to a handful of offenses that are classified as international or universal crimes (e.g. genocide) has led to a great deal of controversy. Those who favor universal jurisdiction argue that certain acts (often crimes) affect all of us, not just the specific individual or group of victims or the country of which the victims are nationals. It is therefore legitimate, they argue, for any state to punish or suppress such acts regardless of any traditional jurisdictional connection between the alleged acts and the state asserting jurisdiction. The availability of universal jurisdiction is premised on the presumed effect of certain crimes on humanity as a whole. Those who commit these offenses are referred to as *hostis humani generis*—enemies of human kind. Skeptics argue that the idea of universal jurisdiction is conceptually incoherent, inconsistent with the principle of political self-determination, and has great potential to be an instrument of political mischief. While they disagree on the conceptual coherence and utility of the notion of universal jurisdiction, both proponents and opponents view its function in purely instrumental terms, to provide the condition for punishing or suppressing certain offenses that affect all of us. This article argues that universal jurisdiction also serves another, less articulated purpose. It has a constitutive function as well. It is partly a process through which the identity of the international community is imagined and enacted. It is an expression of a sense of ourselves (a community of humankind) at

* *Adeno Addis* is the William Ray Forrester Professor of Public and Constitutional Law at Tulane University Law School. He received his B.A. and LL.B (Hons) from Macquarie University (Australia) and an LL.M. and a J.S.D. from Yale.

For helpful comments on an earlier version of this article, I would like to thank Marjorie Kornhauser, Jonathan Nash, Michael Vitiello, Keith Werhan, and Siegfried Wiessner.

given moments of time. This article argues that neglect of this constitutive dimension leads to an incomplete analysis of universal jurisdiction.

I. INTRODUCTION

A great deal of controversy surrounds the concept of universal jurisdiction. Those who favor it argue that certain acts (often crimes)[1] affect all of us, not just the specific individual, group of victims, or country of which the victims are nationals. As such, any state may legitimately prescribe to sanction anyone who allegedly committed any of those acts regardless of any jurisdictional connection between the alleged acts and the state asserting jurisdiction. The availability of universal jurisdiction is, therefore, premised on the presumed effect of those crimes on humanity as a whole. Those who commit these offenses are, we are told, "*hostis humani generis*"—enemies of all mankind.[2] Yet apart from the simple assertion that the international community shares an interest in suppressing or punishing those crimes, the precise connection between those crimes and humanity has never been clearly articulated.

Those who are skeptical of the notion of universal jurisdiction contend that the idea is conceptually incoherent, inconsistent with the principle of political self-determination, and has the potential to be an instrument of political mischief. It is incoherent, they say, because the idea of a crime against humankind is a metaphysical absurdity. Crimes are committed against individuals by individuals, not against an abstract entity known as "humanity," "humankind," or "the international community."[3] The victims and the perpetrators are nationals of a country, not citizens of an international community. As Benjamin Barber notes in his skeptical observation about cosmopolitanism, "No one actually lives 'in the world of which the cos-

1. Although universal jurisdiction has generally been exercised in the form of criminal law, international law does not preclude the application of non-criminal law as part of universal jurisdiction. One, for example, could think of civil remedies for victims of piracy. For the view that the concept of universal jurisdiction "is increasingly finding expression in the civil context," see Beth Van Schaack, *Justice Without Borders: Universal Civil Jurisdiction*, 99 Am. Soc'y Int'l L. Proc. 120, 120 (2005).
2. For a very early use of the term, see 4 William Blackstone, Commentaries 71 (quoting Sir Edward Coke).
3. The position here is analogous to what I have referred to as "methodological individualism" in an earlier article. The methodological individualist, who is hostile to the idea of group rights, contends that only the individual is the ultimate agent of action and therefore the only agent to which a moral right could attach. Groups are merely collections of individual agents and thus the idea of a group right is a metaphysical absurdity. *See* Adeno Addis, *Individualism, Communitarianism, and the Rights of Ethnic Minorities*, 67 Notre Dame L. Rev. 615, 630–31 (1991). The analogy here is clear. States (territorial communities) are viewed as analogous to individuals and thus as the only legitimate sources of rights under international law. The international community is viewed as amorphous and as methodologically absurd as are groups. In the same way that methodological individualists see groups as mere collections of individuals, the international community is seen as a mere collection of states.

mopolitan wishes us to be good citizens.'"[4] That is, to the extent that rights could attach to communities, no such communities or attachments exist at the international level. If the idea of national communities is an abstraction, then the concept of an international community is even more so.[5]

Universal jurisdiction is also inconsistent with the notion of political self- determination, the critics assert, because it allows the institutions of one political community to revise decisions and arrangements made by another political community.[6] A claim of universal jurisdiction may allow one state to intimidate and harass another state (likely a small and politically vulnerable state[7]) or its officials. International politics are then played out in the courts of individual states[8] and critics observe that this is detrimental to international politics, international relations, and the judicial process.[9]

---

4. Benjamin Barber, *Constitutional Faith*, *in* For Love of Country: Debating the Limits of Patriotism 30, 34 (Joshua Cohen ed., 1996). *See also* Michael Walzer, *Spheres of Affection*, *in* For Love of Country, *supra*, at 125, 125 ("I am not even aware that there is a world such that one could be a citizen of it. No one has ever offered me citizenship, or described the naturalization process, or enlisted me in the world's institutional structures, or given me an account of its decision procedures (I hope they are democratic), or provided me with a list of the benefits and obligations of citizenship, or shown me the world's calendar and the common celebrations and commemorations of its citizens.").
5. For an early observation that the international community is a fiction, see Nicolas-Socrate Politis, *Le Problème des limitations de la souveraintè et de la théorie de l'abus des droits dans les rapports internationaux*, 6 R.C.A.D.I. 1, 6 (1925), *quoted in* Nathaniel Berman, *"But the Alternative Is Despair": European Nationalism and the Modern Renewal of International Law*, 106 Harv. L. Rev. 1792, 1807 (1993) ("Behold the vain fiction of the State, there is only one real personality; that is the individual. . . . If the State is a pure abstraction, the international community, as it has been conceived hitherto . . . is an even greater abstraction: an immense sum of fictions.").
6. By "arrangements" I mean to include all kinds of settlements that members of the political community have reached to put their turbulent history behind by either declining to prosecute alleged perpetrators of crimes or by granting amnesty. A good example is the Pinochet situation. *See also* Jeffrey Gettleman, *Uganda Peace Hinges on Amnesty for Brutality*, N.Y. Times, 15 Sep. 2006, at A7.
7. *See* Michael Kirby, *Universal Jurisdiction and Judicial Reluctance: A New "Fourteen Points," in* Universal Jurisdiction: National Courts and the Prosecution of Serious Crimes Under International Law 240, 252 (Stephen Macedo ed., 2004) (Justice Kirby notes "Some judges, concerned about . . . issues of comity, will point out that the assertions of universal jurisdiction before courts have, so far, generally involved the courts of developed countries. . . . However, such judges might question whether this situation would remain the case if judicial assertions of universal jurisdiction became common."). *See also* Kingsley Chiedu Moghalu, Global Justice: The Politics of War Crimes Trials 100 (2006) (There is a "justified concern that [universal jurisdiction] can only be exercised against citizens of weaker nations by the courts of powerful states.").
8. Henry Kissinger, who opposes the idea of universal jurisdiction warns against "judicial tyranny." Henry Kissinger, *The Pitfalls of Universal Jurisdiction: Risking Judicial Tyranny*, Foreign Aff., July–Aug. 2001, at 86 ("The danger [of universal jurisdiction] lies in pushing the effort to extremes that risk substituting the tyranny of judges for that of governments: historically, the dictatorship of the virtuous has often led to inquisitions and even witch-hunts."). One might, of course, think that given his role as the United States Secretary of State during a period where a great deal of human rights violations occurred, especially in Latin America by regimes that were strongly supported by the United States, Kissinger has more than an academic interest in the topic. Indeed, there have been some attempts in Europe and elsewhere to get him indicted for certain international crimes.
9. Ann-Marie Slaughter, *Defining the Limits: Universal Jurisdiction and National Courts*, *in* Universal Jurisdiction, *supra* note 7, at 168, 168 ("The result [of universal jurisdiction] is a

While they disagree on the conceptual coherence and utility of the idea of universal jurisdiction, both proponents and opponents view its function only in instrumental terms—to provide the condition for punishing (and suppressing) certain offenses that are regarded as offenses against all of us. This article argues that universal jurisdiction serves another, less articulated purpose; it has a constitutive function as well. It is partly a process through which the international community imagines its identity.[10] This article argues that neglect of the constitutive dimension of universal jurisdiction has led to an incomplete analysis of the notion of universal jurisdiction.[11]

The idea that jurisdictional issues are partly about constituting and affirming political communities and identities is not new.[12] Jurisdiction, just like the rule of law itself, is not just about getting the substantive or procedural question right, but it is also "an expression of a sense of ourselves as a single, historical community."[13] As this article shows, the crimes that give rise to universal jurisdiction properly so called[14] are simultaneously constitutive and expressive of the international community at given historical moments.

---

potentially dramatic extension of judicial power and a corresponding threat to judicial legitimacy.").

10. As I shall show later, the idea of imagined communities is that of Benedict Anderson's. Benedict Anderson, Imagined Communities: Reflections on the Origin and Spread of Nationalism (2d. ed. 1991). The role of international norms as means of imagining an international community was expressed by Hedley Bull thirty years ago. *See* Hedley Bull, The Anarchic Society: A Study of Order in World Politics 80 (1977) ("[Norms of cosmopolitan justice] are ideas which seek to spell out what is right or good for the world as a whole, for an imagined *civitas maxima* or cosmopolitan society to which all individuals belong and to which their interests should be subordinate.").

11. In this regard I take Joseph Raz's side in his dispute with Ronald Dworkin in relation to whether law is to be understood exclusively as a means of doing (instrumentally) or whether it should also partly be seen as a means of being (as a means of constituting who we are). Dworkin accuses Raz of misunderstanding the nature of law when the latter claims that "[i]n large measure what we study when we study the nature of law is the nature of our own self-understanding." *See* Joseph Raz, *Can There Be a Theory of Law, in* Blackwell Guide to the Philosophy of Law and Legal Theory 324, 331 (Martin P. Golding & William A. Edmundson eds., 2005). Dworkin asserts, somewhat too quickly, that law has no such role. "[I]f we want to study our own self-consciousness we would do much better to turn to fiction, politics, biography, depth psychology , and social sciences. We reflect on the character of law to know what we must do, not what we are." Ronald Dworkin, Justice in Robes 229 (2006). It is somewhat puzzling that Dworkin who has always viewed law as an interpretive enterprise, deeply linked to a particular culture and history, would make the claim that there is a sharp distinction between who we are and what we are supposed to do. What we are to do is to a great extent suggested by who we are. In any case, I shall argue that jurisdiction (and by implication law) is constitutive of who we are as it is a guide of what we are meant to do.

12. Anthony D'Amato, *The Concept of Human Rights in International Law,* 82 Colum. L. Rev. 1110, 1113 (1982).

13. Paul W. Kahn, *Speaking Law to Power: Popular Sovereignty, Human Rights, and the New International Order,* 1 Chi. J. Int'l L. 1, 4 (2000). For the proposition that jurisdiction is about communities and the ability of people to speak as communities, see Robert Cover, *The Folktales of Justice: Tales of Jurisdiction,* 14 Cap. U. L. Rev. 179, 181 (1985).

14. Strictly speaking, universal jurisdiction refers only to the jurisdiction that states are allowed to assert under customary international law. The crimes over which every state is permitted to assert jurisdiction in the absence of any connection between the act being

Scholars from various fields have recognized two different types or categories of norms: regulative and constitutive.[15] While the former order and constrain behavior, the latter create new actors, interests, or categories of actions. Universal jurisdiction norms serve both of these purposes by creating an international community of interest while also regulating the behavior of certain actors within that community. The norm of universal jurisdiction is therefore simultaneously regulative and constitutive.

II. UNIVERSAL JURISDICTION: A BRIEF OUTLINE

It is conventional wisdom among international legal scholars and legal practitioners that international law places a limit on the authority of states to apply their laws extraterritorially.[16] That extraterritorial limitation has, however, been relaxed over the years. States are now allowed to assert prescriptive jurisdiction[17] over acts and issues that have some connection to, or effect on, them even if those acts and issues occurred and arose outside their territories. Thus, a state may regulate not only conduct within its territory but also foreign acts that have substantial or intended effect on its territory.[18] A state may also regulate the conduct of its citizens anywhere in the world.[19] It may pass laws to regulate foreign conduct that threatens its

---

regulated and the regulating state are often listed as genocide, slavery, crimes against humanity, war crimes, piracy, and torture.

15. *See* Martha Finnemore & Kathryn Sikkink, *International Norm Dynamics and Political Change*, 52 INT'L ORG. 887, 891 (1998).
16. *See, e.g.*, RESTATEMENT (THIRD) OF FOREIGN RELATIONS LAW OF THE UNITED STATES §§ 402–404 (1987); Kenneth C. Randal, *Universal Jurisdiction Under International Law*, 66 TEX. L. REV. 785, 785–88 (1988); RESTATEMENT (THIRD) OF FOREIGN RELATIONS LAW OF THE UNITED STATES § 402 (1987) ("[A] state has jurisdiction to prescribe law with respect to conduct that, wholly or in substantial part, takes place within its territory."); IVAN A. SHEARER, STARK'S INTERNATIONAL LAW 184 (1994) ("The exercise of jurisdiction by state over property, persons, acts or events occurring within its territory is clearly conceded by international law to all members of the society of states."); IAN BROWNLIE, PRINCIPLES OF PUBLIC INTERNATIONAL LAW 300–303 (4th ed. 1990). "The principle that the courts of the place where the crime is committed may exercise jurisdiction has received universal recognition . . . ." *Id.* at 300.
17. Prescriptive jurisdiction is "the authority of a state to make its law applicable to persons or activities." RESTATEMENT (THIRD) OF FOREIGN RELATIONS LAW OF THE UNITED STATES pt. IV, introductory note (1987).
18. *See* RESTATEMENT (THIRD) OF FOREIGN RELATIONS LAW OF THE UNITED STATES § 402 (1987) ("[A] state has jurisdiction to prescribe law with respect to . . . conduct outside its territory that has or is intended to have substantial effect within its territory.").
19. This is referred to as the *nationality principle* of prescriptive jurisdiction. *See* RESTATEMENT (THIRD) OF FOREIGN RELATIONS LAW OF THE UNITED STATES § 402 (1987). A state may, for example, prohibit its citizens from fighting in other peoples' wars or from traveling to other countries for the purpose of having sex with minors. The United States prohibits both of these. In relation to the former, see Neutrality Act, 18 U.S.C. § 960 (2006). In relation to the latter, see Prosecutorial Remedies and Other Tools to end the Exploitation of Children Today (PROTECT) Act of 2003 § 105, 18 U.S.C. § 2423 (2006). Another example would be the Foreign Corrupt Practices Act of 1977, 15 U.S.C. § 78dd-2. *See also* BROWNLIE, *supra* note 16, at 303.

national security or the operation of its government.[20] And, although it is less accepted than the bases of extraterritorial jurisdiction outlined above, a state may also assert extraterritorial jurisdiction over certain foreign acts that harm or are intended to harm its nationals.[21]

Put simply, under international law a state is allowed to regulate acts or activities that have some connection with it, although such extraterritorial application of a state's laws is generally said to be subject to a "reasonableness" limitation.[22] These prescriptive jurisdictions are thought to be justified by the existence of what Ronald Dworkin refers to, in another context, as "associative or communal obligations."[23] For there to be valid prescriptive jurisdiction, the regulated person or act must be connected, however thickly or thinly, to the political community we call the state. This is what might be referred to as the political conception of jurisdiction, for the authority is premised on some notion of membership to a political community.[24]

---

20. *Protective principle* is the name given to this basis of jurisdiction. *See* Restatement (Third) of Foreign Relations Law of the United States § 402 cmt. f (1987). *See also* Shearer, *supra* note 16, at 211 ("International law recognizes that each state may exercise jurisdiction over crimes against its security and integrity or its vital economic interests."); Brownlie, *supra* note 16, at 304 ("Nearly all states assume jurisdiction over aliens for acts done abroad which affect the security of the state, a concept which takes in a variety of political offences, but is not necessarily confined to political acts."). There has been some controversy both about the existence and scope of the protective principle, for without more specification the idea of harm could encompass a wide variety of conduct. The resistance may be lessened if the prescriptive authority is limited to how it is described in the text of the essay accompanying this note.
21. This is referred to as the *passive personality* principle.

> The passive personality principle asserts that a state may apply law—particularly criminal law—to an act committed outside its territory by a person not its national where the victim of the act was its national. The principle has not been generally accepted for ordinary torts or crimes, but it is increasingly accepted as applied to terrorists and other organized attacks on a state's nationals by reason of their nationality, or to assassination of a state's diplomatic representatives or other officials.

Restatement (Third) of Foreign Relations Law of the United States § 402 cmt. g (1987). *See also* Brownlie, *supra* note 16, at 303 ("This is the least justifiable, as a general principle, of the various bases of jurisdiction . . . .").
22. *See* Restatement (Third) of Foreign Relations Law § 403 (1987). Whether international law actually requires this limitation is a subject of some controversy. For the negative position, see Phillip R. Trimble, *The Supreme Court and International Law: The Demise of Restatement § 403*, 89 Am. J. Int'l L. 53 (1995). For the affirmative side, see Andreas F. Lowenfeld, International Litigation and the Quest for Reasonableness (1996).
23. Ronald Dworkin, Law's Empire 196 (1986).
24. Noah Feldman uses the phrase "political conception of law" to refer to a theory of law "that makes either consent or some weaker form of communal association a condition of law." Noah Feldman, *Cosmopolitan Law,* 116 Yale L. J. 1023, 1050 (2007). This is what Aristotle referred to as "particular law." Aristotle, Rhetoric bk. 1, ch. 13, line 4–9 (W. Rhys Roberts trans., Dover Publ'g 2004) ("Particular law is that which each community lays down and applies to its own members: this is partly written and partly unwritten. Universal law is the law of nature. For there really is, as every one to some extent divines, a natural justice and injustice that is binding on all men, even those who have no association or covenant with each other."). What

Another category of jurisdiction requires no connection at all between the state asserting jurisdiction and the offense or conduct regulated. When a state asserts authority to prescribe under these circumstances,[25] and without the limitation of the "reasonableness" requirement, it has asserted universal jurisdiction.[26] This is what might be called a cosmopolitan notion of jurisdiction. Unlike the political notion of jurisdiction that informs other bases of prescriptive jurisdiction, the jurisdictional authority in universal jurisdiction does not stem from any connection with the political community we call the state. Political membership, thin or thick, is not a prerequisite.

Some oft-cited examples of the exercise of universal jurisdiction, which sometimes are referred to as "universal jurisdiction plus,"[27] can, however, be explained on the bases of other traditional forms of jurisdiction.[28] These forms of jurisdiction will not be considered universal jurisdiction in this article because they display some basis of political membership, however thin it may be. If something "plus" is present, then the "plus" should be, on its own, a sufficient ground for the assertion of jurisdiction. If, however, the "plus" is insufficient on its own, then there is no traditional jurisdictional connection and universal jurisdiction may apply. The notion of "universal jurisdiction plus" confuses more than it enlightens.

Under international law, states are permitted[29] to assert universal jurisdiction in relation to a handful of offenses. The list of offenses that are subject

---

Aristotle refers to as universal law is what Feldman would call cosmopolitan law, although Feldman (unlike Aristotle) does not rely on natural law for its justification.

25. *See* Restatement (Third) of Foreign Relations Law of the United States § 404 (1987).

26. A good example of a state law asserting universal jurisdiction is found in the German Code of Crimes Against International Law. The Code provides: "This act shall apply to all criminal offences against international law designated under this Act, to serious criminal offences designated therein even when the offence was committed abroad and bears no relation to Germany." Völkerstrafgesetzbuch [VStGB] [Code of Crimes against International Law] 26 June 2002, Bundesgesetzblatt [BGBl. 1] 2002 at 2254, § 1, *translated in* Gerhard Werle, Principles of International Criminal Law 428 (2005).

27. Slaughter, *supra* note 9, at 170.

28. Those who prosecuted Eichmann and Demjanjuk in Israel, for example, cited protective and passive personality principles. *See* CrimC (Jer) 20/61 Israel v. Eichmann [1961] 45 IsrDC 3, *translated in* 36 Int'l L. Rep. 18, 26 (1968) ("From the point of view of international law, the power of the State of Israel to enact the Law in question [Nazis and Nazi Collaborators (Punishment) Law] . . . is based . . . on a dual foundation: the universal character of the crimes in question and their specific character intended to exterminate the Jewish people."). To the extent that Israel could be said to have properly asserted those bases of jurisdiction, then one would not even worry about the question of universal jurisdiction which was also the basis for the claim of prescriptive and adjudicative jurisdiction. The same law was applied to John Demjanjuk, though he was ultimately acquitted on grounds of mistaken identity, CrimA 347/88 Demjanjuk v. Israel [1993] IsrSC 47(4) 221.

29. Some say that states are "obligated" to assert jurisdiction. *See, e.g.*, Geoffrey Robertson, Crimes Against Humanity: The Struggle for Global Justice 291, 311 (3d ed. 2006) ("[T]here is in international law a duty on states to punish crimes against humanity . . . even if this means rejecting or annulling amnesty."). I shall explain later why some people argue that universal jurisdiction ought to be regarded as a duty rather than a right of states.

to universal jurisdiction may develop as a matter of customary international law or by virtue of a treaty regime.[30] This article is mostly concerned with universal jurisdiction that is permitted under customary international law.[31] Currently, states are allowed to assert universal jurisdiction over a handful of crimes as a matter of customary international law: piracy, slave trade, genocide, crimes against humanity, war crimes, and torture. Although there is general agreement that these offenses give rise to universal jurisdiction, it is often not clear why these and not other offenses are on the list. Why, for example, is forced disappearance, the preferred method of Latin American dictators for dealing with opponents in the 1970s and 1980s, not a good candidate for inclusion?[32] What about terrorist offenses?[33] Put simply, what are the criteria by which certain conducts are selected as appropriate for universal jurisdiction? To answer this question, this article will attempt to give a plausible explanation for the existing list and provide for a theory of change that can allow us to add or subtract from it. This task will have a descriptive (positive) and normative dimension to it.

Current accounts of both universal jurisdiction and the list of crimes that are said to give rise to such jurisdiction are unsatisfactory. The next section explores briefly the various justifications that have been or can be suggested for the existence of universal jurisdiction and for the list of international crimes that lead to its assertion. This is followed by the advance of an alternative account that explains more fully both the idea of universal jurisdiction and the offenses that are said to lead to such jurisdiction.

---

30. Customary international law is the law that emerges from customary practices and beliefs of nations. It arises "from a general and consistent practice of states followed by them from a sense of legal obligation" referred to as *opino juris.* Restatement (Third) of the Foreign Relations Law of the United States § 102(2) (1987); Statute of International Court of Justice, art. 38(1)(b), *annexed to* U.N. Charter, *signed* 26 June 1945, 59 Stat. 1055, 1060, T.S. No. 993 (*entered into force* 24 Oct. 1945) (noting that sources of international law applied by the Court include "international custom, as evidence of a general practice accepted as law").
31. The international law of jurisdiction is generally a customary law. As a conceptual matter universal jurisdiction properly so called can only be a matter of customary international law, for a treaty-based jurisdiction can only bind those states which have signed and ratified the treaty. *See* United States v. Yousef, 327 F.3d 56, 96 n.29 (2d. Cir. 2003).
32. Universal Declaration on the Protection of All Persons from Enforced Disappearance, G.A. Res. 47/133, U.N. GAOR, 47th Sess., Agenda Item 97(b), U.N. Doc. A/Res/47/133 (1993) (a non-legally binding document, provides for the exercise of universal jurisdiction for acts of forced disappearance). *See* Mary Robinson, *Preface, in* Universal Jurisdiction, *supra* note 7, at 15, 16. Amnesty International, for example, includes both forced disappearance and extrajudicial killings as conducts subject to universal jurisdiction.
33. *See* Restatement (Third) of Foreign Relations Law § 404 (1987) (referring to "certain acts of terrorism" as crimes that would "perhaps" lead to universal jurisdiction). *See also* United States v. Yunis, 924 F.2d 1086, 1091 (D.C. Cir. 1991) (quoting Restatement (Third) Foreign Relations Law of the United States § 404 (1987)).

III. WHAT MAKES AN OFFENSE ELIGIBLE FOR UNIVERSAL JURISDICTION? EXISTING ACCOUNTS

A. The Power of Practice

One straightforward answer to the question as to why certain offenses are regarded as eligible to universal jurisdiction might be simply because the international community has indicated, either through custom or through conventional law, that these are offenses that deserve such treatment. The authority here is the supposed consensus among member states; the job of the scholar ("publicist," as she is often referred to by international scholars, other legal actors, and international documents)[34] is descriptive and empirical rather than normative. The answer to the question "why this list?" is "because that is what state practice shows." The validity of the practice derives from nothing more than the practice itself. In this sense, Joseph Raz's observation that "practice-based law is self-vindicating" seems to apply.[35]

However, this response is unsatisfactory. Even if one were to assume consensus on the list of offenses—which some doubt, at least in relation to actual practice[36]—it would still be important to explain why there is consensus on this rather than another list. The mere existence of a practice does not tell us much about what informs it or how it may develop over time. While it is true that practice can be self-validating, to the extent that it occurs within permissible moral parameters, we must be careful to note that the reasons for following practice "are not entirely derivable from the

---

34. *See* Statute of the International Court of Justice, art. 38(1)(d), *annexed to* U.N. Charter, *signed* 26 June 1945, 59 Stat. 1055, T.S. No. 993 (*entered into force* 24 Oct. 1945).

35. Joseph Raz, *On the Authority and Interpretation of Constitutions: Some Preliminaries*, *in* Constitutionalism: Philosophical Foundations 152, 173 (Larry Alexander ed., 1998).

36. *See* Luc Reydams, Universal Jurisdiction: International and Municipal Legal Perspectives (2003) (gives a detailed survey of cases in many nations and found only twenty cases in the past ten years). *See also* M. Cherif Bassiouni, *The History of Universal Jurisdiction and Its Place in International Law*, *in* Universal Jurisdiction, *supra* note 7, at 39, 50–54. Referring to three of the most commonly found offenses on customary international law universal jurisdiction list—war crimes, crimes against humanity and genocide—Bassiouni claims that there is no sufficient state practice. In relation to war crimes "there are [so] few [national prosecutions of such cases] that it would be incorrect to conclude that they constitute customary law practice." *Id* at 51. Some have argued that the relevant practice is the fact that "almost two-thirds of all states have some legislation permitting their courts to exercise universal jurisdiction over conduct amounting to genocide, crimes against humanity, war crimes, torture, and other crimes under international law." *See* Lorna McGregor, *Addressing the Relationship Between State Immunity and Jus Cogens Norms: A Comparative Assessment*, *in* International Prosecution of Human Rights Crimes 69, 86 (Wolfgang Kaleck et al. eds., 2007) (citing Amnesty Int'l, Universal Jurisdiction: The Duty of States to Enact and Implement Legislation (2001)). For a response to that contention, see Arrest Warrant of 11 Apr. 2000 (Dem. Rep. Congo v. Belg.), 2002 I.C.J. 3, 63 (14 Feb.) (separate joint opinion of Judges Higgins, Kooijmans & Buergenthal).

fact that [such practice exists]. [Practices] evolve . . . in order to solve a pre-existing social problem."[37] There must be "something valuable in the practice . . . for it to give rise to reasons for action, beyond the fact that [it] is there and just happens to be followed."[38]

Put simply, the notion of practice as a source of authority, even if the practice exists as an empirical matter, does not answer two basic questions: what justifies universal jurisdiction as a conceptual and normative matter, and why do we have this rather than another list of offenses? Perhaps an adequate answer to the first question will help us answer the second.

B. The Heinousness[39] of the Crimes

Another response to the question of what makes an offense eligible for universal jurisdiction is offenses that are so heinous that they offend or diminish all of us to such an extent that every state is entitled to punish or suppress them.[40] Reliance on heinousness as a source of explanation, however, suffers from three

37. *See* Andrei Marmor, *Are Constitutions Legitimate?*, 20 Can. J. L. & Juris. 69, 81 (2007).
38. *Id.* One could argue that customary international law (CIL) of which all of the norms that are said to be subject to universal jurisdiction are a part is not thought to need any explanation for its validity other than the fact that the practice exists. That is true, but the nature of the norms that concern us here (*jus cogens* norms) are a special kind of CIL requiring further explanation and functional justification. After all, unlike other CIL norms, these norms cannot be changed as easily by subsequent practice or even by a subsequent treaty. Only a peremptory norm of similar importance or significance will replace a *jus cogens* norm. Also, to the extent that we are concerned with a radical departure from the normal process of jurisdiction, a functional justification seems to be in order. In any case, it seems to me that all norms, including CIL norms, assume "something valuable in the practice" and it seems important to inquire into the "social problem" which it is adopted to solve.
39. "Heinous" is defined by the Oxford English Dictionary as "highly criminal or wicked, utterly odious or atrocious." The Israeli prosecutor of Adolf Eichmann referred to the crime of which the defendant was accused as "heinous." Hannah Arendt, Eichmann in Jerusalem: A Report on the Banality of Evil 260 (Penguin Books 2006) (1963). *See also* Moghalu, *supra* note 7, at 77.
40. Stephen Macedo, *Introduction, in* Universal Jurisdiction, supra note 7, at 1, 4 ("Universal jurisdiction is the principle that certain crimes are so heinous . . . that a state is entitled or even obliged to undertake legal proceedings without regard to where the crime was committed or the nationality of the perpetrators or the victims."); Peter Weiss, *The Future of Universal Jurisdiction, in* International Prosecution of Human Rights Crimes, *supra* note 36, at 29, 30 ("[E]very act of torture, every violation of what we have come to call a basic human right, diminishes each one of us, no matter by whom or where committed. Universal jurisdiction is [an] expression of this yearning . . . ."); Leila Nadya Sadat, *Redefining Universal Jurisdiction*, 35 New Eng. L. Rev. 241, 244 (2001) ("Application of the theory of universal jurisdiction . . . is predicated largely on the notion that some crimes are so heinous that they offend the interest of all humanity—indeed, imperil civilization itself."); Donald Francis Donovan & Anthea Roberts, *The Emerging Recognition of Universal Civil Jurisdiction*, 100 Am. J. Int'l L. 142, 143 (2006) ("In modern times, universal jurisdiction has been founded on the sheer heinousness of certain crimes, such as genocide and torture, which are universally condemned and which every state has an interest in repressing even in the absence of traditional connecting factors.").

serious shortcomings. First, as a descriptive enterprise it is both under-inclusive and over-inclusive. It is not, for example, clear why piracy, the paradigmatic international crime subject to universal jurisdiction, could be considered heinous on par with slavery and genocide.[41] Indeed, the history of piracy—where government sponsored piracies were tolerated—seems to suggest that it was not the nature of the act but the nature of the actor that mattered.[42] It would stretch any sense of logic to say that heinousness should depend on who engages in a particular act rather than the act itself. It is also under-inclusive to the extent that many crimes that devalue and even destroy human life itself are not part of the list of crimes that are heinous and diminish all of us. Extra-judicial killing, terrorist acts, and forced disappearance are examples.

Second, and perhaps more important, there appear to be no principles by which one could decide as a normative matter which crimes are heinous. Some have used another phrase to describe heinousness—that it shocks the conscience.[43] But that simply gives us another phrase to worry about. Why do these crimes shock the conscience, at least more so than others? Without more guidance it would be hard to defend the existing list and to advocate an addition or subtraction to it. Both for descriptive and transformative[44] purposes, one would need a normative theory.

---

41. *Cf.* Christopher C. Joyner, *Arresting Impunity: The Case for Universal Jurisdiction in Bringing War Criminals to Accountability*, 59 Law & Contemp. Probs. 153, 165 n.48 (1996). Joyner claims that piracy was considered a "particularly heinous and wicked act[] . . . ." It is not quite clear why it would have been thought as such an act in an era when states engaged in far more destructive acts. Even if piracies were properly viewed as heinous in the nineteenth and early twentieth centuries, I am not sure that they could or should be viewed more shocking than many other offenses that are committed now which are not subject to universal jurisdiction.
42. *See* Gerry Simpson, *Piracy and the Origins of Enmity*, *in* Time, History and International Law 219, 228 (Matthew Craven, Malgosia Fitzmaurice & Maria Vogiatzi eds., 2007) ("[I]t is not the quality of the act that is decisive but rather the personality of the actor."). *See also id.* at 226 ("The pirate, then, is not marked by his or her plundering psychology but rather by the absence of public authority."); Eugene Kontorovich, *Implementing* Sosa v. Alvarez-Machain*: What Piracy Reveals About the Limits of the Alien Tort Statute*, 80 Notre Dame L. Rev. 111, 136–45 (2004).
43. Moghalu, *supra* note 7, at 77 ("Universal jurisdiction is a doctrine that asserts that some crimes are so shocking in the affront they represent to all nations that the national courts of any country can and should bring the perpetrators to justice."). *See also* CrimC (Jer) 20/61 Israel v. Eichmann [1961] 45 IsrDC 3, *translated in* 36 Int'l L. Rep. 18, 26 (1968) ("These crimes, which struck at the whole of mankind and shocked the conscience of nations, are grave offences against the law of nations itself (*delicta juris gentium*)."). Sumner B. Twiss, *Torture, Justification, and Human Rights: Toward an Absolute Proscription*, 29 Hum. Rts. Q. 346, 353 (2007) (referring to the debate within the Third Committee during the drafting of the Universal Declaration of Human Rights where participants referred to such Nazi acts as medical experimentation and other maltreatments in the context of Article 4 (torture) as "shocking the conscience of humanity"). M. Cherif Bassiouni, *International Crimes: Jus Cogens and Obligation Erga Omnes*, 59 Law & Contemp. Probs. 63, 69 (1996) (The only way to make sense of *jus cogens* norms is to understand that "certain crimes affect the interests of the world community as a whole because they threaten the peace and security of humankind and they *shock the conscience of humanity*.") (emphasis added).
44. By "transformative" I simply mean adding to or perhaps even subtracting from the list of heinous crimes.

Third, even if one were able to identify which crimes are heinous enough to include on the list, it would not be the end of the problem. One would still need to show a connection between heinousness and the offense to "the interest of all humanity."[45] After all, the suggestion is that these heinous crimes affect all of humanity and are thus of universal concern. What "interests" do they affect and how precisely do they affect them? In a world where the default rule is that a connection to a political community is the legitimate source of prescriptive jurisdictional authority, universal jurisdiction—a radical departure from the default rule—must be defended with good reasons. Yet, those who invoke "heinousness" as a source of justification do not attempt to explain how precisely the notion of heinousness justifies this radical departure.

C. The Probability that the Particular Crime Would Go Unpunished (The Desire for a "No Law-Free Zone")[46]

Perhaps another rationale for designating a crime as appropriate for universal jurisdiction is the assumption that certain crimes, by their very nature, are likely to go unpunished if some form of universal jurisdiction is not available.[47] This argument possesses some merit. To the extent that international law is progressively ushering in a world with no "legal free zone"[48] it makes sense to impose universal jurisdiction for crimes that are likely to go unpunished in the absence of universal jurisdiction.

This may explain why some crimes are included on the list. One may, for example, be able to explain piracy on this ground, given that the crime takes place on the high seas and supposedly beyond the jurisdiction of any state.[49]

45. Sadat, *supra* note 40, at 244.
46. "No place on earth would be treated as a law-free zone." Feldman, *supra* note 24, at 1067.
47. "[T]he rationale of universal jurisdiction is the need to end impunity for heinous conduct." Donald Francis Donovan & Anthea Roberts, *The Emerging Recognition of Universal Civil Jurisdiction*, 100 Am. J. Int'l L. 142, 159 (2006). "Historically, universal jurisdiction was exercised over serious crimes, such as piracy, that were difficult to prosecute using traditional bases of jurisdiction because they occurred beyond state borders, such as on the high seas." *Id.* at 143; Joyner, *supra* note 41, at 153 ("Since war criminals often operate with the knowledge and assistance of local political and legal authorities, domestic law does little to deter these actors. Prevention and punishment of war crimes thus become legal concerns and moral obligations, not just for those governments in whose territory crimes occurred, but for all states."). *See also id.* at 166.
48. Feldman, *supra* note 24, at 1067.
49. It is, however, reasonable to argue that pirates would always be subject to the jurisdiction of a nation under the traditional bases of prescriptive jurisdiction to the extent that the attack will be on a ship registered in a particular country, or on individuals who are citizens of a particular nation or property that belongs to citizens (or government) of a particular country. *See* Kontorovich, *supra* note 42, at 151 ("The flaw [of the 'beyond jurisdictional reach'] explanation is that pirates' crimes did not take place in the water on the high seas—they were committed onboard ships. Maritime vessels have always been considered . . . within the jurisdiction of their home states. In short, traditional jurisdictional concepts appear adequate to deal with piracy without recourse to universality.") (emphasis omitted).

Genocide may be another offense that is likely to escape full punishment within the political community in which it occurred. Under the circumstances of genocide, local political and legal systems are under serious stress, often totally dysfunctional, and unable to dispense justice.[50] Alternatively, governments and/or their supports are so implicated in the genocidal acts that it would be foolhardy to expect that national legal institutions would bring the perpetrators to justice. The complicity of the Sudanese government in the Darfur situation is a very good example. Perhaps one could also think of serious war crimes as likely to go unpunished by the legal system of the political communities whose armed forces are alleged to have committed them, especially when those crimes target internal enemies, those perceived as threats to the established order. The same might go for official torture, another form of waging war on those viewed as a threat to the interest of the political community.[51]

On reflection, however, the "filling the legal gap" rationale does not take us much further than the justifications we explored earlier. First, while it may explain some of the offenses on the universal jurisdiction list, it does not explain why others are left out. For example, it does not seem to be the case that extrajudicial killings or forced disappearances are any more likely to be prosecuted by states of which the accused is a national than are piracy, genocide, torture, crimes against humanity, or serious war crimes. The point is that as a descriptive matter, the likelihood of non-prosecution as a rationale for the kind of crimes we consider as properly subject to universal jurisdiction is under-inclusive. Many crimes may go unpunished in a particular country, but that alone can never be the basis for asserting universal jurisdiction. If the purpose is to ensure against legal gaps (no "law-free zones"),[52] then one would have to show that dealing with these and not other offenses is the proper way to fill the gaps.

Second, even if it were true that universal jurisdiction in relation to these offenses is the appropriate way of dealing with legal gaps, it will still be important to explain why a world where legal gaps are filled by the institutions of individual states is in the interest of the international community.

The idea of a blanket of law, without a hole, over our globe cannot fully explain either the idea of universal jurisdiction or the particular list of offenses that give rise to it. Something more than the possibility of non-prosecution is needed, and perhaps the heinousness of the crime is that "something

50. The Rwandan situation may be an example.

51. Often, it is the interests of the ruling elite that are elevated to the interest of the nation.

52. *See* Feldman, *supra* note 24, at 1066–67 ("The set of global legal systems would be morally illegitimate if it allowed law-free zones in which the accident of place or status meant that there was no law at all. Not all law must reach everywhere, but every place and person must be subject to some law. . . . No place on earth would be treated as a law free-zone.").

more." Conceivably, one could assert that those heinous crimes must not go unpunished when states can punish them via universal jurisdiction at a reasonably acceptable cost, but then we are back to the problem of what constitutes heinousness. Furthermore, when is the cost reasonable or acceptable? After all, critics such as Henry Kissinger base their objection to universal jurisdiction on the ground that the cost is unacceptably high.[53]

D. The Fundamental Nature of the Norm that Is Threatened by These Crimes

Here, the concepts of universal jurisdiction, *jus cogens*, and *erga omnes* come together.[54] What makes an offense subject to universal jurisdiction is not necessarily its heinous status, or because the possibility of it going unpunished without universal jurisdiction is low, but rather because the offense is a violation of a fundamental norm (*jus cogens*)[55] giving rise to obligations (*erga omnes*)[56] that

53. *See* Kissinger, *supra* note 8. *See also* Eugene Kontorovich, *The Inefficiency of Universal Jurisdiction*, 2008 U. Ill. L. Rev. 389, 392 (2008) (arguing that universal jurisdiction greatly increases transaction costs and can therefore prevent "the socially optimal use of prosecutorial entitlements by allowing a few states to block amnesties and similar arrangements even when the states supporting them value such a negotiated outcome more than the dissenting states value prosecution.").

54. Larry May, Crimes Against Humanity: A Normative Account 25 (2005) ("[*J*]*us cogens* norms are universal norms that ground 'universal jurisdiction' in international law . . . . [They] give rise to obligations *erga omnes*, obligations that extend to all people."). *See also* Rosanne van Alebeek, *The Pinochet Case: International Human Rights Law on Trial*, 2000 Brit. Y.B. Int'l L. 29, 34 ("[T]he principle [of universal jurisdiction] should now be seen as having its theoretical basis in the concept of *erga omnes* obligations."). It can therefore be argued that all violations of *jus cogens* norms give rise to universal jurisdiction under customary international law. The only dispute may be in relation to torture, but the ICTY got it right when it declared: "[I]t would seem that one of the consequences of the *jus cogens* character bestowed by the international community upon the prohibition of torture is that every State is entitled to investigate, prosecute and punish or extradite individuals accused of torture, who are present in a territory under its jurisdiction." Prosecutor v. Furundzija, Case No. IT-95-17/1-T, Judgment, ¶ 156 (10 Dec. 1998). *See also* Bassiouni, *International Crimes*, *supra* note 43, at 63, 65.

55. *Jus cogens* is defined by the Vienna Convention on the Law of Treaties as "a norm accepted and recognized by the international community of States as a whole as a norm from which no derogation is permitted and which can be modified only by a subsequent norm of general international law having the same character." Vienna Convention on the Law of Treaties art. 53, U.N. Doc. A/CONF.39/27 (1969), 1155 U.N.T.S. 331 (*entered into force* 27 Jan. 1980), *reprinted in* 8 I.L.M. 679 (1969).

56. The concept of *erga omnes* appeared first in Barcelona Traction, Light and Power Co. Ltd. (Belg. v. Spain), 1970 I.C.J. 3, 32 (5 Feb.). The concept was defined as a situation where a state owes an obligation to the "international community as a whole." The Court gave genocide, slavery and acts of aggression as circumstances in which all States have a legal interest in their prohibition and where every State is said to owe obligation to the international community not to engage in those acts.

extend to all people.[57] The obligation is toward the international community as a whole and is derived from general international law.[58]

Before we explore the issue as to what makes a norm fundamental, let us address the argument, most prominently made by Lori Damrosch, that we ought not to see universal jurisdiction as coterminous with *jus cogens*.[59] The argument is that even though violations of *jus cogens* norms may be subject to universal jurisdiction, universal jurisdiction is not limited to the violation of such norms. It could be, and is, asserted in relation to other offenses. The emergence of universal jurisdiction should thus not be tied to *jus cogens* norms. As a general matter, universal jurisdiction should be delinked from peremptory norms. Some treaties have provided for universal jurisdiction for non-peremptory norms. For the purposes of this article though, universal jurisdiction and *jus cogens* norms are linked in that under customary international law the only offenses that can be subject to universal jurisdiction are violations of peremptory norms. At least that seems to be the consensus, and the separate joint opinion of Judges Higgins, Kooijmans, and Buergenthal in *Congo v. Belgium* makes the point explicitly.[60] It is universal jurisdiction under customary international law that is the focus of this article. As it shall be argued later, it is also important, as a normative matter, that we limit the reach of universal jurisdiction (at least under customary international

---

57. Although the full phrase *obligatio erga omnes* seems to suggest that states are obligated rather than simply permitted to prosecute violators of *jus cogens* norms, there is no consensus on whether there is a duty or a right. *See* Bassiouni, *International Crimes, supra* note 43, at 63, 65. I agree with Bassiouni that if we take the notion of a *jus cogens* norm seriously (their non-derogability), then we must ensure that perpetrators are punished one way or another and that would suggest the imposition of a duty. However, even if there is no consensus on the existence of a duty, it is undeniably the case that there is a right to invoke universal jurisdiction to prosecute such crimes. For my purpose it is sufficient that there is such a right.
58. Affirming the decision of the sentencing judge of the Düsseldorf Court of Appeals (*Oberlandesgericht*), which convicted a Bosnian Serb to life imprisonment for the crime of genocide under the universal jurisdiction of the German Criminal Code, the German Constitutional Court observed: "As [one of] the most serious violations of human rights, . . . genocide is the classic case for application of universal jurisdiction, . . . the function of which is to make possible the most complete possible prosecution of crimes against *particularly important legal values of the international community*." Decision of 12 December 2000, Juristen-Zeitung 2001, at 975 (emphasis added), *cited in* Wolfgang Kaleck, *German International Law in Practice: From Leipzig to Karlsruhe, in* International Prosecution of Human Rights Crimes, *supra* note 36, at 93, 99–100.
59. Lori F. Damrosch, *Comment: Connecting the Threads in the Fabric of International Law, in* Universal Jurisdiction, *supra* note 7, at 91. "The process for adding crimes to the category of universal jurisdiction offenses is not the same as the process for adding to the set of *jus cogens* norms." *Id.* at 95.
60. *See* Arrest Warrant of 11 Apr. 2000 (Dem. Rep. Congo v. Belg.), 2002 I.C.J. 3, 81 (14 Feb.) (separate joint opinion of Judges Higgins, Kooijmans & Buergenthal) ("It is equally necessary that universal criminal jurisdiction be exercised only over those crimes regarded as the most heinous by the international community."). The joint opinion then goes on to describe the crimes that are regarded as violations of *jus cogens* norms.

law) to peremptory norms, over which a wide consensus reigns. Universal jurisdiction is more likely to be utilized if it is limited to offenses regarded as fundamental to the constitution and sustenance of a decent international community.

Now, what makes a norm fundamental? A norm may be so in one of two ways. A norm can be constitutive of our very humanity or identity as human beings (what David Luban calls "humanness").[61] Alternatively, it can be an essential element, or constitutive, of the international community, a core element of the international order that we seek to cultivate and project. On this account, offenses that are considered to be offenses against all of us are violations of identity constituting norms—whether it is the human identity or the identity of the international community. In some ways the two identities may be linked. The international community is defined by those norms that tie us together because we share them as humans. We shall return to that issue in the next section.

Universal jurisdiction is cosmopolitan in two senses. It seeks to capture aspects of the individual that transcend the particular community within which that individual is located and by which he is defined (humanness).[62] We may want to refer to this as individualist cosmopolitanism, meaning that the universalism here seeks to capture the essence of the individual across cultures and social locations. Universal jurisdiction also seeks to imagine and cultivate connections and affiliations among individuals and groups that transcend the traditional political communities known to and defined by traditional international law—states. In this sense, universal jurisdiction is about cultivating an international community. We shall refer to this as communitarian cosmopolitanism. As it shall be clear in the course of the arguments in this article, the two cosmopolitanisms assume one another. In either version, cosmopolitanism suggests that for some purposes and measures, human beings form a single moral community. Further, it suggests that in virtue of this moral community, members of the various territorial (political) communities owe one another certain obligations.[63]

---

61. David Luban, *A Theory of Crimes Against Humanity*, 29 Yale L. J. 85, 86–87 (2004) ("'Humanity' [in crimes against humanity] means both the quality of being human—humanness—and the aggregation of all human beings—humankind."). Humanness, therefore, refers to the idea of what it existentially means to be a human being.
62. For the proposition that torture, a violation of a *jus cogens* norm and subject to universal jurisdiction, could be viewed as a process of destroying what it means to be human, see Louis Michael Seidman, *Torture's Truth*, 72 Yale L. J. 881, 907 (2005) ("The problem with torture is not just that the victim's will is commandeered but that it is commandeered by the dehumanizing realization that all that we associate with being human is an illusion."). What is it that torture takes that is the very essence of humanness, the essence of being human? Seidman claims that it is the individual's "choosing capacity." *Id.* at 901.
63. *See* Pauline Kleingeld, *Six Varieties of Cosmopolitanism in Late Eighteenth-Century Germany*, 60 J. Hist. Ideas 505, 506–08 (1999).

IV. IMAGINING COMMUNITIES AND IDENTITIES: THE CONSTITUTIVE DIMENSION OF UNIVERSAL JURISDICTION

Jurisdictional norms, perhaps more than other norms, play an important role in defining communities. They define what a nation, a state, or a city is.[64] To prescribe jurisdictional rules is, therefore, to constitute an identity—to assert that for certain purposes we deem the particular territorial entity as being a community of interests. Traditional international prescriptive jurisdictions define the authority of every state vis-à-vis other states, and consequently they define the very nature of the territorial community we call the state. Universal jurisdiction, on the other hand, can be seen as one process through which we imagine the international community as a community of interest.

It is important to note that the phrase "imagined communities" is not used to suggest that the international community, as constituted by universal jurisdiction, is false or fabricated. Benedict Anderson, who coined the phrase "imagined community" to describe the nation, observes that "all communities larger than primordial villages of face-to-face contact (and perhaps even these) are imagined."[65] They are *imagined* because members of those communities "will never know their fellow-members, meet them, or even hear of them, yet in the minds of each lives the image of their communion."[66] Communities are imagined or constituted in several ways. As Anderson notes, "Communities are to be distinguished, not by their falsity/genuineness, but by the style in which they are imagined."[67] Universal jurisdiction is one way through which the international community is imagined. The process of imagining here is of two kinds: universal jurisdiction assumes the existence of a community as it simultaneously constitutes that community.[68] What is the nature of the international community that is imagined (assumed and constituted) through the provision and exercise of universal jurisdictions?

---

64. D'Amato, *supra* note 12, at 1113 (Jurisdiction comprises the set of "external rules that have defined [the nation] as a 'nation.'"). One could say the same thing about cities and federal states.
65. Anderson, *supra* note 10, at 6.
66. *Id.*
67. *Id.*
68. This ambiguity is captured by one author when he observes: "The doctrine [universal jurisdiction] assumes the existence of—or at least proposes—a community or a *world* society." Moghalu, *supra* note 7, at 77. This simultaneous action of declaration and constitution was referred to as "performative" by the late, great French social theorist—Pierre Bourdieu. *See* Pierre Bourdieu, Language and Symbolic Power 223 (1991) (Performative discourse attempts "to bring about what it asserts in the very act of asserting it."). For the popular entry of the notion of performative discourse, see J.L. Austin, How to Do Things with Words 94 (Harvard Univ. Press 1st ed. 1962) (famously arguing that language cannot only describe things but actually *do* things). Thus, for example, when the president swings a bottle of champagne at a ship and says "I christen this ship the 'USS New Orleans,'" the president is not describing a christening, but performing one. *See id.* at 5–6. Not surprisingly Austin called these sorts of verbal acts "performatives." *Id.* at 6.

A. Diverse Community

Hannah Arendt argued that the salient characteristic of the human condition is the potential for and the reality of diversity.[69] For Arendt, what made the Nazi crime an attack on the human condition was that it was "an attack upon human diversity as such, that is, upon a characteristic of the 'human status' without which the very words 'mankind' or 'humanity' would be devoid of meaning."[70] Genocide is a good example of an attack on diversity, one designed to cure humanity of its salient characteristic, its "infinite plurality."[71] Genocide is an attack on the very nature of what makes an international community, a community of diverse peoples. How is an attack on human diversity an attack on the international community? The attempt to "cure" this or that community of diversity deprives all of us of various possibilities of being. It diminishes us in the literal as well as in the metaphoric sense.

Genocide and crimes against humanity transgress more than the Kantian categorical imperative of treating humans as ends rather than as means to ends.[72] Rather than merely robbing them of their dignity, these crimes make humans "superfluous" qua humans, to use an Arendtian description.[73] In

69. Arendt, *supra* note 39.
70. *Id.* at 268–269. Michael Ignatieff makes a similar argument:

> What it means to be a human being, what defines the very identity we share as a species, is the fact that we are differentiated by race, religion, ethnicity, and individual difference. These differentiations define our identities both as individuals and as species. No other species differentiates itself in this individualized abundance. A sense of otherness, of distinctness, is the very basis of the consciousness of our individuality, and this consciousness, based in difference, is a constitutive element of what it to be a human being. To attack any of these differences—to round up women because they are women, Jews because they are Jews, whites because they are whites, blacks because they are blacks, gays because they are gay—is to attack the shared element that makes us what we are as a species.

Michael Ignatieff, *Lemkin's Word*, New Republic, 26 Feb. 2001, at 27–28.

71. Hannah Arendt, Vies Politiques 1 (Paris: Tel/Gallimard 1986). *See also* Arendt, Eichmann in Jerusalem, *supra* note 39, at 268–69. *See also* Hannah Arendt, Men in Dark Times 81–94 (1968).
72. Kant's categorical imperative teaches us that we should "act in such a way that [we] always treat humanity, whether in [our] own person or in the person of any other, never simply as a means, but always at the same time as an end." Immanuel Kant, The Moral Law: Groundwork for the Metaphysic of Morals 106–07 (H.J. Paton trans., Routledge 2d ed. 2005) (1785). Kant makes a similar point on another page: "Now I say that man, and in general every rational being, exists as an end in himself, not merely as a means for arbitrary use by this or that will; he must always be viewed at the same time as an end." *Id.* at 105 (emphasis omitted).
73. In a letter to Jaspers, Arendt wrote this about radical evil:

> What radical evil really is I don't know, but it seems to me it somehow has to do with the following phenomenon: making human beings as human beings superfluous (not using them as means to an end, which leaves their essence as humans untouched and impinges only on their human dignity; rather making them superfluous.

See Richard Berstein, *Are Arendt's Reflections on Evil Still Relevant?*, 70 Rev. Pol. 64, 67–68 (2008). *See also* Richard Bernstein, Hannah Arendt and the Jewish Question 97, 139–43 (1996); Hannah Arendt, The Origins of Totalitarianism 433 (1st ed. 1951).

some sense, slavery, another crime subject to universal jurisdiction, fits this category. Slavery does not simply use humans as means, but it denies the slave's very humanity. Slavery is social death,[74] not simply an infringement on human dignity.[75] Thus, to some extent slavery is also about curing us of diversity by denominating a class of people as not fully human and thus not part of us. While genocide is physical extermination of a group, slavery is social extermination of a group on the basis of some characteristics that are taken as indicators of the less than human nature of the particular group. Each—physical and social decimations—tries to define humanity in a way that excludes a portion of humankind. It is in that sense that one could argue that crimes such as genocide, slavery, and crimes against humanity diminish all of us.[76]

In the current global condition, the threat of physical extermination of groups and forms of being, because they are different or look different, is rather high. Likewise, the concern of the international community to prevent or minimize that risk is proper. This is both because most nation-states are multiethnic and multinational and because weapons of mass destruction are becoming more widely available. Consequently, crimes such as genocide and crimes against humanity have emerged as serious threats to the diverse international community we call humankind.[77]

So, one aspect of the international community that is imagined through the provision of universal jurisdiction is a community of diverse peoples and diverse ways of being. This diversity defines not only the international community (the community of communities) but the constituent communities (nation-states) as well. An act that attempts to diminish that diversity diminishes all of us, both literally and metaphorically. Consequently, offenses that are intended to cure us of diversity—such as genocide and crimes against humanity—are the concern of all of us.

---

74. Orlando Patterson, Freedom: Volume I: Freedom in the Making of Western Culture 10 (1991) ("In all societies the three constitutive features of the slave condition [personal domination, natal alienation, perpetual condition of dishonor] add up to a generalized conception of slavery as a state of social death."). *See also* Orlando Patterson, Slavery and Social Death (1982).
75. Almost all extreme offenses deny human dignity but not all deny the humanity (humanness) of the individuals.
76. Apartheid and other institutionalized forms of racism, such as what went on in the United States for a long period of time, are similar to slavery to the extent that they are based on the notion that members of a particular group are, by virtue of their skin color, less than human.
77. The term "crimes against humanity" was apparently coined by an African American, George Washington Williams, to describe "Belgian atrocities against the natives of Congo in the last two decades of the nineteenth century" while "genocide" was "coined by the Jewish-American Raphael Lemkin in 1944 to describe Nazi German atrocities against the Jews." Ramesh Thakur, *Dealing with Guilt Beyond Crime: The Strained Quality of Universal Justice, in* From Sovereign Impunity to International Accountability: The Search for Justice in a World of States 272 (Ramesh Thakur & Peter Malcontent eds., 2004).

The protection of the constitutive norms could come in one of two ways—by recognizing the particular norm as custom or by codifying it in a treaty. Nothing prevents the international community from codifying a customary norm in a treaty and requiring that member states prosecute or extradite while at the same time recognizing the right of all members of the international community to exercise universal jurisdiction over those offenses under customary international law. As noted earlier, in a strict sense, universal jurisdiction is customary in nature, for only then can it be available to all constituent units of the international community. A treaty binds those and only those who become parties to it.

B. A Vulnerable Community

Another defining feature of the current international community is its vulnerability. One could say that the international community consists of communities of equal vulnerability. Globalization and new technologies have increasingly given substance to the body of an international community while at the same time making that community much more vulnerable to destructive threats. The very processes that have made the world a community of communication have also made it an easier target of destructive attacks. Some of the *jus cogens* norms could be understood as directed at protecting the community from these vulnerabilities.

Clearly many threats endanger the well-being and survival of the international community as a whole, but the most immediate source of vulnerability is the threat from terrorism. Every nation—from India to Ethiopia, from Sri Lanka to Russia, from Pakistan to the United States—is vulnerable to terrorist attacks.[78] Although terrorism has been with us for a very long time,[79] the wide-scale threat it poses and the magnitude of the damage it is capable of inflicting are qualitatively different now. It would make sense, then, to recognize universal jurisdiction over offenses—such as terrorism—that are viewed as potential threats to all. Indeed, in some ways the idea of equal vulnerability could explain the recognition of piracy in an earlier era as an international crime subject to universal jurisdiction. One could reasonably argue that piracy only threatened the seafaring powers and their citizens, rather than the international community as a whole, as terrorism appears to do.

78. *See* Paul Kennedy, The Parliament of Man: The Past, Present, and Future of the United Nations 246 (2006) ("no society on the planet is free from random and beastly attack"). Kennedy goes on to make the point that "dealing with terrorism cannot be done by one country alone, however powerful." *Id.*

79. The term "'terrorism' was introduced only in late eighteenth century France, when the young Jacobin government, dominated by Robespierre, initiated a "Reign of Terror" intended to deter perceived counter-revolutionary critics." Alison M. Jaggar, *What Is Terrorism, Why Is It Wrong, and Could It Ever Be Morally Permissible?*, 36 J. Soc. Phil. 202, 202 (2005).

Two lessons may be drawn from the comparison between piracy and terrorism. First, if the common vulnerability posed to the international community (the community of commerce and navigation) was the main justification for subjecting piracy to universal jurisdiction, then clearly terrorism should also be subject to universal jurisdiction. The challenge from terrorism is more global than the historical challenge of piracy. Second, the comparison between terrorism and piracy suggests that a self-defined international community perceives its vulnerabilities as a matter of specific historical conditions. During the seventeenth, eighteenth, nineteenth, and early twentieth centuries, for all practical purposes the sea powers saw themselves as the international community. Thus, vulnerability to their commerce and navigation was seen as vulnerability to the entire community. To the extent that communities are constructed of social meanings and that "[s]ocial meanings are historical in character,"[80] it follows that communities are historical in character. The international community, like any other community, is a creature of specific historical conditions. In that sense, universal jurisdiction is a marker of the international community at a given historical time.

Although terrorism is a candidate for universal jurisdiction because it threatens all nations in the same way that piracy did (and in some sense still does), there is good reason for national courts to continue to be suspicious about treating terrorism as a universal crime under customary international law; there is no agreed upon international definition of terrorism.[81] To be sure, there are movements toward such a definition. The Terrorism Financing Convention of 1999,[82] Security Council Resolution 1566,[83] and the Report

80. Michael Walzer, Spheres of Justice: A Defense of Pluralism and Equality 9 (1983).

81. *See, e.g.*, United States v. Yousef, 327 F.3d 56 (2d. Cir. 2003).

> Unlike those offenses supporting universal jurisdiction under customary international law—that is, piracy, war crimes, and crimes against humanity—that now have fairly precise definitions and that have achieved universal condemnations, "terrorism" is a term as loosely deployed as it is powerfully charged. . . . "[No] consensus has developed on how to properly define 'terrorism' generally."
>
> . . . .
>
> . . . [Such] strenuous disagreement among States about what actions do or do not constitute terrorism . . . [means that] terrorism—unlike piracy, war crimes, and crimes against humanity—does not provide a basis for universal jurisdiction.

Id. at 106–08 (quoting Tel-Oren v. Libyan Arab Rep., 726 F.2d 774, 807 (D.C. Cir 1984) (Bork, J., concurring).

82. Here is how the Convention defines terrorism:

> [An] act intended to cause death or serious bodily injury to a civilian, or to any other person not taking an active part in the hostilities in a situation of armed conflict, when the purpose of such act, by its nature or context, is to intimidate a population, or to compel a government or an international organization to do or to abstain from doing any act.

International Convention for the Suppression of the Financing of Terrorism, *adopted* 9 Dec. 1999, G.A. Res. 54/109, U.N. GAOR, 54th Sess., art. 2(1)(b), U.N. Doc. A/RES/54/109 (2000) (*entered into force* 10 Apr. 2002).

83. The Security Council acting under its Chapter VII authority effectively provided a general definition of terrorism which includes the four important elements that the International

of the High-Level Panel[84] suggest definitions that are more or less similar and could provide the basis for an agreeable account of what constitutes terrorism for the purpose of universal jurisdiction.[85] Despite these challenges, there are specific acts—such as airplane hijacking and bombing—that are regarded as terrorist acts and to which most states are vulnerable. Terrorism of this nature can truly be said to lead to an international community of equal vulnerability. Not surprisingly, states have acted as a community to protect themselves from the common threats posed by these acts.[86]

To summarize, the vulnerability thesis suggests three things. First, the threat of particular crimes or offenses is one to which the overwhelming number of member states of the international community are vulnerable. Crimes such as terrorism threaten most members of the international community to the extent that most political communities contain groups that are dissatisfied with aspects of political or civic life and who may view coercive, political violence as an effective means of advancing their ends. Second, given technological developments and globalization generally, the threat of some crimes is increasingly global (trans-border) in nature. Again, terrorism is a good example. Third, some perpetrators of some crimes, such as terrorism, are no longer localized groups but global entities as well. A global network challenges the global community. A global challenge requires a global response. Cherif Bassiouni has correctly observed that the only way to make sense of *jus cogens* norms is that "certain crimes affect the interest of the world community as a whole because they threaten the peace and security of humankind."[87] This can happen in one of two ways: all constituent members of the international community are vulnerable to

---

Convention for the Suppression of the Financing of Terrorism considers as necessary for denominating an act as terrorist. First, that primary targets are governments, the general population, or international institutions. Second, the intent of the act is to pressure or intimidate primary targets either to do or to abstain from doing a particular act. Third, the pressure or intimidation is accomplished through secondary targets (civilians or others not involved in hostilities) by causing or intending to cause death or serious bodily injury to thee secondary targets. Fourth, the objectives for which the terrorist acts are engaged in are ideological or political rather than personal or private gains. S.C. Res. 1566, U.N. SCOR, 5053th mtg., ¶ 4, U.N. Doc. S/RES/1566 (2004).

84. *Report of the High-Level Panel on Threats, Challenges and Change*, G.A. Res. 59/565, U.N. GAOR, 59th Sess., Agenda Item 55, ¶¶ 157–64, U.N. Doc. A/59/565 (2004).

85. *Id.*

86. *See* Convention on Offenses and Certain Other Acts Committed on Board Aircraft, *adopted* 14 Sep. 1963, 704 U.N.T.S. 220 *(entered into force* 4 Dec. 1969); Convention for the Suppression of Unlawful Seizure of Aircraft, *adopted* 16 Dec. 1970, 860 U.N.T.S. 105 (*entered into force* 14 Oct. 1971); Convention for the Suppression of Unlawful Acts Against the Safety of Civil Aviation, *adopted* 23 Sep. 1971, 974 U.N.T.S. 178 (*entered into force* 26 Jan. 1973).

87. Bassiouni, *International Crimes, supra* note 43, at 63, 69. *See also* Quincy Wright, *War Criminals*, 39 Am. J. Int'l L. 257, 282 (1945) (Universal crimes are those that injure not one nation or peoples but "the community of nations . . . as a juristic community.").

certain crimes such as terrorism or, alternatively, given the globalized nature of our world, an attack on one side of the globe may (and often does) have serious consequences for the rest of it. In this sense, the world has become like a drum—if hit on one end, the whole thing will vibrate.

C. Diversity and Vulnerability: A Recap

The international community's interest in preventing and punishing offenses against *jus cogens* norms rests on the proposition that we live in a world of diversity—of ethnicity, race, and religion—and many of the offenses against *jus cogens* norms specifically target that diversity. Because "almost all nations are patchworks of ethnic, racial, religious, and cultural groups"[88] as a result of globalization and colonialism, an offense that targets people precisely because they belong to any of these groups threatens the very nature of the international community. The magnitude of the threat has increased as a result of new technologies of communication and mass destruction. The technical advances that have made "large-scale, coordinated attacks on civilians possible"[89] have made the international community increasingly a community of equal vulnerability.[90]

V. CONSTITUTING THE COMMUNITY FROM ABOVE AND FROM BELOW

If this account of what constitutes an international crime subject to universal jurisdiction is accurate, then those offenses that undermine the international community could be punished in at least three ways. First, they could be subject to the jurisdiction of an international tribunal, such as the International Criminal Court (ICC). Indeed, the ICC statute gives the Court jurisdiction for violation of most of the *jus cogens* norms.[91]

88. Luban, *supra* note 61, at 138.
89. *Id.* at 139. Reflecting on this issue Luban observes that the "Rwandan genocide could hardly have occurred before the twentieth century." *Id.*
90. In some sense, the two principles that are meant to respond to the facts of diversity and vulnerability—guaranteeing fundamental rights and ensuring basic security—are codified in the UN Charter as the two most important aspirations and purposes of the United Nations. *See* U.N. Charter art. 1, *signed* 26 June 1945, 59 Stat. 1031, T.S. No. 993 (*entered into force* 24 Oct. 1945). *See also* Adeno Addis, *Economic Sanctions and the Problem of Evil*, 25 Hum. Rts. Q. 573, 592 (2003); Larry May, *The International Community, Solidarity and the Duty to Aid*, 38 J. Soc. Phil. 185, 189–90 (2007) "Because of the shared interests in peace and basic human rights protection, of all humans in all political communities, we can speak non-metaphorically about the human or international community.").
91. *See* Rome Statute of the International Criminal Court, art. 5, U.N. Doc. A/CONF.183/9 (1998), *reprinted in* 37 I.L.M. 999.

Second, a convention could require states to either prosecute or extradite those accused of such crimes if they are found in their territory. A number of conventions contain such provisions.[92] Third, those offenses could be subject to the jurisdiction of any country that wishes to assert jurisdiction, even if it lacks traditional jurisdiction—i.e., proper universal jurisdiction. This is what we have referred to as universal jurisdiction properly so called.

As a general matter, there is no reason why a particular offense that is said to undermine the international community could not potentially be subject to all three procedures, even though, prosecution can occur only in one forum. In fact, that is the case now; currently the crimes subject to ICC jurisdiction are also subject (with some modification) to the jurisdiction of every state under customary international law. As a conceptual matter, would it be better to subject crimes that are said to be inconsistent with the very notion of an international community to an international tribunal? That would seem more efficient than to simply authorize each state to assert jurisdiction if it so wishes, or to provide in a convention when a state may assert jurisdiction in relation to a particular crime.

Hannah Arendt thought that truly international crimes, such as crimes against humanity and genocide, should be tried by duly constituted international tribunals. She approvingly quotes Karl Jaspers regarding the Eichmann trial: "the crime against the Jews was also a crime against mankind, and that consequently the verdict can be handed down only by a court of justice representing all mankind."[93] Arendt then asserts that "insofar as the crime [against Jews] was a crime against humanity, it needed an international tribunal to do justice to it."[94] Why is it essential that such crimes be prosecuted before an international tribunal rather than left to the legal systems of the

92. *See, e.g.*, Convention for the Suppression of Unlawful Seizure of Aircraft, *supra* note 86, art. 7:

> The Contracting State in the territory of which the alleged offender is found shall, if it does not extradite him, be obliged, without exception whatsoever and whether or not the offence was committed in its territory, to submit the case to its competent authorities for the purpose of prosecution. Those authorities shall take their decision in the same manner as in the case of any ordinary offence of a serious nature under the law of that State.

Similar provisions are found in other conventions such as the Convention against Torture and Other Cruel, Inhuman, or Degrading Treatment or Punishment, *adopted* 10 Dec. 1984, art. 7, 1465 U.N.T.S. 85 (*entered into force* 26 June 1987); Convention on the Prevention and Punishment of the Crime of Genocide, *adopted* 9 Dec. 1948, art. 4, 78 U.N.T.S. 277 (*entered into force* 12 Jan. 1951).

93. Arendt, Eichmann in Jerusalem, *supra* note 39, at 269 (quoting Karl Jaspers, radio interview later published in *Der Monat*) (internal quotes omitted). Jaspers not only saw crimes such as those committed by the Nazis as crimes against all of us, but interestingly he also saw "solidarity among men as human beings that makes each co-responsible for every wrong and every injustice in the world, especially for crimes committed in his presence or with his knowledge." Karl Jaspers, The Question of German Guilt 32 (E.B. Ashton trans., Capricorn Books 1961) (1947).

94. Arendt, Eichmann in Jerusalem, *supra* note 39, at 269.

constituent parts of the international community? The argument here is that, since the attack is on all of us, only all of us, constituting ourselves in a form of international tribunal, can render a proper verdict. A trial before a state court would minimize the monstrousness of the event[95] and limit the universality of the injury.

One may also add to Arendt's observation a practical concern. The international community (an international tribunal) will more likely ensure not only punishment but just punishment. It will eliminate the real danger that states will misuse the jurisdictional authority for purely partisan and political purposes[96] and consequently undermine the cause of the international community. Rather than contributing to the emergence of an international community, this will do exactly the opposite. It will sow discord and division rather than consensus and solidarity.

Let us first deal with the issue of misuse. This is a serious concern and it has been aired and explored at various fora.[97] Inappropriate assertion of universal jurisdiction could occur in two ways. First, every country may define the particular international crime (e.g., genocide) in its domestic law in a way that is different from the way the crime is understood internationally, thus leading to the prosecution and punishment of defendants for crimes that would not have met international standards. Second, even if the formal standard is consistent with international requirements, the prosecution itself could be politically driven. In relation to the first concern, Anthony Colangelo argues persuasively that if the adjudicative availability of universal jurisdiction is a matter of international law, then the prescriptive substance of the crime that gives rise to such adjudicative competence must also be a matter of international law.[98] In other words, states are not allowed to manipulate the substance of those international crimes. They are instead required to adopt the international definition of crimes that are matters of customary international law.[99] To the extent that the granting of universal jurisdiction

---

95. "The very monstrousness of the events is "minimized" before a tribunal that represents one nation only." *Id.* at 270.
96. *See* Kissinger, *supra* note 8, at 86, 92.
97. *See id.* at 80, 92; Moghalu, *supra* note 7, at 98–101.
98. Anthony J. Colangelo, *The Legal Limits of Universal Jurisdiction*, 47 Va. J. Int'l L. 149, 150 (2006) ("If national courts prosecute on grounds of universal jurisdiction, they must use the international legal definitions—contained in customary international law—of the universal crimes they adjudicate; otherwise, their exercise of universal jurisdiction contradicts the very international law upon which it purports to rely."). *See also* United States v. Yousef, 327 F.3d 56, 87–89 (2d. Cir. 2003) (rejecting terrorism as a universal crime on the account that there is no agreed international definition of the crime. "Unlike those offenses supporting universal jurisdiction under customary international law . . . that now have precise definitions . . . 'terrorism' is a term as loosely deployed as it is powerfully charged.").
99. A good example of an erroneous definition of international crimes is the Ethiopian Penal Code's definition of genocide and crimes against humanity. Ethiopian Penal Code, art. 281 (1957). The specific article, which is titled "Genocide; Crimes Against Humanity," merges

presupposes application of a standardized definition under customary international law, the possibility of misuse will decrease.

As to the second concern, it is true that there are likely to be attempts by one or another segment of a political community to use universal jurisdiction for political purposes. The worry that it would be utilized mainly against citizens and officials of "weak and vulnerable" states is not an unreasonable concern,[100] but the fear may be exaggerated. To begin, the vulnerability of weak states may not be significantly different from their vulnerability to improper imperial interference using other, seemingly more traditional, bases of jurisdiction. Territorial, protective, and nationality jurisdictions could be, and have been, utilized for political purposes as well. Also, there are sufficient political,[101] legal,[102] and

---

genocide and crimes against humanity into one offense and applies the international definition of genocide to that combined offense. The offense of crimes against humanity is essentially deemed to be a form of genocide. In fact, not only does the Penal Code attempt to apply the definition of genocide to crimes against humanity, but its description of what constitutes genocide is contradictory to the accepted international definition of genocide, because the Code's definition of genocide includes political groups as part of the list of groups whose attack may lead to a charge of genocide. Indeed, recently the government convicted members of the opposition for genocide for activities that even if the allegation were true (and it was not) would have not given rise to a charge of genocide under international law. To some extent, the Spanish court's definition of genocide in the Pinochet case was also inconsistent with the international definition to the extent that it included "political groups" in the category of "national groups." Since the 1948 Genocide Convention, *supra* note 92, genocide has been defined to have as victims the following groups only: "national, ethnic, racial or religious groups." For the proposition that the Spanish court mischaracterized the offense of genocide in the Pinochet case, see The Pinochet Papers: The Case of Augusto Pinochet in Spain and Britain 103–104 (Reed Brody & Michael Ratner eds., 2000).

100. Edward Kwakwa, *The Cairo-Arusha Principles on Universal Jurisdiction in Respect of Gross Human Rights Offenses: Developing the Frontiers of the Principle of Universal Jurisdiction*, 2002 Afr. Y.B. Int'l L. 407, 415. *See also* Arrest Warrant of 11 Apr. 2000 (Dem. Rep. Congo v. Belg.), 2002 I.C.J. 3, 43 (14 Feb.) (separate opinion of President Guillaume) (arguing that universal jurisdiction would create "judicial chaos" and that condition would only benefit the powerful). One academic has pithily observed, "What would happen if an African state like Djibouti would prosecute let us say a national of the United States for crimes against humanity? The prosecuting state would either be bombed or will not receive aid from the World Bank." Moghalu, *supra* note 7, at 100. One need not dream up a hypothetical to indicate that citizens of powerful nations are less likely to be indicted by courts of other countries. The quick death of the Belgium universal jurisdiction statute as a result of US pressure for fear that former or current officials could be subject to indictment under the law is a clear example.

101. It is, for example, international political pressure that led to the repeal of the controversial Belgian war crimes statute that asserted universal jurisdiction for certain crimes and under which an arrest warrant against a former official of the Democratic Republic of the Congo was issued. For a postmortem of the statute, see Steven Ratner, *Belgium's War Crimes Statute: A Postmortem*, 97 Am. J. Int'l L. 888 (2003).

102. As I have argued, the jurisdiction should only be available for criminal cases. Civil cases would infinitely multiply the occasions because of the fact that individuals initiate the suits in those cases. But civil cases may also lead to an incoherent and rather chaotic relationship between communities. Unlike the tradition of civilian systems which allow a role for individuals in the initiation of a criminal case, it may be better to adhere to

institutional[103] constraints that will ensure that the occasions of political use of universal jurisdiction are minimized.[104] Indeed, the worry may be that states will continue to be too hesitant to invoke universal jurisdiction rather than that they will be too aggressive and too political about it. Available evidence suggests that to be the case.[105]

If the issue of political misuse is not sufficiently serious to dictate trial before international tribunals only, what about Arendt's observation that only a trial before such a tribunal will capture the seriousness of the crime and its injury to the international community as a whole? A trial before an international tribunal would indeed signal how seriously the crime is taken by the international community, but it is a mistake to think that only such a trial will vindicate the monstrousness of the crime or the injury to all of us.

In fact, normative and strategic reasons argue for proper universal jurisdiction. First, as a strategic matter, we have not yet reached a point where an international tribunal would be allowed to assert jurisdiction over the entire international community in relation to international crimes which customary international law understands as being subject to universal jurisdiction. The compromises needed to create the ICC, and the resulting deference to state sovereignty, are a good example. It is also not clear that even if the tribunal is given jurisdiction over crimes of universal concern, and all states have

---

the common law system leaving the initiation of criminal prosecution to the discretion of state prosecutors. If part of the role of the utilization of universal jurisdiction is one of enabling us to constitute an international community, then it would make sense that constitution would be done not by individuals but by the territorial community personified. In any case, if criminal universal jurisdiction is fully enforced, then the rationale for civil jurisdiction becomes less compelling. Another legal limitation is, of course, the role of the International Court of Justice as it became clear in *Democratic Republic of the Congo*. Indeed, as I shall argue later in the text, the constitution of the international community is going to be partly the result of a dialogue between the International Court and state institutions. *Dem. Rep. Congo*, 2002 I.C.J. 3.

103. As the experience of the German Court suggests, sometimes the fact that evidentiary difficulties (the difficulty of getting all the necessary evidence from the country of origin) may make it difficult for the case to go through, especially when the case is already weak and is only meant as a political statement. A similar point was made by President Guillaume in his separate opinion in *Democratic Republic of the Congo*. Expressing skepticism about the wisdom of unbridled borderless justice that he thought was represented by Belgium's law he observes: "The primary aim of the criminal law is to enable punishment in each country of offences committed in the national territory. That territory is where evidence of the offense can most often be gathered." *Dem. Rep. Congo*, 2002 I.C.J. at 36 (separate opinion of President Guillaume).

104. There are various measures that could be adopted to reduce incidences of political use of universal jurisdiction, such as limiting it to crimes rather than civil cases and only to the violation of peremptory norms.

105. The repeal of the Belgium statute, the reluctance of prosecutors in those countries that have universal jurisdiction statutes in the book such as Germany to pursue foreigners accused of international crimes, and indeed the rarity of adjudicative universal jurisdiction, all indicate that the problem is not going to be aggressive but very rare use of universal jurisdiction. For an account of the German Code of Crimes Against International Law, see Gerhard Werle, Principles of International Law 80–89 (2005). The Code is reproduced as an appendix to the book. *See id.* at 428–33.

signed on (which under the current circumstance is unlikely), that the financial resources would be available for the tribunal to operate effectively. On the other hand, the availability of universal jurisdiction to state institutions will potentially disperse costs and make the financial constraints less relevant.

Second, and more importantly, as a normative matter there is something to be said for the process of constituting a community, in this case an international community, from the bottom up. A community that develops as a result of wider participation of the constituent parts, which universal jurisdiction promises to provide, is likely to be a more defensible one. That will be true partly because the specific applications of the principle of universal jurisdiction by various states would allow for experimentation and adaptation which might provide a glimpse of what works and how it works.[106] Indeed, the notion of universal jurisdiction would gesture simultaneously to the federalist notion of pluralism and the universal ideal of cosmopolitanism. It in fact links the two, each acting on and shaping the other.

The engagement of universalism and localism occurs at two levels. One level is the broad notion of local tribunals applying international norms and principles. The other occurs at a more specific institutional level, the limit the International Court of Justice (ICJ) has attempted to put on the local institutions' and tribunals' understanding of universalism. The ICJ decision in *Democratic Republic of the Congo v. Belgium*[107] is a good example. This decision shows that the exercise of universal jurisdiction by state institutions would be subject to the limits imposed by the Court. One reading of the Court's decision might be that the exercise of universal jurisdiction in the particular case would result not in the shaping of a more just international community, but rather in making it difficult for an international community of interests to emerge. The ICJ seemed to conclude in *Democratic Republic of the Congo* that the exercise of universal jurisdiction over the chief diplomats of other nations would lead to enormous discord.[108] While an

106. This of course is the classic argument in defense of federalism generally. "Experiments in living," as John Stuart Mill puts it, allow citizens to learn from the experiences of other subunits, in this case nation-states. John Stuart Mill, *Utilitarianism and On Liberty*: Including 'Essay on Bentham' and Selections from the Writings of Jeremy Bentham and John Austin 152 (Mary Warnock ed., 2d ed. 2003) (1859).

107. *Dem. Rep. Congo,* 2002 I.C.J. 3. The case involved an arrest warrant that was issued by the Government of Belgium against the foreign minister of the Democratic Republic of the Congo (while the latter was still in office) pursuant to a Belgium statute that granted Belgian courts universal jurisdiction in relation to certain violations of international law. The Court decided that Belgium could not arrest and prosecute the former Foreign Minister because customary international law made him immune. For a description of the Belgium statute, see Ratner, *supra* note 101.

108. But of course as the Court noted, "The *immunity* from jurisdiction enjoyed by incumbent Ministers of Foreign affairs does not mean they enjoy *impunity* in respect of any crimes they might have committed, irrespective of their gravity. Immunity from criminal jurisdiction and individual criminal responsibility are quite separate concepts." *Dem.*

international crimes tribunal would not be subject to such limit from the ICJ, a state court would be. The dialectic between universalism and pluralism is a surer path to the development of a more sustainable and coherent international community.

Third, the notion of universal jurisdiction implicitly accepts the proposition that the tribunals of a state will assert it only if it appears that the states that would have other traditional bases of jurisdiction (such as territorial and nationality) are unable or unwilling to prosecute.[109] One could see this as another level of encounter between universalism and localism. It is an encouragement to political entities with some sort of connection to the act, offense, or offender in question to prosecute by signaling that not doing so will lead to the assertion of jurisdiction by others with no connection at all.[110] The implied priority given to other traditional forms of jurisdictional authorities acknowledges that the injury the offense inflicts is both to the specific political community and to the international community as a whole. The specific community is given priority. We might call this, borrowing a

---

Rep. Congo, 2002 I.C.J. at 25. This means, the ministers could be held liable for their crimes under circumstance that does not adversely affect their performance in their jobs as links between their countries and the rest of the world.

109. *See, e.g.*, Daryl Lindsey, German Prosecutors Won't Pursue Rumsfeld Case, Spiegel Online-Int'l, 10 Feb. 2005, *available at* http://www.spiegel.de/international/0,1518,druck-341131,00.html. The German prosecutor stated that the reason why he was not pursuing Rumsfeld was because "German authorities could only pursue the allegation if US authorities refused to do so—and currently, there is no evidence that they won't." *Id.* Now, even though the German prosecutor has got the general principle right, his assessment that there was no indication that Americans will refuse to pursue the case is rather optimistic. Perhaps the prosecutor's statement could be understood as claiming that the US government has not closed the door of holding some individuals liable for the abuses in Abu Ghraib (as it in fact has already done) and that the German institutions should allow US courts to assign liability in circumstance such as this when liability is not clear outside the directly involved individuals.

110. The ICC is also guided by a similar principle. Under the complementarity principle, "the ICC shall be complementary to national jurisdictions." The ICC cannot accept jurisdiction over a case that is being investigated or prosecuted by a state which has territorial jurisdiction over case unless that state is "unwilling or unable to genuinely carry out the investigation or prosecution." *See* Rome Statute of the International Criminal Court circulated as UN document A/CONF. 183/9 of 17 July 1998 and corrected by proces verbaux of 10 Nov. 1998, 12 July 1999, 30 Nov. 1999, 8 May 2000, 17 Jan. 2001 and 16 Jan. 2002. The statute entered into force on 1 July 2002. The ICC will also decline to accept a case if a state has investigated and declined to prosecute unless that decision stems from unwillingness or inability to prosecute. Of course "unwillingness" is not always an easy attitude or demeanor to ascertain, but a desire to shield the person concerned, because of unjustified delay, or a lack of impartiality. These are all important factors. *See* ICC Statute, art. 17(2), as to "inability" the collapse of the judicial system in the State concerned will clearly indicate that. *See* ICC Statute, art. 17(3). Principle 8 of the Princeton Principles on Universal Jurisdiction also subjects universal jurisdiction to a type of reasonableness standard to give priority to the more closely connected state. *The Princeton Principles on Universal Jurisdiction, adopted* 27 Jan. 2001, *reprinted in The Princeton Principles on Universal Jurisdiction*, in Universal Jurisdiction, *supra* note 9, at 18, 23 [hereinafter *Princeton Principles*].

phrase from Ronald Dworkin in another context, the principle of "local priority."[111] Thus, by acknowledging an international interest, universal jurisdiction does not diminish the value of local interests and relationships. Indeed, it captures more fully the nature of the injury that occurs when a fundamental norm is violated.

There is still the issue of whether the exercise of universal jurisdiction would lead to chaos even if it is accepted that third countries would assert such jurisdiction if and only if the country that has the traditional bases of jurisdiction is unable or unwilling to prosecute. Judge Guillaume in his separate opinion in *Democratic Republic of the Congo* makes the argument that the assertion of multiple universal jurisdictions over a particular offense against a *jus cogens* norm risks "total judicial chaos."[112] This is theoretically possible. Indeed, the *Pinochet* case[113] shows that several countries may be interested in prosecuting a particular violator. David Luban has argued, however, that the possibility of an offense being subject to prosecution under multiple jurisdictions arises even under the traditional bases of jurisdiction. A crime might occur in the territory of one country, but the perpetrator may be a citizen of another country, and the victim a national of a third. Each can assert jurisdiction, with the potential of judicial chaos, but such chaos has generally been avoided and "jurisdictional priority is settled through diplomatic means and the balancing of different states' interests."[114] There is no reason why a similar arrangement could not work in relation to universal jurisdiction.[115]

---

111. *See* Ronald Dworkin, Justice in Robes 70 (2006); Ronald Dworkin, Law's Empire 250–54 (1986).
112. *Dem. Rep. Congo*, 2002 I.C.J. at 43 (separate opinion of President Guillaume).
113. Spain was one of the countries that sought to prosecute Augusto Pinochet for crimes he committed in Chile while president of the country. Spain had issued an arrest warrant against Pinochet and sought an extradition when it learned that Pinochet was in London on a medical visit. The case was heard before English courts, finally reaching the House of Lords. *See* Regina v. Bow St. Metro. Stipendiary Magistrate, *Ex parte* Pinochet Ugarte (No. 3), [2000] 1 A.C. 147 (H.L. 1999) (appeal taken from Eng.). The majority of the Lords held that many of Pinochet's alleged crimes did not satisfy the dual criminality requirement of the British extradition statute (that what he did was a crime both in Britain and Spain at the time the offense was committed). At the end, it fell on the Foreign Secretary, Jack Straw, to decide whether to permit extradition to go ahead or not. And he determined that Pinochet was not in good health to stand trial and thus allowed him to return to Chile. For interests in other countries to pursue Pinochet, see Richard A. Falk, *Assessing the Pinochet Litigation: Whither Universal Jurisdiction?, in* Universal Jurisdiction, *supra* note 7, at 97, 107–10. *See also* Jeffrey L. Dunoff, Steven R. Ratner & David Wippman, International Law: Norms, Actors, Processes 682 (2d ed. 2006) ("Spain's request [for extradition] was followed by similar requests from Belgium, France, and Switzerland, where cases comparable to those in Spain had been filed by other victims of the Pinochet regime.").
114. Luban, *supra* note 61, at 152.
115. Perhaps something akin to the "reasonableness" standard that is applied in relation to the assertion of extraterritorial jurisdictions could be applied in relation to competing assertions of universal jurisdiction. Principle 8 of the Princeton Principle on Universal Jurisdiction suggests a number of factors which may be considered and balanced to

VI. COSMOPOLITAN COMMUNITARIANISM AND UNIVERSAL JURISDICTION: FURTHER THOUGHTS ON THE CONSTITUTIVE DIMENSION OF UNIVERSAL JURISDICTION

I have argued that universal jurisdiction attempts to vindicate norms that must be regarded as minimum cores, what John Rawls refers to as "a special class of urgent rights,"[116] for the emergence and cultivation of an international community of sort. To the extent that the prosecuted individuals or acts have no traditional connection to the prosecuting state, we refer to universal jurisdiction as cosmopolitan. To the extent that the norms that we seek to protect through universal jurisdiction (*jus cogens* norms) are about punishing or suppressing "offenses against humankind" rather than simply defending this or that individual in this or that country, universal jurisdiction is communitarian. It is about protecting or cultivating the international community rather than simply protecting individuals who happen to be citizens or residents of other countries.

This article has argued that universal jurisdiction is simultaneously vindicative and constitutive of the identity of that community. Let us explore the process of constitution a bit more. Identities—individual or group, institutional or personal—are constituted relationally.[117] We define who we are as individuals or as groups partly in relation to the differences we perceive with other individuals or other groups.[118] The act of defining the "Other" is simultaneously one of defining oneself. As William Connolly put it, "Identity requires difference in order to be and it converts difference into otherness in order to secure its own self-certainty."[119] And it is no different with communities, national or international. Communities define their identities in relation to what they regard as the "troublesome or the evil Other."[120]

---

decide jurisdictional priorities in the event that there are competing national jurisdictions. *See Princeton Principles*, *supra* note 110, at 23.

116. John Rawls, The Law of Peoples 79 (1999) (There are "a special class of urgent rights, such as freedom from slavery and serfdom, liberty (but not equal liberty) of conscience, and security of ethnic groups from mass murder and genocide. The violation of this class of rights is equally condemned both by reasonable liberal peoples and decent hierarchical peoples.").

117. *See* Charles Taylor, *The Politics of Recognition*, *in* Multiculturalism: Examining the Politics of Recognition 25, 32–33 (Amy Gutmann ed., 1994); William Connolly, Identity\Difference: Democratic Negotiations of Political Paradox 64 (1991); Martha Minow, Making all the Difference: Inclusion, Exclusion, and American Law (1990); Iris Marion Young, Justice and the Politics of Difference 43 (1990); Paul Ricoeur, The Course of Recognition (David Pellauer trans., 2005).

118. Charles Taylor, The Ethics of Authenticity 47–48 (1991) ("My discovering my identity doesn't mean that I work it out in isolation but that I negotiate it through dialogue, partly overt, partly internalized, with others. . . . My own identity crucially depends on my dialogical relations with others.").

119. Connolly, *supra* note 117, at 64.

120. For the view that nations often use economic sanctions as a process through which they assert their identities, see Addis, *Economic Sanctions and the Problem of Evil*, *supra* note 90, at 578.

Universal jurisdiction is an instrument through which the identity of the international community that constituted or defined. The norms that are protected through universal jurisdiction are those that demarcate the international community from the evil other(s); evils that are regarded as enemies of all of us. The notion of universal jurisdiction is the boundary that outlines the contours of a community which is otherwise difficult to define.[121] In the literal sense, the international community includes all of us in all of our plural guises and therefore cannot contrast itself with other communities for the assertion and certainty of its identity.[122] It is the idea of "enemies of human kind," the notion that certain acts and actors are *beyond* commonly held international norms, that provides the notion of "otherness" necessary for self-definition and self-certainty. The notion of enemies of human kind endows the idea of humankind with the depth of solidarity of which it has never been certain. Defining the enemy is simultaneously defining a category, a community, which stands threatened by this evil.

VII. CONCLUSION

Universal jurisdiction is not merely a technical juridical question about boundaries; it is also about the nature of the international community we seek to constitute and cultivate. Universal jurisdiction seeks to articulate the norms and principles that are minimum cores for the existence of an international community.

This article has referred to universal jurisdiction as communitarian cosmopolitan, for the idea of universal jurisdiction is based on the notion that the interests we attempt to vindicate through it are not merely interests of a particular political community but those of the international community as whole. I use the term "communitarian cosmopolitanism" to distinguish it from what I have chosen to refer to as individualist cosmopolitanism, whose crossing of borders is motivated almost exclusively by the desire to vindicate the rights or interests of individuals from other political communities. Communitarian cosmopolitanism is distinguished from individualist cosmopolitanism on two grounds. First, unlike individualist cosmopolitanism, the communitarian variety is able to explain why certain offenses are regarded as injuries to the *international community* (against all of us, as a corporate entity) rather than simply being offenses against nationals of other

121. Arrest Warrant of 11 Apr. 2000 (Dem. Rep. Congo v. Belg.), 2002 I.C.J. 3, 43 (14 Feb.) (separate joint opinion of President Guillaume) (referring to the notion of international community as "ill-defined").
122. As Roger Scruton put it, "Since there is no 'we' without a 'they,' the possibility of enmity and fragmentation is contained in the very foundation of political existence." Roger Scruton, *The First Person Plural*, *in* Theorizing Nationalism 279 (Ronald Beiner ed., 1999).

political communities whose governments are unable or unwilling to make whole. To view the injuries this way makes the challenges to the assertion of universal jurisdiction less compelling. After all, if the injury is against us, then we have a moral right (or even a duty) to prosecute or suppress offenses that cause those injuries. Second, while individualist cosmopolitanism is simply about maximizing impunity in relation to certain crimes, the notion of communitarian cosmopolitanism is about constituting and protecting a certain kind of international community.

Universal jurisdiction is, of course, not the only process through which member states could defend fundamental norms and in the process define and protect the international community. The obligation of states to the international community as a whole (*obligatio ergo omnes*) can be discharged in a number of other ways: economic and travel sanctions against individuals and states that are violators of fundamental norms (*jus cogens* norms), persuading the Security Council to refer offending individuals to an international tribunal or to sanction offenders, and perhaps military intervention in some exceptional circumstances.[123] But universal jurisdiction is one important way. It is "the attire draped over the naked body of" fundamental norms that are constitutive of the international community.[124]

Universal jurisdiction is thus a form of communitarian cosmopolitanism whose major purpose is the shaping and protection of a certain version of an international community. However, communitarian cosmopolitanism is pursued through a participatory (national) process where national communities apply their coercive laws to persons or activities that pose a threat to the international community we seek to cultivate. In some very interesting ways, universal jurisdiction mediates a number of principles and interests that are often seen as being in tension: specific (individual) versus general (international) injury, individual versus communitarian interests, and specific (national) versus general (international) obligations.

The invocation of universal jurisdiction must proceed in a manner that is likely to be most effective. An effective strategy may have to be selective.[125]

---

123. Michael Reisman argues that "military intervention [may qualify as] a primary technique of enforcing some *erga omnes* norms." Michael Reisman, *Comment, in* THE FUTURE OF INTERNATIONAL LAW ENFORCEMENT: NEW SCENARIOS, NEW LAW? 168, 171 (Jost Delbrück ed., 1993) (clearly, defending *jus cogens* norms qualify as important obligation).

124. Weiss, *supra* note 40, at 30 ("Universal jurisdiction is . . . the attire draped over the naked body of universal norms.").

125. The German approach is interesting in this sense. While Section I of the International Criminal Code establishes universal jurisdiction with no qualification, Section 153f of Criminal Procedure Code apparently gives to the prosecutor a rather wide margin of appreciation in the decision whether or not to initiate investigation. *See* Kai Ambos, *Prosecuting International Crimes at the National and International Level: Between Justice and Realpolitik, in* INTERNATIONAL PROSECUTION OF HUMAN RIGHTS CRIMES 55–68 (Wolfgang Kaleck, Michael Ratner, Tobias Singelnstein & Peter Weiss eds., 2007).

On this account, the NAACP Legal Defense and Educational Fund strategy to dismantle the legal doctrine of "separate but equal," which shielded legal segregation, may be instructive.[126] The Fund chose its cases well (going after the most egregious violators and suing on behalf of the most sympathetic plaintiffs) rather than going across the board and risking failures and backlash.[127] The Fund understood, as should national prosecutors and judicial bodies, that the legal struggle is part of a general strategy of developing a decent community (in our case, an international community), and part of that general strategy is to build public support and to minimize the risk of serious backlash.[128] However attractive universal jurisdiction might be, it is seriously defective if it fails to cultivate attitudes in the various political communities to pursue it.[129] The idea of universal jurisdiction is in its infancy, which means that certain factual realities, limitations, and practical obstacles must be accepted.

126. For an account of the desegregation strategy, see Richard Kluger, Simple Justice: The History of *Brown v. Board of Education* and Black America's Struggle for Equality (1975). *See also* Mark Tushnet, The NAACP: Legal Strategy Against Segregated Education 1925–1950 (2004).
127. For a general litigation strategy of the NAACP, see Tushnet, *supra* note 126.
128. Some components of a strategy that would reduce backlash may include: prosecuting individuals who have no arguable immunity claims; selecting cases which do not pose great evidentiary hurdles; assessing fully the political and legal receptivity of the forum states before filing complaints; assessing the impact of such a trial on new and fragile democracies taking root in the home of the accused; the use of forums in the South as well as in the North so as to reduce the erroneous suspicion that universal jurisdiction is simply a tool the North uses to intimidate the South. The contention that universal jurisdiction is a tool of the North has often puzzled me given the fact that it is victims from the South who have been abused and denied justice who bring their cases to the North. Perhaps a list of formal or informal procedures (best practices) could be developed to guide prosecutors as to how and when to utilize universal jurisdiction.
129. Here I am paraphrasing John Rawls's observation about justice. Rawls writes, "However attractive a conception of justice might be on other grounds, it is seriously defective if the principles of moral psychology are such that it fails to engender in human beings the requisite desire to act upon it." John Rawls, A Theory of Justice 455 (1971).

[9]

The Legal Limits of Universal Jurisdiction

ANTHONY J. COLANGELO*

Despite all the attention it receives from both its supporters and critics, universal jurisdiction remains one of the more confused doctrines of international law. Indeed, while commentary has focused largely and unevenly on policy and normative arguments either favoring or undercutting the desirability of its exercise, a straightforward legal analysis breaking down critical aspects of this extraordinary form of jurisdiction remains conspicuously missing. Yet universal jurisdiction's increased practice by states calls out for such a clear descriptive understanding. The following Essay will engage this under-treated area. It will offer to explicate a basic, but overlooked, feature of the law of universal jurisdiction: If national courts prosecute on grounds of universal jurisdiction, they must use the international legal definitions—contained in customary international law—of the universal crimes they adjudicate; otherwise, their exercise of universal jurisdiction contradicts the very international law upon which it purports to rely. The Essay will argue that this legal feature derives from the distinctively symbiotic nature of universal prescriptive jurisdiction (the power to apply law to certain persons or things) and universal adjudicative jurisdiction (the power to subject certain persons or things to judicial process). Unlike other bases of jurisdiction in international law, the prescriptive substance of universal jurisdiction authorizes and circumscribes universal adjudicative jurisdiction; in other words, it defines not only the universal crimes themselves, but also the judicial competence for all courts wishing to exercise universal jurisdiction.

---

* Associate in Law, Columbia Law School. I would like to thank Rob Sloane, Petros Mavroidis, Tony D'Amato, Tom Lee, and participants in the Associates workshop at Columbia Law School. I would also like to thank Columbia Law librarian Dana Neacsu for her excellent research assistance. Special thanks go to the lovely Carrie Rief.

The Essay will look to chart out some important implications of this thesis for the real-world practice of universal jurisdiction: It will evaluate how most easily to determine the customary definitions of universal crimes, to detect breaches of international law by courts that manipulate subjectively those definitions, and to enforce against such illicit manipulation. The Essay will contend that while some definitional aspects invariably remain to be ironed out by state practice, the provisions of widely-ratified and longstanding international treaties provide generally the best record of the core customary definitions of universal crimes, and accordingly, supply not only a harmonized point of departure for courts wishing properly to exercise universal jurisdiction, but also a useful means for detecting breaches of international law by overzealous courts seeking only to exploit universal jurisdiction for purely political or sensationalist ends. The framework presented thus will address concerns that universal jurisdiction hazards unbridled abuse. As the Essay will argue, the law of universal jurisdiction does not; rather, it prescribes legal limits. And the Essay will conclude that in the end, these limits are enforced not by those states exercising universal jurisdiction, but instead by other jurisdictionally-interested states—that is, most often by those states whose national citizens are the subject of foreign universal jurisdiction proceedings.

I. INTRODUCTION

Unlike other bases of jurisdiction in international law, universal jurisdiction requires no territorial or national nexus to the alleged act or actors over which a state legitimately may claim legal authority.[1] Universal jurisdiction instead is based entirely on the commission of certain "universal crimes."[2] At the present stage of development of international law, this category of crime is generally considered to include piracy, slavery, genocide, crimes against humanity, war crimes, torture, and "perhaps certain acts of terrorism."[3] It is no secret that the near future

1. *See, e.g.*, RESTATEMENT (THIRD) FOREIGN RELATIONS LAW OF THE UNITED STATES § 404 (1987).

2. *See id.* § 404 cmt. a. .

3. *See, e.g.*, United States v. Yunis, 924 F.2d 1086, 1091 (D.C. Cir. 1991) (citing RESTATEMENT (THIRD) FOREIGN RELATIONS LAW OF THE UNITED STATES § 404 (1987)); *see also* THE PRINCETON PRINCIPLES ON UNIVERSAL JURISDICTION 29 (Stephen Macedo ed., Princeton Univ. 2001) [hereinafter THE PRINCETON PRINCIPLES]; Anthony J. Colangelo, *The New Uni-*

may envisage an increased rubric of universal crime that includes, *inter alia*, human sex trafficking, nuclear arms smuggling, and perhaps other characteristically transnational offenses. A "universal jurisdiction" attaches to these crimes, so the argument goes,[4] because they are universally condemned and all states have a shared interest in proscribing such crimes and prosecuting their perpetrators.[5] Accordingly, every state has what is called prescriptive jurisdiction, or lawmaking authority,[6] to proscribe universal crimes wherever they occur and whomever they involve, and adjudicative jurisdiction to subject the alleged universal criminal to its judicial process.[7] Thus if a State *A* national commits a universal crime against another State *A* national in State *A*, all states have jurisdiction to prosecute.

Universal jurisdiction has been the focus of much policy and normative debate: It has been hailed as a catalyst in the global struggle to bring to justice elusive international criminals like tyrants and terrorists, while on the other hand decried as a dangerously pliable tool for hostile states to damage international relations by initiating unfounded proceedings against each other's officials and citizens.[8] Such expansive jurisdiction has in fact provoked sharp backlash from many circles—including former and current U.S. administrations.[9] Yet in the face of some blows to its use,[10] universal jurisdiction is, for the foreseeable future, here to stay.

---

versal Jurisdiction: In Absentia Signaling over Clearly Defined Crimes, 36 GEO. J. INT'L L. 537, 578–602 (2005).

4. This Essay will not address directly the underlying rationale for universal jurisdiction or its extension to certain crimes, but will accept for present purposes its legal existence as well as the generally acknowledged list of crimes. The focus of the Essay instead will be on clearly marking out some important legal parameters that govern how courts must exercise such jurisdiction under international law.

5. RESTATEMENT (THIRD) FOREIGN RELATIONS LAW OF THE UNITED STATES § 404 cmt. a (1987).

6. *Id.* § 401(a).

7. *Id.* § 401(b).

8. For a good primer on the debate, *compare* Henry A. Kissinger, *The Pitfalls of Universal Jurisdiction*, 80 FOREIGN AFF. 86 (2001), *with* Kenneth Roth, *The Case for Universal Jurisdiction*, 80 FOREIGN AFF. 150 (2001). For a progressive, normative restatement of how universal jurisdiction ought to be exercised so as to facilitate its purposes, *see* THE PRINCETON PRINCIPLES, *supra* note 3.

9. Due to pressure from other nations—principally the United States—Belgium restricted the application of its controversially expansive universal jurisdiction law to require, *inter alia*, more traditional links with Belgium, immunity for foreign governmental officials, and an increased role for the public prosecutor. *See* Steven R. Ratner, Editorial Comment, *Belgium's War Crimes Statute: A Postmortem*, 97 AM. J. INT'L L. 888, 891 (2003).

10. *See* Ratner, *supra* note 10; Glenn Frankel, *Belgian War Crimes Law Undone by Its Global*

A number of states' courts have in the past year alone exercised this type of extraordinary jurisdiction,[11] and the recent proliferation of domestic legislation providing for universal jurisdiction[12] signals that the trend will only continue.

But despite the heated political controversy that surrounds it, and its increased use by states, a straightforward legal analysis interrogating some basic features of universal jurisdiction remains strangely lacking. This Essay will engage this under-treated area; it will not ask whether and under what circumstances universal jurisdiction might be a good idea, but rather will seek to discern the international law governing how courts must exercise universal jurisdiction when in fact they pursue such exercises, as well as the international legal consequences of improper exercises of universal jurisdiction. My argument therefore will be primarily a legal one, albeit with important policy implications that will contribute to the larger debate since it goes to the very heart of when and how universal jurisdiction can be exercised under international law. The argument will proceed as follows:

It is presently contrary to international law for one state to extend unilaterally its prescriptive jurisdiction into the territory of another state absent some territorial or national link to the matter over which the first state claims competence—for example, where the act has an impact within that state's territory, involves its nationals, or directly threatens

Reach, WASH. POST, Sept. 30, 2003 at A01.

11. Spain convicted Argentine naval officer Adolfo Scilingo for "crimes against humanity" based on his participation in a program of throwing political prisoners from airplanes during Argentina's "dirty war." Reuters, *Argentine Ex-Officer Convicted in Spain; 'Dirty War' Trial First of Its Kind*, WASH. POST, Apr. 20, 2005, at A17; Giles Tremlett, *'I Don't Try To Justify Myself'*, GUARDIAN, Apr. 21, 2005, at 6. Spain has also issued warrants for three United States soldiers concerning an incident in which a U.S. tank fired on a Baghdad hotel, killing two journalists. Drew Brown, *Spanish Judge Wants 3 Soldiers Arrested in Journalists' Deaths*, SEATTLE TIMES, Oct. 20, 2005, at A16. One of the journalists killed was not a Spanish national; therefore any charges brought based on his death would rely upon the ground of universal jurisdiction. In Britain, London's Central Criminal Court recently convicted Afghan warlord Farayadi Sawar Zardad of torture and hostage taking in Afghanistan between 1991 and 1996. Nikki Tait, *UK Court Convicts Afghan Warlord*, FIN. TIMES, July 19, 2005, at 12. Similarly, Dutch courts have brought charges against two former Afghan generals for war crimes and torture committed during the Soviet occupation of Afghanistan in the 1980s. Marlise Simons, *2 Afghans Face Dutch War-Crimes Charges From 80's Soviet Era*, N.Y. TIMES, Sept. 29, 2005, at A13. Belgium has even resuscitated its "universal jurisdiction law" to grandfather in a case against former Chadian dictator Hissene Habre. Marlise Simons, *Belgium Indicts Chad's Ex-Leader*, N.Y. TIMES, Sept. 30, 2005, at A8.

12. *See infra* notes 83-87 (listing legislation implementing the Statute of the International Criminal Court and providing for universal jurisdiction).

its security.[13] Thus State *B* cannot, without such a link, project its domestic laws onto State *A* and vice versa. Yet, as we have seen, the principle of universal jurisdiction grants all states—including our hypothetical State *B*—jurisdiction to prosecute universal crimes irrespective of where the crimes occur or which state's nationals are involved (either as perpetrators or victims). This immediately raises the important—but thus far neglected—legal question: What prescriptive jurisdiction prescribes universal crimes? In concrete terms, what prescriptive law must national courts apply when they exercise universal adjudicative jurisdiction?

The answer, this Essay will submit, is international prescriptive jurisdiction, and thus in substance, international law. In other words, while a state's national law may not extend unilaterally its prescriptive reach into the territory of another state, international law can, and does, just that with respect to the proscription on universal crime—only in cases of universal jurisdiction, the adjudication of this international legal prohibition occurs through the operation of national courts. Because the international prescriptive substance of universal crimes authorizes a given court's universal jurisdiction, courts must apply that substance—that is, the international legal definitions of the crimes—when they exercise universal jurisdiction, or else their jurisdictional claim contradicts the very international law upon which it purports to rely. The thesis from which I will build my argument therefore is simply that the exercise of universal adjudicative jurisdiction fundamentally depends upon the application of the legal substance of universal prescriptive jurisdiction, and that this prescriptive substance—the definitions of universal crimes—derives from customary international law.

Part II will explain how this thesis brings to light and grounds itself in the uniqueness of universal jurisdiction among the jurisdictional bases generally accepted in international law. For unlike other bases, universal jurisdiction's prescriptive substance at the same time *authorizes* and *circumscribes* courts' adjudicative jurisdiction; it defines not only the universal crimes themselves, but also the judicial competence for all courts wishing to exercise universal jurisdiction. And it is a prescriptive substance common to all states since it can arise only as a matter of customary law, universally binding on them all. My claim thus will place legal limits on the exercise of universal jurisdiction. It is not just the empow-

13. *See infra* note 34, and accompanying text, listing bases of jurisdiction.

erment of states by international law to adjudicate certain matters under any prescriptive law they see fit. Instead, when national courts prosecute on a theory of universal jurisdiction they must apply the international legal definitions of the crimes they adjudicate, or else their jurisdiction conflicts with international law. Part II also will employ this thesis to rebut the claim that because courts typically need some form of domestic authorization to exercise their jurisdiction, universal jurisdiction depends not on international law but on national law.

The thesis raises a number of important questions for the practice of universal jurisdiction that need answering, namely: How are courts to go about determining the definitional substance of what might be dubbed "fuzzy" customary international law? Further, how can states evaluate whether a universal jurisdiction court departs from the customary definition of the crime, thus rendering its underlying jurisdiction contrary to international law? And finally, how can interested states—that is, states on whose territories the universal crimes occurred and/or whose nationals are the subject of universal jurisdiction proceedings—enforce against illegitimate definitional expansions of universal crimes by overzealous courts seeking only to exploit universal jurisdiction for political or sensationalist ends?

In response to these questions, Parts III and IV will offer a basic framework for evaluating the legality of universal jurisdiction exercises under this Essay's thesis. In response to the first question—how to determine the customary definitions of universal crimes—Part III will look to the formation of customary law generally, and will maintain that as to universal crimes in particular, their core substantive elements are set forth quite explicitly in the various treaties and conventions prohibiting the crimes under positive international law. I will not argue that treaty law sets forth definitively the customary definitions of universal crimes, but rather the best *evidence* of what those definitions are. While the contention that treaties may generate customary law is perhaps not entirely free from debate with respect to, for example, the formation of "instant custom" at the moment the treaty enters into force absent opportunity for subsequent international acceptance of or acquiescence in the rules contained therein, or the establishment of custom through only bilateral treaties, I need not go so far for my argument. The treaties proscribing the various universal crimes represent a relatively longstanding consensus not only as to the prohibition on those crimes, but also—necessarily—as to their substance. On this point, the Appendix to this

Essay will critically survey the positive law relating to each of the universal crimes listed above and assay some of the more important definitional provisions which supply a harmonized prescriptive foundation for courts wishing to exercise universal jurisdiction.[14] My purpose in so doing is not to elaborate comprehensively all aspects of the definitions of universal crimes under customary law, but rather to provide courts and international lawyers with a useful point of departure in line with the analytical framework forwarded by this Essay. To be sure, although state practice and *opinio juris* (the two elements that make up customary law) continue to fill in, refine and modify aspects of these customary definitions, for present purposes courts have a clear and workable catalog of core definitions handy, in the form of treaty provisions and legislation transposing those provisions onto domestic law, with which to prosecute universal crimes. In fact, national legislation enabling universal jurisdiction characteristically draws from treaty law to define the relevant offense[15] and courts consequently use that substantive definition to prosecute universal crimes,[16] thus reinforcing custom in this respect.

Next, because treaty provisions largely evidence the core definitions of universal crimes, we might respond to the second question—how to determine when universal jurisdiction courts deviate from the customary definitions of the crimes—by saying initially that there are "easy cases" and "hard cases." Where a court claiming universal jurisdiction clearly departs from the subject crime's core definition—as evidenced by the treaty—absent a showing that customary law has evolved to justify such a departure, the illegitimacy of its jurisdictional claim is easily-identifiable. Especially subject to easy-case categorization are universal crimes with rule-based elements. A quick example here, and one that will be discussed in more detail below,[17] is the Spanish *Audiencia Nacional*'s illegitimate expansion of the victim classes in the definition of genocide to include political groups, which purported to justify the court's assertion of universal jurisdiction over former Chilean dictator Augusto Pinochet.[18] Under this Essay's framework, had the case gone

14. *See* Appendix, *infra*. As the Appendix bears out, the treaties themselves tend to avow either an explicit or implicit purpose to codify or create custom in their respective areas of international lawmaking.

15. *See infra* notes 83–87.

16. *See infra* text accompanying notes 105–17.

17. *See infra* text accompanying notes 105–17.

18. *See infra* text accompanying notes 105–07.

forward on these grounds,[19] Chile—both the territorial and national state—would have had a powerful legal claim to reject Spanish jurisdiction since the definition the court employed was plainly exorbitant. But although treaties strongly evidence the core elements of universal crimes, there invariably will be aspects of the definitions that need to be ironed out further by state practice. Thus, objections to universal jurisdiction that are not based on a court's clear departure from the universal crime's core substantive definition—as evidenced by the treaty—might fall into the "hard case" category. Especially subject to hard-case classification are crimes that depend on the application of standards. Examples here might include whether a specific act constitutes a war crime under standards of target selection and proportionality contained in the Geneva Conventions and their Additional Protocols,[20] or whether a particular interrogation technique constitutes torture under the Torture Convention's widely-accepted definition of the crime.[21] The jurisprudence of international criminal tribunals and of national courts exercising universal jurisdiction—decisions which are not precedent on their own but nonetheless evidence state practice,[22] would be particularly helpful guides here. But in order to illustrate most simply its basic thesis, this Essay admittedly concerns itself more with the easy cases—though the hard cases undoubtedly supply fertile ground for further legal evaluation of universal jurisdiction assertions in line with the framework forwarded here. Indeed, and as Part IV indicates in its enforcement discussion, where territorial and national states—states that have a strong legal interest in a given universal jurisdiction assertion—object to the definition

19. Torture ended up being the relevant crime of extradition for Great Britain, though Pinochet ultimately was not extradited but sent back to Chile because he was determined medically unfit to stand trial. *See* Regina v. Bow St. Metropolitan Stipendiary Magistrate, *ex parte* Pinochet Ugarte, [1999] No. 3, 2 W.L.R. 827, 833–36 (opinion of Lord Browne-Wilkinson), *reprinted in part in* THE PINOCHET PAPERS: THE CASE OF AUGUSTO PINOCHET IN SPAIN AND BRITAIN 255, 268 (Reed Brody & Michael Ratner, eds., 2000) (hereinafter THE PINOCHET PAPERS).

20. I have argued against the use of universal jurisdiction over war crimes generally for this reason. *See* Appendix E, *infra*; Colangelo, *supra* note 3, at 587–94 (observing that these standards afford courts too much latitude to allege war crimes against U.S. forces despite an unprecedented adherence to international humanitarian law in the NATO bombing in the former Yugoslavia and the 2003 invasion of Iraq).

21. Convention Against Torture and Other Cruel, Inhuman or Degrading Treatment or Punishment, G.A. Res. 39/46, art. 1, U.N. GAOR, 39th Sess., Supp. No. 51, U.N. Doc. A/39/51 (Dec. 10, 1984) [hereinafter Torture Convention]; *see also infra* Appendix F (for example, the phrase "severe pain or suffering" is particularly open to interpretation).

22. RESTATEMENT (THIRD) FOREIGN RELATIONS LAW OF THE UNITED STATES § 103 cmt. a, b (1987).

of the crime that purports to justify another state's universal jurisdiction claim, the resolution of that international legal clash will go far toward determining further the customary definition of the crime at issue.

Finally, Part IV will deal with the question of enforcement against a court's illegitimate definitional expansion of a universal crime upon which the court purports to base its jurisdiction. Part IV will explain that the international legal limits of universal jurisdiction are indeed enforceable against such courts, and that the enforcers are those states with concurrent jurisdiction over the alleged crimes—that is, states with territorial or national jurisdiction. As I will show, where jurisdictionally interested states reject an illegitimate universal jurisdiction claim stemming from an improper manipulation of the underlying crime's definition, international law considers the universal jurisdiction claim an enduring breach. In short, it is not the state exercising universal jurisdiction, but most often those states whose nationals are in the dock, that are the enforcers of the legal limits of universal jurisdiction.

II. UNIVERSAL JURISDICTION'S PRESCRIPTIVE-ADJUDICATIVE SYMBIOSIS

Jurisdiction is the central concept in the interface between the nation state and international law; as such, it describes the power allocation both among individual states and between states and international law. A state's jurisdiction, or what some may call "sovereignty,"[23] refers by and large to its authority to make, apply, and enforce law. More distinctly, a state's prescriptive jurisdiction is its authority to apply its law to certain persons or things,[24] and its adjudicative jurisdiction is its authority to

23. Although notoriously opaque, the label "sovereignty" invokes the familiar definition of state power by implying the state's autonomous jurisdictional authority to create, implement, and enforce its own laws; in short, it provides a metric by which changes in a given power dynamic—for purposes of the present discussion, that between the state and international law—may be measured. *See* Marcel Brus, *Bridging the Gap between State Sovereignty and International Governance: The Authority of Law*, *in* STATE, SOVEREIGNTY, AND INTERNATIONAL GOVERNANCE 7–10 (Gerard Kreijen, ed. Oxford 2004). *See generally* John H. Jackson, *Sovereignty-Modern: A New Approach To An Outdated Concept*, 97 AM. J. INT'L L. 782, 786, 789–90 (2003). For a discussion of the evolution of the concept of sovereignty toward a human rights-based, popular sovereignty see W. Michael Reisman, *Sovereignty and Human Rights in Contemporary International Law*, 84 AM. J. INT'L L. 866 (1990).

24. RESTATEMENT (THIRD) FOREIGN RELATIONS LAW OF THE UNITED STATES § 401(a) (1987).

subject persons or things to its judicial process.[25] Importantly, "[j]urisdiction to enforce or adjudicate is dependent on jurisdiction to prescribe."[26] Thus a state has no inherent authority to subject persons or things to its judicial process if that state has no lawmaking authority over those persons or things to begin with.[27]

The international law of jurisdiction is a customary law. That is, it is not based on treaties or other positive agreements among states, but rather on state practice and *opinio juris*, or the state's belief or intent that it is acting with legal purpose[28] (though by these two components, as I

25. *Id.* § 401(b).

26. CHRISTOPHER L. BLAKESLEY ET AL., THE INTERNATIONAL LEGAL SYSTEM 132 (2001); RESTATEMENT § 431 cmt. a.

27. States may, however, agree either formally or informally to delegate among themselves jurisdiction absent territorial or national prescriptive authority—but such an exercise of jurisdiction is only legitimate insofar as it stems from the delegation of jurisdiction by a state with territorial or national prescriptive authority. For example, there is a form of extraterritorial criminal jurisdiction exercised by some European states, in particular Germany, called the "vicarious administration of justice" or "representation" principle which allows for the application of municipal criminal law based only on the custody of a foreign defendant without other territorial or national links. This type of jurisdiction is, however, preconditioned upon "a request from another state to take over criminal proceedings, or either the refusal of an extradition request from another state and its willingness to prosecute or confirmation from another state that it will not request extradition." *Extraterritorial Criminal Jurisdiction*, *in* COUNCIL OF EUROPE, EUROPEAN COMMITTEE ON CRIME PROBLEMS 14 (1990). Unlike universal jurisdiction, the representation principle conforms with the classical sovereignty model under which states have full prescriptive authority regarding conduct within their territories. First, the principle requires some form of agreement or consent between the custodial/prosecuting state and the territorial state. *See id.*

> ([T]he 'representation' principle differs from the principle of universality in that the decision to prosecute is not taken in isolation by the state claiming jurisdiction, but requires a certain understanding, if not agreement, by the other state which is more directly concerned, for instance the state where the offence has been committed.).

Hence, the territorial state permits the custodial state's application of prescriptive jurisdiction, which of course the territorial state has a sovereign prerogative to delegate. Also in this connection, the principle is decidedly subordinate to other principles of jurisdiction, which take priority. *See* Jurgen Meyer, *The Vicarious Administration of Justice: An Overlooked Basis of Jurisdiction*, 31 HARV. INT'L. L.J. 108, 116 (1990). Second, the substantive crime must be virtually indistinguishable as between the custodial and territorial states; the custodial state literally acts as a surrogate for the territorial state. *See id.* at 111

> ([T]he principle of the vicarious administration of justice...implies that it is insufficient to find an applicable norm of the place of conduct which is identical to the [custodial state's] norm; the particular conduct must also satisfy the elements of that norm. Moreover, the grounds of justification and excuse under the law of the place of conduct must be observed....);

see also COUNCIL OF EUROPE, *supra* at 14. In contrast, universal jurisdiction can be exercised irrespective of the permission and *despite* the prescriptive legislation of the territorial state.

28. *See e.g.*, RESTATEMENT (THIRD) OF THE FOREIGN RELATIONS LAW OF THE UNITED STATES § 102(2) (1987) (describing this component as "a sense of legal obligation"); Statute of

show in more detail below, treaties certainly may *inform* or *evidence* the customary law of jurisdiction).[29] While all states may contribute to international custom since it embodies their collective "general practice accepted as law,"[30] custom is an external force on each individual state that makes up part of the international law-making collective.[31] The legal construct of jurisdiction essentially comprises the package of "external rules that have defined [the nation] as a 'nation.'"[32] Presently those rules circumscribe the prescriptive reach of states based principally on their authority over territory and national citizens. Traditional bases therefore hold that a state has jurisdiction over acts that occur—even in part—within its territory (subjective territoriality), may not occur but have an effect within its territory (objective territoriality), involve its national citizens (active and passive personality—based on perpetrator and victim respectively), and are directed against its security (protective principle).[33] Despite an observable allowance for concurrent jurisdiction by multiple states, e.g., a matter occurs (or has an effect) in the territory of one state but involves one or more nationals of another state, and even conflicts between states with concurrent jurisdiction,[34] the jurisdictional

---

the International Court of Justice, June 26, 1945, art. 38, 59 Stat. 1055, 1060, 3 Bevans 1153, 1179 (describing this component as "accepted as law").

29. *See* discussion *infra* note 47.

30. Statute of the International Court of Justice, *supra* note 29, at art. 38.

31. In a recent defense of customary law, George Norman and Joel Trachtman explain this phenomenon in the following manner: while custom is "endogenous to states as a group—meaning that it is not a vertical structure produced outside or above the group of states—it has an independent, exogenous influence on the behavior of each individual state." George Norman & Joel P. Trachtman, *The Customary International Law Game*, 99 AM. J. INT'L L. 541, 542 (2005).

32. Anthony D'Amato, *The Concept of Human Rights in International Law*, 82 COLUM. L. REV. 1110, 1113 (1982) [hereinafter D'Amato, *The Concept of Human Rights*]; Anthony D'Amato, *Is International Law Really "Law"?* 79 NW. U. L. REV. 1293, 1308 (1985)

> (As a construct of international law, a nation is nothing more nor less than a bundle of entitlements, of which the most important ones define and secure its boundaries on a map, while others define its jurisdictional competency and the rights of its citizens when they travel outside its borders.).

33. RESTATEMENT (THIRD) FOREIGN RELATIONS LAW OF THE UNITED STATES § 402 (1987); *see also* Anne-Marie Slaughter, *Defining the Limit: Universal Jurisdiction and National Courts*, *in* UNIVERSAL JURISDICTION 168, 172 (Stephen Macedo, ed., 2004) (noting that like territorial and national bases of jurisdiction, this protective principle is "defined in terms of [a state's] territorial integrity or the safety of its citizens.").

34. *See, e.g.*, Case of S.S. Lotus (Fr. V. Turk.), 1927 P.C.I.J. (ser. A) No. 10, at 30–31 (Sept. 7) (ruling on the collision of a French ship with a Turkish ship, and observing that

> [n]either the exclusive jurisdiction of either State, nor the limitations of the jurisdiction of each to the occurrences which took place on the respective ships would appear calculated to satisfy the requirements of justice and effectively to protect the interests of the

construct provides a relatively practicable and objective measure of the authority of individual states *vis a vis* one another concerning a particular matter. Thus State *B* may apply its prescriptive jurisdiction to persons and things within its territory, and therefore may apply its jurisdiction to a State *A* national within State *B* borders. State *B* may even have a jurisdictional claim over a State *B* national who happens to be in State *A*. But absent some justifying territorial or national nexus (or agreement between the states),[35] State *B* may not project unilaterally its domestic laws onto State *A*. For instance State *B* may not project unilaterally, say, its traffic codes, onto State *A*. That issue is squarely within State *A's* sovereign jurisdiction.[36] It follows that State *B's* courts cannot apply State *B's* traffic code to a State *A* driver, driving only in State *A*, and with no other jurisdictional connection to State *B* since there exists no prescriptive jurisdiction upon which State *B's* adjudicative jurisdiction may rely. It would be as if some British court applied the British rule that drivers must drive on the left side of the road to a U.S. citizen, driving only in the United States and with absolutely no connection to Britain. Such an application plainly would clash with international law.

Yet universal jurisdiction allows State *B's* courts adjudicative authority with respect to an act that occurs entirely within State *A's* borders, has no effect on the territory of State *B*, and involves only State *A* national citizens. If, as we have said, State *B* cannot extend its prescriptive jurisdiction into the territory of State *A*, universal jurisdiction begs the question of what prescriptive jurisdiction authorizes State *B's* courts. In cases of universal jurisdiction that prescriptive jurisdiction is, as a legal matter, international—for as we have seen already, extraterritorial prescriptive jurisdiction of this sort cannot by law be national, e.g., State *B* may not apply unilaterally its municipal law concerning traffic codes to State *A* nationals acting with respect to other State *A* nationals in State *A*. Universal crimes are instead proscribed at the level of international law which, unlike national prescriptive jurisdiction, does extend into the territory of all states.

Universal jurisdiction is therefore quite unique among the bases of in-

two States. It is only natural that each should be able to exercise jurisdiction and to do so in respect of the incident as a whole. It is therefore a case of concurrent jurisdiction.).

35. *See supra* note 28.

36. Indeed, it is difficult to imagine a scenario in which, even with a link to the conduct in question, one state's prescriptive jurisdiction regarding traffic codes could justifiably extend into the territory of another state.

ternational jurisdiction in two discrete but related respects. First, its prescriptive and adjudicative faces are distinctively symbiotic: The prescriptive substance of universal crimes not only defines the crimes themselves, but also authorizes the adjudicative competence for all states engendered by the commission of those crimes. In other words, universal adjudicative jurisdiction depends upon the definitional substance of the crime as prescribed by universal prescriptive jurisdiction.

Second, the legal content of this prescriptive jurisdiction is moored in customary international law. By contrast, a state's jurisdiction over its territory or nationals—while certainly a matter of international law at the edges since it describes the state's authority *vis a vis* other states—is not, at the level of a state's domestic law, necessarily substantiated by the content of international law. International law merely sets the perimeters inside which states have sovereign lawmaking authority (to the extent that they do not legislatively act contrary to international law—by endorsing universal crimes).[37] It follows that states may grant their courts jurisdiction over any subject matter they please within these territorial and national prescriptive perimeters. The same cannot be said of universal jurisdiction—courts' subject matter jurisdiction is circumscribed by the prescriptive substance of the international law outlawing universal crimes. Hence if certain State *A* nationals put into action a program of extermination of other State *A* nationals based on the latter group's race or ethnic identity, courts in State *B* would have the authority, under international law, to prosecute the former group for the universal crime of genocide. But crucially, State *B's* adjudicative jurisdiction would be contingent upon the customary definitional substance of the crime prosecuted, i.e., genocide. Put differently, absent territorial or national links or some other legitimating understanding between the states, State *B* could not prosecute the State *A* actors under its municipal code for a series of homicides; like our traffic code hypothetical, such an application would conflict with international law. In sum, a state's universal adjudicative jurisdiction is empowered not by the state's own domestic prescriptive authority—based on, for instance, its authority over national territory or citizens—but rather, by international law. Consequently, when states exercise universal jurisdiction they are legally constrained to

37. A question arises where the state, through government power, commits universal crimes on a grand scale. Such a state arguably has waived its jurisdiction under international law. For example, it has been suggested that "[a] State that massively violates the rights of an ethnic minority risks forfeiture of its rights to control a given part of its territory." Brus, *supra* note 24, at 13.

adjudicate the prescriptive substance of the crime under international law.

The objection immediately will be made, however, that national courts typically have no authority to pull *sua sponte* from the sky principles of international law according to which they may then adjudicate a matter; instead they must rely upon some domestic law granting them jurisdiction. And thus, the very idea of international prescriptive jurisdiction depends entirely on domestic law. It follows, the argument goes, that (contrary to my stated position) the state court that asserts universal jurisdiction gets its authority not from international law but from that state's domestic legislation. References to what skeptics might sardonically label "so-called international law" may make for nice and popular dicta in the court's opinion, but as a matter of law they are utterly irrelevant.

This position misunderstands the international law of jurisdiction. The principle of universal jurisdiction empowers states *in the first instance* with the capacity to adjudicate certain matters where they otherwise would have no authority to do so. How the sovereign state then authorizes its own judicial bodies to adjudicate the matter is up to the state's domestic law (and thus courts are not randomly pulling from the sky international law). For instance, the domestic law of the state may indeed permit the court to draw directly from international law, or domestic law may incorporate or reflect international law,[38] in which case the state would be using its domestic laws and procedures to adjudicate the substance of international law. But importantly, for cases of universal jurisdiction the substance of the law must accord with the prescriptive juris-

38. These two approaches to international law by national legal systems are called monism and dualism respectively. Under the monist approach to international law,

> [t]he state's constitutional system must recognize the supremacy of international law. The national legislature is bound—constitutionally bound—to respect international law in enacting legislation. The national executive is constitutionally required to take care that international law be faithfully executed, even in the face of inconsistent domestic law. The national judiciary must give effect to international law, notwithstanding inconsistent domestic law, even domestic law of a constitutional character.

LOUIS HENKIN, INTERNATIONAL LAW: POLITICS AND VALUES 64 (Dordrecht 1995). Dualism, on the other hand, views international law as the law between sovereign states, a law that is separate and apart from domestic law. *See* IAN BROWNLIE, PRINCIPLES OF PUBLIC INTERNATIONAL LAW 30 (1990). Thus, for international law to be part of a dualist state's domestic legal system, it must be implemented through domestic legislation. *See* MALCOLM N. SHAW, INTERNATIONAL LAW 107 (1991). Most states incorporate aspects of both approaches with regard to the domestic application of international law.

diction that governs it—that is, it must be international.

III. THE CUSTOMARY LAW OF UNIVERSAL JURISDICTION

If state courts' universal adjudicative jurisdiction depends upon universal prescriptive jurisdiction as defined by international law, then our next question asks how to determine the content of this prescriptive jurisdiction, or the customary definitions of universal crimes. This Part contends that the answer lies in the provisions of the widely-ratified and relatively longstanding multilateral treaties proscribing universal crimes under positive international law. To frame my argument, I begin with two distinctions. The first elaborates upon the distinction between the more procedural law of universal adjudicative jurisdiction and the more substantive law of universal prescriptive jurisdiction. The second, to be clear about the customary character of universal jurisdiction, observes the difference between a treaty-based or "conventional" version of universal jurisdiction, which necessarily confines itself to the states party to the convention that generates such jurisdiction, and the customary law of universal jurisdiction, which extends to all states. I then explain how treaty provisions prescribing universal crimes provide a strong and easily-measurable record of customary law's universal prescription as to those crimes—in other words, the prescriptive jurisdiction that governs state courts' exercises of universal adjudicative jurisdiction.

A. *Adjudicative versus Prescriptive Universal Jurisdiction*

Although universal adjudicative jurisdiction depends upon the substance of universal prescriptive jurisdiction (or conversely, the substance of universal prescriptive jurisdiction authorizes universal adjudicative jurisdiction), the customary rules of universal adjudicative and prescriptive jurisdiction are nonetheless distinct in their character and development. Universal adjudicative jurisdiction essentially outlines the procedural connection needed for courts to assert jurisdiction over the person(s) before it. For universal jurisdiction purposes, this procedural element exceptionally requires no territorial or national nexus to the accused criminal over which a court asserts judicial authority.[39]

39. The conventional or positive law relating to this aspect of jurisdiction is found in treaty provisions establishing states parties' jurisdiction to prosecute, i.e., the provisions determining

My focus here, however, is on universal prescriptive jurisdiction, which relates more to the subject matter over which the court claims competence—that is, the substance of universal crime itself. Due perhaps to a need for legal analysis explaining an increased exercise in the last decade or so of jurisdiction by courts having no territorial or national links to the defendants they seek to prosecute,[40] commentary has concentrated unevenly on the unqualified, and literally global ambit of universal adjudicative jurisdiction,[41] while important aspects of the prescriptive scope and definition of universal crimes themselves have been overlooked. To illustrate, piracy is commonly understood as a core universal crime because throughout international legal history any state's courts could prosecute the pirate absent territorial or national links to him or his piratical acts, and more recently, such adjudicative procedure has been strongly endorsed in conventional law.[42] But the question of what precisely "piracy" is as a matter of customary law has garnered little attention[43]—and yet, as we have seen, this customary definition determines the legal availability of a given court's universal subject matter jurisdiction. To take a more modern and contentious example, "terrorism" has been rejected by courts as a crime of universal jurisdiction. The reason for this rejection stems not from a void of state practice favoring

---

whether states may exercise jurisdiction over acts committed outside their territories, having no effect on their territories and involving non-nationals. *See. e.g.*, the Torture Convention's prosecute-or-extradite provisions set forth *infra*, note 53.

40. *See* LUC REYDAMS, UNIVERSAL JURISDICTION: INTERNATIONAL AND MUNICIPAL LEGAL PERSPECTIVES 1 (2003) (noting that "[m]ore cases of 'universal jurisdiction' have been reported in the past decade than throughout the whole history of modern international law.").

41. Commentary has tended to focus almost exclusively on the availability of universal jurisdiction for courts—i.e., adjudicative jurisdiction, without discussing the substance of the crime itself—i.e., prescriptive jurisdiction. *See, e.g.*, THE PRINCETON PRINCIPLES, *supra* note 3, at 21–25 (listing various universal crimes but not explaining how to define them and dealing largely with procedural issues such as due process, extradition, evidence-gathering, immunities, statutes of limitations, amnesties, resolution of competing jurisdictions, double jeopardy, and settlement of disputes between states with concurrent jurisdictional claims). The author has found one article that discusses universal jurisdiction as a prescriptive jurisdiction, but only to make the point that while a state's universal prescriptive jurisdiction is extraterritorial, jurisdiction to enforce is territorial. *See* Roger O'Keefe, *Universal Jurisdiction – Clarifying the Basic Concept*, 2 J. INT'L CRIM. JUST. 735 (2004) (dealing primarily with the ICJ opinion in the Arrest Warrant case, and not discussing the nature of the prescriptive jurisdiction under the universality principle, the main focus of this Essay).

42. M. Cherif Bassiouni, *The History of Universal Jurisdiction and Its Place in International Law*, *in* UNIVERSAL JURISDICTION 47–48 (Stephen Macedo ed., 2004).

43. For an historical account of the crime that highlights confusion about what set piracy apart from other actions on the high seas, see Eugene Kontorovich, *The Piracy Analogy: Modern Universal Jurisdiction's Hollow Foundation*, 45 HARV. INT'L L.J. 183 (2004).

far-reaching adjudicative jurisdiction over the perpetrators of this type of crime, but rather from the absence of a coherent customary definition of "terrorism."[44] In the words of the United States Court of Appeals for the Second Circuit in the recent *Yousef* opinion:

> Unlike those offenses supporting universal jurisdiction under customary international law—that is, piracy, war crimes, and crimes against humanity—that now have fairly precise definitions and that have achieved universal condemnation, 'terrorism' is a term as loosely deployed as it is powerfully charged.... No consensus has developed on how to properly define 'terrorism' generally.... [Such] strenuous disagreement among States about what actions do or do not constitute terrorism...[means that] terrorism—unlike piracy, war crimes, and crimes against humanity—does not provide a basis for universal jurisdiction.[45]

Thus the answer to the question of how to determine the customary definitional content of universal crimes is of increasing legal and practical importance.

On my view, developed below, that the answer lies in the substnative definitions of treaties, the international crime at issue in *Yousef*, which involved planting and exploding a bomb on a civilian aircraft—not abstractly "terrorism"—clearly would be subject to universal jurisdiction. The relevant international instrument, the 1971 Montreal Convention for the Suppression of Unlawful Acts Against the Safety of Civil Aviation, not only evidences a custom of universal adjudicative jurisdiction by providing for extraterritorial and extra-national jurisdiction over alleged plane-bombers,[46] it fills the prescriptive customary hole that so worried

---

44. United States v. Yousef, 327 F.3d 56 (2d Cir. 2003).

45. *Id.* at 87–89 (internal citation and quotation omitted).

46. Article 5 of the Montreal Convention provides that:

> Each Contracting State shall...take such measures as may be necessary to establish its jurisdiction over the offences [defined]...in the case where the alleged offender is present in its territory and it does not extradite him pursuant to Article 8 to any of the States mentioned in paragraph 1 of this Article.

Article 7 states:

> The Contracting State in the territory of which the alleged offender is found shall, if it does not extradite him, be obliged, without exception whatsoever and whether or not the offence was committed in its territory, to submit the case to its competent authorities for the purpose of prosecution. Those authorities shall take their decision in the same manner as in the case of any ordinary offence of a serious nature under the law of that State.

Convention for the Suppression of Unlawful Acts Against the Safety of Civil Aviation, Sept. 23, 1971, 24 U.S.T. 565, 974 U.N.T.S. 177, 181-82 [hereinafter Montreal

the Second Circuit by prescribing a definite international law articulation of the crime of plane-bombing.[47] Thus while "terrorism" abstractly-labeled may not be subject to universal jurisdiction because of its definitional uncertainty, certain clearly-defined acts of terrorism, like plane-bombing, are.[48]

B. "Conventional" versus Customary Universal Jurisdiction

But treaties and custom are of course essentially different types of law. And like all bases of jurisdiction in international law, "[u]niversal jurisdiction is a fundamentally customary, not treaty-based, law."[49] So before we make the jump from treaty definitions to customary definitions, one more distinction should be made between what might be called treaty-based or "conventional" universal jurisdiction on the one hand, and customary universal jurisdiction on the other. So-called "con-

Convention]. For a discussion of how these provisions evidence custom, see Colangelo, *supra* note 3, at 598:

> A state's entrance into a treaty with other states and commitment to be bound thereby constitutes the maximal expression of state sovereignty and "assent" to the particular rules contained in that treaty; the state's implementing legislation pursuant to the treaty compounds this assent by demonstrating a "general usage and practice" designed to enforce those rules; and finally, "the [state's] judicial decisions recognize and enforce that law" in practice.
>
> The Montreal Convention, which was put into effect in 1971, currently has 173 states parties, which means that in the last thirty years the vast majority of states in the world have agreed to bind themselves to and put into practice through domestic legislation and judicial enforcement the provisions of the treaty. [And while] the Montreal Convention "creates a basis for the assertion of jurisdiction that is moored in a process of formal law-making and that is binding only on the States that accede to it[,]"...it is precisely this process of formal lawmaking between sovereign states, their mutual assent to the rule agreed upon, and their affirmative adoption and implementation of this rule in domestic legislation and judicial decisionmaking that constitutes evidence of the customary rule. What is important to keep in mind is that the treaty, the municipal legislation, and the judicial opinion are not *themselves* customary international law; rather they make up the abs olute best evidence of what a state, the United States, and all other states party to the Montreal Convention consider to be a legally binding practice—and in this respect supply the most powerful evidence possible of customary international law there is.

(internal citation omitted) (emphasis in original).

47. Article 1 of the Montreal Convention defines the offense as:

> unlawfully and intentionally...plac[ing] or caus[ing] to be placed on an aircraft in service, by any means whatsoever, a device or substance which is likely to destroy that aircraft, or to cause damage to it which renders it incapable of flight, or to cause damage to it which is likely to endanger its safety in flight....

Montreal Convention, *supra* note 47, at art. 1

48. Colangelo, *supra* note 3, at 594–603

49. *Id.* at 567; *see also Yousef*, 327 F.3d at 96 n.29.

ventional" universal jurisdiction is somewhat of an oxymoron, or at the least, a misnomer. Because such jurisdiction is rooted in treaty law, it provides neither in fact, nor in law, a truly "universal" jurisdiction.[50] It merely vests a comprehensive jurisdiction for states party to a convention *inter se* with respect to the prosecution of a crime that is the subject of the convention; states party may (and in some cases are obliged to) — under the jurisdictional provisions of the convention—exercise their adjudicative jurisdiction absent territorial or national links to the offense that the convention prescriptively defines and outlaws. Though the convention's prescriptive mandate—i.e., the proscription on the crime—ostensibly binds all states party all the time, conventions tend to limit procedurally the exercise of a state courts' adjudicative jurisdiction, absent territorial or national links to the crime, to instances where the alleged offender is afterwards present or "found" in that state party's territory and it does not extradite him to another state party.[51]

To illustrate, the Torture Convention prescriptively defines and bans the crime of torture for states party to the Convention.[52] And through its prosecute-or-extradite provisions,[53] the Convention provides for an equivalent of universal adjudicative jurisdiction over torture as among the states party. As a matter of positive law, however, both the Convention's prescriptive ban on torture and its grant of extraterritorial and extra-national adjudicative capacity to courts to prosecute torturers comprehend only the jurisdictions of those states party to the Convention.[54]

---

50. *See* ROSALYN HIGGINS, PROBLEMS AND PROCESS: INTERNATIONAL LAW AND HOW WE USE IT 64 (1994) (explaining that treaty-based jurisdiction is never "universal jurisdiction *stricto sensu*" because such jurisdiction concerns only the states parties to the treaty).

51. This provision is commonly referred to as a "prosecute-or-extradite" provision, or *aut dedere aut judicare*.

52. Torture Convention, *supra* note 22, at 197; *see also* Appendix F, *infra*.

53. Torture Convention, *supra* note 22, at 198. Article 5(2) of the convention provides that "[e]ach State Party shall...take such measures as may be necessary to establish its jurisdiction over such offences in cases where the alleged offender is present in any territory under its jurisdiction and it dos not extradite him...." And Article 7(1) provides:

> The State Party in the territory under whose jurisdiction a person alleged to have committed any offence referred to in [the relevant provision] is found shall in the cases contemplated in article 5, if it does not extradite him, submit the case to its competent authorities for the purpose of prosecution.

Id. at 198.

Lori Damrosch has noted that "at a minimum all the prosecute-or-extradite crimes [like torture] are ones as to which there is an *option* to exercise jurisdiction without any link to the crime other than custody of the offender." Lori F. Damrosch, *Connecting the Threads in the Fabric of International Law*, *in* UNIVERSAL JURISDICTION 91, *supra* note 34, at 94 (emphasis in original).

54. For instance, Article 34 of the Vienna Convention on the Law of Treaties provides that

In other words, the Torture Convention does not, on its own, bind non-parties.

By contrast, the customary basis of universal jurisdiction over torture, both in terms of its prescriptive ban on the crime and in terms of its adjudicative scope allowing all states' courts to prosecute the crime, extends beyond those states party to the Torture Convention to contemplate the jurisdiction of all states—making jurisdiction in fact, and in law, "universal." So if State *A* and State *B* are parties to the Torture Convention, and State *B* asserts jurisdiction pursuant to the Convention over a State *A* national found in State *B* for torture committed in State *A* against other State *A* nationals, State *B* is not exercising universal jurisdiction, but is simply discharging its treaty obligations.[55] Similarly, in *Yousef*, while the Second Circuit found that it did not have universal jurisdiction as a matter of *customary law*, it did find jurisdiction under the Montreal Convention and its domestic implementing legislation with respect to acts committed by a Pakistani national, which killed and injured Japanese nationals on a Philippine flag airliner flying from the Philippines to Japan (there was no evidence that a U.S. citizen was even aboard the flight).[56] Critically, in the Torture Convention hypothetical, and in *Yousef*, both the prosecuting and the territorial states were parties to the applicable conventions[57] and the prosecuting states used the prescriptive definitions of the crimes contained in the conventions.[58]

"[a] Treaty does not create either obligations or rights for a third State without its consent," and Article 35 provides that treaties are only binding on non-parties where the non-party "State expressly accepts that obligation in writing." Vienna Convention on the Law of Treaties, May 23, 1969, arts. 34 & 35, 1155 U.N.T.S. 331, 333, 8 I.L.M. 679 (entered into force Jan. 27, 1980).

55. This was essentially the reasoning of Lord Browne-Wilkinson speaking for the English House of Lords in Pinochet III, where he concluded that Pinochet could be extradited to Spain under the Torture Convention since

> the states with the most obvious jurisdiction...do not seek to extradite, the state where the alleged torturer is found must prosecute or, apparently, extradite to another country, i.e. there is universal jurisdiction....Since Chile, Spain and the United Kingdom are all parties to the Convention, they are bound under treaty by its provisions whether or not such provisions would apply in the absence of treaty obligation.

THE PINOCHET PAPERS, *supra* note 20. The Netherlands also recently convicted a torturer absent territorial or national links to his crimes which occurred in the former Zaire (now Democratic Republic of the Congo) based on the Dutch implementation of the Torture Convention's provisions. *See* 51 NETH. INT'L L. REV. 439, 444–49 (2004).

56. *Yousef*, 327 F.3d at 97, 108–110.

57. *Id.* at 109 n.43.

58. *Id.* at 110 (observing that the domestic implementing legislation "carefully tracks the text of the Montreal Convention"). As to the definition of the crime in particular, the Montreal Convention and 18 U.S.C. § 32(b)(3) define the crime in substantively identical terms, see *infra* note

To place the jurisdictional competence of the prosecuting state in the torture hypothetical outside of that vested by the treaty, we would need to make either State *A* (the territorial state), or State *B* (the prosecuting state), or both, non-parties to the Convention. Plainly if either both State *A* and State *B* are non-parties, or just State *B* is a non-party, State *B* cannot pretend to assert jurisdiction based on a treaty to which it is not party, and which accordingly does not vest it with jurisdiction. But what about the scenario in which State *B is* a party to the Convention and State *A* is not? Can State *B* still prosecute a State *A* national for torture committed in State *A* against only State *A* nationals based on the positive law of the Torture Convention? The answer would seem to be no, and the reason is that the Torture Convention, by itself, does not extend its prescriptive jurisdiction outlawing torture into the territory of non-parties, i.e., State *A.* And therefore, State *B,* acting pursuant only to the Convention, would have no *positive* prescriptive jurisdiction authorizing its adjudicative jurisdiction under the Convention.

The State *B* prosecution could, however, rely on the customary law of universal jurisdiction because its prescriptive jurisdiction *does* extend into the territory of all states to proscribe torture, and likewise vests all states with the adjudicative jurisdiction to prosecute the torturer. But State *B's* customary adjudicative jurisdiction would only be valid insofar as it accords with the governing customary prescriptive jurisdiction. And so we come back to the question of how to determine the prescriptive substance of universal crimes under customary law.

C. *Treaties and the Prescriptive Substance of Universal Crimes*

As we have seen, unlike treaties and other positive law instruments that affect only those states that have signed onto them through a formal international lawmaking process, customary law is universal in its application. Moreover, it is evidenced by and evolves organically in light of state practice conditioned by *opinio juris.* Such practice is manifest, for instance, in the state's entrance into a treaty. The idea that generalizable or "norm-creating" treaty provisions—like, for example, proscriptions on internationally agreed-upon crimes—generate customary law is not new[59] and is, in the words of the International Court of Justice, "indeed

---

70.

59. Professor D'Amato first made the argument over forty years ago in his article *Treaties as a Source of General Rules of International Law*, 3 HARV. INT'L L.J. 1 (1962); *see also* ANTHONY

one of the recognized methods by which new rules of customary international law may be formed."[60] Although some might feel the need to temper the formation of custom through treaty by requiring a certain threshold number of states party to the treaty or the passage of a certain amount of time before its provisions could constitute custom,[61] this Essay needs not go so far for its argument. Each of the treaties prohibiting universal crimes enjoys longstanding and widespread acceptance; indeed, and as the Appendix bears out, the treaties themselves even tend to avow either an explicit or implicit purpose to codify or create custom in their respective areas of international lawmaking.[62] That treaties do so is, again, nothing new for international law. The Nuremberg Tribunal, for instance, applied to the accused Nazi war criminals before it, as a matter of customary law, the detailed provisions of the 1907 Hague Convention and the 1929 Geneva Convention on the Prisoners of War.[63] The Tribunal, citing no state practice other than that of states agreeing upon the rules contained in, and entering into, these treaties, observed that the rules were "declaratory of the laws and customs of war."[64] As Anthony D'Amato points out, "[i]t strains credulity to suppose that state practice had become so detailed by 1939—particularly between 1929, the date of the Geneva Convention, and 1939!—that the conventions were merely

A. D'AMATO, THE CONCEPT OF CUSTOM IN INTERNATIONAL LAW 105–66 (1971) [hereinafter D'AMATO, THE CONCEPT OF CUSTOM]; *see also* D'Amato, *The Concept of Human Rights*, *supra* note 33 at 1127–47. *See generally* Arthur M. Weisburd, *Customary International Law: The Problem of Treaties*, 21 VAND. J. TRANSNAT'L L. 1 (1988); Gary L. Scott & Craig L. Carr, *Multilateral Treaties and the Formation of Customary International Law*, 25 DENV. J. INT'L L. & POL'Y 71 (1996).

60. North Sea Continental Shelf (W. Ger. v. Den., W. Ger. v. Neth.), 1969 I.C.J. 3, 41 (Feb. 20); *see also* RESTATEMENT (THIRD) OF THE FOREIGN RELATIONS LAW OF THE UNITED STATES § 102(3) (1987) ("International agreements create law for the states parties thereto and may lead to the creation of customary international law when such agreements are intended for adherence by states generally and are in fact widely accepted.").

61. *See generally* Scott & Carr, *supra* note 60.

62. *See* Appendix, *infra*. The express or implied avowal of generating custom, when buttressed by the history of actions and reactions of states in respect to these treaties, would seem to take care of Dr. Michael Akehurst's concerns that *opinio juris* must accompany a treaty for its provisions to create custom; the ways in which he sees this criterion satisfied are a declaratory statement in the treaty or its preparatory materials to this effect, or by subsequent practice and *opinio juris* supporting the rule. Michael Akehurst, *Custom as a Source of International Law*, *in* THE BRITISH YEAR BOOK OF INTERNATIONAL LAW 1974–1975 1, 45, 49 (R.Y Jennings & Ian Brownlie eds., 1977).

63. *International Military Tribunal Judgment*, *in* NAZI CONSPIRACY AND AGGRESSION: OPINION AND JUDGMENT 83 (1947).

64. *Id.*

'declaratory' of such practice. Rather, the more reasonable interpretation is that the conventions 'declared' what the practice is by virtue of the fact that the signatories undertook to declare that practice operative under the conventions themselves."[65]

The argument from treaty law engages therefore not just the prohibition on the crime but also the articulation of its content. It goes beyond accepting that genocide is prohibited as a matter of international law because the Genocide Convention prohibits it—treaties are the source of most if not all international human rights norms in this regard[66]—to contend that the substantive definition of the crime is reflected in the treaty provisions and, in line with Part II of this Essay, that it is a definition to which courts must adhere in exercising universal jurisdiction. Again, I do not argue that the treaty provisions setting forth penal characteristics constitute themselves definitively the customary definitions of universal crimes; rather, these provisions make up strong *evidence* of what the customary definitions are. It follows too that definitions contained in legislation implementing domestically a state's treaty obligations or simply transposing onto domestic law the treaty's definitional provisions are particularly useful to courts since these domestic-law definitions reproduce, by their very nature, the substance of the conduct prohibited by the treaty.[67] My model necessarily allows for some flexibility in the definitions of the crimes insofar as domestic legislation does not substantively alter the definition of the treaty provision it transforms into domestic law.[68] Even apart from obvious differences that will result

65. D'AMATO, THE CONCEPT OF CUSTOM, *supra* note 60, at 123.

66. *See* D'Amato, *The Concept of Human Rights*, *supra* note 33, at 1128–48.

67. Of course, if the implementing legislation does not reproduce faithfully the crime as set forth in the treaty, the state would be in violation of its treaty obligations, and consequently, the definitions in the implementing legislation would not reflect the customary definitions of the crime (as set forth in the treaty).

68. An example of an improper substantive alteration of a treaty definition is Germany's former Criminal Code § 220a, which translated the definition of genocide contained in the 1948 Genocide Convention into German law. Under the Convention's provisions, the act of genocide is defined as "**[d]eliberately** inflicting on the group conditions of life **calculated** to bring about its physical destruction in whole or in part." The translation in § 220a criminalizes "inflict[ing] on the group conditions **apt** to bring about its physical destruction in whole or in part." Kai Ambos & Steffen Wirth, *Genocide and War Crimes in the Former Yugoslavia Before German Criminal Courts*, *in* INTERNATIONAL AND NATIONAL PROSECUTION OF CRIMES UNDER INTERNATIONAL LAW 769, 784–786 (Horst Fischer et al. eds., 2004) (emphasis in secondary source). Ambos and Wirth explain that the use of the word "apt" in the literal German translation "substantially changes the elements of the inflicting-destructive-conditions-[provision] of genocide with respect to both the ordinary meaning and the *travaux préparatoires* of the Convention." *Id.* at 786

from translating the treaty provisions into different languages for purposes of domestic legislation, slight variations on the language are almost inevitable given the universal prescriptions of treaties as compared to the more state-specific prescriptions of domestic legislation.[69] Using positive international law as the starting point for determining the substance of universal crimes accommodates the modification of definitions through evolutions in customary law regarding the crimes while presently providing courts with harmonized and fairly precise definitions that safeguard, among other things, bedrock criminal law principles of legality, "namely, no crime without a law, no punishment without a law"[70] in the context of international criminal law.[71]

---

69. To take one example, the Montreal Convention, *supra* note 47, provides for the equivalent of universal jurisdiction over anyone who

> unlawfully and intentionally:
>
> ....
>
> places or causes to be placed on an aircraft in service, by any means whatsoever, a device or substance which is likely to destroy that aircraft, or to cause damage to it which renders it incapable of flight, or to cause damage to it which is likely to endanger its safety in flight.

The U.S. implementing legislation, codified at 18 U.S.C. § 32(b)(3) (1996), similarly provides for jurisdiction over

> [w]hoever willfully--
>
> ....
>
> places or causes to be placed on a civil aircraft registered in a country other than the United States while such aircraft is in service, a device or substance which is likely to destroy that aircraft, or to cause damage to that aircraft which renders that aircraft incapable of flight or which is likely to endanger that aircraft's safety in flight.

70. Bassiouni, *supra* note 43, at 45.

71. The history and development of international criminal law has relied on less stringent legality requirements than what might be found under domestic law. *See* Jordan J. Paust, *It's No Defense: Nullum Crimen, International Crime and the Gingerbread Man*, 60 ALB. L. REV. 657, 664–671 (1997); Alfred P. Rubin, *Is International Criminal Law "Universal"?*, 2001 U. CHI. LEGAL F. 351, 357–363 (2001). Thus, so long as states do not expand the definitions of the crimes beyond their customary meanings, states may specify further the definitions of the crime as set forth in a treaty to comport with more stringent domestic legality requirements, as are typical in civil law, code-based systems. For instance, Germany's Code of Crimes Against International Law transforms the ICC crimes into domestic legislation. "Each crime was, however, reformulated into language consistent with German legal terminology, and to ensure that [sic], as required by the German Constitution, the crimes were clearly defined at the time of the commission of the act." Steffen Wirth, *Germany's New International Crimes Code: Bringing a Case to Court*, 1 J. INT'L CRIM. JUST. 151, 153 (2003). The drafters of the ICC evidently were also concerned with specificity problems and therefore agreed to promulgate more specific "Elements of Crimes," which are "non-binding guidelines for the Court, aids for application and interpretation designed to help judges and prosecutors as well as legal counsels appearing in cases before the Court." Wiebke Rückert & Georg Witschel, *Genocide and Crimes Against Humanity in the Elements of Crimes*, *in* INTERNATIONAL AND NATIONAL PROSECUTION OF CRIMES UNDER INTERNATIONAL

There is, however, a circularity problem. How can state practice change the customary definitions of universal crimes if states are legally constrained in their exercise of universal jurisdiction to use, as it were, the customary definitions "as they exist"? This circularity problem tends to afflict customary international law generally.[72] The easy solution for our purposes would be for states to get together and simply change the definition of the crime through an amendment to the relevant treaty, or to create a new instrument relating to that crime. This process has taken place to some extent with respect to crimes spelled out in the statute for the newly-established International Criminal Court and to a lesser degree (since they are not treaties, strictly speaking) in the statutes of various international tribunals created under the auspices of the United Nations. For example, the Charter of the International Military Tribunal under which the Nazis were prosecuted defined crimes against humanity as "murder, extermination, enslavement, deportation, and other inhumane acts committed against any civilian populations…."[73] Although acts such as torture, imprisonment, and rape could potentially fall into the "other inhumane acts" receptacle, they are not set forth explicitly in the Charter and courts using its definitional provisions therefore would be on more precarious ground prosecuting these crimes as universal crimes against humanity than in prosecuting a listed offense such as "extermination" or "enslavement." Yet by the end of the last century, international law evolved such that the statutes of the International Criminal Tribunals for the Former Yugoslavia and Rwanda, and the ICC Statute, do affirmatively list torture, imprisonment and rape as crimes against humanity,[74] thus clarifying or perhaps adding to the customary definitions of crimes against humanity and, in any event, providing courts with firmer prosecutorial footing as to certain of these crimes. Judicial opinions also may contribute to the development or clarification of the

---

LAW, *supra* note 69, at 61.

72. *See, e.g.*, RESTATEMENT (THIRD) OF FOREIGN RELATIONS LAW OF THE UNITED STATES § 102 reporters' note 2 (1987).

73. Agreement for the Prosecution and Punishment of the Major War Criminals of the European Axis art. 6(c), August 8, 1945, 59 Stat. 1544, 82 U.N.T.S. 279.

74. Statute of the International Criminal Tribunal for the Former Yugoslavia, S.C. Res. 827, at art. 5, U.N. SCOR, 48th Sess., 3217th mtg., U.N.Doc. S/RES/827 (May 25, 1993) [hereinafter ICTY Statute]; Statute of the International Criminal Tribunal for Rwanda, S.C. Res. 955, at art. 3, U.N. SCOR, 49th Sess., 3453rd mtg., U.N. Doc. S/RES/955 (Nov. 8, 1994) [hereinafter ICTR Statute]; Rome Statute of the International Criminal Court, art. 7, U.N. Doc. A/CONF.183/9 (July 17, 1998) [hereinafter ICC statute].

definitions under customary law. For example, although the Genocide Convention nowhere explicitly mentions rape in its list of acts that may qualify as genocide when "committed with the intent to destroy, in whole or in part, a national, ethnical, racial or religious group, as such,"[75] international criminal tribunal judgments make clear that acts constituting genocide encompass acts of rape committed with the requisite mens rea.[76]

But all these examples are of legal developments engineered by quintessentially international agreements or institutions. More difficult is the question of when and how national courts advance customary law in domestic proceedings that apply international law, including, naturally, exercises of universal jurisdiction. We can say, for instance, that if the consistent and widespread practice of states prosecuting the international crime of genocide deems intent to destroy a group based on its political self-identification to satisfy the mens rea component of the crime, the customary definition of genocide has expanded to include within its victim class political groups along with the national, ethnic and racial groups carved out by the Genocide Convention. But the first state to extend the definition in this way violates customary law by improperly asserting jurisdiction over a crime that—*at that moment*—prescriptively does not qualify as universal.[77] Yet customary law's recursive constitution may immediately reduce the illegality of that act if interested states—say, the alleged universal criminal's state of national citizenship and/or the state on whose territory the crime occurred—acquiesce in or approve of the universal jurisdictional assertion.[78] And particularly if other states then prosecute genocide in a way that recognizes political groups as victims, the first state's illegal act will have planted a customary "seed,"[79] the cultivation of which, by state practice, will have modi-

75. Convention on the Prevention and Punishment of the Crime of Genocide art. II, Dec. 9, 1948, 78 U.N.T.S. 277.

76. *See* Prosecutor v. Rutaganda, Case No. ICTR-96-3-T, Judgment, ¶ 53 (Dec. 6, 1999); Prosecutor v. Kayishema & Ruzindana, Case No. ICTR-95-1-T, Judgment, ¶ 117 (May 21, 1999); Prosecutor v. Akayesu, Case No. ICTR-96-4-T, Judgment, ¶¶ 507–08 (Sept. 2, 1998).

77. This especially would be the case in this example because including political groups in this victim classification was debated and rejected in the drafting of the Genocide Convention. For a history of the drafting debate on this issue see Beth Van Schaack, Note, *The Crime of Political Genocide: Repairing the Genocide Convention's Blind Spot*, 106 YALE L. J. 2259, 2262–2269 (1997).

78. I discuss this point in more detail, see Part IV, *infra*.

79. Anthony D'Amato, *The Theory Of Customary International Law*, 82 AM. SOC'Y INT'L L. PROC. 242, 246 (1988); D'Amato, *Is International Law Really "Law"?*, *supra* note 33, at 1310–

fied the customary definition of genocide. The possibility of custom evolving beyond treaty definitions was even expressly built into the ICC Statute.[80]

Evolutions in custom likewise may alter and even expand the capacity of states to allow procedurally for universal adjudicative jurisdiction over the perpetrators of international crimes. For instance, while like the Torture Convention, a number of positive instruments dealing with universal crimes provide for extraterritorial and extra-national jurisdiction by state courts over alleged offenders (the conventional equivalent of universal adjudicative jurisdiction), the Genocide Convention does not. In fact, extraterritorial jurisdiction was explicitly rejected in the Convention's drafting.[81] Thus to accept genocide as a universal crime, one must view custom as having expanded the adjudicative scope of jurisdiction as to genocide beyond that envisaged by the treaty to encompass the jurisdiction of all states, irrespective of the place of the crime.

But again, my focus here is on prescriptive jurisdiction, or the substance of the universal crime under international law. Because, as we have seen, treaties furnish neither definitive nor exhaustive definitions of universal crimes due to the organic nature of customary law, courts may not always be obliged to use the precise definitional language of the treaty when exercising universal jurisdiction, though it will often be the case that the treaty definition is the best—not to mention the most readily available—evidence of custom. In fact, the practice of universal jurisdiction evidences this latter point.

To begin with, states' domestic laws facilitating universal jurisdiction flow routinely from the criminalization of the conduct in question at the level of international conventional law. These domestic laws may, for instance, fulfill a state's obligations under a treaty and thus, either through specific implementing legislation (typical in common law countries) or general enabling clauses making the treaty provisions directly applicable (typical in civil law countries),[82] translate into national law

---

1311; D'AMATO, THE CONCEPT OF CUSTOM, *supra* note 60, at 97–98.

80. Rome Statute of the International Criminal Court, art. 10, U.N. Doc. A/CONF.183/9 (July 17, 1998) ("Nothing in this Part shall be interpreted as limiting or prejudicing in any way existing or developing rules of international law for purposes other than this Statute."). For a detailed analysis of Article 10, see Leila Nadya Sadat, *Custom, Codification and Some Thoughts About the Relationship Between the Two: Article 10 of the ICC Statute*, 49 DEPAUL L. REV. 909 (2000).

81. For a detailed and persuasive explanation of this point, see REYDAMS, *supra* note 41, at 48–53.

82. For example, Austria's criminal code provision providing for universal jurisdiction states

the international substance of the crime for courts to prosecute. Prevalent examples include domestic legislation regarding the Torture Convention,[83] the Genocide Convention,[84] and the Geneva Conventions and their Additional Protocol I[85]–this latter legislation has, in a number of states, been substituted for by legislation implementing the newly estab-

that extraterritorial, extra-national jurisdiction applies to "criminal offences, if Austria is under an obligation to prosecute them—even if committed abroad—irrespective of the penal law of the State where they were committed." Strafgestzbuch [StGB] [Penal Code] §64(1)(6) (Austria), *translated in* REYDAMS, *supra* note 41, at 94. "The term 'obligation' in §64(1) subparagraph 6 refers to a treaty obligation." REYDAMS, *supra* note 41, at 97. Another example is Belgium's Code de procédure pénale, titre préliminare, article 12 bis, which has a general enabling clause that reads: "The Belgian courts are competent to take cognizance of offences committed outside the territory of the Kingdom that are the object of an international convention binding on Belgium if the convention obliges in any way to submit the case to the competent authorities for the purpose of prosecution." REYDAMS, *supra* note 41, at 105. Likewise, Denmark's Straffeloven [Strfl] § 8(1)(5) (Denmark), provides: "Acts committed outside the territory of the Danish State, shall also come within Danish criminal jurisdiction, irrespective of the nationality of the perpetrator where the act is covered by an international convention in pursuance of which Denmark is under an obligation to start legal proceedings." REYDAMS, *supra* note 41, at 127. An enabling provision appears also in France's criminal code with respect to self-executing treaties. REYDAMS, *supra* note 41, at 132–33. Somewhat of a departure from this model, the German code, StGB, *supra*, § 6, "Offences Against Internationally Protected Interests or Rights" lists international crimes over which universal jurisdiction exists—all of which, except for one, are directly the subject of an international treaty—and provides a catch-all provision that provides jurisdiction over "acts that are to be prosecuted by the terms of an international treaty binding on the federal republic of Germany even if they are committed outside the country." REYDAMS, *supra* note 41, at 142. Spain's Ley Orgánica del Poder Judicial, article 23.4 follows this model as well, listing offenses prohibited under conventional international law, and providing also for jurisdiction over "any other offence which Spain is obliged to prosecute under an international treaty or convention." REYDAMS, *supra* note 41, at 183. The Netherlands' 2003 International Crimes Act, which amended the Wartime Offenses Act and implements in part the ICC Statute, likewise draws from treaty law to define the offenses over which it provides universal jurisdiction, namely, genocide, crimes against humanity, torture and grave breaches (and even non-grave breaches) of the Geneva Conventions and their Additional Protocol I. *See* International Crimes Act of 19 June 2003, English version *available at* http://www.icrc.org/ihl-nat.nsf/0/fb9070f8fc60c047c1256da30032f0b0?OpenDocument.

83. *See* Australia's Crimes (Torture) Act, 1988, *translated in* REYDAMS *supra* note 41, at 89–90; Uitvoeringswet Folteringsverdrag [The Netherlands' Act Implementing the Torture Convention], *id.* at 167–69.

84. *See* Israel's Crime of Genocide (Prevention and Punishment) Law 1950, see REYDAMS, *supra* note 41, at 160; Switzerland's Code pénal Suisse, title 12bis, Offences Against the Interests of the International Community, *id.* at 195.

85. *See* Australia's Geneva Conventions Act 1957, *translated in* REYDAMS *supra* note 41, at 87–88; Belgium's War Crimes Act, which goes beyond the conventional law to add conduct from Additional Protocol II (non-grave-breaches), and subsequently was amended to add genocide and crimes against humanity, *id.* at 106–107, but implementation of the law has been substantially restricted through amendment due to international pressure, *see supra* note 1; Canada's Geneva Conventions Act, REYDAMS *supra* note 41, at 120; the Netherlands' Crimes in Wartime Act, *id.* at 167; Switzerland's Code pénal militaire, articles 9(1) and 109(1) and Code pénal Suisse, article 6bis, *id.* at 195–196.

lished ICC.[86] Some legislation expressly declares its purpose in this regard. The since-tamed Belgian War Crimes Act,[87] under which Belgian courts have prosecuted a number of Rwandan war criminals for acts committed in Rwanda against Rwandans,[88] had as its purpose "to define three categories of grave breaches of humanitarian law and to integrate them into the Belgian domestic legal order."[89] In fact, "[t]o remain consistent with the definitions used in international law, the Act textually refers to the wording of the relevant provisions of the international conventions."[90] And its definitional provisions even explicitly invoke the relevant conventions by name; for example, the Act sets forth the definition of genocide after stating that the crime is defined "[i]n accordance with the Convention on the Prevention and Punishment of the Crime of Genocide of 9 December 1948."[91]

---

86. *See* Australia's International Criminal Court Act 2002, REYDAMS, *supra* note 41, at 88–89; Canada's Crimes Against Humanity and War Crimes Act which "incorporates the provisions of the ICC Statute into Canadian legislation," *id.* at 122–124; Germany's Code of Crimes Against International Law, "which makes the core ICC crimes offences under domestic law," *id.* at 144; the United Kingdom's International Criminal Court Act 2001, which limits universal jurisdiction to foreigners either resident when the offense was committed, or subsequently become resident and reside in the U.K. at the time proceedings are brought, *id.* at 206. *See* REYDAMS, *supra* note 41, at Part II: Universal Jurisdiction in Municipal Law (discussing the exercise of universal jurisdiction by fourteen states). For specific examples, *see* pg. 87–90 (Australia), 97 (Austria), 105–07 (Belgium), 120–24 (Canada), 127 (Denmark), 132–34 (France), 142–46 (Germany), 159 (Israel), 165–69 (the Netherlands), 183–84 (Spain), 193–96 (Switzerland), 204–06 (United Kingdom).

87. *See* Ratner, *supra* note 10.

88. *See* Luc Reydams, *Belgium's First Application of Universal Jurisdiction: The Butare Four Case*, 1 J. INT'L CRIM. JUST. 428 (2003). Some of these convictions are problematic under international law. For example, as Reydams points out:

> Some of the war crimes of which one of the defendants, Higaniro, was convicted took place when there was no armed conflict at all in Rwanda. The two incendiary reports attributed to him dated from late 1993 and early 1994. Contrary to the prosecutor's assertion, there was no armed conflict in Rwanda between 4 August 1993 (date of the Arusha Peace Accords) and 6 April 1994. While sporadic violent incidents took place during this period they did not reach the threshold of application of the 1949 Geneva Conventions and Additional Protocol II.

Id. at 435.

89. Stefaan Smis & Kim Van der Borght, *Introductory Note* to Belgium: Act Concerning the Punishment of Grave Breaches of International Humanitarian Law, 38 I.L.M. 918, 919 (1999).

90. *Id.*

91. *Id.* at art. 1, § 1. Although the Act formally adopts the prescriptive definitions of the crimes from conventional law, like the Netherlands' International Crimes Act it went beyond conventional law regarding the adjudicative availability of universal jurisdiction over "grave breaches" by including within this category acts that were not committed as part of an international conflict. Smis and Van der Borght explain that

> contrary to the Geneva law, the Belgian Act does not make a distinction between international and non-international conflicts for the purposes of defining grave breaches. In fact,

As a result of this legislative translation of international law into national law, the practice of courts has been to use positive international law (as reflected in national law) to define the subject universal offense when exercising universal jurisdiction. To take one of the earliest and most well-known examples of universal jurisdiction, the definitions of "war crimes" and "crimes against humanity" contained in the Nazi and Nazi Collaborators (Punishment) Law under which the Israeli Supreme Court convicted Nazi war criminal Adolf Eichmann for acts which were—leaving no doubt as to the universal basis of the jurisdiction—committed before Israel was even a state, embodied the definitions of the respective crimes in the Nuremberg Charter.[92] The Israeli Supreme Court justified its competence to judge Eichmann on the grounds that "international law [enforces itself] by authorizing the countries of the world to mete out punishment for the violation of its provisions, which

> pursuant to [the Conventions], the term "grave breaches" is only applicable to international armed conflicts. The violations of humanitarian law in non-international armed conflicts (Additional Protocol II) do not fall within the ambit of the [legislative] undertaking referred to in [connection with grave breaches]. However, considering the number of violations of international humanitarian law that are committed in non-international conflicts, the Belgian legislator found it wise to extend the application of "grave breaches" to violations of the laws of war committed during internal conflicts.

Id. at 920.

92. The Nazi and Nazi Collaborators (Punishment) Law defines the crimes as "crime against humanity" means any of the following acts:

> murder, extermination, enslavement, starvation or deportation and other inhumane acts committed against any civilian population, and persecution on national, racial, religious or political grounds;

"war crime" means any of the following acts:

> murder, ill-treatment or deportation to forced labour or for any other purpose, of civilian population of or in occupied territory; murder or ill-treatment of prisoners of war or persons on the seas; killing of hostages; plunder of public or private property; wanton destruction of cities, towns or villages; and devastation not justified by military necessity.

Demjanjuk v. Petrovsky, 776 F.2d 571, 579 (6th Cir. 1985) (quoting the The Nazi and Nazi Collaborators (Punishment) Law). The Nuremberg Charter defines the crimes as:

> (b) *War Crimes*: namely, violations of the laws or customs of war. Such violations shall include, but not be limited to, murder, ill-treatment or deportation to salve labor or for any other purpose of civilian population of or in occupied territory, murder or ill treatment of prisoners of war or persons on the seas, killing of hostages, plunder of public or private property, wanton destruction of cities, towns or villages, or devastation not justified by military necessity.
>
> (c) *Crimes against humanity*: namely, murder, extermination, enslavement, deportation, and other inhumane acts committed against any civilian population, before or during the war; or persecutions on political, racial or religious grounds....

Agreement for the Prosecution and Punishment of the Major War Criminals of the European Axis, arts. 6(b), 6(c), Aug. 8, 1945, E.A.S. No. 472, 82 U.N.T.S. 280.

is effected by putting these provisions into operation either directly or by virtue of municipal legislation which has adopted and integrated them."[93] Quoting the Nuremberg Tribunal, the Court observed that "the Charter, with all the principles embodied in it—including that of individual responsibility—must be seen as 'the expression of international law existing at the time of its creation; and to that extent (the Charter) is itself a contribution to international law.'"[94] The Charter had, in the words of the Court, "formed part of the customary law of nations."[95] Consequently, through the enactment of the law, the Israeli legislature "gave effect to international law and its objectives."[96] The United States endorsed universal jurisdiction over these precise crimes—as defined under Israeli law—when it subsequently extradited another war criminal, John Demjanjuk, to Israel for prosecution in connection with crimes he had allegedly committed as a World War II concentration camp guard.[97] Ruling the extradition legal under national and international law, the Court of Appeals for the Sixth Circuit examined the definitions of the crimes contained in the Israeli law and held that Israel had universal jurisdiction over war crimes and crimes against humanity.[98] More recently, France's Court of Cassation found jurisdiction over a Rwandan national for crimes committed in Rwanda during that country's civil war based on France's domestic legislation implementing the Torture Convention, and despite the fact that Rwanda was not party to the Convention.[99] The Court held that French courts were competent to "judge persons who could be guilty, in a foreign country, of tortures," under the Torture Convention's definition of the crime,[100] which is incorporated by reference into the French Penal Code through article 689-2 of the Pe-

93. Judgment reproduced in English, 2 LEON FRIEDMAN, THE LAW OF WAR 1664 (Fred L. Israel & William Hansen eds., 1972).

94. *Id.* at 1666 (quoting I.M.T. (1947), vol. 1, 218).

95. *Id.* at 1667.

96. *Id.* at 1668..

97. Demjanjuk was later acquitted by the Israeli Supreme Court on these specific charges due to flaws in the documents identifying him as "Ivan the terrible," the guard against which the charges were directed. Based on evidence that he was nonetheless a concentration camp guard, Demjanjuk's legal battles continue. For a summary see Nathan Guttman, *Demjanjuk To Appeal US Decision To Deport Him*, JERUSALEM POST, Dec. 30, 2005, at 5.

98. *Demjanjuk v. Petrovsky*, 776 F.2d 571, 582–583 (6th Cir. 1985).

99. *See* United Nations, Status of ratification of the Convention against Torture, http://www.ohchr.org/english/law/cat-ratify.htm (last visited, Dec. 21, 2005).

100. Cour de Cassation [Cass. Crim] [highest court of ordinary jurisdiction], Jan. 6, 1998. Nr. X 96-82.491 Pf. Nr. Y 96-82.492, *translated in* 1 YEARBOOK OF INTERNATIONAL HUMANITARIAN LAW 598, 599 (Horst Fischer, et al. eds., 1998).

nal Procedures Code.[101] Furthermore, courts also use the decisions and judgments of international tribunals to inform their application of international law. For example, in convicting on universal jurisdiction grounds Adolfo Scilingo, an Argentine naval captain, for his involvement in "death flights" during Argentina's military rule from 1976-1983, Spain's *Audiencia Nacional* drew from the case law of the ICTY and the text of the ICC to specify, among other things, the elements of crimes against humanity under international law, the character of the civilian population against which the crimes must be directed, the generalized and systematic nature of the crimes, and issues of command responsibility.[102]

Where legislatures or courts depart from the treaties, however, they are obliged to undertake a rigorous and *bona fide* inquiry into the status of customary law to justify the definition they employ. But doesn't this divination of custom just bring us right back to the initial concern of courts subjectively defining universal crimes, leading to the legally unjustified harassment of high-profile individuals for purely political or sensationalist motives? These claims might stick if the real-world practice of courts exercising universal jurisdiction wantonly flouted the legal strictures imposed by universal jurisdiction's prescriptive limits. But in fact the reported cases of universal jurisdiction reveal that courts by and large apply faithfully and responsibly the international legal definitions of universal crimes as evidenced in positive international law.[103] Where courts do not—and have no international legal argument to support their deviation—their violation of international law is readily apparent, and perhaps most importantly, interested states have a strong legal basis to reject such claims.

---

101. Article 689-2 reads:

> Whoever, outside the territory of the Republic, commits acts qualified as a felony or delict, which constitute torture within the meaning of the first article of the convention against torture and other cruel, inhumane, or degrading penalties or treatment, adopted in New York on December 10, 1984, may be prosecuted and tried by French courts if he is found in France.

C. PR. PEN. art. 689-2 (Fr.), *translated in* THE AMERICAN SERIES OF FOREIGN PENAL CODES: 29 THE FRENCH CODE OF CRIMINAL PROCEDURE 294 (Edward M. Wise, ed., Gerald L. Kock & Richard S. Frase trans., 1988) (1964).

102. American Society of International Law, International Law in Brief, *Audiencia Nacional of Spain: Sentence for Crimes Against Humanity in the Case of Adolfo Scilingo* (April 19, 2005), *available at* http://www.asil.org/ilib/2005/04/ilib050426.htm#j3.

103. For a comprehensive cataloging with summaries of exercises of universal jurisdiction in municipal courts, see REYDAMS, UNIVERSAL JURISDICTION, *supra* note 41, at 81–226.

For instance, under this Essay's analysis, Spain's *Audiencia Nacional* defied international law when it upheld jurisdiction over former Chilean dictator Augusto Pinochet for genocide based on crimes allegedly committed against a "national group" by stretching this victim class designation beyond its customary definition to include "a national human group, a differentiated human group, characterized by some trait, and integrated into the larger collectivity."[104] Finding that the acts alleged constituted genocide since they were designed "to destroy a differentiated national group" of political opponents irrespective of their nationalities, i.e., "those who did not fit in [Pinochet's] project of national reorganization...[whether] Chileans or foreigners,"[105] the court effectively (and none-too-subtly) amended the victim groups within the definition of genocide. The court's own conclusory reasoning bespeaks the lack of legal support for its position;[106] genocide has been defined consistently since the 1948 Genocide Convention in the statutes of international courts and treaties to have as victim groups only a "national, ethnical, racial or religious group, *as such*."[107] In the words of the ICTR, "a national group is defined as a collection of people who are perceived to share a legal bond based on common citizenship."[108] The *Audiencia*'s

104. Quoting the English translation in THE PINOCHET PAPERS, *supra* note 20, at 103.

105. *Id.* at 103–04.

106. *Id.* at 100. The court's argument relies principally on the former Spanish legislation in place when the acts allegedly were committed, under which the intent element of genocide encompassed intent to totally or partially destroy a "national ethnic, religious or *social* group," *id.* at 27, 100 (emphasis added), and which was therefore in clear departure from Article 1 of the Genocide Convention which prescribed intent to destroy, in whole or in part, a "national, ethnical, racial or religious group, as such." *See* Appendix C, *infra.*

107. *See* ICTY Statute, *supra* note 75, at art. 4; ICTR Statute, *supra* note 75, at art. 6; ICC Statute, *supra* note 75, at art. 6.

108. Prosecutor v. Akayesu, Case No. ICTR-96-4-T, Judgment, ¶ 512 (Sept. 2, 1998). Notably, the jurisprudence of the ICTR has abandoned the notion expressed in the Tribunal's first finding of genocide in *Akayesu*, at ¶ 516, that the victim class could include "any stable and permanent group"—a definition that would nonetheless still exclude the wholly political group found to be victims in the *Audiencia*'s ruling. Subsequent rulings have determined that the victims of the Rwandan genocide, the Tutsi, were indeed an ethnic group within the meaning of the Statute. Prosecutor v. Musema, Case No. ICTR-96-13-A ¶ 934 (Jan. 27, 2000); Prosecutor v. Kayishema, Case No. ICTR-95-1-T, Judgment, ¶ 95, 98 (May 21, 1999). For an explanation of why the *Akayesu* ruling extending the victim class to "stable and permanent groups" based on the *travaux préparatoires* of the Genocide Convention was wrong, and why the Tutsi constituted a protected class under the correct definition in any event, see William A. Schabas, *The Crime of Genocide in the Jurisprudence of the International Criminal Tribunals for the Former Yugoslavia and Rwanda*, in INTERNATIONAL AND NATIONAL PROSECUTION OF CRIMES UNDER INTERNATIONAL LAW 447, 450–456 (Horst Fischer et al. eds., 2001).

sprawling construction eviscerates the "as such" qualifier[109] and de facto enlarges the class of victims to include potentially any group whatsoever—including, as in the case before it, political groups, which had been explicitly rejected as victims in the drafting of the Genocide Convention.[110] In short, the ruling clashes with one of the more recognizable legal demarcations of the crime of genocide under international law.

In sum, and as the *Audiencia*'s exaggerated ruling shows, positive law articulates not just the substance of universal crimes but also a clear benchmark against which illicit overreaching may be measured. Where such overreaching occurs, the rulings conflict with international law and the exercise of universal jurisdiction is illegitimate. Interested states therefore have a solid legal basis to oppose the exercise of universal jurisdiction in such circumstances. For instance, had the charges concerning Pinochet's extradition from Great Britain—which had arrested the former dictator pursuant to Spain's request—relied on Spanish allegations of genocide (instead of torture, which ended up being the relevant crime of extradition),[111] Chile would have been perfectly justified in protesting the legality of Spain's jurisdiction under international law on the grounds that the basis for jurisdiction—that is, genocide as defined by the *Audiencia*'s ruling—was faulty.[112] The idea of states successfully objecting to the legality of universal jurisdictional assertions is not far-fetched: Congo successfully obtained a World Court ruling invalidating a Belgian claim of universal jurisdiction over Congo's then-Minister of Foreign Affairs on grounds of sovereign immunity,[113] which resulted in Belgium's repeal of the arrest warrant.[114] Indeed, Chile actively considered bringing the Pinochet case to the World Court based on its objections that Pinochet enjoyed immunity[115] (the case was, for practical pur-

109. The "as such" language was added to "implicitly include" a specific motive. Schabas, *supra* note 109, at 458.

110. *See* discussion, *supra* note 78.

111. *See* THE PINOCHET PAPERS, *supra* note 20, at 268.

112. As it turns out, Chile did protest the legality of the jurisdiction, but on grounds of diplomatic and sovereign immunity. *See* Susan Cornwell, *Chilean Visitors Find Pinochet Looking Well*, WASH. POST, Nov. 16, 1998, at A19; Laurie Goering, *Chile's Response to Pinochet Arrest A Gauge of Progress*, CHI. TRIB., Oct. 21, 1998, at 4; *World/Nation Briefs*, NEWSDAY, Nov. 7, 1998, at A12.

113. Concerning the Arrest Warrant of 11 April 2000 (Dem. Rep. Congo v. Belg.), 2002 I.C.J. 121 (Feb. 14).

114. *See* REYDAMS, *supra* note 41, at 116.

115. *See* Goering, *supra* note 113; Ray Moseley, *Chile Will Ask World Court to Intervene for Pinochet; Ex-Dictator Fighting Extradition to Spain*, CHI. TRIB., Sept. 29, 1999, at 6.

poses, resolved when British Secretary of State Jack Straw allowed Pinochet to return to Chile on medical grounds).[116] The legal argument presented here would have been another arrow in Chile's quiver of legal objections to Spanish jurisdiction, and quite a sharp one at that. And although it is certainly the most formal avenue, taking the case to the World Court is by no means the only option among the panoply of mechanisms by which states may express their legal objections and attempt to protect their legal rights or "entitlements" under international law,[117] entitlements such as jurisdictional authority over territory and nationals.

IV. EVOLVING AND ENFORCING THE LIMITS OF UNIVERSAL JURISDICTION

So far this Essay has argued that universal jurisdiction is a customary law which, like all customary law, may evolve by violations that gain acceptance and eventually come to reflect a new consensus of state practice and *opinio juris*. But it has also argued that the treaty-based definitions of universal crimes best evidence custom, and accordingly constrain the legitimate exercise of universal jurisdiction by courts. The tension in these arguments raises perhaps one last question worth addressing: How can we tell whether a violation of international law resulting from a court's expansion of the treaty definition of a universal crime (a) signals a possible shift in customary law, or (b) represents an enduring breach of that law? In other words, how are the legal limits of universal jurisdiction enforced?

Framed broadly, the question of violations blossoming into custom is endemic to all customary law,[118] but in this particular circumstance the proper legal analysis may not be too difficult to discern. The answer lies in the reactions of other jurisdictionally-interested—i.e., national and territorial—states. The protest and acquiescence of states to what amounts to an international legal claim by another state has long been held to be a constitutive element of custom.[119] And a claim of authority

116. Statement of Secretary of State Jack Straw in the House of Commons, March 2, 2000, *reproduced in* THE PINOCHET PAPERS, *supra* note 20, at 481.

117. D'Amato, *Is International Law Really Law?*, *supra* note 33, at 1304–07 (describing legal rights as "entitlements" and applying the terminology to international law); *id.* at 1310–1313 (explaining how countermeasures enforce international law).

118. *See supra* text accompanying note 79.

119. *See* Akehurst, *supra* note 63, at 38–42 (and cases cited therein).

to prescribe and adjudicate foreign conduct by foreign nationals under a theory of universal jurisdiction is as clear an international legal claim as any. Particularly important to the customary calculus are the reactions of states that have a substantial legal interest in the claim at issue, that is, states whose legal rights or entitlements are directly implicated by the claim.[120] In comparison to other areas of international law where it may be hard to identify and measure the various interests of various states implicated by a given claim,[121] the universal jurisdiction scenario presents a relatively clear picture of the interested states and the degree of their interests. The legally interested states are those states that otherwise would have jurisdiction over the acts and persons involved; they are those states whose nationals are the subject of the universal jurisdiction claim and/or whose territories suffered the alleged conduct giving rise to universal jurisdiction.

Accordingly, where a court asserting universal jurisdiction expands the definition of the crime upon which it grounds its competence beyond the crime's customary definition—a definition evidenced largely by treaty law—the reactions of national and territorial states determine the customary status of the universal jurisdiction court's definitional expansion.[122] As we have seen, these states may take a number of measures to repudiate the legality of the universal jurisdiction state's claim; they may, for instance, officially protest,[123] take the case to the World Court

120. *Id.* at 40

(If an act affects the interests of only one State, protest by that State will carry great weight...[and] [t]he extent to which a State's interests are affected varies according to the nature of the act concerned. Failure to protest against an assertion *in abstracto* about the content of customary law is less significant than failure to protest against concrete action taken by a State in a specific case which has an immediate impact on the interests of another State.).

121. *See id.*

122. A non-interested state may try to insulate itself from the definitional expansion of a universal crime by invoking the persistent objector doctrine of international law, which holds that "a state that indicates its dissent from a practice while the law is still in the process of development is not bound by that rule even after it matures." RESTATEMENT (THIRD) OF THE FOREIGN RELATIONS LAW OF THE UNITED STATES § 102 cmt. d (1987). However, "[h]istorically, such dissent and consequent exemption from a principle that became general customary law has been rare." *Id*; *see also* Ted Stein, *The Approach of the Different Drummer: The Principle of the Persistent Objector in International Law*, 26 HARV. INT'L L.J. 457 (1985) (observing that while historically rarely invoked, the principle may play a more instrumental role in modern international lawmaking that occurs through institutional organs such as the United Nations).

123. The contribution of protest alone unaccompanied by some tangible response as a constitutive element of custom is the subject of some controversy. *See* Akehurst, *supra* note 63, at 40–41 (disagreeing with D'Amato's view that unaccompanied protests are not enough to block a new

and, naturally, if the universal jurisdiction is asserted in absentia,[124] refuse to extradite the accused. To enforce the definitional limits of the crime under customary law therefore, states objecting to universal jurisdiction on the grounds set forth above would be well-advised to make explicit their rejection of the universal jurisdiction court's illegitimate definitional expansion upon which the court purports to base its competence.

Consequently, the potential for evolving—or not—the definitions of universal crimes by the process of customary law-violation-turned-new-custom rests not with the state asserting universal jurisdiction, but instead most often with the states whose nationals are in the dock. Where interested states object to the universal jurisdiction assertion by rejecting an illegitimate definitional expansion of the crime that purports to justify the universal jurisdiction court's competence, the court's violation represents an enduring breach of international law. In other words, the objection to jurisdiction effectively blocks a potential shift in customary law as to the definition of the crime. However, if interested states approve of or acquiesce in the court's definitional expansion of the crime, such approval or acquiescence may signal a possible customary shift regarding the definition of the crime in line with the definition adjudicated by the court. Hence if the Pinochet extradition had taken place, and if the Spanish courts had rested their jurisdiction on the universal crime of genocide using their exorbitant definition of the crime—which we know is exorbitant because we can measure it objectively against the treaty definition—Chile would determine, either by approval or rejection of Spanish jurisdiction based on this definition, the *potential* for a customary defini-

---

rule); R.A. Mullerson, *New Thinking by Soviet Scholars: Sources of International Law*, 83 AM. J. INT'L L. 494, 506–07 (1989). In cases of universal jurisdiction, the protest will almost inevitably be accompanied by some form of response, whether it is a suit against the state asserting universal jurisdiction or simply a refusal to extradite.

124. The status of universal jurisdiction in absentia is not yet clear under international law. *See* Colangelo, *supra* note 3, at 548–49

> (Universal jurisdiction in absentia is presently caught in a customary twilight that will witness either the development or the dismissal of the practice depending on the actions and reactions of states in the next part of this century. State practice has not yet worn into the fabric of international law an affirmative custom of universal jurisdiction in absentia assertions. At the same time, however, an incipient trend supporting this type of assertion is emerging, and those who take a permissive view of international law might legitimately submit that custom does not explicitly prohibit universal jurisdiction in absentia.)

(internal citations omitted).

tional expansion of genocide as contrived by the Spanish courts. It should be emphasized that even were Chile to approve of the exorbitant definition and the resulting universal jurisdiction, Spain's jurisdiction would still conflict with international law; one territorial or national state's approval of or acquiescence in a definitional expansion would not be enough to change the customary definition of the crime,[125] especially against the backdrop of a widely-ratified and longstanding treaty to the contrary.

V. CONCLUSION

The purpose of this Essay has been to explicate a basic but overlooked legal feature of universal jurisdiction: If national courts prosecute on grounds of universal jurisdiction, they must use the international legal definitions—as derived from customary law—of the universal crimes they adjudicate. The Essay further has attempted to explain the best way of going about determining what those definitions are, by looking to the provisions of widely-ratified and longstanding international treaties. An important implication of this conclusion addresses concerns that universal jurisdiction hazards unbridled abuse for purely political and sensationalist ends. As I hope to have shown, the international law in this area does not permit such abuse; rather, it prescribes legal limits of universal jurisdiction. These limits are enforced not by those states exercising universal jurisdiction, but principally by those states whose nationals are the subject of foreign universal jurisdiction proceedings. Indeed, should states come to recognize this Essay's thesis, the near future may very well see precisely this type of legal argument being made where universal jurisdiction claims are in dispute.

---

125. A basic definition of the hard-to-pin-down threshold for determining the existence of customary law appears in the Restatement, which states that "[c]ustomary international law results from a *general* and *consistent* practice of states followed by them from a sense of legal obligation." RESTATEMENT (THIRD) OF THE FOREIGN RELATIONS LAW OF THE UNITED STATES § 102(2) (1987) (emphasis added). Whatever view one takes of how much practice achieves the threshold level of generality and consistency necessary to form customary law, one improper assertion of universal jurisdiction accepted as legitimate by an interested state and in the face of a treaty to the contrary would not meet that test.

APPENDIX:
BASIC TREATY PROVISIONS (WITH COMMENTARY) DEFINING UNIVERSAL CRIMES

PIRACY

The Convention on the High Seas, more commonly known as the Geneva Convention on the Law of the Sea, sets forth the substance of the crime of piracy for purposes of customary law. It was first signed in April of 1958, entered into force in 1962, and has 62 states party.[126] The Convention states in its preamble that it was designed to "codify the rules of international law relating to the high seas" and, in so doing, "adopted the following provisions as generally declaratory of established principles of international law,"[127] thus explicitly embodying the custom in this area. The Convention provides that "[a]ll states shall cooperate to the fullest possible extent in the repression of piracy on the high seas or in any other place outside the jurisdiction of any State,"[128] and defines "piracy" as "any of the following acts":

> Any illegal acts of violence, detention or any act of depredation, committed for private ends by the crew or the passengers of a private ship or a private aircraft, and directed:
> On the high seas, against another ship or aircraft, or against persons or property on board such ship or aircraft;
> Against a ship, aircraft, persons or property in a place outside the jurisdiction of any State;
> Any act of voluntary participation in the operation of a ship or of an aircraft with knowledge of facts making it a pirate ship or aircraft;
> Any act of inciting or of intentionally facilitating an act described in subparagraph 1 or subparagraph 2 of this article.[129]

126. United Nations Treaty Collection, Status of Multilateral Treaties Deposited with the Secretary-General,
http://untreaty.un.org/ENGLISH/bible/englishinternetbible/partI/chapterXXI/treaty2.asp (last visited June 14, 2006).

127. Convention on the High Seas pmbl., done Apr. 29, 1958, 1 U.S.T. 2312, 450 U.N.T.S. 82 [hereinafter Geneva Convention on the Law of the Sea].

128. *Id.* at art. 14.

129. *Id.* at art. 15.

Articles 100 and 101 of the more recent Montego Bay Convention on the Law of the Sea, which entered into force in 1994 and has 149 states party,[130] contain a prohibition on and definition of piracy in language virtually identical to that in the Geneva Convention.[131]

SLAVERY

The Geneva and Montego Bay Conventions on the Law of Sea also recognize the criminal nature of slavery as a matter of customary law in their provisions. The conventions provide (again, in essentially identical language) that "[e]very State shall adopt effective measures to prevent and punish the transport of slaves in ships authorized to fly its flag, and to prevent the unlawful use of its flag for that purpose. Any slave taking refuge on board any ship, whatever its flag, shall *ipso facto* be free."[132] There are, however, conventions more specific to the crime that explicate its customary definition. The Slavery Convention, signed at Geneva on September 26, 1926, which has 80 states party[133] and which was amended by a 1957 Protocol (that changes obligations under the Convention in respect of the League of Nations to obligations of the United

130. United Nations Treaty Collection, Status of Multilateral Treaties Deposited with the Secretary-General, http://untreaty.un.org/ENGLISH/bible/englishinternetbible/partI/chapterXXI/treaty6.asp (last visited June 14, 2006).

131. Convention on the Law of the Sea, *opened for signature* Dec. 10, 1982, 516 U.N.T.S. 205, 21 I.L.M. 1261 [hereinafter Montego Bay Convention on the Law of the Sea]. Article 100 states: "All States shall cooperate to the fullest possible extent in the repression of piracy on the high seas or in any other place outside the jurisdiction of any State." And Article 101 states:

> Piracy consists of any of the following acts:
>
> (a) any illegal acts of violence or detention, or any act of depredation, committed for private ends by the crew or the passengers of a private ship or a private aircraft, and directed:
>
> (i) on the high seas, against another ship or aircraft, or against persons or property on board such ship or aircraft;
>
> (ii) against a ship, aircraft, persons or property in a place outside the jurisdiction of any State;
>
> (b) any act of voluntary participation in the operation of a ship or of an aircraft with knowledge of facts making it a pirate ship or aircraft;
>
> (c) any act of inciting or of intentionally facilitating an act described in subparagraph (a) or (b).

132. Geneva Convention on the Law of the Sea, *supra* note 128, at art. 13; *see also* Montego Bay Convention on the Law of the Sea, *supra* note 132, at art. 99.

133. United Nations Treaty Collection, Status of Multilateral Treaties Deposited with the Secretary-General, http://untreaty.un.org/ENGLISH/bible/englishinternetbible/partI/chapterXVIII/treaty3.asp (last visited June 14, 2006).

Nations) that currently has 59 states party[134] expresses in its preamble the universal scope of its "intention of securing the complete suppression of slavery in all its forms and of the slave trade by land and sea," "to find a means of giving practical effect throughout the world to such intentions," and "to conclude to that end more detailed arrangements."[135] The Convention sets forth the following definitions:

> Slavery is the status or condition of a person over whom any or all of the powers attaching to the right of ownership are exercised.
> The slave trade includes all acts involved in the capture, acquisition or disposal of a person with intent to reduce him to slavery; all acts involved in the acquisition of a slave with a view to selling or exchanging him; all acts of disposal by sale or exchange of a slave acquired with a view to being sold or exchanged, and, in general, every act of trade or transport in slaves.[136]

These definitions are further mirrored and reinforced in the Supplementary Convention on the Abolition of Slavery, the Slave Trade, and Institutions and Practices Similar to Slavery, which entered into force in 1957[137] and currently has 119 states party.[138]

---

134. United Nations Treaty Collection, Status of Multilateral Treaties Deposited with the Secretary-General, http://untreaty.un.org/ENGLISH/bible/englishinternetbible/partI/chapterXVIII/treaty1.asp (last visited June 14, 2006).

135. Slavery Convention, pmbl., Sept. 25 1926, 46 Stat. 2183, 60 L.N.T.S. 253, *amended by* Protocol Amending the Slavery Convention, *opened for signature* Dec. 7, 1953, 7 U.S.T. 479, 212 U.N.T.S. 17.

136. *Id.* at art. I.

137. Supplementary Convention on the Abolition of Slavery, the Slave Trade, and Institutions and Practices Similar to Slavery, arts. 1, 7, *done* Sept. 7, 1956, 18 U.S.T. 3201, 266 U.N.T.S. 3. Article 7 in the "Definitions" Section IV of the Convention provides:

> (a) "Slavery" means, as defined in the Slavery Convention of 1926, the status or condition of a person over whom any or all of the powers attaching to the right or ownership are exercised, and "slave" means a person in such condition or status;
> (b) "Slave trade" means and includes all acts involved in the capture, acquisition or disposal of a person with intent to reduce him to slavery; all acts involved in the acquisition of a slave with a view to selling or exchanging him; all acts of disposal by sale of exchange of a person acquired with a view to being sold or exchanged; and, in general, every act of trade or transport in slaves by whatever means of conveyance.

138. United Nations Treaty Collection, Status of Multilateral Treaties Deposited with the Secretary-General, http://untreaty.un.org/ENGLISH/bible/englishinternetbible/partI/chapterXVIII/treaty4.asp (last visited June 14, 2006).

GENOCIDE

The plain language of Article I of the 1948 Genocide Convention, which has 138 states party,[139] firmly entrenches genocide as a crime under international law. It provides: "The Contracting Parties *confirm* that genocide, whether committed in time of peace or in time of war, is a crime under international law which they undertake to prevent and to punish."[140] Article II defines genocide as:

> any of the following acts committed with intent to destroy, in whole or in part, a national, ethnical, racial or religious group, as such:
> Killing members of the group;
> Causing serious bodily or mental harm to members of the group;
> Deliberately inflicting on the group conditions of life calculated to bring about its physical destruction in whole or in part;
> Imposing measures intended to prevent births within the group;
> Forcibly transferring children of the group to another group.[141]

Article III makes illegal "Genocide; Conspiracy to commit genocide; Direct and public incitement to commit genocide; Attempt to commit genocide; [and] Complicity in genocide."[142] This definition has endured unaltered up through present-day conventional law.[143] As noted,[144] judicial gloss has construed certain acts, such as rape, to fall within the definition of acts that can qualify as genocidal.

CRIMES AGAINST HUMANITY

There is no unifying international instrument concerning crimes against humanity, though these crimes have been the subject of watershed instruments of international criminal law. The Charter of the International Military Tribunal at Nuremberg defined crimes against human-

---

139. United Nations Treaty Collection, Status of Multilateral Treaties Deposited with the Secretary-General, http://untreaty.un.org/ENGLISH/bible/englishinternetbible/partI/chapterIV/treaty1.asp (last visited June 14, 2006).

140. Convention on the Prevention and Punishment of the Crime of Genocide art I, Dec. 9, 1948, 78 U.N.T.S. 277 (emphasis added).

141. *Id.* at art. II.

142. *Id.* at art. III.

143. The ICTY, ICTR and ICC all use the Genocide Convention's definition to define the crime. *See* ICC Statute, *supra* note 75, art. 6; ICTR Statute, *supra* note 75, art. 2; ICTY Statute, *supra* note 75, art. 4.

144. *See supra*, discussion accompanying notes 74–76.

ity as:

> murder, extermination, enslavement, deportation, and other inhumane acts committed against any civilian population, before or during the war, or persecutions on political, racial or religious grounds in execution of or in connection with any crime within the jurisdiction of the Tribunal, whether or not in violation of the domestic law of the country where perpetrated.[145]

The Principles of the Charter state that crimes against humanity are crimes irrespective of their legality under domestic law, signifying that they are offenses under international law.[146] Since Nuremberg, a number of international instruments have catalogued crimes against humanity. The most precise and comprehensive of these are the statutes governing international criminal courts. As noted,[147] the statutes of the ICTY and ICTR explicitly include, *inter alia*, imprisonment, torture, and rape among "other inhumane acts."[148] The ICC statute particularizes further the list of crimes against humanity,[149] refines the "other inhumane acts" catch-all with the express requirement that the acts must be "of a similar character [to other crimes against humanity] intentionally causing great suffering, or serious injury to body or to mental or physical health," and provides detailed definitions of the terms and crimes listed as crimes against humanity.[150]

---

145. Charter of the International Military Tribunal art. 6(c), Aug. 8, 1945, 82 U.N.T.S. 280.

146. This reading is confirmed by the Principles of International Law Recognized in the Charter of the Nuremberg Tribunal and in the Judgment of the Tribunal, princ. II, July 29, 1950, U.N. GAOR, 5th Sess., Supp. No. 12, at 11, U.N. Doc. A/1316 (1950).

147. *See supra* discussion accompanying note 75.

148. ICTR Statute, *supra* note 75, art. 3; ICTY Statute, *supra* note 75, art. 5.

149. ICC Statute, *supra* note 75, art. 7. Subsection 1 provides the general definition of crimes against humanity and adds to the explicit list: (in connection with rape) sexual slavery, enforced prostitution, forced pregnancy, enforced sterilization, or any other form of sexual violence of comparable gravity; enforced disappearance of persons; and the crime of apartheid.

150. *Id.* Subsections 2 and 3 define the crimes and terms in Subsection 1. The latter two provisions read:

> For the purpose of paragraph 1:
>
> (a) "Attack directed against any civilian population" means a course of conduct involving the multiple commission of acts referred to in paragraph 1 against any civilian population, pursuant to or in furtherance of a State or organizational policy to commit such attack;
>
> (b) "Extermination" includes the intentional infliction of conditions of life, inter alia the deprivation of access to food and medicine, calculated to bring about the destruction of part of a population;
>
> (c) "Enslavement" means the exercise of any or all of the powers attaching to the right of

WAR CRIMES

War crimes are the subject of more international conventions than any other universal crime. The so-called "Law of the Hague" and "Law of Geneva," referring respectively to the overlapping Hague and Geneva Conventions governing the rules of war, largely account for international law in this area,[151] though the statutes and jurisprudence of international

---

ownership over a person and includes the exercise of such power in the course of trafficking in persons, in particular women and children;
(d) "Deportation or forcible transfer of population" means forced displacement of the persons concerned by expulsion or other coercive acts from the area in which they are lawfully present, without grounds permitted under international law;
(e) "Torture" means the intentional infliction of severe pain or suffering, whether physical or mental, upon a person in the custody or under the control of the accused; except that torture shall not include pain or suffering arising only from, inherent in or incidental to, lawful sanctions;
(f) "Forced pregnancy" means the unlawful confinement of a woman forcibly made pregnant, with the intent of affecting the ethnic composition of any population or carrying out other grave violations of international law. This definition shall not in any way be interpreted as affecting national laws relating to pregnancy;
(g) "Persecution" means the intentional and severe deprivation of fundamental rights contrary to international law by reason of the identity of the group or collectivity;
(h) "The crime of apartheid" means inhumane acts of a character similar to those referred to in paragraph 1, committed in the context of an institutionalized regime of systematic oppression and domination by one racial group over any other racial group or groups and committed with the intention of maintaining that regime;
(i) "Enforced disappearance of persons" means the arrest, detention or abduction of persons by, or with the authorization, support or acquiescence of, a State or a political organization, followed by a refusal to acknowledge that deprivation of freedom or to give information on the fate or whereabouts of those persons, with the intention of removing them from the protection of the law for a prolonged period of time.
3. For the purpose of this Statute, it is understood that the term "gender" refers to the two sexes, male and female, within the context of society. The term "gender" does not indicate any meaning different from the above.

151. *See generally* M. CHERIF BASSIOUNI, INTERNATIONAL CRIMINAL LAW CONVENTIONS AND THEIR PENAL PROVISIONS 285–86 (1997). Among the relevant Hague Conventions here are the: Convention with Respect to the Laws and Customs of War on Land, July 29, 1899, 32 Stat. 1803, and its Regulations Respecting the Laws and Customs of War on Land; Convention Respecting the Laws and Customs of War on Land, Oct. 18, 1907, 36 Stat. 2277, and its Regulations Respecting the Laws and Customs of War on Land. The four Geneva Conventions are: Geneva Convention for the Amelioration of the Condition of the Wounded and Sick in Armed Forces in the Field, Aug. 12, 1949, 6 U.S.T. 3114, 75 U.N.T.S. 31 [hereinafter Geneva Convention for the Amelioration of the Condition of the Wounded and Sick in Armed Forces in the Field]; Geneva Convention for the Amelioration of the Condition of Wounded, Sick and Shipwrecked Members of Armed Forces at Sea, Aug. 12, 1949, 6 U.S.T. 3217, 75 U.N.T.S. 85 (1950) [hereinafter Geneva Convention for the Amelioration of the Condition of the Wounded, Sick and Shipwrecked Members of Armed Forces at Sea]; Geneva Convention Relative to the Treatment of Prisoners of

criminal tribunals also contribute instrumentally to the customary scope and definition of war crimes. I have argued elsewhere against the blanket exercise of universal jurisdiction over war crimes.[152] Two independently persuasive reasons combine to caution strongly against the use of war crimes generally for universal jurisdiction purposes. First, aspects of the law of war are inherently vulnerable to manipulation. For instance, many of the laws of target selection and proportionality boil down to standards invariably encompassing marginal cases,[153] the legality of which in practice will depend largely on the interpretive discretion of the prosecuting court, thus making war crimes allegations and prosecutions vulnerable to massage by politically motivated states for purely sensationalist or propagandist, rather than legal, incentives. This high degree of exposure to political abuse combines to trouble the use of universal jurisdiction over war crimes with the reality that "any armed conflict, no matter how carefully planned and executed and no matter what the justification, will involve instances that can be viewed as war crimes."[154] That is, unlike other universal crimes—e.g., genocide, slavery—these marginal instances that potentially could be viewed as criminal may be, as a practical reality of war, inevitable. Thus, universal jurisdiction over war crimes is both susceptible to political manipulation and available virtually every time an armed conflict takes place, no matter the legality or the desirability of a given military action or, for that matter, its unprecedented adherence to humanitarian law. There is accordingly a real danger that "[t]he usefulness of universal jurisdiction under the right circumstances would be undermined by stretching the category to include wrongful or doubtful circumstances."[155] Furthermore, universal adjudicative jurisdiction is legally flimsy here since no positive instrument concerning the law of armed conflict provides affirmatively in its juris-

War, Aug. 12, 1949, 6 U.S.T. 3316, 75 U.N.T.S. 135 [hereinafter Geneva Convention Relative to the Treatment of Prisoners of War]; Geneva Convention Relative to the Protection of Civilian Persons in Time of War, Aug. 12, 1949, 6 U.S.T. 3516, 75 U.N.T.S. 287 [hereinafter Geneva Convention Relative to the Protection of Civilian Persons in Time of War], and the two Additional Protocols are: Protocol Additional to the Geneva Conventions of 12 August 1949, and Relating to the Protection of Victims of International Armed Conflicts, *adopted* June 8, 1977, 1125 U.N.T.S 3 [hereinafter Protocol I]; and Protocol Additional to the Geneva Conventions of 12 August 1949, and Relating to the Protection of Victims of Non-International Armed Conflicts, *adopted* June 8, 1977, 1125 U.N.T.S. 609.

152. *See* Colangelo, *supra* note 3, at 587–94.

153. *See id.* at 588–92.

154. *Id.* at 593.

155. *Id.* at 592.

dictional provisions for the conventional equivalent of universal jurisdiction.[156]

The most legally sound and practically responsible exercise of universal jurisdiction over war crimes limits the doctrine to "grave breaches" of the Geneva Conventions. A colorable legal argument can be made that "the general obligations to enforce, which include the specific obligations to prevent and repress 'grave breaches' of the 1949 Geneva Conventions and Protocol I, allow states to expand their jurisdiction to include the theory of universality."[157] To the extent that the Conventions condition the existence of a "grave breach" on a *willful* violation of the relevant provision(s),[158] this high *mens rea* prerequisite creates a needed threshold for prosecutions that protects against baseless assertions of universal jurisdiction over marginal cases rooted only in political or sensationalist motives. The relevant articles outlining "grave breaches" in the Conventions are: Article 50 common in the 1949 Geneva Convention for the Amelioration of the Condition of the Wounded and Sick in Armed Forces in the Field and the 1949 Geneva Convention for the Amelioration of the Condition of Wounded, Sick and Shipwrecked Members of Armed Forces at Sea[159] which have 195 states party respectively;[160] Article 130 of the 1949 Geneva Convention Relative to the

---

156. Thus leaving to the state wishing to subject an alleged war criminal to its adjudicative process absent territorial or national links a frail reliance on the permissive nature of jurisdictional assertions generally under international law (since there is conversely nothing in positive law prohibiting such assertions over war crimes). *See* Bassiouni, *supra* note 43, at 51–52.

157. *Id.* at 52.

158. *See* Geneva Convention for the Amelioration of the Condition of the Wounded and Sick in Armed Forces in the Field, *supra* note 152, art. 50; Geneva Convention for the Amelioration of the Condition of Wounded, Sick and Shipwrecked Members of Armed Forces at Sea, *supra* note 152, art. 51; Geneva Convention Relative to the Treatment of Prisoners of War, *supra* note 152, art. 130; Geneva Convention Relative to the Protection of Civilian Persons in Time of War, art. 147; Protocol I, *supra* note 152, arts. 11, 85.

159. They provide in pertinent part:

> Grave breaches...shall be those involving any of the following acts, if committed against persons or property protected by the Convention: wilful killing, torture or inhuman treatment, including biological experiments, wilfully causing great suffering or serious injury to body or health, and extensive destruction and appropriation of property, not justified by military necessity and carried out unlawfully and wantonly.

Geneva Convention for the Amelioration of the Condition of the Wounded and Sick in Armed Forces in the Field, *supra* note 152, art. 50; Geneva Convention for the Amelioration of the Condition of Wounded, Sick and Shipwrecked Members of Armed Forces at Sea, *supra* note 152, art. 51.

160. OFFICE OF THE LEGAL ADVISER, U.S. DEP'T OF STATE, TREATIES IN FORCE 493–94 [hereinafter TREATIES IN FORCE].

Treatment of Prisoners of War,[161] which has 195 states party;[162] Article 147 of the 1949 Geneva Convention Relative to the Protection of Civilian Persons in Time of War,[163] which has 195 states party,[164] and Articles 11 and 85 of the 1977 Protocol Additional to the Geneva Conventions of 12 August 1949, and Relating to the Protection of Victims of International Armed Conflicts,[165] which has 182 states party.[166]

---

161. It provides in pertinent part:

> Grave breaches...shall be those involving any of the following acts, if committed against persons or property protected by the Convention: wilful killing, torture or inhuman treatment, including biological experiments, wilfully causing great suffering or serious injury to body or health, compelling a prisoner of war to serve in the forces of the hostile Power, or wilfully depriving a prisoner of war of the rights of fair and regular trial prescribed in this Convention.

Geneva Convention Relative to the Treatment of Prisoners of War, *supra* note 152, art. 130.

162. TREATIES IN FORCE, *supra* note 161

163. It provides in pertinent part:

> Grave breaches...shall be those involving any of the following acts, if committed against persons or property protected by the present Convention: wilful killing, torture or inhuman treatment, including biological experiments, wilfully causing great suffering or serious injury to body or health, unlawful deportation or transfer or unlawful confinement of a protected person, compelling a protected person to serve in the forces of a hostile Power, or wilfully depriving a protected person of the rights of fair and regular trial prescribed in the present Convention, taking of hostages and extensive destruction and appropriation of property, not justified by military necessity and carried out unlawfully and wantonly.

Geneva Convention Relative to the Protection of Civilian Persons in Time of War, *supra* note 152, art. 147.

164. TREATIES IN FORCE, *supra* note 161..

165. Protocol I provides the most detailed index of grave breaches. Article 11(4), which relates to the physical and mental protection of the wounded, sick and shipwrecked, provides that

> [a]ny wilful act or omission which seriously endangers the physical or mental health of a person who is in the power of a Party other than the one on which he depends and which either violates any of the prohibitions [listed] in paragraphs 1 and 2 [of the Article] or fails to comply with the requirements of paragraph 3 shall be a grave breach of this Protocol.

The "grave breach" provision of Protocol I is, however, Article 85, which provides in full:

> Article 85. Repression of breaches of this Protocol
>
> 1. The provisions of the Conventions relating to the repression of breaches and grave breaches, supplemented by this Section, shall apply to the repression of breaches and grave breaches of this Protocol.
>
> 2. Acts described as grave breaches in the Conventions are grave breaches of this Protocol if committed against persons in the power of an adverse Party protected by Articles 44, 45 and 73 of this Protocol, or against the wounded, sick and shipwrecked of the adverse Party who are protected by this Protocol, or against those medical or religious personnel, medical units or medical transports which are under the control of the adverse Party and are protected by this Protocol.
>
> 3. In addition to the grave breaches defined in Article 11, the following acts shall be regarded as grave breaches of this Protocol, when committed wilfully, in violation of the

TORTURE

The relevant international instrument proscribing the universal crime of torture is the 1984 Convention Against Torture and Other Cruel, Inhuman or Degrading Treatment or Punishment,[167] which currently has 141 states party.[168] The preamble evidences the universal scope of the

---

relevant provisions of this Protocol, and causing death or serious injury to body or health:

(a) Making the civilian population or individual civilians the object of attack;

(b) Launching an indiscriminate attack affecting the civilian population or civilian objects in the knowledge that such attack will cause excessive loss of life, injury to civilians or damage to civilian objects, as defined in Article 57, paragraph 2 (a) (iii);

(c) Launching an attack against works or installations containing dangerous forces in the knowledge that such attack will cause excessive loss of life, injury to civilians or damage to civilian objects, as defined in Article 57, paragraph 2 (a) (iii);

(d) Making non-defended localities and demilitarized zones the object of attack;

(e) Making a person the object of attack in the knowledge that he is hors de combat;

(f) The perfidious use, in violation of Article 37, of the distinctive emblem of the red cross, red crescent or red lion and sun or of other protective signs recognized by the Conventions or this Protocol.

4. In addition to the grave breaches defined in the preceding paragraphs and in the Conventions, the following shall be regarded as grave breaches of this Protocol, when committed wilfully and in violation of the Conventions or the Protocol:

(a) The transfer by the Occupying Power of parts of its own civilian population into the territory it occupies, or the deportation or transfer of all or parts of the population of the occupied territory within or outside this territory, in violation of Article 49 of the Fourth Convention;

(b) Unjustifiable delay in the repatriation of prisoners of war or civilians;

(c) Practices of apartheid and other inhuman and degrading practices involving outrages upon personal dignity, based on racial discrimination;

(d) Making the clearly recognized historic monuments, works of art or places of worship which constitute the cultural or spiritual heritage of peoples and to which special protection has been given by special arrangement, for example, within the framework of a competent international organization, the object of attack, causing as a result extensive destruction thereof, where there is no evidence of the violation by the adverse Party of Article 53, sub-paragraph (b), and when such historic monuments, works of art and places of worship are not located in the immediate proximity of military objectives:

(e) Depriving a person protected by the Conventions or referred to in paragraph 2 of this Article of the rights of fair and regular trial.

5. Without prejudice to the application of the Conventions and of this Protocol, grave breaches of these instruments shall be regarded as war crimes.

Protocol I, *supra* note 152, art 85.

166. States Parties to the Following International Humanitarian Law and Other Related Treaties as of 14-Jun-2006, http://www.icrc.org/IHL.nsf/(SPF)/party_main_treaties/$File/IHL_and_other_related_Treaties.pdf.

167. Torture Convention, *supra* note 22.

168. United Nations Treaty Collection, Status of Multilateral Treaties Deposited with the Sec-

prohibition, which grounds itself in the "recognition of the equal and inalienable rights of all members of the human family" and "universal respect for, and observance of, human rights and fundamental freedoms" necessitating "the struggle against torture and other cruel, inhuman or degrading treatment or punishment throughout the world."[169] To be sure, the chairman-rapporteur of the Working Group established by the U.N. Commission on Human Rights who drew up the Convention, and an author of the initial drafts of the Convention, make clear that the Convention's principal aim was to strengthen enforcement of the existing international ban on torture, not to outlaw it because "the Convention is based upon the recognition that [torture is] already outlawed under international law."[170] Article 1 of the Convention provides:

> For the purposes of this Convention, torture means any act by which severe pain or suffering, whether physical or mental, is intentionally inflicted on a person for such purposes as obtaining from him or a third person information or a confession, punishing him for an act he or a third person has committed or is suspected of having committed, or intimidating or coercing him or a third person, or for any reason based on discrimination of any kind, when such pain or suffering is inflicted by or at the instigation of or with the consent or acquiescence of a public official or other person acting in an official capacity. It does not include pain or suffering arising only from, inherent in or incidental to lawful sanctions.[171]

ACTS OF TERRORISM

As previously discussed,[172] while "terrorism" broadly-labeled is not a crime of universal jurisdiction due to its definitional infirmity, there are certain clearly-defined international crimes most people would consider to be acts of terrorism that are subject to universal jurisdiction. Two examples that come immediately to mind are the hijacking and bombing of

---

retary-General, http://untreaty.un.org/ENGLISH/bible/englishinternetbible/partI/chapterIV/treaty14.asp (last visited June 14, 2006).

169. Torture Convention, *supra* note 22, preamble.

170. J. HERMAN BURGERS & HANS DANELIUS, THE UNITED NATIONS CONVENTION AGAINST TORTURE: A HANDBOOK ON THE CONVENTION AGAINST TORTURE AND OTHER CRUEL, INHUMAN OR DEGRADING TREATMENT OR PUNISHMENT 1 (1988).

171. Torture Convention, *supra* note 22, at art. 1.

172. *See supra*, discussion accompanying notes 44–48.

aircrafts. The main international conventions dealing with these crimes are, respectively, the 1970 Convention for the Suppression of Unlawful Seizure of Aircraft, the Hague Hijacking Convention,[173] which currently has 185 states party,[174] and the 1971 Montreal Convention for the Suppression of Unlawful Acts Against the Safety of Civil Aviation (the Montreal Convention),[175] which currently has 186 states party.[176] Both instruments provide for the conventional equivalent of universal adjudicative jurisdiction in their jurisdictional provisions.[177] As to the definitions of the crimes, under Article 1 of the Hague Hijacking Convention:

> 1. Any person who on board an aircraft in flight:
> unlawfully, by force or threat thereof, or by any other form of intimidation, seizes, or exercises control of, that aircraft, or attempts to perform any such act, or
> is an accomplice of a person who performs or attempts to perform any such act commits an offence (hereinafter referred to as "the offence").[178]

And under Article 1 of the Montreal Convention:

> 1. Any person commits an offense if he unlawfully and intentionally:
> performs an act of violence against a person on board an aircraft in flight if that is likely to endanger the safety of that aircraft; or
> destroys an aircraft in service or causes damage to such an aircraft which renders it incapable of flight or which is likely to en-

173. Convention for the Suppression of Unlawful Seizure of Aircraft, Dec. 16, 1970, 22 U.S.T. 1641, 860 U.N.T.S. 105 [hereinafter Hague Hijacking Convention].

174. TREATIES IN FORCE, *supra* note 161, at 373-74.

175. Montreal Convention, *supra* note 47.

176. TREATIES IN FORCE, *supra* note 161, at 374-75.

177. Article 4 of the Hague Hijacking Convention provides that, in addition to states with territorial or national links to the offense:

> Each Contracting State shall...take such measures as may be necessary to establish its jurisdiction over the offence in the case where the alleged offender is present in its territory and it does not extradite him pursuant to Article 8 to any of the States mentioned in paragraph 1 of this Article.

Hague Hijacking Convention, *supra* note 174, art. 4. Similarly, Article 5 of the Montreal Convention provides that:

> Each Contracting State shall...take such measures as may be necessary to establish its jurisdiction over the offences [defined]...in the case where the alleged offender is present in its territory and it does not extradite him pursuant to Article 8 to any of the States mentioned in paragraph 1 of this Article.

178. Hague Hijacking Convention, *supra* note 174, art. 1.

danger its safety in flight; or
places or causes to be placed on an aircraft in service, by any means whatsoever, a device or substance which is likely to destroy that aircraft, or to cause damage to it which renders it incapable of flight, or to cause damage to it which is likely to endanger its safety in flight; or
destroys or damages air navigation facilities or interferes with their operation, if any such act is likely to endanger the safety of the aircraft in flight; or
communicates information which he knows to be false, thereby endangering the safety of the aircraft in flight.
2. Any person also commits an offence if he:
attempts to commit any of the offences mentioned in paragraph 1 of this Article; or
is an accomplice of a person who commits or attempts to commit any such offense.[179]

179. Montreal Convention, *supra* note 22, art. 1.

Part IV
International Spaces

[10]

Imagine There are No Possessions: Legal and Moral Basis of the Common Heritage Principle in Space Law

GBENGA ODUNTAN*

ABSTRACT

The article examines the legal validity, import and relevance of the concept of 'common heritage of mankind' in relation to outer space territories. The term common heritage of mankind lends itself to a myriad of possible interpretations. Consequently there is a situation where both proponents as well as adversaries of commercial space activities use the term to advance their standpoints. The push by certain states and their private business institutions to begin exploitation of outer space resources for commercial purposes has become more forceful in the dawn of the twenty first century. It becomes imperative to ascertain the legality of appropriation of outer space resources within the context of the overriding principles that outer space is the common heritage of mankind and the province of mankind. The article, therefore, traces the development of the concept of common spaces in international law and draws upon analogies found in parallel regimes of common ownership over other international spaces such as the deep sea bed and Antarctica. The merits and demerits of the existing interpretations of the CHM principle are considered and the author argues that there are sufficient legal, jurisprudential and indeed moral imperatives to adopt the restrictive view that outer space and celestial bodies cannot as of yet be appropriated for profit motives by both states and private bodies. The author also argues in favour of a moratorium over commercial exploitation until an international regime of exploitation is developed taking into account the interests of all mankind and the reality of private commercial operations in outer space.

> *Two things fill my mind with ever-increasing wonder and awe the more often and the more intensely the reflection wells on them: the starry heavens above me and the moral law within me.*
>
> Immanuel Kant (1724-1804)
> Critique of Pure Reason

1. INTRODUCTION

This article examines the legal validity, import and relevance of the concept of 'common heritage of mankind' in relation to outer space territories and in terms of its development in international law. In view of the restiveness of the technologically advanced states to embark on large-scale exploitation of outer space resources the article argues for the development of a progressive utilisation regime for outer space based resources based upon equitable considerations and taking into account the needs of developing countries. Positive examples found under the existing regime of jurisdiction over the high seabed and Antarctica are reviewed and the problematic features of these international regimes are identified in order to highlight the pathways that must be avoided in the development of the utilisation of outer space resources in space law. The argument in favour of recognition of a *de facto* moratorium on mining of the resources based on celestial bodies is made and the jurisprudential basis for the common ownership regime established in space law is explored.

The term common heritage of mankind [1] is one that manages to appear both commonsensical and obscure at the same time. In reality it lends itself to a myriad of possible interpretations. Consequently there is a situation where both proponents as well as adversaries of commercial space activities use the term to advance their standpoints.[2] Analogies of this principle can be found in the legal regime governing virtually all the common spaces. Therefore, it is correct to note that "the common heritage principle has its main impact with respect to the establishment of an international administration for areas open to the use of all states (international commons)".[3] Impetuses for the extension of this principle into outer space would, however, appear to have come from analogies presented in the law of the sea. Though some writers find traces of the contemporary idea of the CHM in the thinking of Francisco de Vitoria[4] and even earlier St. Thomas Aquinas,[5] the more popular opinion is that the CHM principle may have been introduced to the law of the sea as a result of a speech made by Ambassador Parado of Malta to the United Nations General Assembly (UNGA) in which he asserted that the future of the resources of the high seas is best secured if it is recognised as the 'common heritage of mankind'.[6]

The principle consequently received recognition in the UN Declaration of Principles Governing the Seabed and the Ocean Floor, and the Subsoil Thereof, Beyond the Limits of National Jurisdiction.[7] By the time of the completion of the Third United Nations Convention on the Law of the Sea (UNCLOS III) in 1982, it was incorporated in Article 136 of the Law of the Sea Convention that: "the Area and its resources are the common heritage of Mankind".[8] However, it must be admitted that even in the law of the sea the exact legal effect of this principle is subject to much debate.

---

* Ph.D (Law), MA, LLB (hons) BL (hons) BA (hons); Lecturer in Law, Canterbury Christ Church University College, Canterbury North Holmes Road, Canterbury, Kent CT1 1QU, England; Sessional Lecturer in International law, Constitutional and Administrative Law -Kent Law School, University of Kent at Canterbury; Legal Adviser to the Nigerian Government and Member, United Nations-Nigerian/Cameroon Mixed Sub-Commission on the Demarcation of the Boundary between Nigeria and Cameroon. This article is based on central aspects of the author's Ph.D. thesis titled *Sovereignty & Jurisdiction in the Airspace & Outer Space: Legal Criteria for Spatial Delimitation*, submitted at the University of Kent (2002). Many thanks to Professor Nicholas Grief, Head of the School of Finance and Law Bournemouth University, U.K. for his helpful comments and ideas during the completion of this article.

This article is based on central aspects of the author's Ph.D. thesis titled *Sovereignty & Jurisdiction in the Airspace & Outer Space: Legal Criteria for Spatial Delimitation*, submitted at the University of Kent (2002).

[1] To be referred to as the CHM Principle.

[2] Traa-Engelman, *Commercial Utilization of Outer Space: Law and Practice* (London, Martinus Nijhoff Publishers, 1993) p. 27.

[3] Rudiger Wolfrum, 'Common Heritage of Mankind', in Rudolf Bernhardt, Max Planck Institute for Comparative Law, *Encyclopedia of Public International Law*, (Netherlands, Elsevier Science Publishing Company 1989) p. 68.

[4] Sylvia Maureen Williams, 'The Law of Outer Space and Natural Resources', *ICLQ* 36 (1987) p. 144.

[5] *Ibid*; see also. Juan A. Travieso, 'El Patrimonio Comun de la Humanidad en el Nuevo Orden International', Vol. 2 *Revista del Colegio de Abogados de Buernos Aires* (1981).

[6] UNGA Official Records, 22nd Session, Agenda Item 92 (2), Doc. A/6695, 18 August 1967. Article 1 states that: "The sea-bed and ocean floor, and the subsoil thereof, beyond the limits of national jurisdiction (hereinafter referred to as the area), as well as the resources of the area, are the common heritage of mankind".

[7] Reprinted in *International Legal Materials*, 220 (1971) Article 1.

[8] UNCLOS III ILM 1245 (1982).

In relation to Space Law the CHM principle continues to be a subject of intense controversy pitting two forces against each other. As have been pointed out the divide is between the developing states and the developed space faring states. Most of the former are presently incapable of directly reaping the benefits of space exploration, and most of the latter are pushing aggressively for a favourable regime towards the commercialisation of space activities including extensive mining and appropriation rights. Indeed it is right to say that the concept of the Common Heritage of Mankind and its application still keeps the world community divided.[9] Opponents of the concept have ceaselessly attacked its legal validity from the time it was introduced in the law of the sea for predominantly the same reasons that it is today contested in relation to the law governing outer space activities. The chief reason is the incompatibility of the concept with unbridled capitalist exploitation of minerals and resources for private ends in a resource rich zone. That is those states that possess the means to exploit resources in remote places do not see any reason why the spoils should be shared with other states that do not.

Many jurists predominantly of western inclination have criticised any possible suggestion that the phrase expresses a legal concept. This is a very clever approach because once the legal validity in concrete terms has been successfully undermined there exists no need to respect any restrictions on the exercise of property rights. A member of this school of thought argues forcefully but not convincingly that:

> One caution lawyers, diplomats and statesmen should observe is to avoid trying to treat layman's language as if it were formulated in terms of technical legal concepts...on the other hand, the phrase, common heritage of mankind, a layman's formula if ever there was one should be given the greatest respect, while it should not, indeed cannot be viewed as a prescription, it can be accepted as a kind of policy hortatory message, a kind of policy directive...[10]

In similar terms Gorove insists that;

> "common heritage of mankind no matter how well motivated, in a legally binding document carries no clear judicial connotation but belongs to the realm of politics, philosophy or morality and not law".[11]

It, however, appears that on the face of it there is nothing really confusing about the CHM principle. It can also be doubted that the view would ever be popular that outer space and the celestial bodies therein should be appropriated as national territory. The

[9] Engelman *op. cit.*, p.52. See also K. Gorove and E Kamenetskaya, "Tensions in the Development of the Law of Outer Space in *Beyond Confrontation: International Law for the Post-Cold War Era* (Boulder: Westview Press, 1995) *passim*; Gbenga Oduntan, 'The Generational-Technological Gap in Air and Space Law--a Commentary', *Journal of Space Law*, 29 (2003) pp. 185-186, 200-204.

[10] L. Goldie, 'A General International Law Doctrine for Seabed Regimes', *Int'l Lawyer*, 7 (1973) pp. 796, 819.

[11] Gorove, 'The Concept of Common Heritage of Mankind a Political, Moral or Legal Innovation', Vol. 9 *San Diego*, (1996). For further positions stating the alleged indeterminacy of the CHM principle see also Williams, *op. cit.*, p. 144 and Joynes, 'Legal Implications of the Common Heritage of Mankind', *ICLQ*, 35 (1986) p. 190.

real heart of the dispute is whether or not the CHM principle will be able to accommodate an international regime based on commercial principles. That is whether there is a possibility of exclusive rights such as the age-old 'miners right' as argued by M.L. Smith.[12]

To begin with it must be noted that the common heritage principle is fast becoming part of customary international law. It constitutes a distinct basic principle providing general but not specific legal obligations with respect to the utilisation of areas beyond national jurisdiction. It inherently conflicts with the principle of sovereignty since it operates from the basis of regarding an environment as 'international public utility' requiring the obligation to co-operate. [13] The CHM principle was first introduced to cover outer space by the words contained in Article 1 of the Declaration of Legal Principles Governing the Activities of States in the Exploration and Use of Outer Space of 1962.[14]

By the time the Treaty on Principles Governing the Activities of States in the Exploration and Use of Outer Space, including the Moon and Other Celestial Borders (1967)[15] was drafted the resolve of states to render outer space a commons for all humanity had deepened. This led to the formulation of another interesting phraseology. In the discussion of the drafting of Article 1 of the Space Treaty (1967) the choice was between the terms 'province of mankind' and 'common heritage'. Eventually the former phraseology was adopted because it was thought to reflect more closely the principles of the freedom of outer space and the prohibition of appropriation. However, it must be said that introduction of the newer phrase ought not to lead to any confusion nor does this prove that these phraseologies are mere declarations of intention as some writers have mischievously suggested.

Eventually, clear reference to this term was rendered in Article 11 (1) of the Agreement Governing the Activities of States on the Moon and other Celestial Bodies (1979). [16] It provided that: "The moon and its natural resources are the common heritage of mankind". In addition to this, Article 4 (1) of the Moon Agreement combines the two terms in the following manner:

> "The exploration and use of the moon shall be the province of all mankind and shall be carried out for the benefit and in the interests of all countries irrespective of their degree of economic or scientific development".

---

[12] See M.L. Smith, 'The Commercial Exploitation of Mineral Resources in Outer Space', *Space Law View of the Future*, (Deventer, Kluwer Law and Taxation Publishers, 1988) pp. 49-55.

[13] See Wolfrum, *op. cit.*, p.68; see also Said Mahmoudi, *The Law of Deep Sea -Bed Mining*, (Stockholm: Almkvist & Wiksell International, 1987) *et. seq.*

[14] It states: 'The exploration and use of outer space shall be carried on for the benefit and in the interests of all mankind'. UNGA Resolution 1962 (XVIII).

[15] Also known as the Space Treaty. 10 UKTS (1968), 18 UST 2410, 610, U.N.T.S. 205.

[16] Also known as the Moon Agreement. G.A. Res. 34/68, U.N. GAOR, 34th Sess. Supp. No. 46 at 77, U.N. Doc. A/34/664 (1979). Most writers insist on a legalistic interpretation of these provisions and have concluded that the Common Heritage and Province of Mankind principles are two different and distinct legal principles and cannot be used interchangeably. This certainly was the opinion of B. Maiorsky who was the negotiator of the Outer Space Treaty for the Soviet Union. See B. Maiorsky 'A Few Reflections on the Meaning and the Interrelation of 'Province of All Mankind' and 'Common Heritage of Mankind' Notions' in *Proceedings of the 29th Colloquium on the Law of Outer Space*, (1986) pp. 58-61.

It would, therefore, appear that as used in the Moon Agreement (1979) both terms emphasise different things although they are geared towards achieving the same noble objective. Article 4 (1) emphasises the co-operation of states parties in all their undertakings concerning the moon and other celestial bodies; on the other hand Article 11 coupled with Article 5 in particular provide the CHM Principle with legal teeth.[17]

2. OUTER SPACE _*RES NULLIUS* OR *RES EXTRA COMMERCIUM*?

In order to understand the legal status of outer space, it is considered important to determine as much as possible, which of the Latin legal classifications relating to territory apply to it. Particularly reference is made here to the well-tested doctrines of *res nullius* and *res extra commercium*. Christol rightly points out that there may be a need to identify the characteristics of the CHM principle and to distinguish it from such other principles as *res nullius*, *res communis* and *res communis humanitatis.*

[17] Article 5 reads as follows; States Parties shall inform the Secretary-General of the United Nations as well as the public and the international scientific community, to the greatest extent feasible and practicable, of their activities concerned with the exploration and use of the moon. Information on the time, purposes, location, orbital parameters and duration shall be given in respect of each mission to the moon as soon as possible after launching, while information on the results of each mission, including scientific results shall be furnished upon completion of the mission, including scientific results, shall be furnished upon completion of the mission. In the case of a mission lasting more than sixty days, information on conduct of the mission, including any scientific results shall be given periodically at thirty days' interval. For missions lasting more than six months, only significant additions to such information need be reported thereafter. (2). If a State Party becomes aware that another State party plans to operate simultaneously in the same area of or in the same orbit around or trajectory to or around the moon, it shall promptly inform the other State of the timing of and plans for its own operations. 3. In carrying out activities under this Agreement, States Parties shall promptly inform the Secretary-General, as well as the public and the international scientific community, of any phenomena they discover in outer space, including the moon, could endanger human life or health, as well as of any indication of organic life. A question that may immediately suggest itself is -why did the US accept this? A possible answer would be that up till about two decades ago the US policy regarding outer space matters was much less concentrated on commercial aims and more in tune with the realisation that outer space matters are inherently the concern of all states and peoples of the earth. In a piece of very interesting domestic legislation on Extraterrestrial Exposure- (Title 14, Section 1211 of the Code of Federal Regulations,) wherein the US took it upon itself to establish in its space operations: (a) that it is NASA policy, responsibility and authority to guard the Earth against any harmful contamination or adverse changes in its environment resulting from personnel, spacecraft and other property returning to the Earth after landing on or coming within the atmospheric envelope of a celestial body; and (b) other security requirements, restrictions and safeguards that are necessary in the interest of national security. This law makes it mandatory for a quarantine order of indeterminate period, to be issued upon all persons who have experienced extraterrestrial exposure by touching directly or indirectly extraterrestrial matter, or by exposure to the atmosphere of celestial bodies if such person was on NASA manned and unmanned space missions which land or come within the atmospheric envelope of a celestial body and return to the Earth. Whoever willfully violates, attempts to violate, or conspires to violate any provision of regulation or orders issued there under or enters or departs from the limits of a quarantine station in disregard of the quarantine rules or regulations shall be fined not more that $5,000 or imprisoned not more than 1 year, or both. However, in 1991 Part 1211 was removed and reserved by the NASA administrator "since is has served its purpose and is no longer in keeping with current policy". See Fed Regulation, Title 14, Chapter V, Part 1211.104 Policy; see also Code of Federal Regulations, edition of Jan. 1, 1997, Volume14, Part1200 to end, (Cat#AE2.106/3:14/P. 1200-end/997) Part 1211 p. 75.

Indeed there are a host of other principles, which may become relevant to our analysis.[18]

Though it has already been concluded in several places in this work that outer space is *res extra commercium* it remains relevant as ever to examine arguments to the contrary. This exercise will at once reveal the falsity of similar attacks on the settled CHM principle as well as strengthen our arguments in favour of the non-appropriation regime established for outer space.

In subtle attempts to befuddle issues, the suggestion that any of the qualifications *res communis* or *res nullius* or *res extra commercium* or *res communnis omnium* can apply at any time to outer space has been rebuffed as false by writers such as Quadri[19] and later even Lachs. Lachs starts off by accepting that "it is true that some of these definitions have been accepted in other areas of international law". He, however, cleverly sought to dismiss their application to outer space and celestial bodies by stating that their application is conditioned by a reply to a basic question: "Is outer space with the celestial bodies a 'thing' -*res* within the meaning of the law".[20] Quadri also argues that such qualifications are unwarranted because they stem from an assumption that space is a *res* and whichever of the adjectives tacked on lacks legal significance and is at best an indication of the preference of the author or the implications, which the term *res* might suggest. He thinks, "the proper procedure for approaching the question would be to study the possibility of applying the term *res* to space". Proceeding from this reasoning he, thus, concluded that cosmic space is not a *res*.[21]

Such strenuously made distinctions, however, serve no useful purpose. The bold thread that runs through the space treaties is that outer space and its celestial bodies should be explored and exploited in the interest of entire mankind and no one should be allowed to appropriate any parts thereof. In that case it is more sensible to hold that at least for now outer space is *res extra commercium.* It is important to this conclusion that no state has made incursions into space upon the basis of acquisition of territory. In fact the contrary view has always been maintained by all states that have participated in space exploration so far. Therefore, what is clearly property of all cannot be disposed of or used by any particular state or its private citizens (corporate or natural) as private property. Furthermore once the status of *res extra commercium* has been conferred upon any territory it becomes irrelevant to argue for a change in the legal status of the territory in question to make it *res nullius* considering that it already belongs to all.

---

[18] Roman Law distinguished the following *inter alia*: *Res communes*, things owned by no one the use of which was common to all, such as the air, running water, the sea and shores of the sea; *res publicae*, i.e. the property of the state- highways, rivers and harbors; *res universitatis*, property of a city such as theatres or race courses; *res sacrae, religiosae* and *sanctae* were *res nullius divini iuris*-That is no one owned them neither could anyone legally acquire ownership of them; *res nullius humani iuris* were not owned but could be acquired by any one. Examples include abandoned property and wild beasts. See C.Q. Christol, *The Modern International Law of Outer Space*, (1982) *op.cit.* p. 318. See also Roscoe Pound, *Jurisprudence*, Vol. II Part 3 (Minnesota: West Publishing Co. 1959) p.150.

[19] Seara Vazquez, *Cosmic International Law*, (Detroit: Wayne State Univ. Press, 1985) p. 39.

[20] M. Lachs, *The Law of Outer Space: An Experience in Contemporary Law Making*, (Netherlands: Sijthoff Leiden, 1972) p. 48.

[21] *Op. cit.*, p. 39.

Another fine distinction, which has been advanced by proponents of the *res nullius* principle is that under customary international law, resources on the moon and celestial bodies are by their very nature *res nullius,* therefore, appropriation is legally possible. Christol, for instance, is of the opinion that there is a difference between the spatial area of the moon including celestial bodies and their natural resources.[22] To explain this unacceptable position the proponents seek to make a distinction between free space and pathways on the one hand and celestial bodies on the other. With regard to free space it is said that by its very nature and by analogy to the high seas there can be no appropriation since no sovereignty may be claimed without reference to dry land. Thus, the moon and celestial bodies were merely *res nullius* whereas outer space i.e. free space *stricto sensu* was *res extra commercium* and the principles of non-appropriation and free access were valid both before and after the entry into force of the Outer Space Treaty on 10 December 1967.

This view is borne out of the classical but mistaken view of the nature of outer space that lawyers have. It is wrongfully assumed that outer space is a void in which solid celestial bodies float. The easiest way to puncture Christol's argument is to admit that while of course there are geophysical differences between the moon's surface on which natural resources are presently to be found and the gases and cosmic dust which constitutes the other 'spatial territories' he refers to, however, that is the whole point of giving the widest interpretations to, the scope of operation of the CHM principle. We cannot separate the spatial territory from the surface not only because the law as it is written in the Space Treaty (1967) does not do so but because those very rarefied gases, cosmic dust and energy that constitute and fill the void that is known as outer space themselves may one day if not now constitute valuable natural resources. It is not when that day arrives that we would start to develop new laws to include further spheres within the operation of the CHM principle. Therefore, it is better to adopt the view that the CHM principle applies to the whole of outer space including the celestial bodies, as well as their surface and subsurface.[23]

The truth, however, is that the difference between the legal status of celestial bodies and that of free space is a mere academic abstraction in the light of the rules that have so far been treated in both the Outer Space Treaty (1967) and the Moon Agreement (1979). The question that poses itself at this stage is whether *res extra commercium* sufficiently explains the regime governing outer space. Other writers like S.M. Williams persuasively argue that the CHM principles goes even beyond that of *res extra commercium.*[24] The preferable interpretation to give to this is that though *res extra commercium* (literally meaning something, which cannot be the object of commercial trade e.g. tombs under Roman Law) is applicable it lacks the element of pronouncing outer space as the property of all. In that case *res omnium,* (property belonging to all) is better. On the other hand that something belongs to all does not mean that it cannot be sold for profit, say by the agreement of the parties. Thus, if the intention is to find a terminology that reflects both characteristics as closely as possible, then we must be speaking in terms of *res omnium extra communis* (property of all and not subject to sale). Cheng developed this theme even further to the extent

[22] Christol, 1982 *op. cit.*, p. 318.
[23] Christol, 1982 *op. cit.*, p. 318.
[24] Sylvia Maureen Williams, 'The Law of Outer Space and Natural Resources', 36 *ICLQ* (1987) p. 144 *et seq*.

of stating that the CHM principle is a new category to be added to the tripartite division of the world made by traditional law.[25]

The relevance of the two terms, ownership and possession to outer space law has been challenged and a preference for *licence* instead has been denoted. Again it has been stated that there is a need to jettison the term *res nullius* and the insufficiency of even the *res extra commercium* formula has been alluded to. The obvious criticism such sweeping positioning is exposed to is that it may be said that in the enthusiasm of elaborating new terminology, old and tested doctrines of law are being discarded. There is, however, an appropriate defence to this criticism. If indeed new concepts have been created in space law by states in the 20th century in response to new situations which mankind has never faced before, then there is no plausible reason to limit current thinking to older doctrines, which the drafters of the pertinent space treaties had good opportunity to refer to but chose not to and indeed creatively developed alternatives for.

3. THE SCOPE OF APPLICATION OF THE CHM PRINCIPLE IN SPACE LAW

At this stage it is important that the exact scope of the operation of the CHM principle is determined. The rationale for such an exercise cannot be lost to any scholar on the subject who labours to defend the existence and the legal validity of the principle along with its allied principles such as the non-appropriation rule and the absence of a property regime in space. For what will be the use of establishing these rules in space law if it can at any time be successfully argued by a dissenting state or author that a specific celestial body or area of outer space or indeed an entire galaxy is beyond the application of the principle?

It must not be assumed that it is an easy task to determine what part of outer space the existing law covers. The answer as will become apparent has significance in the determination of liability for outer space activities and jurisdiction over space stations. As has been briefly mentioned the formula employed in the drafting of the Moon Agreement (1979) does not lend itself to sufficient exactitude. Admittedly the words of Article 1 limits the provisions contained therein to celestial bodies 'within the solar system'. The implications of this unnecessary limitation include the fact that once any activity takes place outside our solar system it is outside the regime of space law, at least that enunciated in that instrument. The only real beneficiary of such a limitation will be either a rogue state which, seeks to find a part of outer space which is not covered by law over which it can exercise full sovereignty, or another intelligence apart from the human race existing outside the solar system, or both. This suggestion may not be as far fetched as it sounds if we consider the fact that just 50 years ago it was largely held as impossible that man would engage in space flight or step on the moon and that a mere one hundred years ago the first aircraft was built. Thus, only the imagination limits the possibilities of exploration beyond this solar system and the discoveries that the next 50 years might bring. This is the essence of the preference for the view that space law particularly the provisions enunciating the CHM principle, apply not only to the solar system we exist in but to the entire universe of galaxies. Probably the apparent reason for the reference to the solar system in the Moon Agreement 1979 is that as the name of the treaty suggests the principal aim is to make

[25] See Christol, 1982 *op.cit.* p. 318.

legislation for the moon, which is earth's natural satellite and of which there is only one in this solar system.

Let it be assumed that the limitation contained in Article (1) of the Moon Agreement (1979) is accepted. It will be discovered that even then, the clear provisions of the Outer Space Treaty (1967) survive that limitation and still operate to cover (as it reads) "outer space, including the Moon and other celestial bodies" (Article 1). The term 'other celestial bodies' is not limited to any given solar system. The CHM and the Province of Mankind principles, thus, operate to seal forever the hopes of any space explorer to discover any spatial territory to which sovereign or private rights of ownership and control can be legally claimed.

Another way of viewing the scope of application of the CHM principle is to ask if the principle applies to all the contents of empty space. The question is does space law especially the CHM principle apply to the countless mass of meteors, rocks, rarefied gases etc. over and around the earth. The generic terms found in the space treaties (for instance, 'celestial bodies' and 'the moon') make it difficult to tell whether these terms cover all natural objects in outer space irrespective of their size, structure or flight pattern.[26] It was in fact suggested once that smaller bodies should have a different status from outer space proper.[27] In other words only "[t]he Sun and all planets and the moon" were not to be appropriated but "meteorites...any rock in space which can really be used and controlled" should belong to another class.[28]

The stance that smaller natural bodies should be subject to appropriation or regarded as *terra nullius* by virtue of their size is unacceptable. Such a proposition is as absurd as the corresponding theory among some air lawyers to limit sovereignty over national airspace to below dense clouds or those legal theorists that say that icebergs, which flow onto the high seas, should retain the sovereignty of the territory from whence they broke off. In the first place the space treaties, which pronounce the CHM Principle, did not establish this difference. Secondly, it is quite difficult to see how anyone could prescribe the minimum size below which an object would cease to be regarded as a celestial body. The preferred view is that which holds that in the present state of man's knowledge, there is little that can serve as a basis for any distinction between a natural or physical definition of a celestial body, on one hand and a legal definition on the other.[29]

For all relevant purposes, therefore, the CHM principle applies not only to all 'celestial bodies' no matter how small or large and no matter in which solar system in the infinity of space they are found but also to all that may be considered 'free space'

[26] M. Lachs, *op. cit.*, p. 46.
[27] *Ibid.* A list of these proposals was recorded by C.W Jenks in his Report preliminaire Institut du droit international, pp. 109-201; *cf*, also M.G. Markov, 'Moon Landing and International Law', III *Revista di Diritto Aereo*, 1964, No 9 pp. 9 ff.
[28] E.L Fasan, 'Law and Peace for Celestial Bodies', in *Proceedings Fifth Colloquium on the Law of Outer Space, 23-29 September 1962*, pp. 8 f.'; Cocca also believes that "Planets are the only celestial bodies considered from a legal viewpoint; i.e. bodies admitting occupation if they are vacant". See A.A Cocca 'Basic Statute for the Moon and Celestial Bodies', *Revista di diritto Aereo* No. 6, 1963, 2nd quarter, para v. On Meteorites; *cf.* Mc Dougall, Laswell and Vlassic, *Law and Public Order in Space*, (New Haven, 1963) pp 750 ff; J. Machowski, 'The Legal Status of Meteors and Meteorites', *Yearbook A.A.A.*, 39 (1969) pp. 101 ff.
[29] M. Lachs, *op. cit.*, p. 46.

including gases, particles and cosmic dust. The CHM principle, however, is not applicable at all to the airspace above national territory. As regards the airspace over territories on earth over which the CHM principle applies under another body of law such as Antarctica (the World Park concept) or the Area (in the law of the sea) it may be suggested that the legal status of the airspace above those territory cannot be different from the status of the underlying territory.[30] Therefore, the airspace over the area is also the common heritage of mankind but it derives its status in being so not from space law but from the laws of the sea or Antarctic law as the case may be.

Controversial as these positions taken may seem they are rational and in consonance with the legal rule of interpretation particularly that which dictates that laws should be interpreted to give effect to the intention of the drafters and to save it rather than it be destroyed. Lastly on this issue, it must be said that to engage in arguments that seek to limit the geographical or geophysical scope of the CHM principle in outer space as a method of curtailing the potency of the doctrine is a fruitless exercise. However, to engage in the intellectual exercise of determining the legal significance of the CHM principle remains a valid enquiry and is indeed a current legal problem relevant to the current century.

4. THE CHM PRINCIPLE AND THE ARGUMENTS FOR AND AGAINST PROPERTY RIGHTS IN SPACE

No Moon, no planet shall fly a single nations flag.[31]

One of the ways in which certain writers seek to attack and undermine the regime abolishing individual property rights in space is to argue that the CHM principle if ever it has any legal value at all does not in fact operate so as to block property rights in space. This argument thus, necessitates a separate enquiry as to whether CHM principle in any way permits the operation of property over space-based resources. It remains settled law that outer space including the moon and other celestial bodies is not subject to appropriation by claim of sovereignty by means of use or occupation or by any other means. [32]

At this stage, however, it is worth drawing a parallel between the early stages of the development of air transport and that of outer space exploration. In both cases the uncertainties over the unfolding developments helped in different ways to avert the development of legal regimes, which are solely for the interest of one or two states. In the case of air law, the leading air powers recognised the importance of not allowing any one state to have unbridled access to the air space over other national territories.

---

[30] Note our discussions on the application of the CHM Principle and the World Park Concept in Antarctica and the High Seas below. A similar reasoning is found in the argument that the airspace over the high seas should be legally regarded as part of the common heritage of mankind. See further on this theme Nicholas Grief, *Public International Law in the Airspace of the High Seas*, (London, Martinus Nijhoff Publishers, 1994) pp. 9, 12-13.

[31] Committee on the Peaceful Uses of Outer Space, 19 March 1962 A/AC. 105/PV. 2, pp. 13-15.

[32] Article 1 of the Space Treaty (1967) states that the exploration and use of outer space, including the moon and other celestial bodies, shall be carried out for the benefit and in the interests of all countries, irrespective of their degree of economic or scientific development, and shall be the province of all mankind. Article 11 (1) of the Moon Agreement (1979) also provides that 'The moon and its natural resources are the common heritage of mankind'. Note also Article II Outer Space Treaty (1967) and Para. 3 Declaration of Legal Principles (1963).

This was principally to contain the US, which had a clear and distinct technological advantage in the air transport industry. Thus, the theory and practice of exclusive jurisdiction over national airspace by each state was upheld. In the case of space law a similar conclusion as to the undesirability of the entrenchment of hegemonic interests within the new frontier was reached with a different prescription. Rather than grant all states equal sovereignty in outer space no sovereignty was granted at all. The ideological Cold War that was at its height around 1957 produced an effect that was akin to the effects of the First World War on the shaping of air law earlier on in the 20th century. The super powers and the leading states were not sure of the way events arising out of the space activities would turn out in the context of the prevailing cold war. They were equally not certain of the particular benefits accruable from space exploration.

Thus, though the USSR was the first state to put a man in space in 1957, explicit statements were made renouncing all claims to outer space.[33] It was stated that "No human activity on the Moon or any other celestial body could be taken as justification for national appropriation."[34] The US also took this position long before it put a man on the Moon. The position as stated then was "We have rejected the concept of national sovereignty in outer space. No Moon, no planet shall fly a single nation's flag".[35] In the words of US President Johnson "The goals now within reach of the human race are too great to be divided as spoils, too great for the world to waste its efforts in a blind race between competitive nations".[36] These noble postures along with the influence of the majority of developing states facilitated the eventual formulation of the CHM principle.

The problem is that for those states that invest heavily in Space exploratory activities the cost benefit of exploiting extensively space-based resources is quite real.[37] As time goes by and with the inevitable discovery of invaluable space based resources as well as newer and cheaper methods of exploiting them, it is understandable that pressures are on the increase for the law to recognise and permit property rights and the commercialisation of outer space.

It is probably worthy of note that the US would again appear to be at the forefront in the championing of commercialisation of space resources. This is probably comparable to the history of developments in air law where the US developed and actively sponsored the 'open skies' agenda in line with its hegemonic interests.[38] It is,

---

[33] See *Pravda*, 18 November 1959 and United Nations 22 September 1960 (Official Records), p. 48 para, 58.

[34] Legal Sub-committee, 20 October 1966, A/AC. 105/C.2/SR.63.

[35] *Supra* note 24.

[36] See Adlai Stevensen in 1st Comm. statement on; 'International Cooperation in the Peaceful Uses of Outer Space', 2 Dec. 1963, UN Press Release No. 4323, 2 December 1963. Statement also appended to the Educational Progress of NASA, Senate Hearings on Aeronautical and Space Sciences 88th Cong. 1st Sess. 21-22 Nov. 1963. See also S. Bhatt, 'Legal Controls of the Exploration and Use of the Moon and Celestial Bodies', Vol. 8 INJIL (1968) p. 36-38; A Piradov and Y. Rybakov 'First Space Treaty', *International Affairs*, (Moscow: Mar 3 1967) pp. 21-26.

[37] Anderson K. Baca, 'Property Rights in Outer Space', *Journal of Air Law and Commerce*, 58 (1993) pp. 1044-1045.

[38] Starting in 1978 when its own internal aviation market was deregulated, the US has offered very liberal bilateral agreements to other states in furtherance of the open skies agenda. It is worthy of note that up till the present the US still aggressively promotes the principle of 'open skies'. This may, however, not be in the interest of the developing states who are not strategically placed, technologically

therefore, no wonder that the United States National Commission on Space recommended that "steps necessary to undertake the development of ...extra terrestrial resources begin at once". A call was subsequently made for the establishment of pilot mining and production facilities on the Moon by the year 2007.[39] Western scholars such as Kosmo also believe that "the quality of America's future social and economic welfare is inextricably intertwined with the successful commercialisation of space by American private enterprise".[40] Baca pushes the argument to extreme when he insists that

> "...the issue of sovereignty be reconsidered in space, as some form of sovereignty is an absolute necessity to the guarantee of the property rights required for the development of space resources".[41]

Christol, also thinks that there is a distinction between the ban of Article II of the Space Treaty concerning sovereign (i.e. national), appropriation of spatial areas, and the right of legal persons to obtain property. It is also argued that the provisions of Article I, and III in particular, of the Space Treaty (1967) as well as the other Articles allowing free and equal exploration, use and exploitation of the space environment by states, must be contrasted with the rights of other legal persons to engage in such exploration, use and exploitation.[42]

It makes sense to consider at some length the most frequently cited justifications for the position adopted by those writers who believe that the CHM principle (if at all it has a legal value) does allow the existence of property rights in outer space. They are as follows.

(1) That the term Common heritage of mankind lacks any legal or scientific clarity and therefore, means everything and nothing at all.
(2) It is claimed that the preamble to the Outer Space Treaty (1967) in fact recognises the exploitation of outer space.
(3) That Article 1 of the Outer Space Treaty (1967) (which contains the province of mankind formula a necessary adjunct of the CHM principle) is merely 'a statement of general goals' and that the ratification of specialised treaties is necessary to create any

---

capable or which have failing national airlines. The airspace over national territories is becoming freer for the big players in international aviation business; whereas, the possibilities of exploitation of outer space resources is becoming more than ever the exclusive preserve of those very states that benefit most from the predominance of 'open skies'. The current European Union drive towards a common international aviation policy is calculated to reduce even further the fragmentation of both industry and market within Europe so that EU Airlines and their customers will benefit from the full potential of the EU Single Market. This would of course reduce the dominance of their major international rivals particularly American ones. See generally Wybo P. Heere, 'Problems of jurisdiction in Air and Outer Space', *Annals Of Air And Space Law* 72 (1999); Cf. Europa, *Air transport: Why An EU drive towards a common international aviation policy?*, at http://europa.eu.int/comm/transport/air/international/index_en.htm; N.A. Van Antwerp, *The Single European Sky, Air And Space Law* XXVII No.1 April (Feb. 2001); N.A. Van Antwerp *The Single European Sky (2), Air And Space Law* XXVII No.2 (April 2001).

[39] Baca *op. cit.*, p. 1042.

[40] Quoted in C.Q. Christol, (1982) *op.cit*, p. 318.

[41] Baca *op.cit.* p. 1047.

[42] Christol *op. cit.*, p. 318.

specific obligations.[43] In the absence of such treaties Article 1 (1) is seen to be more a moral and philosophical obligation than a legal requirement [44]

(4) That the general principle of non-appropriation is in effect circumscribed to a large extent by treaty provisions designed to facilitate the exploration and use of outer space. In other words, Article 1 specifically makes provision for use of outer space. Because the legal sense of the word, "use" refers to the enjoyment of property often with an advantage or profit arising therefrom, by the occupancy, utilisation or exercise of the property; therefore, some form of appropriation must be permissible in order to facilitate the use contemplated in Article 1.

(5) That since the Outer Space Treaty (1967) does allow for withdrawal, the non-appropriation principle would by the operation of the law of treaties simply not apply to any state that withdraws from it.

(6) That the Moon Agreement (1979), which introduces the CHM concept, has not been ratified by any of the space powers. Also that it has not been signed by many states. Furthermore that it is not binding upon any non-party state and the claim that it represents customary law is not credible.[45]

(7) That in respect of the geostationary orbit the characteristics of that flight path is not analogous to the situation on celestial bodies. Thus, while the CHM principle and non-appropriation rules may work in the former they may be unworkable with respect to a lunar base, where investments will include not only equipment but also site preparation and other modifications. It is argued that in such situations the limited possessory rights and the lack of a power to dispose the property may severely limit the value of any investment. In other words space exploration may eventually suffer from space law to the detriment of mankind.

Such arguments as raised in the seven points delineated above may appear to be formidable and are indeed quite capable of attracting scholarly sympathy but again the correct view is that they are nonetheless insufficient. The arguments certainly do not justify any legal reasoning that limits the operation of the CHM principle in outer space in such a manner as to permit national or private appropriation and to recognise extensive property rights in space. Suggestions that sovereignty be introduced into outer space through a loose interpretation of the CHM principle or in any other form whatsoever is a form of legal heresy and should be dismissed for the following reasons.

In the first place it is merely mischievous to overstate the obscurity of meaning shrouding the term CHM. Doing so is clearly an undisguised attempt to avoid the

---

[43] See N. Jasentuliyana, 'Article 1 of the Outer Space Treaty Revisited', Vol. 17 *Journal of Space Law*, (1989) pp. 129, 139; Baca *op. cit.*, p. 1064.

[44] See 'Settlement and Sovereignty in Outer Space', *U.W. Ont. L. Rev.*, 22 pp. 155, 157-158 (1984).

[45] Baca *op. cit.*, p. 1068. The Moon Agreement entered into force on July 11, 1984 with the ratification by the required fifth state, however, the record of ratification and accession to the Moon Agreement (1979) is indeed quite poor for both developed and developing states. Indeed as at 2001 only 14 states were bound by the Moon Agreement (1979) whereas 123 states are parties to the Outer Space Treaty (1976) and it may be said that developing states particularly have not justified their interest in many of the principles they fought vehemently to have included in the treaty at the conference tables by ratifying it, or by persuading other states to accede to it. It is, however, possible to over emphasise this point because the number of parties is slowly rising and dramatic increases in the number of signatories to the instrument may be easily predicted if any threat to the common understanding states have as to the general nature of the legal regime for outer space emerges or if technological developments make the exploration of the moon easier.

legal validity of the CHM principle. Indeed it may be said with a lot of credence that specific semantic certainty has been afforded to this term in the works of many authors. R.P. Arnold impressively achieves this when he stated as follows:

> "The word heritage suggests property or interests which are reserved to a person by reason of birth, something handed down from one's ancestors or the past. In defining mankind, it is necessary to make a distinction between mankind and man. Mankind refers to the collective group, whereas man refers to individual men and women...Mankind is not yet unified under one government, therefore the collective entity of mankind is represented by the various nations of the world. Thus the exercise of rights to the common heritage of mankind appertains to nations, representing mankind, and not individuals. The use of the phrase common heritage of mankind implies or prescribes worldwide ownership...[46]"

Furthermore, due to the fact that the primary subjects of international law are independent states, it is logical that they should decide together and as a singular community, inclusive of all, fundamental matters that concern all. This is, therefore, what is legalistically referred to as mankind.[47] It has, therefore, become possible to identify some basic elements of the CHM principle:

(a) That the areas constituting a CHM cannot be subject to appropriation.
(b) That the use of such area and the resources thereof shall be subject to a common management system.

(c) That the concept in question implies an active sharing of the benefits derived from the exploration and exploitation of those areas;
(d) That the area be used exclusively for peaceful purposes;
(e) That the area be preserved for future generations in perpetual succession.[48]

In the light of these definitions and assertions it is highly unlikely that any possible interpretation of the CHM principle allows for property rights in space. The allegation that the existing space treaties recognise exploitation of outer space through the provisions permitting space exploration is yet another unsuccessful attempt to befuddle issues. The answer to this is that there is a clear separation in space law between the issue of the use of outer space resources in outer space for scientific experimentation on the one hand and that of exploitation or mining of outer space based resources with a view to repatriating the resources to earth for economic and

---

[46] Rudolph Preston Arnold, 'The Common Heritage of Mankind as a Legal Concept', *Int. Lawyer,* 9 No. 1 p. 154.
[47] Neeru Sehgal, 'The Concept of Common Heritage of Mankind Under the Moon Agreement (1979), 1979', *INJIL* 26 (1986) p. 108; See also Cocca, 'Mankind as New Legal Subject – A New Juridical Dimension Recognized by the United Nations', *Proceedings of the Thirteenth Colloquium on the Law of Outer Space*, (1971) p. 212.
[48] See Williams, 'Outer Space and Natural Resources', *op. cit.*, p. 109; Dekanozov, 'The Common Heritage of Mankind in the 1979 Agreement Governing the Activities of States on the Moon and other Celestial Bodies', *Proceedings of Twenty Fourth Colloquium on the Law of Outer Space*, (1981) p. 186.

monetary gain, on the other hand. Regarding the utilisation of space based resources in outer space itself there is little room for controversy. The reasonable use doctrine has been established in Space Law. The Moon Agreement in Article 6 (2) for instance, permits the usage of minerals and other substances of the Moon in quantities appropriate for the support of their missions. This very much falls short of permitting mining for purely monetary gains. Furthermore as will be later elaborated upon, the right to collect and remove substances and minerals from the moon is limited to "... scientific investigations and in furtherance of the provisions of the agreement" (Article 6 (2) Moon Agreement 1979). The phrase "in furtherance of the provisions of this agreement" covers many things. This includes of course the obligation to have due regard to interests of present and future generations as well as the need to promote higher standards of living and conditions of economic and social progress and development in accordance with the Charter of the United Nations (Article 4, Moon Agreement (1979).

It might indeed be wondered whether the promotion of higher standards of living and economic progress would not be better served if those countries that can afford it were allowed to reap the benefits of their exploration by the granting of substantial mining rights in space law. The answer to this simply is that if that were what was intended, then the space treaties would have expressly stated so. However, what can be found in the treaties particularly within the instruments dictating the CHM principle is an intention not only to maintain outer space and its celestial bodies as common property until an exploitative regime is set up, but an obligation to share very generously benefits derived from scientific knowledge about outer space between all states irrespective of their degree of economic or scientific development (Article 4 (1) Moon Agreement (1979)). This obligation is central to the workings of the CHM/ Province of Mankind principles in space law so much so that states are advised to have regard to the desirability of making a portion of such samples available to other interested states Parties and the international scientific community for scientific investigation (Article 6 (2) Moon Agreement (1979)).

It is, therefore, inevitable to conclude that states are free to determine all aspects of their participation in the exploration and use of outer space. However, for the CHM principle to operate effectively, all states particularly those with relevant space capabilities should contribute to the promoting and fostering of international co-operation. This dictates an abandonment of property claims in outer space as well as the channelling of benefits of space exploration towards the interests of developing countries and countries with incipient space programmes (Declaration 2 and 3, Declaration on International Co-operation (1996).

As to the allegation that the CHM principle does not bind a withdrawing state from the treaties that incorporate it and that it also does not bind any of the Space powers, which does not ratify the Moon Agreement (1979), it must be said that these submissions again are based on an insufficient premise. In any event more and more states have ratified the Moon Agreement (1979) including at least one of the space powers. Furthermore, the regime of equal access to outer space created in the treaties has become part of customary international law. Therefore, a withdrawing party cannot legally gain ownership over what in effect belongs to all. Just as a party to the Chicago Convention (1944) cannot by withdrawing from that treaty unsettle the principle of exclusive sovereignty and jurisdiction of states in their airspace; so also cannot any state(s) undermine the status of outer space as the common heritage of mankind by inopportune withdrawal from treaty law or opportunistic approach to treaty ratification and accession.

6. JURISPRUDENTIAL BASIS FOR COMMON OWNERSHIP, POSSESSION & CONTROL OVER OUTER SPACE

There are certain contradictions in the argument of those writers who expound the legality of unbridled private exploitation of resources on celestial bodies, which must be dispelled. Christol for instance, admits that, "being unable to possess sovereignty, a State may not create exclusive property rights".[49] Yet he goes on to conclude as follows:

> However, those public entities or those private institutions that have the capacity to engage in exploitative activities are fully competent to do so. They are as required by Article VI of the Principles Treaty, to conform to the "authorization and continuing supervision by the appropriate State Party to the Treaty." As a result of this provision it is clear that parties may exercise important jurisdictional controls. Most importantly, the distinction between national sovereignty, and the right of a State to engage in jurisdictional authority, has been recognised. The extent of such jurisdictional authority will depend upon whether a State is bound by either or both of the 1967 Principles and the 1979 Moon treaty.[50]

But the real issue is not whether private organisations can engage in space exploration because of course they can; however, it is clear that no state may grant exploitative or exclusive property rights to public or private entities, which go beyond that which the state itself possesses under the general principles governing space exploration in international law. In fact the authorisation and continuing supervision required of states is there in order to ensure that the conduct of space exploration and exploitation proceeds in consonance with international law. Furthermore it is important to stress that the jurisdictional duties imposed on states are not limited only to the Principles in the Outer Space Treaty (1967) and the Moon Agreement (1979) but also encompass duties that are laid down under the customary international law that has been developed in relation to outer space activities. Thus, the fact that some space faring states particularly the US, Russia, Japan and China have not ratified the Moon Agreement (1979) does not make it possible for them to totally ignore those rules of space law which are central to the regime created for the moon since they serve as evidence of contemporary international law and may in some cases arguably have become part of customary international law.[51]

---

[49] Carl Q. Christol, "The 1979 Moon Agreement: Where Is It Today?", *Journal of Space Law*, 27 No. 1 (1999) p. 4.

[50] *Ibid.*

[51] China for instance has recently been reported to announce plans for a lunar station to exploit valuable resources. Again a distinction may be made between exploitation of infinite resources and those that involve finite mineral resources. The former is typified by the ambition of the Chinese to collect

The effect of both the *res communis* principle adopted in 1967 Space Treaty and the CHM principle adopted in the 1979 Moon Agreement (1979), is to produce a prohibition against the grant of exclusive right to private property. The argument that the *res communis* principle, which prevents a nation from exercising sovereignty on the high seas, but allows their fishermen to exploit fisheries and gives them proprietary rights, also applies to the natural resources in outer space is only correct in the sense that that will be the course the development of the law will have to take once commercial exploitation of outer space resources begins. Moreover, there are important distinctions. Firstly, the practice of exploitation of the high seas for commercial fisheries has been going on for centuries and there is a settled recognition of that fact, prior to the development of treaties regulating the high seas in the last century, whereas the exploitation of outer space resources has hardly begun and the rules contained in the pertinent space treaties are largely in favour of sharing the benefits of exploitation between all states. Secondly as recognised by the United States delegate to the General Assembly conference adopting the Moon Agreement in 1979, even though the Agreement did not specifically put in place a moratorium on the exploitation of natural resources, any such exploitation must be carried out in accordance with Article 11, paragraph 7, and Article 6, paragraph 2.[52]

Article 6 (2) deals principally with the removal of samples for scientific studies. Article 11, paragraph 5 envisages that states parties to the Moon Agreement (1979) will establish an international regime to govern the exploitation of natural resources on the moon and Article 11 (7) provides that the main purposes of the regime shall include: (a) the orderly and safe development of the natural resources of the moon; (b) the rational management of those resources; (c) the expansion of opportunities in the use of those resources; (d) an equitable sharing by all states Parties in the benefits derived from those resources, whereby the interests and needs of the developing countries, as well as the efforts of those countries which have contributed either directly or indirectly to the exploration of the moon, shall be given special consideration. In any case Article 11 (8) very importantly stipulates that all the activities with respect to the natural resources of the moon shall be carried out in a manner compatible with the purposes specified in paragraph 7.

A possible argument that may be presented is that if commercial exploitation can only take place in accordance with Article 11 (7) and that paragraph simply explains what is to be achieved by the envisaged international regime for the exploitation of natural resources on the moon as demanded by Article 11 (5) then commercial exploitation may only begin after that international regime has been put in place.

Even the Outer Space Treaty (1967), which is considered user friendly by the proponents of the theory that exploitation for commercial benefits is currently permitted, expressly stipulates in Article II that,

---

sunlight in orbiting stations and beam either direct light or microwave energy down to earth-based collecting points. See John Gittings and Tim Radford "The Moon –a Giant Leap for the Chinese who Spy a Business Opportunity in Space", *The Guardian*, Tuesday 21 May 2002, p. 3.

[52] UN Doc. A/SPC/34/19, 6, 7 November 1979. Note particularly Article 11 (8) which stipulates; All the activities with respect to the natural resources of the moon shall be carried out in a manner compatible with the purposes specified in paragraph 7 of this article and the provisions of article 6, paragraph 2, of this Agreement.

> "Outer space, including the moon and other celestial bodies, is not subject to national appropriation by claim of sovereignty, by means of use or occupation, or by any other means".

This means that the drafters acknowledge that appropriation may arise by 'use'. Therefore, it may be argued that it is not possible even under this treaty,[53] for any state to exploit resources on the moon for commercial benefits without at least by implication 'appropriating' it.

The requirement in Article IX that a state which is about to conduct an activity which may potentially cause harmful interference with activities of other states parties should undertake appropriate consultation before proceeding with such activity also supports the argument that any state that wants to introduce commercial exploitation must first of all embark upon international consultations. In order words such a state even if not a party to the Moon Agreement (1979) must consult with the parties to that treaty as well as the parties to the Outer Space Treaty (1967) before commercial exploitation begins. In any case one of the most likely candidates for such a move in the near future the United States has already committed itself upon the conclusion of the Moon Agreement (1979) to future participation in negotiations respecting the establishment of an international regime for governing the exploitation of the moon's natural resources.[54]

There is no doubt that the wish of the space faring states is to be able to carry out extensive commercial exploitation of available resources on the moon and eventually on other celestial bodies. This reality also informs the arguments of many writers on the subject. However, it may be said that pretending that the present laws allow unbridled commercial exploitation based upon property rights is not the way to go about it because they clearly do not. The problem is also not with the Moon Agreement (1979) as many writers have sought to argue.[55] The real issue is that further consultations and international negotiations are still required before large-scale exploitation of the moon's resources may begin. This has been envisaged by both treaties that have been considered and cannot be ignored by any state which wants to embark on space mineral exploitation. This is also a reality that must be coped with by both statesmen and writers who advocate the concept of space 'real property rights'.[56] It is, therefore, possible to question the objectivity of views such as those of Professor Bin Cheng when he stated that the Outer Space Treaty (1967),

---

[53] To which very importantly the space faring states that have expressed the wish to embark on commercial exploitation (mainly the US, China and Japan) are parties.

[54] A representative of the US also stated that the US "would, when and if negotiations for such a regime were called for under articles 11 and 18, make a good faith effort to ensure that they are successfully concluded". UN Doc. A/SPC/34/19, 6, 7 November 1979.

[55] See for example Christol *op.cit.*, p. 4. Real danger lies particularly in such views expressed by writers like Kosmo who believes that "the quality of America's future social and economic welfare is inextricably intertwined with the successful commercialisation of space by American private enterprise". Quoted in C.Q. Christol, (1982) op. cit. p. 318. *Cf.* A.K. Baca's view that "...the issue of sovereignty be reconsidered in space, as some form of sovereignty is an absolute necessity to the guarantee of the property rights required for the development of space resources". See Baca *op. cit.* pp. 1044-1045.

[56] See W.N. White, Jr., "Real Property Rights in Space", *Proceedings Colloq. L. Outer Space* 40 (1998) p. 380.

> "while it precludes the space powers from appropriating territorially portions of outer space, the moon and other celestial bodies, leaves them free, *notwithstanding views to the contrary*, nevertheless to appropriate their resources".[57] (Emphasis added).

If indeed the common heritage principle is in any way vague and imprecise then the right to real property on the moon is even more vague as no such thing is mentioned in any treaty.

The Aristotelian analysis of justice may still serve as a crucible into which we may pour the current problems of air and space law of the 20th and 21st Centuries. Thus, it is sensible to adopt the distinction between particular justice and universal justice on one hand and distributive and corrective justice on the other hand.[58] While it may be taken for granted that justice has been achieved with respect to the airspace in that every state has exclusive jurisdiction in its national airspace, the enquiry remains particularly relevant and of contemporary significance with respect to the regime governing control over outer space based resources. There is credibility in the jurisprudential premise that distributive justice is based on the principle that there has to be an equal distribution between equals and that corrective justice restores equality whenever this has been disturbed (for example by a wrongdoing). The relevance of these terms in relation to the ongoing debate about the legal status of outer space and its resources comes into sharper focus in the next few paragraphs.

To start with it may be necessary to recall the principle of the equality of states. Just as in the municipal setting justice connotes the legal equality of all persons so also among nations, equality of states reign supreme. One of the most opportune areas to test the doctrine of state equality and the obligation to take into consideration the interests of other states in resource management is found in relation to the special problem of the geostationary orbit.[59] Note that it has been concluded that there is no basis for excluding the legal nature of that orbit from the legal nature of outer space in general at least for the purposes of application of the CHM principle. The unfortunate situation has arisen in which the geostationary orbit is being clogged up by satellites that belong to a few states. Since the geostationary orbit is a finite resource, the *de facto* commandeering of slots must not be allowed to impede distribution and access to it by a few active states. It is clear that the present position with respect to geostationary orbit use, whereby the orbit is occupied principally by a few countries,

[57] *Ibid*; It is obviously not enough for scholars to adopt the position of the proverbial ostriches that bury their necks in the sand. A lot of intellectual effort has been expended by some writers to proclaim property rights that simply are not there presently. Their position is very well captured in the opening quote to Christol's Article which interestingly attempts to dismiss the formidability of the Moon Agreement (1979) as an obstacle to the concept of space propertisation: It reads: "As I was going up the stair I met a man who wasn't there. He wasn't there again today. I wish, I wish he'd stay away." (Hughes Mearns, 1875) See Christol (1998) op. cit., p. 1.

[58] See Aristotle, *Nicomachean Ethics*, V. trans. Rackham (Cambridge, Harvard University Press, 1968). See also R.W.M. Dias, *Jurisprudence*, fifth ed. (London, Butterworths, 1988) p. 65.

[59] For further discussion of the issues relating to the geostationary orbit see Gbenga Oduntan, *Sovereignty & Jurisdiction in the Airspace & Outer Space: Legal Criteria for Spatial Delimitation*, Ph.D. thesis submitted at the University of Kent (2002). See particularly chapter: 10.4: The Bogota Declaration View. See also the Bogota Declaration of 3rd of December 1976; ITU Document WARC-BS (1977) 81 E of 17 Jan. 1977. Text available in *Journal of Space Law* (1978) pp. 193-196. The parties to the declaration are Brazil, Columbia, Congo, Ecuador, Indonesia, Kenya Uganda and Zaire.

accompanied by prompt replacement of spent satellites with newer satellites is unacceptable. Surely if it continues it may mean that other states may not in the future have orbital positions and related frequencies available.[60]

Significantly the CHM principle in at least this instance also works against the selfish instincts informing the usual positions taken by both developed and developing states. On the one hand, it renders untenable the central thesis of the Bogota Declaration (1976) in that no equatorial state can validly claim sovereignty over the orbit since it is the property of all. On the other hand in line with the corrective aspects of justice the 1985 Report of the Legal Committee on the Peaceful uses of Outer Space (UNCOPUOS) recognises that by reason of their geographical position the equatorial countries should be considered as having special rights to segments of the geostationary orbit superjacent to their territories.[61] Yet there is the likelihood in this century that an equatorial state may wish to launch its own satellite or group of satellites and would be told it cannot do so by the International Telecommunications Union (ITU) because there are no available positions or frequencies for it. The ITU under its present rules may be justified in placing precedence to those states which have already launched satellites in accordance with its 'first come first served' policies. But then, it may well be argued that it would be completely inequitable to expect an equatorial state to accept such a scheme as just. By virtue of geophysical realities there can be no equality of circumstances at least in a factual sense between it and the non-equatorial states, which monopolise the orbit.

A simple way of providing for the interests of these states is to make special slots available for them now and reserve them in perpetuity even if they do not yet have the technological capabilities to exploit the geostationary orbit. This it must be emphasised does not create ownership or sovereignty over the orbit as it is recognised for the airspace. It merely creates a licence to operate geostationary satellites and recognises the importance of justly sharing the finite resource that the geostationary orbit constitutes.

This brings us back to the question of equality. Aristotle claims that justice is equality but only among equals, and inequality is just but only among the unequal. Therefore, he enjoins, that we treat equals equally and the unequal, unequally. Applying this to the regimes governing airspace and outer space, it must be said that both benefits and burdens must be shared equally among states. The benefits of the 'equal' distribution of sovereignty in the airspace include the right to exclude unwanted foreigners, goods, flying objects, the assurance of state security, aviation safety, financial gain through the use of airspace as bargaining chips, etc. The burdens may be said to include the obligation to respect the sovereignty of other states over their own airspace, the duty to observe rules such as the privileges and duties exchanged in the Five Freedoms and Privileges Agreement.[62] In relation to outer space, benefits include the recognition of

[60] The geostationary orbit is a finite resource that can be 'clogged up' in the sense that there is in reality only a few 'parking spaces' in that orbit in which satellites can be placed along the same plane, for efficient coverage of the earth and without interfering or crashing into other satellites. What makes matters worse is that after a number of years some satellites wander off course and can very easily crash into nearby functioning satellites. See further Maurice N. Andem, *International Legal Problems in the Peaceful Exploration and Use of Outer Space*, (Finland, University of Lapland, 1992) p. 162.

[61] See A/AC.105/352 (April 11, 1985) pp.32-34; see further A/AC.105/370, pp.19-27.

[62] The Chicago International Air Transport Agreement 1944. BFSP 1; 171 UNTS 387; In force since 1945. 11 parties; UK not a party.

equal access to outer space (i.e. both orbital flight paths and celestial bodies). An adjunct of the right of access to outer space is the right to ascend into outer space and to descend. This operates as derogation from airspace sovereignty in that the airspace of a state might be traversed for this purpose. Other benefits include the freedom to engage in scientific experimentation and exploration, the removal of samples from celestial bodies, space tourism and the establishment of space stations.

Delineating the burdens to be shared may prove to be more difficult. Presently some developing states seek an active role in different areas of space exploration. These include China, India, Brazil, Argentina, Indonesia, Pakistan, Mexico, Iran, and Nigeria. Nigeria for example, announced with fanfare in 1986 its plans to launch space based telecommunication satellites in the 1990s.[63] In the early months of the year 2000, the President of the country announced that he was sorry but the scheme would have to wait, as there were more pressing priorities of development. Save the obligation to assist in the return of space objects and astronauts which exists in treaty law, most states simply do not stand the chance of bearing the smallest burden neither do they make even the minimal capital outlay towards outer space activities. In this way alone it becomes difficult not to see that following the Aristotelian analysis of justice there may be an amount of injustice in a regime that shares all benefits and burdens equally among transparently unequal states. If some states expend tremendous effort both in financial and intellectual terms in order to engage in outer space activities, it may indeed be argued that they deserve some preferential treatment in the sharing of rights and liabilities. An alternative will be to ensure that all states have an active participation in Outer Space activities, say for example by making equal contributions to a common body, which engages in Space exploration. However, it may be unjust to share such a burden among handicapped or disadvantaged states, which are patently unlikely to possess the necessary capacity to discharge them.

This brings us to the inescapable conclusion that scholars must locate the rationale/ justification for the prevailing regime of common ownership and control over outer space in something else apart from bare reference to the concept of 'equality'. Obviously the CHM principle/ province of mankind formula are based on the idea of distributive justice and as Dias correctly notes justice is a process, a complex and ever shifting balance between differing factors an aspect of which is equality.[64] Therefore, the better view will be to state that the common ownership over outer space is a factor of universal justice. The prevailing principles operate on the basis of the common good of all states. Again it must be reiterated that just as it is makes for world order and peace that all states possess exclusive jurisdiction in national airspace, so also is it equally in the universal interest that all spatial territories above sovereign airspace should not belong to any state. Admittedly this is no more than a value judgment but it is one, which accords with international peace and harmony as well as the general tenor of the development of space law so far.

This reservation of mineral exploitation in outer space until a time in the future when an equitable regime of sharing has been established is a political and legal requirement. The right of all states to contribute to the development of this regime has

[63] Andem *op. cit.*, p. 165.
[64] Dias *op. cit.*, p. 66.

nothing to do with the relative capacities of states to engage in scientific research. It is better to adopt the 'theory of justice'; used by John Rawls, to explain the fact that inequalities of wealth and authority are irrelevant to the imperatives of maintaining compensating benefits for everyone, and in particular for the least advantaged members of society. This is because it is undoubtedly an intuitive idea that everyone's well being depends upon a scheme of co-operation without which no one could have a satisfactory life. The division of advantages should be such as to draw forth the willing co-operation of everyone taking part in it, including if not particularly those who are less well situated.[65] However, much attention must be paid to Dias' view when he wrote that;

> "It is not enough to work out a just scheme of distribution, from whatever point of view but there is the further problem of getting it accepted and keeping it acceptable; which requires constant redistribution according to changing circumstances".[66]

It might be suggested, therefore, that rather than introduce the concepts of sovereignty or property into outer space what may be needed is a realignment of duties with respect to state participation. It may not be enough for states to send delegates to UN fora where legal and policy issues relating to outer space are deliberated upon such as the Committee for Space Research (COSPAR) and the UN Committee on the Peaceful Uses of Outer Space (COPUOS) but they may have to contribute in small ways at least to actual space research and projects. The modalities of this would have to be created under the aegis of the United Nations System.

6. 1. The Significance of Morality

The claim by some writers that there is no room for morality in the creation of international law deserves some consideration. It is thought for instance, that moral considerations are unnecessary in space law since there have been no serious conflicts with respect to outer space. Also connected to this is the argument that the lack of a demarcation between the airspace and outer space has not generated any serious conflicts. Plausible as these arguments may sound they are not acceptable because it is very possible that serious conflicts have been avoided so far as a result of the moral content and equitable considerations inherent in the law. In other words, military and political conflicts may have been defused well ahead by the existence of those very laws which critics of the present regime claim are unnecessary.[67]

The assertion of Sir Harold Nicolson that "[t]here does not exist such a thing as international morality" is inapplicable to air and space law.[68] The preferred view is that held by Arnold Wolfers who wrote; "the 'necessities' in international politics, and

---

[65] John Rawls, (1972) quoted in M.P.A Freeman, (ed.) *Lloyd's Introduction to Jurisprudence*, (London, Sweet and Maxwell Ltd., 1994) p. 466.
[66] Dias *op. cit.*, p. 66.
[67] The relation of law to morals was one of the three subjects most debated by nineteenth –century jurists, the other two being the nature of law and the interpretation of legal history. Jhering called it the Cape Horn of jurisprudence. The juristic navigator who would overcome its perils ran no risk of fatal shipwreck. Roscoe Pound, *op. cit.*, p. 215.
[68] H. Nicolson, *Diplomacy*, 3rd ed. (New York: Oxford University Press, 1973) p. 147. See Arnold Wolfers, *Discourse and Collaboration Essays on International Politics*, (Baltimore, Johns Hopkins University Press, 1973) p. 147.

for that matter in all spheres of life (that states) do not push decision and action beyond the realm of moral judgment". It is an undisputable fact that considerations of morality had an influence on the development of air law. Examples of this include the universal response to the heinous crime of aerial hijack; the formulation of the *aut dedere aut punire* principle in air treaties and Article 3 of the Chicago Convention, which states that states must refrain from the use of weapons against civil aircraft in flight as being incompatible with elementary considerations of humanity (Declaration 4).[69]

Clearly this is one of the reasons why the major air and space treaties are replete with provisions that recognise the imperatives of preventing economic avarice from making an inroad into spatial territories.[70] Rules of law, which permit commercial exploitation for private ends, were not advanced even though the Cold War was raging around the time the first space flight and the first moon landings took place. Indeed the United States delegate after the approval of the Moon Agreement by the COPUOS and Committee Four of the General Assembly in 1979 stated expressly that this 'balanced' and 'reasonable' agreement "would have to meet the approval of the United States Senate".[71] The United States also committed itself to future participation in negotiations respecting the establishment of an international regime for governing the exploitation of the moon's natural resources. International law and politics is, therefore, rooted in ethics. States and non-state actors share a basic moral vocabulary. Therefore, if a sceptic of space law poses the question, what stops a state from acquiring outer space resources solely for its exclusive use and in an unbridled manner, the answer would be "international law forbids it". It may also be asserted that unbridled exploitation of the moon's natural resources without reference to the expectation that it is an international commons also offends international morality. Needless to say any state(s), which disregard this, attacks the rationale of its own peaceful existence. This reasoning is further reinforced by the experience of the

---

[69] Note also the Declaration Adopted by the Council of the International Civil Aviation Organisation at the Ninth Meeting of Its 156th Session on 10 March 1999. Three main multilateral Conventions regulate jurisdiction over criminal acts against civil aviation. They are the Convention on Offences and Certain other Acts Committed on Board Aircraft of September 14, 1963 (The Tokyo Convention, 704 UNTS 219); The Convention for the Suppression of Unlawful Seizure of Aircraft of December 16 1970 (The Hague Convention 860 UNTS 105); and the Convention for the Suppression of Unlawful Acts against the Safety of Civil Aviation of September 23, 1971 (the Montreal Convention 10 ILM 1151). Other multilateral instruments of importance include the United Nations Convention against the Taking of Hostages of December 18, 1979 (18 ILM 1457) The United Nations Convention on the Prevention and Punishment of Crimes against Internationally Protected Persons, including Diplomatic Agents (1973) (1035 UNTS 167) and Annex 17 of the Chicago Convention 1944 which prescribes standards for aviation security. There is also the Protocol for the Suppression of Unlawful Acts of Violence at Airports Serving International Civil Aviation Supplementary to the Convention for the unlawful Acts Against The Safety of Civil Aviation (1971)(Done at Montreal on Sept. 23 1971; ICAO Doc 9518); Reprint also in XVIII-ll *Annals of Air And Space Law* (1993) p. 245; and the Convention On The Marking Of Explosives for the Purpose Of Detection (1991) XVIII-ll *Annals of Air And Space Law* (1993) p. 280. See Further Nanay Douglas Joyner, *Aerial Hijacking As An International Crime* (1974) p. 4; Cheng, Bin. *Aviation, Criminal Jurisdiction and Terrorism: The Hague Extradition? Prosecution Formula And Attacks At Airports* in *Contemporary Problems Of International Law; Essays In Honour Of George Schwarzenberger On His Eightieth Birthday* Cheng, Bin and E.D. Brown eds., (London, Stevens and Sons, 1988) p. 33.

[70] The preamble of the Chicago Convention (1944) for instance stipulates that the development of international civil aviation can greatly help to create and preserve friendship and understanding among the nations and peoples of the world, yet its abuse can become a threat to the general security.

[71] UN Doc. A/SPC/34/19, 6, 7 November 1979.

erstwhile USSR, which was a space power and the pioneer in manned space flight. As events turned out the USSR today exists no more and Russia the main successor to its outer space programmes can hardly fund space exploration. In fact it has recently lost its last independent space station -the Mir station. Fortunately the USSR had from the beginning of its involvement with space activities acknowledged more or less that outer space is *res omnium extra commercium*. If this had not been so, it would have secured for itself a merely transient victory.[72]

It has for long been realised that much of western law, including international law, has developed in response to requirements of western business and civilisation.[73] Although there is generally a conspiracy of silence over this fact it occasionally receives recognition by eminent jurists and has even been expressed by judges on the bench of the International Court of Justice.[74] Any serious inquiry into this particular issue would reveal certain indications that this is a reality even in the fields of air and space law. There are indeed numerous instances in the law and practice of airspace and outer space activities, which arguably constitute evidence of bias in legal development. This does not need to be so and the directive consideration has been explained elsewhere under the theory that there is an imperative to apply the 'interest of mankind' test generally to the regulation of all international air and space activities.[75] As one writer correctly puts it,

> "This notion of 'general interest' is not to be taken for granted and requires to be re-defined in reference to the fast development of modern technology that mostly benefit those (a few hundred million people) who control them while others (billions of people) still creep in the back, fighting for their essentials in life".[76]

---

[72] Note the position taken by Soviet scholars such as Y.A. Korovin. He eloquently submitted: "of possible conception of outer space -either as 'no one's', belonging to no one (*res nullius*) or as an object of common use (*res communis omnium*) we in my opinion, should choose the second one, naturally, if the other states take the same stand." Quite prophetically, he continues; "...proceeding from the conception of outer space as an object of common use for all mankind, it is necessary to recognise that forms and methods of this "common possession" can be established only with the mutual consent of all 'users' i.e., as a result of international agreement among all the states interested in the exploration and use of outer space". Y. A. Korovin, "Conquest of Outer Space and Problems of International Relations", *International Affairs*, (1959), p. 90. See also A.S. Piradov (ed.), *International Space Law*, (Moscow, Progress Publishers, 1976) p. 86.

[73] O.J.Lissitzyn, "International Law in a Divided World", *Int'L Conciliation* (March 1963) at 37.

[74] Judge Amman in the *Barcelona Traction* Case noted that '...certain customs of wide scope became incorporated into positive law when in fact they were the work of five or six powers' Barcelona Traction (Belgium v. Spain), 1958 I.C.J Rep. 308. For wider perspectives of this issue see the following: Wade Mansell et. Al., *A Critical Introduction to Law*, (London: Cavendish Publishers, 1995) pp. 1-27 *et passim*; P. Sinha Surya, *Legal Polycentricity And International Law*, (1996); *N'zatioula Grovogusi Siba, Sovereigns, Quasi Sovereigns and Africans: Race Self Determination In International Law*, (Minnesota: University of Minnesota Press, 1996). As a writer puts it, "a major research theme that unites this diverse anti-colonial intellectual tradition is its primary focus on arguing about the limits within which the newly independent nations of Africa would embrace an international; law that was Eurocentric in its geographic origin." James Thuo Gathii, *Review Essay: International Law and Eurocentricity: Introduction*, 9 *European Journal of International Law* (1997) 184, 187.

[75] See Gbenga Oduntan (2003) *op.cit.* pp. 185- 186, 204 *et passim*.

[76] Patrick Salin, "An Overview of US Commercial Space Legislation and Policies-Present and Future", XXVII *Annals Of Air And Space Law* (2002) note 17, at 209-210.

This is precisely why technological capability or superiority in any sector (aviation, Antarctica, deep-sea bed, or outer space) ought not to be allowed to secure hegemonic interests for any state(s) over and above the general international interest.
In essence to ask whether it is fair and moral that the moon should be free for all nations at all times is to beg the question. Naturally a scholar adopting a capitalist, he-who- dares- wins approach would advance the position that if there is gold on the moon whoever can fetch it should keep it.[77] The truth, however, is that astronomically the moon is the earth's natural satellite. Any adverse changes to the moon's geophysical and environmental state will be of concern to the entire mankind. Its resources may eventually be utilised but at this stage its use must be protected and managed in the interest of both the present and future generations of mankind. Since no one is capable of laying claim to the earth then no one can own the planet's only moon or any of its parts outside the agreement of all concerned. It may indeed be immoral to seek such consent.

Another justification of the morality of the prevailing regime lies in the fact that international law particularly Article 2 (4) of the UN Charter enjoins all states to eschew wars.[78] History has shown that many major wars have arisen from conflicts over territorial conquests.[79] The morale, therefore, is that the moon and other celestial bodes must not become the theatre or subject of conflicts in the future. Andem is correct in noting that:

> "It is logical and rational that anything common and general to all, calls for the general agreement of those concerned to formulate rules regulating its use and disposal...Any exploitation of the moon, for instance, through mining might affect the geophysical structure and composition of the atmosphere surrounding our earth, which would in turn have severe consequences not only on those states now actively engaged in the exploration and exploitation of outer space, but on all other states, developed as well as developing.[80]"

There is no doubt that the entire world has an interest in the development of space activities and that the CHM principle is perhaps the most significant expression of this sustaining interest. This moral and legal force behind this reasoning is well corroborated in the Latin maxim *Quod omnes tangit ab omnes debet approbetur.* In

[77] *Cf.* the views of the erstwhile President Mahithir of Malaysia. He is quoted to have said "I have heard that the South Pole is made of gold and I want my piece of it". Cited in Michael T. Kosmo, 'The Future of the Antarctic Treaty System: An Examination of the 'Common Heritage' and 'World Park' Proposals for an Alternative Antarctic Regime', *Auckland University Law Review*, (1992) p. 117. See also Beck, 'Antarctica at the United Nations 1988: Seeking a Bridge of Understanding', *Polar Records*, 25 (1989) p. 329.
[78] All Members shall refrain in their international relations from the threat or use of force against the territorial integrity or political independence of any state, or in any other manner inconsistent with the purposes of the United Nations. Note also the 1970 General Assembly Declaration on Principles of International laws concerning Friendly Relations and Co-operation among States U.N.G.A Resolution 2625 (XXV); note further Article 2 Moon Agreement (1979).
[79] Particular note must be taken of the wars and conflicts resulting from the expansion of colonial territories by the European powers.
[80] Andem *op. cit.*, p. 95.

other words, what affects all should be approved by all and very evidently common dangers should be the concern of all.

7. CONCLUSIONS

The CHM and the province of mankind terminologies are two sides of the same coin. The principles exist in the space treaties to create legal obligations, which in effect dictate co-operation among states parties in aspects of their undertakings concerning outer space, the Moon and other celestial bodies, and in the sharing of the benefits obtainable therefrom. These principles represent a relatively new category of legal classification for the explanation of jurisdiction and control over international territory. Earlier analogies can be found in the law of the sea and the legal regime governing Antarctica. For all relevant purposes the CHM principle applies not only to all 'celestial bodies' no matter how small or large and no matter in which solar system in the infinity of space they are found but also to all that may be considered 'free space' including gases, particles and cosmic dust. It does not operate over the national airspace presently.

It is probably desirable that the applicability of the CHM principle extends to the airspace over the high seas as well. This is a logical consequence of the declaration of the legal nature of the high sea-bed and ocean floor (excluding the continental shelf) and the subsoil thereof as the common heritage of mankind. Furthermore it is suggested that since the sovereignty and jurisdiction granted to states in their national airspace is delimited *ratione loci* in respect of the space above national territories and not *ratione materiae* in respect of the air, which may at any given time be filling this space. Then there is scope for the separate determination of the legal status of the air itself (i.e. the gaseous envelope surrounding the earth). In that case considering the central and irreplaceable nature of the air to the existence of human beings the sole conclusion that presents itself is that the air (*ratione materiae*) is best assimilated into the concept of CHM. In other words, if there is at least one thing worthy of being regarded as the common heritage of mankind the air that we breathe would certainly qualify.

Of the older classifications known to law the CHM principle is best represented by the classification of *res omnium extra communis*. By virtue of this the area covered belongs to entire mankind as represented by states. Sovereignty cannot in anyway be legally enforced over outer space. Until a regime of exploitation is designed for it as was done in the case of 'the Area' in the law of the sea, outer space and its resources cannot be exploited on a commercial basis. It may indeed be said that it is better that no such regime of commercial exploitation is ever developed if it would inescapably entail environmental degradation or lead to international conflicts.[81]

[81] For a treatment of "impending conflicts over the 'higher grounds' in the near future" see Oduntan (2003) *op.cit.*, pp. 202-204. It suffice to note here that presently there is no shortage of conflicts arising from commercial usages of outer space and there should be a reluctance to create more. These include disagreements over the legality of aerial reconnaissance and remote sensing involving political/economic intelligence gathering at high altitudes and from areas coterminous with state territory (such as from the airspace above the non-sovereign maritime zones); the legality of militarization of outer space (as for instance heralded by the United States' 'Son of Star Wars') and the indeterminacy of what constitutes an aircraft or space craft in legal terms (in view of crafts with hybrid characteristics such as the X15, space shuttles and the privately owned 'spaceshipone' all adaptable for

International space law presently has enshrined the CHM principle and there is no convincing reason to abandon it or limit its applicability qualitatively or quantitatively. The arguments against the legal potency of the CHM Principle are altogether insufficient to credibly cast any doubts as to the necessity and the validity of the principle in present day international law. The argument that it represents no more than a hortatory provision is unsupportable given its inclusion in the substantive parts of the Moon Agreement (1979) (Article 11 (1)). The fact that the principle also has enjoyed legal, obligatory and institutional validity in the law of the sea also proves that it was intended to and indeed has legal effect in space law.

Outer space is the most recent to be conquered in the trilogy of most important international spaces. Before the utilisation of outer space based resources can commence on a large scale or for commercial benefits, an elaborate legal regime would have to be developed. At this stage there is no such regime in place. However, as a result of the CHM principle, which applies to outer space and the celestial bodies, commercial exploitation is presently forbidden. Due to the growing restiveness of certain developed states particularly those states that also have been the keenest to exploit the deep-sea bed and Antarctica, it is imperative that all independent states should consider an exploitation regime shortly. Reasons for this include the potential for damage to the environment and the growing importance of outer space activities in the conduct of technological and scientific development. It is also important to put in place a progressive system before illegal or divergent state practice emerges in terms of space exploration and exploitation.

Before there can be any form of commercial exploitation of resources based in outer space an autonomous regime must be established under space law, with legal bodies of its own and in effective control of all activities. The Enterprise which was created for high sea-bed mining provides a good model upon which a similar organ for space exploitation may be based. The employment of "joint ventures" for outer space mining activities as is designed for the deep-sea mining is also recommended. However, unlike developments in the deep-sea regime the obligation of states Parties to finance an Enterprise mining activities must be retained. The amounts to be contributed may, however, be calculated on means related criteria. In the absence of this regime there can be no legal basis for the introduction of the concept of property or appropriation over resources based in space and on celestial bodies. It is hoped that when eventually such a progressive utilisation regime over space-based resources is put in place there would be scope for active participation in outer space activities, for all states irrespective of size and financial resources. A proportionate contribution system to the common body, which engages in Space exploitation, is desirable. It would clearly be unjust to share equally the burden among handicapped or disadvantaged states.

---

space tourism). Other looming problems the significance of which have been sharpened by the increasing involvement of businesses in space activities include the impending scenario of technological advancement making travel to other universes a possibility; the question of the scope of space law in view of the ambiguity introduced by the 'within the solar system' formula adopted in the Moon Agreement (1979) and not the least of course, the recurrent problem of spatial delimitation of the boundary between airspace and outer space. See further Gbenga Oduntan, "The Never Ending Dispute: Legal Theories on the Spatial Demarcation Boundary Plane between Airspace and Outer Space Vol. 1 *Hertfordshire Law Journal* 02 (Autumn 2003) pp. 81-84.

In terms of environmental concerns it would appear that the emerging space law has a lot to learn from the development of the Antarctic regime. An example, of this is the establishment of the Committee on Environmental Protection. The equivalent of this organ would also be necessary to take control over environmental issues arising from outer space exploration and exploitation. Surely until such a body is created for outer space as well, there can be no assurance of effective policing of the international community's resolve in keeping outer space as free as possible from human contamination and harmful practices. The establishment of such a specialised body is also a *sine qua non* of the commencement of large-scale mineral exploitation of outer space based resources.

It is important that an invidious system of special status for certain states such as the 'consultative party' system that exist under the Antarctic system is not introduced into outer space law. All states must remain equal in all respects possible under the Space Treaties. This is to avert similar hostility to the concept of consultative parties and the hegemony they possess as found in relation to the Antarctic regime. The present system also provides the best possible checks on any potential excesses that may arise in the practice of space exploration. It suffices to repeat that the repercussions of any dangerous activity in space exploration would more likely than not be felt by all states or other states apart from the particular state that conducts the activity. It is not enough to work out a just scheme of distribution, but such a system must be achieved through compromise and negotiation. This will entail getting it accepted and keeping it acceptable. This of course requires constant redistribution according to changing circumstances.

What must be avoided at all costs is a situation whereby a few states and their commercial ventures share the commercial, technological or scientific benefits that accrue from outer space exploration and exploitation between themselves alone without reference to the envisaged regime of international cooperation and equitable sharing stipulated in the major space treaties. Furthermore it may indeed be reiterated that it is better if no commercial exploitation ever takes place on celestial bodies than for severe environmental damage to be done to the earth through the repatriation of resources from outer space. It needs also be considered if indeed human exploitation should be allowed to cause irreversible geophysical or environmental degradation to other celestial bodies all in the cause of generating economic profit for the present generation. It may also be better that a moratorium on exploitation is established to cover the better part of this century somewhat along the lines of the 50-year moratorium placed on the exploitation of Antarctica's natural resources, rather than for the world to be drawn into such international conflicts as was witnessed in the scramble by the colonialists for overseas territories, in Africa, Asia and Latin America. Lastly it must be realised that not all things that can be exploited should be exploited. The fact that technology someday makes it possible to commercially exploit the air we breathe by for instance harnessing it in some form and making it scarce for resale does not mean that the law should lend legitimisation for such an abomination.

The jurisprudential basis for common ownership, possession and control over outer space can be said to be based on the simple logic that what concerns all must be approved by all. The principles of equality of states, justice and the theory of *nemo dat quod non habet* apply to outer space. Therefore, the better view will be to state that the common ownership over outer space is a factor of universal justice. The use of all potentially finite resources must be regulated tightly under an effective international regime. Thus, resources such as the geostationary orbit need to be regulated under more effective laws, which make the *de facto* commandeering of slots impossible, by a few active states. It is clear that the present position with respect to geostationary orbit use, whereby the orbit is occupied principally by a few countries, accompanied by prompt replacement of spent satellites with newer satellites without any allowance for the future interests of developing states is unacceptable and may eventually culminate in friction and disputes among states. It is not difficult to predict that both the technology and ability to place satellites into geostationary orbit will become feasible to very many states within the course of this century. The ITU policy of 'first come first served' may not be adequate to cope with this eventuality and may in fact occasion indirect injustice in certain cases.

There is significant scope for the operation of the precepts of morality by states in their exploratory activities in outer space. Just as certain principles regarding the exercise of jurisdiction and control in the airspace have a moral basis so also there is a moral basis for the CHM and province of mankind principle in space law. International morality does forbid the appropriation of outer space for private ends either by the nation-state or by private individuals and corporate bodies. This is why technological capability or superiority in any sector (aviation, Antarctica, high seas, deep sea bed or outer space) has never been the sole necessary and sufficient reason to secure hegemonic interests over and above the general international interest.

58

[11]

THE COMMON HERITAGE OF MANKIND: AN ADEQUATE REGIME FOR MANAGING THE DEEP SEABED?

EDWARD GUNTRIP*

[The concept of the 'common heritage of mankind' governs the deep seabed. However, the principle of the common heritage of mankind has differing interpretations and consequently lacks legal force. This article attempts to give content to the common heritage of mankind principle, as it applies to the deep seabed, by examining existing principles in international law. It also draws analogies with the principle of the common heritage of mankind as it applies to Antarctica and outer space. The development of international environmental law is considered as a potential model by which the common heritage of mankind principle can develop further legal content.]

CONTENTS

---

* BSc, LLB (Hons) (UWA); Barrister and Solicitor of the High Court of Australia and the Supreme Courts of New South Wales and Western Australia. An earlier version of this article was submitted as part of the author's undergraduate studies at the University of Western Australia.

I INTRODUCTION

In the late 19th century, scientists discovered polymetallic nodules on the deep seabed.[1] The quantities found were large enough to enable commercial mining operations,[2] and in the 1960s, developments in technology meant that accessing these new mineral resources became a real and imminent possibility.[3] The problem, however, was that the deep seabed did not lie within the jurisdiction of any state. Consequently, to regulate access to these resources, a legal regime had to be established. The regime adopted was the 'common heritage of mankind'.

The common heritage of mankind principle consists of four elements. It prohibits states from proclaiming sovereignty over any part of the deep seabed, and requires that states use it for peaceful purposes, sharing its management and the benefits of its exploitation.[4]

Due to the ideological differences of developed and developing states, the common heritage of mankind principle has been interpreted in various ways.[5] These interpretations have not been reconciled and there has been no juridical consideration of the common heritage of mankind principle to clarify them.[6] Therefore, the precise legal requirements of the principle of the common heritage of mankind remain undefined.

Although commercial deep seabed mining is unlikely to commence in the near future, there is still a need to establish an effective legal regime for the deep seabed. This need is demonstrated by, among other issues, the discovery of hydrothermal vents and the potential for military-based activities to occur on the deep seabed.

Hydrothermal vent sites are located on the seabed in areas within and beyond the limits of national jurisdiction.[7] Each site consists of chemical rich waters that

---

1 Jack Barkenbus, *Deep Seabed Resources: Politics and Technology* (1979).

2 Ibid 5.

3 Nico Schrijver, *Sovereignty over Natural Resources: Balancing Rights and Duties* (1997) 215.

4 Martin Harry, 'The Deep Seabed: The Common Heritage of Mankind or Arena for Unilateral Exploitation?' (1992) 40 *Naval Law Review* 207, 226; Said Mahmoudi, *The Law of Deep Sea-Bed Mining: A Study of the Progressive Development of International Law concerning the Management of the Polymetallic Nodules of the Deep Sea-Bed* (1987) 130; Steven Molitor, 'The Provisional Understanding Regarding Deep Seabed Matters: An Ill-Conceived Regime for US Deep Seabed Mining' (1987) 20 *Cornell International Law Journal* 223, 228.

5 Ram Prakash Anand, *Legal Regime of the Deep Sea-Bed and the Developing Countries* (1975) 205.

6 The common heritage of mankind was referred to in *Delimitation of Maritime Areas (St Pierre and Miquelon) (Canada and France)* (1992) 31 ILM 1145, 1172.

7 Lyle Glowka, 'Putting Marine Scientific Research on a Sustainable Footing at Hydrothermal Vents' (2003) 27 *Marine Policy* 303, 304.

support a diverse range of micro-organisms and marine species.[8] Scientific research, the exploitation of mineral deposits and tourism all have the potential to threaten these hydrothermal vent sites.[9]

In order to protect these sites, in January 2003 the World Conservation Union ('IUCN') hosted a workshop in Spain.[10] The workshop's purpose was to try to establish a framework for the protection of these hydrothermal vent sites by establishing Marine Protected Areas ('MPA').[11] Both the IUCN and the World Wildlife Fund recognised that the current legal regime in the areas beyond national jurisdiction left a 'critical gap' in the protected areas system and that high seas protected areas are 'urgently needed'.[12]

The lack of any effective legal regime for the deep seabed also has an impact on potential military uses of the deep seabed as part of the 'revolution in military affairs'[13] and the fight against terrorism. It has been recognised that modern warfare strategy relies on information rather than the mere use of force.[14] A potential source of this information is the use of intelligence gathering devices (such as tracking devices) on the deep seabed. Given that the present threats to global security include terrorism and the proliferation of weapons of mass destruction, the use of the deep seabed to conduct information-gathering activities may become widespread. It is not clear whether the use of information gathering devices on the deep seabed for military purposes conflicts with the common heritage of mankind principle.

These examples illustrate that current concerns about the deep seabed are very different to the concerns that existed in the 1970s regarding deep seabed mining. Previously, the debates over deep seabed mining concerned the right to exploit mineral deposits and the economic consequences of any exploitation.[15] However, mining was, and still is, constrained by both technological and economic factors. Therefore, the context of these discussions was very different to the context of current discussions. The current issues of environmental protection and global concern regarding national security demonstrate that states are now adopting a more holistic approach to the deep seabed. This is because environmental damage may occur from activities that states currently undertake on the deep seabed, and many nations are still coming to terms with the consequences of terrorism on a large scale. Despite this, the differences between the current deep seabed issues and those related to deep seabed mining in the 1970s do not negate the need for a legal regime to govern such activities.

This article examines whether the common heritage of mankind principle has the potential to become a juridical standard capable of managing activities relating to the deep seabed.

---

8 Ibid.

9 Ibid.

10 IUCN News Release, *Deep Thoughts for the High Seas* (2003) <http://www.iucn.org/info_and_news/press/highseas2.pdf> at 1 October 2003.

11 Ibid.

12 Ibid.

13 See generally *The RMA Debate* (2003) <http://www.comw.org/rma/> at 2 September 2003.

14 See, eg, Leonard Litton, *The Information-Based RMA and the Principles of War* (2000) IWS: The Information Warfare Site <http://www.iwar.org.uk/rma/resources/info-rma/litton.htm> at 1 October 2003.

15 See below Part III.

Initially, the development of the common heritage of mankind principle in international law is traced to provide an understanding of how the conflicting interpretations over its substance have arisen. This examination demonstrates the opposing positions taken by developing and developed states, prior to the principle's overall acceptance in the 1994 *Agreement Relating to the Implementation of Part XI of the United Nations Convention on the Law of the Sea.*[16] It also evidences that, despite overall acceptance, the common heritage of mankind principle lacks precise legal obligations.

Subsequently, an attempt is made to give content to each element of the common heritage of mankind principle by considering existing international legal principles drawn from various sources. This demonstrates where the principle currently lacks content. More importantly, it also indicates the elements of the principle that require the most development to allow effective management of the deep seabed.

Finally, this article studies global commons regimes, such as the *Antarctic Treaty*[17] and the *Agreement governing the Activities of States on the Moon and Other Celestial Bodies*,[18] and international environmental law in order to determine by what means the common heritage of mankind principle could evolve into a juridical standard. By contrasting similar principles and regimes that have had varying success, it becomes possible to determine what approach is required to make the common heritage of mankind principle an effective standard.

II THE EVOLUTION OF THE COMMON HERITAGE OF MANKIND PRINCIPLE

The advancement of the common heritage of mankind principle has been hindered by conflicting interpretations on the part of developing and developed states. It was not until the *1994 Agreement* that there arose near universal support for the common heritage of mankind principle. To reach this point, there had been General Assembly resolutions and domestic legislation passed to promote discord and a global convention relating to the law of the sea. This section outlines how the differing approaches of states have shaped the current concept of the common heritage of mankind principle.

A *Initial Proposal*

In 1967, the Secretary-General of the UN included a supplementary item in the agenda of the 22nd session of the General Assembly.[19] This note verbale outlined the need to establish a regime to govern the deep seabed.[20] In order to prevent military competition and technologically advanced states exploiting the

[16] Opened for signature 28 July 1994, 1836 UNTS 3, pt XI (entered into force 28 July 1996) ('*1994 Agreement*').

[17] Opened for signature 1 December 1959, 402 UNTS 71, art IV(1) (entered into force 23 June 1961).

[18] Opened for signature 5 December 1979, 1363 UNTS 3 (entered into force 11 July 1984) ('*Moon Treaty*').

[19] Barkenbus, above n 1, 32; Mahmoudi, above n 4, 119; Yuwen Li, *Transfer of Technology for Deep Sea-Bed Mining: The* 1982 Law of the Sea Convention *and Beyond* (1994) 17; Judge Shigeru Oda, *International Law of the Resources of the Sea* (1979) 109.

[20] Judge Shigeru Oda, *The Law of the Sea in Our Time: Part I — New Developments 1966–1975* (1977) 16.

deep seabed for their own interests, the proposal suggested both an international treaty and an international agency to regulate activities on the deep seabed.[21] The international treaty was to regulate activities on the deep seabed by establishing it as the common heritage of mankind.[22] An international agency was to assume jurisdiction over the deep seabed, regulate and control activities undertaken on the deep seabed and enforce the treaty.[23] Reaction to the proposal was mixed. In general, developing states endorsed the principle and developed states rejected it.

Developing states endorsed the common heritage of mankind principle for two reasons. First, many developing states remain the land-based producers of the minerals found in seabed nodules,[24] while developed states generate the bulk of the world's demand for minerals.[25] Developing states were concerned that if developed states were to mine the deep seabed, the demand for minerals would lessen and, consequently, mineral prices would fall.[26] As the economies of many developing states are heavily reliant upon mineral exports for their income, they perceived the sharing of financial benefits gained from deep seabed mining as a means of recovering any lost income from a fall in mineral prices.

The second, and more influential reason, was the demand for change by developing states embodied in the New International Economic Order ('NIEO').[27] The NIEO aimed to establish a more equitable distribution of resources and income between developed and developing states.[28] By distributing economic benefits from the exploitation of the deep seabed between all parties, the advantages of those developed states with the technology to mine would be shared with developing states. Therefore, many developing states saw

---

21 Barkenbus, above n 1, 32–3; Kathy-Ann Brown, *The Status of the Deep Seabed beyond National Jurisdiction: Legal and Political Realities* (SJD Thesis, York University, 1991) 23; Sofiah Jewa, *How Has the* United Nations Convention on the Law of the Sea *Fared?* (1999) <http://www.mlj.com.my/articles/sofiah.htm> at 1 October 2003; Mahmoudi, above n 4, 119–20.

22 Kathy-Ann Brown, above n 21, 23; Li, above n 19, 17; Mahmoudi, above n 4, 120; Oda, *The Law of the Sea in Our Time*, above n 20, 16.

23 Anand, above n 5, 181–2.

24 Donald Denman, *Markets under the Sea?: A Study of the Potential of Private Property Rights in the Seabed* (1984) 17; Wolfgang Hauser, *The Legal Regime for Deep Seabed Mining under the* Law of the Sea Convention (1983) 14–16; Molitor, above n 4, 226–7.

25 Denman, above n 24, 17; Molitor, above n 4, 226–7.

26 David Hegwood, 'Deep Seabed Mining: Alternative Schemes for Protecting Developing Countries from Adverse Impacts' (1982) 12 *Georgia Journal of International and Comparative Law* 173, 178.

27 The NIEO was outlined at the 1964 UN Conference on Trade and Development by various declarations and was more comprehensively formulated in: *Declaration on the Establishment of a New International Economic Order*, GA Res 3201(S-V1), UN GAOR, 6th special session, 2229th plen mtg, Supp 1, UN Doc A/9599 (1974); *Programme of Action on the Establishment of a New International Economic* Order, GA Res 3202(S-V2), UN GAOR, 2229th plen mtg, Supp 1, UN Doc A/9599 (1974); *Charter of Economic Rights and Duties of States*, GA Res 3281 (XXIX), UN GAOR, 29th sess, 2315th plen mtg, Supp 31, UN Doc A/RES/3281(XXIX) (1975). It has also been included in subsequent multilateral conventions.

28 Bernard Herber, 'The Common Heritage Principle: Antarctica and the Developing Nations' (1991) 50 *American Journal of Economics and Sociology* 391, 391; Lawrence Juda, 'UNCLOS III and the New International Economic Order' (1979) 7 *Ocean Development and International Law Journal* 221, 223–4.

the common heritage of mankind principle as a means of rectifying their economic situation.[29]

Developed states rejected the common heritage of mankind principle on two grounds. First, mainly due to its imprecision, they considered the concept to be devoid of any legal meaning.[30] Second, developed states argued that deep seabed resources could not belong to the world community.[31] Rather, developed states relied upon the freedoms of the high seas, outlined in the 1958 *Geneva Convention on the High Seas*,[32] as the governing regime.[33]

B *General Assembly Resolutions*

To further develop the common heritage of mankind principle, the General Assembly passed *Resolution 2467A*,[34] which created a Committee on the Peaceful Uses of the Seabed and the Ocean Floor beyond the Limits of National Jurisdiction ('Seabed Committee'). The Seabed Committee drafted a number of resolutions, the most important being *Resolution 2574D*[35] and *Resolution 2749*.[36]

1 Moratorium Resolution

The effect of the *Moratorium Resolution* adopted in 1969 was to create a moratorium on deep seabed mining until an international regime had been established. The *Moratorium Resolution* declared that:

1 States and persons, physical or juridical, are bound to refrain from all activities of exploitation of the resources of the area of the sea-bed and ocean floor, and the subsoil thereof, beyond the limits of national jurisdiction;

2 No claim to any part of the area or its resources shall be recognized.

Developing states used the *Moratorium Resolution* to restrict the exploitation of the deep seabed by developed states. The intention behind the *Moratorium Resolution* was to *create legal uncertainty*, stalling any exploitation of the deep seabed.[37] This was to allow for further discussion before the issue was made redundant by the commencement of seabed activities.[38]

---

29 Boleslaw Boczek, 'Ideology and the Law of the Sea: The Challenge of the New International Economic Order' (1984) 7 *Boston College International and Comparative Law Review* 1, 3; Juda, above n 28, 225; Mahmoudi, above n 4, 127.

30 Mahmoudi, above n 4, 124–5; Division for Ocean Affairs and the Law of the Sea, Office of Legal Affairs, UN, *The Law of the Sea: Concept of the Common Heritage of Mankind: Legislative History of Articles 133 to 150 and 311(6) of the* United Nations Convention on the Law of the Sea (1996) 93.

31 Mahmoudi, above n 4, 125.

32 Opened for signature 29 April 1958, 450 UNTS 11 (entered into force 30 September 1962).

33 Mahmoudi, above n 4, 126.

34 GA Res 2467A (XXIII), UN GAOR, 23rd sess, 1752nd plen mtg, UN Doc A/RES/2467 (XXIII) (1968).

35 GA Res 2574D (XXIV), UN GAOR, 24th sess, 1833rd plen mtg, UN Doc A/RES/2574 (XXIV) (1969) ('*Moratorium Resolution*').

36 GA Res 2749 (XXV), UN GAOR, 25th sess, 1933rd plen mtg, UN Doc A/RES/2574 (XXV) (1970) ('*Declaration of Principles*').

37 Kathy-Ann Brown, above n 21, 29; Li, above n 19, 25.

38 Kathy-Ann Brown, above n 21, 29; Mahmoudi, above n 4, 130.

Developed states rejected the binding nature of the *Moratorium Resolution*. John Stevenson, the Legal Advisor of the United States State Department declared, in a letter to the Seabed Committee, the position of the US to be that:

> The *Resolution* is recommendatory and not obligatory. The United States is, therefore, not legally bound by it. The United States is, however, required to give good faith consideration to the *Resolution* in determining its policies ... The United States is not, however, obligated to implement the recommendations and has made clear its opposition to the concept.[39]

Developed states believed that a moratorium would hinder the future development of technologies relating to deep seabed mining.[40] The *Moratorium Resolution* was argued to be counter-productive to the common heritage of mankind principle, as no state could benefit while a moratorium existed.[41] Developed states feared that, to gain access to the nodules, other states would make extended claims of national jurisdiction. This was possible based on the 1958 *Geneva Convention on the Continental Shelf*, which provided that the continental shelf could extend to the depth of any exploitable resources.[42]

2 Declaration of Principles

The General Assembly adopted the *Declaration of Principles* in 1970. This was an attempt to outline the principles governing the use of the deep seabed. It declared the seabed the common heritage of mankind,[43] but it did not resolve the divide between developed and developing states. This was due to two factors. First, the principles outlined in the *Declaration* were ambiguous. It was adopted as a compromise and, consequently, the principles were vague and uncontroversial.[44] This is evidenced by the failure of the *Declaration of Principles* to define the common heritage of mankind principle.[45] Second, states believed that the *Declaration of Principles* had different purposes. The developed states did not consider it to have any binding legal authority. They preferred to regard the common heritage of mankind principle as a facultative concept, which following elaboration, might be capable of governing the resources of the deep seabed. They argued that the lack of legal substance was rectifiable by the international regime.[46] By contrast, the developing states considered the *Declaration of Principles* as the basis of the international regime.[47] Thus, the *Declaration of Principles* had made the common heritage of mankind principle a normative and judicially enforceable means of regulating the deep seabed.

---

39 Edward Brown, *Sea-Bed Energy and Mineral Resources and the Law of the Sea: The Area beyond the Limits of National Jurisdiction* (1986) vol 2, II.2 22.
40 Li, above n 19, 25; Mahmoudi, above n 4, 131.
41 Kathy-Ann Brown, above n 21, 28.
42 Opened for signature 29 April 1958, 499 UNTS 312, art 1 (entered into force 10 June 1964).
43 *Declaration of Principles*, above n 36, [1].
44 Anand, above n 5, 181.
45 See *Declaration of Principles*, above n 36, [1].
46 Li, above n 19, 27; Mahmoudi, above n 4, 135.
47 Ibid.

C UN Convention on the Law of the Sea

Contemporaneous with the *Declaration of Principles*, the General Assembly convened the Third United Nations Conference on the Law of the Sea ('Third Conference').[48] The purpose of this conference was to create a uniform codified regime, covering all aspects of the law of the sea, but in particular the regime governing the deep seabed.[49]

The Third Conference operated according to a 'gentleman's agreement', which provided that no voting would occur until all efforts to reach a consensus had failed.[50] The resulting *UN Convention on the Law of the Sea* also represented a 'package deal'.[51] As 'the problems of ocean space are closely interrelated',[52] states considered all issues simultaneously. Further, arts 309 and 311(6) of *UNCLOS* prohibit reservations. Therefore, states had to accept the *Convention* in its entirety. Laylin recognised that the consequence of these mechanisms was that 'the positions taken by many delegations reflected not their country's view as to the existing law or as to the desirable new law but a trading ploy'.[53] The content of the common heritage of mankind principle became secondary to its strength as a bargaining tool. The principle's subsequent lack of development was evidenced by the provisions of *UNCLOS*, which closely followed the initial proposal and the *Declaration of Principles*.

Part XI of *UNCLOS* embodies the deep seabed provisions. It refers to the seabed as the 'Area', which is defined in art 1(1) as 'the seabed, ocean floor and subsoil thereof, beyond the limits of national jurisdiction'. Article 133 establishes that part XI relates to polymetallic nodules. The Area is governed by the common heritage of mankind.[54] This prevents states claiming or exercising 'sovereignty or sovereign rights' and natural or juridical persons 'appropriating any part thereof.'[55] Article 140(1) provides that all activities must be undertaken for the benefit of mankind as a whole, without regard to whether states are coastal or landlocked, taking into 'particular consideration the interests and needs of developing States'. States must use the Area exclusively for peaceful purposes.[56] The International Seabed Authority ('ISA') is given authority to act on behalf of 'mankind as a whole', in whom the resources of the Area are vested.[57]

Prior to the conclusion of the Third Conference, many developed states indicated that they were not satisfied with the provisions of part XI and would

---

48 Li, above n 19, 37; Ivan Shearer, *Starke's International Law* (11th ed, 1994) 231.

49 Li, above n 19, 37.

50 Bernard Oxman, 'The Law of the Sea' in Christopher Joyner (ed) *The United Nations and International Law* (1997) 321; Hugo Caminos and Michael Molitor, 'Progressive Development of International Law and the Package Deal' (1985) 79 *American Journal of International Law* 871, 874.

51 Opened for signature 10 December 1982, 1836 UNTS 3 (entered into force 16 November 1994) ('*UNCLOS*').

52 Ibid preamble.

53 John Laylin, 'Emerging Customary Law of the Sea' (1976) 10 *International Lawyer* 669, 670.

54 *UNCLOS*, above n 51, art 136.

55 Ibid art 137(1).

56 Ibid art 141.

57 Ibid art 137(2).

not sign *UNCLOS*. The most significant proponent of this attitude was the US. The Reagan administration rejected part XI claiming it would deter future development of deep seabed mineral resources and insisting that there was a lack of certainty regarding the granting of mining contracts.[58] The US government disagreed with artificial limitations placed on seabed production and what it perceived to be burdensome financial requirements.[59] It did not support the structure of the ISA since it would not give the US an adequate role in decision-making processes and would allow amendments to enter into force without US approval.[60] Furthermore, it would provide for the mandatory transfer of technology.[61] The Reagan administration also objected to the ISA on the grounds that a portion of funds received by the Authority might be used to fund national liberation movements.[62]

Consequently, many developed states did not sign *UNCLOS*. This undermined the desired universal acceptance of a codified law of the sea and more specifically, a unified acceptance of the common heritage of mankind principle.

D *Reciprocating States' Regime*

As an interim measure to develop discussion,[63] the US enacted the *Deep Seabed Hard Minerals Resources Act*.[64] France, Italy, Japan, the Soviet Union, the United Kingdom and West Germany passed similar legislation.[65]

The legislation provided for the licensing of any exploration and exploitation occurring on the deep seabed, outside the *UNCLOS* regime.[66] To prevent overlapping licenses, a reciprocating states' regime was entered into in order to recognise licenses issued by other legislating states.[67]

Developing states opposed the legal effect of the legislation and the reciprocating states' regime. In a letter dated 23 April 1979 to the Chairman of the Group of 77,[68] the Group of Legal Experts on the Question of Unilateral Legislation declared that '[t]he adoption of unilateral measures, draft legislation and limited agreements would merely be an event without international legal effect and hence incapable of being invoked vis-à-vis the international

58 *Restatement of the Law (Third) Foreign Relations Law of the United States* (1987) §523.

59 Ibid.

60 Ibid.

61 Ibid.

62 Ibid. The US was particularly concerned about Cuba receiving benefits from the ISA.

63 Edward Brown, above n 39, II.8 5–6; Kathy-Ann Brown, above n 21, 496–7.

64 *Deep Seabed Hard Minerals Resources Act*, 30 USC § 1441 (1980).

65 *Law on the Exploration and Exploitation of Mineral Resources of the Deep Seabed*, 21 ILM 808 (1982) (France); *Law on the Exploration and Exploitation of the Mineral Resources of the Deep Seabed 1985*, 24 ILM 983 (1985) (Italy); *Law on Interim Measures for Deep Seabed Mining*, 22 ILM 102 (1983) (Japan); *Edict on Provisional Measures to Regulate Soviet Enterprises for the Exploration and Exploitation of Mineral Resources*, 21 ILM 551 (1982) (Union of Soviet Socialist Republics); *Deep Sea Mining (Temporary Provisions) Act 1981* (UK) c 53; *Act of Interim Regulation of Deep Seabed Mining*, 20 ILM 393 (1981) (Federal Republic of Germany).

66 Hauser, above n 24, 30.

67 *Agreement concerning Interim Arrangements Relating to Polymetallic Nodules of the Deep Seabed*, opened for signature 2 September 1982, 21 ILM 950 (1982) (entered into force 2 September 1982).

68 The collective body of developing states.

community.'[69] This rejection was based on the argument that the freedoms of the high seas do not apply to the deep seabed, resulting in the *absence* of any legal regime. Consequently, the only applicable law was contained in the *Moratorium Resolution* and the *Declaration of Principles*. The legislation passed by the abovementioned developed states conflicted with these resolutions.[70] These states argued that the General Assembly resolutions were not binding, and that objections had been expressed in voting for both resolutions.[71]

E *The* 1994 Agreement

With the increasing number of ratifications of *UNCLOS* and its imminent entry into force, supporters of a codified law of the sea considered amendments to part XI of *UNCLOS* in order to gain universal support.[72] Consequently, the General Assembly drafted the *1994 Agreement*.[73]

The *1994 Agreement* and part XI are to be interpreted and applied as a single instrument, with the *1994 Agreement* prevailing where inconsistencies arise.[74] Any subsequent ratification of *UNCLOS* also binds a state to the *1994 Agreement*.[75] Further, states cannot accede to the *1994 Agreement* without also adopting *UNCLOS*.[76]

The *1994 Agreement* had the effect of modifying the provisions of *UNCLOS* to which the developed states objected.[77] These included the mandatory transfer of technology,[78] training of personnel[79] and the decision-making process of the ISA. The *1994 Agreement* provides that a review of *UNCLOS* may occur at any time and not only by a review conference.[80] Additionally, modifications have occurred to remove production limitations,[81] to establish an economic assistance fund for land-based producers,[82] and to alter the financial terms of contracts.[83]

---

69 Letter from R Herrera Cáceres, Chairman of the Group of Legal Experts to the Chairman of the Group of 77, 23 April 1979 (1979) 11 *Third United Nations Conference on the Law of the Sea: Official Records* 80–2.

70 Edward Brown, above n 39, II.8 28.

71 Ibid II.2 33.

72 Bernard Oxman, 'The *1994 Agreement* and the *Convention*' (1994) 88 *American Journal of International Law* 687, 688.

73 Jewa, above n 21; L Dolliver Nelson, 'The New Deep Sea-Bed Mining Regime' (1992) 10 *International Journal of Marine and Coastal Law* 189, 192.

74 *1994 Agreement*, above n 16, art 2(1).

75 Ibid art 4(1).

76 Ibid art 4(2).

77 Louis Sohn, 'International Law Implications of the *1994 Agreement*' (1994) 88 *American Journal of International Law* 696, 696.

78 Jewa, above n 21; Nelson, above n 73, 196; see generally Oxman, 'The *1994 Agreement* and the *Convention*' above n 72, 691–3; Bernard Oxman, 'The 1994 *Agreement Relating to the Implementation of Part XI of the UN Convention on the Law of the Sea*' in Davor Vidas and Willy Ostreng (eds), *Order for Oceans at the Turn of the Century* (1999) 24.

79 Nelson, above n 73, 196.

80 Ibid 198–9; see generally Oxman, 'The *1994 Agreement* and the *Convention*', above n 72, 695.

81 Nelson, above n 73, 199; see generally Oxman, 'The *1994 Agreement* and the *Convention*', above n 72, 691; Oxman, 'The 1994 *Agreement Relating to the Implementation of Part XI of the UN Convention on the Law of the Sea*', above n 78, 23.

82 Nelson, above n 73, 199.

The *1994 Agreement* finalised the operations of the Finance Committee[84] and clarified aspects of the Pioneer Investor Scheme.[85] The *1994 Agreement* does not alter the content of the common heritage of mankind principle. It merely reworks the provisions that were preventing universal acceptance.

Developed states were induced to enter into the *1994 Agreement* and consequently into *UNCLOS*. Despite support from the majority of states, Canada has signed both *UNCLOS* and the *1994 Agreement* but has not ratified either.[86] The US has not signed or ratified *UNCLOS* and has signed but not ratified the *1994 Agreement*.[87]

The *1994 Agreement* almost achieved universal acceptance. In order to attain this, developing states had to accede to the demands of developed states over the management of the deep seabed. The common heritage of mankind principle now binds a majority of states through *UNCLOS* and the *1994 Agreement*. However, the *1994 Agreement* has only affected the management regime. It has not altered the *content* of the common heritage of mankind principle. Consequently, the common heritage of mankind principle does apply to the deep seabed, but due to conflicting opinions, the substantive elements of the concept remain vague.

F *Conclusion*

When the common heritage of mankind principle was initially suggested as the regime to govern the deep seabed, developing and developed states took opposing positions. Developing states supported the common heritage of mankind principle as it favoured their economic interests. Developed states had more to gain from utilising pre-existing legal regimes and adapting them to the deep seabed.

The *Moratorium Resolution* and the *Declaration of Principles* did not add to the substance of the elements of the common heritage of mankind principle. The inclusion of the common heritage of mankind principle in *UNCLOS* was undermined by the negotiation processes. The subsequent attitude of the developed states involved in the reciprocating states' regime prevented any significant advances in defining the elements of the common heritage of mankind principle. The *1994 Agreement* did not affect this definition or any elements associated with it. It affected the machinery by which it would operate. As such, the *1994 Agreement* has not resolved the fundamental differences between the interpretation of the developed states and that of the developing states. Therefore, although there is almost uniform acceptance of the principle of

83 Ibid 199–200; see generally Oxman, 'The *1994 Agreement* and the *Convention*', above n 72, 693–4; Oxman, 'The 1994 Agreement Relating to the Implementation of Part XI of the UN Convention on the Law of the Sea', above n 78, 27.

84 Nelson, above n 73, 200; Oxman, 'The 1994 *Agreement Relating to the Implementation of Part XI of the UN Convention on the Law of the Sea*', above n 78, 29.

85 Nelson, above n 73, 200–1; Oxman, 'The *1994 Agreement Relating to the Implementation of Part XI of the UN Convention on the Law of the Sea*', above n 78, 31. The Pioneer Investors Scheme was established for those states that had invested in deep seabed technology. Any investment in deep seabed mining already made by states was factored into the regime governing the exploitation of deep seabed mineral resources.

86 Ibid.

87 Ibid.

the common heritage of mankind, it cannot be said that there is uniformity as to how states interpret the principle. Consequently, the content of the elements of the common heritage of mankind principle has not yet been affirmatively established.

Given that scientific studies are already occurring in relation to hydrothermal vents and that the deep seabed could be subject to widespread intelligence gathering activities, the lack of legal obligations governing these activities is disconcerting for any state wanting to challenge the legality of another state's actions.

III Legal Application of the Common Heritage of Mankind Principle

It would be extremely difficult for a state to argue convincingly that environmental damage or intelligence gathering on the deep seabed did not comply with the common heritage of mankind principle. One approach that states could take would be to try to rely on established principles of international law to provide the basic elements of the principle with some substance.

This part of the article attempts to determine what could constitute a breach of the four elements of the common heritage of mankind principle based on the corpus of international law as it currently stands:

1 the prohibition on the acquisition of the deep seabed;
2 the use of the deep seabed for peaceful purposes;
3 the equitable sharing of benefits gained from deep seabed mining; and
4 the international management regime.

A *Prohibition on the Acquisition of the Deep Seabed*

Article 137(1) of *UNCLOS* provides that:

> No State shall claim or exercise sovereignty or sovereign rights over any part of the Area or its resources, nor shall any State or natural or juridical person appropriate any part thereof. No such claim or exercise of sovereignty or sovereign rights nor such appropriation shall be recognized.

This provision does not address which acts amount to an appropriation or sovereign claim.

1 *Traditional Sovereign Claims*

A state may acquire territory in five recognised ways. These are, by the occupation of *res nullius*, prescription, conquest, accretion and cession.[88] Prescription, conquest and cession are not applicable to the deep seabed as they require a former sovereign, and sovereignty has never existed over the deep seabed. Accretion does not apply to the deep seabed, as it does not undergo the physical processes that would result in it becoming part of a state's territory. As such, the only legal ground for acquiring the deep seabed is by occupying it on the basis that it is *res nullius*.

[88] Tim Hillier, *Sourcebook on Public International Law* (1998) 227; Peter Malanczuk, *Akehurst's Modern Introduction to International Law* (7th ed, 1997) 148–54. See generally Seokwoo Lee, 'Continuing Relevance of Traditional Modes of Territorial Acquisition in International Law and a Modest Proposal' (2000) 16 *Conneticut Journal of International Law* 1, 3–14.

(a) Occupation of Res Nullius

Res nullius refers to property belonging to no-one and exploitable by those who wish to and are capable of doing so.[89] The territory involved must be *res nullius* prior to any occupation.[90]

Res nullius claims over the deep seabed were tested in 1974. An American corporation, Deepsea Ventures Inc ('Deepsea'), filed a notice of discovery and claim of exclusive mining rights to the Clarion Clipperton Zone in the Pacific Ocean.[91] Deepsea asserted exclusive rights to develop, evaluate and mine the resources in an area of 60 000 square kilometres.[92] The company requested diplomatic protection in order to appear before an international tribunal if a dispute arose.[93] The claim was lodged with the US Secretary of State, the Secretary-General of the UN, and the Ambassadors of Australia, Belgium, Bulgaria, Canada, Czechoslovakia, France, Hungary, Japan, Poland and the Soviet Union, the UK, West Germany, as well as multinational corporations.[94]

Accompanying the claim was a legal brief.[95] The brief established the lack of occupation of the seabed as one of the grounds for the claim.[96] It was argued to be analogous to seabed claims occurring prior to the Truman Declaration of 1945.[97] States had previously made exclusive claims to seabed resources, including pearls, oysters, corals and sponges, which were located outside of their territorial jurisdiction.[98] Occupation gave recognition to these claims.[99] Occupation occurred when there had been 'reasonable diligence' in bringing the resources to the commercial market.[100] Deepsea argued that their investment in the project demonstrated occupation.[101]

The claim was not recognised by Australia, Canada, the UK or the US.[102] The US State Department responded by saying that it 'does not grant or recognise

89 Rosalyn Higgins, 'International Law and the Avoidance, Containment and Resolution of Disputes' (1991) 230 *Recueil des Cours* 176; Li, above n 19, 45.

90 *Western Sahara* (*Advisory Opinion*) [1975] ICJ Rep 12 [79].

91 Barkenbus, above n 1, 37; Gonzalo Biggs, 'Deepsea's Adventures: Grotius Revisited' (1975) 9 *International Lawyer* 271, 271; Eduardo Jiménez de Aréchaga, 'International Law in the Past Third of a Century' (1978) 159 *Recueil des Cours* 228; Mahmoudi, above n 4, 98; Markus Schmidt, *Common Heritage or Common Burden?: The United States' Position on the Development of a Regime for Deep Sea-Bed Mining in the Law of the Sea Convention* (1989) 36; Kathryn Surace-Smith, 'United States Activity outside of the *Law of the Sea Convention*: Deep Seabed Mining and Transit Passage' (1984) 84 *Colombia Law Review* 1032, 1045.

92 Barkenbus, above n 1, 37; Jiménez de Aréchaga, above n 91, 228; Mahmoudi, above n 4, 98. See generally Biggs, above n 91, 271–2.

93 Barkenbus, above n 1, 37; Biggs, above n 91, 271–2.

94 Biggs, above n 91, 272.

95 Barkenbus, above n 1, 37.

96 Ibid 37–8; Biggs, above n 91, 273–4; Mahmoudi, above n 4, 99–100.

97 Barkenbus, above n 1, 37.

98 Ibid; Biggs, above n 91, 273.

99 Barkenbus, above n 1, 38.

100 Ibid.

101 Ibid.

102 Ibid; Mahmoudi, above n 4, 101.

exclusive mining rights to the mineral resources of an area of the seabed beyond the limits of national jurisdiction.'[103] Other states ignored the claim.[104]

The rejection of *res nullius* claims may have occurred for two reasons. First, it may have been made to curtail claims over the deep seabed. The rejection militated against developing states making excessive claims over the deep seabed to ensure that nodule rich areas were not within the control of developed states. This would also prohibit private corporations from making large claims over the deep seabed. Either type of claim would have prevented developed states from free access to the deep seabed and its resources. Second, developed states may not have wanted to pre-empt the results of the Third Conference. By suppressing all activities on the deep seabed, the developed states were in a position to assert more influence over both the content of the common heritage of mankind principle and the overall outcome of the Third Conference. The untested potential of the deep seabed increased the bargaining strength of the common heritage of mankind principle.

The effect of these rejections was to dismiss claims that the deep seabed was *res nullius*. Since the deep seabed is not *res nullius*, occupation is not a valid means of acquiring rights over it.

2 *The Compatibility of Sovereign Claims with the Common Heritage of Mankind Principle*

Traditional methods of claiming sovereignty do not appear to apply to the deep seabed. The common heritage of mankind principle excludes these means of acquiring territory by denying the application of other legal principles that allow for appropriation to the deep seabed. Therefore, it would appear that the prohibition on the appropriation of the deep seabed reflects an inherent aspect of the common heritage of mankind principle rather than an individual element that states must adhere to. Consequently, sovereign claims would not form part of any juridical standard that the common heritage of mankind principle embodies for other activities. Therefore, the common heritage of mankind principle is effective in this regard.

B *The Use of the Seabed for Peaceful Purposes*

The phrase 'peaceful purposes' is used in art 141 of *UNCLOS* where it is stated that 'the Area shall be open to use exclusively for peaceful purposes by all States, whether coastal or land-locked, without discrimination and without prejudice to the other provisions of this Part'. This provision reflects one of the main purposes of the original proposal for the deep seabed. However, its practical application has resulted in ambiguity.

1 *Definitions of Peaceful Purposes*

The ambiguities arose in the debates of the Eighteen Nation Disarmament Committee.[105] The purpose of the Committee was to discuss deep seabed related

---

103 Biggs, above n 91, 276; Jiménez de Aréchaga, above n 91, 228; Surace-Smith, above n 91, 1045; Schmidt, above n 91, 37.

104 Barkenbus, above n 1, 38.

military and arms control.[106] Again, the views of the developed and developing states differed. The developed states preferred the approach of the US, which sought an international agreement prohibiting the emplacement of weapons of mass destruction on the seabed and ocean floor, beyond a three nautical mile band.[107] The US thought that complete demilitarisation was not verifiable.[108] The developing states favoured the view of the Soviet Union, which proposed a complete demilitarisation of the seabed, beyond the 12 nautical mile limit.[109]

The compromise agreed to became art 1(1) of the *Emplacement Treaty*, which provides that:

> The States parties to this Treaty undertake not to emplant or emplace on the seabed and the ocean floor and in the subsoil thereof beyond the outer limit of the seabed zone, any nuclear weapons or any other types of weapons of mass destruction as well as structures, launching installations or any other facilities specifically designed for storing, testing or using such weapons.[110]

The utility of this provision is limited. The treaty does not expressly define what peaceful purposes are. 'Non-peaceful' weapons are restricted to nuclear weapons and 'other weapons of mass destruction'. The actions include only the emplacement of devices or facilities designed for the storage, testing or use of such weapons.

It is unclear whether restrictions also apply to other military weapons, and whether other activities may be undertaken for military purposes. Such other activities could include intelligence gathering and the use of tracking devices. This is significant given that intelligence gathering activities on the deep seabed could increase with the 'revolution in military affairs' and the fight against terrorism. The *Emplacement Treaty* does not specify whether the actions have to be for a solely military purpose or whether an incidental military purpose would be sufficient to bring them within the prohibition.

Consequently, the *Emplacement Treaty* insufficiently defines 'peaceful purposes'. Its application is restricted to a narrow range of activities and it is only of limited assistance.

2 *Peaceful Purposes in Analogous Treaties*

'Peaceful purposes' provisions are also contained in the *Antarctic Treaty* and the *Moon Treaty*. The extent to which these provisions can clarify the scope of 'peaceful purposes' in *UNCLOS* is limited.

Article 1 of the *Antarctic Treaty* outlines that 'Antarctica shall be used for peaceful purposes only.' It then prohibits '[i]nter alia, any measures of a military

---

105 The Committee was later known as the Conference on the Committee on Disarmament. A commentary on the Committee's work and the events leading to the conclusion of the *Treaty on the Prohibition of the Emplacement of Nuclear Weapons and Other Weapons of Mass Destruction on the Sea-Bed and the Ocean Floor and in the Subsoil Thereof*, opened for signature 11 February 1971, 955 UNTS 115 (entered into force 18 May 1972) ('*Emplacement Treaty*'), is available at Atomic Archive.com (2003) <http://www.atomicarchive.com/Treaties/Treaty7fulltext.shtml> at 1 October 2003.

106 Atomic Archive.com, above n 105.

107 Ibid.

108 Ibid.

109 Ibid.

110 Above n 105, art 1(1).

nature, such as the establishment of military bases and fortifications, the carrying out of military manoeuvres, as well as the testing of any type of weapons'. Article 3 of the *Moon Treaty* states that:

> (2) Any threat or use of force or any other hostile act or threat of hostile act on the moon is prohibited. It is likewise prohibited to use the moon in order to commit any such act or engage in any such threat in relation to the earth, the moon, spacecraft, the personnel of spacecraft or man-made space objects.
>
> (3) States Parties shall not place in orbit around or trajectory to or around the moon objects carrying nuclear weapons or any other kinds of weapons of mass destruction or place or use such weapons on or in the moon.
>
> (4) The establishment of military bases, installations, fortifications, the testing of any weapons and the conduct of military manoeuvres on the moon shall be forbidden. The use of military personnel for scientific research or any other purposes shall not be prohibited. The use of any equipment or facility necessary for peaceful exploration and the use of the moon shall also not be prohibited.

The *Antarctic Treaty* and the *Moon Treaty* extend the meaning of peaceful purposes to prevent the establishment of military fortifications. This interpretation is wider than the extent of the provision in the *Emplacement Treaty*.

One reason for this distinction may be that the high seas adjacent to the deep seabed *can* be utilised for military activities. While military fortifications are incidental to the use of the high seas for military activities, the storage and testing of weapons on the deep seabed would go beyond what states would consider as incidental to that use. Consequently, states prohibited the storage and testing of weapons. In contrast, neither the *Antarctic Treaty* nor the *Moon Treaty* allows military activities in adjacent areas. Furthermore, the *Moon Treaty* prohibits the transportation of nuclear weapons, and the *Antarctic Treaty* prohibits any military activity on the continent. Therefore, the establishment of a military fortification would automatically contravene the 'peaceful purposes' provisions in these contexts. Consequently, it might be implied from the fact that military activities are allowed adjacent to the deep seabed that the establishment of military fortifications may come within 'peaceful purposes' for the deep seabed.

The *Antarctic Treaty* and *Moon Treaty* also prohibit military manoeuvres. This is less likely to be applicable to the deep seabed, as military manoeuvres are currently subject to the freedoms of the high seas. Therefore, this provision gives little guidance as to what 'peaceful purposes' could mean in the maritime context.

The *Moon Treaty* contains the element of the use of force or threat or use of force. This appears to reflect art 2(4) of the *UN Charter*, which would bind states as a separate obligation. However, in the context of outer space it may also reflect potential attacks on spacecraft and astronauts. Due to the current technology relating to the deep seabed, art 2(4) of the *UN Charter* appears to be a satisfactory means of preventing similar attacks.

The prohibition on carrying nuclear weapons and other weapons of mass destruction, similar to that in the *Moon Treaty*, would be inapplicable. Nuclear marine craft can navigate the high seas above the seabed in accordance with art 90 of *UNCLOS*.[111]

3 *Peaceful Purposes and the Deep Seabed*

Article 1(1) of the *Emplacement Treaty* defines peaceful purposes. However, this provision has a limited scope. When provisions from the *Antarctic Treaty* and the *Moon Treaty* are studied, they provide further examples of what may, in *some* circumstances, constitute peaceful purposes. Yet, upon closer examination, these provisions either do not apply to the seabed or provide only minimal assistance in interpreting art 1(1) of the *Emplacement Treaty*. This creates difficulties for states wishing to undertake activities that could be interpreted as military in nature. However, until further debate occurs, the narrow definition of peaceful purposes in the *Emplacement Treaty* reduces the effectiveness of the common heritage of mankind principle as a legal standard, especially in relation to intelligence gathering devices.

C *Equitable Sharing of Benefits*

The original provisions relating to the distribution of the benefits of deep seabed activities were contained in art 160(2)(f)(i) of *UNCLOS*. The principles are now contained in s 7 of the annex to the *1994 Agreement*. The limits of these principles will only become clear when distribution commences on a case-by-case basis. The criteria applicable will vary depending on the extent to which the distribution of benefits is to assist developing states: it may be limited to direct economic consequences, or could extend to programs that have resulted from cutbacks due to the economic shortfall.

The internal procedure of the ISA governs the distribution of benefits, and litigation over distribution is therefore unlikely to occur. The amount of funding, however, will be a contentious issue that can only be determined when commercial deep seabed activities commence. Until then, the principles provide a useful framework.

D *International Management Regime*

The ISA was set up as the international management regime for the deep seabed. The *1994 Agreement* changed the decision-making system of the ISA, the result of which is a regime that allows the individual interests of states to override the interests of mankind.

The US was opposed to the original system of decision-making as it 'unfairly and unnecessarily granted a disproportionate voice to developing countries that have little or no investment in seabed mining operations'.[112] Other developed states shared this view.[113] Consequently, in order to gain universal acceptance of part XI, it was necessary for the *1994 Agreement* to alter the decision-making process.

---

111 Warships are also immune from the jurisdiction of any state other than that of the flag state: *UNCLOS*, above n 51, art 95.

112 Molitor, above n 4, 226.

113 Ibid.

The ISA is composed of three principal organs: the plenary Assembly, a 36-member Council and a Secretariat.[114] The Assembly serves as the forum for the ISA and its main role is to formally adopt decisions.[115] The Assembly consists of all members of the ISA and each state has one vote.[116] The Council consists of 36 states representing certain categories of states such as consumers, investors and producers, developing states and landlocked states.[117]

The *1994 Agreement* has altered the relationship between the Assembly and the Council, by providing that 'general policies shall be established by the Assembly in collaboration with the Council.'[118] Although the Assembly is the only organ in which all states can participate (and in which the voting system allows for equality of power), where both organs have competence, the Council initiates policies. The Assembly is left with only a residual power to return decisions to the Council.[119] The imbalance between the power of the Council and the Assembly results in states not being able to advocate interpretations of provisions that are likely to benefit them. An additional provision — that the state with the largest economy in terms of GDP is always on the Council — guarantees that the US has an input on the Council. Therefore, the policies of developed states dominate 'mankind'.

This structure represents the proposals initially suggested by the developed states and reduces the involvement of developing states in creating policies and interpreting the provisions of part XI. These changes detract from the management regime reflecting the common heritage of mankind.

E *Conclusion*

The common heritage of mankind principle is composed of various elements to which states should adhere when conducting activities on the deep seabed. However, the content of these elements, and the nature of the activities they permit, is unclear. This is mostly due to the failure of states to fully articulate the scope of these elements.

First, the prohibition on sovereign claims and the appropriation of the deep seabed reflects the inherent nature of the common heritage of mankind principle rather then being an element of it. Second, 'peaceful purposes' is undefined in *UNCLOS* and the *Emplacement Treaty*, while the *Antarctic Treaty* and the *Moon Treaty* have limited definitions. Therefore, further elaboration is required. Third, equitable sharing is yet to commence and consequently there has been no juridical consideration of the guidelines for the distribution of benefits. When this occurs, the extent of assistance may be able to be determined. Fourth, the current distribution of power in the international management regime is inconsistent with the concept of the common heritage of mankind.

These difficulties illustrate that the common heritage of mankind principle is currently unable to effectively govern the resources of the deep seabed. On a

---

114 International Seabed Authority, *About the Authority* (2003) <http://www.isa.org.jm/en/about/default.asp> at 1 October 2003.

115 Ibid.

116 Ibid.

117 Ibid.

118 *1994 Agreement*, above n 16, annex 3(1).

119 Ibid annex 3(4).

more positive note, however, the elements of the principle do establish a *framework* for its future operation. This framework does assist states when undertaking activities on the deep seabed, such as scientific research or intelligence gathering, but fails to provide adequate guidance regarding the legal limitations governing these activities.

IV Global Commons and the Common Heritage of Mankind Principle

For the common heritage of mankind principle to effectively manage activities such as scientific research and intelligence gathering, the content of the principle will need to be developed.

Although the common heritage of mankind principle was initially outlined in the context of the deep seabed, analogous principles have formed the basis of other global commons. In particular, both Antarctic and outer space law have similar foundations. This section compares the common heritage of mankind principle with similar principles in international law, to determine how such a concept develops normative effect. Particular focus is given to the law governing outer space and Antarctica. A comparison of these regimes may highlight legal and structural differences, which may be of assistance in ascertaining whether the common heritage of mankind principle has the potential to effectively govern the deep seabed.

A *Outer Space Law*

In 1959, the UN General Assembly established the UN Committee on the Peaceful Uses of Outer Space ('COPUOS').[120] COPUOS drafted various General Assembly resolutions that, in 1969, became codified in the *Treaty on Principles Governing the Activities of States in the Exploration and Use of Outer Space, Including the Moon and Other Celestial Bodies*.[121] This treaty established a basic framework for the international regime in outer space.[122]

The *Outer Space Treaty* predated the *Declaration of Principles*, which outlined the common heritage of mankind principle's elements. Although the *Outer Space Treaty* does not expressly include the common heritage of mankind principle, it declares that states are to explore and use outer space 'for the benefit and in the interests of all countries' and that outer space 'shall be the province of all mankind.'[123] Article II prohibits any means of appropriating outer space. The exploration and use of outer space is to be in accordance with international law in order to maintain 'international peace and security' and to promote 'international co-operation and understanding.'[124] Article IV prevents the carrying, installation, or stationing of nuclear weapons or other weapons of mass

120 Joseph Bosco, 'International Outer Space Law: A Brief Overview' (1995) 9 *Air and Space Lawyer* 3, 3; Scott Ervin, 'Law in Vacuum: The Common Heritage Doctrine in Outer Space Law' (1984) 7 *Boston College International and Comparative Law Review* 403, 406.

121 Opened for signature 27 January 1967, 610 UNTS 205 (entered into force 10 October 1967) ('*Outer Space Treaty*'). See Ervin, above n 120, 407–8; Heidi Keefe, 'Making the Final Frontier Feasible: A Critical Look at the Current Body of Outer Space Law' (1995) 11 *Santa Clara Computer and High Technology Law Journal* 345, 349.

122 Gennady Danilenko, 'Outer Space and the Multilateral Treaty-Making Process' (1989) 4 *High Technology Law Journal* 217, 218.

123 Ibid art I.

124 Ibid art III.

destruction in orbit. The *Outer Space Treaty* further provides for the liability of states for objects launched into space,[125] and for the principles of cooperation and mutual assistance.[126]

In 1971, Russia and Argentina proposed an agreement for the moon,[127] and COPUOS finalised a draft in 1979.[128] This subsequently became the *Moon Treaty*, the objectives of which are 'the safe development and rational management of lunar resources and the equitable sharing of the benefits derived from those resources'.[129]

Article 11 of the *Moon Treaty* provides that 'the moon and its natural resources are the common heritage of mankind'. Article 11 further specifies that the moon is not subject to appropriation,[130] and that an international regime is to be established when exploitation becomes feasible.[131] Article 11(7)(d) provides for the equitable distribution of benefits derived from these resources. When distribution occurs, special consideration is to be given to developing countries and those countries that have contributed, directly or indirectly, to the exploration of the moon.

The *Moon Treaty* has only been ratified by 10 states,[132] and signed by a further five states.[133] The lack of acceptance, especially by states that promote lunar activities, indicates that it is unlikely that the common heritage of mankind principle in the *Moon Treaty* will be defined. The fact that technological and economic factors currently prevent the exploitation of any mineral resources on the moon further reduces the likelihood that a definition will be formulated. As a result, the common heritage of mankind principle remains an inchoate principle in the context of outer space. This does not preclude the operation of the common heritage of mankind principle in the future. If mining or other systematic activities were to commence, rapid crystallisation of the legal limits might result. However, this has not yet occurred.

This uncertainty parallels the ambiguities present in the common heritage of mankind principle in relation to the deep seabed. For both outer space and the deep seabed, the lack of systematic utilisation has worked against the creation of a specific regime and the articulation of legal restrictions. For this reason, the examination of the common heritage of mankind principle in the context of outer

---

125 Ibid arts VI–VIII, XIII.

126 Ibid arts IX–XII.

127 Ervin, above n 120, 418; Keefe, above n 121, 353.

128 Keefe, above n 121, 353.

129 Barbara Ellen Heim, 'Exploring the Last Frontiers for Mineral Resources: A Comparison of International Law Regarding the Deep Seabed, Outer Space, and Antarctica' (1990) 23 *Vanderbilt Journal of Transnational Law* 819, 833–4.

130 *Moon Treaty*, above n 18, art 11(2).

131 Ibid art 11(5).

132 The treaty has been ratified by Australia, Austria, Chile, Kazakhstan, Mexico, Morocco, Netherlands, Pakistan, Philippines and Uruguay. It has not been ratified by states who have been the principal proponents of lunar activities, such as the US: UN Office for Outer Space Affairs, *Agreement governing the Activities of States on the Moon and Other Celestial Bodies* <http://www.oosa.unvienna.org/SpaceLaw/moon.html> at 1 October 2003.

133 Ibid. The treaty has been signed by France, Guatemala, India, Peru and Romania. It has not been signed by states who have been the principal proponents of lunar activities, such as the US.

space is of little assistance in determining how the principle might develop in the context of the deep seabed.

B *Antarctica*

Prior to the adoption of the *Antarctic Treaty*, seven states had made sovereign claims over sections of Antarctica.[134] These states were Argentina, Australia, Chile, France, New Zealand, Norway and the UK.[135] These states founded their claims on factors including discovery, proclamations of sovereignty, geographical proximity and occupation through the establishment of scientific bases.[136]

During the early part of the Cold War, the US and the Soviet Union expressed interest in the continent due to its potential military significance.[137] This was followed by the establishment of the Scientific Committee on Antarctic Research ('SCAR') and the declaration that 1957–58 was the International Geophysical Year.[138] This led to increased scientific interest in the Antarctic and the negotiation of the *Antarctic Treaty* in 1959.

As issues arose, especially following an increased understanding of the Antarctic ecosystem and the prospect of exploitable mineral resources, new international agreements resulted in the '*Antarctic Treaty* System'. This consists of the *Antarctic Treaty* and Recommendations,[139] the 1972 *Convention for the Conservation of Antarctic Seals*,[140] the 1980 *Convention for the Conservation of Antarctic Marine Living Resources*,[141] the 1988 *Convention on the Regulation of Antarctic Mineral Resource Activities*[142] and the 1991 *Protocol on Environmental Protection to the Antarctic Treaty*.[143]

134 Donald Rothwell, *The Polar Regions and the Development of International Law* (1996) 54; Donald Rothwell, 'The *Antarctic Treaty*: 1961–1991 and Beyond' (1992) 14 *Sydney Law Review* 62, 62; Gillian Triggs, 'Australian Sovereignty in Antarctica' (Pt 1) (1981) 13 *Melbourne University Law Review* 123, 123; Olav Stokke and Davor Vidas, *Governing the Antarctic: The Effectiveness and Legitimacy of the* Antarctic Treaty *System* (1996) 36.

135 Rothwell, *The Polar Regions and the Development of International Law*, above n 140, 54; Rothwell, 'The *Antarctic Treaty*: 1961–1991 and Beyond', above n 134; Triggs, 'Australian Sovereignty in Antarctica: Pt 1', above n 134; see generally Gillian Triggs, 'Australian Sovereignty in Antarctica' (Pt 2) (1982) 13 *Melbourne University Law Review* 302, 302–14; Stokke and Vidas, above n 134, 36.

136 Christopher Joyner, *Governing the Frozen Commons: The Antarctic Regime and Environmental Protection* (1998) 14–19; Rothwell, *The Polar Regions and the Development of International Law*, above n 134, 54–8.

137 Rothwell, *The Polar Regions and the Development of International Law*, above n 134, 63–6; Triggs, 'Australia Sovereignty in Antarctica: Pt 1', above n 134, 124.

138 Rothwell, *The Polar Regions and the Development of International Law*, above n 134, 67.

139 Article IX(1) provides that measures may be taken for the 'furtherance of the principles and objectives of the *Treaty*.' When the measures are approved by the *Antarctic Treaty* Consultative Parties they become recommendations. The subject matter of recommendations is outlined in art IX(4).

140 Opened for signature 1 June 1972, 1080 UNTS 175 (entered into force 11 March 1978).

141 Opened for signature 20 May 1980, 1329 UNTS 247 (entered into force 7 April 1982).

142 Opened for signature 2 June 1988, 27 ILM 868 (1988) (not yet in force).

143 Opened for signature 24 April 1991, 30 ILM 1461 (1991) (not yet in force).

1 *Sovereign Claims*

As mentioned above, seven states have asserted sovereign claims over the Antarctic. While the US and the former Soviet Union have not made such claims, they have indicated their interest in the continent. The basis of the common heritage of mankind principle is that no state can appropriate, or make sovereign claims over, the area governed by the principle. Although all existing and potential claims over the Antarctic are suspended for the duration of the *Antarctic Treaty*,[144] the presence of these claims may undermine the suitability of the Antarctic context for an analysis of the common heritage of mankind principle. However, the Antarctic has a more developed regime than that governing outer space. This is due to the history of cooperation between states and the possibility of feasible development precipitating a regime. Therefore, an examination of the common heritage of mankind principle in the context of Antarctica may provide assistance.

2 *Ban on Mineral Exploitation*

Article 7 of the *Protocol on Environmental Protection to the Antarctic Treaty*[145] states that:

> Any activity relating to mineral resources, other than scientific research, shall be prohibited.

The prohibition on mining is in contrast to the purpose of part XI of *UNCLOS*. The purpose of the common heritage of mankind principle was to equitably share financial benefits from any exploitation. Whilst the permitted activities on Antarctica differ, this does not preclude a comparison between aspects of the regimes that have been successful. The common heritage of mankind principle still applies to the deep seabed and outer space even though no exploitation has occurred. Therefore, the remaining aspect of the international management regime may provide guidance for the common heritage of mankind principle.

3 *Exclusive Membership*

The *Antarctic Treaty* establishes a hierarchy to govern Antarctica. Article IX creates three different groups of state parties, only two of which are entitled to attend Antarctic Treaty Consultative Meetings.[146] These are the 12 states that negotiated the *Antarctic Treaty*, and those states that have acceded to the *Antarctic Treaty* and fulfilled the requirements outlined in art IX(2). Both of these groups comprise the Antarctic Treaty Consultative Parties ('ATCPs').[147] The third group consists of those states that have acceded to the *Antarctic Treaty* but have not fulfilled the requirements of art IX(2).[148]

---

144 *Antarctic Treaty*, above n 17, art IV(2).

145 Opened for signature 4 October 1991, 30 ILM 1461 (entered into force 14 January 1998).

146 Rothwell, *The Polar Regions and the Development of International Law*, above n 134, 86; Stokke and Vidas, above n 134, 45.

147 Rothwell, *The Polar Regions and the Development of International Law*, above n 134, 86–7; Stokke and Vidas, above n 134, 45–6.

148 Rothwell, *The Polar Regions and the Development of International Law*, above n 134, 86–7; Stokke and Vidas, above n 134, 45–6.

This situation has invoked criticisms relating to the management of Antarctica. Many states view the ATCPs as a 'self-designated exclusive club without any clear legal authority to manage Antarctica for the rest of mankind'.[149] This led to the involvement of the UN in 1985. Malaysia introduced a resolution requesting the ATCPs to make information regarding Antarctica generally available to the UN.[150]

In comparison, the common heritage of mankind principle provides that all states are to share in the management of the deep seabed. The *Antarctic Treaty* does not contain the same principle as it was established prior to the enunciation of the common heritage of mankind principle. However, the establishment of a management regime that differentiates between states, and limits their participation, does not represent an equitable model of management envisaged by the common heritage of mankind principle. Consequently, the common heritage of mankind principle should not follow this aspect of the *Antarctic Treaty* nor adopt a similar system, based on the criticisms it has received.

4 *Conclusion*

The *Antarctic Treaty* differs on two of the elements outlined by the common heritage of mankind principle. States have previously made sovereign claims over Antarctica and there is a prohibition on mineral exploitation. However, these differences do not preclude some comparisons as both systems have international management regimes. The creation of the ATCPs was established prior to the common heritage of mankind principle. It does not represent equitable management and has been criticised. Although this does not indicate how the common heritage of mankind principle should proceed to become a workable standard, it does emphasise the aspects that have been less successful in the management of Antarctica. Generally, the *Antarctic Treaty* regime is effective, as it has resulted in international cooperation. It also demonstrates the processes of crystallisation that may occur when development dictates a legal regime. However, the structural and developmental differences make it difficult to transfer this success to the deep seabed.

V International Environmental Law and the Common Heritage of Mankind Principle

Global commons regimes have not, so far, provided guidance in ascertaining whether the common heritage of mankind principle can become a legal standard. The translation of principles from the *Declaration of the United Nations Conference on the Human Environment*[151] and the *United Nations Declaration on Environment and Development*[152] into international law may indicate the future viability of the common heritage of mankind principle as an international legal standard. The *Stockholm Declaration* and the *Rio Declaration* contain principles that relate to the effects of transboundary pollution. These principles

---

149 Joyner, above n 136, 241.

150 *Question of Antarctica*, GA Res 40/156, UN GAOR, 40th sess, 117th plen mtg, Supp 53, UN Doc A/RES/40/156 (1985); Joyner, above n 136, 241.

151 UN Doc A/CONF.48/14/Rev.1 (1973) ('*Stockholm Declaration*').

152 UN Doc A/CONF.151/5/Rev.1 (1992) ('*Rio Declaration*').

lack substantive content like the common heritage of mankind principle, but have nevertheless become effective in international law.

Three factors may indicate why principles from the *Stockholm Declaration* and *Rio Declaration* have been successfully translated into the corpus of international law. First, the negotiation methods of the *Stockholm Declaration* and the *Rio Declaration*, and the conventions that stemmed from the Conferences, differ from the methods adopted for the law of the sea. Second, states have considered international environmental law for a longer period than the common heritage of mankind principle. This has resulted in a substantial body of 'soft law'.[153] Third, judicial consideration has been given to the principles, due to the serious consequences of breaching international environmental law.

A *Development of International Environmental Law*

The development of international environmental law initially proceeded by way of isolated treaties, rather than by a comprehensive study.[154] Subsequent to the *Report on the Problems of the Human Environment* conducted by the Secretary-General of the UN, the UN General Assembly convened the Stockholm Conference on the Human Environment of 1972 ('Stockholm Conference').[155]

The Stockholm Conference was the first conference to deal with environmental issues in a comprehensive manner. The Conference produced:

1 a condemnation of nuclear testing;
2 the creation of World Environment Day;
3 an 'action plan' consisting of recommendations for international action;
4 the adoption of the *Stockholm Declaration*;
5 recommendations for new international machinery (the UN Environment Programme);
6 a recommendation that the draft articles for the *Convention on Ocean Dumping* be referred for adoption; and
7 a decision that a second conference should be convened.[156]

The most important of these outcomes was the adoption of the *Stockholm Declaration*. This consisted of a series of principles intended to influence how states were to conduct activities with regard to the environment.[157]

In 1992, Rio de Janeiro hosted the UN Conference on Environment and Development ('UNCED').[158] This built upon the foundation established by the Stockholm Conference. The main outcomes of UNCED were:[159]

---

153 Soft law refers to general principles of international law that are not necessarily binding upon states, but that restrain state conduct.

154 Wolfgang Burhenne and Richard Tarasofsky, 'Codification and Progressive Development of International Law: An Example from the Field of the Environment' (1998) 28 *Environmental Policy and Law* 77, 77; Shearer, above n 48, 362.

155 Hillier, above n 88, 795; Schrijver, above n 3, 122; Shearer, above n 48, 362.

156 Shearer, above n 48, 364–7; Schrijver, above n 3, 122–5.

157 Shearer, above n 48, 365.

158 Ibid 374; Hillier, above n 88, 804; Schrijver, above n 3, 135.

159 Hillier, above n 88, 805; Shearer, above n 48, 375–6.

1. the creation of the preparatory document *Agenda 21*;
2. the opening for signature of the *UN Framework Convention on Climate Change*;[160]
3. the opening for signature of the *Convention on Biological Diversity*;[161]
4. the adoption of the *Non-Legally Binding Authoritative Statement of Principles for a Global Consensus on the Management, Conservation and Sustainable Development of All Types of Forests*;[162] and
5. the adoption of the *Rio Declaration.*

Both the *Stockholm Declaration* and the *Rio Declaration* contained similar broad-based principles. The international community has generally accepted these principles,[163] despite the fact that they contain undefined terms, and impose obligations upon both developing and developed states.

B *Negotiation Methods in International Environmental Law*

The basis of negotiations at the Stockholm Conference and the UNCED was the 'framework approach'.[164] This process involves defining the scope of the legal obligation in general language, while subsequent protocols outline the specific details.[165] This approach results in a progressive specification of commitments,[166] at a rate that is acceptable to states and allows them to concur on the substance of the obligations. The initial principle acts as a framework, guiding the development of the obligation. Therefore, the legal documentation that UNCED produced merely forms the basis of future regimes.

The *Rio Declaration* demonstrates the effectiveness of the framework approach. General principles were contained in the *Stockholm Declaration*, following the elaboration of which, through treaties and state practice, the content was gradually established. This progressive approach gave states the opportunity to compromise on contentious issues. The *Rio Declaration* further outlined state obligations based on the developments that had occurred. Consequently, the acceptance of the *Rio Declaration* is partly due to the balance of policies of both developed and developing states.[167] By way of compromise, principles such as the precautionary principle[168] and the 'polluter pays' principle[169] were allowed by developing states, while developed states allowed

---

160 Opened for signature 9 May 1992, 1771 UNTS 107 (entered into force 21 March 1994) ('*Framework Convention on Climate Change*').

161 Opened for signature 5 June 1992, 1760 UNTS 79 (entered into force 29 December 1993).

162 *Report of the UN Conference on Environment and Development*, UN Doc A/CONF.151/26(Vol III) (1992) annex III.

163 *Dissemination of the Principles of the Rio Declaration on Environment and Development*, GA Res 49/113, UN GAOR, 49th sess, 92nd plen mtg, UN Doc A/RES/49/113 (1995) refers to the *Rio Declaration* as containing 'fundamental principles for the achievement of sustainable development, based on a new and equitable global partnership.'

164 Peter Sand, 'UNCED and the Development of International Environmental Law' (1992) 3 *Yearbook of International Environmental Law* 3, 6.

165 Ibid.

166 Ibid 7; Burhenne and Tarasofsky, above n 154, 78.

167 Sand, above n 164, 8.

168 *Rio Declaration*, above n 152, principle 15. This imposes a duty on states to prevent environmental damage despite a lack of scientific verification.

169 Ibid principle 16. This imposes a duty on states that cause environmental damage to make reparations for the damage.

'common but differentiated responsibilities'[170] and the right to develop.[171] Such compromise may not have occurred if states had attempted to outline a comprehensive regime in 1972.

In contrast, *UNCLOS* initially established a single comprehensive regime. Obligations were included for the sake of completeness and states could not always achieve compromise on their content. In order to reach agreement on the common heritage of mankind principle, the *1994 Agreement* altered the mechanism by which the principle would operate, rather than develop its content. Consequently, states still have differing interpretations. The aim of universal acceptance led to the difficulty of defining the common heritage of mankind principle.

C *Existence of 'Soft Law'*

The framework approach also has the potential to result in the creation of 'soft law'. States consider the specifics of international environmental law principles, and the resulting resolutions, protocols, and treaties contribute to its corpus. Thus, the combination of formal international environmental law instruments with 'soft law' leads to the establishment of binding international law. Compared with international environmental law, the law relating to the deep seabed has had little consideration. There is, therefore, a lack of 'soft law' governing the deep seabed, which has prevented the common heritage of mankind principle from being fully developed. Combined with the deep seabed's lack of utilisation, the common heritage of mankind principle's negotiation was abstract. Consequently, it remains merely a framework.

D *Judicial Consideration*

Until recently, the abstention by states from undertaking activities on the deep seabed has hindered the development of the common heritage of mankind principle. In contrast, the global community has felt the consequences of activities that have detrimentally affected the environment. This experience has resulted in litigation when states have breached environmental obligations. The subsequent judicial consideration has assisted in the development of international environmental law.

In 1996, two advisory opinions of the International Court of Justice ('ICJ') were sought: *Legality of the Use of Nuclear Weapons in Armed Conflict*[172] and *Legality of the Threat or Use of Nuclear Weapons*.[173] This was followed in 1997 by the decision of the ICJ in *Gabčikovo-Nagymaros Project (Hungary v Slovakia)*.[174]

In the first of these opinions, the ICJ held that it did not have jurisdiction to give an advisory opinion, as had been requested by the World Health

---

170 Ibid principle 7. This concept recognises that the developed states were not subject to the environmental restrictions that currently exist when they were developing. The standard is lowered for developing states on this basis.

171 Ibid principle 3.

172 [1996] ICJ Rep 66 ('*Legality of the Use of Nuclear Weapons*').

173 [1996] ICJ Rep 226 ('*Legality of the Threat or Use of Nuclear Weapons*').

174 [1997] ICJ Rep 7 ('*Danube Dam*').

Organisation. However, in dissent, Judge Weeramantry discussed the progress of international environmental law. He stated that:

> From rather hesitant beginnings, environmental law has progressed rapidly under the combined stimulus of ever more powerful means of inflicting irreversible environmental damage and an ever increasing awareness of the fragility of the environment.[175]

Therefore, the increase in scientific understanding of how the environment operates and the effects of environmental damage were considered as fundamental to the development of international environmental law and provided a context for the development of environmental standards. This can be contrasted with the deep seabed, in the case of which scientific knowledge is still developing and the effects of utilising the deep seabed are not wholly known due to the absence of long term activities.

In the second of these advisory opinions, the ICJ recognised that

> the environment is not an abstraction but represents the living space, the quality of life and the health of human beings, including generations unborn. The existence of the general obligation of States to ensure that activities within their jurisdiction and control respect the environment of other States or of areas beyond national control is now part of the corpus of international law relating to the environment.[176]

The most recent juridical consideration of international environmental law was in *Danube Dam*. Although this case failed to strengthen international environmental law substantially, Judge Weeramantry, in his separate opinion, considered the development of environmental law principles. He considered the past and present sustainable development practices from Sri Lanka, India and Iran. He also referred to international treaties, the *Stockholm Declaration* and the *Rio Declaration*, and domestic environmental law. From this analysis, he outlined two principles: continuing environmental impact assessment and contemporaneity in the application of environmental norms. The principles have emerged as the understanding of the interrelationship between environmental principles and other principles in international law has increased. They require states to further incorporate environmental considerations into their decisions, and they further define the environmental obligations of states by giving more specific content to general concepts, such as sustainable development.

The establishment of these principles was arguably due to the large number of 'soft' and 'hard' law instruments that had resulted from both the framework approach and the previous consideration of environmental principles. Judicial consideration, combined with 'soft law', could similarly enhance the specific content of the common heritage of mankind principle. Such a process has assisted the development of the precautionary principle, as will be discussed below.

---

175 *Legality of the Use of Nuclear Weapons (Advisory Opinion) (Preliminary Objections)* [1996] ICJ Rep 66, 140.

176 *Legality of the Threat or Use of Nuclear Weapons (Advisory Opinion)* [1996] ICJ Rep 226, [29].

E *Precautionary Principle*

The precautionary principle was initially codified at an international level as principle 15 in the *Rio Declaration*. Principle 15 provides that:

> In order to protect the environment, the precautionary approach shall be widely applied by States according to their capabilities. Where there are threats of serious or irreversible damage, lack of full scientific certainty shall not be used as a reason for postponing cost-effective measures to prevent environmental degradation.

The specific obligations encompassed by the precautionary principle are not outlined in the *Rio Declaration*. Their subsequent development is a result of the endorsement of the principle by states in treaties,[177] domestic legislation[178] and domestic court decisions.[179] This endorsement has assisted in the development of a series of standards that indicate whether or not the precautionary principle has been complied with.

Although there is still doubt as to whether the precautionary principle is a principle of customary international law, its content has developed as a result of inclusion in various treaties.[180] In this regard, the precautionary principle has achieved the status of a recognised principle of international environmental law. The same process could be utilised to give content to the common heritage of mankind principle.

F *Conclusion*

The way in which negotiations were conducted at the Stockholm and Rio Conferences resulted in declarations that represented the views of both developed and developing states. This was achieved by working until a compromise was reached, rather than aiming for a complete regime right from the start.[181] This also created a substantial body of legal instruments that have assisted judicial bodies to establish environmental principles in international law. States also have a substantial incentive to incorporate these principles into international environmental law as they will suffer the consequences if they

---

177 These include the *UN Agreement for the Implementation of the Provisions of the UN Convention of the Law of the Sea of 10 December 1982 Relating to the Conservation and Management of Straddling Fish Stocks and Highly Migratory Fish Stocks*, opened for signature 4 December 1995, [2001] ATS 8, art 6 (entered into force 11 December 2001); *Framework Convention on Climate Change*, above n 160, art 3; *UN Convention on Biological Diversity*, above n 161, preamble.

178 See, eg, *Environment Protection and Biodiversity Conservation Act 1999* (Cth) s391; *Environmental Code Act of 1998* (Sweden).

179 See, eg, *Director-General of National Parks and Wildlife Service v Shoalhaven City Council* [1993] NSWLEC 191 (Unreported, Stein J, 23 November 1993).

180 See Owen McIntyre and Thomas Mosedale, 'The Precautionary Principle as a Norm of Customary International Law' (1997) 9 *Journal of Environmental Law* 221, 235:

> Opinion remains divided as to whether the precautionary principle may have crystallized into a binding norm of customary international law. However, the prevalence of the principle in recent environmental treaties, declarations and resolutions ... suggests that it may indeed have attained this status.

See also Arie Trouwborst, *Evolution and Status of the Precautionary Principle in International Law* (2002).

181 Sand, above n 164.

breach environmental obligations. This is reflected by the development of the precautionary principle.

By contrast, the negotiation of part XI of *UNCLOS* did not represent a compromise. Rather, it only reflected the views of both developed and developing states to the extent that both groups recognised the elements of the common heritage of mankind principle. The absence of 'soft law' has prevented the gradual development of the common heritage of mankind principle, and thus the *Moratorium Resolution* and the *Declaration of Principles* have not contributed significantly to development of the principle, particularly as the developed states rejected their content. Inactivity on the deep seabed has also worked against any elaboration of the elements of the common heritage of mankind principle. This inactivity has similarly precluded any juridical consideration of the principle.

Nevertheless, part XI of *UNCLOS* does establish a framework for further development of the common heritage of mankind principle. By utilising this framework, states could reach compromises on each element of the principle, and by convening regular sessions in which to discuss the principle, resolutions and other 'soft law' could develop. Even if states could not initially reach a compromise, this process would establish a body of 'soft law.' Reference to this law would assist in defining the content of the common heritage of mankind principle.

The practical effect of breaches of environmental obligations has been to create judicial statements relating to the status of international law principles. Such a process could only enhance the development of the common heritage of mankind principle.

VI CONCLUSION

Presently, the common heritage of mankind principle is no more than an inchoate concept, consisting of as yet undeveloped standards. Contrasting ideologies and inconsistent interpretations have plagued development of the common heritage of mankind principle. It was not until the adoption of the *1994 Agreement*, which modified *UNCLOS*, that the principle achieved near universal acceptance. However, the *1994 Agreement* did not reconcile the differing approaches of the developed and the developing states; it only modified the administrative aspects of deep seabed activities. Therefore, the common heritage of mankind principle remains undefined.

Established international law does not assist in defining the elements of the common heritage of mankind principle. First, conventional means of claiming sovereignty do not appear to apply to the deep seabed. Therefore, sovereignty becomes an irrelevant consideration. Second, the requirement that the deep seabed is used only for peaceful purposes requires elaboration. Third, the ISA's distribution of the economic benefits is governed by principles that have not yet been tested. Fourth, the decision making procedures of the ISA were altered by the *1994 Agreement* so as to favour the interests of developed states. This has detracted from the international management regime representing the common heritage of mankind. Therefore, although the common heritage of mankind principle has basic elements, they are not sufficiently defined to be a legal standard.

Principles similar to the common heritage of mankind principle have been enunciated in other areas of international law. Both the *Outer Space Treaty* and the *Moon Treaty* contain principles that parallel the common heritage of mankind principle. However, the utility of comparing the deep seabed and outer space is limited as neither has had its legal regimes tested. The *Antarctic Treaty* also contains similar principles to those contained in the common heritage of mankind principle. Although Antarctica differs from the deep seabed in relation to sovereignty and mineral exploitation, this should not automatically preclude the transfer of any relevant principles to the deep seabed. The problems with the international management regime provide guidance for the common heritage of mankind principle. However, neither regime indicates how the common heritage of mankind principle could become a legal standard.

Principles of international environmental law, outlined in the *Stockholm Declaration* and the *Rio Declaration*, may provide a means by which the common heritage of mankind principle can develop. States negotiated the *Stockholm Declaration* and *Rio Declaration* using a framework approach. The Declarations merely outlined general principles. States then discussed the implications of the principles and reached a compromise. Subsequently, much 'soft law' developed to support the principles. This gave them the potential to become workable standards. The influence of judicial consideration also helped to establish these principles. A similar method could be used to determine the substance of the common heritage of mankind principle.

In summary, although the common heritage of mankind principle is not currently a legal standard, it does present a possible means of governing the deep seabed. Consequently, it will need to establish content to be enforceable. This content cannot be drawn from existing international law. Other regimes that use similar principles do not assist in determining the ways in which this can occur. However, the methods used in international environmental law may provide a model for developing the common heritage of mankind principle to a point where it could become an enforceable standard. Even though commercial deep seabed mining is unlikely to commence in the near future, the discovery of hydrothermal vents and the possibility of the widespread use of intelligence gathering devices suggest that other uses may be made of the deep seabed in years to come. That use of the deep seabed is now foreseeable means that a management regime is required that will be able to effectively determine which activities states are permitted to undertake. Consequently, the deep seabed requires a management regime that can effectively determine the activities states are permitted to undertake. The model offered by international environmental law may be one by which the development of an adequate legal regime can occur.

Part V
Environmental Law

[12]

SOLIDARITY, JUSTICE AND CLIMATE CHANGE LAW

ANGELA WILLIAMS*

This think piece examines the concept of solidarity and contemplates the extent to which it is a relevant and valuable mechanism for the promotion of justice within climate change law. In particular, it is suggested that solidarity potentially offers greater depth and maturity than principles such as cooperation, which have previously been the focus of attention, thereby better reflecting the diversity and complexity of our international society. The climate change framework already features solidaristic measures in the form of the principle of 'common but differentiated responsibilities', flexible mechanisms such as the 'clean development mechanism', and the introduction of funding initiatives. It is concluded that whilst solidarity is a mechanism which demonstrates potential for further promoting justice within international climate change law, there remains considerable scope for further development in this area.

CONTENTS

I INTRODUCTION

A welcome shift is occurring within climate change law. Over recent decades we have witnessed the emergence of an international legal framework recognising the environmental and human impacts of climate change, identifying differentiated responsibilities between states, and (mostly) agreeing to initial emission reduction targets. The principle of equity has subtly influenced the development of the international climate change regime, but there now exists a more conscious and overt shift towards promoting ideas of justice and fairness within climate change law. Importantly, this extends not only to the drafting of texts setting out the rights and responsibilities of states but also to the implementation and practical application of climate change mechanisms. The objective of this think piece is to introduce the concept of 'solidarity' and consider the extent to which it is a relevant and valuable mechanism for the promotion of justice within climate change law. Due to the complex and integrated nature of the problem, heavy reliance is placed on the principle of cooperation within climate change law. However, it is argued that solidarity potentially offers a more composite and mature principle that better reflects the diversity and complexity of our international society.

* LLB (Waikato); LLM, PhD (Nottingham); Lecturer in Law, University of Sussex, United Kingdom.

II THE PROBLEM OF CLIMATE CHANGE

As the problems posed by climate change increases, the consequences experienced by both humanity and the natural environment are becoming severe and widespread. In terms of the human impact, a recent report by the Global Humanitarian Forum, whose work specifically focuses on climate justice, indicated that climate change is already responsible for 300 000 deaths each year and is affecting 300 million people worldwide.[1] Furthermore, global economic losses due to climate change amount to more than US$125 billion annually.[2] Unfortunately, however, future forecasts provide greater cause for concern. Current scientific predictions by the Intergovernmental Panel on Climate Change ('IPCC') indicate that average global temperatures are likely to increase during the 21st century by at least 1.8°C, although an increase of more than 5°C is not unlikely.[3] It is widely recognised that one of the key challenges in relation to climate change is the scientific uncertainty surrounding climate modelling and future forecasts.[4] Nevertheless, the estimates provided by the IPCC, the leading scientific climate research body, are (if anything) conservative in terms of predicting environmental change and consequent human impact and thus should be considered the very bare minimum of possible climatic change to be expected.[5]

The effects of rising global temperatures are likely to be experienced across every aspect of human life and will vary depending on the extent of the temperature increase. Whilst a 1°C increase in temperatures may initially support localised advantages — such as modest increases in cereal yields in temperate regions, or a reduction in winter mortality in higher latitude areas of Europe and the United States — there are likely to be equally disadvantageous impacts such as the disappearance of glaciers in the Andes, which would threaten the water supplies of more than 50 million people.[6] In any event, localised benefits are likely to be short-lived before serious negative climate change is experienced.

The availability of water is perhaps one of the most problematic consequences of a changing climate: a temperature increase of 3°C could lead to up to four billion people experiencing water shortages.[7] Some of the most immediate consequences of such water shortages concern food availability and health as agricultural yields decline, placing millions of people at risk of hunger and thereby promoting rates of death from malnutrition. However, whilst severe water shortages develop in some areas, other regions will experience enormous

---

[1] Global Humanitarian Forum, *Human Impact Report: Climate Change — The Anatomy of a Silent Crisis* (Report, 29 May 2009).

[2] Ibid.

[3] IPCC, 'Summary for Policymakers' in Working Group I, IPCC, *Climate Change 2007: The Physical Science Basis* (IPCC Fourth Assessment Report, 2007) 13.

[4] See Richard Kerr, 'Scientists Tell Policymakers We're All Warming the World' (2007) 315 *Science* 754, 754. For a detailed analysis of the modelling techniques currently used by the IPCC, see David Randall et al, 'Climate Models and Their Evaluation' in Working Group I, IPCC, *Climate Change 2007: The Physical Science Basis* (IPCC Fourth Assessment Report, 2007) 589, 589–662.

[5] See, eg, Richard Kerr, 'A Worrying Trend of Less Ice, Higher Seas' (2006) 311 *Science* 1698, 1698–701; Kerr, 'Scientists Tell Policymakers', above n 4, 754–7.

[6] Nicholas Stern, *The Economics of Climate Change: The Stern Review* (2007) 56–7.

[7] Ibid 76.

gains in water, typically in the form of flooding that threatens hundreds of millions of people, particularly those living in coastal areas. In addition to water and food availability, the changing climate has direct consequences for human health. Malnutrition poses perhaps the biggest risk, but the spread of vector-borne diseases demonstrates a considerable threat: a 4°C increase in global temperatures would expose an additional 80 million people to malaria in Africa alone.[8] As such, it is possible to identify an imminent and significant threat to humanity posed by climate change. Moreover, with only very minimal rises in average global temperatures, this threat escalates drastically.

What is perhaps most apparent from this analysis, however, is that the effects of climate change are not going to be distributed evenly across all countries, communities and people. Indeed, it is frequently those who are victim to the most severe of the consequences of climate change that possess the least capacity to adapt and respond to such changes.[9] Communities living amongst the Himalayan glaciers demonstrate one such example. There are 15 000 glaciers in the Himalayan region that provide vital water supplies to millions of people in Pakistan, Nepal, Bhutan, India and Bangladesh.[10] One of the many river basins created by glaciers in the Himalaya Mountains is the Gangetic Basin, which is home to more than 500 million people who depend on inland waterways for their livelihoods but who are, at the same time, vulnerable to flooding. The glaciers feeding river basins, such as the Gangetic, are receding faster than anywhere else in the world and, if the present rate of retreat continues, 'the likelihood of them disappearing by the end of 2035 and perhaps sooner is very high if the Earth keeps warming at the current rate'.[11] The IPCC has recognised that the 'receding and thinning of Himalayan glaciers can be attributed primarily to the global warming due to [an] increase in anthropogenic emission of greenhouse gases'.[12] That is, significant environmental change is occurring as a direct result of increase in greenhouse gas emissions attributed to anthropogenic activities. In this case, whilst those communities living in the vicinity of, and relying on, Himalayan glaciers are clearly the most severely affected, they are also similarly unlikely to have a great deal of capacity to adapt to a rapidly-changing environment. Moreover, these communities are responsible for only a very tiny contribution to the global climate change problem.

Such inequity is similarly evident with respect to Bangladesh, which is also heavily affected by the glacial melt and suffers disproportionate environmental damage. Being one of the most densely-populated countries in the world, as well as being located within a giant river basin, Bangladesh continues to be severely affected by the impacts of climate change.[13] Water, once again, presents the

---

8 Ibid 66.

9 Angela Williams, 'Achieving Justice within the International Legal System: Prospects for Climate Refugees' in Yves Le Bouthillier et al (eds), *Climate Law and Developing Countries: Legal and Policy Challenges for the World Community* (2010) (forthcoming).

10 Rex Victor Cruz et al, 'Asia' in Working Group II, IPCC, *Climate Change 2007: Impacts, Adaptation and Vulnerability* (IPCC Fourth Assessment Report, 2007) 469, 493.

11 Ibid.

12 Ibid.

13 Richard Black et al, 'Demographics and Climate Change: Future Trends and Their Policy Implications for Migration' (Development Research Centre on Migration, Globalisation and Poverty Working Paper No T-27, 2008) 27.

main problem, with accelerated riverbank erosion and increased flooding resulting from both upstream de-glaciation and rising sea levels.[14] Salinity in surface water, ground water and soil is having considerable social and economic impacts as previously extensive and valuable rice fields and agricultural land have become unproductive due to, inter alia, salt contamination and rising sea levels.[15] And Bangladesh is suffering intensified and more frequent storm activity: Cyclone Sidr struck Bangladesh in November 2007, killing more than 2000 people and affecting millions.[16] The Government of Bangladesh reported that the cyclone inundated 32 000 square kilometres; destroyed over 85 000 houses and damaged almost one million; destroyed or partially damaged approximately 1.2 million acres of crops; resulted in the death of 649 people; and created an estimated US$1 billion worth of damage.[17] Whilst this is not the first cyclone to strike Bangladesh (notably Cyclones Gorky in 1991 and Bhola in 1970), anthropogenic climate change will deliver more frequent and severe examples of extreme and destructive weather.

The example of Bangladesh highlights a common experience for many countries still engaged in the process of ongoing economic development. Environmental change occurring as a result of global warming is largely having an inequitable impact on already vulnerable people, communities and countries throughout the world.[18] Whilst climate change is an inherently global problem and will affect people indiscriminately, the ability of both people and states to respond to climate change varies enormously. This differing capacity to adapt is crucial in terms of the resulting inequity and injustice experienced by people, especially in the developing world. What is apparent is that in order for climate change to be equitably and effectively addressed, there needs to be global cooperation for action, underscored by principles of justice. There exists a growing body of literature, particularly within political theory, on the idea of climate justice and the extent to which principles of justice can be integrated into the climate change legal framework.[19] This think piece seeks to engage a much narrower discussion within the climate justice debate by exploring the concept of solidarity as a mechanism for promoting justice in respect of climate change law. The general obligation regarding cooperation is well established.[20] But how might solidarity better contribute to a more effective and just legal framework for climate change? What might inspire countries to cooperate, and how could such

---

14 Ibid.

15 Angela Williams, 'Turning the Tide: Recognizing Climate Change Refugees in International Law' (2008) 30 *Law and Policy* 502, 505.

16 Simon Robinson, 'How Bangladesh Survived a Cyclone', *Time* (New York, US) 19 November 2007.

17 Ministry of Environment and Forests, Bangladesh, *Bangladesh Climate Change Strategy and Action Plan 2008* (2008) 8 <http://www.moef.gov.bd/moef.pdf>.

18 United Nations Development Programme ('UNEP'), *Human Development Report 2007/2008 Fighting Climate Change: Human Solidarity in a Divided World* (UNEP Report, 2007).

19 See, eg, Steve Vanderheiden, *Atmospheric Justice: A Political Theory of Climate Change* (2008); Edward A Page, *Climate Change, Justice and Future Generations* (2006); James Garvey, *The Ethics of Climate Change: Right and Wrong in a Warming World* (2008).

20 *Kyoto Protocol to the United Nations Framework Convention on Climate Change*, opened for signature 16 March 1998, 2303 UNTS 148 (entered into force 16 February 2005) art 3(7) ('*Kyoto Protocol*').

collaboration contribute to greater justice and equity in respect of climate change?

III An Introduction to Solidarity

The concept of solidarity has a long history within political and sociological scholarship.[21] Traditionally associated with the law of obligations, solidarity has emerged to represent a principle of mutual responsibility (or mutuality) focused on the relationship between the individual and society.[22] However, owing to the lack of any 'explicit and coherent theoretical tradition of its use as a systematic term', solidarity is widely used but notoriously difficult to define.[23] In its broadest sense, solidarity describes the relationship or dynamics within a community, and the commitment towards cooperation, support and (re)distribution so as to ensure that less fortunate members of the community are provided for. In this way, solidarity might be viewed as 'the principle that the strength of a society is measured by the extent that its rich members support their vulnerable fellow citizens'.[24] This clearly resonates with the problem presented by climate change where there exists vast inequity in terms of capacity to adapt to and mitigate climate change, along with disparate contributions in terms of greenhouse gas emissions. Thus, on the face of it, the concept of solidarity presents a potential mechanism for the redistribution of resources and responsibilities within the global community so as to achieve a more equitable and justice-orientated response to climate change.

As a sociological idea, solidarity has been discussed and developed alongside the term 'fraternity' to the extent that the former is now commonly considered to have dislodged and replaced the latter.[25] The similarities between the two concepts are clearly evident, however the comparison prompts interesting questions regarding the rationale behind solidarity: what motivates solidaristic behaviour vis-à-vis fraternity? The idea of fraternity inspires notions of kinship and a community with common interests or composed of individuals from the same professional class.[26] Essentially, there tends to be a greater sense of equality within a group when the discourse of fraternity is applied. This is usually quite different from when the concept of solidarity is employed where, despite a common bond uniting a group, there will frequently exist some level of disparity between members. Such disparity is commonly evident when considering issues of climate change, as inequity (be it economic, environmental or otherwise) exists across participants, most notably between developing and industrialised nations. Accordingly, solidarity, rather than fraternity, appears more closely orientated to climate change. Furthermore, greater understanding of the concept of solidarity and its potential application to climate change may be

---

21 For an introduction, see, eg, Steinar Stjernø, *Solidarity in Europe: The History of an Idea* (2005).

22 Kurt Bayertz, 'Four Uses of Solidarity' in Kurt Bayertz (ed), *Solidarity* (1999) 3, 3.

23 Simon Derpmann, 'Solidarity and Cosmopolitanism' (2009) 12 *Ethical Theory and Moral Practice* 303, 304.

24 Robin Cook, 'A Manifesto Like This Would Actually Motivate Our Voters', *Guardian* (London, United Kingdom) 4 February 2005, 24.

25 Bayertz, above n 22, 3; Ulrich Steinvorth, 'The Concept and Possibilities of Solidarity' in Kurt Bayertz (ed), *Solidarity* (1999) 29, 29.

26 Bayertz, above n 22, 3–8.

gleaned from considering the composition of possible groups claiming solidarity and exploring what motivates and inspires solidaristic behaviour.

A *Solidarity amongst Whom?*

As indicated by its heritage in social policy (especially, for example, in France),[27] solidarity is a mechanism for recognising disparity within a community between 'the economically active and the old, between the well and the sick, between those at work and the unemployed', amongst others.[28] Consequently, solidarity is something quite different from fraternity in that it presupposes a disparity that requires cooperation and support (that is, solidaristic measures or behaviour) in order to be resolved. This is clearly the case in respect of climate change, where the capacity of states varies so significantly.

The starting point for solidarity is the presumption of certain shared characteristics (for example, members of a family, a rural community, a nation-state or humanity more broadly), or equality with respect to some social principle (that is, belief in certain fundamental norms or rights), which unites or identifies a group. It is then on this basis that solidarity is identified to represent 'a commitment to some kind of mutual aid or support' for members of that group.[29] It is through the identification of a social bond that solidarity facilitates the provision of support or redistribution within a community. Moreover, the closer the social bond, the greater the level of solidaristic behaviour that is likely to be shown to other members. On the one hand, such an approach might indicate an opportunity for solidarity to be embraced at local levels in response to climate change challenges, whereby transnational and regional solidaristic behaviour reflects the closer social bonds felt by members. This might be evidenced by states accepting neighbouring populations affected by climate displacement, or the creation of national climate initiatives to reduce greenhouse gas emissions with a view to providing a long-term benefit for all members of the solidaristic grouping. However, on the other hand, such an approach could also be considered to undermine international climate change initiatives because global social bonds would be much weaker than the more immediate social bonds experienced by, for example, nationals of a state. It has been suggested that the concept of solidarity is capable of being extended to the universal level, encompassing all humanity, since it is possible to experience solidarity with any human being vulnerable to suffering and humiliation.[30] Indeed, it may be the case that solidaristic behaviour develops and exists in relation to climate change on a number of different levels (local, transnational, regional and global). Whilst these levels may individually reflect varying degrees of strength or weakness (depending on the closeness of the social bond), when viewed collectively, they represents a multifaceted and reinforced culture of solidarity operating at (and reflective of) all levels of the climate change crisis.

---

27 William Outhwaite, 'Who Needs Solidarity?' in Nathalie Karagiannis (ed), *European Solidarity* (2007) 75, 79.

28 Ibid 78.

29 Melissa Llewelyn-Davies, 'Two Contexts of Solidarity among Pastoral Maasai Women' in Patricia Caplan and Janet M Bujra (eds), *Women United, Women Divided: Cross-Cultural Perspectives on Female Solidarity* (1978) 206, 206.

30 Richard Rorty, *Contingency, Irony, and Solidarity* (1989) 192.

Traditionally, solidarity has been identified as being aligned with risk categories and social classes. In these circumstances, solidarity manifests itself in a system whereby 'the poor and risk-prone are the obvious clients of a system that promises to reapportion the effects of uncertainty' (potential redistributive winners and solidaristic groups), whilst conversely the 'affluent and safe' members of society 'have good reason to shun attempts to make them share burdens with the ill-starred' (the redistributive losers and thus, unsolidaristic groups).[31] Such an approach to social policy (and welfare organisation) is commonly viewed as a 'battle between working and middle class, poor and rich, lower and upper', where self interest plays a dominant role.[32] Broadly, this same division can be identified within the international community between industrialised and developing countries. On an international level, many developing countries unite in claims for solidarity and redistribution, identifying common features such as, inter alia, the need for development aid, differentiated responsibilities to global problems (based on prior contributions) and experiences of colonisation. The Group of 77 could be recognised as a collective of developing states such as those envisaged as being 'risk-prone' who are potential redistributive winners in favour of the principle of solidarity.[33]

However, in actual fact, solidarity is not always clearly divided along such traditional class lines but rather, it is possible that one's place within society is subject to variation.[34] Whilst class divisions within a society provide some indication as to solidarity groupings, there is capacity for movement amongst members. This observation is equally relevant in the international context where class divisions are represented by differences between industrialised and developing states. Many oil producing states — as represented by 'OPEC', the Organisation of Petroleum Exporting Countries — could currently be identified as being safe members of society who are typically the redistributive losers and unsolidaristic in nature given the economic wealth and fossil fuel independence experienced by many OPEC nations. However, a global move away from petroleum consumption to renewable energy could see OPEC nations forced to embrace solidaristic measures given their primary reliance on oil production to date. Similar experiences of movement between traditional solidaristic and non-solidaristic groups might also be evident where states (previously reluctant to engage in solidarity measures in response to climate change) are faced with new and significant migration challenges, as displaced populations are forced to migrate. In this way, it is apparent that risk exposure is not, in fact, static and states can transcend different groups that will, in turn, harbour differing opinions and priorities regarding solidarity.[35] However, it is unlikely that states would be motivated toward solidaristic behaviour solely due to a fear that at some future point their risk profile may change and render them less capable to cope and

---

31 Peter Baldwin, *The Politics of Social Solidarity: Class Bases of the European Welfare State 1875–1975* (1990) 14.

32 Ibid.

33 Group of 77, *Joint Declaration of the Seventy-Seven Developing Countries Made at the Conclusion of the United Nations Conference on Trade and Development* (Geneva, 15 June 1964) <http://www.g77.org/doc/Joint%20Declaration.html>.

34 For example, agriculture, at one time considered the safest of occupations, became 'mechanized and perilous' in later years: Baldwin, above n 31, 14–15.

35 Ibid 14.

adapt to climate change. Indeed, it is often difficult to inspire climate change mitigation and adaptation in a state with a seemingly secure future position; the short-term focus of political rhetoric generally surpasses long-term environmental and development policy. Nonetheless, recognition of the risk categories is of interest in highlighting the possible variability within different groups and potential rationale for embracing solidaristic behaviour.

B *Why Solidarity? Motivation and Rationale*

An important aspect of solidarity to be considered is the motivation or inspiration for solidaristic behaviour. The recognition of differing capacities within a community and the need for solidarity raises interesting questions as to *why* members of a group might engage in solidaristic activities. This logic of solidarity has been justified predominately by, on the one hand, self-interest, and on the other, altruism.[36] Justifying solidarity in terms of self-interest recognises that '[r]ationally calculating individuals, aware of society's utility and inter-dependence, maximize their own well-being by improving that of others'.[37] This approach is commonly referenced in economic terms, where redistribution is considered part of a cost–benefit analysis. In this way, some moderate redistribution by more affluent members of society, in favour of less-fortunate members, acts as a type of insurance policy; behaviour that is arguably less to do with solidarity and is, in fact, more economically inspired. Indeed, this may be the case in relation to climate change, whereby the action of industrialised nations supporting developing countries simply represents an attempt to secure their own prosperous future; a kind of insurance policy against future global climate disaster. Nevertheless, it may well be possible for such a self-interested approach to be effective in promoting solidarity. Yet, there are potential pitfalls: an approach motivated by self-interest could create conflict where there is a failure to recognise a problem by members of a group, or alternatively where there is disagreement within the group as to the appropriate level of redistribution required. Both of these hurdles have been evidenced in terms of climate change. So-called 'climate change deniers' have resisted mitigation or adaptation measures, leading to conflict within the international community where solidarity measures have consequently remained unsupported.

Similarly, conflict also arises where there is a lack of agreement within the international community as to the *extent* of any solidaristic behaviour required; this may be in relation to the appropriate level of redistribution (for example, through international development aid), or in relation to the required emission reduction targets (where states continue to debate the appropriate emission reduction target for the benefit of all). Despite such possible shortcomings, solidaristic behaviour, inspired by self-interest, remains constructive in addressing the challenge of climate change. The global nature of the problem means that states need one another in order to work together to achieve a beneficial result; notably, industrialised nations are dependent on states such as China, India and Brazil participating in the international legal framework in order for it to be effective. So, in this way, solidaristic behaviour on the part of

---

[36] Ibid 21.

[37] Ibid 22.

industrialised nations is based on self-interest, but it also represents the classic contractarian analysis of participation in international agreement.

A second justification for solidaristic behaviour is that of altruism, whereby members of a community act out of good faith or a sense of philanthropy. An altruistic rationale for solidarity provokes questions as to *why* members might choose to be altruistic; perhaps a motivation based on a sense of similarity within the group, or recognition of a need for interdependence.[38] However, whilst notions of charity and justice might frame our sense of altruism, it could also well be possible to see such behaviour as, in reality, being little more than economically efficient. This is demonstrated in the assessment made by Nicholas Stern, who explains the cost of developing a low-carbon economy *now* as being considerably more economically effective than delaying action and dealing with the consequences in future years (through needing to treat preventable diseases and replace carbon-intensive energy systems and so on).[39] Whilst seemingly altruistic behaviour may be a reason for solidarity, there could well be consequences that, coincidently or otherwise, happen to also be cost-effective. Accordingly, this creates doubt over altruism as a motivation for solidarity: can any measure be truly altruistic and not be inspired by some form of self-interest? Furthermore, solidaristic behaviour — seemingly motivated by altruism — is most likely to occur in relation to communities demonstrating close bonds: the closer members feel toward each other and empathise with one another's problems, the more willing members will be to engage in solidarity measures. In this way, solidarity can be defined as the 'inner cement holding together a society'.[40] However, there will inevitably be greater cohesion and a sense of moral duty in relation to small groupings of humans (for example, families) than largely indirect and anonymous communities (for example, the 'global community').[41]

The altruistic motivation for solidarity could perhaps be more clearly envisaged where individuals unite in order to represent a common interest. The relationship between solidarity and liberation has emerged to the extent there exists some form of 'emotional cohesion between the members of ... social movements and the mutual support they give each other in their battle for common goals'.[42] This form of solidarity quite overtly embraces ideas of justice to the extent that it is used as a positive action in order to assert a right or benefit for a minority group. Solidarity then becomes part of the process of developing rights and thus, an important source of legal process.[43] This approach potentially could be influential in respect of climate change where the human impacts of such environmental change are directly related to fundamental economic and social rights. In this way, solidarity can be used as a political tool to promote action for mitigation of and adaptation to climate change. However, whilst altruism clearly inspires this liberating form of solidarity, it is possible that there

---

38 Outhwaite, above n 27, 81–2.

39 Stern, *The Stern Review*, above n 6. See also Nicholas Stern, *A Blueprint for a Safer Planet: How to Manage Climate Change and Create a New Era of Progress and Prosperity* (2009).

40 Bayertz, above n 22, 9.

41 Ibid 9–15.

42 Ibid 16.

43 Ibid.

also exists 'overtones of an expectation of potential mutuality and the hope of simultaneously serving one's own interests'.[44] This mutuality is based on the notion that members of a community are willing to embrace solidarity and help those less fortunate because there may come a time where they, in turn, are in need of aid and solidaristic measures from their community (in line with the movement between risk categories described above). Thus, even the most altruistically-inspired behaviour is commonly tinged with notions of self-interest. Climate change exemplifies this sociological explanation: industrialised nations may claim to undertake mitigation measures, for the benefit of all mankind and especially those in the greatest of need with little ability to adapt. However, there ultimately exists an element of self-interest, whereby any resulting benefit in reducing greenhouse gas emissions is enjoyed by everyone.

Perhaps an important question to consider is what kind of motivation for solidarity is most effective in achieving results (that is, mitigating and adapting to climate change)? Ultimately, it would be difficult to deny that both states and individuals are not primarily motivated by a sense of self-interest.[45] Whilst it may be comforting to believe that solidaristic measures are undertaken because of altruistic behaviour, in actual truth, the global community would not demonstrate such vast inequities and extreme poverty if this were the case. Instead, action appears to be most effective where there exists some form of self-interest (for example, addressing climate change so as to reduce the impact to oneself), even if those solidarity measures are cloaked in a form of altruism. Indeed, it could be argued that solidaristic behaviour motivated (at least partly) by self-interest is more reliable than behaviour based on altruism since there is more of a vested interest, rather than simply a possibly wavering sense of benevolence, at stake.

IV SOLIDARITY AND INTERNATIONAL LAW

Many global problems rely on international cooperation in order to achieve any suitable form of remedy or resolution. This is especially the case for environmental problems, such as climate change, that are inherently trans-boundary in character and demonstrate little regard for state borders and the principle of sovereignty. The most basic of ideas within international law — that states have a duty of mutual assistance in order to improve their general situation and relations — seemingly conceives of solidarity as the basic condition for the existence of a community of states.[46] Specifically, it has been considered that:

> Solidarity, as a principle of international law, creates a context for meaningful cooperation that goes beyond the concept of a global welfare state; on the legal plane it reflects and reinforces the broader idea of a world community of interdependent states.[47]

---

44 Ibid 18.

45 For a discussion on the justification for environmental protection in general, see Alexander Gillespie, *International Environmental Law, Policy and Ethics* (2000).

46 Ronald St John Macdonald, 'Solidarity in the Practice and Discourse of Public International Law' (1996) 8 *Pace International Law Review* 259, 260.

47 Ibid.

However, whilst solidarity can be recognised in different forms within international law, it is likely that any specific obligations created by the principle are moral rather than legal and thus, difficult to enforce.[48] Whilst there appears to be some general acceptance as to the existence of the principle of solidarity within international law, there is still a lack of agreement as to the precise nature of the principle. Consequently, a number of different approaches have emerged.[49] Some scholars consider that solidarity creates no additional legal obligations beyond what already exists in treaties and custom, whilst others believe that solidarity does imply an additional legal obligation for industrialised nations to assist less developed countries, or 'at a minimum, not to interfere with the interests of other states'.[50] Finally, some consider solidarity to be a principle that informs the whole system, and is 'a direction in which international law is traveling'.[51] Clearly, the specific meaning of the solidarity principle within the international legal system remains uncertain, however, the essence of the principle is evident in a number of different contexts.

International environmental law can be seen to engage solidarity in different ways. Early principles of non-interference were established in the *Trail Smelter* decision[52] and later endorsed by the 1972 *Stockholm Declaration*,[53] where states agreed to a 'responsibility to ensure that activities within their jurisdiction or control do not cause damage to the environment of other States or of areas beyond the limits of national jurisdiction'.[54] This principle was later reiterated in the 1992 *Rio Declaration*[55] and remains a core principle of modern international environmental law.[56] The principle of cooperation has been, and remains, central to the development of international environmental law. The *Stockholm Declaration* called on states to cooperate to 'develop further international law … for the victims of pollution and other environmental damage'.[57] However, some 20 years later, the *Rio Declaration* developed the principle of cooperation much further by incorporating it into numerous areas of responsibility.[58] Inherent within the *Rio Declaration* is the recognition of the relationship between environment and development, and that the challenges associated with both are inseparable and must be addressed simultaneously. The principle of sustainable development emerged as the mechanism for reconciling environment and development interests and remains a key concept within the international legal

---

48 Ibid 262.

49 These approaches are discussed in greater detail by McDonald: ibid.

50 Ibid.

51 Ibid.

52 *Trail Smelter Arbitration (United States v Canada)* (1941) 3 RIAA 1905.

53 *Report of the United Nations Conference on the Human Environment*, UN Doc A/CONF.48/14/Rev.1 (1 January 1973) ch I (*Declaration of the United Nations Conference on the Human Environment*) ('*Stockholm Declaration*').

54 Ibid principle 21.

55 *Report of the United Nations Conference on Environment and Development*, UN Doc A/CONF.151/26/Rev.1 (Vol I) (12 August 1992) annex I (*Rio Declaration on Environment and Development*) principle 27 ('*Rio Declaration*').

56 Ibid principle 2.

57 *Stockholm Declaration*, above n 53, principle 22.

58 See, eg, *Rio Declaration*, above n 55, principles 5, 7, 9, 12, 14 and 27.

system today.[59] The *Rio Declaration* recognises the varying needs of those within the international community and the importance of addressing environmental and development concerns together by embracing ideas of solidarity. Specifically, it provides that:

> All states and all people shall cooperate in the essential task of eradicating poverty as an indispensible requirement for sustainable development, in order to decrease the disparities in standards of living and better meet the needs of the majority of the people of the world.[60]

Furthermore, the 'special situation and needs of developing countries, particularly the least developed and those most environmentally vulnerable, shall be given special priority'.[61] This represents a clear manifestation of solidarity whereby the international community is called upon to unite and address global poverty with a view to promoting sustainable development.

The principle of sustainable development provides an interesting platform for the examination of solidarity, as it not only strives to obtain cooperation amongst participants across environmental and development interests but it also seeks to achieve a sense of equity between generations.[62] Generational equity — both 'inter' (between current and future generations) and 'intra' (across the current generation) — is inherent to sustainable development, and in many ways articulates the principle of solidarity within international environmental law. Intergenerational equity requires that there is a sense of parity between current and future generations — essentially, that the present does not compromise the ability of future generations to meet their needs. The idea of 'intergenerational solidarity' has been popular in family law and social policy on ageing, although it is now also being examined outside of these contexts. Conversely, intra-generational equity focuses on fairness within the current generation and the need for redistribution of resources and opportunities. In many ways, this principle may be seen as an expression of solidarity in the pursuit of climate justice, given the manner in which it embraces principles of redistribution and equity.

V CLIMATE CHANGE LAW AND SOLIDARITY

The principle of solidarity is evident in different forms throughout the international climate change framework, reflecting the fact that international cooperation is fundamental to the success of any global climate change agreement. However, there are three features of the climate change framework

---

59 World Commission on Environment and Development, *Our Common Future* (1987). On the general concept of sustainable development, see Marie-Claire Cordonier-Segger and Ashfaq Khalfan, *Sustainable Development Law: Principles, Practices and Prospects* (2004).

60 *Rio Declaration*, above n 55, principle 5.

61 Ibid principle 6.

62 For a critique of the concept of sustainable development, see Angela Williams 'Re-assessing Traditional Notions of Sustainable Development' (2006) 18 *Environmental Law and Management* 181.

that are worth highlighting, owing to the way in which the principle of solidarity can be seen to be operating in a practical way. The first is in relation to the principle of 'common but differentiated responsibilities' ('CBDR'), which is based on the need for states to cooperate 'in a spirit of global partnership' in order to conserve and protect the Earth's ecosystem.[63] Specifically, the principle recognises that '[i]n view of the different contributions to global environmental degradation, States have common but differentiated responsibilities'.[64] This means that industrialised states should

> acknowledge the responsibility that they bear in the international pursuit to sustainable development in view of the pressures their societies place on the global environment and of the technologies and financial resources they command.[65]

The CBDR principle represents a clear manifestation of solidarity integrating responsibilities for cooperation, along with recognition of existing disparities within the (in this case, global) community and facilitating support and assistance measures. The *United Nations Framework Convention on Climate Change* ('*UNFCCC*')[66] represents a common agreement on how to respond to the global problem of climate change, but participating states vary enormously in terms of both their contribution to the problem and their capacity to respond. Nevertheless, a global solution and universal participation is imperative if the problem is to be properly addressed. The *UNFCCC* recognises that 'the largest share of historical and current global emissions of greenhouse gases has originated from industrialised countries' and that 'per capita emissions in developing countries are still relatively low'.[67] However, it is similarly acknowledged that 'the global nature of climate change calls for the widest possible cooperation by all countries and their participation in an effective and appropriate international response'.[68] The *UNFCCC* thus adopted the CBDR principle, requiring parties to the Convention to 'protect the climate system for the benefit of present and future generations of humankind, on the basis of equity and in accordance with their common but differentiated responsibilities and respective capabilities'.[69] In light of this, the *UNFCCC* requires industrialised states parties to take the lead in combating climate change, seemingly endorsing solidaristic behaviour.

A second way in which solidarity can be seen to operate within the climate change framework is by way of the flexibility mechanisms, and in particular, the Clean Development Mechanism ('CDM'). One of the unique features of the *Kyoto Protocol* is the introduction of 'flexible mechanisms' created to make it easier, or more cost effective, for Annex I parties (that is, industrialised nations)

63 *Rio Declaration*, above n 55, principle 7.
64 Ibid.
65 Ibid.
66 Opened for signature 4 June 1992, 1771 UNTS 107 (entered into force 21 March 1994).
67 Ibid preamble.
68 Ibid.
69 Ibid art 3(1).

to meet their commitments.[70] Some of the mechanisms are also considered to provide assistance to developing states in respect of ongoing sustainable development and adapting to low-carbon economies. The so-called flexible mechanisms are Joint Implementation,[71] the CDM,[72] and Emissions Trading.[73] Discussion will focus on the CDM, which has received the greatest attention to date from participating states and best demonstrates the application of solidaristic behaviour.

The CDM is considered to embody a dual purpose: first, to assist developing countries in achieving sustainable development and contributing to the overall objective of the *UNFCCC*, and second, to assist industrialised states in achieving compliance with their emission reduction commitments established in the *Kyoto Protocol*.[74] The CDM operates by allowing Annex I parties (that is, the developed states listed in Annex I who have agreed to specific emission reduction targets) to establish project-based activities that reduce anthropogenic greenhouse gas emissions in non-Annex I states. Essentially, the mechanism permits industrialised nations to invest in low-carbon projects in developing country parties. In return for such investment, the Annex I party receives credit by way of Certified Emission Reductions ('CERs') that can be used to contribute to its own emission reduction target. Accordingly, the CDM facilitates solidaristic behaviour by encouraging industrialised states to assist and support developing nations by contributing to the growth of a low-carbon economy. There has been some criticism levelled at the effectiveness of the CDM in promoting justice and equity within the climate change framework.[75] Suggestions that the CDM effectively allows states to 'buy' their way out of meeting their own emission reduction targets have been refuted by highlighting that the use of CERs must be supplemental to domestic action, and that reporting requirements install a sense of transparency and accountability into the process. Indeed, in response to allegations that the CDM remains more focused on alleviating industrialised countries of their anthropogenic emission reduction commitments, one might revisit the differing motivations for solidarity identified earlier. Whilst the CDM can be recognised as solidaristic behaviour, it is clearly not inspired by altruism given the intended dual benefit and the issue of CERs to the investor state. Instead, this form of solidarity is very much conceived of in self-interest to the extent that industrialised states fund projects because they receive a benefit in return. There is no argument to say that the CDM is any less solidaristic because states act out of self-interest rather than a sense of altruism or moral responsibility. On the contrary, the self-interest element could well mean the mechanism is more effective than it might have been otherwise.

---

70 For an overview, see David Freestone and Charlotte Streck (eds), *Legal Aspects of Implementing the Kyoto Protocol* (2005).

71 *Kyoto Protocol*, above n 20, art 6.

72 Ibid art 12.

73 Ibid art 17.

74 Ibid art 12(2).

75 See, eg, Francesca Romanin Jacur, 'Paving the Road to Legitimacy for CDM Institutions and Procedures: Learning from Other Experiences in International Environmental Governance' (2009) 3 *Carbon and Climate Law Review* 69.

A third way in which solidarity appears in terms of international climate change law is by the creation of funding initiatives. The Adaptation Fund was created to finance adaptation projects in developing countries that are especially vulnerable to the adverse effects of climate change.[76] The Special Climate Change Fund, designed to complement other funding mechanisms in the *UNFCCC*, was also established to finance projects relating to adaptation, such as technology transfer and capacity building; 'energy, transport, industry, agriculture, forestry and waste management'; and economic diversification (for example, for oil-exporting countries).[77] In line with the CBDR principle, these funds promote solidarity by encouraging industrialised nations to take the lead and provide support and assistance to less capable states. Thus, analogous with socialist traditions, the concept of solidarity has been employed by the climate change framework as a way of organising our global society and providing a mechanism for social welfare.

VI Concluding Remarks

Climate change law has developed as a complex web of emissions reduction targets, support systems, financial mechanisms, and development initiatives. Cooperation is integral to the success of climate change law and policy not only in terms of unifying states to inspire collective action, but also owing to the diverse and challenging interests that require reconciliation in order for the problem to be effectively addressed. However, cooperation is largely a generalist principle employed in various areas of international law, encouraging states to work together for the purpose of achieving a common goal. It lacks any real appreciation or recognition of varying capacity amongst participants, or the need for redistribution in order to promote a justice-orientated solution. It is suggested here that the principle of solidarity offers a more comprehensive approach that resolves many of the shortcomings identified with a general principle of cooperation. Solidarity may be considered to have greater capacity than cooperation to achieve climate justice, as it is based on and emanates from a moral authority that is absent in relation to cooperation. Indeed, the essence of solidarity can already be identified in a number of different principles and mechanisms present within the legal climate change framework, thus promoting notions of justice and equity. Whilst present throughout much of the international legal system in various forms, the principle of solidarity arguably remains of moral significance only, lacking real clout as a legally enforceable obligation. However, the collaborative nature of solidarity indicates an implied acceptance by states and thus, confirmation as a soft law principle within international environmental law. Moreover, 'soft-law creates the "pull" of legitimacy even without sanctions' through the articulation of common goals,

---

[76] Conference of the Parties ('COP'), UNFCCC, *Report of the Conference of the Parties on Its Seventh Session, Held at Marrakesh from 29 October to 10 November 2001*, UN Doc FCCC/CP/2001/13 (21 January 2002) 52 (*Decision 10/CP.7 — Funding under the Kyoto Protocol*).

[77] Ibid 43 (*Decision 7/CP.7 — Funding under the Convention*).

such as addressing the global climate change problem.[78] This think piece has identified the principle of solidarity as a mechanism for promoting justice within international climate change law and better recognising the needs of developing states so that a fairer and more equitable solution may be achieved. Nevertheless, there remains considerable scope for the further development of solidarity discourse within climate change law.

78 Macdonald, above n 46, 287.

[13]

COMMON CONCERN OF HUMANKIND AND ITS IMPLICATIONS IN INTERNATIONAL ENVIRONMENTAL LAW

JIMENA MURILLO CHÁVARRO*

I INTRODUCTION

Traditionally, international law was conceived to regulate relations between states; those relations are usually based upon the reciprocity principle. However, this traditional approach has not been enough to govern all the new international relations arising from the increase in actors in the international area due to the economic, scientific and technological evolution. These developments have thus generated a more complex relationship between international actors such as states, multinational companies, non-governmental organisations (NGOs) and further between those involved with environment protection.

These developments have shown that states can now cause harm not only to other states but also to the commons. "*Commons*" refers to those areas, resources, or problems involving the community as a whole or where there is no specific state sovereignty.

International environmental law plays an important role here in preserving and conserving the commons, governing the conduct (actions and omissions) of states, and, to an extent, the actions of others actors in relation to the commons.

According to its characteristics, the commons have received the following classification: common areas (property), shared resources, common heritage of mankind and common concern. [1]

---

* Graduate of the Master of Laws in Energy and Environmental Law Programme, convened by the Institute for Energy and Environmental Law (IEEL) of KU Leuven, and law degree of the Universidad Externado de Colombia.

1 Daniel Bodansky, Jutta Bronee and Ellen Hey. *The Oxford Handbook of International Environmental Law*. . (Oxford University Press. 2007), 552. See also R. St. J. Macdonald and Douglas..M. Johnston. *The Structure and Process of International Law*. 2nd ed. (Martinus Nijhoff Publishers 1986). See also Patricia Birnie, and Alan Boyle, *International Law and the Environment*, 2nd ed. (Oxford Univ. Press, 2002), 137.

No clear definition of a common concern of mankind exists, nor does a final decision about its legal implications in international environmental law. Therefore, this essay discusses the concept and the elements of the common heritage of mankind to relate its relation, similitude, or difference with the new concept of common concern to establish its legal implication in this field.

II COMMON HERITAGE OF MANKIND

A *Origin*

It is very difficult to establish exactly when the idea of the common heritage of mankind first emerged in human consciousness. The idea of a commons has always existed. However, the introduction of this concept has been attributed to Ambassador Arvid Pardo of Malta, who in 1967 proposed that the Law of the Sea should be based upon the principle of common heritage of mankind instead of the principle of freedom of the sea.[2]

The main reason of this proposal was related to the fear that some states, seeking to expand their territories, would seek to appropriate the commons areas, especially to exploit their resources. The emerging concept of the 'common heritage of mankind' (hereinafter CHM) has been seen as the effort of the newly independent states (self-governing from the 1960s or 1970s) and developing countries to establish equitable sharing benefits for the exploitation of the resources located beyond national jurisdictions.

The Permanent Mission of Malta submitted a proposal to the United Nations to include a supplementary item in the agenda of the twenty-second session of the General Assembly. It was in this document that the importance of the seabed, the ocean floor and its resources (hereinafter the area) for the community was expressed, and therefore, the necessity to declare the "Area" as common heritage of mankind. It expresses the main reason to define the area as CHM in the following terms:

> In the view of rapid progress in the development of the new techniques by technologically advanced countries, it is feared that the situation will change and that the seabed and the ocean floor, underlying the seas beyond present national jurisdiction, will become progressively and competitively subject to national appropriation and use. This is likely to result in the militarization of the accessible ocean floor through the establishment of fixed military installations and in the exploitation and depletion of resources of immense potential benefit to the world, for the national advantage of technologically developed countries[3].

---

2 http://www.unu.edu/unupress/unupbooks/uu15oe/uu15oe00.htm#Contents. Meter Bautista Payoyo. *Ocean governance: sustainable development of the seas*. (United Nations university Press, 1994) visited on 31 October 2007.

3 Division for Ocean Affairs and the Law of the Sea, Office of Legal Affairs, United Nations. *The Law of the Sea: Concept of the Common Heritage of Mankind: Legislative History of*

With regards to the concept of common heritage of mankind, some delegations, expressed that it was important to establish that the area, as defined by the Law of the Sea, was neither considered *res nullius* nor *res communis omnium,* since these two concepts would open the possibility of claims of national sovereignty, or make the share of the exploitation of the resources located in the area more difficult[4].

In the twenty-third session of the General Assembly in 1968 there was a general acceptance to define the Area, which means the seabed and ocean floor and subsoil thereof beyond the limits of national jurisdiction[5], as a common heritage of mankind. However, this term was only adopted in 1970 in UN General Assembly Resolution 2748. Thereafter it was given legal status in 1979 in the Agreement Governing the Activities of States on the Moon and other Celestial Bodies, and then in 1982 in the Convention of the Law of the Sea.

B *Characteristics of the Common Heritage of Mankind*

The common heritage of mankind has at least four characteristics or elements: the first element is non-appropriation; second, share benefits; third, international management; and fourth, exclusively peaceful use.[6] I will now address each of these characteristics in turn.

Non-appropriation

According to this characteristic, neither state nor natural or juridical person can appropriate, claim, or exercise sovereignty over such an area or its resources. The Moon Treaty, Article 11, only refers to non appropriation by states but the Law of the Sea, in Article 137, goes further and also mentions natural and juridical persons. Additionally, it prescribes that "*all the rights in the resources of the Area are invested in mankind as a whole, on whose behalf the Authority shall act.*" In this sense, it can be said that the 'ownership' of the areas or resources defined as common heritage remain to the whole of humanity[7].

Articles 133 to 150 and 311(6) of the United Nations Convention on the Law of the Sea. (United Nation Publication. 1996), 8.

4 'Ibid' Page 40.

5 United Nations Convention of the Law of the Sea, Part I, article 1.

6 David Hunter, James Salzman and Durwood Zaelke.*International Environmental Law and Policy.* 2nd Ed. (Foundation Press, 2002), 392. See also Daniel Bodansky, Jutta Bronee and Ellen Hey *The Oxford Handbook of International Environmental Law.* (Oxford University Press. 2007), 562. See also Ved P. nanda. *International Environmental Law and Policy.* (Transnational Publishers, Inc. 1995), 12.

7 David Hunter, James Salzman and Durwood Zaelke. *International Environmental Law and Policy.* 2nd Ed. (Foundation Press, 2002), 392.

Shared benefits

As the activities carried out in the common areas should be for the benefit of humankind as a whole, a shared system has been created to benefit all states. This is not only those near the coasts or those with the technology to exploit natural resources in the common areas. This has been the most controversial of all the elements, particularly for some developed countries such as the United States of America, which agreed to sign the Convention of the Law of the Sea (UNCLOS) once the provisions about shared benefit were eliminated.

Both the Law of the Sea Convention, Article 140 (2), and the Moon Treaty Article 11 (7) provide for an *equitable share system*[8] of the benefits perceived from the activities or exploitation of resources in the commons.

In regards to this element, A. Kiss and D. Shelton argue that in the present benefit-sharing has been understood as an *"equitable allocation of revenue"*. Nevertheless, it also means sharing scientific knowledge obtained in the common heritage areas.[9]

Importantly, the above characteristic of the common heritage of mankind will not limit the right of all states to fish in the high seas. As these areas are open to all states, every country has the right of appropriation over the fish captured by them. But, this right is not unlimited since the freedom of fishing is subject to conditions such as those provided by Article 87 (2), which states that *"these freedoms shall be exercised by all States with due regard for the interests of other States in their exercise of the freedom of the high seas, and also with due regard for the rights under this Convention with respect to activities in the Area"*.

International Management

Through international management, it would be possible to achieve the main objectives of CHM. For instance, the Law of the Sea Convention has created an International Authority, established in Article 156 among other functions, to distribute the benefits received from the exploitation of the resources located in the area. Through this authority, the system of equitable share benefits and the protection of the area and its resources will be obtained.

Although, the Moon treaty establishes an international regime *"to govern the exploitation of the natural resources of the moon as such exploitation is about to*

---

8 The Moon treaty says that the moon and its natural resources are the common heritage or mankind. It also states that the main purpose of the international regime to be established shall include an equitable sharing by all States Parties in the benefits derived from those resources, whereby the interests and needs of the developing countries, as well as the efforts of those countries which have contributed either directly – or indirectly to the exploration of the moon, shall be given special consideration.

9 Alexandre Kiss and Dinah Shelton. *International Environmental Law*. 2nd ed. (Transnational Publishers, Inc. 2000), 249

become feasible" (Article 11 (5)), such an international regime has not yet been implemented.

Due to this feature of international management, it is said that the common heritage is a form of trust, where the international community through an international body is the trustee. Some examples are the International Seabed Authority and the Shared administration of Antarctica created by some states under the vigilance of an international body[10].

Exclusively for peaceful use

This element in the Law of the Sea Convention has its origin in the fear of the establishment of fixed military installations in the open sea. This would in turn be implemented in order to have a national economic advantage and the use of the area for defence purposes in the foreseeable future. This exclusive use was established in both the original Outer Space Treaty and then in the Moon Treaty.

C *Weakness of the Concept*

Although the concept of common heritage of mankind has been defined in some treaties and has already been applied within some country parties, there is no general acceptance of its existence. For instance, the United States of America, one of the biggest countries which exercises its right of exploitation in the high sea, resists to recognize or apply the concept.

A second weak point of common heritage is the fact that apart from the LOSC or the Moon Treaty, it has not found application in any other convention or proposal made to extend the concept into other areas. For instance, the idea of introducing the concept of common heritage of mankind in the Convention of the Climate Change and the Convention on Biological Diversity has been generally rejected.

III COMMON CONCERN

A *Origin*

The global consequences of environmental problems are imminent; nowadays there is an avalanche of different natural disasters around the world. Therefore to find a solution to this general problem the cooperation of all states is a necessary requirement. And what is also important in this process is the participation of the political and legal response.

States are working together to come up with new ideas to stop these global problems. An example of the result of their work is the protection of certain areas

10 'Ibid' page 250

and resources throughout the concepts of common heritage, shared resources, and common concern establish in treaties.

The concept of "Common concern" is relatively new and was introduced in the international arena about two decades ago. It was in 1988, through the UN General Assembly Resolution 43/53, that climate change was recognized as a common concern because it is an essential condition to sustain life. Thereafter, the expression has been used in other international documents[11].

One can say that in practice the notion of common concern emerged on the conventions on Climate change and Biodiversity as a reaction to the implications of the common heritage concept. The inclusion of the latter was rejected in both conventions by the countries involved in their negotiations mainly for two reasons. The first, claimed by developing countries, consisted of their fear of a high level of interference or control within their sovereignty by an international body in charge of the commons and its resources. This fear could have materialised if developing countries had lost their sovereignty or ownership over the resources that are within their territories. The second reason was stated by developed countries, which disagreed with the shared benefit system implicit in the common heritage concept. As a result, developed and developing countries decided that it was best to opt for a more ambiguous concept, such as common concern.[12].

Indeed, the concept of common concern has appeared as a solution to the global environmental problems, which are putting the survival of the human race at risk. But it also served as an answer to previous disputes between states which originated from the concept of common heritage, as the common concern is based upon equitable sharing of burdens in the protection of the environment rather than benefits of exploitation from the common resources[13].

B *Aspects of the Common Concern of Mankind*

There are three important facets that compound the notion of common concern of (hu)mankind. Those are the spatial, temporal and social facets, which are going to be subject of study in this essay.

The spatial aspect means that common concern *"implies cooperation of all states on matters being similarly important to all nations, to the whole international*

---

11 UN General Assembly Resolution 44/207 of December 1989, United Nations Framework Convention on climate change 1992 and Convention on Biological diversity.

12 David Hunter, James Salzman, and Durwood Zaelke. *International Environmental Law and Policy*, 2nd ed. (Foundation Press. 2002), 397.

13 http://www.juridicas.unam.mx/publica/librev/rev/iidh/cont/13/doc/doc27.pdf
Note to the Executive Director of UNEP Mostafa K. Tolba to the Group of Legal Experts Meeting> Mata December 13-15, 1990. *the implications of the common concern mankind concept on global environmental issues.* (Revista Instituto Interamericano de Derechos Humanos, Número 13 Enero-Junio 1991), 239 Visited on 8 November 2007.

community"[14]. It is from this aspect that the principle of cooperation becomes visible. As a consequence, all the states should take the appropriate measures to protect the environment according to their own capacities.

It can be stated that this aspect is based upon Principle 7 of the Rio Declaration on Environment and Development which states that *"states shall cooperate in a spirit of global partnership to conserve, protect and restore the health and integrity of the Earth's ecosystem"*. And also based upon the common but differentiated responsibility principle established in the Framework Convention on Climate Change (UNFCCC).

Moving forward within this spatial aspect, it was found that this can be divided into two sub-aspects according to the level of inference of the legal instruments within international and national jurisdiction. As the matter subject to common concern involves the whole community, the protection of the environment is important not only for areas where there is international control, for instance in the Antarctica, but also essential for the protection of the ecosystems located within the jurisdiction of a state.

An example of the latter type of legal instrument, which is an international agreement aiming to protect elements of the environment placed inside national jurisdictions, is the Convention on International Trade in Endangered Species. The principal aim of these treaties is to oblige the states parties to ensure the conservation of the elements of the environment that are under their jurisdiction, since those are considered essential not only for them but for all humanity[15]. Examples of the legal instruments interfering only in areas located beyond states' jurisdiction are the 'Ozone convention or the Antarctica Treaty'.

For the above reason it is possible to say that common concern differs form the CHM because the former is not restricted to the areas beyond national jurisdiction[16].

Regarding the temporal aspect, this has been said to "*arise from the long-term implications of major environmental challenges which affect the rights and obligations not only of the present but also of the future generations*"[17]. According to the complex relations that reign in the world's ecosystem, the effects caused by

---

14 'Ibid', page 239.

15 R. St. J. Macdonald and Douglas. M. Johnston. *The Structure and Process of International Law*. 2nd ed. (Martinus Nijhoff Publishers 1986), 1084.

16 Daniel Bodansky, Jutta Bronee and Ellen Hey. *The Oxford Handbook of International Environmental Law*. (Oxford University Press. 2007), 564. See also http://www.law.mq.edu.au/html/MqJICEL/vol1/vol1-2_4.pdf. Laura Horn, visited on 9 November 2007, pag 244.

17 http://www.juridicas.unam.mx/publica/librev/rev/iidh/cont/13/doc/doc27.pdf
Note to the Executive Director of UNEP Mostafa K. Tolba to the Group of Legal Experts Meeting> Mata December 13-15, 1990. *the implications of the common concern mankind concept on global environmental issues*. (Revista Instituto Interamericano de Derechos Humanos, Número 13 Enero-Junio 1991), 239.

human actions are not immediately perceivable. Therefore, all of the conduct (action and omission) carried out at present will produce their effect in the future. There is thus a moral obligation with the future generation to act now in order to preserve the environment for them.

A third facet of the common concern is the social aspect, this one can be described as *"presuming involvement of all structures and sectors of society in the process of combating global environmental threats, i.e. legislative, judicial and governmental bodies together with private businesses, non-governmental organizations and citizens groups"*[18].

This aspect brings us the opportunity to extend the participant actor in the international law area further than only at state level. The involvement of all sectors of the society is now visible when talking about the action put in motion to prevent the degradation of the environment. However, those actors do not have the possibility to be listen to in courts within the field of International Law. Then, this social aspect of common concern is looking for a dynamic participation of the whole community not only as represented by states but NGOs and citizens groups as well. Consequently the concept of common concern claims a standing for these organizations within the International Environmental Law in front of international courts.

In addition to the aspects of the common concern it is necessary to have a look at the meaning of its wording, as this will incorporate into the concept some elements that one should bear in mind. For instance, the "concern" element invites all states to work in a joint and concerted way when taking decisions or performing actions[19]. The "mankind" element, being the most controversial, could open a new space in the international arena to introduce new actors into this field, since this element represents the link between the present and future generations. As a result, there is a need to establish how the rights of the born and unborn are going to be represented, as well as to determine whether the standing of states is enough to protect areas and resources beyond national jurisdictions.

Finally, there is the "common" element. If we have a look at the notes of the secretariat of the UNEP[20], it is said that this element of the concept would be possible to interpret as is analogous the "common interest", since both involve all the members of the international community. This interpretation is relevant when questions about the hierarchy of interest come into play. As common interest enjoy superiority over the individual states interest, common concern would have the same effect of prevalence in front of other individual interest. One can conclude that the secretariat accepted to give common concern concept a higher status than the others such as common heritage, shared resources and the like. This would lead to the overriding characteristic of the obligations emerging from it.

18 'Ibid', page 239.
19 'Ibid', page 244.
20 'Ibid', page 244.

To summarize, it can be said that the concept of common concern implies for the international community one right and one duty. The former is a legitimate interest in the resources, and the latter a common responsibility to assist in the protection and conservation of those resources[21]. It can also be said that although common concern does not create or imply specific rules, it establishes the general basis for the whole community to act in a matter of international concern[22]. Common concern of (hu)mankind for its ambiguity leaves a door open as an opportunity to build it up as a stronger concept than the ones governing other global commons. It displays for instance the possibility of introducing other sectors of the community within international law to have a more dynamic participation. Furthermore, it allows all states, working jointly, to establish international regulations to preserve resources located within national jurisdictions which confirm that the global environmental problems are the concern of the whole international community.

IV Common Concern and Its Relation with Common Heritage of Mankind

When we talk about global commons we come across with many concepts such as common areas, common heritage, shared resources and the common concern of humankind. Although they may all be related to each other, they have different meanings.

As the differences and limitations between common areas, shared resources and common heritage of humankind are clearer than the relation between the latter with common concern, the step to follow is to compare these two concepts

The first element to study is the territorial scope. While the common heritage applies to areas beyond national jurisdiction and its resources, common concern has a wider scope as it is applied both beyond national jurisdiction but also within the jurisdiction of individual states. It is essential to understand that the environment cannot be divided in geographic sectors according to the borders of each state; the environment is a global ecosystem and it is affected as a whole by the individual actions taken by single countries. Therefore we now need to follow and implement international standards and minimums by all states.

A clear example of this national inference is present in the Convention on Biodiversity, where Article 3 outlines that states have the right to exploit their own

21 O. Yoshida. [A.E. Boyle. "*Remedy Harm to International Common Spaces and Resources: compensation and Other Approaches*" in P. Wetterstein (ed), Harm to the Environment: the Right to Compensation and the Assessment of Damages. (1997), pag 86]. In *The International legal Regime for the Protection of the Stratospheric Ozone Layer.* (Kluwer Law International, 2001), 61.

22 Alexandre Kiss and Dinah Shelton. *International Environmental Law.* 2nd ed.(Transnational Publishers, Inc. 2000), 251.

resources, subject to a limit, which stands *"to ensure that activities within their jurisdiction or control do not cause damage to the environment of other states or of areas beyond the limits of national jurisdiction"*[23].

A second feature of differentiation is, can be referred to here as, the subject of scope. For instance the main focus in common heritage of mankind is related to the areas beyond national jurisdiction and its resources. In contrast, common concern has been focused in matters that are of 'concern' to humanity as a whole. These issues that cause awareness to the humanity are continuously increasing. At present some of those issues are climate change, species in danger and conservation of the biodiversity. But, if we do not stop threatening the environment, the matters of common concern will continue to escalate.

A third dissimilitude, *purported by a group of scholar (who are they?) I decided to call (group of scholars) the authors of the book where I found this interesting point of view like that, if you consider that that is wrong we can change it.* consists of, *"whereas common heritage regimes are concerned with equitable sharing of benefits, common concern regimes focuses on equitable sharing of the burden of cooperation and problem solving"*[24]. They also stated that this burden is summarized in the principle of common but differentiated responsibility.

In conclusion: one can say that the concept of common concern does not add anything to the notion of common heritage. In fact, these concepts are very different, and the former came as a solution to the disagreements between states, to choose the best system to protect and conserve the environment without generating a high interference in their own sovereignty or compromising states to the benefit sharing system established by the common heritage concept.

Although these concepts are different they can also be seen to be related. First, they were created with a similar objective, protection and preservation of the environment regarding a sustainable exploitation. Second, both concepts enjoy of an equitable shared system, one of benefits and the other of burden of cooperation. Thirdly, as common concern has a broader territorial scope and the matters of common concern are of relevance for whole international community it would be possible to say that the former cover some areas to the common heritage. There is for instance a common concern about the extinction of whales, mammals living in the high seas, which is part of the common heritage of mankind. In fact, common concern would be linked with all the global commons and even with resources located within national jurisdictions if those are at risk.

---

23 Convention on Biodiversity, Article 3.

24 Daniel Bodansky, Jutta Bronee and Ellen Hey. *The Oxford Handbook of International Environmental Law*. (Oxford University Press. 2007), 566.

VI Can the Concept of Common Concern Help in the Implementation of the International Environmental Law?

At present common concern of mankind does not imply any legal obligation further than international cooperation[25]. This concept is however still evolving as are its legal implications.

A controversial discussion surrounding the implications of common concern is still going on. On the one hand, we have one branch of academic opinion stating that common concern is a dilute concept; and on the other hand, there is the position of those who declared common concern as an open concept akin to *erga omnes*[26] obligations.

As mentioned above, common concern has been considered by some as a dilute[27] concept when compared with CHM, because it excludes any possibility of common proprietary recognising instead the national sovereignty over the resources located within states jurisdictions. For instance, the Convention on Biodiversity established that States have the sovereign right to exploit their own resources pursuant to their own environmental policies. It has been said that if an international agreement acknowledges state sovereignty over resources located within their jurisdiction, this would limit the interference of the international community in national environmental matters. Although those resources as well as those matters are of significance importance for the whole humanity. According to this group "*the greater the affirmation of sovereignty in a multilateral environmental agreement, the less legitimacy and authority the international regime has when time comes to enforce the stated environmental goals*"[28].

Some scholars do not agree with the above consideration, and instead believe that the concept in study legitimates the whole community to act in the preservation of resources, whereas resources located beyond or within national boundaries create

---

25 David Hunter, James Salzman, and Durwood Zaelke. *International Environmental Law and Policy*, 2nd ed. (Foundation Press. 2002), 398.

26 Erga omnes "obligations derivem for examplem in contemporary international law. from the outlawing acts of aggression, and of genocidem as also from the principles and rules concerning the basic rights of the human personm including protection from slavery and racial discrimination. Some of the corresponding rights of protection have entered into the body of international law; others are conferred by international instruments of a universal or quasiuniversal character" ,,, "The dictum in the Barcelona Traction case identifies two characteristics feature of obligations *erga omnes*. The first one is *Universality*, in the sense that obligations *erga omnes* are binding all States without exception. The second one is *solidarity,* in the sense that every State is deemed to have a legal interest in their protection. Of these two characteristics elements, the second one (solidarity) is linked with wider issues of enforcement and legal standing in international law", http://fds.oup.com/www.oup.co.uk/pdf/0-19-829870-6.pdf, "*The Appearance of the Concept of Obligations Erga Omnes on the Agenda: The Dictum of the International Court in the Barcelon Traction Case",*

27 Jason Schwartz. *"Whose Woods These are Think I know": How Kyoto May Change Who Controls Biodiversity.* (New York University Environmental Law Journal, 2006), Westlaw.

28 'Ibid'

tensions with the principle of state sovereignty. According to this position, prior to the negotiation of the Convention on Biodiversity, states had a clear opinion about their absolute discretion and control over the resources found within their borders. But the widespread awareness about the loss of biodiversity forced a large number of countries to work jointly to find ways for conservation based on the international cooperation. *"In this way, the conservation of biodiversity is no longer viewed as the providence solely of individual states"*[29].

In the same line, there is a tendency to state that the protection and conservation of the environment is a concern of humanity as a whole, thus having the same level of importance as human rights. This position declared common concern akin to *erga onmes* obligations.

A segment of the Draft to the Covenant on Environment and Development (1995)[30], made by the International Union for the Conservation of Nature and Natural Resources (IUCN), is a clear example of this tendency when it states:

The concept of 'common concern' is not new and has been applied in other fields. It forms the basis for international laws relating to human rights, humanitarian relief and international labour relations. Those obligations are now recognized as obligations erga omnes, owed by all States to the entire international community.

This type of obligation owed to all states can be identified as having two elements. The first one is the importance of the right involved, and therefore their observance by every state towards the international community as a whole. The second element is the absence of the reciprocity principle present in the vis-a vis obligations. Recently, the International Court of Justice (ICJ) in the *Gabcikovo-Nagymaros case* declared that *"safeguarding the earth's ecological balance has come to be considered an essential interest of all states, to protect the international community as a whole"*.[31] As this obligation contains the two elements, one could reach the conclusion that safeguarding the earth's ecological balance has the character of *erga omnes obligations.*

So what is an *erga omnes* obligation and what are their implications in the international legal ambit? Those are international norms that due to their importance have to be obeyed by states to the international community as a whole, rather than to individual states. The legal implication arising from the violation of these obligations is the possibility that nation states may choose to formulate a

[29] David Hunter, James Salzman, and Durwood Zaelke. *International Environmental Law and Policy*, 2nd ed. (Foundation Press. 2002), 397.

[30] David Hunter, James Salzman, and Durwood Zaelke. *International Environmental Law and Policy*, 2nd ed. (Foundation Press. 2002), 397.

[31] Alexander Kiss and Dinah Shelton. *International Environmental Law.* 2nd ed. (Transnational Publishers, Inc. 2000), 25.

complaint based on that violation, even if the complaining state has not been injured or been affected by the breach directly[32].

Due to the necessity of the protection and conservation of the world's environment for the whole humanity these general rules, should be equal to those humanitarian obligations and therefore considered as obligations *erga omnes*. As a result, states will be obliged not only by the principle of no harm to any other state, but also to the limit of no harm or degradation to the commons, such as common areas, common heritage, shared resources and matters of common concern. The damage caused to the global commons is therefore an injurious act against the international community[33]. If this theory is accepted the consequence would be that any state could complain for the violation of these rules, even if that state has not been *directly* injured. The reason for the right of standing to all countries is that the violation of *erga omnes* norms indirectly injures every state[34].

Moving forward, I would like to state that common concern of (hu)mankind is a general concept that can be involved or combined with all the other commons if those are threatened. To make it clear, according to its wording, "common concern of mankind" means all matters that are important for humanity, including present and future generations, or every issue that causes awareness for the survival of the human race or puts at risk the global commons. For instance public health, peace, climate change and the conservation of biodiversity have been considered common concern[35].

Common concern is a principle that is part of International Law and as such has been applied in the Environmental field. A good example of this transposition and its evolution from common heritage to common concern is now seen in the application of the Convention of Biodiversity in the specific topic of genetic material. A previous international agreement concerning genetic material, the International Undertaking of Plant Genetic resources, stated that it was "*based on the universally accepted principle that plant genetic resources are a heritage of mankind and consequently should be available without restriction*". Apparently the application of the Undertaking has impeded the protection of these resources by the sovereignty states where they are located. It has also failed in the protection of the plant intellectual property rights of the developed countries and securing the respective compensation for genetic resources of the less developed countries. As a

32 Patricia Birnie, and Alan Boyle, *International Law and the Environment*, 2nd ed. (Oxford Univ. Press, 2002), 99. See also David Hunter, James Salzman, and Durwood Zaelke. *International Environmental Law and Policy*, 2nd ed. (Foundation Press. 2002), 315.

33 Mark Allan Gray. *The International Crime of Ecocide*. in California Western International Law Journal Spring 1996, (California Western School of Law. 1996)

34 David Hunter, James Salzman, and Durwood Zaelke. *International Environmental Law and Policy*, 2nd ed. (Foundation Press. 2002), 315.

35 Christopher D. Ston. *Common but differentiated responsibilities in international law*. (American Journal of International Law April, 2004 by American Society of International Law)

result, the Convention on Biodiversity, trying to amend the error of the Undertaking affirmed the state sovereignty over the biological resources located within their jurisdiction, and also included the principle of common concern of mankind[36].

In fact, the convention states that each country has to take the appropriate measures to regulate biotechnological activities within their territory and to regulate the distribution of its benefits. This example shows how the evolution from one concept to another helps to protect the environment, keeping in mind the development of states.

On this basis, it can be see that that common concern of (hu)mankind is a more advanced principle introduced in the international environmental area than that of common heritage. It is also broader in scope since general concerns can arise within shared resources, common areas, and so on. It is important to clarify that at present common concern does not involve any specific obligations; but it comes along with some legal implications, such as:

- Supremacy of matters of common concern over the individual states interest as a result of its analogy with common interest.
- The character of *erga omnes* to the obligation of protection and conservation of the environment and subsequently the international standing to states in order to make effective the compliance of these obligations.
- Its application within national boundaries and beyond states jurisdiction in all matters of "common concern".
- The opportunity to open a new space, whereas by the establishment of an international environmental court or other means, to allow new actors to participate more actively in the international arena such as NGOs, citizens groups, or the community, since the arising issues are of the concern of humankind.

VI Conclusions

The concept of common concern was brought into the international environmental area as a solution to the disputes originated with the concept of common heritage of mankind. For some the main reason to choose this new concept, that recognized states sovereignty over the resources located within their boundaries, was due to its diluted repercussions. They underestimated common concern since its legal implications have not been clearly established yet.

What is clear is the international cooperation implicit in the concept as according to the capabilities of each country (equitable share of the burden of cooperation), as established by the principle of common but differentiated responsibility. The other

[36] Sara M. Dunn. *From Flav'r sav'r to Environmental saver? Biotechnology and the future of agriculture, international trade, and the environment.* (Colorado Journal of International Environmental Law and Policy, winter, 1998)

implications of the common concern have been stated by the teaching of the most qualified publicists. They mentioned as some of its main characteristics the prevalence of the common interest in the protection of the world's ecosystem in contrast to individual states interest; general standing of states due to the nature of its obligations as *erga omnes*; national and international territorial scope, and an open ended subjective scope, since every new "common concern" can be included in the existing list of matters that are vital for the whole humanity.

Pursuing standing before international environmental courts; for States, NGOs and group of citizens; may allow for the evaluation of new concepts and the opportunity to set up a more pro-active approach in protecting the environment.

[14]

CUSTODIAL SOVEREIGNTY: RECONCILING SOVEREIGNTY AND GLOBAL ENVIRONMENTAL CHALLENGES AMONGST THE VESTIGES OF COLONIALISM

by Werner Scholtz*

1. Introduction
2. The contribution of colonial sovereignty to the international law of inequality
3. Permanent sovereignty *versus* 'eco-imperialism'
4. What to do with sovereignty?
5. Reconciliation through the birth of custodial sovereignty
6. Conclusion

---

* BA *cum laude* LLB (PU for CHE), Dr. jur. (Leiden University), Professor at the Potchefstroom Campus of the North-West University, South Africa. This article was made possible through the generous funding of the *Alexander von Humboldt Stiftung*. I am grateful for the comments of Professor Erika de Wet on a previous draft of this article. Any errors or omissions remain the sole responsibility of the author.

1. INTRODUCTION

The sovereignty and equality of states constitute the basic constitutional doctrine of public international law.[1] The traditional notion of sovereignty is, however, viewed as an impediment to pursuing global solutions to ecological degradation.[2] This implies that the basic doctrine of public international law is challenged by increasing global environmental problems. Camilleri and Falk aptly illustrate the challenge to sovereignty as they opine:

> '[I]t becomes steadily clearer that the "sovereign state" as an institution is not adequately equipped to embody ecological principles. Its approach to the ecological dilemma is confounded by its institutional interests, instrumental role and domain of authority, which are at odds with ecological principles and global ethos required for planetary management. ... [I]t is the system of sovereign states as a whole that is emerging as poorly equipped to meet the challenge posed by mounting ecological disruption.'[3]

How should contemporary public international law respond to the challenges of a global world threatened by ecological deterioration? How could the doctrine of sovereignty rise to the occasion? These questions are the main concern of this article, which intents to formulate a response to these challenges. It is therefore the aim of this article to establish a theory of sovereignty, which is suitable for the challenges presented by a global world. The departure point is the notion of equality included in Article 2 of the Charter of the United Nations.[4] *De*

---

1. I. Brownlie, *Public International Law*, 7th edn. (Oxford, Oxford University Press 2008) p. 289. In general, three elements of sovereignty can be distinguished in contemporary public international law: international legal sovereignty, Westphalian or Vatellian sovereignty and domestic sovereignty. The first element implies that a judicially independent territorial entity has the right to conclude agreements. The second element is also known as the duty of non-intervention in relation to the exclusive jurisdiction of states. Domestic sovereignty refers to the institutions that govern a particular state. See S.D. Krasner, 'The Hole in the Whole: Sovereignty, Shared Sovereignty and International Law', 25 *Mich. JIL* (2003-2004) p. 1077. See also C. Schreuer, 'State Sovereignty and the Duty of States to Cooperate – Two Incompatible Notions (Summary and Comments)', in J. Delbrück, ed., *International Law of Cooperation and State Sovereignty: Proceedings of an International Symposium of the Kiel Walther-Schücking Institute of International Law, May 23-26 2001* (Berlin, Duncker & Humblot 2002) p. 163. In general, sovereignty means that a state is not subjected to the jurisdiction of any other state. The state is, however, subjected to international law, which implies that the latter also might restrict and regulate the exercise of the sovereignty of a state. See also N. Walker, 'Late Sovereignty in the European Union', in N. Walker, ed., *Sovereignty in Transition* (Oxford, Hart 2003) pp. 3-32 at p. 6. See H. Steinberger, 'Sovereignty', in R. Bernhardt, ed., *Encyclopaedia of Public International Law* (Amsterdam, North-Holland 1987) p. 500 at pp. 501-511 for a brief discussion of the historical roots of sovereignty.
2. See, for example: A. Johnson, 'International Environmental Law and State Sovereignty', 3 *Asia Pacific Journal of Environmental Law* (1998) pp. 269-283.
3. J.A. Camilleri and J. Falk, *The End of Sovereignty? The Politics of a Shrinking and Fragmenting World* (Aldershot, Edward Elgar 1992) p. 192.
4. The issue of inequality has not received much attention as a theoretical concept in international law. See B. Kingsbury, 'Sovereignty and Inequality', 9 *EJIL* (1998) p. 599.

jure sovereign equality is a recognized concept, but this form of equality is *de facto* fictional as extreme disparities exist, in particular between developing[5] and developed countries.[6] The unequal situation that exists in international law exhibits a link with colonialism and the usage of sovereignty to exclude 'uncivilized nations'.[7] As a critical Southern scholar I am obliged to take cognizance of the latter fact in order to develop a theory of sovereignty that addresses the realities of a world characterized by extreme inequality between states. The response of developing countries to the effects of exclusive sovereignty, through, *inter alia*, the affirmation of permanent sovereignty, is also important and I accordingly discuss the relevance of this notion in relation to the current problem. In the last part of this article a new approach to sovereignty, which I refer to as custodial sovereignty, will be developed as an answer to the questions raised in this discussion. I conclude the article with brief remarks.

2. THE CONTRIBUTION OF COLONIAL SOVEREIGNTY TO THE INTERNATIONAL LAW OF INEQUALITY

The philosophy of positivism dominated late nineteenth century international law.[8] A central feature of positivism was the distinction that it made between 'civilized' and 'uncivilized' states.[9] International law accordingly was limited to 'civilized nations' which resulted in the possibility to apply different standards to the different categories of people. 'Uncivilized nations' were, therefore, excluded from the claim to sovereignty and the needs of the 'civilized nations' prevailed.[10] The only way in which 'uncivilized nations' could become 'civilized' was to conform to European standards. Thus, the only way in which these nations could win recognition was through submission. The implication of this exclusive approach was that many states could not play an active role in

---

5. No single universal definition of 'developing countries' exists. It must be kept in mind that the developing countries do not constitute a homogeneous group, but consists of a heterogeneous group that adheres to certain criteria of underdevelopment. A low level of GDP mostly is an important indicator of the poor economic growth of developing countries. See M. Bulajić, *Principles of International Development Law: Progressive Development of the Principles of International Law Relating to the New International Economic Order*, 2nd edn. (Dordrecht, Martinus Nijhoff 1993) pp. 168 et seq.

6. See R. Anand, *International Environmental Justice: A North-South Dimension* (Aldershot, Ashgate 2004) pp. 3 et seq.

7. A. Anghie, 'Finding the Peripheries: Sovereignty and Colonialism in Nineteenth-Century International Law', 40 *Harv. ILJ* (1999) p. 22. See also ch. 2 of A. Anghie, *Imperialism, Sovereignty and the Making of International Law* (Cambridge, Cambridge University Press 2004). According to the Cocoyoc Declaration of 1974: 'Much of the world has not yet emerged from the historical consequences of five centuries of colonial control, which concentrated economic power so overwhelmingly in the hands of a small group of nations.'

8. Anghie 1999, *supra* n. 7, p. 10.

9. Ibid., p. 22.

10. Ibid., p. 25.

the development of international law and this resulted in the creation of rules of international law that served as the basis for the economic exploitation of non-European entities. Sovereignty was therefore used to entrench inequality in international law. Various developments, such as decolonization, have changed international law in the twentieth century, but it must be kept in mind that modern international law has inherited the framework of the nineteenth century.[11] Thus, although the racist and paternalistic references were obliterated from the vocabulary of international law, the framework has not been reformed significantly.[12] Anghie therefore remarks:

> '[T]he nineteenth century remains an integral part of contemporary international law. On a material level, the systems of economic and political inequality created by colonialism under the auspices of nineteenth-century international law continue to operate despite the ostensible change of legal regime.'[13]

After the Second World War sovereign equality was used to justify the formal equality of all peoples and, accordingly, decolonization.[14] The focus on equality was necessary to address the exclusive (colonial) sovereignty of the nineteenth century. Sovereign equality included in Article 2(1) of the UN Charter therefore introduced a new era in sovereignty thinking.[15] One may recall the wording of the Friendly Relations Declaration, which reads:

---

11. Treaties that were concluded with indigenous people by way of coercion still are legally binding. The *terra nullius* doctrine is reinterpreted, rather than dismissed altogether on the basis of its racist application. See for instance the application of the doctrine in *Western Sahara*, ICJ, Advisory Opinion, 16 October 1975. Anghie argues that a mere reformulation of offending terminology is not enough to rid international law from the negative effects of colonialism. Anghie 1999, *supra* n. 7, p. 76.

12. Art. 38(1)(c) refers to the 'general principles of law recognized by civilized nations'. The reference to 'civilized states' is, of course, not political correct and it seems that it is treated as non-existent. Cassese, for instance, discusses this source of international law under the heading of 'General principles of international law recognized by the community of nations, as a subsidiary source'. The community of nations of course consisted of Europe and the USA. Cassese recognizes this on p. 190. See A. Cassese, *International Law*, 2nd edn. (Oxford, Oxford University Press 2005) pp. 188 et seq.

13. See Schreuer, *supra* n. 1, p. 164; Anghie 1999, *supra* n. 7, p. 75.

14. See G. Simpson, *Great Powers and Outlaw States: Unequal Sovereigns in the International Legal Order* (Cambridge, Cambridge University Press 2004) pp. 26 et seq. According to Simpson sovereign equality entails three forms of equality. These are formal equality, legislative equality and existential equality.

15. Prior to 1945 the principle of equality was affirmed in the Peace of Westphalia of 1648, but this only applied to Christian states. After the Congress of Vienna (1814-1815), the 'Great Powers' dominated other European states. See B. Fassbender, 'Sovereignty and Constitutionalism in International Law', in Walker, ed., *supra* n. 1, p. 115 at p. 121. See also the discussion of the drafting history of the inclusion of 'sovereign equality' in the UN Charter. Fassbender, ibid., pp. 125 et seq.

> 'All States enjoy sovereign equality. They have equal rights and duties and are equal members of the international community, notwithstanding differences of an economic, social, political or other nature.'[16]

The principle of sovereign equality can, therefore, be understood primarily as securing the rights of states' equality before the law.[17] The equality of states before the law is, of course, not based on the material equality of nations, but relies on a fiction of equality.[18] The commitment to formal equality of all states is also seen as fictional as it is argued that the dependence of developing states on the superior developed states leads to a loss of legal independence as richer states may influence weaker states' actions through coercion.[19] In this regard Kingsbury notes that the commitment to formal equality has lead to various negative results and that the 'traditional sovereignty-based system of international law has proved to be a travesty, in which priorities of ... human welfare were subordinated to a ... commitment to ineffective structures'.[20]

---

16. The Declaration on Principles of International Law Concerning Friendly Relations and Co-operation Among States in accordance with the Charter of the United Nations, hereafter the Friendly Relations Declaration. See UN GA Res. 2625 (XXV) of 20 October 1970. The Declaration furthermore states that:

'In particular, sovereign equality includes the following elements:

(a) States are juridically equal;

(b) Each state enjoys the rights inherent in full sovereignty;

(c) Each state has the duty to respect the personality of other states;

(d) The territorial integrity and political independence of the state are inviolable;

(e) Each state has the right freely to choose and develop its political, social, economic and cultural systems;

(f) Each state has the duty to comply fully and in good faith with its international obligations and to live in peace with other states.'

17. See Fassbender, *supra* n. 15, p. 129. The permanent membership of the five members and the right of veto in terms of Art. 27(3) of the UN Charter is an exception to the sovereign equality of states in the UN. Other exceptions also exist, such as weighted voting in certain international organizations. These exceptions are, however, not constructed as contradicting the principle of sovereign equality as they have been voluntarily consented to. Steinberger, *supra* n. 1, p. 515. See also Simpson, *supra* n. 14, p. 48. See, however, T.M. Franck, *The Power of Legitimacy Among Nations* (Oxford, Oxford University Press 1990) p. 177.

18. See Simpson, *supra* n. 14, p. 39. Equality before the law refers to formal equality. See Simpson, ibid., pp. 42 et seq. Jackson, however, views sovereign equality and the one-nation, one-vote system as 'anti-democratic' in comparison to a system that takes into account factors such as population. J.H. Jackson, 'Sovereignty-Modern: A New Approach to an Outdated Concept', 97 *AJIL* (2003) p. 795.

19. S. Lee, 'A Puzzle of Sovereignty', 27 *California Western ILJ* (1997) p. 255. The problem is that legal positivists make a distinction between law and non-law which results in a situation where the inequalities in the international system become mere social facts and not legal facts. Kingsbury, *supra* n. 4, p. 609. See also Camilleri and Falk, *supra* n. 3, p. 186. Third World countries may be dependent on richer countries and do not always interact on the basis of equality with these states. This results in a situation where poor states may make poor choices that harm the environment. Camilleri and Falk cite the acceptance of toxic chemicals from developed countries as an example.

20. Kingsbury, *supra* n. 4, p. 616. Simpson is, however, of the opinion that '(t)he doctrine of sovereign equality ... is compatible with an array of tolerated social inequalities'. Simpson, *supra*

I am accordingly of the opinion that mere sovereign equality does not suffice in international law. It is therefore necessary to reconcile sovereign equality with the existing *de facto* inequalities that exist in the international order.[21] One of the steps in this regard is to ensure the articulation of sovereignty in a community of states that considers each other as equals.[22] This does not merely entail formal equality, but also some form of material equality which should restrain rich states from pursuing coercion as an option.

3. PERMANENT SOVEREIGNTY *VERSUS* 'ECO-IMPERIALISM'

Sovereignty not only served as an instrument directed against developing countries, but was also used by developing countries pursuant to their objectives. In this regard permanent sovereignty evolved during the decolonization process, which developing countries viewed as an important mechanism to overcome economic disparities and to increase well-being.[23] As such permanent sovereignty was seen to be able to correct the inequalities that existed between developing and developed countries. This concept initially was developed to curtail colonialist interference in the economic affairs of newly independent states and became a central issue in the debate concerning the authority of a host state to nationalize foreign companies exploiting their natural resources.[24] It occupied a central role in the calls made by developing countries for a New International Economic Order.[25] Permanent sovereignty can be defined as the

---

n. 14, p. 56. He is not 'concerned with the banal contrast between juridical equalities and material inequalities'. Simpson, ibid., p. 17.

21. This refers to material equality. This notion should, however, not be taken to the extreme whereby equality implies absolute equality. Material equality is necessary to ensure that all human beings are subjected to fair living conditions. I. Seidl-Hohenveldern, *International Economic Law* (The Hague, Kluwer Law International 2000) p. 21.

22. See J.L. Cohen, 'Whose Sovereignty? Empire *Versus* International Law', 18(3) *Ethics and International Affairs* (2004) p. 20.

23. F.X. Perrez, *Cooperative Sovereignty: From Independence to Interdependence in the Structure of International Environmental Law* (The Hague, Kluwer Law International 2000) p. 95.

24. See in this regard Bulajić, *supra* n. 5, pp. 82-84 and 262 et seq.

25. See the Declaration on the Establishment of a New International Economic Order (Res. 3201-S.VI of 1 May 1974) and the Charter of Economic Rights and Duties of States (Res. 3281-XXIX of 12 December 1974). Art. 2 of the latter resolution deals with permanent sovereignty as it states that '[e]very State has and shall freely exercise full permanent sovereignty, including possession, use and disposal, over all its wealth, natural resources and economic activities'. K. Hossain, 'General Principles, the Charter of Economic Rights and Duties of States, and the NIEO', in K. Hossain, ed., *Legal Aspects of the New International Economic Order* (London, Pinter 1980) p. 1 at pp. 2 et seq. See also the discussion in R.P. Anand, *Confrontation or Cooperation? International Law and the Developing Countries* (Dordrecht, Martinus Nijhoff 1987) pp. 103-128. The Declaration on the Progressive Development of the Principles of Public International Law Relating to a New International Economic Order, which was adopted during a plenary session of the ILA Conference on 30 August 1986, also referred to permanent sovereignty. Para. 5.1 affirms permanent sovereignty as a principle of international law, which emanates from the principle of

right of states to decide freely and independently on the use and exploitation of their natural resources.[26] Permanent sovereignty is viewed as a component of state sovereignty, which is the legal expression of the economic side of political sovereignty and as such refers to economic sovereignty.[27] Today the perception exists that (developing) states use permanent sovereignty as a mechanism to resist international demands for the protection of natural resources against over-exploitation.[28] Developing countries, however, resist the pressure of developed countries as they view the environmental initiatives of the developed world with scepticism and even accuse the developed countries of 'eco-imperialism'.[29] Developing countries fear that the global environmental agenda, which they

---

self-determination. Although various General Assembly resolutions were adopted in relation to the NIEO, these were never really implemented in full and the concept has become nearly obsolete.

26. It is important to recognize that permanent sovereignty is not absolute as it also has the same limitations as sovereignty. Permanent sovereignty, for instance, creates a duty to respect other states' sovereignty over their natural resources. This means that states should not use their natural resources to such an extent as to cause transboundary harm. Perrez, *supra* n. 23, pp. 69 et seq. No uniform agreement exists regarding the exact scope and content of the notion. See also K. Hossain and S.R. Chowdhury, eds., *Permanent Sovereignty over Natural Resources in International Law: Principle and Practice* (New York, St Martin's Press 1984) p. 1. Permanent sovereignty has been formulated and reflected in various resolutions in the General Assembly of the UN. The landmark resolution in this regard is Res. 1803 which affirms the right of states to permanent sovereignty over natural resources but, in addition, requires that permanent sovereignty has to be exercised in the interest of the people and subject to general international law. See UN GA Res. 1803 (XVII) of 14 December of 1962. Other resolutions are, *inter alia*: UN GA Res. 523 (VI) of 12 January 1952; UN GA Res. 626 (VII) of 21 December 1952 and UN GA Res. 2158 (XXI) of 25 November 1966. The Earth Charter of 2000 supports this idea as principle 2 states that 'with the right to own, manage and use natural resources, comes the duty to prevent environmental harm and to protect the rights of the people'. See also N. Schrijver, *Sovereignty over Natural Resources: Balancing Rights and Duties* (Cambridge, Cambridge University Press 1997) pp. 120 et seq. The legal status of permanent sovereignty is dubious. Chowdhury is of the opinion that permanent sovereignty has *jus cogens* status in international law. S.R. Chowdhury, 'Permanent Sovereignty and its Impact on Stabilization Clauses, Standards of Compensation and Patterns of Development Co-operation', in K. Hossain and S. R. Chowdhury, eds., *Permanent Sovereignty over Natural Resources in International Law: Law and Practice* (New York, St Martin's Press 1984) p. 1 at p. 38. It is, however, a view that is not shared by all scholars. See J. Makarczyk, *Principles of a New International Economic Order* (Dordrecht, Nijhoff 1988) p. 352.

27. Perrez, *supra* n. 23, p. 97. This is also not a viewpoint shared by all scholars as they perceive economic sovereignty only as a part of the struggle for economic independence. G. Brehme, *Souveränität der jungen Nationalstaaten über Naturreichtümer. Die ständige Souveränität über die natürlichen Reichtümer und Hilfsquellen (Völkerrechtliche Probleme des Kampfes der jungen Nationalstaaten um ökonomische Unabhängigkeit)* (Berlin, Staatsverlag der Deutschen Demokratischen Republik 1967) p. 8, fn. 9. Brehme acknowledges, however, that he has followed this approach in previous scholarly contributions.

28. Perrez, *supra* n. 23, p. 97.

29. This is of particular importance in relation to the North-South relationship in the WTO. The fears of developing countries that wealthy nations may use trade measures to prohibit the import of goods that are produced according to different environmental standards often are referred to as 'eco-imperialism'. See for instance J.H. Jackson, *The Jurisprudence of GATT and the WTO* (Cambridge, Cambridge University Press 2000) pp. 431 et seq.

perceive as an agenda of the North, may hamper their economic growth.[30] The fears of the developing countries cannot be perceived as mere delusions of paranoia. The international environmental agenda is dominated by the richer developed countries that are plagued by problems of affluence, whereas the developing countries need economic growth and are driven to seek solutions to problems of poverty.[31] The issue of 'eco-imperialism' is evident in the instance of the deforestation of tropical rainforests. The destruction of the Amazonian rainforest in Brazil serves as a particularly good example.[32] It must be borne in mind that deforestation accounts for the elimination of various species as well as the annual release of approximately six billion tons of carbon dioxide in the atmosphere. Thus, Brazil faces a 'catch-22' situation. It is under constant international pressure to repay its international debt as well as under domestic pressure to provide for a population which suffers from the consequences of poverty. Accordingly, deforestation takes place in order to expand industrial and agricultural activities into the rainforest. Developed countries, however, places a higher value on the environmental factors of forest management.[33] They are interested in the global advantages that these forests provide, such as climate stabilization. Some developed countries even consider these forests to be common resources shared by the planet. It is in this regard that developing countries use permanent sovereignty as a 'shield' against the interference of developed countries in order to curb 'eco-imperialism'.

The situation is, however, more complex than it seems. The fact that global environmental initiatives may further the agenda of the rich does not justify ignorance and/or inaction concerning the dire state of the environment. The rapid deterioration of the environment has become a threat to the survival of mankind. Concerted action of all states is required in order to overcome the current problems. Thus, pragmatism dictates that the developing world cannot focus merely on development without taking into account environmental interests. This may serve as an important reason for their participation in international agreements, which address environmental problems for which they do not share historical responsibility.[34] Thus, the developing countries have recognized that they cannot pursue development in the same manner as the developed

---

30. See J.G. Speth, 'International Environmental law: Can it Deal with the Big Issues?', 28 *Vermont L Rev.* (2004) p. 789.

31. A distinction can be made between environmentalism of the South and environmentalism of the North, which may be translated into a difference between 'environmental problems of poverty' and environmental problems deriving from the 'excess of affluence'. See J. Ntambirweki, 'The Developing Countries in the Evolution of an International Environmental Law', 14 *Hastings International and Comparative L Rev* (1990/91) p. 907.

32. See Camilleri and Falk, *supra* n. 3, pp. 193-194.

33. M. Sanwal, 'The Sustainable Development of All Forests', 1 *Review of European Community and International Environmental Law* (1992) p. 289.

34. The Montreal Protocol on Substances that Deplete the Ozone Layer of 1987 serves as a good example.

world.[35] Global environmental protection needs therefore challenge the structure of the international legal system which traditionally has concerned itself with the national interests of state entities. In this regard Bowman remarks:

> '[I]t has become common to observe that the natural environment knows no political boundaries and that the traditional regime of resource exploitation, grounded primarily in the notion of national territorial sovereignty, requires to be replaced by more overtly collectivist approaches.'[36]

The perplexing question that arises is whether sovereignty can respond to the global environmental challenges.

4. WHAT TO DO WITH SOVEREIGNTY?

The ambiguous[37] notion of sovereignty has been the source of much debate in international law and it is neither viable nor necessary to present a detailed discussion in this regard. Sovereignty has been branded a 'mistake' and 'illegitimate offspring'.[38] In the context of globalization, sovereignty is attacked by the thesis that a decentred cosmopolitan world order[39] has emerged which renders

35. Para. 1.4 of the Founex Report reads: 'The developing countries would clearly wish to avoid, as far as is feasible, the mistakes and distortions that have characterized the patterns of development of the industrialized societies.'

36. M. Bowman, 'The Nature, Development and Philosophical Foundations of the Biodiversity Concept in International Law', in M. Bowman and C. Redgewell, eds., *International Law and the Conservation of Biological Diversity* (The Hague, Kluwer Law International 1996) p. 5 at p. 15. Beyerlin is of the opinion that '*[s]taatliche Souveränität und internationale Zusammenarbeit stehen zumal dann in einem Spannungsverhältnis, wenn es um wichtige Gemeinschaftsinteressen geht, die sich nur befriedigen lassen, wenn einzelne Staaten ... ihre eigenen nationalen Interessen hintanstellen*'. U. Beyerlin 'Staatliche Souveränität und internationale Umweltschutzkooperation: Gedanken Zur Entwicklung des Umweltvölkerrechts', in U. Beyerlin, et al., eds., *Recht zwischen Umbruch und Bewahrung. Festschrift für Rudolf Bernhardt* (Berlin, Springer 1995) p. 937. See also K. Odendahl, *Die Umweltpflichtigkeit der Souveränität: Reichweite und Schranken territorialer Souveränitätsrechte über die Umwelt und die Notwendigkeit eines veränderten Verständnisses staatlicher Souveränität* (Berlin, Duncker & Humblot 1998) pp. 96 et seq.

37. Schreuer is of the opinion that sovereignty is 'ubiquitous' and 'elusive'. See Schreuer, *supra* n. 1, p. 163.

38. L. Henkin, 'That "S" Word: Sovereignty, and Globalization, and Human Rights, Et Cetera', 68 *Fordham L Rev.* (1999/2000) pp. 1 and 2.

39. See in this regard: A-M. Slaughter, *A New World Order* (Princeton, NJ, Princeton University Press 2004). Cohen delivers a worthwhile examination of this thesis in order to redeem the discourse on sovereignty in international law. Cohen, *supra* n. 22, pp. 1-24. Cohen rightly rejects this thesis from a normative as well as empirical perspective. Cohen, ibid., pp. 11 et seq. Schrijver also finds that sovereignty is far from irrelevant. N. Schrijver, 'The Changing Nature of State Sovereignty', 70 *BYIL* (1999) pp. 65 and 83. See also A. van Staden and H. Vollaard, 'The Erosion of State Sovereignty: Towards a Post-territorial World?', in G. Kreijen, ed., *State, Sovereignty, and International Governance* (Oxford, Oxford University Press 2002) p. 165 at p. 182; and

the discourse of sovereignty and the role of states irrelevant.[40] I, however, do not bemoan the erosion or demise of sovereignty.[41] I also don't view sovereignty as irrelevant for this discussion. Alternatives to the current international legal system which may lead to a post-sovereignty international law are very ambitious, but the necessary resources do not exist to sustain this.[42] In the aspirational phase of these theories they may even serve as a justification for interventionist actions in other states, such as, for example, the intervention by states to curtail deforestation in developing countries.[43] A new liberal global order also needs a management system in order to address existing inequalities, which does not exist at present. The aspirational phase of these theories accordingly may be used to justify measures that answer to the interests of more powerful states.[44] In accordance with the above discussion, it is not my intent to depart from the notion of sovereignty. It is my point of departure to investigate in which manner sovereignty may be strengthened through international law in order to promote an effective international legal system, which also affirms a shift towards material equality.

Accordingly I am of the view that it is rather necessary to strengthen and develop international law in such a way that sovereignty protects the interests of all peoples.[45] It is possible for sovereignty to adapt to the needs of our current world as it is a dynamic concept of international law. This is illustrated by the fact that the UN Charter introduced a new version of sovereignty that replaced the exclusive form of Westphalian sovereignty.[46] In this regard sovereignty has been revised in order to present a new regime of sovereignty. This presupposes continuity in the sense that the end of one sovereignty regime can be replaced

---

M.R. Fowler and J.M. Bunck, *Law, Power, and the Sovereign State* (University Park, PA, Pennsylvania State University Press 1995).

40. See in this regard Walker, *supra* n. 1, pp. 6 et seq.

41. Lee, *supra* n. 19, pp. 261-263.

42. Kingsbury, *supra* n. 4, p. 624.

43. Cohen, *supra* n. 22, p. 14. Jackson warns against this as it may result in a situation where sovereignty is replaced by 'pure power'. Jackson, *supra* n. 18, p. 801.

44. Cohen, *supra* n. 22, p. 13. The acceptance of a decentred cosmopolitan world order may introduce an imperial project. The USA is extremely hostile towards the UN as well as international law and is the sole superpower of the world with unprecedented military power which it sees fit to invoke in order to enforce human rights and democracy. See M. Hardt and A. Negri, *Empire* (Cambridge, Mass., Harvard University Press 2001) pp. xii, xiv. See also Anghie 2004, *supra* n. 7, p. 279.

45. This statement is in accordance with the idea that sovereignty implies that states have a responsibility to protect their own citizens from avoidable catastrophe, but that when they are unwilling or unable to do so, that responsibility must be borne by the broader community of states. See the Report of the International Commission on Intervention and State Sovereignty (ICISS, 'The Responsibility to Protect' (2001), available at <www.iciss.ca/pdf/Commission-Report.pdf>).

46. It must be borne in mind that Westphalian sovereignty only related to European states. See, however, Simpson, *supra* n. 14, p. 12.

by another.[47] The point of departure in relation to the process of continuity is that sovereignty should not be used as an excuse to frustrate international cooperation on environmental issues. This means that states rather should find ways to cooperate in order to solve environmental problems that originate or occur in the jurisdictions of other states. This assumption affirms the view that sovereignty does not provide states with absolute power.[48] Thus, we should see in 'sovereignty not obstacles, ... but responsibilities and opportunities to secure human values'.[49]

5. RECONCILIATION THROUGH THE BIRTH OF CUSTODIAL SOVEREIGNTY

How should international law develop sovereignty in order to empower states to respond to global environmental needs? It is important to remember that the biosphere does not respect sovereignty as devised by mankind. I have indicated already that it is not necessary to abandon sovereignty, but to ensure that it is strengthened and adapted to the current problems of the international community. What is needed is some form of permanent sovereignty in order to ensure that developing states can have the freedom to choose sustainable development and protect their environment from, for instance, toxic dumping by developed countries. On the other hand, it is clear that cooperation is required and that a communal effort is of vital importance to promote global ecological security.[50] A collective approach is of particular importance to assist developing countries to pursue sustainable development in order to promote economic growth and combat poverty without mismanaging the environment. Developing countries

47. According to Walker, 'we may answer the charge of actual or anticipated redundancy by suggesting that the dynamic of transformation within late sovereignty will involve the continuous evolution rather than the demise of sovereignty'. Walker, *supra* n. 1, p. 28. Jackson also opines that traditional sovereignty concepts should evolve rather than disband the notion of sovereignty. See Jackson, *supra* n. 18, p. 801. Schrijver views sovereignty as a dynamic concept which 'can have a different meaning in different historical periods although certain essential characteristics remain'. Schrijver, *supra* n. 39, p. 70. Van Staden and Vollaard opine that sovereignty has undergone change and that at present it entails duties and obligations towards the subjects of a state, other states and other bodies. Van Staden and Vollaard, *supra* n. 39, p. 182.

48. Sovereignty is absolute, but not power. See Lee, *supra* n. 19, pp. 242 et seq. See also in this regard Steinberger, *supra* n. 1, p. 518 which states: 'The problem of "absoluteness" of sovereignty is ultimately a problem of the source of the validity of international law.' Jackson in this regard states: 'The old "Westphalian" concept in the context of a nation-state's "right" to monopolize certain exercises of power ... has been discredited in many ways.' Jackson, *supra* n. 18, p. 801. See also Schrijver, *supra* n. 39, p. 71.

49. Henkin, *supra* n. 38.

50. See P. Mische, 'National Sovereignty and Environmental Law', in S. Bilderbeek, ed., *Biodiversity and International Law: The Effectiveness of International Environmental Law* (Amsterdam, IOS Press 1992) pp. 105-114.

are facing various obstacles, such as foreign debt.[51] What is needed, accordingly, is to reconcile the concept of sovereignty with the need for a global approach to the problems of an environmental nature. This approach needs to take cognizance of the dynamics of the North-South relationship.[52]

The reconciliation of sovereignty and the global cooperative approach to environmental problems is, for instance, resembled in the Convention on Biological Diversity of 1992 (CBD). The notion of 'common concern' included in the Preamble of the CBD implies a common responsibility of the international community in relation to the important issue of the management of the global environment in a sustainable fashion. This does not, however, negate the importance of (permanent) sovereignty as Article 3 of the CBD replicates principle 21 of the Stockholm Declaration, which affirms the rights of states to exploit their own natural resources. Furthermore, Article 15 of the CBD refers to the sovereign rights of states over their natural resources as the basis of the authority to determine access to genetic resources.[53] Articles 3 and 15 are reminiscent of the notion of the permanent sovereignty of states over their natural resources. The Preamble of the United Nations Framework Convention on Climate Change of 1992 (UNFCCC) also reaffirms the sovereignty of states and in addition recalls the sovereign right of states to exploit their own resources.

It is interesting to consider to what extent the emphasis on state sovereignty could be balanced against the notion of common concern, as sovereignty is not absolute and the common concern notion further moulds the notion of sovereignty. The inclusion of the notion of common concern in the CBD and the UNFCCC must be understood in the context of the evolution which permanent sovereignty has undergone in recent years. A modern understanding of sovereignty must acknowledge the importance of co-operation and interdependence in accordance with global reality and should not focus on the fiction of absolute independence.[54]

---

51. T. Johnston, 'The Role of Intergenerational Equity in a Sustainable Future: The Continuing Problem of Third World Debt and Development', 6 *Buffalo Environmental Law Journal* (1998/99) pp. 36-83. Johnston discusses factors that are responsible for the inequitable relationship between the North and South and convincingly argues that third world debt plays a major role in this regard.

52. See K. Mickelson, 'South, North, International Environmental Law and International Environmental Lawyers', 11 *Yearbook of International Environmental Law* (2000) pp. 52-81; Ntambirweki, *supra* n. 31, pp. 905-928; U. Beyerlin, 'Bridging the North-South Divide in International Environmental Law', 66 *Zeitschrift für ausländisches und öffentliches Recht und Völkerrecht* (2006) pp. 259-296.

53. The CBD is the first international instrument which expressly affirms the sovereign rights of states over their genetic resources. The Preamble of the UNFCCC also affirms the notion of sovereignty of states.

54. The focus is on the positive obligations. However, this statement does not imply that states have no independence. States still must be able to invoke sovereignty where another, for instance, attempts to exploit its natural resources.

Although the exact meaning and status of common concern of mankind (CCM) is not clear in international law, it is not to say that it does not have any implications for states.[55] It is the common interests of states, which refers to the survival of humankind[56] that results in the birth of the CCM in relation to, for instance, biodiversity and the atmosphere. The notion of common concern indicates that the global environment is the responsibility and interest of all states. No state may, therefore, take actions autonomously that may be detrimental to the global environment. It is not wholly unthinkable that certain issues that are of common concern may evolve into obligations *erga omnes*.[57] The Hague Recommendations furthermore suggests that the designation of the global

---

55. F. Biermann, '"Common Concern of Humankind": The Emergence of a New Concept of International Environmental Law', 34 *Archiv Des Völkerrechts* (1996) p. 431. See also A.S. Timoshenko, 'Responses to Environmental Challenges: UNEP Experience', in N.M. Al-Nauimi and R. Meese, eds., *International Legal Issues Arising under the United Nations Decade of International Law* (The Hague, Nijhoff 1995) pp. 169-170.

56. According to Brunnée, 'common interest' is a generic term. In some instances 'common interest' may result in an international law rule that entails certain duties. In these instances '(w)e are faced with the phenomenon of a common interest so compelling that it alone formulates the rule and coincides with the rule's content'. It is only in these cases that it is correct to use the term CCM. This means that CCM is a facet of 'common interest'. 'Common interest' therefore serves as a driving force in the development of rules. 'Common interest' is the product of the coinciding individual state interests, which implies that it is characterized by egocentric (anthropocentric) rather than altruistic features. J. Brunnée, '"Common Interest" – Echoes from an Empty Shell? Some Thoughts on Common Interest and International Environmental Law', 37 *Zeitschrift für ausländisches und öffentliches Recht und Völkerrecht* (1989) pp. 791-808. Some scholars, however, argue that the issue is not if the Earth as such will survive. In terms of the Gaia theory the Earth will adapt and take care of itself. The question is rather whether humans can survive the changes that the Earth effects in response to the actions of humans. See Mische, *supra* n. 50, p. 106. We are, therefore, not necessarily 'killing the world', but changing it and thereby 'killing' its inhabitants.

57. See the *Case concerning the Barcelona Traction, Light and Power Company Limited* (Second Phase), ICJ, 5 February 1970. See B.H. Oxman, 'The International Commons, the International Public Interest and New Modes of International Lawmaking', in J. Delbrück, ed., *New Trends in International Lawmaking – International 'Legislation' in the Public Interest: Proceedings of an International Symposium of the Kiel Walther-Schücking-Institute of International Law, March 6 to 8, 1996* (Berlin, Duncker & Humblot 1997) pp. 21-60. See further: M. Ragazzi, *The Concept of International Obligations Erga Omnes* (Oxford, Clarendon Press 1997) and C.J. Tams, *Enforcing Obligations Erga Omnes in International Law* (Cambridge, Cambridge University Press 2005). I think that it is, of course, questionable whether *erga omnes* obligations would give rise to adjudication by the ICJ concerning international environmental matters as states are reluctant to be subjected to the jurisdiction of the court. This is, however, a matter which I do not intent to discuss in this article. See P.W. Birnie and A.E. Boyle, *International Law and the Environment* (Oxford, Oxford University Press 2002) pp. 220-233 for a general overview of international environmental adjudication. The Report of the International Law Commission acknowledges the need to establish a more detailed definition of the meaning of an obligation *erga omnes* concerning the high seas, outer space and ozone layer. Report of the International Law Commission on the work of its forty-third session, 29 April-19 July 1991, Official Records of the General Assembly, Forty-sixth session, Supplement No. 10, p. 118, available at <www.un.org/law/ilc/index.htm> (25 September 2007).

environment as a CCM may be that the 'costs should be shared equitably among states, taking into account historic responsibilities and present technical and financial capabilities'.[58] This implies that all states have a common interest and, accordingly, common responsibilities in order to address global environmental problems. The contributions of the various states, however, need to differ in the light of their culpabilities and capabilities in relation to the problem at hand.

It is important in this regard to take note of the arguments of Glennon. According to Glennon, a global environmental resource is described as a 'natural resource located within the territory of one country, but broadly enjoyed and arguably needed, by the world community as a whole'.[59] A global environmental right arises in relation to a global environmental resource which creates the expectation that the resource will be protected by all states. States therefore are likened to trustees. A breach of this obligation by a state constitutes an injury to all the other states since the obligation is owed to the whole community. Glennon furthermore states that a global environmental obligation exists which refers to the duty of states 'to share in preserving global environmental resources'.[60] He makes a distinction between custodial obligations (the obligations of the location state to preserve the resources) and support obligations (the duty of other states to contribute to the custodial obligations of states *via*, for instance, financial support).[61] The financial support either could be of a multilateral nature through the establishment of international funds or unilaterally through 'debt-swap' or 'debt through nature'-agreements whereby lenders to developing countries forego all or a portion of a debt repayment in return for the implementation of environmental protective measures by the developing country.

I am, however, of the opinion that one should introduce the notion of 'custodial sovereignty' in relation to 'global environmental resources' as this notion reflects the progressive development that sovereignty and permanent sovereignty has undergone in relation to international environmental law in recent years.[62] Custodial sovereignty accordingly implies that a state is the custodian of

58. Para. 3 of The Hague Recommendations on International Environmental Law, Peace Palace, The Hague of 16 Augustus 1991. In Bilderbeek, ed., *supra* n. 50, pp. 194-202.

59. M.J. Glennon, 'Has International Law Failed the Elephant?', 84 *AJIL* (1990) p. 34.

60. Ibid., p. 35.

61. Financial assistance pertaining to the elephant issue refers to the compensation for forgoing the sale of ivory of elephant, which die naturally and the confiscation of ivory as well as costs of the measures of conservation.

62. I previously have coined the term in relation to the issue of elephant culling but have not expanded on the theoretical premises of this notion in international law as the previous article for the most part dealt with the application of the notion in relation to the *casus* of elephant culling. See W. Scholtz, 'Animal Culling: a Sustainable Approach or Anthropocentric Atrocity: Issues of Biodiversity and Custodial Sovereignty?', 2 *Macquarie Journal of International and Comparative Environmental Law* (2005) pp. 9-30. Other authors have also developed theories concerning the role of sovereignty and the threat to the global environment. See A.D. Tarlock, 'Exclusive Sovereignty *versus* Sustainable Development of a Shared Resource: The Dilemma of Latin American

its global environmental resources and that other states have an expectation that the relevant state will protect these resources for the whole of mankind. Other states are burdened with the duty to support the custodial state to fulfil its obligations. The custodial state is still entitled to exploit its resources in accordance with its (permanent) sovereignty, but the latter is restricted by the expectation interests of other states. The sovereignty of the custodial state further enables it to deter unwanted interference by other states regarding its resources and presents it with the opportunity to pursue sustainable development. Underlying the notion of custodial sovereignty is two fundamental elements. The first element concerns the common (global) responsibility of all states for the protection of global environmental resources. The second element concerns the differentiated responsibilities of states' contribution to the protection of these resources. Custodial sovereignty entails the implementation of differential treatment in relation to developing countries.[63] Thus, elements of custodial sovereignty are encapsulated best by the principle of common but differentiated responsibilities (CBDR).[64] The CBDR principle is therefore of great importance

---

Rainforest Management', 32 *Texas ILJ* (1997) pp. 37-66. See furthermore: P. Birnie, 'The Role of International Law in Solving Certain Environmental Conflicts', in J.E. Carroll, ed., *International Environmental Diplomacy: The Management and Resolution of Transfrontier Environmental Problems* (Cambridge, Cambridge University Press 1990) p. 95 at p. 104. She accordingly proposes that sovereignty should be replaced by the concept of 'planetary citizenship'. Another suggestion is that of 'decentralized planetary sovereignty' which means the acceptance of functional sovereignty instead of territorial sovereignty. This idea makes provision for the internationalization of resources on the basis of the common heritage of mankind (CHM). International organizations have a very important role to play in this regard. See J. Tinbergen, *Reshaping the International Order: A Report to the Club of Rome* (London, Hutchinson 1977) para. 5.8. Another interesting approach to the management of global environmental resources is the application of the 'public trust' doctrine. See P.H. Sand, 'Sovereignty Bounded: Public Trusteeship for Common Pool Resources?', 4 *Global Environmental Politics* (2004) pp. 47-71. See also: T. Gebel, *Der Treuhandgedanke und die Bewahrung der biologischen Vielfalt. Einschränkung der territorialen Souveränität durch treuhänderische Verwaltung von lebenden Umweltressourcen?* (Sinzheim, Pro Universitate Verlag 1998) and V.P. Nanda and W.K. Ris, Jr., 'The Public Trust Doctrine: A Viable Approach to International Environmental Protection', 5 *Ecology Law Quarterly* (1975/76) pp. 292-319. It is not possible to discuss the differences between my suggestion and the above. The main difference is, however, that 'custodial sovereignty' is found on the acknowledgement of the colonial history of international law as well as the inequality that exists between states.

63. Cullet defines differential treatment 'as the instances where the principle of sovereign equality is sidelined to accommodate extraneous factors, such as divergences in levels of economic development or unequal capacities to tackle a given problem'. P. Cullet, 'Differential Treatment in International Law: Towards a New Paradigm of Inter-state Relations', 10 *EJIL* (1999) p. 551. See furthermore: L. Rajamani, *Differential Treatment in International Environmental Law* (Oxford, Oxford University Press 2006) and D. French, 'Developing States and International Environmental Law: The Importance of Differentiated Responsibilities', 49 *ICLQ* (2000) p. 46.

64. See M-C. Cordonier Segger, et al., 'Prospects for Principles of International Sustainable Development Law after the WSSD: Common but Differentiated Responsibilities, Precaution and Participation', 12 *RECIEL* (2003) p. 54 at p. 56. The New Delhi Principles recognizes the CBDR principle as one of the seven leading law principles of sustainable development law. This principle has been included in various treaties.

for the notion of custodial sovereignty.[65] In this regard, measures relating to financial and technology transfer are very important.[66] The Global Environmental Facility (GEF) has a particularly important role to play in order to address the global environmental problems of common interest.[67] The GEF is the primary mechanism that must facilitate the flow of financial resources.

In terms of the notion of custodial sovereignty, common concern exists in relation to global environmental resources.[68] But what exactly are global environmental resources? I think it is wise to amend the definition of Glennon. In my opinion, a global environmental resource is a *renewable* natural resource of which a part or the whole of the resource is located in the territory of a state, but which is needed and enjoyed by the whole of mankind.[69] The mismanagement

---

65. I have dissected the CBDR principle in a forthcoming article in order to gain an understanding of the role of this principle in relation to custodial sovereignty.

66. It is not my intent to provide a detailed analysis of this issue. Rather, I shall present examples and briefly reflect on this issue. See L. Gündling, 'Compliance Assistance in International Environmental Law: Capacity-Building Through Financial and Technology Transfer', 56 *Zeitschrift für ausländisches und öffentliches Recht und Völkerrecht* (1996) pp. 796-809. His discussion on the difficulties relating to technical and financial assistance is of particular importance. See F. Biermann, *Financing Environmental Policies in the South: An Analysis of the Multilateral Ozone Fund and the Concept of 'Full Incremental Costs'* (Berlin, WZB 1996). See also: UNEP, *Handbook for the International Treaties Protecting the Ozone Layer* (Nairobi, UNEP 2003). Various international treaties contain provisions pertaining to financial and technical assistance. Art. 10 of the Montreal Protocol establishes a Multilateral Fund which makes provision for financial and technical assistance, including the transfer of technologies, to developing countries. The UNFCCC also contains numerous provisions concerning the transfer of finances and technology. Arts. 4(3)-(5) provide for the assistance of developing countries in the fulfilment of their obligations through financial resources, the transfer of technology and know-how. Art. 16 of the CBD reads that 'transfer of technology ... to developing countries shall be provided and/or facilitated under fair and most favourable terms, including on concessional and preferential terms'. Under Art. 18(2) technical and scientific cooperation, in particular with developing parties, shall be promoted. Art. 19 deals with the handling of biotechnology and distribution of its benefits and also makes mention of developing countries. Arts. 20, 21 and 39 of the CBD deal with the transfer of financial resources. Art. 39 designates the GEF as the interim institutional structure for the period between the entry into force of the CBD and the first meeting of the Conference of the Parties. In terms of Decision I/2 of the Conference of Parties, the GEF shall remain the institutional structure to operate the financial mechanism.

67. See S.A. Silard, 'The Global Environment Facility: A New Development in International Law and Organization', 28 *George Washington Journal of International Law and Economics* (1995) pp. 607-654. Other funds may also be of importance in this regard. See B.B. Röben and V. Röben, 'Institutional Aspects of Financing Sustainable Development After the Johannesburg Summit of 2002', 63 *Zeitschrift für ausländisches und öffentliches Recht und Völkerrecht* (2003) pp. 517-520.

68. I borrow the term 'global environmental resources' from Glennon. See Glennon, *supra* n. 59, pp. 1-43.

69. This means that fossil fuels are excluded from this definition. Incorporating fossil fuels in this definition will be met by fierce resistance from oil producing countries and may serve as the basis for further interventionist policies by developed countries. It must be borne in mind that non-renewable resources also can become depleted if they are used in an unsustainable manner. See J.M. Conrad, *Resource Economics* (Cambridge, Cambridge University Press 1999) p. 1.

of global environmental resources may give rise to a common interest that these resources should be managed in a more sustainable manner. I am of the opinion that biological sources fit the definition of a global environmental resource.[70] The more difficult question is whether the global atmosphere my also be classified as such.[71] The classification of the atmosphere is more difficult. A distinction needs to be made between the atmosphere and the airspace of a state. The airspace above a state's land and sea territory forms part of the exclusive sovereignty of the state.[72] The atmosphere refers to the layer of air above the territory of a state. The rights and duties concerning the atmosphere must therefore be separated from the sovereignty over the airspace of a state. The status of the atmosphere is not clear as it is a distinct category in international law. It is not the same as airspace as the latter refers merely to a spatial dimension whereas the atmosphere consists of a fluctuating and dynamic air mass.[73] It can also not be classified as part of the global commons as it may overlap with territorial sovereignty.[74] The possibility to utilize the concept of 'shared resources' in order to define the rights and duties of states concerning the atmosphere is not appropriate as the notion of 'shared resources' is more relevant in

70. Biological resources are the tangible biotic components of ecosystems. Art. 2 of the CBD states that biological resources 'include genetic resources, organisms or parts thereof, populations, or any other biotic component of ecosystems with actual or potential use or value for humanity'. Examples of biological resources are real entities, such as maize, elephants, elephant tusks or fish. In contrast, biodiversity is not the sum of ecosystems, species and genetic material, but rather the variability within and among them. Biodiversity is an attribute to life. L. Glowka, et al., *A Guide to the Convention on Biological Diversity* (Gland, IUCN, the World Conservation Union 1994) p. 15.

71. I have considered if one should not declare the components of the biosphere in the broadest geophysical sense as global environmental resources. This, then, would include the global ecological system integrating all living beings and their relationships, including their interaction with the elements of the lithosphere (rocks), hydrosphere (water) and atmosphere (air). This is, however, stretching things too far as this merely means that 'everything' is a global environmental resource.

72. F. Biermann, *Saving the Atmosphere: International Law, Developing Countries and Air Pollution* (Frankfurt-on-Main, Lang 1995) p. 5.

73. The sovereignty over territorial airspace is not unrestricted as it is limited in height and extends to the point where the airspace meets space itself. The Outer Space Treaty of 1967 (Treaty on Principles Governing the Activities of States in the Exploration and Use of Outer Space, including the Moon and Other Celestial Bodies) does not establish a precise boundary between airspace and outer space. The Moon Treaty of 1979 (Agreement Governing the Activities of States on the Moon and Other Celestial Bodies), which has recalled the latter, also does not clearly define this issue. See P. Sands, *Principles of International Environmental Law* (Cambridge, Cambridge University Press 2003) p. 14.

74. Vogler, however, treats it as part of the global commons. J. Vogler, *The Global Commons: A Regime Analysis* (Chichester, Wiley & Sons 1995) pp. 2 et seq. This also seems to be the approach that the International Law Commission favours. See Report of the International Law Commission, *supra* n. 57, p. 118. The problem further is illustrated by the Vienna Convention for the Protection of the Ozone Layer of 1985. Art. 1(1) defines the ozone layer as 'the layer of atmospheric ozone above the planetary boundary layer'. It is difficult to apply the notions of sovereignty or shared resources in this regard.

situations of bilateral or regional transboundary pollution.[75] I am therefore of the opinion that the global atmosphere also constitutes a global environmental resource as it is a *renewable*[76] natural resource of which a part or the whole of the resource is located in the territory of a state, but which is needed and enjoyed by the whole of mankind.

6. CONCLUSION

The doctrine of sovereignty is not obsolete. It still functions as the basic constitutional doctrine of public international law and accordingly as a point of departure for this discussion. Sovereignty is a dynamic concept, which needs to answer to the challenges of the international community. The notion must be moulded and shaped in order to reflect the needs of the international community. Sovereignty, and especially permanent sovereignty, is still of importance in international law. Developing countries need sovereignty in order to ensure their development and to be able to withstand the coercion of developed countries that wish to pursue their own agendas under the disguise of worthy causes, such as the protection of the environment. Furthermore, various alternatives to the traditional international legal system may serve as a basis for hegemony and domination of certain developing countries. This does, however, not mean that developing states may do with their environmental resources as they please. The threat of environmental destruction is a threat that is faced by the whole of mankind. The traditional notion of sovereignty, and more specifically permanent sovereignty, does not reflect the reality of the biosphere as an organism which is oblivious to borders created by man. The earth functions as a single organism and the destruction of, for instance, biological resources in one state will have an impact on the biosphere and, accordingly, mankind as such. Mankind has a common interest in the protection of the global environment as this will safeguard the survival of all humans. All states therefore have a common concern regarding the protection of the global environment.

What does the above-mentioned mean, therefore, in relation to the notion of sovereignty? Sovereignty needs to undergo changes in order to address past (and current) injustices. I have also pointed out that sovereignty must answer to the needs of the international community, which is the common concern of states concerning the protection of the global environment. The fusion of the above-mentioned notions leads me to a notion which I refer to as 'custodial sovereignty'. Custodial sovereignty dictates the importance of the implementation of provisions relating to the transfer of technology and financial resources. It embodies indirectly the acceptance of the responsibility of developed

75. See in this regard Biermann, *supra* n. 72, pp. 9-10.

76. I think that one indeed may view the atmosphere as a natural renewable resource as it consists of, *inter alia*, 20.95 per cent oxygen, which is listed as a renewable resource.

countries for past pollution without overemphasizing the issue of reparations for wrongful conduct, which developed countries have resisted. The more cumbersome obligations of the developed world are especially focused on the common interest of all states, which is the survival of mankind. This means that the transfer of technology and finances in order to assist the developing world to meet their environmental obligations is not mere charity, but an investment in the future of developed countries. Thus, developing countries may be in favour of custodial sovereignty as it satisfies their call for equity and assists them to pursue development that is sustainable. This implies that they can provide at least basic living standards for their current and future citizens. The acceptance of custodial sovereignty therefore entails responsibilities for both developed and developing countries as the governments of developing countries must facilitate usage of the financial resources for the intended purpose.[77] Custodial sovereignty adheres to the idea that sovereignty endows states with responsibilities as this form of sovereignty not only provide states with rights to exploit natural resources and deter unwarranted interference, but focuses on the obligations of states to ensure the protection of global environmental resources in a cooperative fashion for all mankind.

Further, the inclusion of differential treatment provisions in important international environmental treaties may serve as evidence of the acceptance of the main tenets of custodial sovereignty. This implies that the theory of custodial sovereignty doesn't impose a radical alteration of accepted public international law, but rather describes a current trend and explains the theoretical tenets thereof.

In summary, the notion of custodial sovereignty takes cognizance of the colonial history of sovereignty as it acknowledges the lack of material equality between states and affirms differential treatment. It furthermore acknowledges the importance of sovereignty to enable developing states to pursue development and counter eco-imperialism. The recognition of this form of sovereignty, however, displays pragmatic realism as it responds to the need to address global environmental threats. It is accordingly not false to say that custodial sovereignty represents the sustainable development side of modern sovereignty.

---

77. See in this regard K. Ginther, E. Denters and P.J.I.M. de Waart, *Sustainable Development and Good Governance* (Dordrecht, Nijhoff 1995).

Part VI
Cultural Heritage

[15]

BEYOND STATE SOVEREIGNTY: THE PROTECTION OF CULTURAL HERITAGE AS A SHARED INTEREST OF HUMANITY

*Francesco Francioni**

Introduction

It is a great pleasure for me to take part in this symposium marking the twenty-fifth anniversary of the Michigan Journal of International Law. During these years, the journal has contributed to the development of the science of international law and, with the Michigan Law School, has played a distinct role in promoting trans-Atlantic dialogue between the United State and Europe. Judging from the participants, this symposium is another manifestation of this on-going dialogue.

The general topic on which we are called to make contributions concerns diversity and fragmentation of the international legal order. This is certainly an important and timely theme since international law is becoming ever more complex both at a normative level, with an increasing variety of specialized branches of law, and at the institutional level, with the proliferation of courts and tribunals, agencies and organizations posing the problem of overlapping competences and possible conflicts of jurisdiction. The specific topic I am proposing to address in this presentation concerns culture and the way in which its products and processes—what I call cultural heritage—have stimulated the emergence of new norms and new actors in international law. Culture represents a manifestation of diversity among the States that compose the international community. At the same time culture is also an element of diversity within the State. To the extent that culturally distinct groups exist within a State, the enjoyment of their own culture contributes to the pluralism of national societies and to the articulation of the State in a multiplicity of social actors that often seek international recognition if

* Professor of International Law and Human Rights, European University Institute, Firenze, and University of Siena.

not a true international legal status. Such new actors include ethnically distinct communities, minorities, indigenous peoples, non-governmental organisations (NGOs) and religious groups to mention just a few examples. With the removal or at least the reduction of governmental barriers to the free flow of cultural communication and exchange between different States, the international role of these non-state actors has increased. Hence, the problem arises, as indicated in the title of this symposium, whether the emergence of these different voices onto the international plane is likely to increase diversity or cause cacophony, which is a different word for saying disharmony, discord, or even anarchy. This is a much debated subject today, and legal literature, including some contributions in this symposium, has abundantly covered the implications of the emergence of private actors, such as individuals, NGOs and transnational corporations, as participants in the law making process, tenants of rights and as potential addresses of international obligations. The role of these non-state actors has been analysed both in terms of contributions that they may bring toward a more democratic governance of human society,[1] but also in terms of increased risks that a culturally oriented deconstruction of the general category of citizenship may pose for the unity of the State and the orderly management of international relations.

In this paper I will try to explore the topic from a different perspective: i.e. the emergence of cultural heritage as part of the shared interest of humanity, with the consequent need for international law to safeguard it in its material and living manifestations, including the cultural communities that create, perform and maintain it. Culture in itself is not extraneous to the formation of the modern nation State. Especially in the history of nineteenth century Europe, culture as language, religion, literary and artistic traditions provided the cement and the legitimizing element to support the claim to independent statehood. In the second part of the twentieth century it provided the political foundation for the right of self-determination of peoples striving to form their independent State. This history has also influenced the language of international law where the link between individuals and the State has been identified in terms of nationality rather than citizenship. However, in the contemporary world the case of a State totally coinciding with a culturally homogeneous nation is the exception rather than the rule. Today, within most States there is co-existence of different cultures, traditions, minorities. In some States these cultural differences are filtered and distilled into a higher idea of a common polity, attracting a superior allegiance from the people. In others, diversity is maintained through a constitutional equilibrium of

1. *See* Ernst-Ulrich Petersmann, *Theories of Justice, Human Rights and the Constitution of International Markets*, 37 Loy. L.A. L. Rev. 407 (2003).

power-sharing (as in Switzerland) or through the integration of diversity into a true multicultural society founded on constitutional guarantees of fundamental freedoms and human rights (as in the United States). In other cases, culture can become the source of intolerance, claims for separation, and sometimes for violent oppression and ethnic conflict.

International law has not remained indifferent to this dynamic of culture within the State and between the States. Protection of minorities, as addressed in post World War I peace treaties and *ad hoc* treaties, has helped deconstruct the sovereign State by legitimizing the claim to an international status of culturally distinct groups.[2] Universal human rights law has confirmed this status with Article 27 of the Covenant on Civil and Political Rights,[3] and has provided the foundation for the gradual building up of a movement toward the recognition of a distinct and enhanced status of indigenous peoples.[4] At the same time, international law has played a constructive role in furnishing the intellectual basis to models of supranational integration (as in Europe) which build upon a common core of traditions, democracy, human rights, the rule of law, and economic freedoms. From this common core of cultural values a proto-federal structure transcending the nation State and a new transnational constitution[5] is currently developing.

2. *See, e.g.*, Treaty between the United States, the British Empire, France, Italy, Japan, and Poland, signed in Versailles, June 28, 1919 (so-called Polish Minorities Treaty), *available at* http://www.austlii.edu.au/au/other/dfat/treaties/1920/12.html, which sets the pattern for all of the other post-World War I treaties on minorities, including e.g.; Paris Treaty between the Principal Allied and Associated Powers and Romania, Dec. 9, 1919 (so-called Romanian Minorities Treaty), *available at* http://www.austlii.edu.au/au/other/dfat/treaties/1920/13.html; Sèvres Treaty between the Principal Allied and Associated Powers, and Greece, concerning Thrace, Aug. 10, 1920, *available at* http://www.lib.byu.edu/~rdh/wwi/versa/sevres1.html. In recent times, the movement for the recognition of the rights of culturally distinct groups has led to the adoption of relevant international legal instruments, both of binding character (*see*, Convention Concerning Indigenous and Tribal Peoples in Independent Countries, International Labor Organization Convention No. 169, 72 ILO Official Bull. 59 (1989), entered into force Sept. 5, 1991, *available at* http://www1.umn.edu/humanrts/instree/r1citp.htm) and non-binding character (*see, e.g.*, the United Nations Declaration on the Rights of Persons Belonging to National or Ethnic, Religious and Linguistic Minorities, G.A. Res. 47/135, U.N. GAOR, 47th Sess., Agenda Item 97(b), U.N. Doc. A/RES/47/135 (1993)).

3. Article 27 of the International Covenant on Civil and Political Rights states that: "[i]n those States in which ethnic, religious or linguistic minorities exist, persons belonging to such minorities shall not be denied the right, in community with the other members of their group, to enjoy their own culture, to profess and practise their own religion, or to use their own language." International Covenant on Civil and Political Rights, Dec. 16, 1966, 999 U.N.T.S. 171, 179, 6 I.L.M. 368, 375-76.

4. This movement has especially led to the adoption of the Convention Concerning Indigenous and Tribal Peoples in Independent Countries, *supra* note 2.

5. The term "transnational constitution" in relation to the evolving system of community law was used by an eminent member of the Michigan Law School Faculty, Professor Eric Stein, in his seminal article; Eric Stein, *Lawyers, Judges, and the Making of a Transnational Constitution*, 75 AM. J. INT'L L. 1 (1981).

Given this very broad and complex background, an examination of the manifold manifestations in which culture creates an international entitlement for human groups (non-state actors) would occupy much more space and time than what I am allowed. So, I will concentrate my analysis on the more technical aspects of the way in which international law has articulated the relevance of cultural heritage in normative terms. I will identify three separate facets of such articulation: 1) the protection of cultural heritage and cultural groups as part of the protection of human rights; 2) the emergence of the concept of individual criminal responsibility for cultural crimes; 3) the emerging notion of "cultural diversity" as a general interest for whose protection the international community "as a whole" must mobilize.

I. Cultural Heritage and Human Rights

The UN Charter does not contain specific clauses connecting culture to human rights. In 1948 the UN General Assembly rejected the notion of "cultural genocide."[6] Yet, the development of international law since then provides evidence that the protection of human rights, now part of positive international law, extends to culture and cultural heritage of peoples.

First, the concept of human dignity, which informs the human rights provisions of the Charter and of the Universal Declaration (" . . . recognition of the inherent dignity and of the equal and inalienable rights of all members of the human family . . . ")[7] includes peoples entitlement to the respect of the cultural heritage that forms an integral part of their identity, history and civilization. Destruction or desecration of symbolic objects and sites that are essential to the enactment of a people's culture (be it a library, a place of worship, a sacred site for indigenous peoples) is a violation of their collective dignity no less than a violation of their personal dignity.

Second, Article 22 of the Universal Declaration states that everyone " . . . is entitled to realization . . . of . . . cultural rights indispensable for his dignity."[8] Article 18 guarantees the right to freedom of conscience and religion which is an integral part of one's culture.[9] Article 27 pro-

6. *See* U.N. GAOR, 6th Comm., 83d mtg., U.N. Doc. A/C.6/SR.83 (1948). *See also Background Paper Genocide*, ST/DPI/ SER.A/68 (Nov. 1951).

7. Universal Declaration of Human Rights, G.A. Res. 217A, U.N. GAOR, 3rd Sess., Pt. I, Resolutions, at 71, at pmbl., U.N. Doc. A/810 (1948).

8. *Id.* at art. 22.

9. *Id.* at art. 18 (stating that "[e]veryone has the right to freedom of thought, conscience and religion; this right includes freedom to change his religion or belief, and freedom,

claims the " . . . right freely to participate in the cultural life of the community . . . " and " . . . to enjoy the arts and to share in scientific advancement and its benefits."[10] These rights have been confirmed by Article 15 of the International Covenant on Economic, Social and Cultural Rights.[11] Article 27 of the International Covenant on Civil and Political Rights has been interpreted by the Human Rights Committee in a way to ensure special entitlement to minorities and indigenous peoples to have access to natural resources.[12] It goes without saying that these provisions create not only a negative obligation not to interfere with cultural freedoms, but also a positive obligation to take steps to protect cultural groups and communities in their exercise of such freedoms and, in particular, to protect cultural and religious property which provide the indispensable situs for the practice of such freedoms. Destruction of mosques and libraries in Bosnia, and subsequent destruction of Orthodox churches in Kosovo after NATO "liberation," stand as dramatic evidence of the linkage between human rights and cultural heritage. This linkage was well identified and stressed by the Special Rapporteur of the Commission on Human Rights in his report on the situation of human rights in Yugoslavia.[13]

Third, the exponential growth of international cultural property law in the past fifty years bears witness to the emergence of a new principle according to which parts of cultural heritage of international relevance are to be protected as the common heritage of humanity. This principle is valid both in the event of armed conflict and in peacetime. During armed conflict, the 1954 Hague Convention,[14] now ratified by 109

---

either alone or in community with others and in public or private, to manifest his religion or belief in teaching, practice, worship and observance.")

10. *Id.* at art. 27.

11. International Covenant on Economic, Social and Cultural Rights, Dec. 16, 1966, 993 U.N.T.S. 3. Article 15(1)(a) states that "[t]he State Parties to the present Covenant recognize the right of everyone: to take part in cultural life. . . ."

12. *See* Lubicon Lake Band v. Canada, Communication No. 167/1984 (Mar. 26 1990), *available at* http://www1.umn.edu/humanrts/undocs/session45/167-1984.htm.

13. See the Report on the situation of human rights in former Yugoslavia prepared by T. Mazowiecki pursuant to Commission resolution 1992/S-1 of Aug. 14, 1992, where he writes:

> [a]lthough the conflict in Bosnia and Herzegovina is not regarded as a religious one, it has been characterized by the systematic destruction and profanation of mosques, Catholic churches and other places of worship, as well as other sites of cultural heritage. This has been reported to be the case particularly in areas currently or previously under the control of Serb forces . . . Some Orthodox churches have been destroyed in areas of central Bosnia and Herzegovina which were or are under the control of the Government and/or Croat forces.

U.N. Doc. E/CN.4/1993/50, Feb. 10 1993, para. 106.

14. *See* Convention on the Protection of Cultural Property in the Event of Armed Conflict, Aug. 7, 1956, 249 U.N.T.S. 240 [hereinafter Hague Convention].

States[15] and *de facto* applied by many non-parties as expression of general principles of international law,[16] recognizes that "... damage to cultural property belonging to any people whatsoever means damage to the cultural heritage of all mankind, since each people makes its contribution to the culture of the world."[17] In peacetime, the 1972 World Heritage Convention, whose parties are now numbering 172, confirms the same principle with respect to cultural and natural heritage as an outstanding universal value and requires that the "State Parties to this Convention recognize that such heritage constitutes a world heritage for whose protection it is the duty of the international community as a whole to co-operate."[18]

Fourth, the relevance of this treaty practice for the present discussion is further proven by the fact that cultural rights of individuals, groups and of humanity as a whole are guaranteed not only in inter-state relations, as in the case of international conflicts, but also in relation to purely domestic situations where the issue of the protection of cultural heritage arises within the territory of the State. The destruction in 2001 of the great Buddhas of Bamyian, as part of the Taliban's delirium of cultural cleansing, attracted protests and condemnation by States, including Islamic States, the UN, UNESCO, the EU, and other international organizations.[19] The mobilization of shame against such act has led to the adoption by the UNESCO General Conference in October, 2003 of the Declaration on Intentional Destruction of Cultural Heritage, which is intended to prevent the repetition of such acts in the future.[20]

15. The updated list of State parties is available at http://erc.unesco.org/cp/convention.asp?KO=13637&language=E.

16. The United States, whose ratification has been pending in the Senate for the past ten years, has applied the Hague principles in its military manuals. The Operational Law Handbook treats the Hague rules as norms of customary law and the international section of the legal office of the department of defence systematically trains military personnel on the respect for cultural property, on the prohibition of their use for hostile purposes, on the interpretation of military necessity and prior warning in case of unavoidable use of force.

17. Hague Convention, *supra* note 14, at pmbl.

18. Convention for the Protection of the World Cultural and Natural Heritage, Nov. 16, 1975, art. 6, para. 1, 1037 U.N.T.S. 151.

19. See the practice cited in Roger O'Keefe, *World Cultural Heritage: Obligations to the International Community as a Whole?*, 53 INT'L & COMP. LQ. 189, 195–202 (2004).

20. *See* UNESCO Declaration Concerning the Intentional Destruction of Cultural Heritage, UNESCO General Cong., 32d Sess. (adopted by consensus Oct. 17 2003). On the destruction of the Buddhas of Bamiyan, see Francesco Francioni & Federico Lenzerini, *The Destruction of the Buddhas of Bamiyan and International Law,* 14 EUR. J. INT'L. L. 619 (2003) (this article was part of a larger study commissioned by UNESCO to Professor Francioni with the view of defining the legal framework for the adoption of the above Declaration). For a reductionist and State oriented view of international law on the subject, see O'Keefe, *supra* note 19, who recognizes that wanton destruction of cultural heritage of great importance may not be shielded by domestic jurisdiction but, contradictorily, fails to recognize that such

II. CULTURE AND INTERNATIONAL RESPONSIBILITY

While it is clear that today the violation of international standards on the protection of cultural heritage of any people may attract State responsibility,[21] it is especially with regard to individual criminal responsibility that one can find the most significant developments in contemporary practice. At the time of this writing, *Prosecutor v. Strugar*[22] is pending before the International Criminal Tribunal for Yugoslavia (ICTY). This legal action is based on an indictment that charged the defendant with violations of the laws and customs of war and in particular with "unjustified devastation, unlawful attacks on civilian objects, destruction or wilful damage to institutions dedicated to religion, charity and education, the arts and sciences, historic monuments and works of art and science."[23] This case is especially interesting because it concerns the bombing of the old city of Dubrovnik, a site inscribed in the UNESCO World Heritage List, which makes it of indisputable universal relevance for humanity as a whole. Strugar, in his capacity as commander of the Yugoslavian army, was responsible for the bombing of the city of Dubrovnik. He was indicted for intentional destruction of cultural property of great interest for humanity as a whole.

In March, 2004, the ICTY enacted its judgment on another case regarding the shelling of the old town of Dubrovnik perpetrated in 1991, holding that "the crime of destruction or wilful damage done to institutions dedicated to religion, charity, education, and the arts and sciences, and to historic monuments and works of art and science . . .

---

destruction may constitute an international wrongful act just because of the general interest of the international community in preventing such discriminatory and arbitrary destruction.

21. The principle of State responsibility for intentional destruction of cultural heritage of importance to humanity is included in paragraph VI of the UNESCO Declaration Concerning the Intentional Destruction of Cultural Heritage, *supra* note 20, which reads: "[a] State that intentionally destroys or intentionally fails to take appropriate measures to prohibit, prevent, stop, and punish any intentional destruction of cultural heritage of great importance for humanity, whether or not it is inscribed on a list maintained by UNESCO or another international organization, bears the responsibility for such destruction, to the extent provided for by international law." International responsibility for violations of the rules on the protection of cultural heritage has also been spelled out in Article 38 of the Second Protocol to the Hague Convention for the Protection of Cultural Property in the Event Of Armed Conflict, Mar. 26, 1999, *available at* http://www.unesco.org/culture/laws/hague/html_eng/protocol2.shtml (hereinafter Second Protocol) which includes "the duty to provide reparation." Article 31 of the Second Protocol provides also that the Parties undertake to act, jointly through the Committee (the treaty body established to oversee the implementation of the Protocol), or individually, in cooperation with UNESCO and the United Nations, and in conformity with the Charter of the United Nations. *See id.* at art. 31. Thus, Article 31 implies the possibility of enforcing State responsibility through sanctions.

22. Prosecutor v. Strugar, ICTY Case No. IT-01-42-PT (ICTY Judgment, third amended indictment filed Dec. 10, 2003).

23. *See id.* at Counts 4–6.

represents a violation of values especially protected by the international community."[24] The ICTY added that such crime, being perpetrated against a site protected by the World Heritage List on behalf of humankind as a whole, "is . . . of even greater seriousness" since it was directed "on an especially protected site . . ."[25]

But what is the legal basis for affirming the responsibility of the individual for cultural crimes? Since 1954 the principle that serious violations of norms relating to the protection of cultural heritage may entail international criminal liability has been recognized in various international instruments. The 1954 Hague Convention recognizes this principle at Article 28.[26] The 1977 Protocol I additional to the Geneva Convention contains a specific provision extending the obligation to suppress grave breaches of the 1949 Geneva Convention to acts of "extensive destruction" of cultural property to which special protection has been accorded within the framework of a competent international organization.[27] The Statute of the International Criminal Tribunal for Yugoslavia has expanded the scope of individual criminal liability for cultural crimes by including such crimes in the category of violations of the laws and customs of war.[28] Similarly, the 1998 Rome Statute of the International Criminal Court includes attacks on cultural heritage in the category of war crimes.[29]

The most advanced and detailed provisions on individual criminal liability for serious violations of international norms on the protection of cultural heritage are to be found in the 1999 Protocol additional to the

---

24. Prosecutor v. Jokić, Judgments Int'l Trib. for the Prosecution of Persons Responsible for Serious Violations of Int'l Humanitarian Law Committed in the Territory of the Former Yugoslavia since 1991, Case No. IT-01-42/1-S, at para. 46 (Mar. 18, 2004).

25. *Id.* at para. 53.

26. *See* Hague Convention, *supra* note 14, art. 28 (stating that "[t]he High Contracting Parties undertake to take, within the framework of their ordinary criminal jurisdiction, all necessary steps to prosecute and impose penal or disciplinary sanctions upon those persons, of whatever nationality, who commit or order to be committed a breach of the present Convention)."

27. *See* Protocol Additional to the Geneva Conventions of 12 August 1949, and Relating to the Protection of Victims of International Armed Conflicts (Protocol I), June 8, 1977, art. 85, para. 4(d), 1125 U.N.T.S. 3 (hereinafter Protocol I). *See also, id.* at art. 53 (prohibiting attacks, military use of, as well as reprisals against, cultural heritage).

28. Statute for the International Criminal Tribunal for the Former Yugoslavia, *as amended* May 19, 2003 by Resolution 1481, *available at* http://www.un.org/icty/legaldoc/index.htm (hereinafter ICTY Statute). Article 3(d) provides that violations of the laws and customs of war shall include "seizure of, destruction or wilful damage done to institutions dedicated to religion, charity and education, the arts and sciences, historic monuments and works of art and science." *Id.* at art. 3(d).

29. The Rome Statute of the International Criminal Court, *circulated as document* July 17, 1998, art. 8(2)(b)(ix)(applicable to international armed conflicts) and art. 8(2)(e)(iv) (applicable to armed conflicts not of an international character), *available at* http://www.icc-cpi.int/library/basicdocuments/rome_statute(e).pdf.

1954 Hague Convention.[30] This protocol was negotiated and adopted in order to reinforce the rather weak system of the Hague Convention in the face of the devastation brought upon cultural heritage in the conflicts of the 1980s and 1990s, especially the Iraq-Iran war and the Balkan conflict.[31] This protocol applies in its entirety to international and non-international armed conflicts and it is entering into force just at the time of this symposium.[32] Chapter 4 of the Protocol introduces the principle of universal jurisdiction over the most "serious violations" of the norms protecting cultural heritage.[33] Article 17 obliges the party in whose territory the offender is present to prosecute or extradite that person regardless of his or her nationality or of the place where the offence was committed.

The link between the international protection of cultural heritage and individual criminal responsibility has not remained confined to its mere enunciation in conventional and statutory provisions in international instruments. It has been increasingly articulated and fleshed out in the case law of international courts and tribunals, especially of the ICTY. Besides the case of *Prosecutor v. Jokić*,[34] where cultural crimes have been recognized as independent counts of criminal liability under the laws and customs of war, several precedents can be identified which elaborate a typology of connections between cultural heritage and individual criminal responsibility. Thus, the act of destruction of cultural property with discriminatory intent toward a culturally distinct group, besides being capable of autonomously falling under the rubric of war crimes, has been considered to be an element of crimes against humanity, specifically of the crime of persecution within the meaning of Article 5(h) of the ICTY Statute. This principle has been applied in the 2001 decision of *Prosecutor v. Kordic & Cerkez*. Addressing the acts of deliberate destruction of ancient mosques in Bosnia Herzegovina, the ICTY held that:

30. *See* Second Protocol, *supra* note 21.

31. *See* Patrick J. Boylan, Review of the Convention for the Protection of Cultural Property in the Event of Armed Conflict, http://unesdoc.unesco.org/Images/0010/001001/100159eo.pdf (1993).

32. Article 43 states that the protocol "shall enter into force three months after twenty instruments of ratification, acceptance, approval or accession have been deposited." Second Protocol, *supra* note 21, art. 43. The twentieth instrument of ratification or accession was deposited (by Costa Rica) on Dec. 9, 2003, thus the Protocol entered into force on Mar. 9 2004. The States parties are at present 24. *See supra* note 21, http://erc.unesco.org/cp/ convention.asp?KO=15207&language=E.

33. Under article 15, these include the attack upon internationally protected cultural property, the use of such property in support of military action, and the extensive destruction or appropriation of cultural property. *Supra* note 21, art. 15.

34. Jokić, *supra* note 24, at para. 53.

> ... when perpetrated with the requisite discriminatory intent, [the destruction] amounts to an attack on the very religious identity of the people. As such it manifests a nearly pure expression of the notion of 'crimes against humanity' for all of humanity is indeed injured by the destruction of a unique religious culture and its concomitant cultural objects.[35]

This decision is notable also for its recognition that acts of destruction or wilful damage to cultural property dedicated to religion has been "... criminalized under customary international law."[36] In an earlier decision, in the *Blaskic* case,[37] the threshold of persecution set by the Tribunal in relation to acts of wilful destruction of cultural heritage was set quite high: the acts must be re-iterated or systematic and must reveal a pattern of gross violations. Thus not every single act of destruction of cultural heritage, even of wanton destruction, amounts to the crime of persecution.

Another important aspect of the intersection between cultural heritage and individual criminal responsibility is the finding by the Trial Chamber of the ICTY that deliberate destruction of cultural heritage of a given ethnic group may constitute evidence of the element of *mens rea* required for the commission of the crime of genocide.[38] This places new emphasis on the social existence of a group, as opposed to its purely biological existence, with the consequences that the systematic destruction of symbolic places and buildings of their culture and religion may reveal, under appropriate circumstances, the specific intent to destroy in whole or in part such group within the meaning of genocide under the 1948 Convention.[39]

---

35. Prosecutor v. Kordic & Cerkez, ICTY Case No. IT-95-14/2-T, (ICTY Judgment, Feb. 26, 2001) at para. 207, *available at* http://www.un.org/icty/kordic/trialc/judgement/kor-tj010226e.pdf.

36. *Id.* at para. 206.

37. Prosecutor v. Blaskic, ICTY Case No. IT-95-14-T, (ICTY TC Judgment, Mar. 3, 2000), *available at* http://www.un.org/icty/blaskic/trialc1/judgements (concerning *inter alia* acts of destruction of cultural property by Croatian leaders).

38. Prosecutor v. Krstic, ICTY Case No. IT-98-33-T, (ICTY TC Judgment, Aug. 2, 2001), *available at* http://www.un.org/icty/krstic/TrialC1/judgement/krs-tj010802e.pdf. This judgment concerned the massacres committed by military and paramilitary forces of the Serbs of Bosnia in the city of Srebrenica. The appellate chamber has confirmed the unprecedented finding that such massacres amounted to genocide in Prosecutor v. Krstic, ICTY Case No. IT-98-33-4 (ICTY Appeals, Apr. 19 2004), *available at* http://www.un.org/icty/krstic/Appeal/judgement/krs-aj040419e.pdf.

39. *See id.* at para. 579 (citing Dec. 12, 2000 decision of the BundesVerfassungsgerichthof (the German Federal Constitutional Court) that the definition of the crime of genocide "defends a supra-individual object of legal protection ... and extends beyond the physical and biological extermination)."

Of course, the limit of this jurisprudence, and of the international norms thereby applied, is that it concerns situations of armed conflict where protection of cultural heritage is somehow becoming part and parcel of humanitarian law and the international protection is a consequence of the fundamental distinction between military and non-military objectives. However, at least with regard to gross violations of the international obligation to respect cultural heritage—such as the intentional destruction of monuments of universal importance—it seems that an *opinio juris* as to their unlawful character also in peace time is emerging. This is witnessed by the world-wide condemnation of the acts of destruction by the Taliban of the great Buddha of Bamyam in 2001.[40] It is confirmed by the resolve manifested within the UN and UNESCO to clarify that international law does not tolerate such acts of barbarity, a resolve that has led to the unanimous adoption in 2003 of the UNESCO Declaration Concerning Intentional Destruction of Cultural Heritage. This declaration is an instrument of soft law.[41] It is not a binding treaty. Yet, the fact that it represents the legal follow-up to a specific act of cultural devastation, together with the nature of the declaration as the product of the will of the international community as a whole—because the whole world is represented in the UNESCO General Conference–[42] makes such instrument a particularly relevant indicator of the sense of obligation that wilful destruction of cultural heritage, whether in armed conflict or in peacetime, may entail State responsibility and individual criminal liability.[43]

In addition to the practice developed in the ICTY and UNESCO, the linkage between protection of cultural heritage and international responsibility for violations of fundamental rights of individuals and groups has influenced the case law of specific human rights courts. In a 1999 decision in the case of *Islamic Community of Bosnia v. Rep. Srpska,* the Human Rights Chamber for Bosnia referred to Article 9 of the European Convention on Human Rights to support its conclusion that freedom of religion in

40. *See supra* text accompanying note 21.

41. On the relevance of soft law in contemporary international law, see Francesco Francioni, *International 'Soft Law': A Contemporary Assessment,* in FIFTY YEARS OF THE INTERNATIONAL COURT OF JUSTICE 167 (Lowe &Fitzmaurice eds., 1996); *see also* P.M. Dupuy, *Soft Law and the International Law of the Environment,* 12 MICH. J. INT'L L. 420 (1991).

42. The universal character of the General Conference at the time of the adoption of this Declaration is all the more evident by the re-joining of the United States to the Organization. Today, the only country that appears to be absent from UNESCO is Singapore.

43. *See supra* note 19, at paras. VI, VII.

a given community cannot be achieved unless peaceful enjoyment of the places and buildings dedicated to worship is guaranteed to the people.[44]

III. International Law and Cultural Diversity

The developments analyzed in the preceding sections show that, under appropriate circumstances, cultural heritage in the territory of any State may be considered an element of the general interest of the international community, and, as such, it must be protected even against the wishes of the territorial State. This new form of protection entails that, today, States are bound to tolerate scrutiny and intervention, especially by competent international organizations, when they wilfully engage in, or intentionally fail to prevent, the destruction of, or serious damage to, cultural heritage of significant value for humanity. While this conclusion leaves open the question of what is the threshold of the "value" of the item of cultural heritage in order for it to reach the level of common concern for humanity, it is clear that the increasing number of lists, registers and inventories established and maintained by competent international organizations, notably UNESCO,[45] are capable of providing objective parameters of evaluation and a *prima facie* certification of the international significance of a given item of cultural heritage. In this sense, culture as the common patrimony of humankind becomes an important tool to counterbalance sovereignty, understood as the complete and undisturbed dominion over a territorial space, and to foreclose the objection of "domestic jurisdiction" so often invoked to preserve the power monopoly of the sovereign State.[46]

44. *See* The Islamic Community in Bosnia and Herzegovina v. The Republika Srpska, Case No. CH/96/29, Human Rights Chamber for Bosnia and Herzegovina, 38 ILM 534 (1999).

45. There are now at least three different instruments aimed at cataloguing cultural heritage of exceptional importance: the World Heritage List, under the 1972 World Heritage Convention, which now contains 754 cultural items, *available at* http://whc.unesco.org/heritage.htm; the register under the special protection regime of the 1954 Hague Convention, now updated with the new list for "enhanced protection" under the 1999 Protocol to the Convention, Second Protocol, *supra* note 21 art. 11; and, finally, the Representative List of the Intangible Cultural Heritage of Humanity and the List of Intangible Cultural Heritage in Need of Urgent Safeguarding provided for by, respectively, articles 16 and 17 of the Convention for the Safeguarding of Intangible Cultural Heritage, Oct. 17, 2003, art. 16-7, *available at* http://www.unesco.org.

46. U.N. Charter art. 2, para. 7 (stating that "[n]othing contained in the present Charter shall authorize the United Nations to intervene in matters which are essentially within the domestic jurisdiction of any state or shall require the Members to submit such matters to settlement under the present Charter; but this principle shall not prejudice the application of enforcement measures under Chapter VII."

But the impact of the international concern with cultural heritage goes beyond the territorial dimension of sovereignty. As we have shown in the preceding sections, cultural heritage is linked to the human element. It represents the symbolic continuity of a society beyond its contingent biological existence. Thus, the obligation to respect cultural heritage is closely linked with the obligation to respect human rights and to sanction its most serious breaches with individual criminal liability under international law.

The recognition of this human dimension of cultural heritage raises the problem whether international law should shift from a protection of cultural heritage as the purely material products of the creativity of a given people or group to the more ambitious goal of safeguarding the very social structures and processes that permit the generation and transmission of such products. This brings us to the subject of cultural diversity as a value to be safeguarded in itself and beyond the value of the single cultural object.

As is known, contemporary international law has already recognized "biological diversity" as the common concern of humankind. The 1992 Convention on Biological Diversity[47] transcends the traditional approach based on conservation of individual species and recognizes the interconnected nature of the different components of the global ecosystem. Hence, the convention recognizes that it is the interest of humanity to preserve biological diversity as a value in itself, beyond the value of the single species to be protected.

Should a similar development take place also with respect to cultural diversity? In addressing this question, certainly one cannot ignore that there is a difference between culture and nature. Biological diversity, which finds expression in the infinite variety of forms of life in the biosphere, is more permanent and resilient; it is subject only to the slow pace of mutation according to the laws of evolution, save for the destructive impact of human activities. Culture, by contrast is more adaptable. It is subject to constant exchange and its evolution may be measured within the span of generations rather than millennia.

While these differences are real, there is no plausible reason for holding that the more dynamic and adaptable character of culture should be an obstacle to the legal recognition of the value of cultural diversity and of the need to safeguard such diversity as a general interest of humanity.

On the contrary, the evolutionary character of culture requires the maintenance of robust cultural traditions whose richness and diversity

47. *See* Convention on Biological Diversity, June 5, 1992, *available at* http://www.biodiv.org/convention/larticles.asp.

permit fruitful exchange and interaction between different peoples and world views. International law cannot remain indifferent to this task. First, because the present state of economic globalization is generating an increasing concern with the prospect of a uniform commercial monoculture and with the destabilizing effects that this may entail in terms of loss of social cohesion and identity in national societies. Second, because only international law, rather than individual sovereign States, may perform the pedagogical role needed to bridge the gap of diffidence and hostility between different civilizations and world views that globalization has unleashed and that we urgently need to re-compose today in the complex puzzle of shared humanity. How badly we need international law in pursuing this goal is proven, unfortunately, by the current increase in violent conflict and terrorism as a consequence of the attempt to unilaterally transplant, by force, democracy and free market in countries where different social structures and complex cultural traditions prevail.[48]

Thus, if international law has a role to play in the safeguarding of cultural diversity,[49] how has this role been performed and what results have been achieved so far? I shall try to respond to this question by examining two important developments that are currently contributing to the emergence in international law of a common concern for the safeguarding of cultural diversity. I refer to the recent movement toward the adoption of an international regime for the protection of the immaterial elements of living cultures, what we call intangible cultural heritage, and the present effort toward the adoption of a universal treaty on cultural diversity.

A. *Intangible Cultural Heritage*

The concept of "intangible cultural heritage" covers an infinite variety of manifestations of a living culture as opposed to the material products—movable or immovable—that have been the object of international protection in the past.[50] As possible examples, one may think of

48. Iraq is only the latest and most tragic example. On the link between unilateral exportation of democracy and the rise of violence and conflict see A. Chua, World on Fire: How Exporting Free Market Democracy Breeds Ethnic Hatred and Global Instability (2002).

49. On this matter, see F. Lenzerini, *Riflessioni sul valore della diversità culturale nel diritto internazionale*, 46 Comunità Internazionale 671 (2001).

50. *See, e.g.*, Convention on the Protection of the Underwater Cultural Heritage, Nov. 2, 2001, *available at* http://www.unesco.org/culture.laws/underwater/html_eng/convention.shtml; UNIDROIT Convention on Stolen or Illegally Exported Cultural Objects, June 24, 1995, *available at* http://www.unidroit.org/english/conventions/c-cult.htm; Convention for the Protection of the World Cultural and Natural Heritage, *supra* note 18; Convention on the Means of Prohibiting and Preventing the Illicit Import, Export and Transfer of Ownership of Cultural

typical forms of musical expression: literary and oral traditions; poetry, languages, theatre, dance and mime; religious traditions and rituals; crafts and skills; choreography and costumes; agricultural practices; indigenous medicinal practices linked with knowledge of plants; social methods of dispute settlement and other forms of traditional creativity that anthropologists generally catalogue as "folklife." So many forms of immaterial cultural heritage have one feature in common; all of them provide elements to define the identity of a cultural community with its specific social and intellectual processes and distinct world view. This specificity characterizes the relevant cultural community in relation to the broader framework of the sovereign State; its speciality or uniqueness becomes an appealing symbol of community identity.

An early recognition of the international relevance of these living aspects of culture was the UNESCO Recommendation on the Safeguarding of Traditional Culture and Folklore.[51] This recommendation was adopted by the General Conference in 1989 after several years of difficult deliberations mainly due to the dilemma whether to protect traditional culture by way of intellectual property rights or through a separate normative instrument. The 1989 Recommendation shunned this dilemma by limiting its role to the enunciation of a set of general principles and guidelines of a non-binding character.[52]

In the period immediately following the adoption of the UNESCO Recommendation little progress was made toward effective protection of intangible cultural heritage. The implementation of the UNESCO Recommendation in domestic law was generally inadequate. Many countries continued to have no laws, administrative measures or customary rules to specially safeguard intangible cultural heritage. Identification and cataloguing of traditional culture remained lacking thus preventing the very visibility of such culture for the purpose of its legal protection. In response to these shortcomings, in the mid 1990's a new interest and a new approach began to emerge. In 1994, UNESCO adopted the Guidelines on Living Human Treasures,[53] which, following the example set in Asia by countries such as Japan and Korea, aimed at developing incentives and legislation to support the survival of old craft skills which, although not capable of generating sufficient income in a market economy, are

---

Property, Nov. 14 1970, *available at* http://www.unesco.org; Hague Convention, *supra* note 14.

51. Recommendation on the Safeguarding of Traditional Culture and Folklore, Nov. 15, 1989, *available at* http://www.unesco.org.

52. The principles are grouped in six parts: A. Definition of Folklore; B. Identification; C. Conservation; D. Preservation; E. Dissemination; F. Protection; G. International Cooperation. *Id.*

53. Guidelines on Living Human Treasures, *at* http://www.unesco.org/culture/heritage/intangible/treasures/html_eng/method.shtml.

nevertheless an important component of the social fabric and an essential condition for the maintenance and restoration of the material heritage. In 1997, UNESCO launched another initiative relevant to intangible heritage via the program entitled, Proclamation of Masterpieces of Oral and Intangible Heritage. This program was specifically aimed at the recognition and listing of outstanding forms and traditional culture. The first round took place in 2001 and led to the proclamation of some extremely valuable forms of intangible cultural heritage in the different cultural regions of the world,[54] as well as the second proclamation, which took place in 2003.[55]

Building on these two initiatives, as well as on a series of regional seminars, UNESCO and the Smithsonian Institution organized in 1999 in Washington, D.C. a conference entitled "A Global Assessment of the 1989 Recommendation on the Safeguarding of Traditional Culture and Folklore: Local Empowerment and International Cooperation."[56] The conclusions of the Washington conference contained substantive recommendations and an operational resolution. The recommendations reiterated the necessity of adopting a more inclusive definition of intangible cultural heritage, going beyond the concepts of folklore and of popular culture used in the 1989 UNESCO Recommendation. More important, it highlighted the need to put at the center of the system of protection the peoples, groups and communities that are the creators and bearers of intangible cultural heritage. This represented an important shift as compared to the approach adopted in the past of giving overriding priority to the interest of scientific research thus relegating cultural communities to mere objects of study and investigation. The operational resolution consisted in a request to UNESCO to undertake a feasibility

54. For example, among the nineteen masterpieces proclaimed in 2001, the following were selected: Kunqu Opera from China; The Cultural Space of the Brotherhood of the Holy Spirit of the Congos of Villa Mella from Dominican Republic; The Oral Heritage and Cultural Manifestations of the Zápara People from Ecuador and Peru; Georgian Polyphonic Singing from Georgia; Kuttiyattam Sanskrit Theatre from India; Opera dei Pupi, Sicilian Puppet Theatre from Italy; Nôgaku Theatre from Japan; Cross Crafting and its Symbolism from Lithuania; The Cultural Space of Djamaa el-Fna Square from Morocco. List of Masterpieces of the Oral and Intangible Heritage of Humanity, *at* http://www.portal.unesco.org/culture/en/ev.php-URL_ID=21274&URL_DO=DO_Topic&URL_Section=201.html.

55. Among the twenty-eight masterpieces selected in 2003, one may cite the oral traditions of the Aka Pygmies of Central Africa from Central African Republic, The Baltic Song and Dance Celebrations from Estonia, Latvia and Lithuania, The Andean Cosmovision of the Kallawaya from Bolivia, the Iraqi Maqam, The Royal Ballet of Cambodia and the Vanuatu Sand Drawings. *Id.*

56. A Global Assessment of the 1989 Recommendation on the Safeguarding of Traditional Culture and Folklore: Local Empowerment and International Cooperation, *at* http://www.folklife.si.edu/resources/unesco.

study in view of the adoption of a new normative instrument on the safeguarding of traditional culture.

It is against this background that between 2001 and 2003, negotiations were undertaken within the framework of UNESCO. In October, 2003, a new Convention on the Safeguarding of Intangible Cultural heritage was adopted unanimously by the General Conference.[57] This convention defines intangible cultural heritage as "the practices, representations, expressions, knowledge, skills—as well as the instruments, objects, artefacts and cultural spaces associated therewith—that communities, groups and, in some cases, individuals recognize as part of their cultural heritage."[58] The rationale of the convention lies in the idea that the protection of intangible cultural heritage has not only the purpose of safeguarding national interests belonging to each sovereign State, but, particularly, the value of such heritage "as a mainspring of cultural diversity,"[59] corresponding to a "common concern" of the international community as a whole.[60] In this sense, the close interrelation between cultural diversity and intangible heritage is stressed by the second part of the definition, according to which "[such] heritage, transmitted from generation to generation, is constantly recreated by communities and groups in response to their environment, their interaction with nature and their history, and provides them with a sense of identity and continuity, thus promoting respect for cultural diversity and human creativity."[61] Consistently, the convention text emphasizes the role "of communities, groups and, where appropriate, individuals that create, maintain and transmit [intangible cultural] heritage,"[62] stressing the necessity that their participation is ensured "[w]ithin the framework of [each State Party] safeguarding activities of [such] heritage"[63] and in the context of the identification and definition of its various elements.[64] It is nevertheless regrettable that representatives of the above communities and groups are not included among the members of the Intergovernmental Committee for the Safeguarding of the Intangible Cultural Heritage, which is only

57. Convention on the Safeguarding of Intangible Cultural Heritage, *supra* note 45.

58. *Id.* at art. 2. This definition was elaborated by a group of independent experts, chaired by the present writer, who met in Grinzane Cavour, Turin, Italy, in March, 2001. This meeting, organized by UNESCO, was meant to be, and actually was, the first step of the work which led to the adoption of the Convention by the UNESCO General Conference in October 2003.

59. *Id.* at pmbl.

60. *Id.*

61. *Id.* at art. 2.

62. *Id.* at art. 15.

63. *Id.*

64. *See id.* at art. 11(b).

composed of State representatives.[65] The Committee has the competence, *inter alia*, of selecting the items of intangible heritage to be safeguarded at the international level according to Chapter IV of the convention. This circumstance is capable of weakening the role played by the peoples concerned in the operation of the convention and, *a fortiori*, its proper functioning and effectiveness, since only such peoples own the appropriate knowledge, skills and ability for properly managing and safeguarding the intangible heritage they have created and transmitted from generation to generation.

B. *Diversity of Cultural Contents and Artistic Expressions*

While the concept of intangible cultural heritage operates directly within the sphere of national sovereignty in that it entails empowering non-state actors, i.e. peoples and local communities, with a claim to legal protection under international law, the concept of cultural diversity takes this process a step further and introduces the concept of "humanity" as the new "non-state actor" entitled to the safeguarding of cultural diversity as a common patrimony to be preserved in the public interest to be transmitted to future generations. Although no binding treaty has been adopted yet to directly protect and promote cultural diversity, several soft law instruments have already occupied the field and a new convention is now being negotiated within the framework of UNESCO.

The first instrument to be mentioned is the 1966 UNESCO Declaration of the Principles of International Cultural Cooperation,[66] whose Article 1 proclaims that "in their rich variety and diversity, and in the reciprocal influences they exert on one another, all cultures form part of the common heritage belonging to all mankind." The 1992 UN General Assembly Declaration on the Rights of Persons Belonging to National or Ethnic, Religious and Linguistic Minorities[67] reiterated at Articles 1 and 4 that pluralism and cultural diversity form part of the general interest of humanity. Finally, in 2001, the General Conference of UNESCO adopted the Universal Declaration on Cultural Diversity,[68] whose Article 1 expressly states that "as a source of exchange, innovation and creativity, cultural diversity is as necessary for humankind as biodiversity is for nature: in this sense, it is the common heritage of humanity and should be recognized and affirmed for the benefit of the present and future gen-

---

65. *See id.* at art. 5.

66. Declaration of the Principles of International Cultural Cooperation, Nov. 4, 1966, UNESCO, art. 1, *available at* http://www.unesco.org.

67. *See supra* note 2.

68. UNESCO Universal Declaration on Cultural Diversity, Oct. 23, 2001, art. 1, *available at* http://www.unesco.org.

erations." On the basis of this statement, the declaration stresses the inseparability of the defense of cultural diversity from human rights, both in the sense that the former implies a commitment to the fulfilment of human rights and fundamental freedoms, in particular of minorities and indigenous peoples, and in the sense that cultural diversity may not be invoked as an excuse to infringe upon human rights guaranteed by international law.[69] Further, the declaration proclaims cultural heritage as the "wellspring of creativity" because "creation draws on the roots of cultural tradition, but flourishes in contact with other cultures. For this reason, heritage in all its forms must be preserved, enhanced and handed on to future generations as a record of human experience and aspirations, so as to foster creativity in all its diversity."[70] This entails that cultural products and services should be treated not as mere commodities but as "vectors of identity, values and meaning" and that in the present context of globalization the free flow of ideas and works should be made compatible with "... the production and dissemination of diversified cultural goods and services through cultural industries that have the means to assert themselves at the local and global level."[71]

As often happens in international law, the adoption of a soft law instrument is only the first step toward the establishment of a binding legal regime. This has happened also with the Universal Declaration on Cultural Diversity. In October, 2003, the UNESCO General Conference, on the basis of a comprehensive preliminary study on the technical and legal aspects relating to the desirability of a standard setting-instrument on cultural diversity, approved a resolution deciding that the question of cultural diversity "must be regulated by an international convention." It was mandating that the UNESCO Director-General submit to the 33rd Session of the General Conference (Fall, 2005) a report on the negotiating progress and a first draft of a Convention on the Protection of the Diversity of Cultural Contents and Artistic Expressions.[72]

The protection of cultural diversity as the common heritage of humanity is now on the international agenda. The negotiations currently taking place[73] are not likely to produce a quick result. Opposition still

69. *See id.* at art. 4 (stating, *inter alia*, that "[n]o one may invoke cultural diversity to infringe upon human rights guaranteed by international law, nor to limit their scope)."

70. *See id.*

71. *See id.* at art. 9.

72. *See* Desirability of Drawing Up an International Standard-Setting Instrument on Cultural Diversity, July 1, 2003, UNESCO General Conference, Resolution 32C/52, para. 25, *available at* http://unesdoc.unesco.org/images/0013/001307/130798e.pdf.

73. At the time of this writing (April 2004), two rounds of negotiations of governmental experts have taken place and have mostly concentrated on the scope of the future convention. *See* http://portal.unesco.org/culture/en/ev.php@URL_ID=2450&URL_DO=DO_TOPIC&URL_SECTION=201.html.

remains from certain powerful States based on the fear that the future Convention may allow States to raise barriers to the free circulation of cultural products and services.[74] A difficult challenge lies ahead in terms of tuning the UNESCO work with the existing commitment of its members with the WTO and the TRIPS agreements.[75] But in spite of these uncertainties, for the purpose of our discussion, the work of UNESCO and the international practice developing in connection with it has made abundantly clear that the international community has recognized cultural diversity as the common heritage of humanity. By doing so, it has removed cultural heritage from the exclusive control of national sovereignty; it has empowered the non-state actors represented by the peoples and communities who are the bearers of such heritage to claim international protection, if necessary, even against their national State or against third parties. Ultimately, it has made humanity as such the title holder of the general interest to the protection and transmission of cultural diversity as the common and indivisible patrimony of human civilization.

74. *See* The Intervention by the United States Delegation at the UNESCO 32nd General Conference, Meeting of the Committee on Culture, Oct. 13, 2003.

75. One should not forget that all WTO Members are also members of UNESCO (with the only extravagant exception of Singapore). On the interaction between culture and trade, see Bruno De Witte, *Trade in Culture: International Legal Regimes and EU Constitutional Values*, in THE EU AND THE WTO: LEGAL AND CONSTITUTIONAL ISSUES 237 (De Burca & Scott eds., 2001).

[16]

WORLD CULTURAL HERITAGE: OBLIGATIONS TO THE INTERNATIONAL COMMUNITY AS A WHOLE?

ROGER O'KEEFE

I. INTRODUCTION

The preamble to the Convention concerning the Protection of the World Cultural and Natural Heritage 1972 (the 'World Heritage Convention'),[1] adopted 30 years ago, testifies to the conviction of the States Parties 'that deterioration or disappearance of any item of the cultural . . . heritage constitutes a harmful impoverishment of the heritage of all the nations of the world'.[2] It speaks of the recognized 'importance, for all the peoples of the world, of safeguarding this unique and irreplaceable property, to whatever people it may belong'[3] and declares 'that parts of the cultural . . . heritage . . . of outstanding interest . . . need to be preserved as part of the world heritage of mankind as a whole'.[4]

Motivated by this awareness of a universal interest in 'the conservation and protection of the world's heritage',[5] each State Party to the Convention, by virtue of Article 4, recognizes its 'duty of ensuring the identification, protection, conservation, presentation and transmission to future generations'[6] of cultural heritage situated on its territory, 'cultural heritage' being defined as monuments, groups of buildings and sites 'of outstanding universal value'.[7] It undertakes to 'do all it can to this end, to the utmost

[1] 16 Nov 1972, 1037 UNTS 151 ['WHC'].

[2] WHC, preamble, second recital.

[3] Ibid, fifth recital.

[4] Ibid, sixth recital. Contrary perhaps to common assumption, the phrase 'the world heritage of mankind as a whole' found in this preambular recital refers to all cultural and natural heritage covered by the Convention, and not merely to those select properties inscribed on the so-called 'World Heritage List' pursuant to Art 11 (2). Cf, for example, Art 6 (1), where the term 'world heritage' is used to denote 'the cultural and natural heritage mentioned in Articles 1 and 2' (viz all heritage protected by the Convention), as distinct from 'the cultural and natural heritage referred to in paragraphs 2 and 4 of Article 11' (viz only heritage included in the World Heritage List and the 'List of World Heritage in Danger' respectively), as found in Arts 6 (2) and 12. See, in this regard, *Richardson v Forestry Commission* (1987–8) 77 ALR 237/90 ILR 58, High Court of Australia, at 242/63, per Mason CJ and Brennan J.

[5] WHC, fourth recital.

[6] Ibid, Art 4.

[7] Ibid, Art 1. The obligation imposed by Art 4 arises regardless of whether the cultural heritage in question is inscribed on the World Heritage List. Art 4—like Arts 6 (1) and 6 (3)—speaks of 'the cultural and natural heritage referred to in Articles 1 and 2', rather than 'the cultural and natural heritage referred to in paragraphs 2 and 4 of Article 11', as used in Arts 6 (2) and 12; and Art 12 makes it clear that '[t]he fact that a property belonging to the cultural or natural heritage has not been included in [the World Heritage List] shall in no way be construed to mean that it does not have an outstanding universal value for purposes other than those resulting from inclusion in [the List].' In practical terms, the obligation laid down in Art 4 applies to all cultural and natural heritage either inscribed on the World Heritage List, included in a so-called 'tentative list' submitted by the State Party on whose territory it is situated in accordance with Art 11 (1), or otherwise identified and delineated by that State Party in accordance with Art 3. See, eg, *Queensland v Commonwealth of Australia* (1989) 86 ALR 519/90 ILR 115 at 524–6/129–31, per Mason CJ, Brennan, Deane, Toohey, Gaudron & McHugh JJ, and especially at 134/528, per Dawson J; see also *Richardson v Forestry Commission*, above, n 4, where a conclusion to this effect is implicit in the various judgments.

of its own resources and, where appropriate, with any international assistance and cooperation . . . it may be able to obtain'.[8]

By virtue of its non-synallagmatic nature, and of the Convention's express textual references to a universal interest in the preservation of the cultural heritage in question, the obligation laid down in Article 4 is an obligation owed to all States Parties to the Convention and 'established for the protection of a collective interest of the group', in the words of Article 48 (1)(a) of the International Law Commission's Articles on the Responsibility of States for Internationally Wrongful Acts.[9] It is an obligation *erga omnes partes*, to use the traditional terminology. As such, it is an obligation enforceable, in principle, by all of those Parties: in the event that a State Party fails to fulfil it, each of the other States Parties, jointly or severally, enjoys the right to compel performance—or, in the words of Article 48 (2)(a) of the ILC's Articles, to claim 'cessation of the internationally wrongful act'—ultimately by way of judicial proceedings, where possible, or perhaps even countermeasures.[10]

But what about States not party to the Convention? Is it not the case that the monuments, groups of buildings and sites protected by the Convention are expressly characterized in its preamble as 'the world heritage of mankind as a whole'? And are not States Parties and non-States Parties together the legal representatives on the international

[8] WHC, Art 4. In fulfilment of Art 4's general duty, each State Party subscribes in Art 5 to a set of specific obligations in respect of cultural heritage situated on its territory, 'in so far as possible, and as appropriate for each country' (ibid, Art 5, chapeau). Additionally, States Parties recognize in Art 6 (1) that 'such heritage constitutes a world heritage for whose protection it is the duty of the international community as a whole to co-operate', and undertake in Art 6 (3) 'not to take any deliberate measures which might damage directly or indirectly the cultural . . . heritage . . . situated on the territory of other States Parties to [the] Convention'.

[9] Articles on Responsibility of States for Internationally Wrongful Acts, annexed to GA res 56/83, 12 Dec 2001 ['ARSIWA']. The States Parties to the WHC obviously constitute 'a group of States' within the meaning of Art 48 (1)(a). See also International Law Commission ['ILC'], *Report on the work of its fifty-third session (23 April–1 June and 2 July–10 August 2001)*, UN Doc A/56/10, commentary to ARSIWA Art 48, paras (6) & (7), 320–1. The obligations falling within the scope of Art 48 (1)(a) 'are not limited to arrangements established only in the interest of the member States but would extend to agreements established by a group of States in some wider common interest': ibid, para (7), 320–1; see also J Crawford, *The International Law Commission's Articles on State Responsibility. Introduction, Text and Commentaries* (Cambridge Cambridge University Press 2002) 43.

[10] The lawfulness of countermeasures by non-injured States is an open question: see Conclusion, below n 117, for more. In addition, both countermeasures and judicial proceedings face formidable obstacles in practice, and not just those considered in the Conclusion, below. For a start, it is not always easy to identify a breach of the Convention. The obligations laid down by Art 4 are couched in terms ('all it can do', 'to the utmost of its own resources', 'where appropriate') which allow State Parties such a measure of implementing discretion as to make 'second guessing' tricky for other States; and while conventional discretions of this nature must, in the final analysis, be subject to the requirement of application in good faith (see Vienna Convention on the Law of Treaties 1969, 1155 UNTS 331 ['VCLT'], Art 26, as declaratory of general international law, and *Gabcikovo-Nagymaros Project (Hungary/Slovakia)*, Judgment, ICJ Rep 1997, 7, at para 142), it is understandable and proper that other States should be reluctant to substitute their appreciation of the possibility and appropriateness of action for that of the state on which Art 4 is incumbent. In practice, formal invocation of responsibility is only foreseeable (and only then with a strong dose of optimism) in flagrant cases of deliberate destruction. A similar hurdle is posed, *mutatis mutandis*, by the fact that the characterization of property as being 'of outstanding universal value' within the meaning of Art 1, and hence covered by the Convention in the first place, falls by virtue of Art 3 to the state on whose territory the property is situated.

plane of 'mankind as a whole'? As such, is it not possible to argue that the obligation imposed by Article 4 of the Convention is owed not merely to States Parties but to 'the international community as a whole', as the term is used in Article 48 (1)(b) of the ILC's Articles,[11] with the result that *any* State, regardless of whether it is party to the Convention, has the right—whether individually or in concert with other States—to compel a State Party's performance?

II. THE CONVENTION AND THE *PACTA TERTIIS* RULE

Despite its invocation of the interest of 'mankind as a whole' in the protection of the world's cultural heritage, the Convention is still a treaty. And, as a general rule, treaties do not create rights for third States:[12] *pacta tertiis nec prosunt nec nocent*. In this light, the right to invoke a State Party's responsibility for breach of the duty imposed by Article 4 is prima facie a right enjoyed by the other States Parties alone.[13] The obligation arising from this provision might be explicitly for the benefit of all humanity; but, on the face of it, only States Parties are entitled to compel its performance.

It is, of course, possible for a treaty to create third-party rights with the consent of those third parties.[14] Such rights can be accorded to a single State, or to a group of States, or—as is relevant here—to all States.[15] While there is no indication that the non-States Parties to the Convention have in fact consented to the according of such rights, assent would be presumed as long as the contrary is not indicated, given the absence of any conventional provision otherwise.[16]

But a treaty can only accord third-party rights if the States Parties intend this to be the case,[17] and there is no sign that the States Parties to the Convention so intended. No operative provision of the Convention indicates such an intention, and the unspecific implications of the preamble are insufficient in this regard.[18]

[11] See also *Barcelona Traction, Light and Power Company, Limited, Second Phase*, ICJ Rep 1970 3, at para 33, which also refers synonymously to 'obligations *erga omnes*'. 'All States are by definition members of the international community as a whole . . .': ILC, above, n 9, commentary to ARSIWA Art 48, para (10), 322. Note that the identical term 'the international community as a whole' is found in WHC, Art 6 (1). Needless to say, neither 'the international community as a whole' nor, for that matter, 'mankind as a whole' enjoys international legal personality in its own right: see, eg, *Legal Consequences for States of the Continued Presence of South Africa in Namibia (South West Africa) notwithstanding Security Council Resolution 276 (1970)*, Advisory Opinion, ICJ Rep 1971, 16, diss op Fitzmaurice at para 33; J Crawford, 'Responsibility to the International Community as a Whole', in J Crawford, *International Law as an Open System. Selected Essays* (London 2002) 341 et seq, at 344.

[12] See VCLT, Art 34, as declaratory of general international law on point. An exception appears to exist as regards treaties establishing an international status or regime: see, generally, R Jennings and A Watts (eds) *Oppenheim's International Law. Volume 1. Peace* (9th edn London 1996), parts 2–4, 1205–6; A McNair, *The Law of Treaties* (Oxford Oxford University Press 1961), 265–71; P Cahier, 'Le problème des effets des traités à l'égard des Etats tiers', 143 RCADI (1974–III) 589 at 660–77. Despite the superficial attraction of the argument, however, the WHC is not such a treaty.

[13] Strictly speaking, it is breach of the Convention, not the Convention itself, which would create the right to invoke responsibility. But it is reasonable, for present purposes, to assimilate the former to the latter.

[14] See VCLT, Arts 34 and 36.

[15] See ibid, Art 36 (1).

[16] See ibid.

[17] See ibid.

[18] Moreover, it seems inequitable that non-States Parties, in their capacity as members of 'the international community as a whole', should benefit from the right enjoyed by States Parties to compel performance of the Convention without sharing the duty imposed on the same

By way of aside, the same tension between the language of universal interest and the *pacta tertiis* rule is manifest in the obligation to preserve cultural heritage situated on its territory imposed on a State Party to the International Covenant on Economic, Social and Cultural Rights by Article 15 (1)(a)—the right to take part in cultural life—of the Covenant.[19] The Committee on Economic, Social, and Cultural Rights speaks of States Parties' duty of '[p]reservation and presentation of mankind's cultural heritage';[20] and, for example, the Special Representative of the Secretary-General on the situation of human rights in Cambodia, characterizing the vandalism and looting of the Khmer temple complex at Angkor Wat as an issue going to Article 15 of the ICESCR,[21] has written that 'Angkor and Angkorian artefacts must be preserved and protected for all Cambodians, and the world'.[22] But the obligations imposed by Article 15 (1)(a) of the ICESCR, while owed *erga omnes partes*, are not obligations *erga omnes simpliciter*, as it were. Although reference is made to 'mankind's' cultural heritage, the Covenant is nonetheless a treaty, and can have no third-party effect unless this is clearly intended by States Parties and consented to by third States. Neither is the case here.

'international community as a whole', by Art 6 (1), to cooperate in the protection of the world cultural and natural heritage: see, in this light, *North Sea Continental Shelf Cases* (Federal Republic of Germany/Denmark; Federal Republic of Germany/Netherlands), ICJ Rep 1969 3, at para 28; and a third party's consent to the incurring of a treaty obligation must be express and expressed in writing: see VCLT, Art 35. No such written assent has been given by any of the non-State Parties to the WHC. (As it is, there is no indication that the States Parties intended to create third-party obligations anyway.)

[19] International Covenant on Economic, Social and Cultural Rights, 993 UNTS 3 [hereafter, 'ICESCR']. Art 15 provides in relevant part:

> 1. The States Parties to the present Covenant recognize the right of everyone:
> (a) To take part in cultural life . . .

See also General Discussion on the Right to Take Part in Cultural Life as recognized in Article 15 of the International Covenant on Economic, Social and Cultural Rights, UN Doc E/1993/22, Chap VII [hereafter, 'General Discussion']. Article 15 of the ICESCR embodies in binding treaty form 'the right freely to participate in the cultural life of the community' recognized by Art 27 of the Universal Declaration of Human Rights, GA res 217 A (III), 10 Dec 1948. As interpreted by the Committee on Economic, Social and Cultural Rights, in an illustration of the wider normative influence of the WHC, Art 15 (1)(a) of the ICESCR encompasses a positive duty to preserve the physical state of cultural heritage: see, eg, the Committee's comments at UN Docs E/1991/23, para 79; E/1992/23, paras 310, 312; E/1993/22, para 186. This duty encompasses an obligation to protect such heritage from vandalism and theft (see E/1993/22, para 186), as well as a prohibition on its deliberate destruction (see E/1995/22, para 136).

[20] See Revised Guidelines regarding the Form and Contents of Reports to be submitted by States Parties under Arts 16 and 17 of the International Covenant on Economic, Social and Cultural Rights, UN Doc E/1991/23, 88 at 108, para 1 (f); General Discussion, above, n 19, para 213.

[21] See UN Doc E/CN.4/1994/73, paras 118–22.

[22] Ibid, para 120. The UN Commission on Human Rights took note of the Special Representative's report, and his recommendations and conclusions, 'with interest'—'in particular the identification of priority areas requiring urgent attention': Commission on Human Rights res 1994/61, 4 Mar 1994, para 8, chapeau. The first of these priority areas was '[t]he devotion of proper resources . . . for [inter alia] the defence of cultural treasures, especially Angkor Wat': ibid, para 8 (a).

III. THE CONVENTION'S CORE OBLIGATION AND GENERAL INTERNATIONAL LAW

A. Overview

Might it be said, however, that the core obligation of protection, conservation, and transmission to future generations incumbent on a State Party to the World Heritage Convention in respect of monuments, groups of buildings and sites of outstanding universal value situated on its territory is now an obligation recognized by general international law, with the result that its performance may be compelled not just by other States Parties, but by any or all of the international community as a whole?[23] The question calls for a review of relevant State practice.[24]

B. Outline of the Evidence

1. 'Soft' law

Several non-binding standard-setting instruments adopted by States in the context of the General Conference of UNESCO embody norms relevant to States' putative customary obligations in respect of cultural heritage situated on their territory.[25]

On the same day it adopted the World Heritage Convention, the General Conference of UNESCO also adopted the Recommendation concerning the Protection, at National Level, of the Cultural and Natural Heritage.[26] Considering 'that . . . the cultural and natural heritage . . . constitute[s] an essential feature of mankind's heritage'[27] and 'that every country in whose territory there are components of the cultural and natural heritage has an obligation to safeguard this part of mankind's heritage and to ensure that it is handed down to future generations',[28] the General

[23] If they were to exist, such obligations would, of course, arise whether or not a State was a Party to the WHC. That is, they would be owed not simply *to* but also *by* all States.

[24] Note that it is the practice of States alone that is relevant to the formation of a customary international rule, at least in this context. As such, the diplomatic activity and statements of the UN Secretary-General and of the Director-General of UNESCO in relation to the Buddhas of Bamiyan, as well as the statement made by the Chairperson of the World Heritage Committee in this regard, can—for strict legal purposes—be ignored. The same goes for statements made about the Buddhas by various non-governmental organisations. Note also that the extremely widespread and representative participation of states in the World Heritage Convention itself (a treaty which, when drafted, was clearly not declaratory of existing custom) does not, in itself, indicate that the obligations embodied therein have emerged as rules of general international law: see RR Baxter, 'Treaties and Custom', 129 RCADI (1970) 25 at 64 and 73.

[25] For a brief explanation of the workings and institutional status of UNESCO recommendations and declarations, see O Lefranc, 'Les problèmes juridiques posés devant la XIIe session de la Conférence Générale de l'UNESCO (Novembre–Décembre 1962)' (1962) 8 AFDI 638 at 657–8, 662–6; H Saba, 'Unesco and Human Rights', in K Vasak and P Alston (eds) *The International Dimensions of Human Rights. Volume 2* (Westport/Paris 1982), 401 ff, at 402–3; SP Marks, 'Education, Science, Culture and Information', in O Schachter and CC Joyner (eds) *United Nations Legal Order. Volume 2* (Cambridge Cambridge University Press 1995), 577 ff, at 578–82, 621–5.

[26] Recommendation concerning the Protection, at National Level, of the Cultural and Natural Heritage, 16 Nov 1972, reproduced in *Conventions and Recommendations of Unesco concerning the protection of the cultural heritage* (Paris 1985).

[27] Ibid, preamble, third recital.

[28] Ibid, preamble, fifth recital.

Conference enunciated norms and principles applicable to cultural heritage, defined as monuments, groups of buildings and sites 'of special value'.[29] The most fundamental of the Recommendation's general principles is that 'the protection, conservation and presentation of [the cultural heritage] impose responsibilities on the States in whose territory it is situated, both vis-à-vis their own nationals and vis-à-vis the international community as a whole', in fulfilment of which 'Member States should take such action as may be necessary . . .'.[30]

Four years later, the General Conference of UNESCO adopted the Recommendation on Participation by the People at Large in Cultural Life and their Contribution to It.[31] Recalling, inter alia, Article 27 of the Universal Declaration of Human Rights (viz the right to take part in cultural life, as embodied in binding form in Article 15 (1)(a) of the ICESCR),[32] this instrument recommends that Member States 'adopt legislation or regulations . . . in order to . . . protect and enhance the heritage of the past, and particularly ancient monuments . . .'.[33]

In 1997, '[m]indful of the will of the peoples . . . to safeguard the values and principles enshrined in the Universal Declaration of Human Rights, and all other relevant instruments of international law',[34] '[c]onsidering the provisions of [inter alia] the International Covenant on Economic, Social and Cultural Rights . . .',[35] and '[c]onvinced that there is a moral obligation to formulate behavioural guidelines for the present generations within a broad, future-oriented perspective',[36] the General Conference adopted the Declaration on the Responsibilities of the Present Generations Towards Future Generations. Article 7 of the Declaration states in part that '[t]he present generations have the responsibility to identify, protect and safeguard the tangible . . . cultural heritage and to transmit this common heritage to future generations.'

Finally, in 2001, the General Conference adopted the UNESCO Universal Declaration on Cultural Diversity.[37] The preamble to the Declaration declares the General Conference to be '[c]ommitted to the full implementation of the human rights . . . proclaimed in the Universal Declaration of Human Rights and other universally recognized legal instruments, such as the two International Covenants of 1966 . . .';[38] and it '[r]efer[s] to the provisions relating to cultural diversity and the exercise of cultural rights in the international instruments enacted by UNESCO',[39] citing by way of footnote the World Heritage Convention, among others.[40] Article 7 of the Declaration states that 'heritage in all its forms must be preserved, enhanced and handed on to future generations . . .'.

29 Ibid, Art 1.

30 Ibid, Art 4.

31 Recommendation on Participation by the People at Large in Cultural Life and their Contribution to It, 26 Nov 1976, UNESCO Doc 19C/Resolutions, Annex I, 29.

32 Ibid, preamble, first recital. Art 27 (1) of the Universal Declaration of Human Rights, GA res 217 A (III), 10 Dec 1948, states: 'Everyone has the right freely to participate in the cultural life of the community . . .'.

33 Recommendation on Participation in Cultural Life, above, n 31, Art 4, chapeau and subsection (q)(i).

34 Declaration on the Responsibilities of the Present Generations Towards Future Generations, 12 Nov 1997, UNESCO Doc 29C/Res 44, preamble, first recital.

35 Ibid, preamble, second recital.

36 Ibid, preamble, twelfth recital.

37 UNESCO Universal Declaration on Cultural Diversity, 2 Nov 2001, UNESCO Doc 31C/Res 25, Annex I.

38 Ibid, preamble, first recital.

39 Ibid, preamble, fourth recital.

40 See ibid, n 1.

2. State practice in relation to the Buddhas of Bamiyan

(a) Preface

A solid body of relevant practice comes in the form of reactions by States, jointly and severally, to the damage inflicted in 1998 and 1999 on the great statues of the Buddha at Bamiyan in Afghanistan by the country's then-Taliban government,[41] as well as—more tellingly—to the Taliban's destruction of the Buddhas in 2001. In this regard, it should be borne in mind that the Taliban's treatment of the Buddhas was not governed by the laws of armed conflict. While sporadic warfare continued in the far north-east of Afghanistan, the Bamiyan valley and the rest of the country were, at all relevant times, free of hostilities and securely under the Taliban government's control—in other words, the Buddhas were not destroyed in the fighting.[42] Nor is there a legal state of belligerent occupation in non-international armed conflict.[43] It is also worth noting by way of aside that the Taliban's acts constituted flagrant violations of the World Heritage Convention itself,[44] even if many States and commentators were confused as to the applicability of the Convention to the facts.[45]

[41] For a chronology of the events in question, and some of the international reaction to them, see UNESCO Doc WHC-01/CONF.208/23, 4–11.

[42] See also T Georgopoulos, 'Avez-vous bien dit "crime contre la culture"? La protection internationale des monuments historiques' (2001) 54 RHDI 459 at 471–2. For this reason, it is impossible to agree with Francioni and Lenzerini's assertion that the laws of armed conflict were applicable to the situation: see F Francioni and F Lenzerini, *The Destruction of the Buddhas of Bamyan and International Law* (2002), copy on file with author, 23–5, 28–30.

[43] The apparent assertion to the contrary by the Director of UNESCO's Division of Cultural Heritage, Sector for Culture (Bureau of the World Heritage Committee, Twenty-Fifth Session, 25–30 June 2001, Report of the Rapporteur, UNESCO Doc WHC-2001/CONF.205/10 para I.9) is without merit. The reality is that, while Art 19 of the 1954 Hague Convention for the Protection of Cultural Property in the Event of Armed Conflict, 249 UNTS 240, gives the Convention limited applicability during armed conflicts not of an international character, the concept of belligerent occupation is limited to the occupation of foreign territory during international armed conflict.

[44] Afghanistan ratified the Convention on 20 Mar 1979. On 21 Dec 1981, it nominated the monuments of the Bamiyan valley for inclusion in the World Heritage List. The nomination was received by the Sector for Culture of the Division of Cultural Heritage of UNESCO on 14 Apr 1982. See UNESCO Doc WHC-01/CONF.208/23, 2. This nomination had the legal effect of rendering the Convention applicable to the Buddhas of Bamiyan (see above, n 7), and the wilful damage and eventual destruction of the Buddhas were clear breaches of the obligation imposed by Art 4.

[45] It was suggested by the Director of UNESCO's Division of Cultural Heritage, Sector for Culture that the Convention 'does not apply to civil conflicts': Bureau of the World Heritage Committee, Twenty-Fifth Session, 25–30 June 2001, Report of the Rapporteur, above n 43 para I.9. It is true that, in the context of hostilities, the international humanitarian law applicable to non-international armed conflicts serves as *lex specialis* to the *lex generalis* of the World Heritage Convention. But no provision of the Convention states that it does not apply as such in the event of armed conflict. Moreover, as stated above, there were no hostilities in Bamiyan at the times in question; and if the Convention were inapplicable whenever there is a non-international armed conflict somewhere on the territory of a State Party, it would not have applied to Westminster Abbey during the Troubles in Northern Ireland or to the historic areas of Istanbul during the fighting in the Kurdish regions of Turkey—an absurd proposition. As for the legal effect of the absence of the Buddhas from the World Heritage List, see above, ns 7 and 44. Finally, *pace* the Director of UNESCO's Division of Cultural Heritage, Sector for Culture (ibid), the fact that the Taliban remained unrecognized as the Government of Afghanistan by all but three states and was not the government accredited to the UN is irrelevant to the State responsibility of Afghanistan: see also Francioni and Lenzerini, above n 42, 19–20.

(b) General Assembly of States Parties to the World Heritage Convention

Several months after the demolition of the Buddhas in March 2001, the General Assembly of the States Parties to the World Heritage Convention adopted a resolution on the protection of the cultural heritage of Afghanistan.[46] Noting, in the preamble, the various international legal instruments on the protection of the cultural heritage adopted under the aegis of UNESCO and UNIDROIT respectively, the resolution '[c]ondemn[ed] the wilful destruction of the cultural heritage of Afghanistan by the Taliban forces, particularly the statues of Bamiyan, as "crime[s] against the common heritage of humanity" '. It went on to appeal to States Parties to the Convention to become party, where they had not already done so, to the other conventions noted in the preamble; to invite the World Heritage Committee to consider ways and means by which the implementation of the Convention could be reinforced, 'especially in relation to the other relevant UNESCO Conventions for the protection of the cultural heritage'; and to invite the Director-General of UNESCO 'to inform the Secretary-General of the United Nations when the common heritage of humanity is threatened with wilful destruction so that he/she may propose necessary actions to protect this heritage'.

(c) General Conference of UNESCO

A few days later, at its thirty-first session and the first after the destruction of the Buddhas, the General Conference of UNESCO adopted a resolution entitled 'Acts constituting a crime against the common heritage of humanity'.[47] Calling on all Member States of the Organization 'and all other States of the world' to become parties to the cultural heritage conventions adopted under the aegis of UNESCO and UNIDROIT respectively 'in order to maximize the protection of the cultural heritage of humanity, . . . in particular, against destructive acts',[48] the General Conference noted and reiterated 'the fundamental principles included in these instruments to prevent the destruction of the cultural heritage . . .'.[49] The resolution concluded by inviting the Director-General of UNESCO to formulate, on the basis of these principles, 'a Draft Declaration concerning the Intentional Destruction of Cultural Heritage'.[50]

(d) United Nations organs

In late 1998, after the Taliban's first attack on the Buddhas,[51] the General Assembly of

[46] Resolution on the protection of the cultural heritage of Afghanistan adopted by the General Assembly of States Parties to the World Heritage Convention at its thirteenth session (Paris, 30–31 Oct 2001), reproduced at UNESCO Doc WHC-01/CONF.208/23, 12.

[47] UNESCO Doc 31C/Res 26, 2 Nov 2001.

[48] Ibid, para 1.

[49] Ibid, paras 2 and 3. Such destruction was declared to include looting and illicit excavations.

[50] Ibid, para 4.

[51] As well as expressing its concern over the vandalism and destruction of Afghan monuments, the General Assembly addressed the looting of Afghanistan's cultural heritage. It 'call[ed] upon all Afghan parties, in particular the Taliban, to protect the cultural and historic relics . . . of Afghanistan from acts of . . . theft, and request[ed] all Member States to take appropriate measures to prevent the looting of cultural artifacts and to ensure their return to Afghanistan': see GA res 53/203A, 18 Dec 1998, para 21; GA res 54/189A, 17 Dec 1999, para 30; and GA res 55/174A, 19 Dec 2000, para 30. Similarly, it '[e]xpresse[d] its deep concern at reports of . . . looting of cultural artifacts in Afghanistan' and once again 'request[ed] all Member States to take appropriate measures to prevent the looting of cultural artifacts and to ensure their return to Afghanistan': see

the United Nations[52]—in a resolution headed 'Situation of human rights in Afghanistan'[53]—'[e]xpresse[d] its deep concern at reports of attacks on . . . cultural artifacts in Afghanistan' and 'emphasize[d] that all parties share[d] the responsibility to protect their common heritage . . .'.[54] These statements were repeated verbatim in further resolutions adopted in 1999[55] and 2000[56] under the heading 'Question of human rights in Afghanistan'. All three resolutions, adopted without a vote, made preambular reference to the Universal Declaration of Human Rights and to the International Covenants on Human Rights.[57] Precisely the same preambular and operative formulae were used by the Commission on Human Rights in a resolution of 2000 entitled 'Situation of human rights in Afghanistan'.[58] Earlier resolutions adopted by the Commission under the same rubric, also referring to the Universal Declaration and to the Covenants,[59] '[n]ote[d] with deep concern . . . [r]eports of the destruction . . . of the cultural and historic heritage of Afghanistan'[60] and '[a]ppeal[ed] to Member States and to the international community . . . [t]o take urgent measures to prevent the demolition . . . of cultural artefacts'.[61] The Commission adopted all three resolutions without a vote.

Similarly, in another resolution of late 1998,[62] the General Assembly '[r]eiterate[d] that the cultural and historic relics and monuments of Afghanistan belong to the common heritage of mankind' and 'call[ed] upon all Afghan parties, in particular the Taliban, to protect the cultural and historic relics and monuments of Afghanistan from acts of vandalism [and] damage . . .'. It repeated this verbatim in resolutions of 1999[63] and 2000.[64] Finally, on 9 March 2001, before the destruction of the Buddhas of Bamiyan had been confirmed, the General Assembly adopted Resolution 55/243, entitled 'The destruction of relics and monuments in Afghanistan'.[65] 'Bearing in mind the International Covenant on Economic, Social and Cultural Rights and the need to respect the common heritage of humankind'; '[d]eeply concerned and appalled by the Taliban edict of 26 February 2001, ordering the destruction of all statues and non-Islamic shrines in Afghanistan, and by the deliberate ongoing destruction of these relics

GA res 53/165, 9 Dec 1998, para 16; GA res 54/185, 17 Dec 1999, para 16; and GA res 55/119, 4 Dec 2000, para 19; see too, almost identically, GA res 52/145, 12 Dec 1997, para 17.

[52] In parallel with the General Assembly's activities, the Security Council—which Member States, in accordance with Art 24 (1) of the Charter, recognize as acting on their behalf—reaffirmed in the preamble to SC res 1214 (1998) 'its respect for [Afghanistan's] cultural and historical heritage'. It repeated this reaffirmation in the respective preambles to SC res 1267 (1999) and SC res 1333 (2000).

[53] GA res 53/165, 9 Dec 1998 (adopted without a vote).

[54] Ibid, para 16.

[55] GA res 54/185, 17 Dec 1999 (adopted without a vote), para 16.

[56] GA res 55/119, 4 Dec 2000 (adopted without a vote), para 19.

[57] See the first recital of each respective preamble.

[58] See Commission on Human Rights res 2000/18, 18 Apr 2000 (adopted without a vote), preamble, first recital and para 14.

[59] Commission on Human Rights res 1998/70, 21 Apr 1998 (adopted without a vote), preamble, first recital; Commission on Human Rights res 1999/9, 23 Apr 1999 (adopted without a vote), preamble, first recital.

[60] Commission on Human Rights res 1998/70, para 2, chapeau and subpara (g).

[61] Commission on Human Rights res 1999/9, para 12, chapeau and subpara (e).

[62] GA res 53/203A, 18 Dec 1998 (adopted without a vote), para 21.

[63] GA res 54/189A, 17 Dec 1999 (adopted without a vote), para 30.

[64] GA res 55/174A, 19 Dec 2000 (adopted without a vote), para 30.

[65] GA res 55/243, 9 Mar 2001 (adopted without a vote).

and monuments which belong to the common heritage of humankind'; and '[n]oting that the destruction of the statues in Afghanistan, in particular of the unique Buddhist sculptures in Bamiyan, would be an irreparable loss for humanity as a whole',[66] the General Assembly

> 1. *Strongly call[ed] upon* the Taliban to abide by their previous commitments to protect the cultural heritage of Afghanistan from all acts of vandalism, damage and theft;
> 2. *Strongly urge[d]* the Taliban to review their edict of 26 February 2001 and to stop its implementation;
> 3. *Also strongly urge[d]* the Taliban to take immediate action to prevent the further destruction of the irreplaceable relics, monuments or artefacts of the cultural heritage of Afghanistan ...

The resolution's final paragraph '[c]all[ed] upon Member States to help, through appropriate technical measures, to safeguard the sculptures, including, if necessary, their temporary relocation or removal from public view'.

All the above resolutions were adopted without a vote. Not a single preambular or other reference was made in any of the resolutions to Afghanistan's obligations under the World Heritage Convention, the mention of the Taliban's 'previous commitments to protect the cultural heritage of Afghanistan' being a reference to unilateral statements by the regime.[67] In the debate in the General Assembly before the adoption of resolution 55/243, Ukraine was alone in characterising the Buddhas's destruction as a breach of the Convention.[68]

(e) Regional groupings

At the regional level, the Presidency of the European Union, speaking on behalf of EU Member States, reacted with 'dismay and shock' to news of the Taliban edict ordering the destruction of all statues and non-Islamic shrines in Afghanistan, describing 'Afghanistan's rich cultural heritage' as being 'of priceless historic value' and 'of vital importance not only to Afghanistan but to the world as a whole'. The EU 'strongly urge[d]' the Taliban leadership not to implement its decision.[69] Cyprus, Malta, Turkey, and the Central and Eastern European countries associated with the European Union, along with the EFTA States Members of the European Economic Area, aligned themselves with the EU declaration.[70] Similarly, the Secretary General of the Council of Europe, referring to 'respect for human rights ... and awareness of our common cultural heritage ...', 'expressed his dismay' at the ensuing destruction, declaring that ' "[n]o political or religious power has the right to deliberately destroy cultural property

[66] Ibid, preamble, second, fourth, and sixth recitals respectively.

[67] See UNESCO Doc WHC-01/CONF.208/23, 5; 'Welcome to our beautiful country... Mullahs bid to attract tourists to tragic Afghanistan', *Observer*, 5 Nov 2000; 'Lost treasures of Kabul', *Guardian*, 17 Nov 2000.

[68] See UN GAOR, Fifty-fifth Session, 94th Plenary Meeting, 9 Mar 2001, UN Doc A/55/PV.94, 12. It is possible that the Ukrainian ambassador to the General Assembly was using the phrase 'in particular' in the sense of 'specifically'.

[69] Declaration by the Presidency on behalf of the European Union on destruction of all statues in Afghanistan, Brussels, 1 Mar 2001 <http://www.eu2001.se/eu2001/news/news_read.asp?iInformationID=12480>. This statement was repeated verbatim by the Swedish ambassador to the UN General Assembly, speaking on behalf of the EU: see UN GAOR, above, n 68, 2–3.

[70] Declaration by the Presidency on behalf of the European Union, ibid. In addition, in the UN General Assembly, Ukraine aligned itself with the EU's statement: see UN GAOR, ibid, 11–12.

that belongs to humankind, or to deprive future generations of a heritage which is simply not the prerogative of a single group, ideology or faith" '. He invited international organisations and institutions 'to take concerted action with a view to safeguarding this common heritage . . .'.[71]

For their part, the Ambassadors to UNESCO of the fifty-four Member States of the Organization of the Islamic Conference 'unanimously came together' at the time of the destruction of the Buddhas 'in vigorous condemnation of these unacceptable attacks on humanity's common heritage', 'determined to join [UNESCO] in taking concrete action'.[72] The Arab Group of countries represented at UNESCO condemned the destruction, which 'represent[ed] the Heritage of humanity as a whole', and demanded its immediate cessation, calling for concrete international action to protect these 'inestimable treasures of the universal Heritage'.[73] The Asia Pacific Group of countries represented at the Organization, characterizing Afghanistan's cultural heritage as 'of exceptional universal value', 'expresse[d] its strong condemnation' of what it called 'an inadmissible attack on . . . an irreplaceable civilisational inheritance of all mankind'. It called upon the Taliban 'immediately [to] stop the destruction and vandalism of all cultural and historic monuments and relics of Afghanistan, including in particular the ancient statutes of Buddha in Bamiyan', and 'strongly endorse[d]' the action taken by the UNESCO Director-General to protect this heritage.[74]

Again, no mention was made in any of these statements of Afghanistan's obligations under the World Heritage Convention.

(f) Individual States

Finally, at the bilateral level, the United States of America, numbering the Buddhas 'among the world's great cultural treasures', joined the UN and other States 'in urging the Taliban to halt [the] desecration of Afghanistan's cultural heritage'.[75] In the event, it 'strongly condemn[ed] this destruction of the irreplaceable world heritage', with the Secretary of State calling it 'a crime against humankind'.[76] Russia was said to be 'seriously concerned' at the Taliban's 'encroachment on the cultural-historic heritage of not only the Afghan people, but all world civilization'; it expressed the hope that the regime would heed worldwide appeals 'to rescind [its] odious edict', and appealed to the international community 'to do all it [could] in the name of the preservation of the unique monuments of the past, the destruction of which would cause irreparable damage to all humankind'.[77] France called on the Taliban to renounce its decision,

[71] 'Council of Europe Secretary General appalled by cultural heritage destruction in Afghanistan', Council of Europe Press Service, Strasbourg, 2 Mar 2001 <http://press.coe.int/cp/2001/146a(2001).htm>.

[72] 'UNESCO envoy sent to Afghanistan', UNESCO Press Release No 2001–31, Paris, 2 Mar 2001 <http://www.unesco.org/bpi/eng/unescopress/2001/01-31e.shtml>.

[73] Communiqué du Groupe Arabe auprès de l'UNESCO, Paris, 2 Mar 2001 <http://www.unesco.org/bpi/eng/unescopress/2001/grouparabvf.shtml> [author's translation].

[74] Asia Pacific Group of countries represented at UNESCO, Statement on Afghanistan, Paris, 9 Mar 2001 <http://www.unesco.org/opi/eng/unescopress/2001/apac.shtml>.

[75] US Department of State (Philip T Reeker, Deputy Spokesman), Press Statement, Washington, DC, 27 Feb 2001 <http://www.state.gov/r/pa/prs/ps/2001/960.htm>.

[76] US Department of State (Richard Boucher, Spokesman), Daily Briefing, Washington, DC, 12 Mar 2001 <http://www.state.gov/r/pa/prs/dpb/2001/1191.htm>.

[77] 'Taliban Edict to Destroy Non-Islamic Relics in Afghanistan', Ministry of Foreign Affairs of the Russian Federation, Daily News Bulletin, Moscow, 1 Mar 2001 <http://www.ln.mid.ru/Bl.nsf/arh/A96C78D751D9F58443256A03003132D7?OpenDocument>.

which 'would endanger ... part of the world's cultural heritage',[78] and President Chirac endorsed UNESCO's efforts to mobilize the international community to prevent the execution of the Taliban's edict.[79] The French government 'solemnly condemn[ed]' the Buddhas' eventual destruction.[80] The German Foreign Minister declared his government to be 'horrified by the wanton destruction of irreplaceable cultural artifacts in Afghanistan', noting that damage to the Buddhas in particular 'would be an irreparable loss for humanity'; he emphasized that Afghanistan '[bore] great responsibility for preserving the world cultural heritage on its territory', and 'strongly support[ed]' calls to the Taliban 'not to damage, [let alone] destroy, Afghanistan's cultural heritage'.[81] For its part, Australia urged the Taliban to heed international calls to ensure the safety of the Buddhas, which were 'of outstanding cultural ... significance, not just for Afghanistan, but for the international community as a whole'.[82]

States with significant Buddhist populations were especially vocal in their condemnation of the Taliban's acts. The Indian Minister of External Affairs, referring to the Buddhas of Bamiyan as 'incomparable and unique,' called for a halt to 'the destruction of these precious manifestations of the cultural heritage of humankind', describing it as 'a grave wrong, indeed, a sacrilege to humanity, to the civilisational and cultural inheritance of all mankind ...';[83] and in a joint resolution of both Houses, the Indian Parliament 'unanimously condemn[ed] ... in the strongest possible terms' what it described as 'an appalling act of cultural vandalism' against 'one of the greatest examples of human creativity', expressing the hope that 'the world community and especially the United Nations' would 'prevail upon the Taliban regime in Afghanistan to desist from this senseless, destructive act'.[84] Japan 'expresse[d] its deepest concern'

78 'Destruction of pre-Islamic statues in Afghanistan', Ministry of Foreign Affairs of France, Statement by the Ministry of Foreign Affairs Spokesperson, Paris, 28 Feb 2001 <http://www.diplomatie.gouv.fr/actu/article.GB.asp?art=10511>.

79 Letter, President of the French Republic to Director-General of UNESCO, Paris, 1 Mar 2001 <http://www.unesco.org/bpi/eng/unescopress/2001/chirac.shtml>.

80 'Destruction of pre-Islamic statues in Afghanistan', Ministry of Foreign Affairs of France, Statement by the Ministry of Foreign Affairs Spokesperson, Paris, 13 Mar 2001 <http://www.diplomatie.gouv.fr/actu/ article.GB.asp?art=10511>.

81 'Federal Government appeals to the Taliban Government in Kabul: Afghanistan bears responsibility for preserving the cultural heritage', German Foreign Office, Berlin, 1 Mar 2001 <http://www.auswaertiges-amt.de/www/en/infoservice/presse/index_html?bereich_id=9&type_id=2&archiv_id=1272&detail=1>. Germany was instrumental in drafting GA res 55/243, and introduced it to the General Assembly: see UN GAOR, above, n 68, 1. In the ensuing debate, Germany 'strongly condemn[ed]' the Taliban's acts, which 'destroy[ed] the cultural heritage of humanity': ibid, 1 and 2 respectively.

82 'Destruction of Buddhist Statues in Afghanistan', Australian Minister for Foreign Affairs, Media Release, 2 Mar 2001 <http://www.dfat.gov.au/media/releases/foreign/2001/fa024_01.html>.

83 'External Affairs Minister, Shri Jaswant Singh's Statement in Parliament on March 2, 2001', Ministry of External Affairs of India, Press Release, New Delhi, 2 Mar 2001 <http://www.meadev.nic.in/news/official/20010302/official.htm>. The Minister concluded: 'If the Taliban do not wish to retain this inheritance, India would be happy to arrange for the transfer of all these artifacts to India where they would be kept safely and preserved for all mankind, in the full knowledge and clear understanding that they are, in the first place and above all, treasures of the Afghan people themselves'. The above phrases were repeated verbatim and elaborated on by the Indian representative to the UN General Assembly: see UN GAOR, above, n 68, 6–8.

84 'Resolution Adopted by both Houses of Parliament', Ministry of External Affairs of India, Press Release, New Delhi, 2 Mar 2001 <http://www.meadev.nic.in/news/official/20010302/

over the Taliban edict, considering it 'internationally recognized that [the Buddhas] should be preserved', and 'preserved as common heritages [sic] of . . . Humanity'.[85] It urged the Taliban to review the edict and to take 'proper measures for the preservation of cultural treasures'.[86] Nepal too condemned the destruction and 'call[ed] upon the international community to join hands to preserve and safeguard the Buddhist monuments'.[87] Thailand and Sri Lanka each expressed their alarm,[88] and appealed to the Taliban to halt the demolition.[89] The latter described the statues as 'of universal cultural and artistic value', and their preservation as 'of interest not only to the Buddhist countries but to the world at large'.[90]

Nor were Islamic States silent. Iran condemned the Taliban's decision,[91] stating that the Buddhas were part of Afghanistan's 'cultural and national heritage and belong[ed] to the history of the region's civilization in which all humanity has a share'.[92] Even

official.htm>. Similarly, the Indian Prime Minister—writing to the leaders of Japan, South Korea, Cambodia, Sri Lanka, Bhutan, Thailand, Laos, Cambodia, Myanmar, USA, UK, France, Russia, and China, as well as to the UN Secretary-General—spoke of the Taliban decree as 'an assault . . . upon an irreplaceable civilisational inheritance of all mankind', and urged that the matter be taken up 'with those countries that ha[d] influence with the Taliban, so that they, too, could intervene to seek the withdrawal of the decree': Ministry of External Affairs of India, Press Release (Untitled), New Delhi, 2 Mar 2001 <http://www.meadev.nic.in/news/official/20010302/official.htm>.

85 'Statement by the Press Secretary/Director-General for Press and Public Relations, Ministry of Foreign Affairs, on the Taliban's Edict to Destroy Statues', Ministry of Foreign Affairs of Japan, Press Release, Tokyo, 1 Mar 2001 <http://www.mofa.go.jp/announce/announce/2001/3/0301.html>.

86 'Japan's Response to Taliban's Edict to Destroy Statues', Ministry of Foreign Affairs of Japan, Press Release, Tokyo, 7 Mar 2001 <http://www.mofa.go.jp/announce/announce/2001/3/0307.html>. For further measures taken by Japan, see ibid. In the UN General Assembly, Japan 'deplore[d] the destruction of the historical statues and monuments of Afghanistan', which were 'truly the common heritage of all humankind': UN GAOR, above, n 68. 4. Similarly, the South Korean representative to the General Assembly characterized the Buddhas as 'an irreplaceable part of the cultural heritage of mankind', and affirmed that his country 'would fully participate in the efforts of the international community to protect the common heritage of mankind': ibid, 9.

87 'Taliban Fire Mortars at Afghan Buddha Statues', Reuters, Kabul, 2 Mar 2001. The Nepalese ambassador to the UN General Assembly described the Buddhas as 'invaluable treasures of [the] world cultural heritage': UN GAOR, ibid, 12.

88 'Taliban Gather Explosives to Smash Afghan Statues', Reuters, Kabul, 2 Mar 2001.

89 'Afghans Smash Ancient Statues, Defy World Appeals', Reuters, Islamabad, 1 Mar 2001.

90 'Foreign Minister Expresses Concern on [sic] the Threat to the World Famous Buddha Statues in Afghanistan', Ministry of Foreign Affairs of Sri Lanka, *Sri Lanka News Update*, 2 Mar 2001 <http://www.lanka.net/lankaupdate/02%20March%202001.html#lkupdate2>. Similarly, in the UN General Assembly, Thailand called the Buddhas 'an invaluable part of Afghanistan's rich cultural heritage, and indeed of the common cultural heritage of mankind': UN GAOR, above, n 68, 11; Bhutan, 'strongly condemn[ing]' their destruction, 'consider[ed] the unique Buddha statues of Bamiyan to be not only a priceless heritage of the Afghan people but also a common heritage of humankind': ibid, 6; and Cambodia decried the destruction of the Buddhas as 'a great loss to Afghanistan [and] an irreparable loss to humanity as a whole', since they were 'the cultural heritage of mankind': ibid, 13.

91 'Taliban demolish ancient statues. Afghani leaders ignore global pleas to preserve giant Buddha figures', MSNBC News Services, 3 Mar 2001.

92 'Museums Interested in Plan to Save Afghan Art', Reuters, New York, 2 Mar 2001. In the UN General Assembly, the Iranian representative described the Buddhas as 'part of the cultural heritage of humanity', which should be 'preserved for the benefit of present and future generations': UN GAOR, above, n 68, 10 and 11 respectively. Similarly, the Egyptian ambassador to the

Pakistan, the Taliban's closest ally, 'appeal[ed] to the Afghan Government to take measures to fully protect Afghanistan's rich historical monuments, sites and artifacts which are part of [the] world's cultural heritage'.[93] The Pakistani Minister of the Interior was dispatched to Afghanistan in a vain attempt to dissuade the Taliban leader, Mullah Omar, from destroying the Buddhas.[94]

Once more, not every State that condemned the Taliban's acts was a Party to the World Heritage Convention. Nor was any explicit reference was made to Afghanistan's conventional obligations.

C. *Analysis of the evidence*

Each of the elements of State practice outlined above calls for separate analysis before general conclusions can be drawn as to the law.

Starting with the four non-binding standard-setting instruments adopted by the General Conference of UNESCO, none of these affords compelling evidence of customary rules regarding states' obligations in respect of cultural heritage situated on their territory. The terminology and other language employed denies them the fundamentally norm-creating character that is a prerequisite for the formation of a rule of general international law,[95] although this is less unequivocally so in the case of the Universal Declaration on Cultural Diversity.[96] As regards both the Recommendation concerning the Protection, at National Level, of the Cultural and Natural Heritage and the Recommendation on Participation by the People at Large in Cultural Life and their Contribution to It, the designation 'Recommendation', the hortatory language used in the relevant provisions[97] and their express applicability only to the Member States of UNESCO[98] (rather than to States generally) all indicate that neither instrument reflects a belief on the part of its adopters that the norms it embodies are customary rules of law. Both the former Recommendation and the Declaration on the Responsibilities of

General Assembly expressed the conviction that 'the historical heritage of the various civilizations belongs to all humanity, which should seek to safeguard and to ensure its continuity . . .': ibid, 9.

[93] Ministry of Foreign Affairs of Pakistan, Press Release, Islamabad, 1 Mar 2001 <http://www.forisb.org/pr/ 2001/PR01–51.htm>; see also 'Statement by Mr Abdul Sattar, Foreign Minister of Pakistan', Ministry of Foreign Affairs of Pakistan, Press Release, Jeddah, 2 Mar 2001 <http://www.forisb.org/pr/2001/PR01–51a.htm>. Pakistan recalled this appeal verbatim in the UN General Assembly: UN GAOR, ibid, 10.

[94] Ministry of Foreign Affairs of Pakistan, Press Release, Islamabad, 10 Mar 2001 <http://www.forisb.org/pr/ 2001/PR01–56.htm>.

[95] See *North Sea Continental Shelf Cases*, above, n 18, at para 72.

[96] Rather than the hortatory '. . . should . . .' or 'It is recommended that . . .', Art 7 of the Declaration on Cultural Diversity, above, n 37, uses the mandatory 'must' (even if '. . . shall . . .' is more unambiguously legal). At the same time, it employs the passive construction 'heritage . . . must be preserved', rather than the more typical active construction 'States have a duty . . .' or the like, suggesting an effort on the part of the General Conference to avoid the phraseology of law.

[97] See Recommendation concerning the Protection, at National Level, of the Cultural and Natural Heritage, above, n 26, Art 4 ('should'); Recommendation on Participation by the People at Large in Cultural Life and their Contribution to It, above, n 31, Art 4 ('It is recommended that . . .').

[98] See Recommendation concerning the Protection, at National Level, of the Cultural and Natural Heritage, ibid, Art 4; Recommendation on Participation by the People at Large in Cultural Life and their Contribution to It, ibid, Art 4.

the Present Generations Towards Future Generations speak of a 'responsibility' towards the cultural heritage,[99] a subtle but significant avoidance of the formal legal terms 'obligation' and 'duty',[100] and a semantic ploy common to diplomatic drafting. The fact that the responsibilities asserted by the latter instrument are incumbent on 'the present generations', as opposed to States, further implies that the General Conference was not declaring what it saw as existing international law; indeed, the preamble to the Declaration refers to its provisions as 'behavioural guidelines'.[101]

Turning to the reactions of States to the destruction of the Buddhas of Bamiyan, the resolution adopted by the General Assembly of the States Parties to the World Heritage Convention provides very little support for the existence of customary obligations in respect of cultural heritage situated on a state's territory. The quotation marks around the phrase ' "crimes against the common heritage of humanity" ' immediately suggest that the use of this term to condemn the wilful destruction of the statues was intended by way of rhetorical device, rather than formal legal characterization. And in the unlikely event that it was, in fact, intended as a statement of law, the phrase is too vague and ambiguous to give rise to a rule, since it is unclear whether the term 'crime' was intended to denote State or individual responsibility.[102] The former intention is unlikely, in light of the well-publicized omission (at least *eo nomine*) of the very concept of State criminal responsibility from the Articles on the Responsibility of States for Internationally Wrongful Acts adopted by the International Law Commission in August 2001, prior to the adoption of the resolution in question[103]—unless, that is, the notion of a 'State crime' was inaccurately conflated with the breach of a *delictual* obligation owed to the international community as a whole. Alternatively, if individual criminal responsibility were intended, the assertion of this is without prejudice, and hence irrelevant, to the question of Afghanistan's putative (delictual) responsibility for demolishing the Buddhas.[104] Either way, the opaque phrase ' "crimes against the common heritage of humanity" ' lacks the fundamental norm-creating quality required of a rule of general international law.

As for the resolution of the General Conference of UNESCO on 'Acts constituting

[99] See Recommendation concerning the Protection, at National Level, of the Cultural and Natural Heritage, ibid, Art 4; Declaration on the Responsibilities of the Present Generations Towards Future Generations, above, n 34, Art 7.

[100] In international legal terms, 'responsibility' is the result of breaching an 'obligation'. It is not the obligation itself.

[101] Declaration on the Responsibilities of the Present Generations Towards Future Generations, above, n 34, preamble (twelfth recital).

[102] The two are unhelpfully confused in Georgopoulos, above n 42, at 468–9 and 474–5. The fact that neither is plausible as a statement of custom contemporaneous with the Taliban's acts increases, in turn, the probability that the States Parties' intention was purely rhetorical. Nor, given the general principle of criminal law expressed in the maxim *nullum crimen sine lege*, is it probable that the General Assembly of States Parties was positing *ex post facto* a novel customary rule to the effect that the wilful destruction of at least certain monuments in peacetime gives rise either to State or individual criminal responsibility.

[103] See above, n 9. It is conceded that this point might assume too much by way of international legal expertise of the delegates to the General Assembly of the States Parties to the Convention.

[104] See, eg, Art 4 of the ILC's Draft Code of Crimes against the Peace and Security of Mankind, *Yearbook of the International Law Commission 1996*, Vol II (2). The distinction is reflected in Art 25 (4) of the Rome Statute of the International Criminal Court, UN Doc A/CONF.183/9, English text as corrected.

a crime against the common heritage of humanity', this does no more than note and reiterate 'the fundamental principles' of a range of cultural heritage conventions, and invite the Director-General of UNESCO to formulate a 'Draft Declaration concerning the Intentional Destruction of Cultural Heritage'.[105] It does not expressly characterize the destruction of the Buddhas of Bamiyan as such a crime, whatever that might mean.

For their part, even if their lack of reference to the World Heritage Convention is conducive to this, the various resolutions of the UN General Assembly and Commission on Human Rights evidence no clearer a belief in the existence of States' customary obligations in respect of cultural heritage situated in their territory than do the resolutions and standard-setting instruments already discussed. The resolutions on the situation of human rights in Afghanistan eschew legal idiom: the talk is again of 'responsibility', rather than 'obligation' or 'duty'. Similarly, the preamble to General Assembly Resolution 55/243 refers merely to the 'need' to respect the common heritage of humankind. As for paragraph 1 of the latter, it stresses the Taliban's previous unilateral undertakings to preserve the Buddhas, rather than any putative obligation under general international law. Moreover, in debate prior to the adoption of the resolution, only the representative of Ukraine characterized the destruction of the Buddhas as a violation of international law, and even then he added the ambiguous rider 'in particular of the United Nations Educational, Scientific and Cultural Organization (UNESCO) Convention Concerning the Protection of the World Cultural and Natural Heritage'.[106]

Nor does the plethora of statements by regional groupings and individual States in response to the Taliban's acts furnish any clear *opinio juris* to the effect that Afghanistan was obliged by customary international law to spare the Buddhas of Bamiyan. While an impressive array of States jointly and severally condemned the Taliban's actions, none of them unambiguously characterized it as a violation of a legal obligation, let alone a customary one. The US Secretary of State's ambiguous reference to a 'crime against humankind' was almost certainly wholly rhetorical.[107] India's mention of a 'grave wrong' is opaque, and any legal content it might conceivably have is undermined by the obviously rhetorical words that follow.[108] Japan, for its part, did think it 'internationally recognized' that the Buddhas 'should be preserved . . . as common heritages [sic] of . . . Humanity . . .'; but it is uncertain, given the hortatory 'should', whether this posits a legal duty and, if so, whether it refers to customary international law or to Afghanistan's obligations under the World Heritage Convention. Germany's statement that Afghanistan '[bore] great

[105] That this Draft Declaration is not intended to assert a customary prohibition on the peacetime destruction of cultural heritage is foreshadowed in the background paper to the resolution: see UNESCO Doc 31 C/46, 12 Sept 2001, para 6 (c).

[106] See UN GAOR, above, n 68, 12. The rider is ambiguous to the extent that the phrase 'in particular' can be used to mean 'specifically'.

[107] It is highly unlikely that it was intended as a formal reference to State criminal responsibility, for the reasons outlined above and in light of the US's consistent opposition to the concept of State criminal responsibility. It is equally unlikely that individual criminal responsibility was being suggested, again for reasons already discussed and given the semantically significant divergence between the chosen phrase 'crime against humankind' and the legal term of art 'crime against humanity'.

[108] '. . . indeed, a sacrilege to humanity, to the civilisational and cultural inheritance of all mankind . . .'.

responsibility for preserving the world cultural heritage on its territory' is not dissimilar.[109]

Finally, it should be noted that the consistent endorsement, in the above resolutions and statements, of cultural heritage as a common heritage of humankind is not to be equated with the assertion of a customary obligation to preserve this heritage. Such an obligation might be suggested by way of corollary. But a corollary is insufficiently norm-creating in itself to form the basis of a rule of law.

All in all, the relevant State practice attests to a remarkable universal consensus that the destruction of the Buddhas of Bamiyan was condemnable as a matter of policy, being harmful to the interests of the Afghan people and of humanity as a whole. But none of it supports the conclusion that a State is presently under a customary legal obligation, in time of peace, to protect, conserve and transmit to future generations cultural heritage situated on its territory, either straightforwardly or as a function of a human right. The requisite *opinio juris* is just not evident.

This does not mean, however, that the evidence supports no legal conclusions whatsoever.

While it may not suggest customary legal duties on the part of the State on whose territory cultural heritage is situated, the above evidence provides cogent and conclusive support for the view that—as a matter of general international law—diplomatic condemnation[110] of a State's mistreatment of at least certain monuments situated on its territory, along with diplomatic efforts to prevent or halt it, does not amount to an impermissible interference in that State's domestic affairs.[111] Every State and regional grouping quoted above clearly felt legally entitled to intervene diplomatically in

[109] Two things suggest a rhetorical import. First, in formal legal terms Afghanistan would bear responsibility not 'for preserving the world cultural heritage on its territory' but for failing to do so. Secondly one does not speak of 'great' State responsibility: a State is responsible or it is not, regardless of the extent of reparation owed. (Nor is it irrelevant that the German representative in the UN General Assembly, in 'strongly condemn[ing]' the Taliban's deeds, characterized them merely as 'irresponsible acts of religious intolerance' and as 'barbarism': see UN GAOR, above, n 68, 1 and 2 respectively.) Moreover, even if a legal meaning was intended, it is unclear whether the responsibility asserted is referable to custom or to the Convention. The use of the phrase 'world cultural heritage' would perhaps imply the latter.

[110] Note that, even where an international obligation is implicated, protest and other forms of diplomatic censure do not amount to the invocation of State responsibility, so that even States not entitled to invoke such responsibility under either Art 42 or Art 48 of the ILC's Articles are nonetheless entitled to have their say, as it were: see ILC, above, n 9, commentary to ARSIWA Art 42, para (2), 294–5; and Crawford, above, n 9, 42. *A fortiori* if, as here, no international obligation is involved.

[111] For the prohibition on intervention, see Declaration on the Inadmissibility of Intervention in the Domestic Affairs of States and the Protection of Their Independence and Sovereignty, GA res 2131 (XX), 21 Dec 1965; Declaration on Principles of International Law concerning Friendly Relations and Co-operation Among States in accordance with the Charter of the United Nations, GA res 2625 (XXV), 24 Oct 1970, third section; Declaration on the Strengthening of International Security, GA res 2734 (XXV), 16 Dec 1970, paras 2, 4, and 5; Declaration on the Inadmissibility of Intervention and Interference in the Internal Affairs of States, GA res 36/103, 9 Dec 1981. The prohibition on intervention, a corollary of the sovereign equality of States, was held to be a rule of general international law in *Military and Paramilitary Activities In and Against Nicaragua (Nicaragua v United States of America)*, Merits, Judgment, ICJ Rep 1986, 14, at para 202. In the context of the UN, see UN Charter, Art 2 (7); and, as specifically regards UNESCO, see Constitution of the United Nations Educational, Scientific and Cultural Organization, Art I (3).

defence of the Buddhas of Bamiyan. Although the relevant practice derives from a single incident, it is extensive and virtually uniform,[112] and could be said to manifest customary international law. Additionally, in the specific context of UN organs such as the General Assembly and the Commission on Human Rights,[113] the practice reveals unequivocally that criticism by these organs of a State's conduct towards at least certain monuments, and their mobilisation to influence it for the better, is not to be considered an impermissible intervention 'in matters which are essentially within the domestic jurisdiction of [that] State', within the meaning of Article 2 (7) of the UN Charter. Moreover, insofar as the 'target' State in question was a Member of the General Conference of UNESCO when the latter adopted, without a vote in each case, the Recommendations and Declarations cited above, it could be said to have acknowledged by its conduct that cultural heritage situated on its territory is a proper subject of international concern;[114] *a fortiori* where that State is a party to the World Heritage Convention.

This leaves open the question of the scope of application *ratione materiae* of these rights of intervention. Specifically, just how culturally significant must given heritage be before States and the UN can intervene? In this regard, it will be recalled that General Assembly Resolution 55/243 spoke of the Buddhas of Bamiyan as 'unique' and 'irreplaceable'; the European Union described them as 'of priceless historic value' and 'of vital importance . . . to the world as a whole'; the US placed them 'among the world's great cultural treasures'; Australia characterized them as 'of outstanding cultural . . . significance, not just for Afghanistan, but for the international community as a whole'; and India referred to them as 'one of the greatest examples of human creativity'. At the same time, there is no indication that these epithets were invoked as formal criteria, let alone legal minima for intervention. For its part, the Recommendation concerning the Protection, at National Level, of the Cultural and Natural Heritage defines as 'cultural heritage' monuments, groups of buildings and sites 'of special value'. The Declaration on the Responsibilities of the Present Generations Towards Future Generations speaks simply of 'cultural heritage', without elaborating, and the Universal Declaration on Cultural Diversity refers similarly to 'heritage'.[115]

In the end, however, it is not actually necessary to specify a priori the degree of cultural significance demanded before a given monument, building or site is considered cultural heritage in respect of which States and the UN are entitled to intervene. It need

[112] See *North Sea Continental Shelf Cases*, above, n 18, at para 74.

[113] As for UNESCO, a UN specialized agency, it is clear that the constitutional prohibition on its intervention 'in matters which are essentially within [a Member State's] domestic jurisdiction' (Constitution of the United Nations Educational, Scientific and Cultural Organization, Art I (3)) does not prevent it from intervening to 'assur[e] the conservation and protection of the world's inheritance of . . . works of art and monuments of history', in accordance with the mandate accorded it by Art I (2)(c) of its Constitution. In cases involving non-States Members of the Organization, the general permissive rule discussed in the text would still permit such intervention.

[114] In the words of Baxter, once a matter has become the subject of even a 'soft' international norm, it 'can no longer be asserted to be one within the reserved domain or domestic jurisdiction of the State': RR Baxter, 'International Law in "Her Infinite Variety" ' (1980) 29 ICLQ 549, at 565.

[115] The Recommendation on Participation by the People at Large in Cultural Life and their Contribution to It, above, n 31, Art 4, chapeau and subsection (q)(i), limits itself to 'the heritage of the past, and particularly ancient monuments', excluding the architectural and artistic heritage.

simply be stated by way of a rule that States and the organs of the United Nations are not prevented by the prohibition on interference in the domestic affairs of a State from intervening diplomatically in defence of 'cultural heritage', as such, situated on that State's territory. The threshold of cultural value demanded before a given monument, group of buildings or site is considered 'cultural heritage' for the purposes of the rule can be left as a matter of appreciation in each case. It is not fatal to the requisite norm-creating character of a rule that its applicability be a matter of judgment. Such is the case with countless rules; indeed, such is the case with the 'outstanding universal value' required by the World Heritage Convention.

The upshot is that, although it cannot be concluded that a State currently owes obligations to the international community as a whole in respect of cultural heritage situated on its territory, the international community as a whole, jointly and severally, is permitted by general international law to subject a State's peacetime treatment of such heritage to scrutiny, comment and, where appropriate, criticism.

IV. CONCLUSION

In the event, then, all States—whether singly, in regional fora, or in the context of UNESCO or of UN organs—may intervene diplomatically if another State fails in time of peace to protect, conserve and transmit to future generations cultural heritage situated on its territory, regardless of whether they, or that State, are Parties to the World Heritage Convention. They may call on that State to care for this heritage, and protest if it fails to do so. They may not, however, compel preservation through judicial proceedings or countermeasures. The world's cultural heritage is the proper concern of the international community as a whole but it is not yet, in peacetime, the object of obligations owed to that community.

The practical consequences of the distinction are, however, slight. As it is, the law of State responsibility is, in practice, an unlikely and ill-adapted mechanism for compelling a State to preserve cultural heritage situated on its territory. Jurisdictional hurdles make judicial proceedings notoriously difficult. As for countermeasures, it is unresolved whether they are available at all to those States invoking responsibility solely under Article 48 of the ILC's Articles;[116] and even if this were so, assessing proportionality[117] might pose a bar, given that simple reciprocity,[118] in the form of damage by other States to cultural heritage found on their respective territories, would be preposterous and possibly impermissible.[119] Finally,

[116] See ARSIWA, Art 54 and ILC, above, n 9, commentary to ARSIWA Art 54, 350–5; Crawford, above, n 9, 54–6; M Koskenniemi, 'Solidarity Measures: State Responsibility as a New International Order?' (2001) 72 BYIL 337.

[117] See ARSIWA, Art 51: 'Countermeasures must be commensurate with the injury suffered, taking into account the gravity of the internationally wrongful act and the rights in question.'

[118] Proportionality does not necessarily equate with reciprocity. That is, countermeasures need not involve the breach of an identical obligation. At the same time, reciprocity obviously makes the assessment of proportionality more straightforward.

[119] Recall that deliberate damage by a state to cultural heritage situated on its territory constitutes a violation of the right to take part in cultural life recognized in Art 27 of the Universal Declaration and Art 15 of the ICESCR. In this light, depending on the interpretation of the word 'fundamental', countermeasures involving damage to cultural heritage might—although, it has to be said, probably would not—fall foul of the stipulation in ARSIWA, Art 50 (1)(b) that

and perhaps most saliently, a State's responsibility can only be invoked once it has breached the relevant international obligation, and by then, in most cases of damage to or destruction of cultural heritage, it is too late.[120] In light of all this, in the great majority of cases, diplomatic pressure would be the only practicable option. As such, given that States not party to the World Heritage Convention are, it appears, permitted to intervene diplomatically if another State fails, in time of peace, to preserve elements of the world's cultural heritage situated on its territory, it scarcely matters in practice that they are not entitled to compel preservation through the invocation of State responsibility. Indeed, in practice, since diplomatic coercion is the only realistic course of action, it is perhaps immaterial that States which *are* Parties to the World Heritage Convention may, in principle, invoke another's responsibility for failing to preserve this heritage.

POSTSCRIPT

At its 32nd session (29 September–17 October 2003), the General Conference of UNESCO adopted the Declaration concerning the Intentional Destruction of Cultural Heritage,[121] as foreshadowed in its resolution of 2001 entitled 'Acts constituting a crime against the common heritage of humanity'.[122] Recalling both 'the tragic destruction of the Buddhas of Bamiyan that affected the international community as a whole' and 'the principles of all UNESCO's conventions, recommendations [and] declarations . . . for the protection of cultural heritage'; mindful 'that . . . intentional destruction [of cultural heritage] may have adverse consequences on human dignity and human rights'; and mindful 'of the development of rules of customary international law . . . related to the protection of cultural heritage in peacetime . . .', the General Conference resolves in paragraph III (1) that States 'should take all appropriate measures to prevent, avoid, stop and suppress acts of intentional destruction of cultural heritage, wherever such heritage is located'. It declares in paragraph VI that '[a] State that intentionally destroys or intentionally fails to take appropriate measures to prohibit, prevent, stop, and punish intentional destruction of cultural heritage of great importance for humanity, whether or not it is inscribed on a list maintained by UNESCO or another international organization, bears the responsibility for such destruction, to the extent provided for by international law'. The phrase 'crimes against the common heritage of humanity' is not founded in the text, although paragraph VII recommends that States 'should', in accordance with international law', provide for individual criminal responsibility in respect of the relevant acts. The Declaration's hortatory language and Article VI's use, in the light of the *travaux préparatoires*,[123] of the phrase 'to the extent provided for by international

'[c]ountermeasures shall not affect . . . obligations for the protection of fundamental human rights'.

[120] Although perhaps not too late to stop damage becoming destruction, in cases of deterioration or piecemeal harm.

[121] Text on file with author.

[122] See above, at 180.

[123] See the resolution 'Acts constituting a crime against the common heritage of humanity', above at 180. More specifically, UNESCO Doc 31 C/46, para 6 (c) states that the Declaration 'would not be intended to create obligations for States, but would restate the fundamental principles of the existing legal instruments . . .'.

law' make it clear that the General Conference is not suggesting that States currently owe customary peacetime obligations in respect of cultural heritage situated on their territory; rather, the Declaration is a restatement of the conventional *droit acquis* (as well as a resounding affirmation of an emergent political consensus). At the same time, by calling on States—and not just Member States—to prevent and stop intentional destruction of cultural heritage 'wherever such heritage is located', the Declaration recognizes that diplomatic mobilization for the benefit heritage threatened in a given State does not amount to unlawful intervention in that State's domestic affairs.[124]

Roger O'Keefe*

[124] In support of UNESCO's own right to intervene, the preamble (third recital) to the Declaration cites Art I (2)(c) of the Organization's Constitution.

* University Lecturer & Deputy Director, Lauterpacht Research Centre for International Law, University of Cambridge; Fellow, Magdalene College, Cambridge. The article is a more detailed version of a presentation made by the author at 'Legal Tools for World Heritage Conservation', an international workshop on the occasion of the thirtieth anniversary of the World Heritage Convention held on 11–12 November 2002 in Siena, Italy and organized by the UNESCO World Heritage Centre and the Faculty of Law of the University of Siena.

Part VII
Human Rights and Development

[17]

Correcting Globalisation in Health: Transnational Entitlements versus the Ethical Imperative of Reducing Aid-Dependency

Gorik Ooms* and Rachel Hammonds
Institute of Tropical Medicine, Antwerp

*Corresponding author: Gorik Ooms, Department of Public Health, Institute of Tropical Medicine, Nationalestraat 155, 2000 Antwerp, Belgium. Tel.: +32-3-247.66.66, Fax: +32-3-216.14.31, E-mail: gooms@itg.be

There is growing tension between arguments for increasing foreign assistance to achieve the Millennium Development Goals and arguments for reducing foreign assistance so as to avoid a new form of colonisation. This essay argues that the impact of the global economy on access to healthcare in developing countries requires global corrective measures. It acknowledges the risk of foreign assistance being used for illegitimate purposes, but argues that if foreign assistance were provided within a human rights framework of rights-holders and duty-bearers, this risk can be mitigated. It analyses the current development aid paradigm, and how the fight against AIDS has begun to change it. It also examines why access to essential healthcare is a human right creating national and transnational entitlements and argues that foreign assistance responding to these entitlements is not a matter of discretionary spending; it is a matter of meeting legal obligations. It explores the legal implications of the core content of the right to health and its relationship with the obligation to provide assistance. It concludes with a review of two different but complementary proposals to create a global approach to the realisation of the right to health: the Global Health Fund and the Health Impact Fund Initiative.

The Ethical Imperative of Reducing Aid-Dependency?

'Needless to say, that apart from fanning corruption, aid plays to the advantage of the giver—the richer nations of the world which keep the poor mineral-rich countries dependent and in many ways, economically colonized' commented Moses Sserwanga (2007) of *The Monitor* (Kampala, Uganda) calling for the November 2007 Commonwealth Heads of Government Meeting to endorse and pursue fair trade, not aid as the route to human development.

Sserwanga is not alone in this view. Captured by the slogan 'Trade, Not Aid', the ethical imperative of reducing aid-dependency is increasingly supported by well-intended voices from the so-called 'global South' as well as from the 'global North' (Jenkins, 2002; Vidal, 2002; Preble and Tupy, 2005). Development aid is perceived as undesirable, at best as a necessary evil that should be consigned to the history books as soon as possible.

We also support efforts to make international trade 'fairer'. However, we do not understand why both claims are linked and treated as mutually exclusive: why 'trade, not aid' instead of 'trade, and aid'? Is there anything intrinsically wrong with global, transnational solidarity, loosely defined as the ethical responsibilities of all human beings towards one another? Does all aid deserve to be termed 'economic colonisation'?

The ethical imperative of reducing aid-dependency is not benign. In the absence of an alternative domestic source of financing, reducing the aid-dependency of developing countries' health sectors simply means reducing health expenditure, which decreases access to healthcare for most of the population and in particular for poor and vulnerable groups. It leads to extremely difficult ethical choices for health practitioners in developing countries, such as withholding lifesaving treatment from some people because the same amount of money can 'buy' more human lives if spent on cheaper treatments for other diseases (and other people). Of course, those choices exist in developed countries as well, but in countries with an annual government health budget of less than US$15 per person, they take a far crueller form than in developed countries where governments' annual health budgets exceed US$2000 per person.

Those who oppose aid-dependence will argue that they do not want people to be denied access to healthcare or life-saving treatment and consequently die. In fact, their arguments probably do not address the issue of African AIDS patients becoming dependent on open-ended assistance to finance their treatment. They concern themselves with African states becoming dependent on foreign assistance. As such, they limit the scope of 'fairness' in transnational interactions to economic transactions only: once economic fairness has been established, the well-being and the dignity of individual people is a purely national or domestic matter. Solidarity between people is thus confined to the borders of the state.

We do not share this view. Firstly, we believe that the ethical responsibility of human beings towards one another transcends national borders. Furthermore, as economic globalisation has an impact on the well-being and the dignity of all people, corrective measures must be taken at a global level as well. But we acknowledge that foreign assistance can take the form of economic colonisation, whereby, for example, donor countries obtain favourable conditions for exporting mineral resources from a recipient country in return for much needed assistance in fighting deadly epidemics. While we do not endorse the ethical imperative of reducing aid-dependency as such, we do endorse the ethical imperative of avoiding a new form of colonisation.

We acknowledge the tension between the ethical imperative of avoiding new forms of colonisation and promoting the well-being of all human beings, wherever they live. We can overcome this tension by understanding foreign assistance as a transnational legal obligation and providing it as such, not as condition-laden charity. The risks of economic colonisation can be mitigated by rooting foreign assistance in the ethical imperative of transnational solidarity and administering it within a human rights framework with ensuing transnational duties and entitlements, creating rights-holders and duty-bearers, rather than the dominant aid framework of discretionary giving.

The evolution from condition-laden discretionary giving to a new aid paradigm based on duties and entitlements is already taking place, but it requires both further theoretical deepening and the development of tools for practical implementation.

In this essay, we will:

- Examine how globalisation affects health in developing countries, and why the impact of the global economy on access to healthcare in those countries requires global corrective measures;
- Explore the health development paradigm and its failures, and how the fight against AIDS has started changing it;
- Examine the right to health as an international right; the core content of the right to health and its relationship with the obligation to provide assistance;
- Analyse two different but complementary proposals to create a global approach to the realisation of the right to health: the Global Health Fund and the Health Impact Fund Initiative.

The Impact of Globalisation on Health in Developing Countries

We have heard that the world is becoming a global village so many times that it is becoming a meaningless truism. Yet for the Mozambican woman picking cashew nuts from the few trees she owns, globalisation is a reality. She used to pick, roast and peel the nuts. Now she does not roast and peel any more because World Bank economists have convinced her government that her comparative advantage is not to roast and peel nuts.

As the BBC (Loyn, 2003) reported: 'The new winds of economic reform were designed to enable Mozambique to enter the world economy, winning debt forgiveness and new international funding. But the result instead was that 10,000 people who were directly employed by the [cashew] industry lost their jobs, another million nut collectors lost an income, and Mozambique remains resolutely close to the bottom in league tables of world poverty.'

One million Mozambican nut collectors lost an income (McMillan *et al.*, 2002; De Renzio and Hanlon, 2007). But that is not the only way in which globalisation affected their lives. Most of them have children and, like all children, they get sick and need treatment.

About 40 per cent of Mozambican households do not seek treatment when a family member gets ill because either the nearest health centre is too far away, or they cannot afford the user fees (Chao and Kostermans, 2002). Those who seek treatment might find a health centre without appropriately trained staff. According to estimates by the Joint Learning Initiative, and endorsed by the World Health Organization (WHO), 'countries with fewer than 2.5 health care professionals (counting only doctors, nurses and midwives) per 1000 population failed to achieve an 80 per cent coverage rate for deliveries by skilled birth attendants or for measles immunization' (World Health Organization, 2006). Mozambique, with its population of about 20 million people, would need 50,000 health professionals. In 2004, it had 514 doctors; 3974 nurses and 2236 midwives: a shortage of more than 86 per cent, or more than 43,000 health professionals (WHO, 2007a). Here, globalisation plays a role as well. There is a free and open global market for trained health workers: a Mozambican nurse will compare the salary offered by the Health Ministry with the salary offered by the South African or British public health systems. Fortunately, for Mozambicans seeking healthcare, the damage from this aspect of globalisation remains limited. Most Mozambican health workers speak their native language and Portuguese, not English. But this is probably a temporary protection, as English conquers the world as the lingua franca, future generations of Mozambican health workers will be attracted by the pull factors of globalisation.

Now imagine the former nut collector, out of a job, fortunate enough to live close to a health centre, fortunate enough to live close to a health centre with a trained health worker and fortunate enough to be able to pay the fee. Chances are that she will not receive the appropriate medicines for her children. This might well be a consequence of globalisation too. Until recently, Mozambique did not offer patent protection for medicines. The Mozambican Health Ministry purchased most medicines from India, where patent protection for medicines did not yet exist either and manufacturers produced cheap generic versions of new and effective medicines.

Nowadays, the heralds of a global unrestricted market want medicines available in India and Mozambique to be available in Europe and North America as well. At the same time, they want the extraordinary profits generated by new medicines—which depend on patent protection and the legal monopolies they create; the opposite of an unrestricted market—to be protected; they do not want generic medicines manufactured in India to be sold on European and North American markets. Rather than strengthening barriers between rich and poor markets, they have tried to ban generics from the poor markets. And, to a large extent, they have succeeded. To become or to maintain membership in the World Trade Organization (WTO), countries like India and Mozambique were required to adopt patent protection for medicines.

As globalisation rendered many poor Mozambicans poorer, and health workers and medicines more expensive, one might expect the heralds of globalisation to promote corrective or protective global solutions to Mozambique's health crises. The opposite is true. When it comes to healthcare—and other social services—the heralds of globalisation suddenly plead national self-reliance or the importance of local solutions. Global interdependence is good when it comes to trade, but when it comes to healthcare it is undesirable aid-dependency.

The Current Aid Paradigm, and how the Fight against AIDS has Started Changing it

In a global market, the provision of social services requires a global approach as well. Yet, to take one example, at present the International Monetary Fund (IMF) is unwilling or unable to imagine open-ended global financing mechanisms for social services. The IMF believes its role is to 'prepare countries for an orderly exit from long-term reliance on aid' (International Monetary Fund, 2007a: 7).

The consequences of aiming for 'an orderly exit from long-term reliance on aid'—national self-reliance or reducing aid-dependency—are quite dramatic. Primarily, it creates a type of mental brake on increasing foreign assistance for social services: if the ultimate aim is national self-reliance, too much aid could hinder or delay the achievement of this goal. Some will argue that the real reason for insufficient foreign assistance is selfishness on behalf of wealthier countries, and that the aim of national self-reliance is at best a weak excuse for reduced aid. But this seems to be contradicted by the fact that billions of dollars of presently available foreign assistance are not used to improve health or educational services but are instead used to increase developing countries' dollar reserves.

According to Terry McKinley of the United Nations Development Program (UNDP), 'significant proportions of [Official Development Assistance] have been diverted into reserves, aborting the transfer of real resources into developing countries' (McKinley, 2005: 8). In sub-Saharan Africa alone, the total amount of dollar reserves increased from US$32 billion in 2000 to US$58 billion in 2004.

Although McKinley blames this phenomenon on the fear of aid-induced 'Dutch disease', the IMF has gradually replaced 'Dutch disease' warnings as with the concept of 'fiscal space' or 'fiscal sustainability' as the new rationale for recipient countries to stockpile and not use foreign assistance. What is fiscal space or fiscal sustainability? According to Pablo Gottret and George Schieber of the World Bank it is 'a country's capacity to accommodate expenditures financed with aid within the domestic budget constraint in a reasonable period of time' (Gottret and Schieber, 2006: 139).

What happens when donors are willing to fund expenditures that are higher than what the 'domestic budget constraint in a reasonable period of time' allows? Rather than refusing the 'excess' foreign assistance, governments might be tempted—and are encouraged by the IMF—to accept this assistance, but to divert it to dollar reserves and not spend it improving health or education services.

Thus it appears that the aim of sustainability at the national level is the main obstacle to a substantial increase in foreign assistance for healthcare: it inhibits donor countries' willingness to increase foreign assistance, and even if they did, chances are the additional assistance would not be spent. However, if we view foreign assistance for healthcare in the same way as we view social security transfers within a country then we would not have to concern ourselves with calculating when and if developing countries will develop the capacity to finance basic healthcare without foreign assistance. Instead we would accept that many developing countries need to rely, to varying degrees, on continued financial assistance for several decades. At the very least this change in mindset may allow for the full use of the foreign assistance that is currently available, rather than diverting substantial parts to dollar reserves.

We believe that the fight against AIDS has already created a new aid paradigm. The low-income countries highly affected by AIDS are unable to finance AIDS treatment themselves. Recognising this the Global Fund to fight AIDS, Tuberculosis and Malaria (Global Fund, 2007: Section 4.5.5) has abandoned the conventional approach to sustainability: 'Applicants are not required to demonstrate financial self-sufficiency for the targeted interventions by the end of the proposal term' (Global Fund, 2007: Section 4.5.5).

Furthermore, AIDS activists from wealthy countries are pushing their governments to finance the Global Fund in accordance with an 'equitable contributions framework', based on the relative size of their economies (France *et al.*, 2002). This effort has had some success, and has turned the Global Fund into an embryonic global social security mechanism (with a limited mandate): high-income countries contribute in accordance with their wealth; low-income countries obtain entitlements in accordance with their needs.

Finally, grants from the Global Fund come without political strings attached. Proposals are reviewed by the Global Fund's Technical Review Panel, composed of independent experts, and are approved for funding by the Board of the Global Fund, composed of representatives of donor and recipient countries, United Nations agencies and civil society.

Mead Over, former Lead Health Economist of the World Bank's Development Research Group and currently a Senior Fellow at the Center for Global Development, attributes the 'single-minded focus on AIDS treatment and prevention' to the success of AIDS activists in transforming foreign assistance from charity (or 'discretionary spending') into entitlement spending. 'By effectively converting foreign assistance from discretionary to entitlement spending, the "success" of existing AIDS treatment programs has already locked us into a new aid paradigm. To the extent that the international community heeds the UNAIDS' call, entitlement spending will greatly increase in the next few years, both in absolute terms and, unless total assistance expands at the same phenomenal rate, as a percentage of total assistance' (Over, 2007). We agree with Over on this point: AIDS activists have helped usher in a new aid paradigm by transforming what was perceived as charitable, discretionary spending into entitlement spending.

In the next sections of this essay, we will argue that this new aid paradigm is firmly rooted in the right to health and in the national and transnational entitlements it creates. As such it is a way in which high-income countries can move towards complying with their international obligations with regard to the right to health in the developing world. It should not remain the exception applicable only to the fight against AIDS, tuberculosis and malaria: it should become the standard for global health aid and for other global aid to realise essential social rights whenever the aim of sustainability at national level is unrealistic.

The Right to Health

Ethics and values lie at the heart of the formal framework of international human rights law. The relationship between ethics and human rights is complex and has already been richly explored by many others (Archer, 2003). In this essay, we only aim to explore the extent to which the formal framework of international human rights law provides a foundation for an alternative aid paradigm, in which foreign assistance becomes a duty, responding to an entitlement, thus avoiding foreign assistance being used as a new form of colonisation.

The 1948 Universal Declaration of Human Rights (United Nations, 1948) (UDHR) is the foundation of the modern human rights movement, and although not a legally binding document in itself, later multilateral international human rights treaties elaborating the content of the UDHR do give rise to legally binding obligations on governments. The two key treaties arising from the UDHR, the International Covenant on Civil and Political Rights (United Nations, 1966a) (ICPR) and the International Covenant on Economic, Social and Cultural Rights (United Nations, 1966b) (ICESCR) contain legally binding obligations for the states that ratify them.

The artificial split and elaboration in two different covenants has led some commentators to claim that one set of rights should be prioritised. One critique of social rights like the right to health stems from the fact that they require state action to be implemented. The perception that civil and political rights can be secured without state action or funding and simply require that the state not abuse its power is clearly erroneous, and is not a persuasive argument for favouring one set of rights over the other. The legitimacy of claiming a right to health has also been questioned by commentators who challenge the justiciability of all economic, social and cultural rights, claiming they are 'merely' programmatic rights (Vierdag, 1978). This justiciability critique is rebutted by numerous commentators (Arambulo, 1999). The political and academic debates surrounding the two different sets of rights continue despite the fact that human rights experts and the international community have affirmed that human rights are indivisible and cannot be fulfilled in isolation from one another.[1]

Article 12 of the ICESCR defines the right to health as 'the right to the highest attainable standard of physical and mental health' and corresponding state obligations encompass the provision of medical services and the underlying preconditions necessary to health. This bare bones definition has been affirmed and expanded on in later international conventions (United Nations, 1979, 1989) and other national and international legislation. The nature of states' obligations in achieving economic, social and cultural rights, including the right to health, has been specified more precisely by the United Nations Committee on Economic, Social and Cultural Rights (the Committee), as will be discussed below.

Core Obligations and the Obligation to Provide Assistance

In 1986, Esin Örücü elaborated the notion of the 'core content' of a human right: the essential substance of a right, its raison d'être, without which it would have no meaning (Örücü, 1986). The concept of 'core content' was endorsed by the Committee in General Comment No. 3 (Committee on Economic, Social and Cultural Rights, 1990). It clarified that there are limits to the compromises that states can make with regard to realising economic, social and cultural rights by invoking the explicitly acknowledged impossibility of realising all of them completely and at once. Further, there is a minimum threshold, a minimum essential level or a core content, which must be realised without further delay.

Toebes' work defining the core content of the right to health classified the elements that contribute to the health status of persons dividing them into two sub-groups: elements of healthcare and the underlying preconditions for health (Toebes, 1999). One year later, the Committee's General Comment No. 14 on the right to health affirmed the existence of a minimum essential level of the right to health (Committee on Economic, Social and Cultural Rights, 2000a).

Like Toebes, the Committee defined the minimum essential level of the right to health indirectly, through the definition of the core obligations of States parties with regards to the right to health. The list includes an obligation to ensure access, to health facilities, goods and services as well as basic shelter, housing, safe and potable water and ensuring freedom from hunger through ensuring access to minimum essential food. The core obligations also include the obligation to provide essential drugs, as from time to time defined under the WHO Action Programme on Essential Drugs. The fundamental importance of non-discrimination is emphasised throughout as is the obligation for a state to pay particular attention to vulnerable or marginalised groups (Committee on Economic, Social and Cultural Rights, 2000a: para. 43).

The Committee further clarified that neither resource constraints nor progressive realisation can excuse non-compliance with the core obligations noting that the burden rests with the State to demonstrate that it has used all available resources to satisfy its core obligations, which are non-derogable (Committee on Economic, Social and Cultural Rights, 2000a).

For most health practitioners with experience in developing countries, this definition of the minimum essential level of the right to health is a distant dream. In 37 of the world's 54 low-income countries, as classified by the World Bank, public health expenditure was less than US$10 per person per year in 2004 (Ooms *et al.*, 2006). The inadequacy of this level of spending is glaring when compared with the Commission on Macroeconomics and Health's (CMH) estimate of US$38 per person per year in 2015, needed for an adequate package of healthcare interventions including AIDS treatment (Commission on Macroeconomics and Health, 2001).

In light of this shortfall, at a May 2000 Committee session Paul Hunt remarked: 'if the Committee decided to approve the list of core obligations, it would be unfair not to insist also that richer countries fulfil their obligations relating to international cooperation under article 2, paragraph 1, of the Covenant. The two sets of obligations should be seen as two halves of a package.' (Committee on Economic, Social and Cultural Rights, 2000b:

para 27) Later, in reporting on his Mozambique mission Hunt re-emphasised this point stressing that financial and technical assistance is an international responsibility under the ICESCR and the International Convention on the Rights of the Child. (Hunt, 2006).

However, as Skogly argues, the legal force of obligations of international cooperation in human rights instruments has not been settled. It is debated 'whether there is an obligation to provide international assistance (as in official development assistance) by rich countries, and on the other hand, whether there is a right to receive international assistance on part of the poorer countries.' (Skogly, 2006).

We argue that the principle of international cooperation is becoming part of customary international law as evidenced in founding documents of several international bodies. For example, articles 55 and 56 of the Charter of the United Nations (1945) affirm the principle of cooperation among states. The necessity of international cooperation to realise the right to health in particular was confirmed in the preamble to the Constitution of the WHO: 'The enjoyment of the highest attainable standard of health is one of the fundamental rights of every human being without distinction of race, religion, political belief, economic or social condition. The health of all peoples is fundamental to the attainment of peace and security and is dependent upon the fullest co-operation of individuals and States.' (World Health Organization, 1946). Article 2(1) of the ICESCR creates an obligation on States parties to provide international assistance and cooperation to the maximum of their available resources (United Nations, 1966b). Further, in General Comment No. 3, the Committee clarified that the ICESCR's drafters intended the phrased 'to the maximum of its available resources' to refer to both a State's resources and those available through international cooperation and assistance (Committee on Economic, Social and Cultural Rights, 1990).

In debating the nature of international obligations, Philip Alston argues that repeated inclusion of these commitments in international institutions will demonstrate their status as customary law. 'It will be difficult for countries to insist that they have persistently objected to such an evolution if they continue to affirm in so many contexts their commitment to assisting developing country governments to achieve targets as tangible and clearly achievable as the MDGs. The correlative obligation would, of course, be confined to situations in which a developing country had demonstrated its best efforts to meet the Goals and its inability to do so because of lack of financial resources '(Alston, 2005: 778).

In our opinion, even more important than the 'reiteration of such commitments' is the fact that some countries cannot realise the core content of the right to health, having demonstrated their 'best efforts' and their 'inability to do so because of lack of financial resources'. If the right to health is in itself meaningless without the realisation of at least the core content, and if some countries lack the resources to realise the core content of the right to health, then the right to health cannot be realised on a global scale without the obligation to provide assistance. In turn, this legal obligation only takes effect when developing countries have demonstrated their 'best efforts' to fulfill their obligations.

The Right to Health and Access to Essential Medicines

In recent years attempts by civil society activists to improve access to essential medicines for disadvantaged and vulnerable groups, in particular the world's poor, have further energised the debate surrounding the right to health. The issue of access to essential medicines is an excellent example of how local and international factors interact and essentially shape local market access. It is an unfortunate example of how failure to respect the core obligation to provide essential medicines, on the part of both developing nations and those in a position to assist, costs the lives of millions of the world's disadvantaged and vulnerable people.

The 2005 Montreal Statement on the Human Right to Essential Medicines (the Montreal Statement) (Pogge, 2005), adopted by a group of experts, academics and international organisations, reiterated that access to essential medicines has a key role to play in realising the right to health. It is pertinent here because it addresses the effect that lending, trade and aid policy, and the international organisations involved in these fields, have on access to essential medicines in the developing world and consequently the right to health.

Articles 9 and 10 of the Montreal Statement are explicit about the direct link between policies advanced by the developed world, through bilateral and multilateral action (e.g. through the IMF and World Bank), and the impact on health in the developing world. Article 11 calls on states to place the right to health above trade concerns and notes 'that States are entitled and obliged to take all reasonable and feasible steps to enable access to essential medicines, including adopting trade practices and using trade flexibilities and safeguards, such as compulsory licensing and parallel importing.' Article 13 calls on international institutions and their members to comply with their duty to respect and actively promote the right to health by ensuring that international agreements relating to the protection of intellectual property are in conformity with human rights obligations.

The Political Declaration by Governments, adopted at the June 2006 United Nations General Assembly High Level Meeting on AIDS (marking the fifth anniversary of the adoption of the Declaration of Commitment on HIV/AIDS by the United Nations General Assembly (United Nations, 2001)) echoed Article 11 of the Montreal Statement. It included the proclamation 'that access to medication is one of the fundamental elements to achieve the right to health, and the WTO TRIPS Agreement does not and should not prevent States from taking measures now and in the future to protect public health.' (United Nations, 2006).

Transforming a Collective Obligation into Individual Transnational Entitlements: The Global Health Fund

We have argued that an alternative global health aid paradigm, based on legal entitlements and duties, can overcome the tension between the ethical imperatives of avoiding a new form of colonisation and of promoting the well-being and the dignity of all human beings. However, when trying to move from theory to practice, we are confronted with a complex scheme of rights-holders and duty-bearers. We have argued above that developing countries have a right to assistance to achieve the core content of a right when they can prove that they have made their 'best effort' but cannot achieve the core content of a right due to financial constraints. But who must assist whom? There are many countries in need of assistance and many countries in a position to assist. The correlative duties need to be distributed among states in some way.

Perhaps an international court of social justice, where low-income states could make high-income states comply with their duties, would solve the problem. Such a court could apply principles of equity and fairness to establish individual states' entitlements and duties. However, no such court exists. This is a problem, but not an insurmountable one. For example, AIDS activists pressured the international community to create the Global Fund, which—when viewed through a human rights lens—is nothing other than a tool for compliance with the transnational obligation to fulfill an essential part of the core content of the right to health. The existence of the Global Fund exerted pressure on governments of states in need of assistance to develop AIDS treatment plans and on governments of states in a position to assist to provide the needed assistance. It created individual states' entitlements, and to some extent—the 'equitable contributions framework' already mentioned—individual states' duties.

But it is difficult to achieve progress in the fight against a single disease (or even three diseases) without addressing the fragility of public health systems in developing countries. To address this fundamental problem the world needs a Global Fund to fight poor health, including AIDS treatment but not excluding other essential healthcare, or a Global Health Fund to realise the core content of the right to health. What would be required to transform the Global Fund into a Global Health Fund, firmly rooted in a human rights approach, or a 'Framework Convention on Global Health' (Gostin, 2008)?

First of all, a Global Health Fund would have to acknowledge that the primary responsibility for realising the right to health remains with the state. It would have to establish a benchmark for the domestic contribution to healthcare that can be expected from developing countries. That would in fact require a double benchmark:

- One benchmark to estimate the amount of domestic resources a developing country can reasonably mobilise for government expenditure;
- A second benchmark to estimate the share of its domestic resources a developing country can reasonably allocate to healthcare.

We examine these benchmarks below, but before looking at the details and the figures, we want to emphasise that we are looking for a method, not for precise estimates. The figures need only be sufficiently realistic to demonstrate the feasibility of a Global Health Fund, as a method to transpose collective entitlements and duties into individual states' entitlements and duties, and not to provide precise estimates.

In order to make a realistic proposal for the first benchmark, we examined present levels of government revenue excluding grants in low-income countries of Sub-Saharan Africa, as estimated by the IMF in its Regional Economic Outlook report for Sub-Saharan Africa of October 2007 (International Monetary Fund, 2007b: 51). These countries managed to increase government revenue excluding grants from 15.6 per cent of GDP in 2003 to 17.8 per cent of GDP in 2008. This is an increase of 0.44 per cent of GDP per year. At this rate, by 2015, government revenue excluding grants could be 20 per cent of GDP.

For the second benchmark, we propose using the pledge made by African Heads of State and Government in the 2001 Abuja Declaration (Organisation of African

Unity, 2001) according to which 15 per cent of the budget should be allocated to health.

The combination of these two benchmarks leads to a general benchmark: low-income countries should mobilise and allocate to healthcare the equivalent of 3 per cent of their GDP before they can say they have made all reasonable efforts to realise the core content of the right to health.

How well are low-income countries performing against this combined benchmark? When we calculate present (figures for 2004) government expenditure on health, the median result is 1.9 per cent of GDP. The weighted average, however, is only 1.1 per cent GDP. India, whose economy accounts for more than half of the combined GDP of low-income countries and whose government expenditure on health is only 0.9 per cent of GDP, brings the average down. Without India, the weighted average would be 1.5 per cent of GDP. But even if we exclude India, low-income countries would have to double their government health expenditure, on average, before they can claim foreign assistance.

Even if this increase in expenditure would double or triple domestic resources for health, it would not be sufficient to realise the core content of the right to health. When we look at IMF estimates about real GDP per capita for the same countries, and assume that 3 per cent of GDP is how much governments of these countries can spend on health without foreign assistance, none of them can spend even half of the US$38 per person per year target recommended by the CMH. In as much as we can consider this US$38 per person per year target an indicator of what these countries need to spend to realise the core content of the right to health, we can consider the difference between US$38 and 3 per cent of real GDP per capita as these countries' entitlement from a Global Health Fund, per inhabitant. These 52 countries together (excluding Somalia and the Democratic Republic of Korea, for which no reliable figures are available) would have an entitlement of about US$51 billion to a Global Health Fund: *not* a collective entitlement, but the sum of 52 *individual* states' entitlements. India alone would have an entitlement of US$21 billion; the other 51 countries would together have an entitlement of US$30 billion.

From where would a Global Health Fund obtain its funding? Again, following human rights logic, 'states in a position to assist' have a duty to assist the countries mentioned in Table 1. But which states are 'states in a position to assist'? At the very least, the 30 member states of the Organisation for Economic Co-operation and Development (OECD) have, by joining the OECD admitted that they are states in a position to assist. How much assistance should they provide? On this question, the Committee provides some guidance. In its concluding observations, the Committee regularly commends states for their level of foreign assistance if it exceeds the equivalent of 0.7 per cent of their GDP, and encourages states to allocate a bigger part of their budget to foreign assistance if the state in question does not attain the level of 0.7 per cent of GDP. For example, Denmark was commended for achieving the target, and on the same day Italy was encouraged to improve its performance (Committee on Economic, Social and Cultural Rights, 2004a,b). The 0.7 per cent of GDP target was first affirmed in a 1970 UN General Assembly Resolution (United Nations, 1970: para. 43). It has since been regularly reaffirmed in international documents and increasing the number of countries committed to reaching this target is central to achieving the UN Millennium Development Goals (UN Millennium Project website). The 0.7 per cent of GDP target was first affirmed in a 1970 UN General Assembly Resolution (United Nations, 1970: para. 43). It has since been regularly reaffirmed in international documents; increasing the number of countries committed to reaching this target is central to achieving the UN Millennium Development Goals (UN Millennium Project website).

We can therefore assume that states in a position to assist have an obligation to allocate the equivalent of 0.7 per cent of their GDP to foreign assistance. However, health is not the only human right for which they have an obligation to provide assistance. What share of foreign assistance would be available for global health aid? We assumed that if states in need of assistance should allocate 15 per cent of their domestic resources, states in a position to assist should also allocate 15 per cent of foreign assistance to health. That would mean 15 per cent of 0.7 per cent of GDP, or 0.1 per cent of GDP. This approach allows us to calculate individual states' duties to a Global Health Fund. As the combined GDP of OECD member states was about US$30,000 billion in 2004, the sum of their duties would be about US$30 billion.

How are 'states in a position to assist' performing against this benchmark? In 2004, global health aid stood at US$12 billion, while it should have been at least US$30 billion, if OECD member states had allocated 0.1 per cent of their GDP to global health aid. It appears that when measured according to the above criteria 'states in a position to assist' are performing as badly as 'states in need of assistance'. As with 'states in need of assistance' those 'states in a position to assist' would almost have to triple their domestic resource allocation to health. If low-income countries increased their government health expenditure to 3 per cent of GDP, and if OECD members increased their foreign assistance for health to 0.1 per cent would there be enough financial resources to realise the

Table 1. Government health expenditure in low-income countries

A Low-income countries	B Total health expenditure, percentage of GDP (World Health Organization, 2004)	C Government health expenditure, percentage of total health expenditure (World Health Organization, 2007b, estimates for 2004)	D Government health expenditure, percentage of GDP (calculation by authors)	E GDP, billion US$ (International Monetary Fund, 2004)	F Government health expenditure, million US$ (calculation by authors)	G GDP per capita (International Monetary Fund, 2004)	H Government health expenditure, per capita, if it were 3% of GDP, in US$ (calculation by authors)	I Foreign assistance needed to achieve government health expenditure of US$38 per capita per year; millions US$ (calculation by authors)
Somalia	n/a	n/a	n/a	n/a	n/a	n/a	n/a	n/a
São Tomé and Principe	11.5	86.2	9.9	0.1	7.1	706.8	21.2	1.7
Malawi	12.9	74.7	9.6	2.6	253.0	208.2	6.2	400.3
Timor-Leste	11.2	78.9	8.8	0.3	30.0	353.8	10.6	26.2
Solomon Islands	5.9	94.5	5.6	0.3	14.8	566.4	17.0	9.8
Rwanda	7.5	56.8	4.3	1.8	78.2	213.6	6.4	271.4
Mongolia	6.0	66.6	4.0	1.8	72.6	716.8	21.5	41.8
Liberia	5.6	63.9	3.6	0.5	16.5	137.4	4.1	113.5
Zimbabwe	7.5	46.1	3.5	4.7	162.5	400.7	12.0	304.8
Zambia	6.3	54.7	3.4	5.4	187.5	480.4	14.4	267.1
Kyrgyz Republic	5.6	59.8	3.3	2.2	74.2	435.2	13.1	127.0
Burkina Faso	6.1	54.8	3.3	5.1	171.0	399.4	12.0	333.2
Mali	6.6	49.2	3.2	4.9	160.5	405.3	12.2	315.2
Papua New Guinea	3.6	84.3	3.0	3.9	119.2	695.5	20.9	96.8
Korea, Dem. Rep.	3.5	85.6	3.0	n/a	n/a	n/a	n/a	n/a
Bhutan	4.6	64.2	3.0	0.7	20.9	944.3	28.3	7.3
Haiti	7.6	38.5	2.9	3.5	103.3	431.6	12.9	204.9
Ghana	6.7	42.2	2.8	8.9	250.8	435.6	13.1	507.8
Mozambique	4.0	68.4	2.7	5.9	161.5	308.7	9.3	549.8
Ethiopia	5.3	51.5	2.7	9.5	258.9	133.5	4.0	2,414.9
Benin	4.9	51.2	2.5	4.1	101.7	564.3	16.9	151.4
Uganda	7.6	32.7	2.5	6.8	169.4	245.1	7.4	852.6

Senegal	5.9	40.3	2.4	8.0	190.8	704.8	21.1	191.9
Uzbekistan	5.1	46.6	2.4	12.0	285.2	464.0	13.9	622.8
Niger	4.2	52.5	2.2	2.9	64.0	238.2	7.1	375.9
Mauritania	2.9	69.4	2.0	1.5	30.1	542.0	16.3	60.0
Sierra Leone	3.3	59.0	1.9	1.1	20.9	202.0	6.1	169.7
Yemen, Rep.	5.0	38.3	1.9	13.9	265.7	682.4	20.5	356.3
Gambia	6.8	27.1	1.8	0.3	5.0	184.0	5.5	47.8
Madagascar	3.0	59.1	1.8	4.4	77.3	240.4	7.2	558.3
Eritrea	4.5	39.2	1.8	0.6	11.2	140.4	4.2	152.8
Kenya	4.1	42.7	1.8	16.2	284.5	495.3	14.9	759.3
Tanzania	4.0	43.6	1.7	11.3	197.8	309.0	9.3	1,054.5
Cambodia	6.7	25.8	1.7	5.3	92.3	393.9	11.8	354.8
Comoros	2.8	56.9	1.6	0.4	5.8	604.7	18.1	11.9
Chad	4.2	36.9	1.5	4.4	68.5	501.5	15.0	202.4
Central African Republic	4.1	36.8	1.5	1.3	19.8	325.4	9.8	113.6
Vietnam	5.5	27.1	1.5	45.5	678.9	555.2	16.7	1,750.8
Nepal	5.6	26.3	1.5	6.8	99.5	292.1	8.8	676.4
Sudan	4.1	35.4	1.5	21.7	314.7	629.0	18.9	659.5
Nigeria	4.6	30.4	1.4	71.5	1,000.3	501.4	15.0	3,274.9
Guinea-Bissau	4.8	27.3	1.3	0.3	3.5	175.5	5.3	50.4

Table 1. (Continued)

A Low-income countries	B Total health expenditure, percentage of GDP (World Health Organization, 2004)	C Government health expenditure, percentage of total health expenditure (World Health Organization, 2007b, estimates for 2004)	D Government health expenditure, percentage of GDP (calculation by authors)	E GDP, billion US$ (International Monetary Fund, 2004)	F Government health expenditure, million US$ (calculation by authors)	G GDP per capita (International Monetary Fund, 2004)	H Government health expenditure, per capita, if it were 3% of GDP, in US$ (calculation by authors)	I Foreign assistance needed to achieve government health expenditure of US$38 per capita per year; millions US$ (calculation by authors)
Togo	5.5	20.7	1.1	1.9	22.1	323.9	9.7	169.4
Congo, Dem. Rep.	4.0	28.1	1.1	6.5	73.5	117.1	3.5	1,926.1
Tajikistan	4.4	21.6	1.0	2.1	19.7	328.8	9.9	177.4
Côte d'Ivoire	3.8	23.8	0.9	15.5	140.2	867.4	26.0	214.1
Bangladesh	3.1	28.1	0.9	59.1	515.0	392.8	11.8	3,946.4
India	5.0	17.3	0.9	666.3	5,763.5	617.5	18.5	21,012.8
Burundi	3.2	26.2	0.8	0.7	5.6	90.5	2.7	258.9
Lao PDR	3.9	20.5	0.8	2.5	20.1	433.0	13.0	144.9
Afghanistan	4.4	16.9	0.7	6.0	44.4	541.5	16.2	239.9
Guinea	5.3	13.2	0.7	3.9	27.6	437.9	13.1	223.6
Pakistan	2.2	19.6	0.4	98.1	423.0	655.5	19.7	2,743.9
Myanmar	2.2	12.9	0.3	10.8	30.6	198.6	6.0	1,739.9
Total				1,176.0	13,214.3			51,238.7
Total excluding India				509.7	7,450.8			30,225.9

n/a, not available.

core content of right to health on a global scale. At first sight, there would not. A Global Health Fund would need US$51 billion, and OECD member states would have to contribute 'only' US$30 billion. However, between 2004 (the year on which these estimates are based) and 2015 (the year in which the US$38 health expenditure level should be achieved), economies will continue to grow. 'States in need of assistance' will need less than US$51 billion, and 'states in a position to assist' will have to contribute more than US$30 billion.

We can debate at length the appropriateness of all the percentages used. We can debate the definitions of states in need of assistance and states in a position to assist. We can debate the US$38 per person per year target. Furthermore, as the details of a Global Health Fund would take years to be agreed upon, and more years to be implemented, economies will grow (both the economies of states in a position to assist and states in need of assistance), populations will grow, and new diseases might appear or new medicines might be invented. These would all be factors that would change the parameters of a Global Health Fund. We simply want to offer a method that allows for transforming collective duties and entitlements into individual states' duties and entitlements.

Transforming a Collective Obligation into Individual Transnational Entitlements: The Health Impact Fund (HIF) Initiative

As explained above, developing countries had somewhat easier access to new medicines because many of them did not grant patent protection to new medicines. As soon as a new medicine reached the market, pharmaceutical companies in India and elsewhere could start reverse engineering and produce generic copies. Countries like Mozambique were then able to buy the cheaper generic version rather than the expensive original.

This situation was far from satisfactory. Private pharmaceutical companies do not have a legal obligation to fulfil the right to health (they do have an obligation to respect the right to health). However, public institutions funding research and development (R&D) based in states in a position to assist do have a transnational obligation to fulfil the right to health. A Médecins Sans Frontières (MSF) report argues that the pressure to pursue the commercialisation of research findings is increasing in the developed world (Médecins Sans Frontières, 2001: 20). The same report notes that basic research leading to the discovery of potential drug leads generally occurs at publicly funded universities, in-house government facilities or research institute in North America, Europe and Japan. At the very least, they should allocate a part of their research and development budgets to diseases that are common in the developing world, even if uncommon in their own countries. But they do not.

Of the 1393 new drugs approved between 1975 and 1999, only 13 were specifically indicated for tropical diseases and, of these 13, five were by-products of veterinary research and two had been commissioned by the military (Médecins Sans Frontières, 2001; Trouiller *et al.*, 2002). An additional three drugs were indicated for tuberculosis. The next five years brought 163 new drugs of which five were for tropical diseases and none for tuberculosis, which together account for 12 per cent of the total disease burden (Chirac and Torreele, 2006).

To make matters worse, globalisation forced developing countries to adopt stringent intellectual property protection measures in their national legislation, as a condition for attaining or retaining WTO membership. Although this was clearly not in their interest or to their advantage, losing the benefits of WTO membership might have been worse. Furthermore, Joseph Stiglitz describes it as follows: 'As the [Trade Related Aspects of Intellectual Property Rights (TRIPS)] agreement was being negotiated in Geneva in 1993, the Council of Economic Advisers and the Office of Science and Technology Policy in the White House tried to make American negotiators understand our deep reservations. What the United States was asking was, we thought, not in the interests of the advancement of science, and was certainly not in the interest of developing countries. But American and European negotiators adopted the positions of the drug and entertainment industries, and others who simply wanted the strongest intellectual property rights' (Stiglitz, 2006: 116).

Nonetheless, the TRIPS Agreement came into force, allowing little or no real leeway for developing countries. If a new medicine is brought to the market today—and if it is a real innovation—it can be protected by a patent in all countries that have the capacity to produce generic copies for at least 20 years. Developing countries are thus at the mercy of pharmaceutical companies, which may or may not offer them an affordable price.

From a human rights and entitlements point of view, if the new medicine treats a common disease effectively—for example it cures tuberculosis after a week's treatment—patients needing this medicine could legitimately claim it as part of the core content of their right to health. If they live in a state in need of assistance, their government could 'pass the buck' to states in a position to assist. Rather than aiming for a US$38 per person per year expenditure level, the Global Health Fund might then have to aim for US$45, for example, and the annual bill for states in a position to assist would increase accordingly.

Unfortunately, the Global Health Fund does not exist, and even if it existed, it is unlikely that it would automatically increase its grants simple because a new medicine has been developed. A simple reality check shows that the Global Fund continued to fund the highly ineffective chloroquine treatment for several years despite the existence of a more effective treatment—artemisinin-based combination therapy or ACT, which was not even patent-protected. In answering critics of this policy the Global Fund claimed that it continued to fund chloroquine treatment if a country specifically requested it arguing that it was a funding mechanism that relied on the WHO for technical support. Critics claimed that the Global Fund was doing a poor job of peer-reviewing proposals and that the WHO was failing to provide the appropriate technical leadership (Yamey, 2003).

Therefore, even a Global Health Fund as ambitious as that proposed above is unlikely to be a sufficient solution allowing us to realise the core content of the right to health. A different and complementary solution will have to be found to finance the research and development of new medicines, especially medicines relevant to developing countries.

Sharing the costs of existing medicines is an intervention at the end of the cycle of the development of medicines. Increasing the health sector budgets of developing countries, even quadrupling them, would create a new market for medicines, but it would remain a small market. North America, Europe and Japan accounted for 80 per cent of the world pharmaceutical market in 2002 (with a total projected world value of $406 billion), while Africa, Asia, Latin America and the Middle East, representing 80 per cent of the world's population, accounted for only 20 per cent of the pharmaceutical market (Médecins Sans Frontières, 2001).

From a human rights perspective, we are looking for a mechanism that values all human lives as equal. One Disability-Adjusted Life Year (DALY) saved in Mozambique should be honoured with the same reward as one DALY saved in India, the European Union or the USA. The burden of paying for those rewards should be shared among states in accordance with their capacity to share it, or their relative wealth. Even if we can make the case that states in a position to assist share a collective obligation to foster the development of new medicines needed by people living in developing countries, and that individuals living in developing countries have an entitlement allowing them to claim global investments in the development of medicines they need, we are again confronted with the dilemma of collective obligations. It is easier to say that states in a position to assist share a collective obligation to invest in new medicines most needed by all human beings, than to translate this into measurable obligations for each state.

No matter how utopian this may sound, a solution that addresses both of the abovementioned dilemmas—valuing all human lives as equally important, and sharing the burden in accordance with relative wealth—has already been 'invented'. As the HIF Initiative will be presented elsewhere in this issue of Public Health Ethics, we will limit ourselves to quoting this brief description: 'We propose a complement to the current patent system, a Health Impact Fund, that rewards innovators in proportion to the global health impact of their interventions via treaty-backed payments. To access this payment stream, holders would allow the open manufacture, distribution and sale of their products. With this option in place, diseases that do great harm mainly among the poor become profitable targets of R&D. By choosing this option for a specific medicine, innovators make it immediately available for competitive manufacture, which reduces its price to near marginal cost of production. Patients benefit further from additional incentives a registered innovator has to collaborate with generic producers and to help upgrade health services in poor areas.' (Incentives for Global Health, 2007).

Under article 31 of the TRIPS Agreement, states can allow the use of patent-protected innovation without the permission of the patent-owner 'if, prior to such use, the proposed user has made efforts to obtain authorization from the right holder on reasonable commercial terms and conditions and that such efforts have not been successful within a reasonable period of time' (World Trade Organization, 1994: 333). This is such an ambiguous statement that the patent-owner can easily argue that the proposed conditions are unreasonable. But article 31 also foresees an exceptional remedy: 'This requirement may be waived by a Member in the case of a national emergency or other circumstances of extreme urgency or in cases of public noncommercial use'. This is the essence of compulsory licenses: in case of 'national emergency', governments can allow a pharmaceutical manufacturer to make a generic equivalent of the much needed but unaffordable medicine.

But how to decide if a situation is a national emergency? A lot of situations will be clear-cut: either the medicine is not essential (the medicine does not treat or cure a common disease, or there are other medicines available), or the medicine is essential (the medicine does treat or cure a common disease, and there are no other medicines available). But there is an overlap—situations in which there is an obvious public health need, but perhaps not important enough to call it a national emergency—which could also be considered as a gap. In some situations, neither the customary solution (patent protection), nor the exceptional remedy (compulsory license) is appropriate: patent protections leads to unaffordable prices, while the systematic use of compulsory licenses would become a strong counter-incentive for pharmaceutical companies to invest in the research and development of medicines that might be of use in developing countries, and therefore likely to be hit by a series of compulsory licenses.

Here, the HIF would fill a gap. Pharmaceutical companies investing in the research and development of medicines that might be of use in developing countries would have an alternative for the 'double or nothing' gamble that applying for a patent would mean: double if the patent stands, nothing if it is overruled by a series of compulsory licenses. The HIF option would provide them with a reasonably rewarding alternative: not 'double', not 'nothing'.

The existence of an alternative might also facilitate the use of compulsory licenses. At present, a patent-owner hit by a compulsory license is generally perceived as a victim: a rightful owner of intellectual property who has been robbed. But if the patent-owner had the alternative of obtaining a reasonable reward through the HIF, and decided not to use it, then the exceptional remedy of a compulsory license would seem more equitable.

Thus the HIF would provide a solution to the dilemma of essential but patent-protected medicines. As they are essential medicines, states have an obligation to provide them, and if states in need of assistance cannot afford them, then states in a position to assist have an obligation to provide assistance. As they are patent-protected, the patent-owner can charge exorbitant prices, knowing that states have a legal obligation to purchase these medicines. But if patent-owners had a reasonable alternative, and chose not to use it, the solution is simple: any essential medicine not registering with the HIF could immediately be hit with a worldwide series of compulsory licenses.

Furthermore, even if the treaty (or treaties) backing the HIF would be based on voluntary contributions, it is highly probable that the size of the contributions would be in accordance with the relative wealth of participating states. All countries would benefit from this proposal—as some new medicines registered with the HIF would also benefit patients in high-income countries—but the countries with the greatest needs would benefit most. As such, the HIF would also create a form of a global social security mechanism and fit within the alternative global health aid paradigm, creating transnational entitlements, rather than aiming for reduced aid-dependency.

Finally, the benefits of the HIF would also come without political strings attached. Developing countries would be able to purchase the new medicines, at a much lower price than if they were patent-protected, without having to return favours to donor countries.

Conclusion

Does all aid deserve to be termed 'economic colonisation'? We do not think so. If foreign assistance is based on charity only, with no obligation for donor countries other than to satisfy the moral obligations of their constituencies, it may come with strings that primarily serve the donor countries' own interests. Then foreign assistance might well be deserving of this characterisation. However, if foreign assistance is based on transnational entitlements rooted in international human rights, and perceived and considered as such by both states in a position to assist and states in need of assistance, it is not economic colonisation. It is merely a correction to economic globalisation and in that sense is needed to transform economic globalisation from colonisation to interdependency.

The proposals explained in this essay illustrate the feasibility of a new global health aid paradigm; they might not be the best solutions but at least they promote some much-needed thinking 'outside of the box'. Although some development experts might regret it, the new global health aid paradigm is already a reality. And it needs to be further developed.

Notes

1. The indivisibility of all human rights means that an analysis based on a single right is artificial and limited. We acknowledge the limitations of our approach, as it is clear that aggregate improvements in funding will do little to improve the health status of individuals subject to racial or gender discrimination or social exclusion. The merit of our approach is that the focus on a single right helps to simplify the case for a new aid paradigm.

Acknowledgements

The authors wish to thank Paul Hunt and Thomas Pogge for their useful suggestions on improving their arguments.

References

Alston, P. (2005). Ships Passing in the Night: The Current State of the Human Rights and Development Debate Seen Through the Lens of the Millennium Development Goals. *Human Rights Quarterly*, **27**, 755–829.

Arambulo, K. (1999). *Strengthening the Supervision of the International Covenant on Economic, Social and Cultural Rights.* Antwerpen/Groningen/Oxford: Intersentia/Hart.

Archer, R. (2003). *Duties sans Frontières: Human Rights and Global Social Justice.* Versoix: International Council on Human Rights Policy.

Chao, S. and Kostermans, K. (2002). Improving Health for the Poor in Mozambique: The Fight Continues. World Bank, *HPN Discussion Paper.* Available: http://siteresources.worldbank.org/HEALTHNUTRITIONANDPOPULATION/Resources/281627–1095698140167/Chao-ImprovingHealth-whole.pdf [accessed December 31, 2007].

Chirac, P. and Torreele, E. (2006). Global Framework on Essential Health R&D. *Lancet*, **367**, 1560–1561.

Commission on Macroeconomics and Health. (2001). *Macroeconomics and Health: Investing in Health for Economic Development.* Geneva: WHO. Available: http://www.cid.harvard.edu/archive/cmh/cmhreport.pdf [accessed December 31, 2007].

Committee on Economic, Social and Cultural Rights. (1990). *General Comment No. 3. The Nature of States Parties Obligations.* Geneva: Office of the High Commissioner for Human rights. Available: http://www.unhchr.ch/tbs/doc.nsf/(symbol)/CESCR±General±comment±3.En?OpenDocument [accessed December 31, 2007].

Committee on Economic, Social and Cultural Rights. (2000a). *General Comment No. 14. The Right to the Highest Attainable Standard of Health.* Geneva: Office of the High Commissioner for Human rights. Available: http://www.unhchr.ch/tbs/doc.nsf/(symbol)/E.C.12.2000.4.En?OpenDocument [accessed December 31, 2007].

Committee on Economic, Social and Cultural Rights. (2000b). *Summary Record of the 10th Meeting.* Geneva: Office of the High Commissioner for Human Rights. Available: http://www.unhchr.ch/tbs/doc. nsf/(Symbol)/d8711da53e337f75802568d90-03bc930?Opendocument [accessed December 31, 2007].

Committee on Economic, Social and Cultural Rights. (2004a). *Concluding Observations of the Committee on Economic, Social and Cultural Rights: Denmark.* Geneva: Committee on Economic, Social and Cultural Rights. Available: http://www.unhchr.ch/tbs/doc.nsf/(Symbol)/E.C.12.1.Add.102.En?Opendocument [accessed December 31, 2007].

Committee on Economic, Social and Cultural Rights. (2004b). *Concluding Observations of the Committee on Economic, Social and Cultural Rights: Italy.* Geneva: Committee on Economic, Social and Cultural Rights. Available: http://www.unhchr.ch/tbs/doc.nsf/(Symbol)/E.C.12.1.Add.103.En?Opendocument [accessed December 31, 2007].

De Renzio, P. and Hanlon, J. (2007). Contested Sovereignty in Mozambique: The Dilemmas of Aid Dependence. Oxford University, Department of Politics and International Relations, *Global Economic Governance Programme Working Paper.* Available: http://www.globaleconomicgovernance.org/docs/Derenzio%20and%20Hanlon_Mozambique%20paper%20rev%20120107.pdf [accessed December 31, 2007].

France, T., Ooms, G. and Rivers, B. (2002). The GFATM: Which Countries Owe, and How Much? *IAPAC Monthly*, **8**, 138–141. Available: http://www.hawaii.edu/hivandaids/IAPAC%%202002.pdf [accessed December 31, 2007].

Global Fund to Fight AIDS, Tuberculosis and Malaria. (2007). *Proposal Form–Round 7.* Geneva: Global Fund to fight AIDS, Tuberculosis and Malaria. Available: http://www.theglobalfund.org/en/files//R7_Proposal_Form_en.doc [accessed December 31, 2007].

Gostin, L. (2008). Global Health: Meeting Basic Survival Needs of the World's Least Healthy People: Towards a Framework Convention on Global Health. *Georgetown Law Journal*, **96**, 331–392.

Gottret, P. and Schieber, G. (2006). *Health Financing Revisited: A Practitioner's Guide.* Washington, DC: The World Bank. Available: http://siteresources.worldbank.org/INTHSD/Resources/topics/Health-Financing /HFRFull.pdf, December 31, 2007.

Hunt, P. (2006). *Report of the Special Rapporteur, Paul Hunt, to the Sixty-fist session of the Commission on Human Rights Council. Addendum: Mi*: United Nations, Economic and Social Council. Available: http://www2.essex.ac.uk /human_rights_centre /rth/docs/mozambique.pdf [accessed December 31, 2007].

Incentives for Global Health, HIF Initiative. Website. Available http://www.patent2.org/files/a_page_on_track2.doc [accessed December 31, 2007].

International Monetary Fund. (2007a). *Fiscal Policy Response to Scaled-Up Aid.* Available: http://www.imf.org/external/np/pp/2007/eng/060507.pdf [accessed December 31, 2007].

International Monetary Fund. (2007b). *World Economic and Financial Surveys: Regional Economic Outlook, Sub-Saharan African*. Available: http://www.imf.org/external/pubs/ft/reo/2007/AFR/ENG/sreo-0407.pdf [accessed December 31, 2007].

Jenkins, S. (2002). *Don't Patronize Africa, Give Trade Not Aid*. Available: http://www.thirdworldtraveler.com/Africa/Don't_Patronize_Africa.html [accessed December 31, 2007].

Loyn, D. (2003). Mozambique's Lost Cashew Nut Industry. *British Broadcasting Corporation*. Available: http://news.bbc.co.uk/2/hi/africa/3082316.stm [accessed December 31, 2007].

McKinley, T. (2005). *Why is 'Dutch Disease' Always a Disease? The Macroeconomic Consequences of Scaling Up ODA*. New York: United Nations Development Programme. *United Nations Development Programme Working Paper*. Available: http://www.undp.org/povertycentre/newsletters/WorkingPaper10.pdf [accessed December 31, 2007].

McMillan, M., Rodrik, D. and Horn Welch, K. (2002). *When Economic Reform Goes Wrong: Cashews in Mozambique*. Cambridge, MA: John F. Kennedy School of Government. *Faculty Research Working Papers Series*. Available: http://ksgnotes1.harvard.edu/research/wpaper.nsf/rwp/RWP02–028/$File/rwp02_028_rodrik.pdf [accessed December 31, 2007].

Médecins Sans Frontières. (2001). *Fatal Imbalance: The Crisis in Research and Development for Drugs for Neglected Diseases*. Geneva: Médecins Sans Frontières. Available: www.msf.org/source/access/2001/fatal/fatal.pdf [accessed December 31, 2007].

Ooms, G., Derderian, K. and Melody, D. (2006). Do We Need a World Health Insurance to Realise the Right to Health? *PLoS Med*, **3**: e530.

Organisation of African Unity. (2001). *Abuja Declaration on HIV/AIDS, Tuberculosis and Other Related Infectious Diseases*. Available: http://www.un.org/ecosocdev/geninfo/afrec/vol15no1/151aids5.htm.

Örücü, E. (1986). The Core of Rights and Freedoms: The Limits of Limits. In Campbell, T. (ed.), *Human Rights: From Rhetoric to Reality*. New York:Blackwell.

Over, M. (2007). *AIDS Treatment as an International Entitlement: Are We Ready for a Global Welfare Paradigm*? Center for Global Health Policy. Available http://blogs.cgdev.org/globalhealth/2007/09/aids_treatment_as_an.php [accessed December 31, 2007].

Preble, C. and Tupy L. (2005). Trade, Not Aid. *Reason Online*, Available: http://www.cato.org/pub_display.php?pub_id=3873 [accessed December 31, 2007].

Pogge, T. (2005). *Montréal Statement on the Human Right to Essential Medicines*. Statement by the participants of the International Seminar on Human Rights and Access to Essential Medicines, Montréal, Canada, September 30–October 2, 2005. Available: http://www.ethics.harvard.edu/download/pogge2.pdf [accessed December 31, 2007].

Skogly, S. (2006). *Beyond National Borders: States' Human Rights Obligations in International Cooperation*. Antwerpen/Oxford: Intersentia.

Sserwanga, M. (2007). Uganda: CHOGM We Want Fair Trade, Not Aid. *The Monitor (Kampala)*, Available: http://allafrica.com/stories/200711191593.html [accessed December 31, 2007].

Stiglitz, J. (2006). *Making Globalization Work*. London: Penguin Books.

Toebes, B. (1999). *The Right to Health as a Human Right in International Law*. Antwerpen/Groningen/Oxford: Intersentia/Hart.

Trouiller, P., Olliaro, P., Torreele, E., Orbinski, J., Laing, R. and Ford, N. (2002). Drug Development for Neglected Diseases: A Deficient Market and a Public-Health Policy Failure. *Lancet*, **359**, 2188–2194.

United Nations. (1945). Charter of the United Nations. Available: http://www.un.org/aboutun/charter/ [accessed December 31, 2007].

United Nations. (1948). Universal Declaration of Human Rights. UN Doc. A/810 at 71 (1948). Available: http://www.un.org/Overview/rights.html [accessed December 31, 2007].

United Nations. (1966a). International Covenant on Civil and Political Rights. UN Doc. A/6316 (1966). Available: http://www.unhchr.ch/html/menu3/b/a_cpr.htm [accessed December 31, 2007].

United Nations. (1966b). International Covenant on Economic, Social and Cultural Rights. UN Doc. A/6316 (1966). Available: http:// www.unhchr.ch/html/menu3/b/a_cescr.htm [accessed December 31, 2007].

United Nations. (1970). General Assembly Resolution 2626 (XXV) October 24, 1970. Available: http://www.un-documents.net/a25r2626. htm [accessed December 31, 2007].

United Nations. (1979). Convention on the Elimination of All Forms of Discrimination against Women. U.N. Doc. A/34/46, at 193 (1979). Available: http://www.ohchr.org/english/law/cedaw.htm [accessed December 31, 2007].

United Nations. (1989). Convention on the Rights of the Child. U.N. Doc. A/44/49, at 166 (1989). Available: http://www.ohchr.org/english/law/crc.htm [accessed December 31, 2007].

United Nations. (2001). Declaration of Commitment on HIV/AIDS. General Assembly Special Session Resolution A/RES/S-26/2 of June 27, 2001. Available: http://www.un.org/ga/aids/docs/aress262.pdf [accessed December 31, 2007].

United Nations. (2006). Political Declaration on HIV/AIDS. Available: http://data.unaids.org/pub/Report/2006/20060615_HLM_PoliticalDeclaration_ARES60-262_en.pdf [accessed December 31, 2007].

United Nations Millennium Project Website. Available: http://www.unmillenniumproject.org/press/07.htm [accessed December 31, 2007].

Vierdag, E. (1978). The Nature of the Rights Granted by the International Covenant on Economic, Social and Cultural Rights. *Netherlands Yearbook of International Law*, **9**, 69–105.

Vidal, J. (2002). Trade Not Aid. *The Guardian*, Available: http://www.guardian.co.uk/globalisation/story/0,7369,722865,00.html [accessed December 31, 2007].

World Health Organization. (1946). *Constitution of the World Health Organization.* Geneva: World Health Organization. Available: http://www.searo.who.int/LinkFiles/About_SEARO_const.pdf [accessed December 31, 2007].

World Health Organization. (2006). Working Together for Health. Available: http://www.who.int/whr/2006/whr06_en.pdf [accessed December 31, 2007].

World Health Organization. (2007a). 'Core Health Indicators: Mozambique.' Geneva: World Health Organization. Available: http://www.who.int/whosis/database/core/core_select_process.cfmcountry=moz&indicators=healthpersonnel [accessed December 31, 2007].

World Health Organization. (2007b). 'National Health Accounts.' Geneva: World Health Organization. Available: http://www.who.int/nha/country/Annex1&2,%20March%205,%202007.xls [accessed December 31, 2007].

World Trade Organization. (1994). The Agreement on Trade Related Aspects of Intellectual Property Rights (TRIPS). Available: http://www.wto.org/English/docs_e/legal_e/27-trips.pdf [accessed December 31, 2007].

Yamey, G. (2003). Malaria researchers say global fund is buying 'Useless Drugs.' *BMJ*, **327**, 1188. Available: http://www.pubmedcentral.nih.gov/articlerender.fcgi? artid=300784 [accessed December 31, 2007].

[18]

Human Rights, the Millennium Development Goals, and the Future of Development Cooperation

PAUL J. NELSON *
University of Pittsburgh, USA

Summary. — This paper examines the distinct approaches to poverty contained in the human rights movement and the Millennium Development Goals (MDG). MDG advocates and many in the human rights community assert that the goals are consistent with, and indeed a means of operationalizing, human rights standards and principles. This paper finds fundamental differences in the two initiatives' conceptual approaches to poverty reduction, in the policy recommendations they support on key social policy issues, and in the social actors they have been able to mobilize. The research is based on documentary research, and on an examination of 40 development NGOs and social movements.

Key words — poverty, human rights, millennium development goals, accountability, social movements, NGOs

1. INTRODUCTION

At the end of the 1990s, it seemed that social theory had done much to clarify the nature of extreme poverty, and the conditions under which it could be effectively reduced. Sen (1999) had persuaded many that poverty should be understood as a multi-dimensional condition, shaped by constraints on individuals' freedoms and capabilities, and perpetuated by discriminatory institutions and failed political systems. Social capital theory had persuaded actors across the political spectrum of the central roles of "norms and networks that enable people to act collectively" (Woolcock & Narayan, 2000).

At the same time, two initiatives were in process to refocus development cooperation, and these two map out two distinctly different paths and futures for development cooperation. The Millennium Development Goals (MDG) propose to improve the health, nutrition, and well-being of some of the 1.2 billion humans who live on less than the equivalent of a dollar a day. Endorsed by 189 governments at the Millennium Summit and supported by the World Bank, United Nations, and all of the major donor governments, the MDGs mobilize the classic development sector tools: donor pledges, goals and benchmarks, multi-volume reports, and sophisticated monitoring by United Nations agencies and other major donors.

At the same time, there is growing interest in the implications of human rights—economic, social, and cultural (ESC) rights as well as civil and political rights—for development practice, and a movement toward human rights-based or "rights-based" approaches (RBA) to development cooperation. The RBA rests not on the workings of markets and the generosity of donors, but on internationally recognized human rights standards and principles, to which governments and donors are obliged to adhere.

The MDGs and rights-based approaches both attempt in different ways to refocus and perhaps reinvigorate the development enterprise. The MDGs are a careful restatement of poverty-related development challenges, in language that avoids reference to rights; they are a donor country interpretation of the key issues, for a donor-country audience. Rights-based

* For comments and insights on earlier versions of this paper, the author is grateful to participants in the Workshop on Health, Inequality and Society, University of Pittsburgh; to Dr. Ellen Dorsey; and to two anonymous referees. Final revision accepted: February 1, 2007.

approaches, by contrast, seek to link the development enterprise to social movements' demands for human rights and inclusion, and to tie development to the rhetorical and legal power of internationally recognized human rights.

This article tests two widely held positions: that the MDGs mirror and complement human rights approaches to social policy; and that a global initiative such as the MDGs can mobilize a united system of states, donors, NGOs, and social movements. MDG advocates contend that human rights and the MDGs are complimentary: human rights establish broad principles and standards, and the MDGs create operational goals, indicators, and benchmarks. Both are organized around aspects of well-being (health, nutrition, education, etc.), and the Millennium Declaration that frames the MDGs emphasizes their ties to the Universal Declaration of Human Rights. But despite their arrival at the same juncture in the development of development, the MDGs and human rights-based approaches have less in common than appears at first glance. This paper asks how important the differences are, and what can be done to reconcile them. After introducing the MDGs and human rights approaches in Part One, I compare the two initiatives across three dimensions: conceptual, policy, and mobilization.

First, there are important conceptual differences between the MDGs and human rights, having to do with agency, accountability, the analysis of causes, and symptoms of poverty, including political and civic freedoms. The differences, analyzed in Part Two, have important implications for the strategies and policies they embrace. Second, the two tend to be associated with contrasting sets of preferred policies. The differences over health and water policies analyzed in Part Three are among the most heated debates in contemporary development policy, and they suggest that the consensus around a "new poverty agenda" is much less solid than it sometimes appears.

Finally, human rights and the MDGs have provoked distinctly different responses from international organizations (NGOs and intergovernmental), on the one hand, and from social movements and NGOs based in the poor countries, on the other. The ability of domestic constituencies to hold government accountable to anti-poverty commitments is key to rapid and sustained reductions in poverty, and here a final difference between human rights and the MDGs emerges: human rights have been an important mobilizing resource and source of leverage for social movements and local citizen organizations in demanding government action to protect, respect, and fulfill their rights; the MDGs have not proven to be a motivating force or source of political leverage for such citizen action.

The paper draws on research carried out in 2005, relying on documentary sources and a review of 40 NGO and social movement organizations. Following the three sections outlined above, a concluding section reflects on the significance of the MDG and human rights movements for the global governance of economic and social relations, and for participants in international development cooperation.

2. MDGS, HUMAN RIGHTS, AND DEVELOPMENT

(a) *MDGs*

Building on social policy goals articulated in the 1980s and 1990s, the MDGs are written and institutionalized to mobilize support from the donor countries and their citizens, to accomplish concrete and important tasks. The goals, summarized in Figure 1, are monitored by many United Nations and other donor agencies, and focus largely on the symptoms of underdevelopment: Goals 2 (education), 4 (child mortality), 5 (maternal mortality), and 6 (access to safe drinking water) all propose to extend coverage of minimum social services, a task that aid agencies have often financed effectively.

The goals can be traced to the 1995 World Summit on Social Development (WSSD), which enjoys great legitimacy among NGO and activists from much of the world, thanks to the broad involvement of governmental and NGO participants in the WSSD preparations and negotiations (Bissio, 2003). But unlike the 1995 WSSD, the 1996 "Shaping the 21st Century" document that became a foundation for the MDGs emerged from the OECD's Development Assistance Committee (DAC), involving little such input. Former DAC Director James Michel argues that the MDGs were "based largely on the formulation recommended in *Shaping the 21st Century* and in the World Bank/IMF 2000 paper "A Better World for All," a fact that took the MDGs "from being disparate findings in various Uni-

Goal 1 Eradicate extreme poverty and hunger

Target 1: Halve (1990 to 2015) the proportion of people whose income is less than one dollar/day
Target 2: Halve (1990 to 2015) the proportion of people who suffer from hunger

Goal 2 Achieve universal primary education

Target 3: Ensure that, by 2015, children everywhere, boys and girls alike, will be able to complete a full course of primary schooling

Goal 3 Promote gender equality and empower women

Target 4: Eliminate gender disparity in primary and secondary education, preferably by 2005, and in all levels of education no later than 2015

Goal 4 Reduce child mortality

Target 5: Reduce by two thirds (1990 to 2015) the under-five mortality rate

Goal 5 Improve maternal health

Target 6: Reduce by three quarters (1990 to 2015) the maternal mortality ratio

Goal 6 Combat HIV/AIDS, malaria and other diseases

Target 7: Halt by 2015 and have begun to reverse the spread of HIV/AIDS
Target 8: Halt by 2015 and have begun to reverse the incidence of malaria, other major diseases

Goal 7 Ensure environmental sustainability

Target 9: Integrate the principles of sustainable development into country policies and programs and reverse the loss of environmental resources
Target 10: Halve, by 2015, the proportion of people without sustainable access to safe drinking water and basic sanitation
Target 11: By 2020 achieve significant improvement in the lives of at least 100 mn slum dwellers

Goal 8 Develop a global partnership for development

Target 12: open, rule-based, predictable, non-discriminatory trading and financial system.
Target 13: Address needs of least developed countries: tariff and quota-free access for exports; enhanced debt relief; more generous ODA for countries committed to poverty reduction
Target 14: …needs of landlocked developing countries and small island states
Target 15: …measures in order to make debt sustainable in the long term
Target 16: …implement strategies for decent and productive work for youth
Target 17: …provide access to affordable essential drugs…
Target 18: …make available the benefits of new [information and communication] technologies

Figure 1. *Millennium development goals and targets. (Source: United Nations Statistics Division. Millennium indicators database.) (http://millenniumindicators.un.org).*

ted Nations conferences to becoming a unified set of DAC recommendations to the international community…" (Michel, 2005). For this reason, many NGO activists see the MDGs as a product of the OECD governments and the international financial institutions (Bissio, 2003; Tomlinson, 2005), a perception that compromises the MDGs' ability to mobilize social and political actors.

Scholars and practitioners have raised concerns about the MDGs. Critics see them as insufficiently attentive to past development failures (Sanderson, 2004; Saith, 2006) and unlikely to be met (Clemens, Kenny, & Moss, 2007), particularly in Africa (Sahn & Stifel, 2003). Pogge (2004) argues that back-dating the poverty goal to a base year of 1990, which permitted the MDGs to work from the same baseline as had other goals declared during the 1990s, also meant that the rapid poverty reduction in China in the early 1990s made only an additional 19% real reduction in the incidence of extreme poverty was required to meet the global goal. Clemens et al. (2007), on the other hand, argue that the goals are too ambitious, and that they encourage the illusion that their targets and objectives could be met simply by mobilizing enough additional aid.

(b) *Human rights-based approaches*

Practitioners in human rights and development have led a resurgence of interest in the linkages between human rights and development practice since the mid-1990s. Amnesty International and Human Rights Watch, whose work has come to define human rights, have begun to expand their focus from traditional advocacy on civil and political rights to include ESC rights. A new global network on ESC rights links NGOs working on economic and social human rights worldwide (ESCR-net.org).

Among major development donors, UNDP, UNICEF, and other United Nations agencies, Swedish Sida, Norwegian Norad, British DFID, and the Australian aid agency have adopted rights-based (in Sida's case, human rights and democracy) approaches. The UN agencies' experience is analyzed in Darrow and Tomas (2005), and recent studies including Plipat (2005) document bilateral and NGO experiences. UNDP and UNICEF have played central roles in framing human rights-based approaches, and specialized NGOs such as the Centre on Housing Rights and Evictions (COHRE), Food Information and Action Network (FIAN), Center for Economic and Social Rights (CESR), and the International Women's Health Coalition (IWHC) have taken the lead on many issues Nelson and Dorsey (2003).

Proponents see human rights as a new development framework that can "lend moral legitimacy and the principle of social justice" to human development (UNDP, 2000, p. 3). At Oxfam-America, a rights-based approach addresses discontent with "welfare-based" models of development, unifies diverse development initiatives, and "has proven appealing to the global media..." (Offenheiser & Holcombe, 2003, pp. 4, 18).

Human rights approaches, however, are also subject to criticism. Like the MDGs, human rights are a potential source of legitimacy for aid donors, which are eager to occupy the "high moral ground" (Uvin, 2002, pp. 1–2). Uvin, who is skeptical of the intentions behind development donors' rhetoric, argues that "incorporating human rights terminology into development discourse" is a rhetorical gesture that need not change how policies are adopted and promoted or projects identified, financed, or evaluated.

The difficulty of enforcing state compliance with ESC rights has limited their use to shape social policy (Gauri, 2004), although enforcing these obligations through international human rights mechanisms is not central to most development agency strategies. The imprecision of some standards, bemoaned by some human rights practitioners (Fidler, 1999), is a limiting factor in applying ESC rights; development practice has a stronger record of devising measurable targets and monitoring systems.

Human rights-based approaches have been an undercurrent throughout the history of development, largely within UN agencies and committees. But the present interest is more widespread, applied, and specific, and often linked to social movement campaigns in the poor countries, giving the human rights approach a second, political dimension. NGOs and social movements, for example, advocate for broader access to essential medicines, particularly for those affected by HIV/AIDS. Advocacy for the right to HIV/AIDS treatment has involved close cooperation with poor-country governments, and appeals to ESC rights standards as a counterweight to corporate power and to liberal trade rules (Nelson & Dorsey, 2007). Friedman and Mottiar's (2005) study of the Treatment Action Campaign's (TAC) mobilization strategies in South Africa demonstrate the ability of rights-based advocacy strategies to motivate major changes in social policy.

To understand the differences between these parallel and contemporaneous movements, I now turn to three conceptual differences that separate them.

3. GOALS, PLEDGES, AND RIGHTS: THE CONCEPTUAL GAPS

Goals and rights are associated with distinct traditions in ethics and political philosophy. Goals are distinctly utilitarian, calculated to maximize welfare gains. Rights make a normative claim, that human dignity entitles each person to certain kinds of treatment, and to protection from others. For development, three sharp conceptual differences are those related to agency (to whom do the rights/goals belong?); the nature of accountability; and the attention given to root causes of poverty.

(a) *Whose goals and whose rights?*

Goals and rights differ in theory, and these differences are fundamental to understanding the politics of the MDGs and human rights. The differences reviewed here relate to two characteristics: agency and the "possession" of rights and goals; and the nature of the obligations or duties associated with them.

Human rights in some cases designate and adhere to groups (children, women, and indigenous people), but the broad range of human rights contained in the UDHR, and in the International Covenants on ESC Rights (ICESCR) and on Civil and Political Rights (ICCPR), are rights of individuals. Goals, on the other hand, belong to states and the international organizations in which they are negotiated. They *refer* to the people who suffer the indignities of poverty, but those individuals are the objects of the goals, not their agents. The facts that governments adopt as a goal the halving of the number of people living in extreme poverty does not give any particular destitute person a right or a claim on her government. (The Millennium Development Campaign hopes to build ownership of the goals among civil societies, but there is an important difference between this metaphorical use of "ownership" and the literal possession of human rights.) The MDGs are not any individual citizen's goals in the same sense that the right to food or to information is that individual's right.

Rights, unlike goals, inherently create duties, and these duties give them their political significance. The claim, for example, that every person has the right to adequate food, even in time of famine, by virtue of their dignity as a human being, is a meaningful statement in the abstract: human dignity calls for freedom from hunger. But the statement has meaning for policy because it is associated with duties and obligations, and the definition of those duties is among the most difficult and politically charged challenges for human rights. In this case, the duty to respond to acute malnutrition clearly extends, under Article two of the ICESCR, to states and international agencies that are in a position to provide assistance, although the government continues to hold the principal responsibility to assure that resources are marshaled to protect its people.

(b) *Accountability: pledges, goals, and rights*

MDG advocates refer to the goals' capacity to strengthen accountability, but the meaning of that accountability is rarely clear. Fukuda-Parr (2004) argues that because the MDGs "can be monitored," they create a "framework for accountability," empowered by benchmarks, and a "systematic procedure for global monitoring and support" maintained by the United Nations. According to Fukuda-Parr, data collected by the UNDP makes monitoring possible at the "international, national and local levels" (p. 397). Indeed, the MDGs have spawned "an industry of costing, planning, and campaigning in the UN system, among donor governments, the IFIs and many CSOs" (Tomlinson, 2005).

But monitoring does not equal accountability, and accountability "outward" to a donor agency is rarely enough to promote the kind of social change envisioned in the MDGs. Such change requires local and national institutions and practices that make governments accountable to organized citizens, and to an electorate as a whole.

The logic and politics of the MDGs have much more in common with donor pledging than with human rights. One of the principal features of development assistance since the 1970s has been a series of international commitments to soft goals and objectives. In 1974 participants in the World Food Conference pledged their countries' support for a global effort to eradicate hunger in ten years' time. Following numerous global meetings and other pledges in the 1980s, the UN-sponsored global conferences of the 1990s again captured significant public attention Jolly (2004). Among these global conferences and the agendas they set, the goals of the 1995 Copenhagen World Social Summit are linked most directly to the MDGs. Many other meetings have also produced resolutions and pledges, but the MDGs are the best articulated, widest ranging, and most sustained campaign, with a broad UN commitment and a Millennium Development Campaign designed to promote them.

Pledging processes for emergency response, international special initiatives, and global conference agendas rarely feature any meaningful accountability mechanisms, and the MDGs are no exception. Mild, informal "shaming" among donors for failures to deliver on pledged resources has been generally ineffective, and a review of the record of payment on humanitarian pledges is "anything but reassuring" (Walker, Wisner, Leaning, & Minear, 2005). After Hurricane Mitch devastated parts of three Central American countries in 1998, $9 billion was pledged; five years later, $4.5 billion had been delivered. The 2003 earthquake that destroyed the ancient city of Bam, Iran, provoked $1 billion in pledges, but $130 million had been paid in June 2005 (Patrick, 1998; Walker et al., 2005).

In theory, human rights standards establish much stronger accountability, through periodic self-reporting by governments to UN committees, which have (limited) authority to mount investigations and publicize reports that "name and shame" violators. But in practice, neither ESC rights nor the MDGs has an effective means of holding donors or governments accountable to their pledges or policies. ESC rights and states' obligations theoretically have the same legal authority as civil and political human rights, but suffer from the weakness of the institutions that monitor them within the United Nations (Felice, 1999). Much of the oversight of economic and social rights depends on the effectiveness of individual special rapporteurs and experts designated by the human rights committee, and on reporting by a handful of NGOs that specialize in ESC rights.

The MDGs, on the other hand, call for greater generosity by the rich countries and commitment by the poor countries, but they introduce no mechanism for accountability by either. Domestic, internal mechanisms in the poor countries, then, are the key to effective political leverage in support of either the MDGs or ESC rights. UNDP Administrator Mark Malloch Brown (2002) argues that while the MDG's "unique global authority" comes from their endorsement by 189 states, progress will come when "everyone from a politician here in Berlin to a farmer in Bangladesh or a shop-keeper in Burkina Faso can understand and push for further action by their own governments...." The campaign, he continues, depends on national and global organizing to "build on the success of global campaigns like the debt relief and land mines movements..." (p. 6).

In the absence of meaningful international authority and sanctions, Malloch Brown is correct: if the MDGs are to stimulate change in policies, institutions and spending priorities in the poor countries, they must be able to mobilize community organizations, social movements, local NGOs, and others to generate accountability within national political systems. We return to this issue in Part four.

(c) *Quick impact versus root causes*

Human rights-based approaches tend to call for attention to the *causes and multiple dimensions* of poverty, and to the linkages between poverty and civil and political freedoms; the MDGs are output indicators that aim primarily for progress in some of the worst *symptoms* of poverty. Both in principle and in the practice of many agencies, human rights approaches to social and economic policy have involved tracing the social, economic, political, and other causes of rights deprivation. In theory, this is true because human rights principles call for attention to patterns of discrimination in law, institutions, and policy, because they emphasize the interrelatedness of political and civil freedoms with economic and social rights, and because they emphasize the need to establish effective legal and institutional protections for groups that are subject to discriminatory treatment (Nowak, 2005, esp. pp. 28–29).

In practice, while agencies' implementation of RBA is uneven, prominent agencies such as CARE, Sida, and ActionAid, among others, affirm that one of the principal advantages of a human rights framework is a structured means of tracing the often multiple causes of poverty, and social exclusion. While for ActionAid this emphasis on causal analysis is largely tied to policy, other agencies stress the applications of human rights principles to understanding causes of poverty in program and project identification and design. In Sida, this practice refers largely to the country-level analysis of poverty and its causes (Sida, 2001). Some CARE programs ground their situation analysis and monitoring in human rights principles and standards. A country study of CARE-Burundi shows how national staff analyzed patterns of discrimination against the Batwa minority, and their "systematic marginalization," in devising community development initiatives (Rand, 2002, pp. 30–37). The lesson for program planning, according to CARE, is that "the key was to keep asking *why* [emphasis in original]. Once staff got the knack of capturing the trail of logic, [and] learned to ask *why* certain people had no land or what had happened to the land they previously had, local politics and power relations began to surface" (Rand, 2002). Similarly, CARE has developed methodologies such as a "rights-based monitoring tool" produced for CARE Malawi, which relies on an analysis of discrimination in legal, political, and social institutions and practices to understand what restricts rural households' access to land, credit, and agricultural inputs (Picard, 2004).

The MDGs and human rights approaches differ in their attention to structural and socio-political factors that cause and perpetuate poverty. The only attention given in the MDGs to discrimination or uneven coverage is in the call for eliminating gender disparities in school enrollment rates (Goal 2, Target 3). Of the structural factors underlying poverty and wealth in poor countries—access to land, labor, wages, credit, and (some would add) entrepreneurial opportunity—none is mentioned by the MDGs. This diversion of attention from difficult, structural features of poverty and inequality should be added to the concerns raised by Maxwell (2001) about the perverse impacts of targets on decision-making by donors and governments.

The MDGs' proponents argue that because the goals are output measures, not strategies, they do not exclude strategies that expand opportunities and access to productive resources (Malloch Brown, 2003), and critics of the MDGs have called for just this kind of broader effort to address the causes of poverty (Social Watch, 2005). But embracing this strategy for a global anti-poverty initiative does mean that other possible strategies are omitted or de-emphasized.

The MDGs create incentives for donors and governments to favor quick impact over addressing complex social systems. This tendency appears most clearly in the "quick wins" strategy outlined in the 2005 UN report on investing to advance the MDGs, which calls for funding for "high potential, short-term impact" initiatives that can yield "breathtaking results within three or fewer years..." and "start countries on the path to the Goals" (p. 25). These measures include, for example, mosquito bed nets for malaria protection, MDG model villages, immunizations, school meals, and water purification devices. Such investments have two kinds of payoff: they begin to drive down key indicators for the goals, and they offer the prospect of quick impact that can mobilize donors' aid funds. Most of them involve not systemic change but delivering individual health and education benefits. These "quick win" strategies are not the sole approach of the UN agencies, but the UN Millennium Project (2005) has made them central to its campaign, and to its call for "scaled-up" investment in development assistance. Because they are attractive to donor agencies and their domestic constituencies, they attract aid funds and therefore the attention of poor country governments.

Pragmatically, this feature can be seen as a strength of the MDGs: the goals establish benchmarks with attainable levels of progress, and they rely on interventions that can be accomplished without even attempting to address the thorny social and political causes of inequality and deprivation. Accomplishing the goals would mean real improvement in quality of life for some of the world's poor. But these incentives also imply a quiet retreat from important trends in recent development cooperation toward greater recognition of the right of people affected by development policies to participate influentially in shaping them, and the need to guarantee political freedoms in order to make poverty reduction politically sustainable.

These differences appear at first to be matters of strategy, but upon closer examination, the MDG and human rights-based approaches differ more fundamentally. This is true because most MDG strategies are neither societal nor systematic: the strategy invests in measures that benefit individuals and households, for the most part, without creating social or institutional changes that give reason to hope for follow-on benefits for those not reached. Second, because the MDGs do not call for an analysis of the causes of poverty and its manifestations, they generally do not directly address the structural factors that human rights analysis points to as root causes, nor do they incorporate work toward political and civil freedoms. Third, the MDG campaign has not produced coherent aid and trade policy among the donors, and is associated with positions and strategies on several economic and social policy issues that are inimical to the ESC rights agenda. I now turn to these substantive policy clashes.

4. POLICY AND POLITICS: THE DIVIDE BETWEEN MDGS AND HUMAN RIGHTS

If, despite these conceptual differences between the MDGs and human rights approaches, they promoted a consistent global set of humane policy initiatives, the differences might be primarily of theoretical interest. Some human rights and development agencies take this position: Oxfam, Action Aid, Christian Aid, Misereor, and many UN agencies have aligned themselves with rights-based approaches, and advocate the MDGs as a step toward the broader realization of these rights. Shetty (2005) articulates this view on behalf of the UN-sponsored Millennium Development Campaign, calling the MDGs the link between human rights and "mainstream economic decisions-making processes" of the international financial institutions. Philip Alston, Advisor to the High Commissioner on Human Rights, also emphasizes the potential for harmonization and coordination, even as his analytic comments highlight the MDGs' failures to emphasize their grounding in international human rights (Alston, 2005).

But the debates over water privatization and the provision of medicines for HIV treatment reveal stark policy differences of two kinds. First, the aid and trade policies associated with the MDGs are themselves incoherent and contradictory. Goal 8, which calls for creating a global partnership for development, envisions a coherent set of aid, trade and financial institutions and arrangements. (Goal 8 is also the one goal for which donor nations are primarily responsible, and the one goal without benchmarks or deadlines.) Rather than a coherent package, however, while the MDGs focus on aid, rules and institutions on trade, intellectual property and finance are being dominated by the commercial and investment interests of the industrial country governments.

Second, the policy differences demonstrate the strong tendency of social actors affiliated with the MDG process and advocates of human rights approaches to square off on opposite sides of these issues. This brief discussion of the water and HIV/AIDS debates illustrates these two dynamics among the organizations and actors being mobilized by the human rights and MDG efforts.

(a) *Water* [1]

MDG advocates call for donors to step up their assistance for water and sanitation, and the major donors have complied. New resources for potable water are being invested through country programs that generally deemphasize project funding, instead providing system-wide support to improve and expand water systems. Donor aid from the World Bank and bilateral donors, including British DFID, USAID, and EU agencies, emphasizes a shift to private sector provision, through contracts, franchises, or outright ownership of formerly public water utilities. The 2005 Commission on Financing Water for All, headed by Michel Camdessus, argued that the way to finance "water for all" is to expand and facilitate corporate management of water and sanitation systems (Winpenny, 2005). Although reports of the UN Task Force on the MDG water target carefully avoids taking a position on the question of privatization (UN Millennium Project Taskforce on Water and Sanitation, 2005), the Camdessus report and the advocates of privatization rely heavily on the MDG target to demonstrate the need for public measures to facilitate, insure, and reward private investment. Moreover, the report has been treated as an authoritative statement for financing the MDG target by the Asian Development Bank, World Bank, European Union Water Initiative, and other major donors (Asian Development Bank, 2006; Water Aid, 2005; World Bank, 2003).

Human rights scholarships and activism approaches privatization in an entirely different manner. Social movements of consumers and human rights activists favoring publicly managed solutions call for human rights-based resistance to privatization and commoditization of water. Although water provision by private firms is a longstanding arrangement in a few countries, the present rapid move toward private provision has its origins in the late 1980s. "By the end of 2000, at least 93 countries had partially privatized water or wastewater services...but less than ten percent of all water is currently managed by the private sector" (Snitow & Kaufmann, 2004).

Water provokes and inspires human rights claims directly and urgently: it is arguably a fundamental right upon which other guarantees depend. In addition to the fundamental question of price and affordability for low-income citizen-consumers, the issue that has produced the deepest controversy is the corporate preference for prepayment arrangements when service contracts include low-income or otherwise high-risk consumers. Profitability is the key to all the arguments for private sector provision—efficiency, incentives to improve infrastructure, and incentives to conserve—and companies have negotiated arrangements to ensure payment from a high percentage of consumers, at relatively low transaction costs. The favored approach has been meters that operate on pre-paid cards or keys, a mechanism that has ignited strong human rights-based opposition, as in South Africa (Anti-Privatisation Forum, 2003; Marvin, Laurie, & Napier, 2001; SAMWU, 2000).

Across Asia, Africa, and famously in some Latin American countries, social movements led by consumers, human rights advocates, unions, and environmentalists have sought to block or modify corporate contracts, invoking human rights. Conca's (2005) survey of global water advocacy confirms that human rights have become a dominant frame for social movement activism, and several cases illustrate this pattern of human rights-based opposition to privatization. In Ghana, the Coalition against Privatization of Water in Ghana brings together consumers, trade unions, and NGOs and invokes international human rights (Ghana National Coalition Against the Privatisation of Water, 2001). In South Africa, national guarantees, contained in provisions of the 1996 constitution that embraced many of the internationally recognized human rights standards, have allowed a powerful domestic challenge to privatization efforts.

The now-famous resistance to corporate water contracts in several Bolivian cities, and Argentina's quieter disputes, are among many recent setbacks for the privatization movement (Picolotti, 2003). In India, human rights arguments figure prominently in legal and political challenges to the National Water Policy of 2002, which provided for private ownership and management of water systems (Pant, 2003); and in opposition to transnational beverage bottlers' use of water resources (India Resource Center, 2005).

A growing set of UN agencies and international NGO advocates are supporting these movements, particularly since the United Nations Human Rights Committee's finding in November 2003 that clarify the legal basis for a human right to water. The New York-based Committee on Economic and Social Rights (CESR, 2001), International Water Working Group (2004), and the UK-based NGO Water Aid are among many agencies employing a human rights approach to water policy advocacy (Water Aid, n.d.). Amnesty International (2003), the Centre on Housing Rights and Evictions (COHRE) (2004), 2005, the World Health Organization (WHO) (2000), WHO, COHRE and the American Association for the Advancement of Science (2004), and several others have launched new reports or initiatives on the human right to water since 2003.

This is not a difference only of emphasis or strategy, it is a disagreement over ownership or control of water systems, and the fundamental principles and mechanisms on which water systems are to be based.

(b) *HIV/AIDS*

The MDGs (Goal 6) and human rights advocates have made malaria and HIV/AIDS important priorities for action. Donor performance on increasing and targeting aid to the health sector, and to these diseases in particular, has been mixed, and there is much debate over the real amount and adequacy of some governments' new commitments to the Global Fund (LaFraniere, 2004). But more fundamentally, the major donors and the trade rule-making process at the WTO have again been at odds with human rights-based prescriptions for improved response to the HIV/AIDS pandemic.

The trade- and aid-related actions of the rich countries are significant here because they are a measure of the MDGs' capacity to mobilize not only generous aid support for the AIDS pandemic but also their seriousness about Goal 8, whose "global partnership for development" is to include trade policy (targets 12 and 13) and debt (target 15).

While donors declare their support for innovative support to patients with HIV, major aid donors and WTO provisions have continued to insist on patent protections for commercial drugs that drive up the cost of treatment. AIDS activists' partial victory in 2001, when the Ministerial Meeting at Doha affirmed that governments' right to act in a public health emergency superseded trade-related intellectual property rights (TRIPs), and made a temporary exception to the TRIPs rules for HIV/AIDS drugs, opened a further debate over the mechanisms by which poor country governments can act. For countries that cannot produce their own generic anti-retroviral drugs, a low-cost and efficient mechanism for trade in these generic drugs is essential, and there is heated debate over a temporary mechanism created in August 2003 and adopted in December 2005 by the Ministerial Meeting in Hong Kong. Critics argue that the case-by-case approval approach is a cumbersome mechanism that violates the spirit of the 2001 agreement. The US- and EU-supported solution, one letter argues, locks in a "burdensome and unworkable" solution, in the interests of ensuring that no generic drugs find their way into industrial country markets ("Joint Statement by NGOs" 2005).

The MDGs are not, of course, responsible for the failings of TRIPs, nor of other WTO negotiations. But when WTO rulings are evaluated against the MDG goal of producing a coherent global development partnership, the MDGs appear to be an ineffective instrument for mobilizing and motivating change in the wealthy industrial countries' positions. Trade issues, as Vandemootele, Malhotra, and Lim (2003) argue, are essential to accomplishing the MDGs, yet the goals have not afforded any actors the power needed to insist on real concessions and innovations needed to create the "development partnerships" called for in Goal 8.

5. MOBILIZATION: INTERNATIONAL AND DOMESTIC CONSTITUENCIES

How significant are the MDGs to national and local NGOs and social movements that have the potential to mobilize political support? While the MDGs are coordinated and monitored by a range of inter-governmental agencies, the political impetus for creating enduring changes in priorities, policies, and institutions largely depends on the mobilization of domestic political support. This section reports on a survey of international development NGOs, social movements, and NGOs in the poor countries.

UN Millennium Campaign-sponsored surveys report that many poor-country civil society organizations are on board the MDG campaign, and the Global Call to Action Against Poverty, whose agenda is tied to the MDGs, lists some 840 civil society organizations "already supporting the Global Call to Action" (2006). But although poor-country NGOs answer "yes" when asked if they are working on the MDG goals—that is, doing work on education, malaria prevention, child health, etc. (Foster & Wells, 2004)—the critical question is whether citizen organizations are mobilizing to hold their governments accountable to these objectives, and here the answer is different.

The position of Social Watch, the primary NGO effort to monitor the MDGs, is revealing. Social Watch, whose secretariat is located in the Third World Network in Montevideo, Uruguay, emerged from NGO participation in the 1995 WSSD and has member organizations and affiliates in more than 60 countries. Social Watch's comments on the MDGs are contained in a March 2005 "Benchmark" statement that amounts to a systematic critique of the MDGs. It argues, in brief, that the goals should be extended from reducing the incidence of poverty to eradicating it, and deepened from their focus on symptoms to embrace the language of guaranteeing rights, diminishing inequality, reducing social exclusion, and promoting justice (Social Watch, 2005). Social Watch engages with the MDGs, in other words, not by using the goals to leverage policy change, but by arguing that they be transformed into a broader set of structural goals.

To make a broader assessment of the relevance of the MDGs to social movements and NGOs based in the poor countries, I have examined how and whether such organizations make use of the MDGs and of human rights to advance their work. An inspection of publications, press releases, and website documents of 40 NGOs provides some evidence of how relevant the MDGs are to major social movements and development NGOs based in Southern societies. [2] Twenty Southern-based NGOs and social movement organizations and 20 international NGOs based in the industrial countries were investigated. In each case, five were selected from major national-level NGOs involved in poverty, employment, and health; five more were selected from smaller NGOs working in health-related fields; ten more were chosen at random from the Global Call to Action against Poverty list of supporting civil society organizations.

The Southern NGOs and social movements include large NGOs such as Bangladesh Rural Action Committee (BRAC), the South African

Treatment Action Campaign, and the Self-Employed Women's Association in India; as well as many smaller NGOs working in health, agriculture, gender, and income generation.

The results are summarized in Figure 2, which reports, for 40 organizations, whether their publications and advocacy strategies refer to the MDGs, to human rights, to both, or to neither. The contrast between international NGOs and the Southern NGOs and social movements is striking. While 18 of the 20 international NGOs mention the MDGs prominently, only four of the Southern NGOs make any reference at all. In some cases the MDG references are far from prominent: there is a single reference to the MDG in AMREF documents, in an interview with the foundation's malaria program director. Only the Latin American Llamado Nacional makes reference to the MDGs as a source of policy leverage. Compared to the MDGs, Southern NGOs refer to human rights more frequently (11 of 20), international NGOs somewhat less (10 of 20).

These results suggest that while the United Nations and MDG organizers have had some success in reaching the interested and concerned population in the United States and Europe, the MDGs have not become salient to major organizations and networks based in poor countries. This divide may be a matter of concern for observers of NGOs; for current purposes, it demonstrates the limitations of such goals as tools for internal political leverage over government policies.

6. CONCLUSIONS: DIRECTIONS FOR DEVELOPMENT COOPERATION

The MDGs and human rights approaches to development are divided in theory, in the policy approaches they promote for reducing poverty, and in the social actors they mobilize. These differences are often obscured, rhetorically, by development practitioners, but when the MDG campaign and the human rights-based approaches are considered as ideal types, it is difficult to avoid the conclusion that these two trends are being embraced by actors with divergent visions of development, and are becoming normative sources of support for two conflicting development agendas.

The MDG variant envisions a future driven by output goals and challenges to address the symptoms of extreme poverty. Donors are mobilized by the challenge to meet these goals, pledging aid or other forms of support for a variety of humanitarian, commercial and other foreign policy objectives. The coalition of donors is broad: debates over neo-liberal strategies, trade rules and other points of contention are secondary to the shared objectives of donors from the World Bank to the most progressive of the international NGOs, to build support for improvements in the human condition.

The rights-based approach begins, like the MDGs, from aspects of human well-being: health, nutrition, education, and other desirable conditions. For human rights-based practitioners, however, these are in turn grounded in internationally agreed standards, contained in human rights covenants and treaties. The first difference, then, is philosophical: the human rights standards are not indicators or goals but legally binding statements about rights to which humans are entitled by virtue of their humanity.

These statements are also broader in their coverage, and this difference is significant, not because the human rights agreements include a longer "list" of rights (they do), but because of the nature of those rights, which include the right to be free from discrimination, and civil and political rights such as the right to information and to freedom of expression, that have proven to be preconditions of success for pro-poor movements. The rights-based approach is more conflictive, mobilizing, and providing support to social movements that assert and claim international human rights.

There is considerable evidence that human rights are a more effective means of mobilizing the organized electorate than are donor-supported goals. The MDGs, on the other hand, have other advantages, including the targets, benchmarks, and monitoring systems familiar to development donors. There would seem to be good reason, based both in social theory and in recent experience, to integrate the MDGs more deeply with human rights guarantees. Although the MDGs are framed to avoid the obligations associated with economic and social rights, individual donors could readily tie their work on specific goals much more explicitly to the relevant human rights guarantees.

A starting point for any effort to make this link would be for donors to take seriously the 2002 Draft Guidelines for the application of human rights to poverty reduction strategies. The guidelines, developed by the UN High Commissioner for Human Rights, designate nine rights

NGO's name and country	Refers to MDG	Refers to HR	Refers to neither
Ashwinikumar Medical Relief Society (India)			x
Asian Pacific Network on Food Sovereignty		x	
African Medical and Research Foundation (Kenya)	x		
BRAC Bangladesh			x
Children in Need India (CINI)			x
Cambodian Human Rights Association		x	
Center for Science and the Environment (India)			x
CONADES (Peru)		x	
Feminist Dalit Organisation (Nepal)		x	
Greenbelt Movement (Kenya)		x	
Forum for Forest Workers (India)		x	
Llamado Nacional a la Accion Contra Pobreza (Peru)	x		
MST (Brazil)		x	
Rwanda Women's Network		x	
People's Health Movement (Bangladesh)		x	
Philippines Rural Reconstruction Movement			x
Self-Employed Women's Association (India)		x	
Social Watch	x		
Treatment Action Campaign (South Africa)		x	
Uganda Coalition for Sustainable Development	x		
Southern NGOs and Social Movements	**4**	**11**	**5**
Accion International (US)			x
Action Aid (South Africa/UK)	x	x	
CARE (US)	x		
Caritas (Italy)	x		
Catholic Relief Services (US)	x		
CIDSE	x		
Doctors Without Borders	x	x	
Global Campaign for Education	x	x	
Halifax Initiative (Canada)	x	x	
Healthlink Worldwide	x		
International Women's Health Coalition (US)	x	x	
Lutheran World Federation (Switzerland)	x	x	
Mercy Corps (US)	x		
Oxfam (UK)	x	x	
Physicians for Human Rights (US)	x	x	
Project Hope (US)			x
Save the Children (US)	x	x	
Tearfund (Ireland)	x		
Water Aid (UK)	x	x	
World Vision (US)	x		
Northern NGOs	**18**	**10**	**2**

Figure 2. *International and Southern NGOs: links to human rights and MDGs. Sources: Organizations' annual reports and websites.*

as central to poverty reduction strategies, and outline a framework for their application to the process of developing, implementing, and monitoring national poverty reduction strategies (UN Draft Guidelines, 2002).

MDG-inspired effort to finance education, pre- and post-natal care and improved housing for slum dwellers (to take three examples) could be coupled with equally determined efforts to encourage legislation and institutions that allow citizens to assert their rights to these services. The MDGs' "quick-win" strategies could be part of an effort to move as rapidly as possible toward state, voluntary and market mechanisms that effectively guarantee citizens access to the minimum levels of services and well-being guaranteed in the ICESCR. But quick-win strategies without an informed and organized public, able to assert its rights, may well mean that gains in the MDGs' indicators last only as long as the UN-sponsored campaign keeps donor funds flowing.

NOTES

1. Portions of the analysis of water and of HIV/AIDS have been reported in Nelson and Dorsey (2007).

2. The investigation was based on the NGOs' worldwide web pages. Because some organizations (Thailand's Assembly of the Poor, for example) have no web presence, this method may bias the survey toward organizations *more* likely to be engaged with international processes. For each organization, the website's internal search engine was first used to search for pages and documents with the keywords "millennium" and "millennium development goals." Next, links to "publications," "campaigns," "our work," and similar sections were followed. For websites without an internal search function, these links were used exclusively.

REFERENCES

Alston, P. (2005). Ships passing in the night: the current state of the human rights and development debate seen through the lens of the millennium development goals. *Human Rights Quarterly, 27*, 755–829.

Amnesty International (2003). World Water Forum, on file with authors.

Anti-Privatisation Forum (2003). The struggle against pre-paid water meters in Soweto, 10 September 2003. <http://www.labournet.net/world/0309/sawater1.html>.

Asian Development Bank (2006). Gurria panel searching for demand-supply equilibrium in water financing. <http://www.asiandevbank.org/water/Articles/gurria.asp>.

Bissio, R. (2003). Civil society and the MDGs. *UNDP Development Policy Journal, 3*(April), 2003.

Clemens, M., Kenny, C., & Moss, T. (2007). The Trouble with the MDGs: confronting expectations of aid and development success. *World Development, 35*(5), 735–751.

CESR (2001). Right to water fact sheet #1: global statistics. <www.cesr.org>.

COHRE (2004). Legal resources for the right to water: national and international standards, Geneva: COHRE. <http://www.cohre.org/downloads/water_res_8.pdf>.

Conca, K. (2005). *Governing water: Contentious transnational politics and global institution building*. Cambridge: MIT.

Darrow, M., & Tomas, A. (2005). Power, capture, and conflict: a call for human rights accountability in development cooperation. *Human Rights Quarterly, 27*(2), 471–538.

Fukuda-Parr, S. (2004). Millennium development goals: why they matter. *Global Governance, 10*, 395–402.

Felice, W. F. (1999). The viability of the UN approach to economic and social human rights in a globalized economy. *International Affairs, 3*, 563–598.

Fidler, D. P. (1999). *International law and infectious diseases*. Oxford: Oxford University Press.

Foster, J., & Wells, P. (2004). *We the peoples: A call to action for the UN millennium declaration*. Ottawa: North South Institute and the World Federation of United Nations Associations.

Friedman, S., & Mottiar, S. (2005). A rewarding engagement: the treatment action campaign and the politics of HIV/AIDS. *Politics & Society, 33*, 511–565.

Gauri, V. (2004). Social rights and economics: claims to health care and education in developing countries. *World Development, 32*(3), 465–477.

Ghana National coalition against the privatisation of water (2001). Accra declaration on the right to water. <http://www.isodec.org.gh/Papers/accradeclaration.PDF>.

Global call to action against poverty (2006). Global call to action against poverty. <http://www.whiteband.org/Lib/about_sup/en>.

India Resource Center. 2005. Coca-Cola challenged on human rights abuses, press release, April 20, 2005. <http://www.indiaresource.org/campaigns/coke/2005/cokechallenged.html>.

International Water Working Group (2004). Water is a human right, say "no" to prepaid water meters. <http://www.citizen.org/cmep/Water/cmep_Water/>.

Joint statement by NGOs on TRIPS and public health (2005). <http://www.cptech.org/ip/wto/p6/ngos12032005.html> (December 2005).

Jolly, R. (2004). Global development goals: UN experience. *Journal of Human Development, 5*(1), 69–95.

LaFraniere, S. (2004). UN fund for halting diseases faces money woes. *New York Times*, April 17, 2004.

Malloch Brown, M. (2002). Meeting the millennium challenge: a strategy for helping achieve the united nations millennium development goals. <http://www. inwent.org/ef-texte/mdg/brown.htm>.

Malloch Brown, M. (2003). Millennium development goals, poverty reduction strategy papers and the new global development agenda, Address by the UNDP Administrator, New York, 14 February 2003. <http://www.undp.org/dpa/statements/administ/2003/february/14feb03.html>.

Marvin, S., Laurie, N., & Napier, M. (2001). Pre-payment: emerging pathways to water services. <http://www.aguabolivia.org/newcastle/documentos/Nina-Marvin-southAfrica.htm>.

Maxwell, S. (2001). Heaven or hubris: reflections on the new 'new poverty agenda'. *Development Policy Review, 21*(1), 5–25.

Michel, J. (2005). The birth of the MDGs, DACNews, September–October 2005. <http://www.oecd.org/document/34/0,2340,en_2649_33721_35295778_1_1_1_1,00.html>.

Nelson, P., & Dorsey, E. (2003). At the nexus of human rights and development: new methods and strategies of global NGOs. *World Development, 31*(12), 2013–2026.

Nelson, P., & Dorsey, E. (2007). New rights advocacy in a global public domain. *European Journal of International Relations, 13*(2), 187–216.

Nowak, M. (2005). A human rights approach to poverty. In *Human rights in development yearbook 2002. Empowerment, participation, accountability and non-discrimination: Operationalising a human rights-based approach to development* (pp. 15–36). Leiden: Martinus Nijhoff Publishers.

Offenheiser, R. C., & Holcombe, S. (2003). Challenges and opportunities in implementing a rights-based approach to development: an Oxfam America perspective. *Nonprofit and Voluntary Sector Quarterly, 32*(2), 268–306.

Pant, R. (2003). From communities hands to MNCs' BOOTs: A case study from india on right to water. Right to water project of rights and humanity, UK. <http://www.righttowater.org.uk/pdfs/india_cs.pdf>.

Patrick, S. (1998). The check is in the mail: Improving the delivery and coordination of post-conflict assistance, Working Paper, NYU Center on International Cooperation. <http://www.ciaonet.org/wps/pas01/>.

Picard, M. (2004). Measurement and methodological challenges to CARE International's rights-based programming. <http://www.enterpriseimpact.org.uk/pdf/EINAug04.pdf>.

Picolotti, J. M. (2003). The right to water in Argentina, report prepared for rights and humanity, November 5, 2003. <http://www.cedha.org.ar/docs/doc175-eng.doc>.

Plipat, S. (2005). Developmentizing human rights: how development NGOs interpret and implement a human rights-based approach to development policy, Unpublished doctoral dissertation, University of Pittsburgh.

Pogge, Thomas (2004). The first United National millennium development goal: a cause for celebration?. *Journal of Human Development, 5*(3), 377–397.

Rand, J. (2002). Care's experience with adoption of a rights-based approach: five case studies. <http://www.crin.org/docs/resources/publications/hrbap/AREexperiences_case_studies.doc>.

Sahn, D. A., & Stifel, D. C. (2003). Progress toward the millennium development goals in Africa. *World Development, 31*(1), 33–52.

Saith, A. (2006). From:universal values to millennium development goals: lost in translation. *Development and Change, 37*(6), 1167–1199.

SAMWU (2000). Joint rural development services network and South African Municipal Workers Union (SAMWU) statement, Johannesburg, August 21, 2000, on the South African Water Services Act, on file with the author.

Sanderson, S. (2004). Poverty and conservation: the new century's 'peasant question?' *World Development, 33*(2), 323–332.

Sen, A. (1999). *Development as freedom*. New York: Random House.

Shetty, S. (2005). Making rights real: the challenge in meeting the MDGs, 2005. Public presentation, 24 March, 2005, London. Notes on file with the author.

Sida (2001). *Country strategy development: Guide for country analysis from a democratic governance and human rights perspective*. Stockholm: Sida.

Snitow, A. & Kaufmann, D. (2004) The new economy of water. <http://www.pbs.org/pov/pov2004/thirst/special_neweconomy.html>.

Social Watch (2005). A civil society benchmark for the 5-year review of the millennium declaration. <http://www.socialwatch.org/en/noticias/documentos/Benchmark_2005_eng.doc>.

Tomlinson, B. (2005). The politics of the millennium development goals. <http://www.realityofaid.org/themeshow.php?id=14>.

UN draft guidelines: a human rights approach to poverty reduction strategies. <http://www.unhchr.ch/development/povertyfinal.html>.

UNDP (2000). *Human development report 2000*. New York: Oxford University Press.

UNICEF (n.d.). Human rights for children and women: How UNICEF helps make them a Reality. <http://www.unicef.org/pubsgen/humanrights-children/humanrightseng.pdf>.

UN Millennium Project Task Force on Water and Sanitation (2005). Final Report, Health, Dignity, and Development: What Will It Take? <http://www.unmillenniumproject.org/documents/What_Will_It_Take.pdf>.

UN Millennium Project (2005). A practical plan to achieve the millennium development goals. <http://www.unmillenniumproject.org/reports/fullreport.htm>.

Uvin, P. (2002). On high moral ground: the incorporation of human rights by the development enterprise. *Praxis, 17*, 1–11.

Uvin, P. (2004). *Rights and Development*. Westport, CT: Kumarian.

Vandemootele, J., Malhotra, K. & Lim, J. A. (2003). Is MDG 8 on track as a global deal for human development? UNDP Bureau for Development Policy. <http://www.undp.org/povertycentre/publications/mdg/MDG8_OnTrack-UNDP-Jun03.pdf>.

Walker, P., Wisner, B., Leaning, J., & Minear, L. (2005). Smoke and mirrors: deficiencies in disaster funding. *BMJ, 330*(January), 247–250.

Water Aid (n.d.). Human rights approach to development. <http://www.righttowater.org.uk/code/HR_approach.asp>.

Water Aid (2005). An empty glass: The EU Water Initiative's contribution to the water and sanitation Millennium targets. <http://www.wateraid.org/documents/an_empty_glass.pdf>.

Winpenny, J. (2005). Financing water for all: report of the world panel on financing water infrastructure. Chaired by Michel Camdessus, March 2003. <www.gwpforum.org/servlet/PSP>.

Woolcock, M., & Narayan, D. (2000). Social capital: implications for development theory, research, and policy. *World Bank Research Observer, 15*(2).

World Bank (2003). World Bank Group Response to the Report of the World Panel on Financing Water Infrastructure Chaired by Mr. Michel Camdessus, July 14, 2003. <http://www.financingwaterforall.org/fileadmin/Financing_water_for_all/Stakeholders_responses/WBG_Response_to_Camdessus_Report.pdf>.

World Health Organization, *Right to Water*, 2000. <http://www.who.int/water_sanitation_health/rightowater/en/>.

World Health Organization, COHRE and American Association for Advancement of Science (2004). Manual on the right to water. <http://www.cohre.org/downloads/water_flyer.pdf>.

[19]

Transnational Human Rights Obligations

Sigrun I. Skogly & Mark Gibney***

I. INTRODUCTION

In the Trail Smelter case, *United States vs. Canada*, the Court held that:

> Under the principles of international law . . . no State has the right to use or permit the use of its territory in such a manner as to cause injury by fumes in or to the territory of another or the properties or persons therein, when the case is of serious consequence and the injury is established by clear and convincing evidence.[1]

This case was heard close to a century ago, yet little has developed in terms of states' obligations or responsibility for transnational effects of their actions. This is true for international law generally, and for international human rights law more specifically.

The topic of transnational human rights obligations for states has not been widely explored.[2] By transnational obligations, we imply the possibility that states may have obligations relating to the human rights effects of their external activities, such as trade, development cooperation, participation in international organizations, and security activities. Most work of human

---

* *Sigrun I. Skogly* is Lecturer of Law at Lancaster University, United Kingdom. She holds an LL.M. from Essex University, and a Ph.D. in Law from University of Oslo. Her work in recent years has focused on human rights obligations, in particularly non-state actors. She is the author of the book *The Human Rights Obligations of the World Bank and the International Monetary Fund.* She is currently working on a book project on states' human rights obligations in foreign affairs.

** *Mark Gibney* is the Belk Distinguished Professor at the University of North Carolina–Asheville.

An earlier version of this article was presented at the International Studies Association's Annual meeting in Chicago, Illinois, Feb. 2001.

1. Trail Smelter Case (*United States v. Canada*), 3 R.I.A.A. 1905 (1941). *See also* Mark Gibney, Katarina Tomasěvski, & Jens Vedsted-Hansen, *Transnational State Responsibility for Violations of Human Rights,* 12 HARVARD HUM. RTS. J. 273 (1999).
2. *See* Gibney, Tomasěvski, & Vedsted-Hansen, *supra* note 1 (one of the few works in this field).

rights institutions focuses on the national or internal obligations that states have and how states that have ratified the various human rights instruments implement these provisions within their national borders. Although human rights guarantees stem from international treaties and the obligations, therefore, are of an international nature, the subjects of the human rights protection are normally the state's own nationals and residents. International human rights law is part of the general regime of international law in that its sources stem from treaty law, customary international law, and general principles of law. International human rights law, however, is different from other areas of international law because the implementation of the provisions of these treaties, or the norms of customary international law in this field, commonly is done domestically. Thus, there is a vertical relationship between a state and its subjects, rather than a horizontal relationship among states.[3]

Accepting that this is the main thrust of international human rights law obligations, this article will challenge the notion that this is the *only sphere* in which states have obligations pertaining to this part of international law. In this article, we will address the following questions:

- In which areas do states' trans- or cross-border operations play a role in terms of human rights enjoyment?
- What are the legal foundations for obligations in this field?
- What are the experiences of the international bodies responsible for human rights monitoring and international judicial bodies in dealing with cross-border obligations?
- Are there implications in terms of "obligations of result" and "obligations of conduct"?
- What is the sovereignty paradox that this approach may imply?

3. Allan Rosas holds that "[t]he Universal Declaration offers a paradigmatic challenge to the Hobbesian strand of the Westfalian legacy, which has seen their international system as a horizontal inter-state system based on the sovereign equality of states." This is because the Universal Declaration:
   - concerns matters between the state and its own population (*vertical* approach) other than inter-state relations;
   - concerns all *human beings*, who, in the words of Article 1 of the Declaration, "are born free and equal in dignity and rights," rather than the nationals (citizens) of a given state;
   - is a proclamation and interpretation of *universal values*, rather than a negotiated compromise between the different wills (interests) of states.

   Allan Rosas, *State Sovereignty and Human Rights: Towards a Global Constitutional Project,* XLIII Pol. Stud. 61, 62–63 (footnote omitted) (1995). *See also* Harry J. Steiner & Philip Alston, International Human Rights in Context: Law, Politics and Morals 57 ff. (2d ed. 2000).

This article will only address the effects of states' direct involvement in transnational activities. Although interesting and important, we will not be able to address the extent to which states are under obligations to regulate the transnational conduct of private parties under their jurisdiction (third party regulation). This should not be taken to imply that we regard it as less important, but rather a choice of focus for this article.

II. TRANSNATIONAL ACTIVITIES

In these times of globalization, the role of the individual state has changed and, in some measure, diminished.[4] The role of the state in guiding economic policy, which may enhance or threaten human rights enjoyment, is largely reduced.[5] International forces increasingly determine national decision making, particularly in smaller states and poorer states, and the power of private international forces, such as transnational corporations (TNCs), often imply that governments' scope of choice is limited.[6] This reality has not only been recognized by academics but also has been acknowledged by the United Nations. In his study from 1992 on the realization of economic, social, and cultural rights, the UN Special Rapporteur, Danilo Türk argues:

> The legal basis upon which economic, social and cultural rights rest, essentially assumes the presence of a "strong" State as the motor behind realizing these rights, combined with a correlative national approach toward this category of legal entitlement. This view, however, is clearly at odds with the prevailing political realities of a majority of States, as well as views of the allegedly "appropriate role" of the State.[7]

Writing almost ten years later, the UN Secretary General expressed very similar opinions when commenting on the benefits and challenges of globalization:

---

4. *See* Sigrun Skogly, *Democracy and Human Rights: The Role of the International Donor Community in Africa,* 2, 1 J. Third World Spectrum 81 (1995) (discusses the paradox of state human rights obligations in times of globalization).
5. In an article on globalization and human rights, Virginia Leary states, "[u]nder structural adjustment programmes, governments are less able to freely adopt economic and social policies; international financial institutions and transnational corporations are often the real influences in the adoption of such national policies." Virginia Leary, *Globalisation and Human Rights in* Human Rights: New Dimensions and Challenges 265–266, 281 (Janusz Symonides ed., 1998).
6. *See generally* Human Rights Standards and the Responsibility of Transnational Corporations (Michael K. Addo ed., 1999).
7. Danilo Türk, Special Rapporteur, United Nations, Economic and Social Council, *The Realization of Economic, Social and Cultural Rights—Final Report,* UN Doc. E/CN.4/Sub.2/1992/16, 3 July 1992, at 23, ¶ 85.

> Weak states are one of the main impediments to effective governance today, at national and international levels alike. For the good of their own people and for the sake of our common aims, we must help to strengthen the capacity of those states to govern, not undermine them further. . . . By the same token, states need to develop a deeper awareness of their dual role in our global world. In addition to the separate responsibilities each state bears toward its own society, states are, collectively, the custodians of our common life on this planet—a life the citizens of *all* countries share. Notwithstanding the institutional turmoil that is often associated with globalisation, there exists no other entity that competes with or can substitute for the state. Successfully managing globalisation, therefore, requires—first and foremost—that states act in a manner consistent with their dual role.[8]

Thus, the crucial role of a strong and organized state is recognized by commentators on globalization and the fulfillment of human rights. Concurrently, it is recognized that the forces of globalization in their present form may reduce the strength of the state. It is also acknowledged that states are involved in more international activities than ever before, not least through their work in intergovernmental organizations and in their attempts to liberalize international trade.

In terms of transnational human rights obligations, all of these activities become important. Human rights are commonly divided into five groups: civil, political, economic, social, and cultural. Although emphasis is constantly placed the interdependence and indivisibility of all categories of human rights (and rightly so), the actual effect of transnational operations by states may be more common and visible in the area of economic and social rights.[9] This effect may be explained by the nature of states' transnational activities at the beginning of the twenty-first century. States are commonly involved in international security issues, in development assistance, in trade relations, and in work with intergovernmental organizations, all of which promote international economic and social development. Thus, they are involved in activities that influence people's financial and material resources, through employment opportunities (and employment conditions), through the advancement of liberalized trade, agricultural developments and advancement, educational opportunities, and also through arms sales, which can greatly influence the resources available for economic and social development necessary for the improvement in levels of human rights enjoyment.

We are not saying that it is only economic and social rights that require

8. Kofi Annan, The Role of the United Nations in the 21st Century, Report presented by the Secretary-General on 4 Apr. 2000, at 11.
9. This statement needs qualification. In the article by Gibney, Tomasěvski, and Vedsted-Hansen, the authors document serious issues in relationship to civil and political rights as well, not least in terms of granting export licenses to companies producing torture equipment. *See* Gibney, Tomasěvski, & Vedsted-Hansen, *supra* note 1, at 271–72.

financial resources from the state. To the contrary, such provisions are absolutely necessary to the fulfillment of civil and political rights as well. In a recent report, the International Council on Human Rights Policy documented how important resources are—both domestic (internal) and international (external)—for the establishment and running of an adequate system for the administration of justice.[10] Nevertheless, the most frequent, and most direct, influence on the enjoyment of human rights by foreign states' activities is most likely to be seen in the area of economic and social rights. Thus, without making any normative judgment as to the relative importance of human rights in general, the main focus of this article will be on economic and social rights.

In order to illustrate where transnational activities may influence human rights, it may be of interest to look at the approaches of two countries. In a recent White Paper, the Norwegian government called for a strengthening of Norway's promotion of internationally recognized human rights beyond its own borders. It stated, "Human rights are for all individuals, whether or not they live in Norway or in other parts of the world. This universality principle gives a moral and legal imperative for all to contribute to a global human rights protection."[11] The Norwegian government wants to focus its attention through development cooperation, work through the human rights sections in the United Nations, and in other international human rights organizations.[12] Differing slightly from this is a Swedish Government White Paper from 1998 in which the approach to human rights in a transnational setting was more extensive. This Swedish White Paper emphasized that an integrated human rights policy shall be an integral part of the entirety of Swedish foreign policy, including development assistance, trade relations, military and security cooperation, voting in intergovernmental organizations, and refugee policy.[13] Thus, this approach brings human rights to *all* elements of Swedish foreign policy, while the Norwegian approach limits its foreign policy to only part of its transnational operations. Notwithstanding the differences between these two countries, however, both illustrate that there is now a growing recognition that the promotion of human rights implies more than ensuring that human rights are not violated in each state's domestic setting, but also that activities the state is engaged in abroad may have human rights implications.

---

10. *See* International Council on Human Rights Policy, *Local Perspectives: Foreign Aid to the Justice Sector*, Geneva, International Council on Human Rights Policy, June 2000.
11. Det Norske Storting, St. Meld. Nr. 21 (1999–2000), *Menneskereverd i Sentrum* (The Norwegian Parliament, White Paper No. 21, 1999–2000 Human Dignity in Focus—author's translation), Ch. 2, *available at* <http://odin.dep.no/repub/99-00/stmld/21> [hereinafter: Norwegian White Paper].
12. *See id.*
13. *See* The Swedish Government, Human Rights in Swedish Foreign Policy, White Paper 1997/98:89, at 12 (Original Title Regeringens skrivelse 1997/98:89: Mänskliga rättigheter i svensk utrikespolitik, author's translation).

III. LEGAL FOUNDATION FOR TRANSNATIONAL HUMAN RIGHTS OBLIGATIONS

Any discussion of the implementation or the promotion of human rights obligations beyond national borders needs first to establish the legal foundations for these claims. The basis for any such obligation would be found not only in international human rights covenants and conventions but also in the UN Charter. As members of the United Nations, states have pledged themselves to "achieve international cooperation in solving international problems. . . . And in promoting and encouraging respect for human rights and for fundamental freedoms. . . ."[14] Further, in Article 56, UN members "pledge themselves to take joint and separate action in cooperation with the Organisation for the achievement" of "universal respect for, and observance of, human rights and fundamental freedoms."[15] These provisions, seen in conjunction with Article 103, which states that obligations under the Charter will prevail over other obligations in international law,[16] imply that member-states of the UN will be under an obligation to operate in accordance with respect for human rights. By the very inclusion of human rights in the UN Charter, they became a matter of international concern.[17]

The UN Charter by itself, however, may not be enough to claim that states have legal obligations to ensure that their own transnational activities do not jeopardize human rights in other countries. In fact, whether the wording in Articles 55 and 56 represents a legal obligation upon states to cooperate in the international community to attain the goals of the United Nations has been disputed.[18] In order to assess the extent to which such legal obligations exist, the provisions of the UN Charter need to be seen in light of the developments in international human rights law in the latter half of the last century.

Compared to the present day, the UN Charter was drafted in an era with strong nation-states, centralized control of power, and limited international interaction. The technological facilities for international interaction were

14. U.N. Charter, art. 1(3), *signed* 26 June 1945, 59 Stat. 1031, T.S. No. 993, 3 Bevans 1153 (*entered into force* 24 Oct. 1945).
15. *Id.* art. 55.
16. Article 103 of the UN Charter reads: "In the event of a conflict between the obligations of the members of the United Nations under the present Charter and their obligations under any other international agreement, their obligations under the present Charter shall prevail." *Id.*
17. *See* Hersh Lauterpacht, International Law and Human Rights 146 (1950).
18. See generally Lauterpacht, *supra* note 17; Egon Schwelb, The Influence of the Universal Declaration on Human Rights on International and National Law, Am. Soc. Int'l L. Proceedings, 1959; The Charter of the United Nations: A Commentary (Bruno Simma ed., 1994); Louis B. Sohn, *The Human Rights Law of the Charter* 12 Texas Int'l L. J. (1977).

limited to the telephone, and air traffic for business purposes was in its early days. In this situation, national authorities retained a strong hand in the internal development of their respective states through capital control, control over the movement of people, and restrictions on international investment. In the last two decades, marked by the massive opening up of markets and globalization in general, many governments' abilities to control what their own subjects are doing as well as to influence foreign actors, whether natural or legal persons, has been reduced. In this climate, where free market competition has been the guiding principle in the foreign affairs of the dominant states in the international society, it is easy to forget the possible negative human effects of these activities.

To discuss these legal arguments, it is necessary to look at the sources of international law, both in terms of *de lege lata* and what may be in the process of development. This section will be divided into three separate parts: a) customary international law; b) treaty law; and c) soft law.

A. Customary International Law

There are many controversial areas of customary international law in regards to human rights that will not be dealt within this article. Due to the recent inclusion of human rights law in international law, it is difficult to use the traditional "test" in determining the existence of customary rules in this field.[19] Nevertheless, there seems to be a general consensus that at least certain parts of international human rights law have gained status as customary international law, and as such, are binding upon all states.[20] Some commentators claim that all of the Universal Declaration of Human Rights (Universal Declaration) represents international customary law,[21] while others take a more cautious attitude and include only a few of the rights or certain elements of the rights contained in the Universal Declaration.[22] All states are under an obligation to respect the rights that have this status. The question becomes whether this obligation to states is related only

19. It is common to require that a norm fulfill the following criteria in order to be established as customary international law: a consistent state practice for a period of time, followed by an *opinio juris*. *See generally* ROSALYN HIGGINS, PROBLEMS AND PROCESS: INTERNATIONAL LAW AND HOW WE USE IT (1993).
20. *See* THEODOR MERON, HUMAN RIGHTS AND HUMANITARIAN NORMS AS CUSTOMARY LAW 80 (1989).
21. This view has been advocated by Sohn: "The Declaration, as an authoritative listing of human rights, has become a basic component of international customary law, binding on all states, not only on members of the United Nations." Louis Sohn, *The New International Law: Protection of the Rights of Individuals Rather than States* 32 AM. UNIV. L. REV. 17 (1982), *quoted in* MERON, *supra note* 20, at 82.
22. Oscar Schachter, *International Human Rights*, HAGUE ACADEMY OF INT'L LAW, RECEUILS DES COURS, 334–35 (1982).

to their own population, or whether indeed states have obligations in relationship to the subjects of other states as well.

Due to the relatively restrictive nature of the content of customary international norms in the field of human rights, some commentators imply that these norms carry mainly negative obligations. These commentators argue that states' obligations pertaining to customary international human rights law will be regarded as obligations not to interfere, not to violate—or rather that these obligations will be fulfilled if the state refrains from acting. To illustrate, the prohibition of torture is a recognized rule of customary international law by which states are under an obligation to refrain from torturous practices. The more positive obligations to train police personnel not to carry out torture or to ensure that torture victims receive adequate treatment may not be part of the customary element of this right. Similarly, the right to food and the right to life may have customary international law elements to them in that states are under an obligation not to deliberately starve people by removing their food supply. However, the more positive elements of these rights, such as the obligation to ensure that people have access to food in quantities and qualities that are sufficient for their mental and physical development in a manner that is culturally acceptable,[23] may not be of a customary nature. Thus, the wider content of these rights—beyond the customary elements—may be seen to be of a positive nature, and will be of firmer obligations based on treaty law to which only the states that have ratified the treaties can be held accountable.

Thus, in terms of transnational obligations based on customary international law, it would be fair to assume that the content of the obligation would be of a negative nature—states should refrain from actions in their international or transnational operations that will fail to respect the human rights of people in other states. To illustrate, there may be an obligation not to supply a foreign state with torture equipment. There is, however, no obligation to send personnel to train the police in non-torturous practices, although a state could do so legitimately if the foreign state agreed.

As customary human rights law develops, the national boundaries for obligations pertaining to these norms will be weakened. We have seen this weakening in the application of universal jurisdiction for certain violations of human rights, particularly in terms of torture, extrajudicial killings, and crimes against humanity.[24] It is pertinent to assume that in a globalized

23. *See* UN Committee on Economic, Social and Cultural Rights, General Comment No. 12, Right to Adequate Food, U.N. Doc. No. E/C.12/1999/5, at ¶ 11.
24. *See* Regina v. Bartle and the Commissioner of Police for the Metropolis and Others Ex Parte Pinochet (House of Lords Mar. 24, 1999); Filartiga v. Pena-Irala, 630 F.2d 876 (2nd Cir. 1980); Attorney General of Israel v. Eichmann, 36 INT'L. L. REP. 277 (Sup. Ct. Israel 1962).

world where individual citizens' lives are heavily influenced by operations by actors beyond one's national borders, the obligation to respect customary international human rights law in transnational operations will be considerably strengthened. It will be increasingly recognized that, not only are there governments that are unwilling to ameliorate the human rights effects of foreign actors within their own borders, but also that they are unable to do so, due to political and economic inequalities, in the international community as well.

In terms of transnational obligations, the principle would be that states would have a duty to act in accordance with customary international human rights law in their international operations to the extent that people in a foreign state do not suffer as a result of the first state's action. In fact, principles of diplomatic protection and state responsibility could be used as an analogy in this setting. It is a recognized principle that states shall refrain from causing harm to another state.[25] Another principle holds that if a state harms another state's national, this action in international law terms is seen to cause harm to the second state.[26] If one state harms the national of another state when this national still is in his or her own state, however, the issues of diplomatic protection or state responsibility do not seem to be carried as far. For example, if an agent of a state travels to another state and assassinates one of that state's nationals, quite obviously, a case of responsibility will be triggered. If the first state gives an export licence for torture equipment to be sold to the second state and citizens of the second state die from torture, however, the issue of responsibility is not as clear.[27]

The customary norm is a prohibition of torture, but the implementation of this prohibition so far has been seen to be of a rather strict internal operation (apart from cases such as the Pinochet case, but in that case, it was the prosecution that was abroad, not the effects of the state's actions).[28] In the torture equipment example, one could easily argue that the importer state is to blame, as it was this state that chose to use the equipment. It is also a valid argument, however, that by making torture equipment available, the first state is at least an accomplice to the crime of torture and should assume part of the responsibility. Similarly, if a state was asked to grant credit guarantees for investment in another state, and this guarantee would

25. *See* Trail Smelter Case, *supra* note 1.
26. *See* Malcolm N. Shaw, International Law 562 (4th ed. 1997).
27. *See* Gibney, Tomasěvski, & Vedsted-Hansen, *supra* note 1, at 271–72.
28. There is now, however, a new take on this case. There is now a possibility that General Pinochet will be indicted in the United States for his involvement in the murder of Orlando Letelier and a colleague in Washington DC in 1976. Letielier was a former Chilean Ambassador to the United States and a prominent opponent of Pinochet. *See* Fredric L. Kirgis, *Possible Indictment of Pinochet in the United States,* Am. Soc. Int'l Law Insights (Mar. 2000), *available at* <http://www.asil.org/insights.htm>.

only be granted on the condition that trade unions were outlawed in the industry in which investment was sought, human rights issues would be at play, but rarely invoked. In this scenario, the deliberate act of the credit-guaranteeing state would infringe upon the rights of the population in the receiver state.

B. Treaty Law

In addition to the already mentioned provisions of the UN Charter, there are a number of other treaty provisions that may be of relevance in international human rights law. The most prominent instruments from which transnational human rights obligations may be established are the International Covenant on Economic, Social, and Cultural Rights (ICESCR),[29] and the International Covenant on Civil and Political Rights (ICCPR).[30] In respect to transnational obligations, there may be a rather substantive difference between the two Covenants. The general obligation provisions can be found in Article 2 of both Covenants. Article 2 of the ICESCR contains the following passage:

> 1. Each State Party to the present Covenant undertakes to take steps, *individually and through international assistance and co-operation,* . . . with a view to achieving progressively the full realisation of the rights recognised in the present Covenant. (Emphasis added.)

Article 2 of the ICCPR is rather different in that it states:

> 1. Each State Party to the present Covenant undertakes to respect and to ensure to *all individuals within its territory and subject to its jurisdiction* the rights recognised in the present Covenant. (Emphasis added.)

These texts seem to indicate that the obligations upon the ratifying states are tied more firmly to national borders in terms of civil and political rights than for economic and social rights. Civil and political rights are guaranteed within the ratifying state's territory and for individuals over whom it exercises jurisdiction. On the other hand, economic, social, and cultural rights shall be achieved individually and "through international assistance and cooperation," without specifying a territorial or jurisdictional

---

29. International Covenant on Economic, Social and Cultural Rights, *adopted* 16 Dec. 1966, G.A. Res. 2200 (XXI), U.N. GAOR, 21st Sess., Supp. No. 16, U.N. Doc. A/6316 (1966), 993 U.N.T.S. 3 (*entered into force* 3 Jan. 1976). Current ratifications: 143 (as of Jan. 2001).
30. International Covenant on Civil and Political Rights, *adopted* 16 Dec. 1966, G.A. Res. 2200 (XXI), U.N. GAOR, 21st Sess., Supp. No. 16, U.N. Doc. A/6316 (1966), 999 U.N.T.S. 171 (*entered into force* 23 Mar. 1976). Current ratifications: 147 (as of Jan. 2001).

limitation. Without going into detail on the specifics of the various aspects of the obligations as provided by the two Articles 2, it seems that a preliminary conclusion can be drawn that the drafters of the ICESCR have envisioned that the fulfillment of these rights has transnational dimensions as well as domestic ones.[31]

This vision is also evidenced in other articles of the ICESCR, particularly in Article 23, which states, *inter alia,* that:

> The States Parties to the present Covenant agree that *international action* for the achievement of the rights recognized in the present Covenant *includes such methods as* the conclusion of conventions, the adoption of recommendations, the furnishing of technical assistance, etc. (Emphasis added.)

This article is seemingly rather weak in the role it envisions for transnational operations, in terms of promoting economic, social, and cultural rights. It is significant in this endeavor, however, that the ICESCR specifically recognizes the role of not *only* the ratifying state, but also states outside national borders. It should also be noted that the listing of activities that other states are supposed to engage in to achieve the rights listed in the ICESCR are examples and cannot be read as an exhaustive list, as the article itself uses the term "such methods as."

C. Soft Law

The final section under the legal basis for obligations concerns "soft law," a term that includes decisions of international bodies and UN organs, such as Convention-based Committees.[32] In their work on the various human rights conventions and covenants, these Committees have produced authoritative interpretations of the substantive content of rights, as well as the procedural and substantive obligations of the state parties. In this regard, the Committees have assisted in clarifying the understanding of international human rights law within their specific areas of expertise.

---

31. It should be noted that, although the ICESCR seems clearer in respect to transnational obligations, this should not lead to a conclusion that such obligations only pertain to these specific rights. Clearly, as was discussed in the above section, transnational human rights obligations based on customary law (civil, political, cultural, economic, and social) will be applicable to this comprehensive set of rights.
32. The implementation of the following human rights conventions and covenants are supervised by expert Committees: the ICCPR, the ICESCR, the Convention on the Elimination of All forms of Racial Discrimination, the Convention on the Elimination of Discrimination against Women, the Convention Against Torture and Other Cruel, Inhuman or Degrading Treatment or Punishment, and the Convention on the Rights of the Child.

In terms of transnational obligations, the Committee of Economic, Social, and Cultural Rights[33] has issued several interesting statements. For instance, in May 1999, this Committee passed General Comments on The Right to Adequate Food, as recognized in Article 11 of the ICESCR.[34] In this General Comment, the Committee stated:

> States Parties should recognise the essential role of international cooperation and comply with their commitment to take joint and separate action to achieve the full realisation of the right to adequate food. In implementing this commitment, State parties should take steps to respect the enjoyment of the right to food in other countries, to protect that right, to facilitate access to food and to provide the necessary aid when required.[35]

In the most recent General Comment from the same UN Committee, the General Comment on the Right to Health, the statements of transnational obligations seem to be even clearer. The Committee here states:

> To comply with their international obligations in relation to article 12, States parties have to respect the enjoyment of the right to health in other countries, and to prevent third parties from violating the right in other countries, if they are able to influence these third parties by way of legal or political means, in accordance with the Charter of the United Nations and applicable international law. Depending on the availability of resources, States should facilitate access to essential health facilities, goods and services in other countries, wherever possible and provide the necessary aid when required.[36]

Compared to some earlier instruments dealing with economic and social rights and the obligations pertaining to them, this is a clear enhancement of international obligations of states. For example, in the *Maastricht Guidelines*,[37] adopted by a group of experts in 1997, the section on transnational

33. This is the only treaty-related committee that was not established through the treaty text itself. This committee was established in 1986, based on the model of the already existing expert committees established by the individual conventions.
34. UN Committee On Economic, Social and Cultural Rights, General Comment 12 (UN Doc. E/C.12/1999/5), 12 May 1999.
35. Id. ¶ 36. The legal basis for this statement is referred to in UN Charter, article 56. The specific provisions contained in articles 11, 21, & 23 of the International Covenant on Economic, Social and Cultural Rights, and the Rome Declaration of the World Food Summit. *Id.*
36. UN Committee on Economic, Social and Cultural Rights, General Comment No. 14, *The Right to Health*, U.N. Doc. No. E/C.12/1999/5, at ¶ 39.
37. The Maastricht Guidelines on Violations of Economic, Social and Cultural Rights, adopted by a group of thirty experts in Maastricht, 22–26 Jan. 1997. The objective of this meeting was to "elaborate on the Limburg Principles as regards the nature and scope of violations of economic, social and cultural rights and appropriate responses and remedies." INTERNATIONAL COMMISSION OF JURISTS, MAASTRICHT GUIDELINES, *Introduction* 81 (Nov. 1997). (The Limburg Principles on the Implementation of the International Covenant on Economic, Social and Cultural Rights, were adopted by a group of distinguished experts

obligations is weak because the obligations generally are seen to be of a national character.[38]

However, addressing the role of international financial institutions, the UN Committee on Economic, Social and Cultural Rights, in General Comment no. 2 dealing with structural adjustment programs, held:

> [A]djustment programmes endeavours to protect the most basic economic, social and cultural rights become more, rather than less, urgent. States parties to the Covenant, as well as the relevant United Nations agencies, should thus make a particular effort to ensure that such protection is, to the maximum extent possible, built-in to programmes and policies designed to promote adjustment.[39]

On a more general level, the Vienna Declaration and Programme of Action Part I, paragraph 13 confirms that "[t]here is a need for States and international organisations, in cooperation with non-governmental organisations, to create favorable conditions at the national, regional and international levels to ensure the full and effective enjoyment of human rights."

Thus, in customary international law, treaty law, and in a variety of soft law expressions, the role of the state beyond its national borders in protecting human rights is clearly recognized. As a result, it is quite a paradox that so-called international human rights should only have a national dimension.

IV. CASE LAW

The introduction to this article started by a reference to the Trail Smelter case, in which the state's responsibility for negative effects on another state's territory is quite clearly established. In terms of human rights case law, however, this area continues to evolve, and the international jurisprudence is by no means consistent. It seems that the main issue that the courts or committees have problems with is in determining the direct link between state actions and the resulting human rights violations in other countries. There are, however, some interesting decisions that illustrate the different approaches.

In *Loizidou v. Turkey*, the European Court of Human Rights stated that

---

in international law, in Maastricht on 2–6 June, 1986, International Commission of Jurists, Limburg Principles 65 (Nov. 1997).

38. *The Maastricht Guidelines, supra* note 37, ¶ 16 reads "The violations referred to in section II are in principle imputable to the State within whose the jurisdiction they occur. As a consequence, the State responsible must establish mechanisms to correct such violations, including monitoring investigation, prosecution, and remedies for victims."

39. General Comment No. 2 (1990), International Technical Assistance Measures, Covenant, art. 22, *supra* note 29, E/1990/23, at 86–88.

responsibility for one's own acts can reach outside its jurisdiction.[40] In this case, which concerned the confiscation of property in the Turkey-occupied areas of Northern Cyprus, the court held that the responsibility of contracting parties can be involved because of acts of their authorities, whether performed within or outside national boundaries, which produce effects outside their own territory.[41]

Similarly, in cases concerning the extradition of people to countries where they may face torture or capital punishment, the European Court of Human Rights has consistently held that this would be a violation of Article 3 of the European Convention for the Protection of Human Rights and Fundamental Freedoms. This was held, *inter alia,* in *Soering v. United Kingdom.*[42] A similar, although more limited, application of this principle has been acknowledged by the UN Human Rights Committee in *Ng v. Canada.*[43] In *Ng,* the applicant had been extradited from Canada to the United States to stand trial in California where he was likely to face the death penalty by gas asphyxiation. The Committee held that this would be a violation of Article 7 of the ICCPR, as the execution of a capital punishment sentence must be "carried out in such a way as to cause the least possible physical and mental suffering."[44] Thus, the UN Human Rights Committee held that, even if capital punishment is not prohibited by the ICCPR, the likely punishment that this applicant would face would be in contravention of the ICCPR, and therefore, Canada's extradition was in violation of the ICCPR.[45]

There is also some recognition that states have a responsibility to control criminals and terrorists on their territory who may cause harm in another state. This responsibility has been confirmed in *Lawless v. Ireland,*[46] and *McCann v. United Kingdom.*[47] In *McCann,* which dealt with the use of

40. Judgment, *Loizidou v. Turkey,* Series A. no. 310, at 24, ¶ 62 (ECHR 23 Mar. 1995), *available at* <http://hudoc.echr.coe.int/Hudoc1doc/HEJUD/sift/505.txt> (visited 29 Apr. 2002).
41. *Id.*
42. Judgment, *Soering v. United Kingdom,* Series A. no. 161 (ECHR 7 July 1989), *available at* <http://hudoc.echr.coe.int/hudoc/>.
43. Complaint No. 469/1991, Human Rights Committee, Views of the Committee, 5 Nov. 1993, UN Doc. A/49/40, Vol. II.
44. *Id.* ¶ 16.4. It should be noted that the Committee found that this case was in violation of article 7 because the mode with which the person would be subjected to capital punishment would constitute cruel and inhuman treatment. The Committee, however, did not find a violation of article 6, which guarantees the right to life because "[t]he Committee notes that article 6, paragraph 1, must be read together with article 6, paragraph 2, which does not prohibit the imposition of the death penalty for the most serious crimes." *Id.* ¶ 15.3.
45. *Id.* ¶ 17.
46. European Commission on Human Rights, *Lawless v. Ireland,* Comm. Report 19.12.59, Eur. Court H.R., series B., no. 1, at 237–41.
47. *McCann and Others Judgment,* 27 Sept. 1995, Series A., no. 324.

special SAS forces to prevent terrorist attacks in Gibraltar that lead to the death of three people, the court held that the government is "required to have regard to their duty to protect the lives of the people in Gibraltar including their own military personnel."[48]

In other cases, however, the problem of demonstrating a close degree of proximity for the violation has been a ground for dismissal. For instance, in *Puccini v. Italy*,[49] which dealt with the sale of antipersonnel mines, the European Commission on Human Rights found the case inadmissible. Thus, it can be seen that the scope of states' transnational obligations and responsibility is still an underdeveloped area of international jurisprudence.

V. IMPLICATIONS OF "OBLIGATIONS OF RESULT" AND "OBLIGATIONS OF CONDUCT"

One of the questions that remains to be addressed is what kind of obligations may be advanced to states in their transnational operations. It would be neither pertinent, nor practical, to imply that all states are responsible for all human rights enjoyment everywhere. Rather, there has to be a relatively direct link to activities of the state across borders. One distinction of obligations that has gained some acceptance in international human rights law discourse is the distinction between the *obligation of conduct* and the *obligation of result.* In the words of the International Law Commission in their Draft Articles on state responsibility, this distinction implies that "[t]here is a breach by a State of an international obligation requiring it to adopt a particular course of conduct when the conduct of that State is not in conformity with that required of it by that obligation."[50] Furthermore, "[t]here is a breach by a State of an international obligation requiring it to achieve, by means of its own choice, a specified result if, by the conduct adopted, the State does not achieve the result required of it by that obligation."[51] These two definitions of obligation of conduct and obligation of result, respectively, imply that international law accepts that obligations may be fulfilled through a state's behavior and/or the end result of this behavior.

To use an example where both of these obligations are applied, one could again look at the principle that states cannot extradite a person to a

48. *Id.* ¶ 192.
49. European Commission of Human Rights, Commission's report of 6 Sept. 1994 on the application (no. 20208/92). This decision was later upheld by the Court, see Court decision, 13 Sept. 1995.
50. Y.B. INT'L L. COMM., U.N. Doc. A/CN.4/SER.a/1996 (Draft Article 20 of the International Law Commission Draft Articles on State Responsibility).
51. *Id.* Draft art. 21.

country where that individual is likely to face capital punishment. In this example, the obligation of conduct would be the obligation not to extradite (relating to the state's conduct), while the obligation of result would be that no individual under a state's jurisdiction should be subject to torture, even if the torture would be inflicted in a foreign country.

Looking more generally to the transnational obligations, it seems prudent to emphasize both an obligation of conduct, and of result. In other words, what is emphasized is an obligation related to "best practice" as well as the end result of their actions. By emphasizing best practice, there is a realization that there are many variables that influence the human rights enjoyment of people, and it may at times be impossible to demand from foreign states that the results of their actions may never be linked to situations of human rights violations. If states observed an obligation of conduct, to the extent that human rights effects of their transnational activities were in focus, a large number of negative human rights implications would be avoided. However, this does not mean that states should not look to the end result; indeed, the end result would guide the conduct. States should, nevertheless, be "judged" on their conduct rather more carefully than on the end result of transnational operations.

What is the sovereignty paradox that this approach may imply? Finally, we would like to address how these transnational obligations may influence the very fundamental principle in international law of state sovereignty. Possibly the main reason why the developments in this field have been slow is that the sovereignty principle is so strong, and every time international law tries to address issues of a national character the sovereignty threshold has to be overcome. We have seen this in traditional human rights law, and also to a large extent in international environmental law.

However, there is a paradox in the sovereignty argument when facing transnational obligations. Upon the ratification of the UN Charter, human rights became an issue of legitimate international concern—but it was uncertain how far it could penetrate national sovereignty. Through the development in international human rights law in the last fifty years, this has become clearer, and it is constantly developing. It is now quite accepted that gross human rights violations receive widespread international attention and condemnation by the United Nations; economic sanctions and even humanitarian intervention have become increasingly accepted as reactions to severe human rights situations. On another level, interstate complaint procedures are contained in most of the major human rights conventions, and they have been extensively used in the European Convention of human rights system.

Nevertheless, the idea that one state's activities might have some kind of influence on the human rights situation in another state runs directly contrary to the sovereignty issue. The argument that is often advanced is that one state cannot dictate how other states use their resources or conduct their international affairs, whether domestic in origin or international. Thus, selling arms to another state that is likely to use such weapons to oppress internal opposition, or shipping anti-personnel mines to a state where their use is much more likely to harm civilian rather than military populations, or investing in industry that is likely to cause health problems or to deprive people of their land and leave them destitute, these issues are rarely (if ever) addressed in terms of human rights. The receiving state takes the view that the consequences of these arms or mines, or indeed the internal effect of the industry, is simply part of the sovereign decisions of the national government, which also means that there is no accountability on part of the state that provides the weaponry or the financial investment. Yet, it seems to be acceptable from a sovereignty perspective to grant development assistance for agricultural production, for example, with the specified condition that the necessary technical equipment is purchased in the assisting state. However, apparently it is contrary to the principle of sovereignty to put in a condition that the agricultural workers should have a right of association, even if the granting state and the recipient state both have ratified human rights conventions guaranteeing the right of association. The reciprocity of international obligations, which is a fundamental principle in international law, does not seem to apply in these cases.

Realistically, the sovereignty principle is a major hurdle to overcome, as sovereignty is fundamental in the international law discourse. It goes to the core of how states interact in terms of international law. No state can dictate to another state how it should behave. International law, apart from certain elements of customary law, is based on consensus and voluntary adherence. This is quite obvious in the discussions and application of obligations *erga omnes*. It seems to be an accepted element of international law that certain principles are of such fundamental importance that breaches of these are seen as breaches of obligations that run equally to all other states, and every state has the right to help protect the corresponding rights. When a state breaches an obligation *erga omnes* it injures every state, including those not specifically affected. As a victim of a violation of the international legal order, every state is therefore competent to bring actions against the breaching state.[52]

Nevertheless, even if there is a breach of an obligation *erga omnes*, there is no duty upon any state to prosecute. The breach of international law is of such severity that any state will have jurisdiction to prosecute, but due to the respect for sovereignty and comity of each and every state, there is no obligation to act. Thus, if a state blatantly violates human rights in another

52. *See* Meron, *supra* note 20.

state through its transnational operations (it could be military support, direct support for oppressive regimes, etc.) no state—neither the assisting state, the receiver state, or a third state—is obligated (at least in terms of international law as it is presently constituted) to prosecute or otherwise try to remedy the situation. In fact, the paradox becomes that if the state itself is responsible for massive human rights abuses, it is of a concern to the international community. But if human rights problems or neglect is a result of the involvement of foreign states, all of a sudden, the sovereignty argument carries far more weight.

VI. CONCLUSION

The topic of transnational obligations is not well developed in international human rights law. In fact, it is in its early stages, largely helped by the occurrences of humanitarian intervention in Kosovo, and the attempted prosecution of General Pinochet. Even if the outcomes of these cases may have represented failures in some respects, they both pointed to weaknesses or discrepancies in current international human rights law which urgently need to be addressed. Increased globalization and the tremendous inequality in terms of state power around the world will increase the call for state accountability, not only domestically but also transnationally. So far, the emphasis has very much been on the respect level of obligations, thus looking at states' direct actions which may in fact cause human rights violations, such as torture or executions. But this needs to be expanded to other areas, including the obligation to protect against harmful activities carried out by third parties. This is a field of study that needs far greater attention from academics, practitioners, and by inter- and non-governmental organizations in the years to come. The call for accountability across borders is only going to be stronger as the borders become weaker.

Part VIII
Global Society

[20]

Writing about impunity and environment: the 'silver jubilee' of the Bhopal catastrophe

Upendra Baxi
Professor of Law in Development, University of Warwick, UK and University of Delhi, India

Addressing the 'silver jubilee' of the Bhopal catastrophe, this article interrogates a set of serial corporate and juridical failures to bring redress for the profound suffering and violation experienced by those ravaged by the Bhopal event. Presenting the catastrophe as a series of interlinked catastrophes, including the failure to deliver retributive justice for the Bhopal-violated, the author suggests the inadequacy of some existing narrative strategies concerning Bhopal to respond to the 'geographies of injustice' intimated by the lived actuality of human, social and environmental suffering produced by mass disasters. Identifying a politics of naming fully complicit in the discursive diminution of the incomprehensible levels of human and nonhuman sentient suffering caused by the failures of the Union Carbide Corporation (UCC), the author engages 'the practice of suffering thought', locating his discussion in critical notions of biopower and recent Marxian insights. Lamenting the radical failure of response to the fundamental violation enacted (and now globally symbolized) by Bhopal and the corporate impunity of the UCC, the author celebrates the rise of new social movement solidarity in the face of Bhopal – global subaltern movement affinities now inaugurating a 'new jurisprudence of human solidarity' and alternate possible futures lying beyond the contemporary global corporate colonization of human rights discourse.

Keywords: *Bhopal, Bhopal-violated, impunity, environment, juridicalization, biopower/biopolitics, human rights, injustice and critical solidarities*

1 PREFATORY REMARKS

Writing about the Bhopal catastrophe – a massive lethal release of 47 tonnes of methyl isocyanate (MIC) on 3 December 1984, killing more than 10,000 people, imposing various degrees of suffering and disability on nearly a quarter of a million human beings and creating extensive environmental damage – is a necessary but difficult enterprise. If understanding the causes and consequences of the catastrophe remains critical for envisioning a better future for the integrity of the environment and of human rights, this may not proceed undialectically – merely accentuating some new histories of impunity for multinational corporate conduct without any serious regard for the active agency of the survivors, which also provides a complex register of the movement toward emancipatory politics. Further, *writing* about the Bhopal catastrophe, or any mass disaster, becomes *violence* when insensitive to the continuing suffering of affected peoples and sentient beings and entities in nature. Ways of avoiding epistemic violence are not readily available, on the one hand, in rational presentations of the catastrophe – which often register an overdrive of practical reason (according to which canon only the 'rational' constitutes the 'real') nor, on the other hand, in the dramaturgy inherent to articulatory practices of sentimental reason. Indeed, the on-the-one-hand/on-the-other-hand binaries of thought all too often privilege practices of epistemic violence, as the theory, practice and movement in the spheres of human rights and environment so constantly reveal. *Writing* Bhopal, even on the eve of its silver jubilee, thus invites practices of suffering thought – a poignant narrative performance seeking to grasp the cascading orders of human rightlessness and social suffering – continually imposed by the rational real as it exists and continues to proliferate – while according full dignity to the disarticulated voices of sentient environmental suffering. In the Bhopal saga, the latter features merely as a figuration of environmental pollution and toxic degradation; the death and suffering of nonhuman sentient beings continues to emerge in legal/juridical languages as claims over 'damage' to 'agricultural livestock'. Such discursive habitus or dispositifs concerning mass disasters contain little or no conversation with the theory and movement for 'animal' rights or any deep ecology-type narratives of suffering in nature. In this particular respect, this present contribution in itself offers only a partial vignette of the Bhopal catastrophe. The state of art concerning mass disasters/catastrophes in general – and Bhopal in particular – does not foreground these concerns, and I fully acknowledge that my preferred way of speaking about the 'Bhopal-violated', avoiding the conventional language of 'victims', only partially redeems this not so benign neglect of wide-ranging environmental concerns. *Faute de mieux*, a brief outline of strategies of understanding must here suffice, and I may here offer only a somewhat random description.

First, increasingly, the birth of a multidisciplinary field named as disaster management now provides frameworks for understanding Bhopal. Grasping the prehistories (or the causal itineraries) of the catastrophe remains, of course, important for the tasks of disaster management and for future prevention – as far as is humanly possible – but the primary focus here remains on disaster preparedness, that is, on coordination of, and control over, the situation of a particular disaster event and directed towards the expeditious and effective management rehabilitation and relief of affected populations and the marginal amelioration of environmental harm. All disasters – whether 'natural', 'man-made' (a term fortunately impossible to feminize!) or 'political' – are accorded equal treatment in disaster management discourse. This discursive equality has the merit of situating an understanding of all disasters across human historical time.[1] However, historical and comparative disaster research fails to accord dignity of discourse to larger complex events of mass disaster such as the practices of colonization, the histories of the Cold War – or wars generally – and episodes/events of genocidal political formations – in short, to the narratives of political cruelty and mass atrocity and narratives of the destruction of natural resources and ecological heritage.[2] In its contemporary moment, especially in the post 9/11 United States, disaster research remains coequally directed towards efficient management of catastrophic terror attacks and natural catastrophes. In this genre, notable advances are made in the framing

1. For example, AM Gunn, *The Encyclopedia of Disasters: Environmental Catastrophes and Human Tragedies* (Westport, Connecticut 2008) in a two-volume narrative of 184 disasters begins with the supervolcano, Toba, Indonesia, 74000 BC and ends with the Greensburg, Kansas, tornado, 2007, assigning Bhopal catastrophe 155th place.
2. Ibid. Gunn no doubt includes Srebrenica and Rwanda in his narrative, but the histories of colonialism/imperialism do not find a mention. See, in contrast, E Galeano, *Open Veins of Latin America: Five Centuries of the Pillage of a Continent* (Monthly Review Press, New York 1997); W Rodney, *How Europe Underdeveloped Africa* (Bogle-L'Ouverture Publications, London 1983); D Naroji, *Poverty and Un-British Rule in India* (1901; republished by Ministry of Information and Broadcasting, Government of India, 1988); P Dove, *The Catastrophe of Modernity: Tragedy and the Nation in Latin American Literature* (Bucknell University Press, Lewisburg 2004) and, of course, the notable corpus of Noam Chomsky.

categories, especially those that distinguish 'accidents' from 'disasters' and the latter from 'catastrophes'.[3] The multifarious notion of 'disaster-preparedness' remains especially crucial, significantly networking federal and state government agencies,[4] although conjointly with the labours of various social action groups, the mass media and practices of social philanthropy. Furthermore, these otherwise inclusive notions of disaster and management/governance regimes do not embrace structurally imposed deprivation and injustices such as impoverishment and violent practices of social exclusion which have the same, if not a more pervasive, blighting impact on human and environmental conditions than the discourse of disaster management may ever *fully* convey. Obviously, then, a certain *politics of naming* remains at work. I may not say more than to point out that even the various global policy enunciations directed towards the alleviation of the conditions of mass poverty (such as the UN Millennial Developmental Goals declarations and programmes of action) and, the current wave of literature insisting that impoverishment constitutes the serial and cumulative violation of contemporary human rights norms, standards and values, while offering different narrative pathways than those available in disaster-preparedness and management research, still remain inadequate from the perspectives of the suffering peoples and the communities of resistance.

The *second* approach engages some global macrosociological narratives, especially exemplified by – and since – the emergence of what Ulrich Beck famously names as a 'global risk society'[5] – the activities, agencies and enterprises that produce, distribute and manage risks. In this formation, there occur not merely ecological contentions and conflicts assuming 'the form of doctrinal struggles … towards a proper road to modernity',[6] as well as 'definitional struggles over the scale, degree and urgency of risks', but also engagements with ways of 'opening up of the political' towards some kind of 'democratization of technoeconomic development'.[7] Notable as this perspective (variously problematizing conventional modes of risk-analysis and management) and prognosis ('reflexive modernization' somehow coping with the specifically political resolution of dilemmas posed by relatively autonomous technoscientific development and rights-oriented governance) remains, it also carries, at the same time, a tendency to renormalize risk production and distribution, conveyed by Beck's famous aphorism: we all live in an 'age of side effects'.[8]

3. See, eg, H Rodriguez, E Quarantelli and R Dynes (eds), *Handbook of Disaster Research* (Springer, London 2006); R Perry and EL Quarantelli (eds), *What Is a Disaster? New Answers to Old Questions* (Xlibris Books, Philadelphia 2005).
4. In the wake of the Katrina disaster, much concern was expressed at the Stafford Act (the Federal Disaster Relief and Emergency Assistance Act, PL 100-707, signed into law 23 November 1988), which classified the eligibility of federal funding into two categories: 'emergencies' and 'major disasters', the latter capping federal assistance at US$5 million. The Act has been further supplemented by Public Law 109-205, 4 October 2006 concerned with homeland security management. Some regard disasters as 'regulation catalysts': see ME Kahn, 'Environmental Disasters as Risk Regulation Catalysts? The Role of Bhopal, Chernobyl, Exxon Valdez, Love Canal, and Three Mile Island in Shaping U.S. Environmental Law' (2007) 35 J Risk Uncertain 37.
5. U Beck, *Global Risk Society: Towards a New Modernity* (Sage, London 2002).
6. Ibid 40.
7. Ibid 237–50.
8. U Beck, A Giddens and S Lash (eds), *Reflexive Modernization* (Stanford University Press, Stanford 1994) 175; see also the contribution by Anthony Giddens, 'Living in Post-traditional Society' in the same volume, at 84.

Distribution is, as we learn – or ought to relearn – from 'Uncle' Marx, not an epiphenomenon but rather integral to (and decreed by) the mode of production. The imageries of the side-effects remain, though perhaps not entirely, the actual states/estates of human and social suffering produced by mass disasters – what I name as 'geographies of injustice'.[9] These paradigmatically vary across global North and global South – and indeed, across peoples who constitute the South in the North and the North in the South. The saga of Bhopal would have thus been very different had the initial location of the plant (strongly favoured by the Union Carbide Corporation [UCC]) been in South Mumbai rather than its terminal location in the city of Bhopal, the capital of Madhya Pradesh (MP)! Or, to illustrate this in a different way (and as has been often noted in the Bhopal discourse), had the wind direction on that fateful day engulfed not the areas of the urban impoverished but the super-citizenry habitats of the urban affluent!

Further, even in terms of Michel Burawoy's evocative metaphor, while modern risk society entails forms of 'politics of production' as well as 'production of politics',[10] both these forms of politics often consign to irrelevance the catastrophic sufferings of people and the devastation of the environment. Massive denials of the right to be human and to continue to remain human occupy but an obscure space in this narrative genre. What matters from the perspectives of global justice, now constitutively informed by concerns with the logics, paralogics and languages of contemporary human rights, is not so much the question of the inherent and inevitable production of risks and hazards in the name of social and economic development but rather the problem of the uneven distribution of risk exposure and embodied/lived experience. While it is true to say that the global risk society creates catastrophic events that respect *no* national frontiers, ideological divides or concerns for national sovereignty (after all, the Bhopal catastrophe occurred in the space-time of 18 months that also witnessed Chernobyl and the Sandoz chemical factory fire at Basle), all the available evidences suggest that impoverished populations everywhere bear a disproportionate burden of human harm and hurt and remain most adversely affected by environmental damage and deterioration arising out of mass industrial disasters.[11] Both for Third-World humanity as a whole on a global level and for peoples within nations subjected to combined and uneven practices of 'development', the risk society emerges as a kind of political fate, best described by Kwame Nkrumah in the imagery of neocolonialism as '*power without responsibility and exploitation without redress*'.[12]

A *third* and related narrative strategy speaks, in the main, to what has been termed (in some heavy Foucaldian/post-Foucaldian languages) as *environmental/ecological*

9. U Baxi, 'Geographies of Injustice: Human Rights at the Altar of Convenience' in R Craig (ed), *Torture as Tort: Comparative Perspectives on the Development of Transnational Human Rights Litigation* (Hart, Oxford 2001) 197–212.

10. M Burawoy, *The Politics of Production: Factory Regimes Under Capitalism and Socialism* (Verso, London 1985).

11. It is this awareness that marks ongoing attempts at articulating sustainable development as an integral part of the human right to development and the further quest to develop the right to development itself. See U Baxi, *Human Rights in a Posthuman World: Critical Essays* (OUP, New Delhi 2007) Chs 3 and 4.

12. K Nkrumah, *Neo-Colonialism: The Last Stage of Imperialism* (Thomas Nelson and Sons Ltd, London 1965, emphasis added). See, as to the practices of environmental racism, L Westra and BE Lawson (eds), *Faces of Environmental Racism: Confronting Issues of Global Justice* (2nd edn Rowman and Littlefield Publishers, Lanham 2001).

govermentality.[13] In a sense, this refers to 'technopolitics', understood not just in the sense of the mediation of political power by technological development but more specifically as 'rule by experts'.[14] Further theoretical contexts are provided via some specific notions of biopower, especially in new constellations of the technoscientific prowess of global capital.[15] In another narrative vein, the question here concerns the 'production of nature' now emerging from critical developments in Marxian approaches to human and social geography.[16] This essay marks a small beginning towards situating Bhopal within these perspectives.

A *fourth* narrative strategy relegates the archetypal Bhopal catastrophe to some new ways of inventing new approaches to 'business ethics', in themselves often constituting a further set of aggravating and hazardous neologisms – at least from the perspectives of suffering humanity. Several generations of the languages of corporate social responsibility still remain premised on the view that human rights responsibilities do not directly or *even* indirectly attach to the state-*like* but still *non-state* multinational corporate actors.[17] Space constraints forbid a detailed analysis of this narrative strategy, save for saying that the Bhopal catastrophe marks a savage amniocentesis of any endeavour aimed at relating contemporary human rights discourse to multinational corporate governance conduct.[18]

A *fifth* narrative strategy directs close attention to pedagogies arising from mass disasters and catastrophes. In sum, as concerns the Bhopal catastrophe, this narrative

13. See P Rutherford, 'The Entry of Life into History' in E Darier (ed), *Discourses of the Environment* (Blackwell, Oxford 1999) 1–34; P Rutherford, 'Ecological Modernization and Environmental Risk' in the same volume at 95–118; TW Luke, 'Environmentality as Green Governmentality' in the same volume at 121–51.

14. See, especially, T Mitchell, *Rule of Experts: Egypt, Techno-Politics, Modernity* (University of California Press, Berkeley 2002); B Latour, *Reassembling the Social: an Introduction to Actor-Network-Theory* (OUP, Oxford 2007); J Ferguson, *The Anti-politics Machine: Development, Depoliticization and Bureaucratic Power in Lesotho* (University of Minnesota Press, Minnesota 1994).

15. The recently available work of Roberto Esposito remains precious for deciphering emergent forms of biopower and biopolitics, especially in the insistence on affirmative biopolitics. See, especially, R Esposito (T Campbell (trans)), *Biopolitics and Philosophy* (University of Minnesota Press, Minneapolis 2007). See also T Campbell, 'Bios, Immunity, Life: the Thought of Roberto Esposito' (2006) Diacritics 2.

16. See, especially, D Harvey, *Justice, Nature and the Geography of Difference* (Blackwell, Oxford 1996); N Smith, *Uneven Development: Nature, Capital, and Production of Space* (3rd edn Georgia University Press, Athens 2008); A Schmidt, *The Concept of Nature in Marx* (New Left Books, London 1971); N Thrift, 'From Born to Made: Technology, Biology and Space' (2006) 30 (4) Trans Inst Br Geogr 463. In this sense (and with Neil Smith), we may speak of the evolution of the second nature: the universes of politics and regulation over those that already produce 'nature' as a human creation.

17. See U Baxi, *The Future of Human Rights* (3rd edn OUP, New Delhi 2008) Ch 9. See further L Bormann-Larsen and O Wiggen, *Responsibility in World Business: Managing Side-Effects of Corporate Activity* (United Nations University, Tokyo 2004) and specifically U Baxi 'The "Just War" for Profit and Power: the Bhopal Catastrophe and the Principle of Double Effect' in the same volume, 175–201; R McCorquodale, 'An Inclusive International Legal System' (2004) 17 Leiden J Int'l Law 477–504.

18. The recent determined reversal by Jonathan Ruggie, the UN Special Representative on Business and Human Rights, marks a significant diminution of the valiant accomplishments that marked the inaugural advent of the UN Norms of Human Rights Responsibilities of Multinational Corporations and Related Business Entities, analysed fully in Baxi, ibid.

move, far from scrupulously attending to the wider general histories of 'toxic capitalism',[19] proceeds to 'learning lessons' from the specific instance of each and every mass disaster. The Bhopal catastrophe, in particular, spawns yet more specific narratives of causal itineraries of the histories of contemporary ultrahazardous chemical industries.

While a post-Bhopal world promises some superior understanding of the importance of industry-'wise' specific aetiologies of mass disasters and catastrophes and also counters this 'trend' in some future histories for the development of 'best industry standards' – thus thwarting the further potential of future Bhopals[20] – the probability of the risk management of future genetic/biotech Bhopals also remains hazardously uncertain. By this, I refer (and of course here, necessarily, without voluminous citations to relevant literature) to an entire array of the migration of biohazards under the auspices of Northern strategic biotech industries to some Third World locations if only to fully avoid the regimes of any advanced regulation of such risks established in the United States or the European Union. Unlike the manifest and manifold hazards systemically produced by the global chemical industry, the globally strategic biotech industries, as is now well known, pose a wave of socially and scientifically invisible biohazards replete with further long-term risks to humans *in* – and even *as* environment – no matter how one may privilege the languages of 'sustainable development' (even in this era of febrile talk of global warming).

Finally, and without being exhaustive, we encounter specific interfaces between technoscience and new social movements – including human rights and 'surface' and 'deep' ecology movements.[21] I have pondered elsewhere[22] the tensions between 'new' and 'old' social movements and between new social movements and human rights movements in terms both of politics of *knowing* and *being*. The Bhopal catastrophe marks the rise of new social movements in the light of the fact that the otherwise powerful trade union movements necessarily had to place industrial safety struggles over employment creation and sustenance. I may not here elaborate this complex remark concerning the relative decline of the historic roles of labour movements (in India and elsewhere) save for saying that Bhopal-violated humanity furnish some new 'histories' of militant subjectivity disanchored from trade union militancy and leading towards an extraordinary congregation of global subaltern movement affinities and social solidarities across borders, comprising social

19. See F Pearce and S Tombs, *Toxic Capitalism: Corporate Crime and the Chemical Industry* (Dartmouth, Aldershot 1998).
20. See I Eckerman, 'The Bhopal Gas Leak: Analyses of Causes and Consequences by Three Different Models' (2005) 18 J Loss Prev Process Indust 213; I Eckerman, *The Bhopal Saga: Causes and Consequences of the World's Largest Industrial Disaster* (Universities Press (India) Private Limited/New Delhi, Orient Longmans, Hyderabad 2004). See also, D Lapierre and J Moro, *It Was Five Minutes Past Midnight in Bhopal* (Full Circle, Delhi 2001); D Kurzman, *A Killing Wind: Inside Union Carbide* (McGraw Hill, New York 1987); D Weir, *The Bhopal Syndrome: Pesticides, Environment, and Health* (Sierra Club Books, San Francisco 1984); P Shrivastava, *Bhopal: Anatomy of a Crisis* (Ballinger, Cambridge 1987); S Hazarika, *Bhopal: The Lessons of a Tragedy* (Penguin, New York 1987).
21. See, especially, K Eder, *New Politics of Class: Social Movements and Cultural Dynamics in Advanced Societies* (Sage, London 1993).
22. Baxi, *Future* (n 17) Ch 7.

networks of biomedical, juridical and ethical social action communities[23] fully deferential to the perspectives of the movements-on-the-ground. This movement fully places in view the Bhopal catastrophe, not as a single event but as a series of catastrophic events.

To this narrative strategy, I must of course add the dimension of the theory, practice and movement that legalizes, as well as juridicalizes, mass disasters or catastrophes. By 'legalization', I here signify ways in which legislative and judicial remedies are fashioned to assure justice according to the law to the victims of 'mass torts', where the numbers of people, as well as injuries they suffer, remain indeterminate.[24] 'Juridicalization', in my lexicon, signifies ways in which the communities of suffering human beings and peoples in resistance reinvent responsive law and jurisprudence towards a more emancipatory and dialogical openness of adjudicatory and legislative power. The relationship between 'legalization' and 'juridicalization' remains complex as well as contradictory; the hard-won gains of the latter often stand cancelled by the former. Even so, this contribution highlights the ways in which the Bhopal-violated humanity (and their next of kin – the fluctuating consortia of human rights and environmental activists) have sought to achieve the juridicalization of catastrophe, even when profoundly haunted by some terminal forms of legalization.

2 IS THE BHOPAL CATASTROPHE A 'POLITICAL EVENT'? – A NECESSARY DIGRESSION

Writing in the shadow of now intergenerational sufferings of the Bhopal-violated humanity, it remains necessary to attend to the fact that 'it' continues to articulate an uncanny production of the Will to Truth pitted against the Nietszchean Will to Power of the forces, agents and managers of global capital – including the Indian state managers. The Bhopal-violated have continually exposed the hollowness of the reiterated claims of the immunity and impunity of the UCC and its successor-in-interest, Dow Chemicals.[25] They manifest an extraordinary series of performative/agentative acts, simply incredible in the face of their unnameable sufferings, via conflicted yet collective acts authoring (as I note fully later) the subsequent juridical itineraries of Bhopal litigation both in the United States and India seeking to 'discipline and punish' the UCC.

Yet, a conceptual limit, or threshold difficulty, must now be fully faced in terms of the political 'eventness' of the Bhopal catastrophe. Leaving aside the poignant fact that the discourse of the contemporary club of progressive A-to-Z (Agamben to Zizek) thinkers continue to write as if the Bhopal catastrophe *never* happened, their

23. Reflected variously in the exertions of the International Campaign for Bhopal Victims and the four hearings/listenings conducted under the auspices of the Permanent People's Tribunal that establish ways of communication of linkages between industrial hazards and human rights violations.
24. See U Baxi, *Mass Torts, Multinational Enterprise Liability and Private International Law, Recueil des cours 276* (Martinus Nijhoff, The Hague 1999, 2000) 305–427, and the literature cited therein.
25. See the as yet unreported decision of Justice K Chandru, Madras High Court, 2009, which repudiated all claims of economic loss and damage for defamation filed by Dow Chemicals concerning demonstrations by Bhopal activists outside its corporate office premises valiantly upholding their constitutional right to protest against the residual toxic pollution which, according to them, rightly imposed duties of toxic cleanup on the successor company.

theoretical constructions of what may count as a 'political' event almost compel the addressal of the Bhopal catastrophe as a political *nonevent*. Thus, writing Bhopal must ethically counter this erasure of the event from the contemporary discourse of human rights, justice and people's movement – a task that may not render altogether inapt an extension to Bhopal-violated humanity of Alain Badiou's remark – that theirs is the authentic resolve to become 'something other than a victim, other than a being-for-death, and thus *something other than a mortal being*'.[26] The Bhopal-violated fully testify to Badiou's observation that 'if the "rights of man" exist surely they are not rights of life against death, or rights of survival against misery' but rather 'they are the rights of the Immortal, affirmed in their own right, or the rights of the Infinite exercised over the contingency of suffering and death'.[27] Further, this movement of suffering peoples and communities in resistance carries a larger narrative message, recrafting the discourse of environment and human rights, lifting us beyond the languages of victimage/victimhood and beckoning/reckoning towards a 'political situation, one that calls for a political thought-practice, one that is peopled by its own authentic actors … '.[28] Indeed, the 'valiant victims' of Bhopal[29] remain 'faithful' to the event of the catastrophe, treating it '*right to the limit of the possible*'.[30] Put another way, they 'draw from this situation, to the greatest possible extent, the affirmative humanity it contains … to try to be the immortal of the situation'.[31]

What constitutes a political event for Badiou remains a contested terrain,[32] and the Bhopal catastrophe and attendant struggles for rights and justice may still not qualify as a 'political event', if only because these do not compel 'the subject to invent a new way of being or acting in the situation'.[33] Despite this, I prefer to read (with profound apologies to Badiou) the Bhopal 'eventness' as marking the birth of new subjectivities questioning modes of primitive accumulation in late capitalism, reading the event as

> a kind of epistemic free radical that can migrate through many strata, the analysis of which reveals to us a sphere of the absolutely possible, of hitherto suppressed possibilities, previously undisclosed openings, and unimagined, unrealized unsuspected futures. While this is the sphere of hopes and dreams, it is no less the sphere of monsters and nightmares, since nothing guarantees that the unsuspected or undreamt of will not be unexpectedly terrible.[34]

The reference to 'free radical' remains deeply pertinent; to be sure the runaway reaction of the MIC remained as such for their global corporate producers. These now chafe at the 'epistemic free radicals' in turn produced by the protest of the

26. A Badiou, *Ethics: An Essay on the Understanding of Evil* (Verso, London 2001) 12.
27. Ibid 12.
28. Ibid 13.
29. U Baxi and A Dhanda (eds), *Valiant Victims and Lethal Litigation: The Bhopal Case* (NM Tripathi, Bombay; The Indian Law Institute, New Delhi 1990), U Baxi, 'Introduction'.
30. Badiou (n 26) 15.
31. Ibid 30.
32. See I Mackenzie, 'What is a Political Event?' (2008) 11 (3) *Theory and Event* (available at <http://muse.jhu.edu/journals/theory_and_event/v011/11.3.mackenzie.html> (last accessed 12 November 2009). See also A Johnston, 'The Quick and the Dead: Alain Badiou and the Split Speeds of Transformation' (2007) 1 (2) IJZS 56; R Saleci, 'The Nature of Event in Late Capitalism' (2008) 29 (5) Cardozo L Rev 2333.
33. Badiou (n 26) 42.
34. See J De Caputo, 'Bodies Still Unrisen, Events Still Unsaid' (2007) 12 (1) Angelaki 73, 73.

Bhopal-violated humanity. The globally-constituted corporate world regards the dreams of justice of the Bhopal-violated as the 'sphere of monsters and nightmares'. Yet, it is in this *not* entirely 'postmetaphysical' footloose and fancy-free narrative move that I now proceed to silhouette some histories of the juridicalization of the eventness of the Bhopal catastrophe. I proceed to do so from a deeply anguished activist and engaged perspective, yet not (hopefully and honestly) surrendering in any way the sense of narrative complexity and contradiction.

3 A BRIEF HISTORY OF THE FIRST BHOPAL CATASTROPHE

The first catastrophe occurred on 3 December 1984 and remains attributable to some key operational decisions of the UCC which controlled its Indian subsidiary, Union Carbide India Limited (UCIL). The pre-trial discovery documents established several incontrovertible truths. The first phase of Bhopal litigation before Judge Keenan fully confirmed the fact that UCC failed to follow the best industrial practice standards in the manufacture and storage of large quantities of MIC for the production of two brand insecticides/pesticides in a factory located in a densely populated area of the capital city of the state of MP. Second, it was also fully established that UCC also preferred systematically to ignore early warning signals of the potential of massive toxic release, specially demonstrated by the 1982 gas 'leak' that killed two workers, and the subsequent in-house safety audit report that stressed the urgency of the need for adequate safety systems at the Bhopal factory. UCC failed to take measures to prevent the subsequent lethal release by replicating the state of art digitalized safety systems installed at its own plant in West Virginia, which produced and stored minuscule amounts of MIC compared with the Bhopal plant. Third, considerations of 'efficient' corporate governance led to the closure of the refrigeration plant – essential to the prevention of a runaway chemical reaction. *Fourth*, in the first weeks of the event, the UCC and the UCIL media operations moved swiftly to minimize the risk-exposure, denying that what was released was MIC and insisting that it was merely harmless phosgene – and also providing misinformation concerning remedial measures, thus further aggravating the plight of the suffering.[35]

For those who *still continue* to take the languages of corporate social responsibility seriously, it remains important to note that UCC has never fully explained why it

35. See U Baxi and T Paul (eds), *Mass Disasters and Multinational Liability: The Bhopal Case* (NM Tripathi, Bombay; Indian Law Institute, New Delhi 1985); U Baxi (ed), *Inconvenient Forum and Convenient Catastrophe: the Bhopal Case* (NM Tripathi, Bombay; Indian Law Institute, Delhi 1986); U Baxi and A Dhanda (n 29). See further J Cassels, *The Uncertain Promise of Law: Lessons from Bhopal* (University of Toronto Press, Toronto 1993); U Baxi (n 24); D Dembo, W Morehouse and L Wykle, *Abuse of Power: Social Performance of Multinational Corporations: the Case of Union Carbide* (New Horizons Press, New York 1990); Amnesty International, *Clouds of Injustice: Bhopal Disaster 20 Years On* (Amnesty International Publications, London 2004).

Additionally, see also for a poignant literary and existential narrative, Lapierre and Moro, *Five Minutes Past Midnight* (n 20); for early accounts, see Kurzman, *A Killing Wind* (n 20); Weir, *The Bhopal Syndrome* (n 20); Shrivastava, *Bhopal: Anatomy of a Crisis* (n 20); Hazarika, *Bhopal: Lessons of a Tragedy* (n 20). A most useful periodic contemporary analysis by Will Lepowski appears in several issues of *Chemical and Engineering News* and periodic publications of the International Council of Public Affairs and International Centre for Law and Development, New York.

needed to produce and store in such large quantities a known lethal chemical substance at the Bhopal factory; nor has it placed in the public domain – despite insistent activist demand[36] – the epidemiological and toxicological information concerning MIC over which UCC possesses a global knowledge monopoly. It is perhaps no overstatement to say, at least from the standpoint of still *unnameable* and ongoing future human and environmental harms, that this toxic immunity/impunity of continuing nondisclosure constitutes a full indictment of the limitations of the elements currently constituting 'crimes against humanity'.

The Bhopal saga provides a cruel testimony to the fact that as concerns the entirely disposable peoples and environments in the Third World, there is as yet simply *no* functional equivalent of the right to information, or governance transparency, worth mentioning – even in the otherwise proliferating contexts of so-called business ethics or global corporate 'governance'. Thus, in respect of the world's 'largest peacetime industrial disaster', as Judge Keenan was to describe it in the first phase of Bhopal litigation, neither the sufferings nor the human rights of the Bhopal-violated have been taken seriously.

Yet, a singular focus on these corporate governance misdeeds and mayhems must be placed within the larger context of the ideology of developmentalism, which led the Union of India (UOI) to invite UCC to establish such ultrahazardous manufacture at Bhopal in the first place. This furnishes a complex story with several subplots, a story not lending itself to the summary analysis which has, however, perforce to suffice here. An immediate motif stands furnished by India's quest for self-sufficiency in food-grain production animated by import-substitution strategies. A larger motif is provided by the Indian leadership of 'nonaligned nations'' complex mediation of Cold War global politics via its own distinctive genre of planned economy, privileging self-reliant agrarian development entailing a lesser dependence on American overseas aid programmes. More at centre-stage is, of course, the literally fantastic reproduction of nature mirrored in early breakthroughs of R-DNA plant technologies which ushered in high-yielding, multicrop seed and plant varieties. This first 'Green Revolution' occurred worldwide, be it recalled, before the advent of global environmental/deep ecology movements, providing unrivalled governmental opportunities for what we today grasp as biopower and biopolitical governance.

The political ecology of the first Bhopal catastrophe still awaits the emergence of new Foucaldian labours deciphering Third World biopolitical governance, perhaps best summated by a gifted phrase of Vandana Shiva: the first 'Green Revolution' did not merely foster plant monocultures but also further propagated the 'monocultures of mind'.[37] However, recourse to a wider contextual understanding remains far from exculpatory of the immediate contexts of the secular sins of commission

36. I raised this in my address at the Annual General Meeting of UCC, as a proxy shareholder for the American Union of Baptist Churches, on the eve of the 15th anniversary of the catastrophe, insisting that no justification remained at hand for nondisclosure given the settlement orders which fully exculpated UCC from any legal liability and also given the UCC public relations gesture accepting – in part – 'moral responsibility' for the event. Not only did the CEO representative chairing the event not respond, but when the meeting ended, as Ward Morehouse, Clarence Das and myself (all representing Bhopal-violated) began to leave, the shareholders made way for us with gesticulations, one of them saying loudly, *'Beware of the fumes of Bhopal'*!

37. V Shiva, *Monocultures of the Mind: Perspectives on Biodiversity and Biotechnology* (Zed Books, London 1993).

and omission by UCC and its normative cohorts. The tragedy of the first Bhopal catastrophe lies precisely – at least from the perspectives of the Bhopal-violated – at the not-too-distant doorstep of the UCC, although the violated also variously regard the UOI and MP governments as completely complicit in their still unending agony.

Importantly, from the first anniversary of the Bhopal catastrophe until today, demands for retributive justice are combined with those of distributive justice. The mammoth outcry – *'Union Carbide Ko Phansi Do'* – *'Hang the UCC'* – still resonates and conveys a crucial message: restorative justice in situations of the catastrophic imposition of human and social suffering remains ethically inadequate outside retributive justice. For the entire span of about 25 years now, the multifarious 'victim' groups, each with their own distinctive agendum for relief and rehabilitation, still speak with one voice about the extradition of the ex-CEO of UCC (Warren Anderson), previously declared by the Bhopal court as an absconder or fugitive from justice. Though momentarily arrested and detained, Anderson still continues to be a 'fugitive felon', thanks to lackadaisical pursuit of extradition proceedings by the UOI, in part abetted by the disinclination of the US State and Justice Departments. The issue, of course, is not about a particular named individual but rather concerns modes of extradition of the ways of reckless corporate governance; the Bhopal-violated engaged in this hot pursuit represent a more finely tuned sense, compared with the nascent theorists, of global reparative justice. If, as happened in the course of the Nuremburg Tribunal, a few German corporations were held guilty of connivance with genocide, there is little reason or justification (outside the *realpolitik* of the United States) for continued impunity for multinational enterprises that now enact crimes against humanity – already made analogously punishable by the Rome Treaty establishing the International Criminal Court.[38]

4 JURIDICAL INNOVATIONS: PROMISES, PERPLEXITIES AND PERILS

4.1 The quest for justice

The quest for justice for the violated peoples was not an easy one by any means, and divergent Bhopal-based social action groups[39] offered different approaches concerning what should be done. Justice assumed wider meaning than justice according to the law – contained in the unanimous demand for retributive justice and the varying alternative legal strategies for the pursuit of effective compensation and rehabilitation. Healthcare justice and economic justice remained the central preoccupation of all the Bhopal activist groups. Indeed, legal strategies were always viewed by 'victim' groups from the wider perspectives of healthcare and economic justice. The languages of justice, rather than of human rights, were thus always privileged. In all my association with the Bhopal-violated activists until now, it was never in doubt that rights-languages were not, for them, important in themselves but only important as a means

38. See A Ramsastry, 'Corporate Complicity: from Nuremburg to Rangoon' (2002) 20 Berkeley J Intl L 91.

39. These major groups are Bhopal Gas Peedit Mahila Udyog Sangathan ('BGPMUS'); Bhopal Gas Peedit Mahila Stationery Karmachari Sangh ('BGPMSKS'); Bhopal Gas Peedit Sangharsh Sahayog Samiti; ('BGPSSS') Bhopal Group for Information and Action ('BGIA'); The International Campaign for Justice in Bhopal (ICJIB); the Medico Friends Circle, Forum; the Jan Swasthya Kendra and Sambhavana Trust Clinic. Fortunately, this listing remains far from exhaustive.

to the ends of justice. And 'justice' for the Bhopal activists was a matter of struggle, of people's impassioned politics and of direct action fully and constantly geared towards naming and shaming the producers of social indifference, including state managers and agents and their normative cohorts – comprising the commentariat – 'learned' professions, public intellectuals and the 24/7 mass media pundits. The Bhopal-violated humanity's movement for justice furnishes a rare instance of a quest for human and ecological justice (at least in India since her independence) of the formation of militant justice-consistencies, or those now named – in some postmodern political phrase-regimes – as 'counterpublics'.

One way, surely, to narrate this agonizing movement for justice remains best provided (to evoke a profound notion from the philosopher Maurice Merleau-Ponty) by the vivid discourse of justice in/of the flesh – the experience of lived individual bodies, and not of any abstract or species bodies.[40] And in many senses (which I may not elaborate here), the human right to health 'talk', while important, does not quite measure up to the imperatives of justice in/of the flesh.

The imperatives, of course, are rather easily stated, in practical terms of pressing problems in the domain of healthcare justice (where they still sadly continue to lie). Not only were the available healthcare facilities in government hospitals, in terms of expert diagnosis and treatment, woefully limited, but the lack of important information concerning the toxicological impact of MIC prevented effective care management, even by dedicated and radical health activist groups in Bhopal, Delhi and elsewhere. The Indian Supreme Court's judicial arithmetic classification of compensable injuries into various categories (as late as 4 May 1989) relegated as many as 150,000 out of more than 200,000 'victims' to only bearing 'minor injuries' and restricted the category of severe injury to a cruelly ludicrous figure of 2000 people![41] This outrageous pronouncement bears no relation to the manifest existential suffering of the survivors or to the record in the archives of as many as 15,000 additional deaths between 1985 and 2003.[42] Apart from the immediate adverse health impacts such as pulmonary malfunctioning and deterioration, corneal opacity and posttraumatic stress syndrome – all of which had direct disruptive effects on the livelihood opportunities of the affected peoples – there exist very few studies of the median and long-term effects of the catastrophe (such as immune system damage, neurological and neurovascular harm, cardiovascular damage, gynaecological impairment, carcinogenic impacts and psychic ill-effects[43]). The International Medical Commission Bhopal (IMCB) identified these further effects in a 1994 study.[44] I mention all this briefly here to expose the fact that the pioneering

40. See a recent interesting account by SP Thomas, 'Through the Lens of Merleau-Ponty: Advancing the Phenomenological Approach to Nursing Research' (2005) 6 Nurs Philos 63–76. See also B Flynn, 'Textuality and the Flesh: Derrida and Merleau-Ponty' (1984) 15 J Brit Soc Phenom 164–79; T Carman, 'The Body in Husserl and Merleau-Ponty' (1999) 27 Philosophical Topics 206–226.

41. U Baxi and A Dhanda (n 29) lv.

42. Amnesty International (n 35) 12.

43. Ibid 14–8.

44. See S Acquilla and others, 'Aftermath of the World's Worst Chemical Disaster, Bhopal, December 1984' (2005) 18 J Loss Prev Process Ind 268. The Indian Council for Medical Research (ICMR) began a systematic study of the health impacts beginning in 1985 but abandoned it, suddenly and inexplicably in 1993. See also C Sathyamala, N Vohra and K Satish, *Against All Odds: Continuing Effects of the Toxic Gases on the Health Status of the Surviving Population in Bhopal* (The Centre for Community Health and Social Medicine, Bhopal and Delhi 1989).

juridical innovations (analysed later) were never fully adequate to the dimension of healthcare justice, partially crystallized by the human right to health.

It remains all the more important to note that the issues of soil and water pollution have been effectively raised recently before American courts (further reinforced thanks again to a Bhopal-violated initiative that now energizes some active members of the US Congress). Indeed, the latter now concede that these issues were not finally settled by any judicial proceeding in India, and further, that the UCC, and even its successor-in-interest, the Dow Chemicals Corporation, may still be fully legally liable and ethically accountable.[45]

The leading voices at Bhopal that initially opposed judicial recourse as an impediment to struggle for healthcare justice have, unfortunately, been fully proved right and at a colossal cost of human and social suffering. Much the same may be said concerning the human rights to life and means of livelihood; as despite our sincere efforts, no significant micro-regional employment opportunities/strategies consistent with decimated bodies were ever fully planned by the state and national governments.[46]

4.2 Perplexities surrounding the choice of legal action

Among those who favoured some kinds of legal/juridical strategies – strategies that I was especially privileged to coordinate in the wake of the catastrophe – the manifest concerns led to no clear agreement on what should be done. Some activist groups preferred militant legal action against the UCC; some others were in favour of holding the Indian state fully legally liable and morally responsible; some others preferred a sustained social militant action programme of direct action against a state held hostage by global capital. In the event, a menu of strategies evolved: support for pursuing and prosecuting UCC by whatever legal means possible; devising strategies of stringent legal action holding the national and state governments fully legally liable and the pursuit of militant direct action strategies in aid of both these courses of action. Yet, as I know as a self-elected servant of these diverse groups, some incommensurable ideological differences also persisted. I might add that these remain distant from the forbidding prose of the high priests of the critical legal studies movement! I have involuntarily learnt a great deal, and more vividly – in particular about the truths of popular distrust of state law in general and the ambivalences of counter-hegemonic movements of suffering peoples. Further, there was a good deal of reflection (though obviously not thus expressed) concerning ways in which the imperial techniques of emergent green governmentality may, after all, construct a future regime of law reform and environmental governance in a parasitical relation to the actual sufferings of the Bhopal-violated. The catastrophe did indeed act as a 'risk regulation catalyst'

45. See, as to the US proceedings, the decision of the US Court of Appeals, 2nd Circuit, in *Sajjida Bano and Others v UCC and Warren Anderson* 17 March 2004, which still leaves open some possibilities of appropriate judicial action. See further the call made by several United States Congressmen in a letter dated 16 June 2009 urging the Chairperson and the Board of Directors of Dow Chemicals at least to assume, in the context of environmental degradation, the same order of responsibility as it did for the predecessor UCC, setting aside $2.2 billion in 2002 to put towards Union Carbide's pending asbestos liabilities in the United States as for the Bhopal-violated, rather than disowning and evading any further 'liabilities it inherited from Bhopal'. See further T Edwards, 'Contamination of Community Water Sources in Bhopal, India', 20 October 2005 (on file with the author) and Amnesty International (n 35) Ch 3.
46. Amnesty International (n 35) Ch 2. See also C Sathyamala, N Vohra and K Satish (n 44).

resulting in a wide range of legal and administrative reform measures.[47] However, this regulatory boom did little to ameliorate the plight of the Bhopal-violated.

Moreover, there was precious concern for the autonomy of Bhopal activism. Indeed, initially this concern went so far as to enable the more radical elements to indict some others wishing to pursue legal strategies as collaborators with the Indian state and even as 'stooges' of UCC! This tension was painfully evident on the very first anniversary of Bhopal and required difficult negotiation throughout the process of devising a common framework for legal action. This story must await another day, save for saying here that the creative jurisprudence of suffering peoples and communities in resistance emerges via a constant and often agonizing reflexive vigilance.

In the event, there was broad understanding that pursuing UCC entailed the creative cooptation of the contingent Indian forms of govermentality. This understanding, endlessly ridden with perplexities, provided limited activist endorsement of two specific strategies, each one of which, in turn, constituted a moment of promise as well as peril. Briefly put, all this contained a 'temporary suspension of disbelief' (to evoke poet William Coleridge's expression) in the possibility of a benign state.

The first constitutive element of the promise of justice for Bhopal-violated was the creative adaptation of the doctrine of *parens patriae* by the sovereign Indian democratic state. The Bhopal Act 1985 (supported, and mainly authored, by some Bhopal-violated peoples and some activists, including myself) by which the Indian Parliament authorized the UOI to pursue mass disaster litigation as a victim surrogate before US judicial fora, marks the first step in the proverbial journey of a thousand miles towards a daring articulation of Indian environmental govermentality.

In a sense, perhaps, this remained entirely reducible to a technical rather than any profoundly ethical state/law innovation. Technical, because it aimed first at establishing jurisdiction over the UCC in US judicial fora, since the UCC otherwise remained entirely outside Indian jurisdictional borders and boundaries; second, it was aimed at the short-changing of the Bhopal-violated peoples by the 'Kings of Torts' – the swarm of US contingency fee lawyers, who had initiated as many as 144 legal proceedings in the US courts for varying amounts of damages[48] – and thereby to secure complete justice for them. Even so, and in howsoever exigent and normatively messy and untidy modes, India thus emerged, inaugurally, as a postcolonial sovereign plaintiff in hot pursuit of a mighty multinational corporation. Incidentally, the first two objectives were largely fulfilled in the proceedings before Judge Keenan; even when the United States was not held to be a convenient forum for the trial of the suit,[49] Judge Keenan obligated UCC to submit to Indian jurisdiction and to accord full discovery of all relevant documentation.

More crucial, though, was the foundational principle inaugurally enunciated as the principle of absolute multinational enterprise liability. The Indian complaint before Judge Keenan maintained as follows:

47. Too numerous to survey here – even when especially worthy of summary mention – remain the terms of the recasting of the colonial Factories Act and the innovatory measures of the Public Liability Insurance Act (providing for interim compensation of the those violated by hazardous industries and the tightening of air and water pollution legal regimes).

48. The first suit was filed within four days of the catastrophe: see, *Dawani et al v Union Carbide Corporation, SDW Va.* (7 December 1984).

49. See U Baxi, *Inconvenient Forum* (n 35) 34–69 for the text of Judge Keenan's decision dated 12 May 1986; my critique in the Introduction to that work 1–34 and (n 24) Ch 2. For a more favourable approach to Keenan, see J Cassels (n 35) Ch 6.

> A multinational corporation has *a primary, absolute and non-delegable duty to the persons and country in which it has in any manner caused to be undertaken any ultrahazardous or inherently dangerous activity.* This includes a duty to provide that all ultrahazardous or inherently dangerous activities are *conducted with the highest standards of safety and to provide all necessary information and warnings regarding the activity involved.*
>
> Defendant multinational Union Carbide breached this *primary, absolute, and non-delegable duty* through its undertaking of an ultrahazardous and inherently dangerous activity posing *unacceptable risks* at its plant in Bhopal, and the resultant escape of lethal MIC from that plant. Defendant Union Carbide *further failed to provide that its Bhopal plant met the highest standards of safety and failed to inform the Union of India and its peoples of the dangers therein.* Defendant Union Carbide is primarily and absolutely liable for any and all damages caused or contributed to by the escape of lethal MIC from its Bhopal plant.[50]

It needs stressing that these manifold enunciative performatives go above and beyond the extant global law and jurisprudence. Conventional approaches suggest that tort law remedies are private, not public, law remedies;[51] the Bhopal juristic innovations transcend these limits, relating tort law to human rights and environmental violations. Furthermore, in accentuating a *network* conception of the integrity of multinational corporate governance, the innovation adds value to a sustained critique in the name of global justice, fully confronting the awesome consolidation of the global

50. (Emphasis added). See the Indian complaint before the United States District Court, filed 8 April 1985 Southern District of New York, reproduced in U Baxi and T Paul, *Mass Disasters* (n 35) 4–5. Further, India maintained that:

> Multinational corporations by virtue of their global purpose, structure, organization, technology, finances and resources have it within their power to make decisions and take actions that can result in industrial disasters of catastrophic proportion and magnitude. This is particularly true with respect to those activities of the multinationals which are ultrahazardous or inherently dangerous.
>
> Key management personnel of multinationals exercise a closely-held power which is neither restricted by national boundaries nor effectively controlled by international law. The complex corporate structure of the multinational, with networks of subsidiaries and divisions, makes it exceedingly difficult or even impossible to pinpoint responsibility for the damage caused by the enterprise to discrete corporate units or individuals. In reality, there is but one entity, the monolithic multinational, which is responsible for the design, development and dissemination of information and technology worldwide, acting through a forged network of interlocking directors, common operating systems, global distribution and marketing systems, financial and other controls. In this manner, the multinational carries out its global purpose through thousands of daily actions, by a multitude of employees and agents. Persons harmed by the acts of a multinational corporation are not in a position to isolate which unit of the enterprise caused the harm, yet it is evident that the multinational enterprise that caused the harm is liable for such harm. The multinational must necessarily assume this responsibility, for it alone has the resources to discover and guard against hazards and to provide warnings of potential hazards. This inherent duty of the multinational is the only effective way to promote safety and assure that information is shared with all sectors of its organization and with the nations in which it operates.

See further the Amended Consolidated Complaint and the Jury Demand filed by plaintiffs on 8 July 1985; U Baxi and T Paul, *Mass Disasters* (n 35) 148–60.

51. But see PM Shuck (ed), *Tort Law and the Public Interest: Competition, Innovation, and Consumer Welfare* (WH Norton, New York 1991) and the literature referred to in U Baxi (n 24).

risk society and its 'principled' regimes of immunity and impunity for predatory formations of multinational enterprises and their related business entities.

Further, this daring enunciation of the principle of absolute multinational enterprise liability was soon extended by the Supreme Court to hazardous industry, manufacture or process carried out by Indian corporations and business entities and, even during the Bhopal case interim proceedings, further held as binding on Indian courts in a judgment of MP High Court awarding interim 250 million US dollars compensation for Bhopal-violated.[52] The Bhopal case stands 'settled' in an appeal from this very latter affirmation; UCC, having already stalled various Indian judicial proceedings, now needs to act, not only on its behalf but also in a fiduciary capacity/role as a vessel and vehicle of global multinational capital.

UCC accomplishes this role rather remarkably in comparison to the performatives of the Indian State's *parens patriae* obligations. First, UCC denies the very existence of any networked conception of a monolithic global corporation as any real (or actually existing) or any imaginable entity. Second, UCC redraws the corporate veil, resisting its prizing open in the name both of good corporate governance and human rights. Third, UCC contests the Indian enunciation of the principle of absolute multinational enterprise liability in various ways, though never fully explicitly, as its forensic strategies are directed in the main towards the avoidance of any determination concerning its liability.

Granting all these awesome forensic strategies, reading through several submissions made before the US and Indian courts makes it abundantly clear that UCC contested the principle on the ground that it violates the basic and time-tested principles of civil liability for injurious acts – the doctrines of negligence or fault liability which crystallize justice and fair play in the realm of tort liability – even to the extent of problematizing articulations of legislative standards of strict/no-fault liability. Manifestly then it remained easy for UCC to claim that any assertion of absolute liability that allows *no* scope for defence is simply unjust.[53] Further, UCC severally claimed that the Indian enunciation of absolute multinational enterprise liability conflates the identity and responsibility of both the 'parent' and the 'subsidiary' company.[54] UCC maintained vigorously throughout that if any entity was responsible for the relevant acts or omissions, it was the UCIL, its Indian subsidiary. By contrast, the UOI interrogated the justice quality of the conventional tenets of tort and corporation law on a higher platform – that of the standards of protection and promotion of human rights and environmental integrity applicable for owners and operators of ultrahazardous manufacture, processes or applications. The quantification of overall actual damages for human and environmental harm, pegged at 3 billion US dollars including claims for punitive damages,

52. See *M.C. Mehta and others v Shriram Food and Fertilizer Industries and Union of India* (Oleum Gas Leak Case) AIR 1987 SC 1026 and the 4 April 1998 decision of the MP High Court reproduced in U Baxi and A Dhanda (n 29) 338–83.

53. This may appear as axiomatic, until we realize that the principle of absolute multinational liability is not obviously designed to extend to situations of *force majeure* or Acts of God. No one would rationally and reasonably seek to extend the principle to situations of natural disasters such as floods, cyclones, earthquakes and tsunami, or even to an act of war, were these actually to cause the runaway MIC reaction. The UCC trivialized its potential critique of the principle via vague assertions that a militant Sikh group named 'Black June' had claimed responsibly for the Bhopal catastrophe! This strained even the credibility of an otherwise sympathetic Judge Keenan!

54. Baxi, *Valiant Victims* (n 35) 32–5.

remained critical, as well as triggering the future of environmentally sensitive and human-rights friendly corporate governance.

5 THE SECOND BHOPAL CATASTROPHE

The betrayal of the promise of the new principle constitutes the second Bhopal catastrophe, in which the Indian state, in complete amnesia concerning its claimed *parens patriae* role, proceeded to persuade the Indian Supreme Court in chamber (nonpublic) proceedings towards the settlement of the dispute for a meagre amount of 470 million US dollars. The brief judicial settlement order, animated by a rhetorical concern for the urgent need to respond to the sufferings of the Bhopal victims, constitutes a judicial scandal for a variety of reasons. First, the settlement orders were passed in gross violation of the Court's finely-honed jurisprudence of natural justice because the Bhopal-violated petitioners were not given any opportunity of hearing in the proceedings. In a subsequent review petition, the Court itself acknowledged this foundational error, only to treat that proceeding as an instance of postdecisional hearing which in the end sustained the settlement amount! Further, the original settlement orders went so far as to impose obligations upon the UOI to defend the UCC in India and worldwide in any civil action arising from the first catastrophe and to confer a blanket immunity on all criminal actions against the UCC in India, subsequently and meagrely lifted in the review petition. I ponder, speculatively though, in the concluding section, the practice of some sentimental reason that guided the Court in proceeding towards the settlement (out of an ostensible regard for 'justice' to the victims) which in turn governed a somewhat unfeeling juridical aftermath.

Aggravating all this, the Supreme Court decision in the review petition proceeded to quantify damage awards for deaths, estimated at a conservative figure of 2000 fatalities, and arbitrarily to classify the toxic and epidemiological injuries into 'minor' and 'severe' impairments, further fixing the floor as well as the ceiling for compensation and rehabilitation.[55] The Bhopal-violated were thus judicially and juridically shortchanged, offering an instance not noted by the A-to-Z thinkers, of the constitution of *adjudicatory biopower/biopolitics*.

The Supreme Court of India proceeded to justify the settlement via the rhetoric of the dire need to provide some relief to 'victims' but in the process also proceeded to recompose their surviving bodies in terms of classification of compensable injuries into categories of death, permanent total disability, temporary total or partial disability, injuries of utmost severity, minor injuries and loss of livestock, and by the establishment of 'specialized medical centres' for treatment and therapy.[56] Adjudicatory biopower/biopolitics thus creates and circulates 'politicized bodies' of collective

55. The space constraints of this contribution require me to forsake voluminous case law citations and to refer you instead to my critique of these extraordinary adjudicative exertions of power, in my 'Introduction' (n 29) and the textual materials fully archived in that volume. I must here at least add that the review petitions, as drafted by me and questioning the unreason of the settlement orders, were signed individually by eminent citizens from the worlds of the humanities, education, science, technology, and active public citizens. The ethical weight carried by these names at least induced the Supreme Court of India to 'unpack' the settlement and to acknowledge the error of its ways.
56. See the Table in *Valiant Victims* (n 35), lv.

subjects of mass industrial disasters.[57] I suggest that once we regard relatively autonomous adjudicative deliberation as a site for production of the *political* (that is, production of conflicted conceptions of the truths of human rights and justice), juridical biopower emerges as an integral aspect of diverse activist constructions of, and for, the narratives of biopolitics/biosovereignty.

6 THE THIRD BHOPAL CATASTROPHE

Because of space constraints, and because also there is nothing further that may be said about India's callous governance response to the Bhopal-violated, I here provide a summary statement of what must be described as the still continuing third Bhopal catastrophe, in which the inaugural promise of the daring juristic innovations emerges as a full order of perils for the Bhopal-violated. The Supreme Court of India's chaotic 'nomos' justifying the unjustifiable settlement orders[58] constitutes a story in which the 'victims' stand 'revictimized' all over again (in the words of victims) and forever.

That 'justification' of the settlement amount was based, as the Court said, on certain '*assumptions of truth*'.[59] What remained decisive was the judicial view of uncommitted/impartial justice pitted against 'different opinions of the interpretation of laws or on questions of policy or even on what may be considered wise or unwise', because (as the Court said) when 'one speaks of justice and truth, these words mean the same thing to all men whose judgement is uncommitted'.[60]

It did not judicially matter, after all, that the Supreme Court's settlement orders were preceded by shoddy and inadequate record-keeping of deaths and serious injuries[61] and followed by the multifarious, even nefarious 'bureaucratization of justice'.[62] Nor did it matter, furthermore, that the tribunals established for the disbursement of compensation made impossible demands for evidence of 'genuine' claims, as opposed to 'fake' ones; for a while, this even required full evidence of death due to the MIC exposure – paperwork entailing evidence of death certificates and of participants at the funerals! Subsequently, the tribunals sought strict proof of the nature and extent of the injury from the survivors! This resulted in frequent activist demands for Supreme Court invigilation of the administration of disbursement

57. See in this context an extraordinary anthropological analysis by V Adams, 'Suffering the Winds of Lhasa: Politicized Bodies, Human Rights, Cultural Difference, and Humanism in Tibet' (1998) 12 (1) Med Anthropol Q 74. I find poignant the reference to 'winds' in this discourse as relating to the killing wind direction of the Bhopal catastrophe. Although not so naming it, the work of Anna Grear on embodiment/disembodiment via the discourse of corporate legal personhood remains here also compelling for any discourse of the juridical biopolitical constitution of human rights and social suffering. See, especially, the insightful discussion in A Grear, 'Challenging Corporate "Humanity": Legal Disembodiment, Embodiment and Human Rights' (2007) 7 Hum Rts L Rev 511–43. See also A Grear, 'Human Rights, Human Bodies? Some Reflections on Corporate Human Rights Distortion, the Legal Subject, Embodiment and Human Rights Theory' (2006) 17 Law and Critique 171–99 and A Grear, *Re-Directing Human Rights: Facing the Challenge of Corporate Legal Humanity* (Palgrave MacMillan, Basingstoke 2010 forthcoming).
58. *Union Carbide Corporation v Union of India and Ors* [1989] 1 SCR 730.
59. Ibid para 30.
60. Ibid.
61. J Cassels (n 35) 155–62; see also Amnesty International (n 35) Ch 4.
62. J Cassels (n 35) Ch 8.

relief, but even this window of opportunity was finally and cruelly shut down by a Bhopal-weary Court in 2007[63] in an untoward fidelity to a judicial conception of justice that finally rings down the curtain on any just and humane treatment and regard for the Bhopal-violated.

7 CONCLUDING THE INCONCLUDABLE?

In a sense, while the stories of juridicalization of the Bhopal catastrophe have for the most part ended, the saga of suffering still remains, unfolding toxic continuities across now the second generation of the Bhopal-violated. Yet, the spirit of resistance and struggle that accompanies their suffering even in a vastly changed world constituted by the globalizing postmodern condition lives on, despite the second and third Bhopal catastrophes, which signify what I have named as the *structural adjustment* of Indian judicial activism – an integral aspect of now rampant judicial and juridical globalization.

In the main, and in terms of resistance to the juridicalization of their sufferings, the Bhopal movement still continues to struggle to unpack the settlement orders judicially granting extraordinary impunity to UCC. These, incidentally, still remain altogether inexplicable outside my working hypothesis that the judicial abdication occurred out of a 'fine' regard for the self-image of the institutional integrity of the Indian Supreme Court. By this, I refer to a possible state of anxiety generated by the otherwise gifted leaders of the Indian Bar, suborned by UCC, who may have fully exploited (in chamber hearings) the apprehension that any final decision of the Court might be impugned and set aside by an inferior US Court on the ground that the final Indian judgment failed to accord UCC the dignity of due process of law. Judge Keenan had previously laid the foundations for this apprehension concerning the subjection to a US 'due process' requirement of any Indian final judgment by heaping lavish praise on the Indian judiciary, saying: 'The Union of India is a world power in 1986, and its courts have a proven capacity to mete out fair and equal justice' and that, accordingly, to decide the Bhopal case in a US Court would be to deprive the 'Indian judiciary of this opportunity to stand tall before the world and to pass judgment on behalf of its own people … '; to do so, would be further to 'revive a history of subservience and subjugation from which India has emerged'.[64] On this scenario, any refusal to recognize and enforce an Indian damages award by a small causes court in New York may have amounted not so much to an act of legal imperialism but to a performance of adjudicatory pathology of a Third World summit Court unable to decipher the entailments/ requirements of the rule of law doctrine, otherwise the same thing as rule by global capital. The Indian Supreme Court may thus stand tall in the world but only with high heels of 'due process' fashioned by the designer goods produced by the American judicial and juridical markets!

Given the fact that the Bhopal-violated petitioners had successfully stymied all suggestions of unconscionable extrajudicial settlement (ranging from 100 million US dollars to, finally, 250 million US dollars, UCC insured damage), some non-'victim' articulators of public opinion, in India and elsewhere, hailed the settlement as eminently 'just'. By contrast, the Bhopal-violated, overcoming the moment of

63. *Bhopal Gas Peedith Mahila Udyog Sanghathan and Anr. v Union of India (UOI) and Ors* (2007) 9 SCC 707.

64. U Baxi, *Inconvenient Forum* (n 35) 69; see my Introduction critiquing these observations.

desolate despair, soon enough recovered resilience with the demand that since the UOI was a party to the judicial settlement orders, it must now make 'good' the deficit between the settlement award of 470 million US dollars and India's original claim for 3 billion US dollars in their favour – a demand that still echoes in various civil suits against the UOI and the MP Government. All this, while reinforcing the suspicions of the Bhopal-violated concerning recourse to the state/law combines, also suggests acts of popular resistance against their reduction to states of nonbeing via the settlement orders and their aftermaths.

In the process marking an anguished recovery of the collective self of the Bhopal-violated, the only way of escaping legal liability and moral responsibility known to the Northern corporate world – the way of merger and amalgamation and of divestiture of assets to successors-in-interest – stands further severely challenged.[65] Creatively adapting Mahatma Gandhi's famous 'Quit India' movement that, after all, germinated an inaugural movement asserting the human right to self-determination of colonized peoples everywhere, the contemporary Bhopal-violated movement now marshals the symbolic powers of a 'Dow, Quit India' movement,[66] further innovating the politics of direct action and mass civil disobedience. This furnishes, indeed, a movement for deglobalization set against the rampant injustices and violations of a globalizing world.

Notable on this register remains a 'walk for justice' (*Padayatra*) from Bhopal to Delhi led by 39 survivors of the first catastrophe, amongst many hundred others. This walk articulated six demands for justice,[67] the pertinence of which is not one bit diminished by the progressive hearing-impaired ears of India's single-minded globalizing state managers. These demands rearticulate a *complete code of justice*, transcending the juridicalization of the first Bhopal catastrophe and seeking a complete reversal of the impacts of the second and third catastrophes.

The rate and direction of policy response to the demands will, understandably, be based on the perceptions of threats posed to the new comity of concerns established, since the Bhopal settlement, between globalizing Indian state managers and the consortia of global capital. There is, in the 'nature of things', as it were, no assurance that the intransigence of the organic intellectuals of the Bhopal-violated movement (not an

65. Leaving aside, here, the narratives of alternative of recourse to bankruptcy proceedings, a favourite device of US multinational enterprises routinely adopted to escape large damage awards.

66. See the archive on http://www.studentsforbhopal.org/?q=node/4 (last accessed 12 November 2009).

67. These included the demand for the setting up of a national commission on Bhopal with the funds and authority to administer health care, research, economic rehabilitation and social support for the survivors; provision of safe drinking water to those affected by the contaminated ground water of the Union Carbide factory; establishment of a special prosecution cell to prosecute the case against Union Carbide Corporation and its former chairman, Warren Anderson; ensuring scientific assessment of the toxic contamination of the factory and surrounding areas and forcing Union Carbide's owner, The Dow Chemical Company, to clean up and compensate for the damage; the blacklisting of Dow and Union Carbide's products and technologies in India and the halting of the expansion of Dow's business; the declaration of December 3rd as a national day of mourning for victims of industrial disasters and pollution and the undertaking that the Bhopal disaster be included in school and college curricula.

Incidentally, and without the slightest trace of any pride of authorship, it warms my aging though activist human heart that my plea for a high-powered commission for relief and rehabilitation for the Bhopal-violated (U Baxi, *Inconvenient Forum* (n 35) 34) now stands thus creatively adapted on the eve of the silver jubilee of Bhopal.

entirely a vanishing breed yet an already endangered species) and the wider networks of international activist solidarity may yield any determinate results for the Bhopal-violated humanity in the immediate future.

Even so, the very name 'Bhopal' continues to haunt the votaries of globalization in India, at least, as a profound moral nuisance. By frequent recourse to direct action strategies inviting incredible state repression, the Bhopal-violated constantly tease – and test – the tactics, tricks, and treacheries of green govermentality and further ensure that the injustices suffered by them will remain more than 'remembrance of things past'. In this, they seek to ensure that such orders of anti-human rights and eco-unfriendly trade-offs may never occur again.[68]

To listen, and even to yield to, the new movement of the Bhopal-violated is thus to flout the imperatives of India's emergence – if no longer as the ethical voice of the postcolony of the nonaligned nations – at least as an equal 'Davos-type' emergent 'Asian giant' as important as the People's Republic of China. This new form of 'gigantochomachy' is precisely at stake in the Bhopal-violated movement, not thus far fully ingested by some de-globalizing 'new' social and human rights movements.

The conclusionary space of this tormented narrative offers little room for any detailed analysis of the new politics now reconstructing new forms of sovereign bio-politics, save for briefly noting a few trends. First, the democratization of people's knowledge now stands fully combated by continuing practices of the nationalization of truth and the politics of denial, a not uncommon occurrence in the worldwide histories of recent mass disasters, and yet still countered by Bhopal-violated practices of resistance.[69] Second, justifications for a new ideology of developmentalism under which contemporary neocolonialism goes – as it were – global, now need to be continually refurbished in the languages recreating new modes of primitive accumulation within the very heart of what is otherwise described as 'postmodern' capitalism.[70] Third, the state/law combine must in the face of the Bhopal-violated movement still continue to 'impersonate' the standards of that human rights civility[71] which has marked policy and adjudication responses as somehow still concern-full acts of 'justice' for the Bhopal-violated![72]

68. Which here include constitutionally enshrined human rights further developed by an otherwise activist Supreme Court of India and the internationally obligatory human rights norms and standards accepted by India and at times also crafted by UN mediation.
69. Thus, for example, the entirely ungrudging reception of the UCC successor-in-interest Dow Chemicals, without even as much regard for restoration of human rights and claims of justice as urged by the Bhopal movement as shown even by the letter dated 16 June 2009 from leading US legislators to Dow Chemicals (n 45), which now leads UOI to defend the presence and actions of the successor company.
70. India's Eleventh Plan enunciation now replaces the imagery of *equitable development* (based on human rights and social justice) with inclusive *growth* (based on consideration of global trade and economic competitiveness) in which a flexible labour market is considered a new imperative for anticonstitutional Indian development; see Planning Commission, Government of India, *Eleventh Five Year Plan, 2007-12, Volume 1,* at paras 1:15, 4:70 (OUP, New Delhi 2008).
71. I adapt this phrase from the gifted work of D Fischlin and M Nandorfy, *Eduardo Galeano: Through A Looking Glass* (Black Rose, Montreal 2002) 31–42.
72. And, in a different mode, the Indian state managers insist on heavily coopting the languages of ILO talk of 'fair globalization', further affirming the potential of affirmative practices of biopower/biopolitics. ILO: *Decent Work* (Geneva 1999).

The Bhopal-violated re-emerge Phoenix-like, to mix metaphors, compellingly from their own MIC ashes. They interrogate (to adapt a phrase from Nietzsche) the 'superficiality' of the 'profundity'[73] of so many critical modes of legal/juridical and even human rights nihilism. Adapting a further Nietzschean phrase – and to entirely invert the contexts of the author's intent – the movement of the Bhopal-violated manifests the 'courage of all strong spirits to *know* their own immortality'.[74]

Thus, reaching towards the improbability of a conclusion may be all that matters. At the conclusion of his great novel *Tess of the d'Urbevilles,* Thomas Hardy poignantly writes that '"Justice" was done, and the President of the Immortals, in the Aeschylean phrase, had ended his sport with Tess'. While it may be true to say that that the binational (the common community of the Indian and United States justices) presidents of the judicial immortals may have thus rendered 'justice' by decreeing a judicial fate for the Bhopal-violated, their continuing struggles constitute at least a reminder of a different genre of 'immortality' spoken of by Alain Badiou (quoted earlier) – as 'the rights of the Immortal, affirmed in their own right, or the rights of the Infinite exercised over the contingency of suffering and death'.

Put differently, the continuing movement of the Bhopal-violated beckons a new jurisprudence of human solidarity in a runaway globalizing world. Their movement more fully revitalizes India's original intent in devising the principle of absolute multinational enterprise liability for ultrahazardous industry, process and application when seeking compensation for the 'enormity of the Bhopal disaster'[75] (even when lost in translation), via this jurisprudence of solidarity. The contemporary Bhopal movement reiterates India's original pleading before Judge Keenan that *no* regime of multinational capital impunity ought to be allowed to go so far as altogether erasing this 'unimaginable and unforgettable catastrophe', of 'pain, suffering, and emotional distress of immense proportion' resulting in the 'virtual destruction of [their] entire world'.[76]

In this, the Bhopal-violated movement constantly interrogates the assassins of collective memory and further enacts a jurisprudence of critical human and social solidarity, paralleled perhaps only in the contemporary world by the commemorative moments of Hiroshima–Nagasaki survivors and next of kin.

Perhaps, then, I may 'conclude' here by adapting the phrase-regime of Richard Rorty that such jurisprudence is not 'discovered by reflection but created ... *by increasing our sensitivity to particular details of pain and humiliation and other unfamiliar sorts of people*'.[77] The message of Bhopal, in the main, thus constructs some new alternate futures beyond the new paradigm of trade-related, market friendly and environmentally hostile human rights.[78]

73. F Nietzsche, *The Genealogy of Morality, Preface* at 4, as quoted in B Leiter, *Nietzsche on Morality* (Routledge, London 2002) 42.
74. Quoted in Leiter (n 73) 48.
75. U Baxi and T Paul, *Mass Disasters* (n 35) 9.
76. Ibid 8.
77. R Rorty, *Contingency, Irony and Solidarity* (Cambridge University Press, Cambridge 1989) 16.
78. Baxi, *Future* (n 17) Ch 8.

[21]

International Law and Social Movements: Challenges of Theorizing Resistance

BALAKRISHNAN RAJAGOPAL*

This Article offers an analysis of the key theoretical challenges that arise from the impact of local and transnational social movement action—as witnessed in Seattle in 1999—on international law and institutions. In spite of a vast scholarly literature in the social sciences on social movements and their relationship to the state and other actors, international lawyers have not engaged this literature so far. Given the increasing importance of non-state and individual action in international affairs, this Article suggests that it is now timely to engage with this literature. This Article presents the outlines of a larger project to rethink international law through social movements rather than through states or individuals, as realists and liberals do. At the heart of the analysis in this article is the question of how international lawyers can understand the mass resistance around the world to

---

* Ford International Assistant Professor of Law and Development and Director, Program on Human Rights and Justice, Massachusetts Institute of Technology. SJD (Harvard Law School, 2000); LLM (The American University, 1992); BL (University of Madras, 1990). I wish to thank Obiora Okafor and Anthony Anghie for conversations and comments. I also wish to thank Nathaniel Berman, Richard Falk, James Gathii, David Kennedy and Martti Koskenniemi for conversations and debates about various issues during the past two years. A version of this article was presented at the University of Toronto Law Faculty Legal Theory Colloquium in March 2002, and I thank Kerry Rittich for her enormous enthusiasm and support. Some ideas from this article have also been presented at the Conference of the Law and Society Association and the Research Committee on the Sociology of Law, Budapest, Hungary, July 4, 2001; the Conference on The "Third" World and the International Order: Law, Politics and Globalization, Osgoode Hall Law School, York University, Oct. 12–13, 2001; and at the Opening Plenary, Latcrit Conference on "Coalitional Theory and Praxis: Social Justice Movements and Latcrit Community," University of Oregon Law School, May 2, 2002. The usual caveats apply. This article presents some key themes from my forthcoming book to be published by Cambridge University Press, INTERNATIONAL LAW FROM BELOW: DEVELOPMENT, SOCIAL MOVEMENTS AND THIRD WORLD RESISTANCE (forthcoming 2003).

global legal structures. The article argues that international lawyers need a theory of resistance, not simply one of governance, to ensure that the voices of the ordinary people, who are increasingly marginalized by the current global order, are properly heard. After outlining some of the key theoretical barriers in international law that prevent a real engagement with social movements, the Article explores some possible foundations for a cultural politics of international law that would enable international legal scholarship to pay proper regard to the empirical reality of international relations and to remain committed to the best cosmopolitan ideals of the discipline.

"A focus on social movements with restructuring agendas itself incorporates a political judgment on how drastic global reform can best be achieved at this stage of history."[1]

1. Richard Falk, *The Global Promise of Social Movements: Explorations at the Edge*

I. INTRODUCTION

The much-maligned "anti-globalization" protests in Seattle, Genoa, and Washington, D.C., as well as the World Social Summit meeting in Porto Allegre, Brazil, have ignited an interest in understanding mass action on a global scale. Concerted social movement action has driven several recent international legal developments (including the Ottawa Convention on Anti-Personnel Landmines,[2] the establishment of the World Bank Complaints Panel,[3] the establishment of the World Commission on Dams,[4] the Doha Declaration regarding the World Trade Organization's Agreement on Trade-Related Aspects of Intellectual Property Rights ("TRIPS") and Public Health,[5] an advisory opinion of the International Court of Justice regarding the threat or use of nuclear weapons)[6] and the emergence of new soft law standards for corporate social responsibility.[7] In most, if not all, of these actions, well-organized social movements in the Third World have formed alliances with those in the West and have transformed the political space[8] of

of Time, 12 ALTERNATIVES 173, 173 (1987).

2. Convention on the Prohibition of the Use, Stockpiling, Production and Transfer of Anti-Personnel Mines and on Their Destruction, signed Sept. 18, 1997, 36 I.L.M. 1507, (entered into force Mar. 1, 1999) [hereinafter Ottawa Convention]. *See also* THE BANNING OF ANTI-PERSONNEL LANDMINES: THE LEGAL CONTRIBUTION OF THE INTERNATIONAL COMMITTEE OF THE RED CROSS (Louis Maresca & Stuart Maslen eds., 2000).

3. On the World Bank Complaints Panel, see http://wbln0018.worldbank.org/ipn/ipnweb.nsf. *See* Daniel Bradlow, *International Organizations and Private Complaints: The Case of the World Bank Inspection Panel*, 34 VA. J. INT'L L. 553 (1994).

4. On the World Commission on Dams, see http://www.dams.org/default.php. See also the symposium issue *in* Kader Asmal, *Introduction: World Commission on Dams Report, Dams and Development*, 16 AM. U. INT'L L. REV. 1411 (2001).

5. *See Doha Declaration on the TRIPS Agreement and Public Health*, WT/MIN(01)/Dec/2 Para. 4 (Nov. 14, 2001). This Declaration was partly the result of grassroots pressure to reinterpret the TRIPS Agreement so as to allow the sale of generic HIV/AIDS drugs.

6. *See* Legality of the Threat or Use of Nuclear Weapons, 1996 I.C.J. 95 (note, in particular, Justice Weeramantry's dissent). This advisory opinion was the result of a global movement against nuclear weapons. For a perceptive analysis of the role played by global civil society in making this case possible, see RICHARD FALK, *The Nuclear Weapons Advisory Opinion and the New Jurisprudence of Global Civil Society*, *in* LAW IN AN EMERGING GLOBAL VILLAGE 165–88 (1998).

7. *See Business and Human Rights*, *in* HUMAN RIGHTS WATCH WORLD REPORT (2001); HUMAN RIGHTS—IS IT ANY OF YOUR BUSINESS? (2000) *available at* http://www.iblf.org/csr/csrwebassist.nsf/content/f1d2a3a4c5.html#1. On soft law norms, see COMMITMENT AND COMPLIANCE: THE ROLE OF NON-BINDING NORMS IN THE INTERNATIONAL LEGAL SYSTEM (Dinah Shelton ed., 2000).

8. For the purposes of this article, "political space" refers to the sanctioned—but contested—boundaries within which normative evolution and compliance occur.

rulemaking and implementation in international law. Indeed, global norms are increasingly being produced and shaped through an interaction between States, international institutions, and rebellious networks of peasants, farmers, women, and environmentalists, while legal enforcement is increasingly influenced by the everyday resistance of ordinary people. Despite these developments, international law does not yet have a theory of resistance. This article proposes that international law requires a theory of resistance to remain relevant, both to the empirical reality of international relations, and to the cosmopolitan values, such as human dignity, equality, and peace, that have traditionally attracted the Third World states to international law. This theory of resistance must take Third World social movements seriously. While taking social movements seriously has never been an easy task for international lawyers, in the aftermath of the attacks on September 11, 2001 and the subsequent war on "terror," they have a greater responsibility to pay close attention to social movements and to ensure that legitimate protests are not also labeled as "terrorism."[9] Nevertheless, international law can no longer pretend that mass resistance from the Third World does not fundamentally shape its domain. Indeed, the central focus of the inquiry here must be: how does one write this resistance into international law?

The articulation of a theory of resistance in international law will both compel a fundamental rethinking of the very meaning of the term "Third World" as a collection of States in international law[10] and raise profound theoretical challenges to the international legal order as it presently stands. In the following four Parts, this article presents the outlines of an undertaking to consider international law through social movements, rather than through States or individuals.[11] In Part II, the author presents some of the causes for the inability or unwillingness of international lawyers to seriously consider social movements and review some recent literature that suggests ways to overcome this tendency. In Part III, the author suggests some preliminary ways to think about a theory of politics for an

9. The Italian Prime Minister is reputed to have remarked, in the aftermath of the September 11th attacks, that the protestors against the World Economic Forum in Genoa were also terrorists.

10. For a detailed argument to this effect, see Balakrishnan Rajagopal, *Locating the Third World in Cultural Geography*, THIRD WORLD LEGAL STUD. 1 (1998–99).

11. The broader project is forthcoming, as noted above, as a book by Cambridge University Press in 2003. For a preview of some of the themes and issues contained in the broader project, see Balakrishnan Rajagopal, *From Resistance to Renewal: The Third World, Social Movements and the Expansion of International Institutions*, 41 HARV. INT'L L.J. 529 (2000).

international law that takes into serious consideration the resistance of Third World social movements in contrast to the traditional international law approach to politics. To do so, this article introduces a series of conceptual tools from literature on social movements and links those tools to international legal debates. It further suggests that analyzing international law through the lens of social movements is much more rewarding than analyzing it exclusively from the perspectives of either states (as realists/positivists do) or individuals (as liberals/naturalists do). International law needs to de-center itself from the unitary conception of the political sphere on which it is based, which takes the state or the individual as the principal political actor. In Part IV, the author attempts to articulate some bases for a theory of resistance in international law by drawing on the work of Michel Foucault, Antonio Gramsci, Frantz Fanon, and Partha Chatterjee. Part V is a brief conclusion.

II. INTERNATIONAL LAW AND SOCIAL MOVEMENTS: SEEING PAST EACH OTHER

Despite the fact that international relations is no stranger to mass action—epochal twentieth century developments, after all, were catalyzed through mass action (e.g., nationalism, anti-colonialism, Marxism, identity-based mobilizations, and pro-democracy movements)—international lawyers traditionally have neither attempted to interpret mass actions nor engage the rich literature on social movements.[12] International and domestic lawyers are traditionally interested in governance, not resistance. As a result of professional training, intellectual orientation, political and class alignment, and tradition, lawyers focus on various kinds of governmental and private institutions. With this focus, they tend to ask different sets of questions about social change and the role of law in it. For instance, in domestic law, lawyers examine the "contribution" of courts to the civil rights movement in the United States by studying landmark cases such as *Brown v. Board of Education.*[13] Such "technical" or "legal" discussions filter out the contributions of the masses from historical transformations and highlight the roles played by judges and lawyers. In this clinical reduction of facts, the case itself becomes the historical event, so that

12. For a discussion, see *infra* Part III and note 40 for literature.

13. Brown v. Bd. of Educ., 347 U.S. 483 (1954).

legal history is reduced to a cataloguing of factually abstracted episodes that bear little relation to each other.

This traditional tendency in Western domestic law to ignore the contribution of the masses is a result of many factors that are too complex to examine here, but two that are discussed below are relevant to international law; they are problems of source and method.[14] With regard to the problem of source, lawyers tend to have a juro-centric approach that focuses on the texts emerging from public institutions such as legislatures, courts such as the International Court of Justice, the United Nations, and the World Trade Organization's Dispute Settlement Authority. In this approach, there is no space for "texts of resistance"[15]—i.e., either informal or explicitly illegal interpretive acts by individuals and groups that are contrary to institutional interpretations of the law. Thus, for lawyers, the source of normative legitimacy and authority is consistently the statist institutions. For example, environmental lawyers are more concerned with the regulatory behavior of the state than with the rise of environmental consciousness or the mass action that may have led to the regulatory behavior of the state. This has the result of ignoring the social origins of legal rules and institutions and, therefore, the role of laypeople in legal analysis.

Regarding the problem of method, much of legal analysis is focused entirely on the cogency and the internal logical structure of the language of the law. As such, the prescriptive stance of legal analysis focuses on figuring out the gaps, conflicts and ambiguities in the language of the law, even if to reveal the existence of ideology.[16] While this focus is enormously valuable for many purposes, merely revealing the structural flaws in legal reasoning does nothing to ground it in particular social and political contexts and makes the law look surprisingly static.[17] Furthermore, although a revelation of the internal incoherence of law may undermine the authority of law, it does not offer an indication of how it should be reformed.

14. *See* Symposium, *Passing Through the Door: Social Movement Literature and Legal Scholarship*, 150 U. PA. L. REV. 1, 54–55 (2001).

15. This term is borrowed from Robert M. Cover, *The Supreme Court, 1982 Term: Foreward: Nomos and Narrative*, 97 HARV. L. REV. 4, 45–50 (1983).

16. This is a classic stance adopted by critical legal studies scholars. *See, e.g.*, DUNCAN KENNEDY, A CRITIQUE OF ADJUDICATION: FIN DE SIÈCLE 113–214 (1997). Even here, the focus is not on the massive regulatory apparatus of the state, which is the source of so much "law" in the Third World, but on judge-made law. As the title of this book indicates, it is adjudication, not regulation, that is critiqued.

17. For a recent acknowledgement from a leading critical scholar, see MARTTI KOSKENNIEMI, THE GENTLE CIVILIZER OF NATIONS: THE RISE AND FALL OF INTERNATIONAL LAW 1870–1960 2 (2002).

Incorporating the social dimensions of law into legal analysis—e.g., viewing the history of the sex discrimination doctrine in U.S. constitutional law as one that arose from a larger women's suffrage movement rather than from the Fourteenth Amendment[18]—has vast consequences for legal reasoning, broader social reform, and the role that law plays in reform. In international law, such incorporation leads to a mode of legal analysis that places much more significance on the consequences of particular legal rules and doctrines for those who do not have a voice or power in the legal system[19] and that, importantly, does not shy away from acknowledging the need to reinterpret international law in order to account for their interests.

The tendency in Western domestic law to ignore the contribution of the masses has been criticized by at least two camps in recent years. One camp within the United States, a group of critical race theorists, feminists, and gay-lesbian theorists, has criticized this decontextualized, technocratic-rational model of law and legal history on the ground that it ignores both the role that law plays in everyday life and empowerment and the role played by ordinary people as agents of legal transformation.[20] For them, the liberal legal model[21] that has remained dominant in the United States so far is fatally flawed due to these blind spots, among others, and needs to be fundamentally reconceptualized. Although some of their writings

18. Reva Siegal, *She the People: The Nineteenth Amendment, Sex Equality, Federalism, and the Family*, 115 HARV. L. REV. 947 (2002).

19. The jurisprudence of Justice C.G. Weeramantry stands out as a shining example. See, in particular, his dissent in Legality of the Threat or Use of Nuclear Weapons, 1996 I.C.J. 95.

20. For examples of critical race scholarship, see CRITICAL RACE THEORY: THE KEY WRITINGS THAT FORMED THE MOVEMENT (Kimberlé Crenshaw et al. eds., 1995); PATRICIA WILLIAMS, THE ALCHEMY OF RACE AND RIGHTS (1991); Kimberlé Williams Crenshaw, *Race, Reform and Retrenchment: Transformation and Legitimation in Anti-Discrimination Law*, 101 HARV. L. REV. 1331 (1988). Examples of feminist legal scholarship include CATHERINE A. MACKINNON, TOWARD A FEMINIST THEORY OF THE STATE (1989); MARTHA MINOW, MAKING ALL THE DIFFERENCE: INCLUSION, EXCLUSION AND AMERICAN LAW (1990); Katherine Bartlett, *Feminist Legal Methods*, 103 HARV. L. REV. 829 (1990); Ann Scales, *The Emergence of a Feminist Jurisprudence: An Essay*, 95 YALE L.J. 1373 (1986); Robin West, *Jurisprudence and Gender*, 55 U. CHI. L. REV. 1 (1988). For recent gay-lesbian legal scholarship, see WILLIAM ESKRIDGE JR., GAYLAW: CHALLENGING THE APARTHEID OF THE CLOSET (1999); Janet Halley, *Gay Rights and Identity Imitation: Issues in the Ethics of Representation*, *in* THE POLITICS OF LAW: A PROGRESSIVE CRITIQUE 115 (David Kairys ed., 1998); Kendall Thomas, *Beyond the Privacy Principle*, 92 COLUM. L. REV. 1431 (1992).

21. In the domestic legal context, liberal legalism is said to consist of a set of premises that are supposed to underlie a specific mode of analyzing legal (and human) relations. These include the notion of the atomistic individual, the distinction between public and private spheres, and law as a neutral and impartial mechanism for resolving disputes between atomistic individuals. For a classic critique of liberalism, see ROBERTO UNGER, KNOWLEDGE AND POLITICS (1975).

allude to social movements, they do not explicitly engage social movement literature.[22] They draw inspiration, inter alia, from the legal theoretical work of Robert Cover, which posits the notion of "interpretive communities"[23] that create law and give it meaning through their personal experiences.

The other camp, a small number of socio-legal theorists and comparativists from the United States and Europe, along with several constitutional scholars from non-Western countries, has engaged in important critiques of liberal theories of rights, justice, and democracy, sometimes by engaging social movements literature. These critiques include the works of: Joel Handler on civil rights, welfare, and other movements in the United States;[24] Austin Sarat on identity and rights and cause lawyering;[25] Jüergen Habermas on social movements, democracy, and rights;[26] Alan Hunt and Neil Stammers on human rights;[27] Sousa Santos on legal theory and human rights;[28] Upendra Baxi on democracy, rights, and justice;[29] and more recently, Diane Otto on human rights and postcolonial theory[30] and Julie Mertus on transnational civil society.[31] These critiques have pointed

22. Although critical scholarship has not directly engaged it so far, some recent developments indicate an increasing interest in social movement literature. The Latcrit conference for the year 2002 has taken social movements as its main theme and the University of Pennsylvania Law Review recently held a symposium on "Social Movements and Law Reform." *See* Symposium, *Social Movements and Law Reform: Passing Through the Door: Social Movement Literature and Legal Scholarship*, 150 U. PA. L. REV. 1 (2001).

23. Cover, *supra* note 15, at 40.

24. JOEL HANDLER, SOCIAL MOVEMENTS AND THE LEGAL SYSTEM: A THEORY OF LAW REFORM AND SOCIAL CHANGE (1978).

25. IDENTITIES, POLITICS AND RIGHTS (Austin Sarat & Thomas Kearns eds., 1995); CAUSE LAWYERING (Austin Sarat & Stuart Scheingold eds., 1998).

26. JÜERGEN HABERMAS, BETWEEN FACTS AND NORMS: CONTRIBUTIONS TO A DISCOURSE THEORY OF LAW AND DEMOCRACY (1996); Jüergen Habermas, *New Social Movements*, 49 TELOS 33–37 (1981).

27. Alan Hunt, *Rights and Social Movements: Counter-Hegemonic Strategies*, 17 J.L. & SOC'Y 309, 309–28 (1990); Neil Stammers, *A Critique of Social Approaches to Human Rights*, 17 HUM. RTS. Q. 488 (1995).

28. BOAVENTURA DE SOUSA SANTOS, TOWARD A NEW COMMON SENSE: LAW, SCIENCE AND POLITICS IN THE PARADIGMATIC TRANSITION (1995).

29. THE RIGHTS OF SUBORDINATED PEOPLES (Oliver Mendelsohn & Upendra Baxi eds., 1994); Upendra Baxi, *Taking Suffering Seriously: Social Action Litigation Before the Supreme Court of India*, *in* JUDGES AND JUDICIAL POWER: ESSAYS IN HONOUR OF JUSTICE V. R. KRISHNA IYER (Rajeev Dhavan et al. eds., 1985); Upendra Baxi, *Voices of Suffering and the Future of Human Rights*, 8 TRANSNAT'L L. & CONTEMP. PROBS. 125 (1998).

30. Diane Otto, *Rethinking the "Universality" of Human Rights Law*, 29 COLUM. HUM. RTS. L. REV. 1 (1997); Diane Otto, *Subalternity and International Law: The Problems of Global Community and the Incommensurability of Difference*, 5 SOC. & LEGAL STUD. 337 (1996).

31. Julie Mertus, *From Legal Transplants to Transformative Justice: Human Rights*

out the elitist bias of extant rights theories and conceptions of democracy and have attempted to formulate general conceptions of law that would accommodate the role of subaltern communities and individuals.

A central aspect of the two camps of literature discussed above has been a scrutiny of the role that law plays in regulating power in everyday life and, in turn, the impact of everyday practices on the law itself.[32] This study of the dynamic between the institutional and extra-institutional aspects of social life and of the importance of extra-institutional mobilization for the success or failure of institutions, has injected new elements into an understanding of law. Indeed, one of the main distinguishing characteristics of social movements literature has been this emphasis on the interconnectedness, at both the national and global levels, between everyday forms of power struggles and institutional politics.[33] Stated differently, a social movement perspective emphasizes the importance of extra-institutional forms of mobilization for the "success" or "failure" of institutional forms.[34] In this sense, these extra-institutional forms of mobilization constitute important arenas of resistance that remain beyond the cognitive boundaries of international law's sole, approved discourse of resistance—human rights.

Few of these perspectives have yet permeated international law despite recent scholarship in international relations that seriously considers social movements.[35] International law remains trapped in a

and the Promise of Transnational Civil Society, 14 AM. U. INT'L L. REV. 1335 (1999).

32. This is the understanding of power that Michel Foucault has advanced—i.e., power is not confined to the institutional, political arenas, but "circulates" through all spheres of life as a relational phenomenon. *See* MICHEL FOUCAULT, POWER/KNOWLEDGE: SELECTED INTERVIEWS AND OTHER WRITINGS, 1972–1977 (1980).

33. *See, e.g.*, Falk, *supra* note 1.

34. This is what Rajni Kothari calls "non-party political process," and Claus Offe calls "noninstitutional politics." Rajni Kothari, *Masses, Classes and the State*, *in* NEW SOCIAL MOVEMENTS IN THE SOUTH: EMPOWERING THE PEOPLE 59 (Ponna Wignaraja ed., 1993); Claus Offe, *New Social Movements: Challenging the Boundaries of Institutional Politics*, 52 SOC. RES. 817 (1985).

35. *See, e.g.*, ROGER BURBACH ET AL., GLOBALIZATION AND ITS DISCONTENTS: THE RISE OF POSTMODERN SOCIALISMS (1997); ROBERT O'BRIEN ET AL., CONTESTING GLOBAL GOVERNANCE: MULTILATERAL ECONOMIC INSTITUTIONS AND GLOBAL SOCIAL MOVEMENTS (2000); KATHRYN SIKKINK AND MARGARET KECK, ACTIVISTS BEYOND BORDERS: ADVOCACY NETWORKS IN INTERNATIONAL POLITICS (1998); TRANSNATIONAL SOCIAL MOVEMENTS AND GLOBAL POLITICS: SOLIDARITY BEYOND THE STATE (Jackie Smith et al. eds., 1997); Paul Ghils, *International Civil Society: International Non-Governmental Organizations in the International System*, 44 INT'L SOC. SCI. J. 417 (1992); Ronnie D. Lipschutz, *Reconstructing World Politics: The Emergence of Global Civil Society*, 21 MILLENIUM 389 (1992); Martin Shaw, *Global Society and Global Responsibility: The Theoretical, Historical, and Political*

version of politics that is narrowly focused on institutional practice and an understanding of the "social" that accepts the unity of the agent as a given. This has resulted in an artificially narrow outlook in international law. Some leading scholars, aware of this, have attempted to construct a broader approach to international law, mainly by identifying non-state actors as "international" actors[36] and by arguing for a right to personal identity that would permit international law to accommodate a plurality of social agents (on the basis of class, gender, race, ethnicity, etc.).[37] Despite this attempt, much of what occurs in extra-institutional spaces in the Third World remains invisible to international law. Indeed, the limitations of liberal categories such as rights, employed to represent social movements, are part of the reason that such blind spots continue to exist. While this argument cannot be pursued here, it is important to recognize that it is difficult to acknowledge the role of mass action in international law because of its institutionalist bias, jurocentrism, and elitism. Given that most Third World social movements consist of the urban poor, peasants, workers in the informal sector, illiterate women, and indigenous peoples whose resources are being destroyed, the legal categories—such as human rights—that are being used to represent "voices" of suffering[38] tend to have elitist blind spots.

Limits of "International Society," 21 MILLENIUM 421 (1992); Kathryn Sikkink, *Human Rights, Principled Issue-Networks and Sovereignty in Latin America*, 47 INT'L ORG. 411 (1993); Paul Wapner, *Environmental Activism and Global Civil Society*, 41 DISSENT 389 (1994); Peter J. Spiro, *New Global Communities: Nongovernmental Organizations in International Decision-Making Institutions*, 18 WASH. Q. 45 (1995).

36. This has a rich pedigree in international law. The first wave of scholarship argued for the recognition of international institutions and multinational corporations as legal actors. *See* WOLFGANG FRIEDMANN, THE CHANGING STRUCTURE OF INTERNATIONAL LAW (1964); WILFRED JENKS, THE COMMON LAW OF MANKIND (1958); PHILIP JESSUP, TRANSNATIONAL LAW (1956); Percy Corbett, *What is the League of Nations*, *in* BRITISH YEAR BOOK OF INT'L L. 119–48 (1924). A second wave argued for the recognition of individuals, peoples, and liberation movements as legal actors. *See* HERSCH LAUTERPACHT, INTERNATIONAL LAW AND HUMAN RIGHTS (1950); CHRISTOPHER QUAYE, LIBERATION STRUGGLES IN INTERNATIONAL LAW (1991); Louis Sohn, *The New International Law: Protection of the Rights of Individuals Rather Than States*, 32 AM. U. L. REV. 1 (1982). A third wave has now been arguing for recognition of NGOs as international legal actors. *See* Steve Charnovitz, *Two Centuries of Participation: NGOs and International Governance*, 18 MICH. J. INT'L L. 183 (1997); Spiro, *supra* note 35. Richard Falk has been calling for a post-Westphalian world order based on the emergence of a "globalization from below." *See* RICHARD FALK, LAW IN AN EMERGING GLOBAL VILLAGE: A POST-WESTPHALIAN PERSPECTIVE (1998).

37. Thomas Franck, *Clan and Super Clan: Loyalty, Identity and Community in Law and Practice*, 90 AM. J. INT'L L. 359 (1996).

38. *See* Baxi, *Voices of Suffering and the Future of Human Rights*, *supra* note 29.

III. RETHINKING THE POLITICAL IN INTERNATIONAL LAW: BEYOND LIBERALISM AND MARXISM

This Part will first provide a contextual introduction to the theoretical challenges that arise when we adopt a social movement perspective toward international law. The current interest in social movements must be traced to the historical context in which forms of popular mobilizations began to transform the Third World. During the 1950s and 1960s, the principal forms of popular mobilizations in the Third World were organized around the "nation," aimed mainly at national liberation from colonial rule, and around "class," aimed at a structural transformation of the colonial/comprador economic and social orders within Third World countries.[39] Such mass radicalism lay behind the elite Third World radicalism one witnessed at the United Nations, calling for a New International Economic Order ("NIEO"). This mass radicalism was accompanied and followed by large public mobilizations in Western countries, such as: movements involving civil rights, black nationalism, women's rights, and gay and lesbian rights in the United States; the Green movement in West Germany; and the 1968 student protests in France.[40] In the early 1970s, however, after the engineered "fall" of Allende in Chile, the splintering of the Third World coalition, the containment of nationalist and class movements by the two Super Powers, and the genuine grassroots disillusionment with the violence of the nation-building project in many Third World countries, new forms of popular mobilization began to emerge, based on novel forms of domination and exploitation (such as migrant labor, urban squatters, and women). These mobilizations began to transform the political, economic, and social landscape of many Third World countries. Yet, they could not be analyzed within the Marxist paradigm, which had provided the tools for interpreting radical social change in the Third World for several decades. Literature on social movements emerged largely as a response to these new forms of mobilizations, even as it sought to explicate the exhaustion of leftist ideology. This explains

39. *See generally* FRANTZ FANON, THE WRETCHED OF THE EARTH (1963); FRANK FUREDI, COLONIAL WARS AND THE POLITICS OF THIRD WORLD NATIONALISM (1994).

40. The literature on these movements is vast. For a sample, see DOUG MCADAM ET AL., DYNAMICS OF CONTENTION (2001); ALBERTO MELUCCI, NOMADS OF THE PRESENT: SOCIAL MOVEMENTS AND INDIVIDUAL NEEDS IN CONTEMPORARY SOCIETY (1989); FRANCES FOX PIVEN & RICHARD CLOWARD, POOR PEOPLES' MOVEMENTS: WHY THEY SUCCEED, HOW THEY FAIL (1977); EDWARD SHORTER & CHARLES TILLY, STRIKES IN FRANCE, 1830-1968 (1974); SIDNEY TARROW, POWER IN MOVEMENT: SOCIAL MOVEMENTS AND CONTENTIOUS POLITICS (1998); CHARLES TILLY, THE FORMATION OF NATIONAL STATES IN WESTERN EUROPE (1975).

the attempt to distinguish the new forms of popular mobilizations as "new social movements" (based on identity politics), as opposed to presumably "old" social movements (based on national liberation or class).[41] By the end of the 1990s, identity-based movements ran out of steam and became subject to severe questioning from post-Marxists, among others.[42] This followed the discovery that the "move to markets" in development policy in the early 1990s conveniently coincided with the move away from class to identity. The whole spectrum of literature that discusses the above political and social developments is what this article refers to broadly as social movements literature. This literature is complex, varied, and dispersed across several disciplines including sociology, comparative politics, anthropology, and critical development studies.[43]

Social movements literature contains a multitude of views about what constitutes a social movement and what distinguishes a "new" from an "old" movement. To take one example, Mario Diani identifies the following general elements in a social movement: (1) they involve networks of informal interactions between a plurality of actors; (2) they are engaged in political or cultural conflicts; and (3) they organize on the basis of shared beliefs and collective identities.[44] This definition raises several important issues.

First is the issue of what causes one movement to mobilize more successfully than another—that is, what kinds of networks of interaction are necessary to convert popular discontent or sporadic disaffection into a viable movement. A general answer is that "social

---

41. For a good example of this analysis, see Jüergen Habermas, *New Social Movements*, 49 TELOS 33 (1981).

42. It is important to recognize that, in the social sciences, the debate about the newness of the "new" social movements is now sterile and ignored. *See, e.g.*, David Plotke, *What's So New About New Social Movements?*, 20 SOC. REV. 81, 81–102 (1990).

43. For recent works on social movements, see CULTURES OF POLITICS/POLITICS OF CULTURES: RE-VISIONING LATIN AMERICAN SOCIAL MOVEMENTS (Sonia E. Alvarez et al. eds., 1998) [hereinafter CULTURES OF POLITICS/POLITICS OF CULTURES]; KLAUS EDER, THE NEW POLITICS OF CLASS: SOCIAL MOVEMENTS AND CULTURAL DYNAMICS IN ADVANCED SOCIETY (1993); RAMACHANDRA GUHA, THE UNQUIET WOODS: ECOLOGICAL CHANGE AND PEASANT RESISTANCE IN THE HIMALAYAS (1989); NEW SOCIAL MOVEMENTS AND THE STATE IN LATIN AMERICA (David Slater ed., 1985); NEW SOCIAL MOVEMENTS IN THE SOUTH (Ponna Wignaraja ed., 1993); ANTHONY OBERSCHALL, SOCIAL MOVEMENTS: IDEOLOGIES, INTERESTS AND IDENTITIES (1993); GAIL OMVEDT, REINVENTING REVOLUTION: NEW SOCIAL MOVEMENTS AND THE SOCIALIST TRADITION IN INDIA (1993); SIDNEY G. TARROW, POWER IN MOVEMENT: SOCIAL MOVEMENTS, COLLECTIVE ACTION AND POLITICS (1994); THE CHALLENGE OF LOCAL FEMINISMS (Amrita Basu ed., 1995); THE MAKING OF SOCIAL MOVEMENTS IN LATIN AMERICA: IDENTITY, STRATEGY AND DEMOCRACY (Arturo Escobar et al. eds., 1992) [hereinafter THE MAKING OF SOCIAL MOVEMENTS IN LATIN AMERICA]; ALAIN TOURAINE, RETURN OF THE ACTOR: SOCIAL THEORY IN POST INDUSTRIAL SOCIETY (1988).

44. Mario Diani, *The Concept of Social Movement*, 40 SOC. REV. 1 (1992).

movement organizations," such as non-governmental organizations ("NGOs"), provide the glue for the coordination of actors with multiple motives to join the movement.[45] This does not mean, however, that NGOs lead social movements[46] nor that they, themselves, constitute social movements.[47] Amnesty International, for example, is not a social movement, but may form a part of specific social movements, such as the movement against capital punishment, in particular locations. This basic insight is often lost in international law and international relations scholarship that confuses social movements with NGOs[48] or conflates NGOs with civil society.[49] One major reason for this confusion is, as noted in Part II, the institutionalist bias in legal scholarship, which compels notice of mass action only when it is institutionalized either by emergence as a state or by registration as an NGO. While a lack of institutionalization is an Achilles' heel of social movements, legal scholarship misses much of social reality when it focuses only on institutions.

The second issue raised by Diani's definition of a social movement involves the plurality of actors in social movements including organizations, groups of individuals, and individuals, all of whom may have different motivations for joining the movements. The "anti-globalization" movement—recently witnessed in Seattle in 1999 and in Washington, D.C. and Genoa in 2000—is an example of this plurality. Members of the movement include an eclectic mix of Western labor activists worried about the loss of jobs, unions that push for protectionism, environmental activists concerned about the ecological damage of global business practices, human rights activists who worry about the unaccountability of corporations and international organizations, governments who exploit these fears to promote geopolitical interests, Third World social movements for whom the struggle against globalization is a struggle to live, and a number of other hangers-on who may lack an immediate stake but who still desire to be a part of the activity. Exploring and understanding these different motivations is crucial to a proper appreciation of how international legal norms and processes work in practice.

45. TARROW, *supra* note 43, at 15.

46. As Tarrow asserts, a "bimodal relationship between leaders and followers . . . is absent from movements." *Id.*

47. Diani, *supra* note 44, at 13–14. *See* William Fisher, *Doing Good? The Politics and Antipolitics of NGOs Practices*, 26 ANN. REV. ANTHROPOLOGY 439, 436–64 (1997).

48. *See, e.g.*, Spiro, *supra* note 35.

49. *See, e.g.*, Charnovitz, *supra* note 36.

A third issue noted by Diani is that different scholars understand the notion of conflict in different ways.[50] Some view the notion of conflict as primarily interpersonal and cultural,[51] while others view it as one directed toward economic and political change.[52] In the context of the Third World, most social movements emerge through a conflict with capitalist development. As Barry Adam points out:

> To ignore the dynamics of capitalist development, the role of the labour markets in reorganizing spatial and familial relations, and the interaction of new and traditional categories of people with dis/employment patterns is to ignore the structural prerequisites which have made the new social movements not only possible, but predictable.[53]

The literature on social movements also notes that how a conflict plays out (e.g., the strategies used, the means deployed and shunned, and, simply, what gets counted as "political") will depend upon each society's own historical methods of protest—what Tarrow refers to as "contention by convention."[54] This calls for a very contextual understanding of resistance, unlike the totalizing category of rights, which presumes that resistance is expressed only in the secular, rational, and bureaucratic arenas of the modern state, particularly through the judiciary. Thus, Parisians build barricades[55] and Indians stage dharnas and satyagrahas. "Political culture," as a concept, is critical for understanding what gets counted as "political" when conflicts arise in particular societies. International law and law in general, however, reduce complex conflicts in non-Western societies to the "rationalist, universalist and individualist" political culture of the West.[56]

The final element of Diani's definition of a social movement

---

50. Diani, *supra* note 44, at 10.

51. ALBERTO MELUCCI, NOMADS OF THE PRESENT: SOCIAL MOVEMENTS AND INDIVIDUAL NEEDS IN CONTEMPORARY SOCIETY (1989).

52. Sidney Tarrow theorizes that movements respond to political opportunity and advance their causes through direct confrontation with formal political spheres. *See* TARROW, *supra* note 43, at 18. Post-Marxists emphasize how movements emerge through their ongoing struggles with the state and capital. *See* Barry Adam, *Post-Marxism and the New Social Movements*, 30 CAN. REV. SOC. & ANTHROPOLOGY 316 (1993).

53. Adam, *supra* note 52, at 322.

54. TARROW, *supra* note 43, at 18.

55. *Id.* at 19.

56. CHANTAL MOUFFE, THE RETURN OF THE POLITICAL 2 (1993).

is that it is organized on the basis of shared beliefs and collective identities. This raises the fourth, and final, issue of how such identities are initially formed. Some suggest that "consensus mobilization" is an on-going part of a movement's formation,[57] while others acknowledge that irreconcilable differences lead to a "process of realignment and negotiation between actors."[58] It appears that both of these processes occur in many social movements, often simultaneously. As gaps between different actors widen and consensus eludes them, realignment of identities begins to occur. This process is wholly different from the "right to identity" approach adopted by international law, which looks at identity as merely an individual choice.

A. Beyond Liberalism

For a number of reasons, the new forms of mobilization in the Third World cannot be analyzed using liberal categories such as rights. First, liberal theory assumes a sharp distinction between public and private, privileging only that which belongs to the public sphere for legal protection.[59] As the feminist slogan "personal is political" vividly showed, this assumption simply fails to take into account the relations of power in the domestic or private arenas. The distinction between public and private was based on a sharply delimited arena of the "political," which feminists, among others, have shown to be inadequate.[60]

Second, liberal theory assumes all legitimate power to be united in a "sovereign will" and all political activity to be conducted through institutional arenas such as legislatures and through institutions such as political parties.[61] Third World mass movements

---

57. TARROW, *supra* note 43, at 22–23.

58. Diani, *supra* note 44, at 9 (citing D.C. Snow et al., *Frame Alignment Processes, Micromobilization, and Movement Participation*, 51 AM. SOC. REV. 464 (1986)).

59. *See* Frances Olsen, *Constitutional Law: Feminist Critiques of the Public/Private Distinction*, 10 CONST. COMMENT. 319 (1993). For an analysis in international law, see Karen Engle, *After the Collapse of the Public/Private Distinction: Strategizing Women's Rights*, *in* RECONCEIVING REALITY: WOMEN AND INTERNATIONAL LAW 143 (Dorinda G. Dallmeyer ed., 1993).

60. *See* J. Oloka-Onyango & Sylvia Tamale, *"The Personal is Political" or Why Women's Rights are Indeed Human Rights: An African Perspective on International Feminism*, 17 HUM. RTS. Q. 691 (1995); Celina Romany, *Women as Aliens: A Feminist Critique of the Public/Private Distinction in International Human Rights Law*, 6 HARV. HUM. RTS. J. 87 (1993); Olsen, *supra* note 59.

61. Thus, even while describing his "law of peoples," John Rawls imposes the requirement of a constitutional democratic government through which liberal people act as he

experienced this assumption as too restrictive because it excluded other arenas of doing politics and promoted a corrupt version of statism. European social theorists, particularly Jüergen Habermas, Alain Touraine, Claus Offe, and Alberto Melucci, criticized this liberal tendency to unify the political space.[62] Habermas, in particular, theorized about new social movements, drawing on the experience of German Green movements, and postulated the idea of a "public sphere" where opinion formation takes place prior to will formation in the sanctioned political arenas.[63] This "public sphere" has been a useful tool for conceptualizing social movements.

Third, liberal theory assumes the unity of the social actor (as a consumer, producer, citizen, etc.) and creates formal arenas where the interests of such social actors would be represented.[64] The praxis of social movements in the Third World shows that the heterogeneity and plurality of the social actor is an essential feature of mass mobilization, which the representational model is unable to accommodate without doing violence to its heterogeneous character.[65]

Fourth, liberal theory assumes a harmonious view toward economic growth, as it assumes that the post-World War II welfare state would shoulder the responsibility of humanizing it. This assumption is based on the Weberian understanding that the contradictions created by the institutions of civil society—property, market, the family, etc.—would be "neutrally" resolved by the State.[66] Instead of achieving this result, however, the State simply colonized civil society and, indeed, all life spaces.[67] This was particularly true in Latin America and Asia, which followed State-led industrialization as part of an import-substitution strategy in the decades following World War II. Thus, social movements in the Third World have

tries to balance the law of peoples with the law of states. *See* JOHN RAWLS, THE LAW OF PEOPLES 23–24 (1999).

62. *See* sources cited *supra* notes 40 and 43.

63. *See* JÜERGEN HABERMAS, BETWEEN FACTS AND NORMS: CONTRIBUTIONS TO A DISCOURSE THEORY OF LAW AND DEMOCRACY (1996). Admittedly, Habermas' theory is entirely domestically-focused and does not examine international politics. Nevertheless, his theory has been influential in thinking about civil society in democratic transitions, and it offers a model for contemplating global civil society.

64. For a critique, see Chantol Mouffe, *Democracy, Power and the "Political," in* SEYLA BENHABIB, DEMOCRACY AND DIFFERENCE: CONTESTING THE BOUNDARIES OF THE POLITICAL 245–56 (1996).

65. See CULTURES OF POLITICS/POLITICS OF CULTURES, *supra* note 43, at 10–14.

66. In Weberian terms, this meant the bureaucracy and the law. *See* FROM MAX WEBER: ESSAYS IN SOCIOLOGY (H.H. Gerth & C.W. Mills eds., 1946).

67. For an analysis, see Ashis Nandy, *State, in* DEVELOPMENT DICTIONARY: A GUIDE TO KNOWLEDGE AS POWER (Wolfgang Sachs ed., 1992).

arisen partly as an attempt to liberate these life spaces from the State and partly to politicize the very institutions of civil society so that it is no longer dependent upon increasing regulation and control.

B. Beyond Marxism

What is the role of Marxist theory in the new forms of Third World mobilization? After all, Marxism provided theoretical tools for analyzing social conflicts in the Third World for almost half a century. The short answer is that social movements in the Third World emerged substantially as a response to the failure of Marxism as a discourse of liberation. This was due to many factors. First, Marxism assumes the identity of social agents (peasant, labor, etc.) through fixed social structures that privileges some categories over others (for example, the proletariat as the vanguard).[68] This means, for example, that a struggle that lacks a "real" class basis—e.g., "bourgeois feminism" or "kulak farmers"—cannot be comprehended. Thus, Marxism became marginal to the most important social struggles in the Third World that were organized around, for example, environmental degradation, the oppression of women, and dispossession of labor and assets from farmers.

Second, Marxism is wedded to an evolutionary view of society and, for example, tends to interpret all social struggles in terms of a move from feudalism to capitalism.[69] Besides being rigid and essentialistic, this historical determinism misses the real nature of many Third World social movements, which combine struggles over material aspects (economic struggles) with struggles over symbolic meanings (cultural struggles).[70] In addition, the evolutionary view borders on ethnocentrism as it automatically assumes the superiority of specific forms of Western modernity over non-Western tradition. This was rejected by several social movements in the Third World, such as the Zapatistas, that organized around a particularly strong

68. *See* Karl Marx & Friedrich Engels, *Manifesto of the Communist Party*, *in* THE MARX-ENGELS READER 469–500 (Robert C. Tucker ed., 1978).

69. *See e.g.*, Karl Marx, *On Imperialism in India*, *in* THE MARX-ENGELS READER, *supra* note 68, at 653–64. For a critique, see Balakrishnan Rajagopal, *Locating the Third World in Cultural Geography*, THIRD WORLD LEGAL STUD. 1, 17–18 (1998–99).

70. For a good discussion of the theoretical issues in the context of the Latin American feminist movement, see Norma Stoltz Chinchilla, *Marxism, Feminism and the Struggle for Democracy in Latin America*, *in* THE MAKING OF SOCIAL MOVEMENTS IN LATIN AMERICA, *supra* note 43, at 37–51.

cultural identity.[71]

Third, Marxism shares with liberal theory the understanding of a unified political space and, thus, the State as the main agent of social and economic change.[72] Consequently, the purpose of mass mobilization, as theorized, is the capture of state power. This understanding was reinforced by the statism of Third World development models in the post-World War II period, such as import-substitution and export-promotion. Social movements, on the other hand, reject the State as the main agent of socio-political transformation and do not seek state power as an end in itself. Instead, they seek to obtain their own political space in which they can set the pace and direction of economic change.[73]

Fourth, with globalization, Marxism began to lose touch with new forms of economic arrangements and new forms of struggles that accompanied them, not only in advanced industrial societies, but also in the Third World. These new economies, demonstrated most clearly by the emergence of foreign direct investment, trade, and capital markets, began to reveal that the sphere of capital accumulation and its processes were wider than those of commodity production and exchange. It was wider in at least two ways: (1) capital accumulation increasingly took place on a global scale, whereas commodity production had been theorized within the boundaries of the nation-state; and (2) capital accumulation began to include substantial amounts of labor (domestic labor and informal immigrant labor in low-wage apparel industries) and wealth (natural resources) that were not included in commodity production and exchange. In short, there was a global economy in the making. Marxism was simply unable to supply the theoretical tools to comprehend and respond to it. The social movements that emerged in the Third World surfaced largely as a response to the new, harsh forms of global economy.[74] Indigenous peoples' movements, fishworkers' movements, farmers' movements, and "anti-globalization" protests are a result of the failure of Marxism

71. *See* George Yudice, *The Globalization of Culture and the New Civil Society*, *in* CULTURES OF POLITICS/POLITICS OF CULTURES, *supra* note 43, at 367–68.

72. This was most clearly manifested in the way Marxism differentiated itself from anarchism. *See* Friedrich Engels, *Versus the Anarchists*, *in* THE MARX-ENGELS READER *supra* note 68, at 728–29. For a critique, see PARTHA CHATTERJEE, THE NATION AND ITS FRAGMENTS (1993).

73. *See* Gustavo Esteva, *Regenerating Peoples' Space*, 12 ALTERNATIVES 125 (1987).

74. *See generally* Samir Amin, *Social Movements at the Periphery*, *in* NEW SOCIAL MOVEMENTS IN THE SOUTH, *supra* note 43, at 76–100; David Slater, *Rethinking the Spatialities of Social Movements: Questions of (B)orders, Culture and Politics in Global Times*, *in* CULTURES OF POLITICS/POLITICS OF CULTURES, *supra* note 43, at 380–404.

as a coherent leftist doctrine. To follow Gail Omvedt,[75] what is needed is a historical materialism of all groups adversely affected by the new global economy.

C. Toward a "Cultural Politics"

Social movements arise as a challenge to liberalism, Marxism and, by extension, to extant theories of international law. These theories extend from the utopian (liberal/Western/naturalist) to the apologist (Marxist/Third World/positivist/Realist).[76] The utopians imagine a world without sovereignty (but not necessarily without the state) in which the individual is the primary political actor. Alternatively, the apologists take the political community of the nation-state as the primary political actor and seek to imagine an international legal order that is simultaneously created and constrained by its sovereignty.

Social movements differ from both the utopian and apologist approaches of conceptualizing an international order. Social movements seek to preserve the autonomy implied in the positivist vision, but to abandon the nation-state as the collectivity that would guarantee such autonomy. They also share the naturalists' deep suspicion of the leviathan, but allow a multiplicity of arenas, including the community (rather than the individual), as political actors. Instead of accepting the unified political space propounded by these extant theories, social movements seek to redefine the very boundaries of what is properly "political."

Indeed, most social movements enact a unique form of politics that the author would label "cultural politics." This label is not meant to privilege those movements that are more clearly cultural as "authentic." In the past, this focus on culture resulted in a false dichotomy between "new" and "old" social movements. The former focused on identity and new forms of politics (involving, e.g., human rights, sexual orientation, environment, etc.), whereas the latter movements focused on the struggle for resources to cope with the contradictions of a capitalist economy (such as urban squatters', peasants', and fishworkers' movements). Rather, for all of these movements, identity is strongly associated with survival strategies.

75. OMVEDT, *supra* note 43, at xvi.

76. The apology versus utopia contrast is borrowed from Martti Koskenniemi's path-breaking book, FROM APOLOGY TO UTOPIA: THE STRUCTURE OF INTERNATIONAL LEGAL ARGUMENT (1989).

This gives rise to a much richer, contextual, and relational form of politics. As the introduction to an important, recent collection of essays noted:

> We interpret cultural politics as the process enacted when sets of social actors shaped by, and embodying, different cultural meanings and practices come into conflict with each other.... Culture is political because meanings are constitutive of processes that, implicitly or explicitly, seek to redefine social power. That is, when movements deploy alternative conceptions of women, nature, race, economy, democracy, or citizenship that unsettle dominant cultural meanings, they enact a cultural politics.[77]

The above definition of cultural politics makes it clear that politics is much more than a set of actions taken in formal political arenas (such as legislatures). Rather, it is a decentralized phenomenon that encompasses power struggles enacted in private, social, economic, and cultural arenas, in addition to the formal arenas. By challenging and redefining what counts as political and who defines what is political, social movements foster alternative conceptions of the political itself.

To illustrate more clearly what the rich, relational definition of the "political" in cultural politics means for international law, an outline of its elements is as follows:

> Politics goes beyond what we do in formal arenas, and therefore beyond formal voting rights and representation. Human rights law and mainstream political science, however, continue to focus on what happens in the formal institutions to the exclusion of non-institutional mobilizations. For example, a leading democracy theorist states that political institutionalization is "the single most important and urgent factor in the consolidation of democracy."[78]

This narrow outlook governs several areas of international law including peacekeeping and peacebuilding, international economic law, good governance, and humanitarian interventions to save "failed states."

---

77. CULTURES OF POLITICS/POLITICS OF CULTURES, *supra* note 43, at 7.

78. *See* CAPITALISM, SOCIALISM, AND DEMOCRACY REVISITED (Larry Diamond & Marc F. Plattner eds., 1993).

Struggles over meanings and values in the domain of culture are also political. The personal is finally political. This reverses a bias against culture that international law has historically exhibited.

Political struggles are relational; they are not individual. This abandons the "billiard ball" model of politics that has governed liberal rights theory and realist international legal theory. These theories assume that individuals and States are rational self-maximizing actors and therefore focus on their "right to choose" alternative political paths. A social movements approach, by contrast, focuses on the actual way political choices are shaped in collective settings, thereby allowing analyses to either "scale up" from the level of individuals, or to "scale down" from the level of states.

Conflict is at the heart of politics. This element, borrowed from Marxism, reverses the liberal theory's presumption in favor of harmony between social classes (and resultant covering-up of underlying conflicts). These conflicts, which arise at both the material and symbolic levels, are not among nation-states, but among classes. Such a focus on conflict can then aid in infusing a notion of social justice into the analysis of legal rules and institutions in areas such as international economic law.

By positing a cultural politics, social movements effectively foster alternative modernities. As Fernando Calderon puts it, some movements focus on the question of how to be both modern and different.[79] By mobilizing meanings that cannot be defined within standard paradigms of Western modernity, such movements challenge the authority of international law to speak on what is modern and traditional.

Finally, identities do not result merely from individual choice, but from relational activities among a group of people who unite to achieve a common purpose in the form of a movement. In this sense, the "rights" to identity may be inherently relational.[80] This notion is entirely foreign to both the utopian and apologist approaches to international law described above.[81]

---

79. Fernando Calderon, *quoted in* CULTURES OF POLITICS/POLITICS OF CULTURES, *supra* note 43, at 9.

80. Recent rights and property scholarship in North America has moved to articulate a social relations approach. *See, e.g.*, JOSEPH WILLIAM SINGER, ENTITLEMENT: THE PARADOXES OF PROPERTY (2000); Jennifer Nedelsky, *Reconceiving Rights as Relationship*, 1 REV. CONS. STUD. 1 (1993); Joseph Singer, *The Reliance Interest in Property*, 40 STAN. L. REV. 611 (1988); Joseph Singer & Jack Beerman, *The Social Origins of Property*, 6 CAN. J.L. & JUR. 217 (1993).

81. *See supra* note 76 and accompanying text.

It may appear then that the praxes of social movements centrally challenge the very foundations of international law, and provide a more realistic and promising means of imagining a post-Westphalian order, as Richard Falk has labeled it.[82] Instead of defending the "universal" categories of sovereignty and rights, social movements offer a "pluriversal" defense of local communities. In doing so, they reveal the limitations of both a Kantian liberal world order, based primarily on individual autonomy and rights, and also a realist world order based primarily on State sovereignty.

IV. RESISTANCE AS AN ANALYTICAL CATEGORY IN INTERNATIONAL LAW

Traditional international law is unconcerned with mass action unless it is directed at the creation of states in the form of movements that assert the right to self-determination. Even in such cases, international law usually leaves the murky terrain of mass action and "returns" only to welcome the victor as a legitimate representative of State sovereignty.[83] This doctrinal position enabled European and American colonial empires to defeat the legal claims of Third World, anti-colonial, and nationalist movements for independence under international law. Regardless of how much "resistance" such groups posed—for example, during the Mau Mau rebellion in British Kenya—traditional international law has no vocabulary for understanding and accommodating it. This enabled the colonial authorities to treat anti-colonial resistance as criminal acts and to deal with it through law enforcement measures, especially through the doctrine of emergency. Indeed, traditional international law is notorious for the ease with which it has sanctioned violence against non-Western peoples. As Professor Anthony Anghie has emphasized so eloquently about nineteenth-century positivism:

> The violence of positivist language in relation to non-European peoples is hard to overlook. Positivists

---

82. RICHARD FALK, LAW IN AN EMERGING GLOBAL VILLAGE: A POST-WESTPHALIAN PERSPECTIVE (1998).

83. *See* LEAGUE OF NATIONS O.J. Spec. Supp. 3, at 6 (1920) (stating that when a state undergoes a transformation of dissolution, its legal status is uncertain). For a trenchant critique of this case and the self-determination doctrine, see Nathaniel Berman, *Sovereignty in Abeyance: Self-Determination and International Law*, 7 WIS. INT'L L.J. 51 (1988). *See also* Anthony Carroll & B. Rajagopal, *The Case for the Independent Statehood of Somaliland*, 8 AM. U. J. INT'L L. & POL'Y 653, 666–74 (1992).

> developed an elaborate vocabulary for denigrating these peoples, presenting them as suitable objects for conquest, and legitimizing the most extreme violence against them, all in the furtherance of the civilizing mission—the discharge of the white man's burden.[84]

The hope that formal political independence for the colonized territories would quickly lead to the creation of a new international law was dashed as the efforts by the newly independent countries to create a NIEO in the 1970s grounded to a halt.[85] During the last couple of decades, it has become increasingly difficult to place much hope in the capacity of Third World states to act as effective guarantors of the democratic aspirations of the masses in the Third World. State sovereignty has been parceled both upwards (to international institutions such as the World Trade Organization and Bretton Woods institutions) and downwards (to market actors and NGOs). The idea of development, with its catching-up rationale that provided the motivation for nation-building in the post-World War II period, has come to be seen as an ideological enterprise with profoundly dangerous implications for the most vulnerable and voiceless in society.[86] In addition, the Third World State has come to colonize all life spaces in civil society and has effectively championed the interests of the global elite that control the world economy. The democratic deficit experienced by global governance processes has been exacerbated due to the democratic deficit of Third World States that act as the agents of the "globalitarian" class.[87] The reformist sensibility in international law during the post-World War II period, which revolved around a commitment to individual human rights and an expanded concept of international development including the law of "welfare," also failed to reverse the rot in the system. Though the

84. Antony Anghie, *Finding the Peripheries: Sovereignty and Colonialism in Nineteenth Century International Law*, 40 HARV. INT'L L.J. 1, 7 (1999).

85. This effort by newly independent countries took the form of a number of U.N. General Assembly resolutions and declarations, which legal status was contested by Western international lawyers. *See Charter of Economic Rights and Duties of States*, G.A. Res. 3281, U.N. GAOR, 29th Sess., Supp. No. 30, at 50, U.N. Doc. A/9030 (1974); *Declaration on the Establishment of a New International Economic Order*, G.A. Res. 3201, U.N. GAOR, 6th Special Sess., Supp. No. 1, at 3, U.N. Doc. A/9559 (1974). On the NIEO, see MOHAMMED BEDJAOUI, TOWARDS A NEW INTERNATIONAL ECONOMIC ORDER (1977).

86. For an analysis, see Balakrishnan Rajagopal, *International Law and the Development Encounter: Violence and Resistance at the Margins*, 93 A.S.I.L. PROC. 16 (1999).

87. *See generally* DAVID HELD, DEMOCRACY AND THE GLOBAL ORDER: FROM THE MODERN STATE TO COSMOPOLITAN GOVERNANCE (1995).

causes of this are too complex to examine here,[88] it may be noted that the idea of human rights has proven to be too Western, disciplinary, and anti-political. At the same time, the idea of development has proven to be associated with the containment of mass resistance (especially anti-communist peasant) and a destructive modernity (destructive as in having a devastating impact on natural resources and livelihoods). The post-World War II "settlement" of the colonial question through the grant of political sovereignty did not end mass movements in the Third World. Instead, this resistance took myriad other forms, through social movement action, that have not been sufficiently understood by international lawyers, partly due to the disciplinary limitations discussed above. It is now becoming obvious that Third World social movements represent the cutting edge of resistance in the Third World to antidemocratic and destructive developments. It is important for international lawyers to seek to develop a theory of resistance that would enable them to, at least partially, respond to the political challenge to assure a just and stable world order.

In what ways may a theory of resistance be articulated in international law? We may begin with the elements of the new notion of cultural politics, outlined in Part III above. If politics goes beyond what we do in representative arenas and encompasses civil society, if struggles over symbolic values and meanings matter as much as those over resources, if political struggles and identities are inherently relational, if conflict is central to politics, and if alternative modernities may be fostered by alternative conceptions of the political, then a theory of resistance must begin by questioning many elements of the existing theories of international law and relations. It must cease treating the state and the ideology of development with irrational reverence. It must develop a more flexible and dynamic conception of the dialectic between institutions and extra-institutional mass action. It must pay diligent and honest attention to the social origin of the rules of international law. It must rethink the relationship between international law-making and domestic enforcement. It must pay much closer attention to the actual workings of norms and institutions by studying the everyday forms of power struggles in which they are implicated. It must be reinvigorated by a new, Third World identity that allows new and more useful coalitions of states and social movements to be built, for

88. For a detailed examination of the encounter between post-World War II international lawyers' new sensibility to reconstruct international law and the emergence of a new discourse of development to foster growth and reduce poverty in the Third World, see Rajagopal, *supra* note 86.

example on issues such as agricultural subsidies or health and trade issues.

A. Inspirations for Formulating a Theory of Resistance

A theory of resistance in international law must pay particular attention to the rearticulation of four issues: (1) against what? (the nature of the exercise of power in current international society, including the exercise of power by the modern state); (2) toward what end? (the nature of human liberation that is sought, including the relationship between resistance and the psychology of deprivation); (3) using what strategies? (the relationship between reformist and radical resistance); and (4) what should be the role of the postcolonial state in resistance? (the state as a plural, fragmented, and contested terrain). While this project has not yet truly begun, the writings of some prominent theorists such as Michel Foucault, Frantz Fanon, Antonio Gramsci, and Partha Chatterjee may offer some potential inspirations for building such a theory of resistance and addressing each of the above four issues.

1. Michel Foucault

The first such source of inspiration is the notion of governmentality or governmental rationality, expounded by Michel Foucault in a series of lectures in the late 1970s.[89] This notion aids in a better understanding of the nature of particular exercises of power upon which a theory of resistance must focus. As defined by Foucault, governmentality means:

> The ensemble formed by the institutions, procedures, analyses and reflections, the calculations and tactics that allow the exercise of this very specific albeit complex form of power, which has as its target population, as its principal form of knowledge political economy, and as its essential technical means apparatuses of security.
>
> The tendency which, over a long period and throughout the West, has steadily led toward the pre-eminence over all other forms (sovereignty, discipline,

89. *See* THE FOUCAULT EFFECT: STUDIES IN GOVERNMENTALITY (Graham Burchell et al. eds., 1991).

> etc.) of this type of power which may be termed government, resulting, on the one hand, in the formation of a whole series of specific governmental apparatuses, and on the other, in the development of a whole complex of *savoirs*.
>
> The process, or rather the result of the process, through which the state of justice of the Middle Ages, transformed into the administrative state during the fifteenth and sixteenth centuries, gradually becomes "governmentalized."[90]

The nature of the exercise of power in the Third World makes it clear that it is a mistake to regard the power emerging from the State as the principal power. Rather, most effective power has shifted to apparatuses of government that are both above and below the state, as well as to both domestic and transnational private actors. As such, there needs to be a theory of power in the Third World that is broader than that which emerges from state institutions. Also, the form of the exercise of power in the Third World has a particularly bureaucratic aspect to it, consisting of techniques designed to observe, monitor, shape, and control the behavior of individuals situated within the state. This focus on the population is particularly intense with regard to the indigent, who constitute the primary object of the exercise of governmental rationality. This is not new, of course. As a mid-nineteenth-century French author wrote, "assisting the poor is a means of government, a potent way of containing the most difficult section of the population and improving all other sections."[91] Poverty alleviation is currently perhaps the most important motivation behind the operation of international institutions and significant areas of international law.[92] At a time of more intense social mobilization in the Third World, this focus on poverty alleviation raises troubling questions regarding the ideological nature of international law and institutions.

Foucault's definition is useful for developing a theory of resistance that departs from the treatment of the state as an obsession.

---

90. *Id.* at 102–03.

91. *Id.* at 151 (quoting Firmin Marbeau, *Du paupérisme en France et des moyens d'y rémédier au principles d'économic charitable*, Paris, 1847).

92. *See, e.g.*, WORLD DEVELOPMENT REPORT 2001/2002: ATTACKING POVERTY (2000) *available at* http://www.worldbank.org/poverty/wdrpoverty/report/. Even the IMF has reframed its mission with the umbrella of poverty alleviation, renaming, for instance, the Enhanced Structural Adjustment Facility (ESAF) as the Poverty Reduction and Growth Facility (PRGF). *See* IMF website *at* www.imf.org.

Traditional state theory in the Third World, influenced by Marxism, holds that the modern activities of government must be deduced from the properties and propensities of the state.[93] Foucault reverses that presumption and suggests that the nature of state institutions is a function of changes in the practice of government. This reversal has the salutary effect of moving the focus of political theory away from an excessive attention on institutions and toward practices.[94]

Finally, Foucault's definition allows for a focus on both the micropolitics of power relations and their strategic reversibility. The former permits a theory of resistance to take into account how individuals and groups experience power relations, thereby enabling international law to accommodate the feminist slogan, "personal is political" without theoretical discomfort.[95] The latter, strategic reversibility of power relations, essentially shows the contestability of seemingly entrenched power structures by demonstrating how governmental practices themselves can be turned into a focus of resistance in what Foucault calls the "history of dissenting 'counter-conducts.'"[96] This focus on micropolitics and strategic reversibility offers a richer basis for articulating a theory of resistance that focuses on social movements.

2. Frantz Fanon

A second issue in the articulation of a theory of resistance is toward what end the resistance must aim. In two of his well-known essays, *Concerning Violence*, and *The Pitfalls of National Consciousness*,[97] Fanon lays out the psychological aspects of colonialism as well as those of anti-colonial resistance. Three themes, discussed below, arising from his work are relevant to the articulation of a theory of resistance that engages Third World social movement action.

The first theme is that a complete view of human liberation cannot be confined to the nationalist paradigm. As Amilcar Cabral

93. *See* THE FOUCAULT EFFECT: STUDIES IN GOVERNMENTALITY, *supra* note 89, at 4.

94. *Id.*

95. *See* Fernando Teson, *Feminism and International Law: A Reply*, 33 VA. J. INT'L L. 647 (1993) (discussing an example of discomfort with feminist approaches to international law).

96. THE FOUCALT EFFECT: STUDIES IN GOVERNMENTALITY, *supra* note 89, at 5.

97. FRANTZ FANON, THE WRETCHED OF THE EARTH 35–106, 148–205 (Constance Farrington trans., 1963).

stated, "national liberation is an act of culture."[98] This basic lesson is amply illustrated by the emergence of thousands of social movements of farmers, peasants, urban poor, indigenous peoples, women, and workers, who have felt excluded by the nation-building project during the postcolonial period. The idea that nationalism is a sufficient response to colonialism has proven to be inadequate. As Fanon says, "[h]istory teaches us that the battle against colonialism does not run straight away along the lines of nationalism."[99] Instead, he advocates a range of measures that can be adopted to avoid the dangers of nationalist consciousness, including the danger of that singular postcolonial institution, the political party, the ideological underpinnings of which rest on the Western assumption that the masses are incapable of governing themselves.[100] These views have profound importance for articulating the ends of mass resistance in already-independent nation states as they move away from the ends, such as secession, that are traditionally postulated for mass movements in international law. Indeed, the practice of several social movements, such as the Zapatistas in Mexico and the National Alliance for Tribal Self Rule ("NATSR") in India, has moved away from nationalist framings of their demands.[101] Nevertheless, these movements often see their strategies as contributing to a vision of human liberation that is as profound as anti-colonial nationalism. As Pradip Prabhu, one of the conveners of the NATSR, remarked about the passage of a law in India in 1996 that extended village self-rule to tribal areas, "it is the first serious nail in the coffin of colonialism."[102]

The second theme that emerges from the work of Fanon relates to resistance and economic power. A traditional understanding of mass action holds that, to be viable, mass action must rest on economic strength. This economic theory of violence is derived from Marxist theory, which holds that economic substructure determines all social outcomes. As Engels states:

> To put it briefly, the triumph of violence depends upon the production of armaments, and this in its turn depends on production in general, and thus . . . on

98. Amilcar Cabral, *National Liberation and Culture*, *in* RETURN TO THE SOURCE: SELECTED SPEECHES (1974).

99. FANON, *supra* note 97, at 148.

100. *Id.* at 187–88.

101. *See* George Yudice, *The Globalization of Culture and the New Civil Society*, *in* CULTURES OF POLITICS/POLITICS OF CULTURES, *supra* note 43, at 353–79 (analyzing Zapatista culture).

102. Personal communication, Fall 1997.

> economic strength, on the economy of the State and in the last resort on the material means which that violence commands.[103]

This logic often drives the accumulation of economic power by nation-states and forms the core of the catching-up rationale in the development paradigm. It also underlies the traditional Third World lawyer's response to colonialism as a peculiar economic exploitation (as opposed to racial or religious domination) that could, they believed, be reversed through doctrines such as Permanent Sovereignty Over Natural Resources.[104] As suggested above, however, mass action in the Third World is often a combination of struggles over material resources and symbolic meanings. It is simultaneously cultural and economic. Fanon recognizes the importance of this aspect. On the one hand, he bluntly states that, "[i]n the colonies, the economic substructure is also the superstructure. The cause is the consequence; you are rich because you are white, you are white because you are rich."[105] In the postcolonial context, the intersection between economic dominance and caste, racial, ethnic, or religious dominance is a fact of life. It is also a fact of life in international relations. On the other hand, Fanon notes that even economic and military dominance has not historically assured colonial countries of victories over the colonized peoples, partly due to tactics such as guerilla warfare.[106] Fanon's theory avoids the underestimation of mass resistance in a non-hegemonic context, a context in which most social movements operate.

Finally, the third theme that is relevant to a theory of resistance is Fanon's understanding that the new forms of capitalism in the Third World have transformed the political space for governance and resistance. Although he was writing well before the advent of the new global economy, Fanon notes that, as the colony is transformed from a sphere of exploitation to a market for goods, blind domination of the natives based on slavery is replaced by a desire to protect the market, including the "legitimate interests," of the colonial business elite.[107] In his view, this transformation creates a "detached

103. *Cited in* FANON, *supra* note 97, at 64.

104. G.A. Res. 1803, U.N. GAOR, 17th Sess., Supp. No. 17 at 15, U.N. Doc. A/5217 (1962). *See also* PERMANENT SOVEREIGNTY OVER NATURAL RESOURCES IN INTERNATIONAL LAW (Kamal Hossain & Subrata Roy Chowdhury eds., 1984).

105. FANON, *supra* note 97, at 40.

106. *Id.* at 64–65.

107. *Id.* at 65.

complicity" between capitalism and anti-colonial resistance.[108] In addition, the creation of a work force in the colony leads to a politics of reformism wherein strikes and boycotts take the place of anti-colonial rebellion.[109] This analysis contributes significantly to an understanding of how global capitalism works and how resistance to it is structured. Global capitalism works to create and protect markets and, increasingly the "rights," of the consumers. Its presence in Third World societies results in workers and others who directly benefit from it and whose politics are aimed at reformism. This analysis reveals how the spread of free markets is so often equated with the spread of freedom in general. For articulating a theory of resistance under conditions of globalization, there must be an acute understanding of how globalization structures opportunities for resistance. Fanon's work offers some clues with regard to how to proceed.

3. Antonio Gramsci

A third inspiration for a theory of resistance in international law is the well-known work of Antonio Gramsci in *The Prison Notebooks*.[110] Though Eurocentric[111] like his contemporaries, Gramsci postulates three ideas that are of enormous value for articulating a theory of resistance that focuses on the practice of social movements.

The first is his notion of "hegemony," which, as defined by Gramsci, means:

> The spontaneous consent given by the great masses of the population to the general direction imposed on social life by the dominant fundamental group; this consent is "historically" caused by the prestige (and consequent confidence) which the dominant group enjoys because of its position and function in the world of production;
>
> [t]he apparatus of state coercive power which "legally"

108. *Id.*

109. *Id.* at 66.

110. ANTONIO GRAMSCI, SELECTIONS FROM THE PRISON NOTEBOOKS OF ANTONIO GRAMSCI (Quintin Hoare & Geoffrey Nowell Smith eds. and trans., 1971).

111. *Id.* at 416 (noting the "[h]egemony of Western Culture over the whole World Culture" and certifying that European culture is the only "historically and concretely universal culture").

> enforces discipline on those groups who do not "consent" either actively or passively. This apparatus is, however, constituted for the whole of society in anticipation of moments of crisis of command and direction when spontaneous consent has failed.[112]

Hegemony to Gramsci, then, is an active process involving the production, reproduction, and mobilization of popular consent, which can be constructed by any "dominant group" that takes hold of and uses it. This meaning is different from the more common understanding of "hegemony" as domination through force, and corresponds realistically to the global process of governance that rests, not only on brute military force, but also on the confluence between force and moral ideas. Thus, it is the case that the interests of great powers are sought to be justified by the language of "humanitarian intervention," and that containment of mass resistance is justified through "poverty alleviation." As such, the "consent" given by the international society of states to the general direction imposed on world affairs is a function of the domination of the force and ideas of the West.

For several centuries, the West's hegemony was unshakeable. After decolonization and the rise in the economic power of Asia, as well as the emergence of multiple voices of dissent from within Western societies, however, opportunities have existed for some decades for creative political and legal strategies for the Third World. Social movements, including both those directed at corporate accountability for environmental and human rights abuses and single-issue movements, such as those for banning anti-personnel landmines, have attempted to manufacture the consent of the population for alternative paths of sustainable development, peace, or democracy. While these movements continue to lack the state's coercive apparatus for enforcing discipline on those who do not consent, it is arguable that this part of Gramsci's definition does not apply and has never applied to international affairs because international relations has always lacked an enforcement mechanism. It is plausible that in international law and relations, the conditions under which "spontaneous consent" may be manufactured are as, if not more, important than the existence of forceful enforcement mechanisms. One can understand this idea in the disciplinary sensibility that states obey most rules of international law most of the time, even in the absence of enforcement[113] or in the recognition of the increasingly

112. *Id.* at 12.

113. *See* LOUIS HENKIN, HOW NATIONS BEHAVE (1979). Admittedly, the reason given

important role that transnational advocacy networks play in international politics.[114]

The second idea articulated by Gramsci relates to the definition of "passive revolution" and the distinction between "war of position" and "war of movement/maneuver." This theme is critical for understanding the relationship between civil society and the state broadly, and for theorizing about the tactical efforts of social movements to influence global law and policy. He defines passive revolution in two ways: (1) as a revolution without mass participation; and (2) as a "molecular" social transformation that occurs beneath the surface of society where the progressive class cannot advance openly.[115] The latter definition, for which he cites Gandhi's non-violent movement against British rule as an example,[116] helps to introduce into political theory the everyday forms of resistance to economic and political hegemony. Although he is critical of passive revolution as a political program, he uses the term broadly enough to indicate that when a frontal attack may be impossible, a passive revolution may occur despite the surface stability of particular regimes or even the global order. Class and other forms of struggle may continue, even if only at an interpersonal level.[117] This perspective is important for expanding the analysis of international law and politics to include extensive descriptions of the micro-politics of change. Without engaging social movement literature and the tools of anthropological analysis that it provides, international law and relations cannot hope to accomplish this type of analysis.

It is important to note the distinction between "war of position" and "war of movement/maneuver" in Gramscian thought. Gramsci uses the term "war of position" to mean a muted form of political struggle that is only possible during periods of relatively stable equilibrium between fundamental classes.[118] In particular, he emphasizes that this struggle takes the form of triumph over civil

for this does not rest on a Gramscian framework, but on an understanding of legal process. Nevertheless, this perspective recognizes the value of maintaining Western "hegemony" through the application of a legal process that produces consent. *See also* Harold Koh, *Why Do Nations Obey International Law?*, 106 YALE L.J. 2599 (1997).

114. *See* SIKKINK & KECK, *supra* note 35.

115. GRAMSCI, *supra* note 110, at 46. (Note that Gramsci is critical of passive revolution.).

116. *Id.* at 107.

117. *Id.* at 47. Partha Chatterjee suggests that passive revolution is, in fact, the general framework of capitalist transformation in societies where bourgeois hegemony has not been accomplished in the classical way. *See* CHATTERJEE, *supra* note 72, at 212.

118. CHATTERJEE, *supra* note 72, at 206.

society before engaging the state. As he puts it, "a social group can, and indeed must, already exercise 'leadership' before winning governmental power (this indeed is one of the principal conditions for winning of such power)."[119] A "war of movement/maneuver," on the other hand, is a frontal attack that aims to seize the institutions of hegemony. Boycotts are a form of a war of position, strikes a form of a war of movement.[120] The same struggle may constitute both a war of position and war of movement. Thus, he notes that Gandhi's passive resistance is a war of position which, at certain times, became a war of movement and, at other times, underground warfare.[121] Social movement action is mostly a passive revolution, which can, at times, be a war of position (as when transnational movements press demands for boycotts of brands or insist on eco-labeling) or a war of movement (as when ethical investors divest stocks of companies that are deemed by social movement actors to be unfriendly to environmental or human rights concerns). A political theory of international law that ignores the role of passive revolution or war of position is in danger of becoming irrelevant or, worse, being blind to the role of non-state groups that do not qualify as NGOs.

The third and final idea that is important to a theory of resistance is that of the relationship between the masses and intellectuals. Several social movements that arose during the 1990s have revealed the existence of a symbiotic relationship between mass action, on the one hand, and movement intellectuals, on the other, who act as mediators between the movements and the global cosmopolitan class. Some intellectuals have assumed leadership positions themselves in various social movements. Examples include Gustavo Esteva (Zapatistas), Pradip Prabhu (NATSR), Vandana Shiva (ecological feminism) and Arundhati Roy (Narmada Bachao Andolan in India). However, there are few, if any, international lawyers who are associated with social movements. This regrettable fact causes even progressive international lawyers to seem rather clubby and elitist with no real connection to the most important mass struggles of our time. This is especially the case in the Third World, where international lawyers have an ethical responsibility to the masses, but remain committed to highly formalistic and statist analyses of the international order. This leads them to take positions on international legal issues that reflect state positions and ignore social reality. An example is the ready acceptance by Third World

119. *Id.* at 57.

120. *Id.* at 229.

121. *Id.*

international lawyers in the 1970s of the developing countries' position that environmental concerns were those of the rich and that poverty was the greatest polluter. This position entirely overlooked the existence of environmental movements in their own societies.[122] It also overlooked the exclusive focus of Western international lawyers on NGOs as the only legitimate non-governmental actors.[123]

Gramsci's analysis assists in formulating a theory about the proper relationship between international lawyers (as intellectuals) and social movements. He explains that the supremacy of the social group manifests itself in two ways—as "domination" and as "intellectual and moral leadership."[124] It is imperative that a struggle capture at least some intellectual and moral leadership and this opens a role for intellectuals. Agreeing with Lenin that the division of labor between intellectuals and the working class is false,[125] Gramsci suggests that the working class is capable of developing from within itself "organic intellectuals" with a dual role—that of production and organization of work and that of a "directive political" role.[126] This approach has the salutary effect of drawing attention to the class character and other ruling characteristics of international lawyers while recognizing the connection between their role in "producing" legal knowledge and the dominant group of which they are a part. It is imperative that a theory of resistance in international law pay close attention to these aspects of elite/non-elite and law/social interaction to remain effective and credible.

4. Partha Chatterjee

Of primary importance to the articulation of a theory of resistance in international law is the role of the state. The sanctioned language of resistance in international law, i.e., human rights, is generally thought to be an anti-state discourse, though this is increasingly recognized as an inaccurate description.[127] Given that

122. *See, e.g.*, R.P. Anand, *Development and Environment: The Case of the Developing Countries*, 24 INDIAN J. INT'L L. 1 (1980). Several environmental movements such as Chipko had already been taking place in India since the early 1970s. *See* GUHA, *supra* note 43.

123. *See, e.g.*, Charnovitz, *supra* note 36.

124. GRAMSCI, *supra* note 110, at 57.

125. *Id.* at 3–4.

126. *Id.* at 4.

127. This is due to the increasing salience of economic, social, and cultural rights that require an active role for the State, as well as the recognition that effective protection of human rights and the rule of law sometimes requires state-building. On the first, see UNDP, *Human Development Report: Human Rights and Human Development* (2000). On the

many social movements arose as a result of the pathologies of the developmental state, as suggested above,[128] what is and what should be the relationship between resistance and the state? Should the state be a target or an ally? It is impossible to answer this question in the abstract as it depends upon the particular relationship between states and social movements on particular issues. Nevertheless, Partha Chatterjee's work[129] on the nature of the postcolonial state provides some clues on how social movements relate to Third World states.

The first theme that Partha Chatterjee develops is the centrality of the ideology of development for the very self-definition of the postcolonial state.[130] This resulted directly from an economic critique of colonial rule that attacked the legitimacy of such rule because it resulted in the exploitation of the colonized nation.[131] As Chatterjee discusses this critique, the state represents the only legitimate form of the exercise of power because it is a necessary condition for the development of the nation. The legitimacy of the state, then, does not come merely from elections; rather it derives from its rational character to direct a program of economic development for the nation.[132] As a result, the challenge posed by social movements to the developmental ideology of the state, whether it be through environmental or human rights critiques of its developmental activities, is seen as anti-national.[133] What is instead required is a theory of resistance that questions the developmental ideology of the state and seeks to build alternative sources of legitimacy for the state.

A second theme relates to the assumed neutrality of the state in the development process. The postcolonial goal was to establish a Hegelian rational state that would engage in the planning for and implementation of development. This soon proved to be difficult as the state itself proved to be a contested terrain where the power relations that it sought to reorder through development planning were

second, see Gregory Fox, *Strengthening the State*, 7 IND. J. GLOB. LEGAL STUD. 35–77 (1999).

128. See the initial discussion *supra* Part III.

129. *See* CHATTERJEE, *supra* note 72.

130. *Id.* at 202–05.

131. *Id.* at 202.

132. *Id.*

133. For example, the critics of the Narmada dam project in India have been dubbed by its Home Minister as foreign elements. *See* Balakrishnan Rajagopal, *Opinion, The Supreme Court & Human Rights*, THE HINDU (Dec. 6, 2000), *available at* http://www.hindu.com/2000/12/06/stories/05062524.htm.

already shaping the very identity of the state[134] and that of civil society. This means that the objects and subjects of planning merge into each other and that politics is never just an external constraint on the state in the development process.[135] Rather, politics deeply penetrates the state even as the state constitutes itself as the chief agent of development. This insight has deep implications for international law since it, also, assumes a neutral state that undertakes to execute legal obligations in a technical and rational manner with respect to the objects of intervention that are located in politics. A theory of resistance in international law must allow for the interpenetration of state and society, of domestic and international, and of law and politics. In fact, social movement practice demonstrates that this has already been happening. For example, the leaders of social movements and the state agencies in Latin America in areas such as environment and women's rights continually switch jobs and blur the lines between the state and the objects of its intervention. Often, social movements and the states have complex, interpenetrative relationships, as exemplified by the Servicio Nacional de la Mujer (SERNAM) in Chile,[136] which is the National Women's Bureau (a government agency), or the Venezuelan ecology movement that began with a state Organic Law on the Environment in 1976.[137] This complexity indicates that a theory of resistance in international law must treat the state as a plural and fragmented terrain of contestation rather than as a monolith.

V. CONCLUSION

The call for a theory of resistance that addresses the need to understand social movement action should not be misunderstood as a call for a rejection of international legal order. Rather, international law and institutions provide important arenas for social movement action, as they expand the political space available for transformative politics. For international lawyers, engaging social movement literature and developing the sensibility of concerned activists, who

134. CHATTERJEE, *supra* note 72, at 207–08.

135. *Id.* at 208.

136. *See* Veronica Schild, *New Subjects of Rights? Women's Movements and the Construction of Citizenship in the "New Democracies," in* CULTURES OF POLITICS/POLITICS OF CULTURES, *supra* note 43, at 91–117.

137. Maria Pilar Garcia, *The Venezuelan Ecology Movement: Symbolic Effectiveness, Social Practices and Political Strategies, in* THE MAKING OF SOCIAL MOVEMENTS IN LATIN AMERICA, *supra* note 43, at 151.

are motivated by the best cosmopolitan ideals of the discipline, awaits. Mass action is a social reality in contemporary society, and international lawyers cannot remain ignorant of it. A new Third World approach to international law will need to engage social movements to transcend the impasse in which it finds itself. This new international law has the potential to contribute to a new understanding of not only the doctrines and ideas of international law, but also the very ethical purpose of the discipline.

This article has traced some of the theoretical challenges faced by international lawyers as they seek to understand their encounter with social movements. It has also suggested some preliminary considerations for articulating a theory of cultural politics that could ground a theory of resistance in international law. During most of its existence, international law has remained too Western, elitist, male-centered, and imperial, and an encounter with social movements offers an opportunity for it to fundamentally transform.

Name Index